THE CANADIAN POLITY

A COMPARATIVE INTRODUCTION

THIRD EDITION

Ronald G. Landes

Saint Mary's University

Prentice-Hall Canada Inc., Scarborough, Ontario

To my wife, Peggy,
and our children,
Megan and Donny

Canadian Cataloguing in Publication Data

Landes, Ronald G., 1945–
  The Canadian polity

3rd ed.
Includes bibliographical references.
ISBN 0-13-116740-5

1. Canada — Politics and government.   I. Title.

JL65   1983.L3   1991   320.971   C90-094171-5

Prentice-Hall Inc., Englewood Cliffs, New Jersey
Prentice-Hall International, Inc., London
Prentice-Hall of Australia, Pty., Ltd., Sydney
Prentice-Hall of India Pvt., Ltd., New Delhi
Prentice-Hall of Japan, Inc., Tokyo
Prentice-Hall of Southeast Asia (Pte.) Ltd., Singapore
Editora Prentice-Hall do Brasil Ltda., Rio de Janeiro
Prentice-Hall Hispanoamericana, S.A., Mexico

ISBN 0-13-116740-5

Copy Editor: Maura Brown
Coordinating Editor: Kelly Dickson
Production Coordinator: Florence Rousseau
Cover Design: Sue Boehler
Typesetter: Q Composition Inc.

   2 3 4   AGC   94 93 92 91

Printed and bound in the USA by Arcata Graphics Company

Contents

Preface to the Third Edition *ix*
Preface for Students *xi*
Preface for Instructors *xiii*
Acknowledgments *xvi*

PART ONE: THE NATURE OF GOVERNMENT AND POLITICS

1   *The Comparative Study of Canadian Government*   *2*

    The Nature of Government   *5*
    A Comparative Perspective on Canadian Government   *24*
    Summary   *26*
    Recommended Readings   *26*

2   *Political Analysis: Concepts and Principles*   *29*

    The Nature of Politics   *32*
    Basic Concepts of Political Analysis   *40*
    Basic Principles of Political Analysis   *51*
    Comparative Political Analysis   *57*
    Summary   *60*
    Recommended Readings   *60*

PART TWO: THE POLITICAL STRUCTURE OF THE CANADIAN POLITY

3   *The Constitution Federalism: Operation and Reform*   *64*

    Characteristics of Constitutional Government   *65*
    The Canadian Constitution   *67*
    British Constitutional Practice   *84*
    The American Constitutional Experience   *87*
    Comparing Constitutions   *92*
    Summary   *93*
    Recommended Readings   *94*

4   *The Executive Branch of Government: The Facade and Reality of Political Power*   97

The Nature and Growth of Executive Power   *98*
The Formal Executive in Canada   *101*
The Political Executive in Canada   *108*
The British Parliamentary Executive   *121*
The American Presidential Executive   *125*
Comparing Executives   *129*
Summary   *131*
Recommended Readings   *131*

5   *The Bureaucracy and Policy-Making*   *135*

The Nature of Bureaucracy   *136*
Models of Decision-Making   *139*
The Bureaucracy-Policy Nexus in Canada   *142*
The British Bureaucracy: The Role of Whitehall   *152*
Policy-Making in the American Presidential System   *154*
Comparing Bureaucracies   *157*
Summary   *158*
Recommended Readings   *159*

6   *The Legislative Branch of Government: Representation and Legitimation*   *162*

The Development of Legislatures   *163*
Exercising Legislative Power: The Role of the Canadian House of Commons   *166*
The Legislature in Great Britain   *191*
The American Legislature   *196*
Comparing Legislatures   *201*
Summary   *203*
Recommended Readings   *204*

7   *The Judicial Branch of Government: The Reluctant Exercise of Power*   *207*

The Nature of Judicial Power   *208*
The Canadian Judicial System   *212*
The Court System in Britain   *221*
The American Judiciary   *222*
Comparing Judiciaries   *227*
Summary   *228*
Recommended Readings   *229*

PART THREE: POLITICAL PROCESSES AND POLITICAL BEHAVIOUR

8   *Political Culture: The Beliefs and Values of the Polity*   232

Political Culture: Definition and Types   *233*
The Canadian Political Culture   *235*
The British Political Culture   *249*
The American Political Culture   *251*
Comparing Political Cultures   *254*
Summary   *255*
Recommended Readings   *255*

9   *Political Parties: The Acquisition and Retention of Political Power*   259

The Nature of Political Parties   *260*
The Canadian Party System   *267*
Comparing Parties and Party Systems   *296*
Political Opposition and Party Futures   *308*
Summary   *309*
Recommended Readings   *310*

10   *The Electoral Process: Political Recruitment and Elections*   314

The Nature of Elections and Political Recruitment   *315*
Political Recruitment in Canada   *318*
The Election Process in Canada   *323*
Britain's Electoral Process   *330*
American Elections   *333*
Comparing Electoral Processes   *336*
Summary   *337*
Recommended Readings   *337*

11   *Comparing Electoral Systems*   341

The Significance of Electoral Systems   *342*
Types of Electoral Systems   *344*
The Canadian Electoral System   *347*
The British Electoral System   *351*
The American Electoral System   *354*
Comparing Electoral Systems   *357*
Summary   *360*
Recommended Readings   *361*

12   *Political Behaviour: Socialization and Participation*   *363*

   Acquiring Political Beliefs: The Political Socialization
      Process   *365*
   Citizen Participation: Voting Behaviour   *370*
   Summary   *380*
   Recommended Readings   *380*

13   *Political Behaviour: Interest Groups*   *383*

   The Nature of Interest Groups   *384*
   Interest Groups Triumphant: The American Pattern   *388*
   Interest Groups in Canada   *394*
   The Pattern of British Interests   *400*
   Comparing Interest Groups   *403*
   Summary   *404*
   Recommended Readings   *405*

PART FOUR: EVALUATING THE CANADIAN POLITICAL EXPERIMENT

14   *Canadian Politics at Work: The 1982 Canada Act*   *408*

   1982 Canada Act: Major Provisions   *409*
   Passage of the Canada Act: A Political Analysis   *416*
   The Impact of the 1982 Constitution Act   *430*
   The Meech Lake Accord   *437*
   Recommended Readings   *445*

15   *The Canadian Polity: A Comparative Assessment*   *447*

   Comparing the Canadian, British, and American Political
      Systems   *448*
   The Liberal-Democratic Nature of the Canadian Polity: Prospects
      for Reform   *452*

Constitution Act, 1982–
   Part I: The Canadian Charter of Rights and Freedoms   *457*

Constitutional Accord, 1987   *462*

Bibliography   *469*

Subject Index   *487*

Name Index   *494*

List of Tables and Figures

FIGURE 1.1   Government Take from a Bottle of Liquor   *10*

FIGURE 1.2   National Government Expenditures in Canada 1984–1985   *12*

TABLE 1.1   Parliamentary and Presidential Governments   *23*

TABLE 1.2   A Combined Classification of Democratic Governments   *23*

FIGURE 3.1   Schematic Portrayal of Separate Institutions Sharing Power   *90*

TABLE 4.1   The Canadian Federal Cabinet Structure (January 1989)   *111*

FIGURE 4.1   Canada's Executive Branch of Government   *120*

FIGURE 5.1   Federal Cabinet Structure (January 1989)   *147*

TABLE 7.1   The Canadian Supreme Court 1990   *217*

TABLE 7.2   The American Supreme Court 1990   *226*

TABLE 9.1   Officially Registered Political Parties — Canadian Election 1988   *265*

TABLE 9.2   1980 Federal Election Results   *275*

TABLE 9.3   1988 Canadian Federal Election Results   *276*

TABLE 9.4   1983 Conservative Leadership Convention   *286*

TABLE 9.5   1984 Liberal Leadership Convention   *286*

TABLE 9.6   1990 Liberal Leadership Convention   *287*

TABLE 9.7   1989 NDP Leadership Convention   *289*

TABLE 9.8   British Conservative Party Leadership Selection — 1975   *299*

TABLE 9.9   British Labour Party Leadership Selection — 1983   *300*

TABLE 10.1   1988 Canadian Election Results   *324*

TABLE 10.2   Provincial Seats in the House of Commons   *328*

TABLE 10.3   1987 British Election Results   *333*

TABLE 11.1   Plurality Formula — Majority Victory   *345*

TABLE 11.2   Plurality Formula — Plurality Victory   *346*

TABLE 11.3   Canadian Election Results — 1974, 1979, 1980, 1984, 1988   *348*

TABLE 11.4   Alternative Electoral Systems 1988 (Seats)   *350*

TABLE 11.5   British Election Results — 1974, 1979, 1983, 1987   *352*

TABLE 11.6   Electoral College — Minimal Winning Coalition   *355*

TABLE 11.7   Electoral College — Creating Majorities   *357*

TABLE 14.1   Basic Provisions of the Canada Act   *411*

TABLE 14.2 Passage of the Canada Act   *418-419*
TABLE 14.3 Process of the Meech Lake Accord   *440-441*
TABLE 15.1 Governmental and Political Characteristics of the
Canadian, British, and American Polities   *449-451*

Preface to the Third Edition

To the casual observer, the pace of Canadian politics might seem to be inexorably slow. However, to an author, the pace seems to resemble a downhill racer out of control. Even before the ink on the manuscript of one edition is dry, the revision process becomes necessary again. For example, here are a few of the major events which have occurred in Canadian politics since the second edition was published: in November, 1988 the Conservatives won their second majority victory; a free trade agreement with the United States was negotiated and implemented; a proposed constitutional amendment, the Meech Lake accord of 1987, became a focal point on the domestic political agenda; the Liberal party witnessed a resurgence in the provincial arena, especially in Manitoba and the Atlantic provinces; and the Liberal and New Democratic parties have selected new national leaders. At the same time, significant changes have also been evident in both the British and American polities.

Thus, the third edition of *The Canadian Polity* seeks to make the coverage of recent political events as current as possible. The basic structure of the second edition remains in place. Throughout, we have updated examples and have expanded the theoretical material. At the request of a number of users, more extensive recommended reading lists have been presented. Finally, cartoons and supplementary materials have also been employed in this edition. Quotations, tables, and cartoons have been included in each chapter to increase student interest, as well as to expand on and illustrate the material in the text.

While the number of specific changes are too numerous to list here, a few examples might be instructive. In Chapter 1, the concept of privatization is discussed in relation to the expansive nature of government. An extended discussion of ideology has been added in Chapter 2. The recent elections in Canada (1988), Britain (1987), and the United States (1988) are analyzed, as well as changes in the party systems of each country. The failed Meech Lake agreement is discussed in detail in Chapter 14, as well as recent Supreme Court decisions regarding the Canadian Charter of Rights and Freedoms. The defeat of the Robert Bork nomination to the American Supreme Court and the resurgence of the Labour Party in

British politics are discussed as well. In other words, a thorough updating of the text has taken place in this new edition.

The enthusiastic reception of the first two editions of *The Canadian Polity*, by both students and instructors, has been most gratifying. Many have taken the time and effort to offer suggestions for this third edition. While not all of their ideas have been incorporated, the author is certainly appreciative of the efforts of the book's "attentive public."

Preface for Students

Studying the politics of one's own country should be an exciting experience, for politics and government determine not only our present condition, but our future survival. To that end we have sought to provide an interesting examination of how the Canadian political system operates. We begin with an overview of the nature of government and politics (Part One), proceed to a consideration of basic political institutions (Part Two), investigate political processes and political behaviour (Part Three), and conclude with an assessment of the workings of the Canadian polity (Part Four). In considering such topics, we seek to introduce the student to three main areas of investigation: first, the nature of political analysis; second, the fundamentals of Canadian government; and third, the study of comparative government. These three goals are intertwined throughout the text and should be borne in mind by students as they read the various chapters.

Several suggestions concerning the use of this text may be helpful before proceeding. Each title page presents one or more quotations which express that chapter's main theme. Upon completion of each unit, the student should return to these opening ideas and think about them. Second, at the end of each chapter we have provided a list of recommended readings. These items include several of the most important classic works on each topic, along with more current publications. Except in a few cases, these works should be accessible in most university libraries and intellectually rewarding for the beginning student. Finally, a footnote style different from what you may be used to is employed throughout the text. Instead of footnote numbers with references at the bottom of the page or at the end of the chapter or book, relevant bibliographical information is included in the body of the text itself. The first item refers to the author's last name, the second to the year of publication of the work cited, and the third to the page number, if the reference is to a particular passage. This format does not break the reader's train of thought, but allows him or her to see immediately whose work is being quoted. Full reference information for each item cited is contained in the bibliography at the end of the book. For major historical works, the original date of publication is given in the text, with both the original and later edition dates included in the bibliography.

Since the text is written for undergraduate students, the author encourages you to write to him with your comments or suggestions for improvement. Please send your views to the Political Science Department, Saint Mary's University, Halifax, Nova Scotia, Canada, B3H 3C3.

Preface for Instructors

Many instructors approach the introductory course in political science with considerable apprehension. Too often, the initial politics course at the university level is seen as either a burden to be endured or an affliction to be avoided assiduously in the future. This reaction is, unfortunately, fairly typical: we are socialized in graduate school to be specialists in ever-narrowing subfields of increasing irrelevance. Not surprising, then, is the negative reaction to the task of giving a "general overview" of the discipline to beginning students.

This pattern, to put it bluntly, is a mistake. For one thing, it deprives the student of a chance to learn from those who should know the most about the discipline. Too often it is forgotten that probably half of all the students enrolled in political science courses across the country take only the beginning political science option. If we do not teach them an understanding of politics at that level, we never will. Avoidance of the introductory course is also a mistake from the instructor's perspective, for it relieves him or her of the responsibility to teach the most difficult of all courses. Contrary to a myth of the profession, we would contend that the easiest courses to teach are the advanced ones, for the quite simple reason that students will learn in spite of what we do. In the introductory course we have the opportunity to motivate people to learn about politics, at least in part, because of what we do. If we cannot communicate effectively with beginning university students, it is doubtful that we can do so with our colleagues either.

The downplaying of the introductory course is clearly evident in the available teaching materials — few, if any, works are designed with the beginning Canadian politics student in mind. The purpose of this book is to fill this gap by providing a readable and informative text that introduces students to both the Canadian and comparative politics areas. While the major emphasis is on an introduction to Canadian politics (approximately 60 percent of the material), included as well are detailed analyses of the politics of Britain and the United States and general concepts from the field of comparative politics (approximately 40 percent). Thus, the text has three basic goals: first, to serve as an introduction to the craft of political analysis; second, to provide an introduction to the study of Canadian government; and third, to offer students a look at the practice of comparing political systems. Part One introduces students to the nature of government (Chapter 1) and to the basic concepts and principles of political analysis (Chapter 2). Quite likely, students will find Chapter 2 the most difficult in the book. As a result, if it is to be successful, Chapter 2 may require particular attention from the instructor. Chapter 2 is significant because it lays the basis for the way the various political institutions and processes are analyzed in Parts Two and Three.

The basic institutions of Canadian government (constitution, executives, bureaucracy, legislatures, and judiciaries) are analyzed in Chapters 3 through 7. Having set the institutional context of government, we then proceed to an analysis of political processes and political behaviour in Part Three. Chapter 8 expands the context of politics by introducing the student to the concept of political culture. Chapter 9 investigates the nature of political parties and party systems. The electoral process is dealt with in the next three units: Chapter 10 looks at the nature of elections and political recruitment; Chapter 11 discusses the topic of electoral systems; and Chapter 12 considers how the individual learns to participate and does participate in the political process. Particular attention is given to the role of interest groups in Chapter 13.

Part Four of the text seeks to place the nature of Canadian government in sharper focus by analyzing how it works in practice (Chapter 14) and how it relates to the concept of classical democracy (Chapter 15). This serves as a basis for recommending some needed areas of political reform. Chapter 14 tries to connect the various topics by analyzing the content and passage of the 1982 Canada Act, including the failed Meech Lake accord of 1987.

Since each instructor probably has a particular way of structuring the introductory course, no order of chapters is likely to satisfy everyone. We have tried to make each chapter a self-contained unit, so that the instructor might rearrange the order in Parts Two and Three without seriously hampering the flow of analysis. Each chapter in Parts Two and Three begins with a brief introduction and consideration of basic concepts relating to the specific topic, applies these ideas to Canadian, British, and American polities, and ends with a look at the key areas for comparing how the various political institutions and processes operate. A point-form summary and list of recommended readings is also provided for Chapters 1 through 14. This chapter structure should allow the smooth incorporation of a discussion of any other countries of particular interest to an instructor through the use of lecture material. While aimed at the introductory level, this text may also be of use as required reading in second- and third-year Canadian and Comparative Government courses.

The ideological bias of the author is that of a liberal-democrat. A variety of approaches are utilized throughout the text, including historical, institutional, and behavioural perspectives.

Any suggestions or comments concerning this text would be most appreciated by the author, especially those that might be incorporated into future editions. Please send your views to the Political Science Department, Saint Mary's University, Halifax, Nova Scotia, Canada, B3H 3C3.

Acknowledgments

In writing this textbook, an author quickly realizes how much he depends on others. Over the years, numerous teachers, students, and researchers have contributed in their own way to *The Canadian Polity*. Their help is hereby gratefully acknowledged.

Others have also been essential in the development of the three editions of this work. Saint Mary's University aided in a number of ways, in particular, by granting a sabbatical leave in 1979–80, during which time this book began to take shape. For the first edition, Laurie Wheeler, political science secretary, managed to turn handwritten scrawls into a first-draft manuscript. The wizardry of Shirley Buckler and Sharon Whitefield on the word processor artfully transformed numerous revisions into a finished manuscript. For the second edition, Laurie Jonah typed the manuscript in its initial stages, while Cathy Lane handled the numerous revisions which produced a final product. Most of the work for the third edition was completed while on sabbatical leave during 1988–89. Once again, Cathy Lane handled the word processing task; to her much credit should be given. Several friends provided helpful comments and encouragement throughout the revision process for the third edition: particular thanks are owed to Peter Dale and Don Naulls. Finally, I also wish to thank the reviewers for their helpful and informed comments: J.E. Crimmins of Huron College, Peter McCormick of the University of Lethbridge, Henry Jacek of McMaster University, Agar Adamson of Acadia University, and Daniel Madar of Brock University.

Various individuals at Prentice-Hall have been essential to the completion of this project. Along with Prentice-Hall's then local representative, Don Blair, the late Frank Hintenberger signed the book in December of 1980. Cliff Newman and Marta Tomins have guided the manuscript throughout its first two editions. For the latest edition, particular thanks should be given to Pat Ferrier and his staff.

Finally, recognition must be given to my loving family, without whose cooperation this project would not have been possible. Somehow, my family managed to endure all three editions of this book — and to them it is, once again, lovingly dedicated.

PART ONE

The Nature of Government and Politics

The overall responsibility of power is to govern as reasonably as possible in the interest of the state and its citizens. A duty in that process is to keep well-informed, to heed information, to keep mind and judgment open and to resist the insidious spell of wooden-headedness. If the mind is open enough to perceive that a given policy is harming rather than serving self-interest, and self-confident enough to acknowledge it, and wise enough to reverse it, that is a summit in the art of government (Tuchman, 1984: 32).

Technology and civilization may be the necessary condition for human welfare; they are not a sufficient one. The missing element is the nature of the polity (Finer, 1983: 4).

To put it in simplest terms, politics defines what people want; government decides what they get. For democracy to work, government must respond to politics (Shogan, 1982: 5).

CHAPTER 1 The Comparative Study of Canadian Government

To compare is a natural way of thinking. Nothing is more natural than to study people, ideas, or institutions in relation to other people, ideas or institutions. We gain knowledge through reference (Dogan and Pelassy, 1984: 1).

The study of comparative politics, to borrow a phrase from Guys and Dolls, *is the "oldest established permanent floating crap game" in the social sciences. It moves freely across the boundaries of academic disciplines as well as nation-states. The pioneers of comparative politics, from Aristotle to Alexis de Tocqueville, were born too long ago to have had their thoughts confined by the narrow boundaries of a single academic discipline, or by a single national culture (Rose and Peters, 1978: xi).*

In the development of its political institutions Canada has been, placed as it is between the United States and Britain, more like the ham in the sandwich than the link between the two. Our political structure and processes are based on the examples of both other countries (Franks, 1983: 201).

CONSIDER FOR A MOMENT the following events from the past several decades of Canadian politics:

1. *October 1970*: Canada is shocked when the FLQ abducts and later releases British Trade Commissioner James Cross and then kidnaps and later murders Pierre Laporte, Quebec Minister of Labour, House Leader of the Quebec Government, and senior colleague of Premier Robert Bourassa. Apprehending an insurrection, the federal cabinet, at the request of the Montreal and Quebec governments, imposes the War Measures Act. For nearly two months the federal government exercises a vast arsenal of emergency powers and for an additional five months utilizes slightly less power under the Public Order Temporary Measures Act. The police forces conduct 5 000 raids and arrest 465 people, many in the middle of the night. Included in the roundup are mainly separatist sympathizers in Quebec, among them many academics and artists.

2. *November 15, 1976*: Nine years after resigning as provincial Liberal cabinet minister and eight years after the founding of the Parti Québécois, René Lévesque, in his third try for elective office as leader of the Parti Québécois, gathers 41 percent of the popular vote and 69 of the 110 seats in the Quebec National Assembly. For the first time in Canadian history, a major provincial government is controlled by an avowedly separatist political party. As a prelude to Quebec's possible secession from the century-old Canadian Confederation, the Parti Québécois promises a future referendum in Quebec on Lévesque's blueprint for "sovereignty-association."

3. *May 22, 1979*: Prime Minister Pierre Elliott Trudeau, Canada's leader for 11 years and survivor of three previous general elections, is defeated by Joe Clark, a result that leads the *Toronto Star* to proclaim, "Now Joe Who really is a somebody!" At age 39, Canada's youngest Prime Minister, Clark ends 16 years of Liberal government in Ottawa. Gaining only 36 percent of the popular vote (4 percent less than the defeated Liberals on a national basis) and 136 seats in the House of Commons (six short of a majority government), Clark, with minimal representation from Quebec, is faced with the task of forming Canada's fourth minority government in 17 years.

4. *December 13, 1979*: After only six months in office and two days after presenting its first budget, the new Tory government faces an NDP non-confidence motion in the House of Commons. With the small Social Credit caucus abstaining, and with the combined opposition of the Liberal and NDP caucuses, the Conservatives are defeated by a vote of 139 to 133. A dissolution of Parliament is granted by the Governor General on December 14, with the election writs issued for February 18, 1980. Canada's 32nd general election aborts the nine-month old minority Tory government and reestablishes a majority Liberal government under the resurrected tutelage of Pierre Trudeau. Joe Clark becomes Canada's youngest former prime minister.

5. *May 20, 1980*: The Parti Québécois, in an attempt to gain public support for negotiating sovereignty-association with Ottawa, holds its long-awaited referendum. After an extremely hard-fought, emotional, and at times bitter campaign, 60 percent of the Quebec electorate refuse to grant the Parti Québécois its desired mandate. The federal Liberal government, in an attempt to seize the political initiative, quickly begins another round of constitutional talks, with new constitutional proposals to be ready by September 1980. René Lévesque postpones calling a provincial election in Quebec and indicates his willingness to participate in the new series of constitutional deliberations.

6. *April 17, 1982*: After two years of intense political conflict between the federal and

provincial governments and 115 years after Confederation, Canada becomes, in all respects, an independent country. The proclamation of the 1982 Constitution Act by Queen Elizabeth II in Ottawa adds a Charter of Rights and a series of amending formulas to the existing Canadian Constitution.

7. *February 29, 1984*: On the night before, a solitary figure contemplates his future while wending his way along the streets of Ottawa through a winter storm. The next day Pierre Trudeau, Canadian Prime Minister for a decade-and-a-half, announces his intention of retiring from politics. (Given that 1984 is a leap year, critics assume that the date was chosen to prevent an annual celebration of the blessed event.) A leadership convention is called for June, at which John Turner defeats Jean Chrétien. With a strong lead in the polls (the first time the Liberals are in front in three years), Prime Minister Turner seeks his own mandate from the Canadian people.

8. *September 4, 1984*: The Conservative party of Canada, having replaced in June of 1983 its former leader Joe Clark with the relative unknown Brian Mulroney, sweeps to the largest party win in Canadian history. In an unprecedented electoral victory, the first Conservative majority government in 25 years, the Tories seize 211 out of 282 seats in the House of Commons. In full public view the Liberal party, quite arguably the most successful democratic political party in the Western World, commits political hari-kari. The Liberal caucus is reduced to 40, with the NDP barely trailing with 30 seats. With the Tory breakthrough in Quebec (58 of

75 seats compared to only 1 in 1980), a major realignment of the Canadian party system seems possible.

9. *April 30, 1987*: To the surprise of most Canadians, and probably to themselves as well, the First Ministers announce an initial, unanimous agreement on yet another "new" constitution for Canada. Primarily the result of trying to bring Quebec back into the Canadian constitutional family, since it was the only province that did not sign the 1982 Canada Act, the proposed Constitution Act of 1987 (popularly known as the Meech Lake accord) recognizes Quebec as a "distinct society." In addition, significant changes are proposed with respect to Supreme Court and Senate appointments, the federal spending power, the amending formula, and the future agenda of constitutional reform. The initial response to the Meech Lake accord is positive. However, as time goes on, doubts are raised, as provincial governments in Manitoba and New Brunswick — and later Newfoundland, demand changes.

10. *June 22, 1990*: After months of increasingly acrimonious political debate and negotiations among the First Ministers and general public, the Meech Lake accord dies when the Newfoundland legislature refuses to take a vote on the matter. French-English relations are seriously damaged — perhaps irreparably, as support for sovereignty-association grows in Quebec. Canada's constitutional future, once again, is thrown into doubt.

The above examples tend to belie the often-made charge that Canadian government and politics are uninteresting. One reason students have found Canadian politics less than exciting is that many introductory textbooks place a great, if not exclusive, emphasis on the analysis of political structures and institutions. Much time is spent on the "nuts and bolts" of governmental structure and organization (e.g., how many senators there are from each province,

> I listened to my heart and saw if there were any signs of my destiny in the sky, and there were none—there were just snowflakes (Pierre Elliott Trudeau, February 29, 1984).

their method of appointment, their length of tenure). Therefore, there is often a neglect of political processes (e.g., elections, federal-provincial relations).

A person attempting to understand the debates surrounding the various reform efforts in relation to the Canadian Constitution, for example, would quickly see the importance of both political structures and political processes. Before one could understand the significance of proposed constitutional changes, it would be necessary to have a knowledge of the components of the current constitutional system. An historical perspective on how the Canadian Constitution has evolved from 1867 to the present would provide additional insights into the need for various constitutional reform proposals. However, to know what the Constitution is and to comprehend the nature of the proposed changes would still leave much unsaid. An appreciation of the amendment process (i.e., how amendments are proposed and adopted) would also be crucial. As is so often the case in politics, these two factors of structure and process intermingle and influence each other. An understanding of Canadian politics requires knowledge and insight into both political institutions and political processes.

A second reason why students often seem bored by Canadian government is that our system is treated in relative isolation from other political systems. The injunction "to know ourselves" (Symons, 1978) should be a call for understanding, not parochialism. A fundamental assumption of the analysis in this book is that Canadian government and politics can be best understood and appreciated in a comparative context. The problems encountered by the Canadian system are not necessarily unique, and in most cases are not at all unique. Many countries face problems of regionalism, secessionist threats, minority governments, and constitutional change. Not only do comparisons with other countries teach us about other political systems, but they provide us with a basis for assessing the strengths and weaknesses, advantages and disadvantages of the Canadian political experiment.

The Nature of Government

In beginning our analysis of the Canadian **polity** or **political system**, we will first consider the nature of government. Much of what political science knows about the nature of government that is worth knowing can be summarized as follows: government is ubiquitous, multiple, expansive, necessary, and varied.

THE UBIQUITOUS NATURE OF GOVERNMENT

Government is ubiquitous in both geographical and practical terms. Territorially the world is divided among governmental units called nation-states (170 of them by 1990). All earthly domain is claimed by these nation-states — there is literally no place on earth that one can go to get away from governing authority. If people emigrate from one country to another, they do not rid themselves of government, but merely exchange one governing authority for another. Attempts to create utopias of one kind or another may seek to do away with government, but they do so on territory claimed by the government of a nation-state and are usually allowed to exist only as long as they present no immediate threat to existing political

The history of the West, from the time of Europe's fragmentation into sovereign states, shows us an almost uninterrupted advance in the growth of governmental power (de Jouvenel, 1962: 127).

> *Joseph Howe on the Nature of Government:*
> It is the first duty of a government to take
> the front rank in every noble enterprise; to
> be in advance of the social, political, and
> industrial energies, which they have under-
> taken to lead (Howe, quoted in Beck,
> 1964: 124).

institutions. Even the possible escape to outer space appears to be unlikely without the monetary and technological support of an existing government.

Government is also ubiquitous in practical terms: little we do in life is free from government control and regulation. The extent of governmental regulation in Canada was summarized by then Justice Minister Jacques Flynn in August 1979, in a speech to the Canadian Bar Association, when he pointed out that a listing of federal regulations came to over 15 000 pages. In addition, the Law Reform Commission of Canada has found that federal laws have created 30 000 offences, while provincial laws have added another 20 000. Similarly, in Ontario during the period 1984–1988, over 3800 new regulations were proclaimed, producing over 13 000 pages of regulatory detail (McMonagle, 1988). Given these numbers, it is little wonder that most aspects of our lives are touched by governmental authority. The taxes we pay, the conditions of our workplaces, the nature of the products we buy, our medical treatment, the procedures of birth, marriage, and death are all regulated by government. On a larger scale, governments decide questions of war, peace, and environmental protection, the consequences of which determine whether we live or die, as individuals and as a planet.

Although government is ubiquitous, it is difficult to define. This difficulty stems from the fact that government is a summary concept that organizes our perception of reality: we usually see the manifestations or results of government (e.g., taxes, laws), not government itself. One can physically see governmental buildings (such as the Parliament building in Ottawa), governmental personnel (cabinet officers, civil servants such as deputy ministers), and governmental processes (passage of a piece of legislation through Parliament, a federal-provincial First Ministers' Conference). Yet there is no single place where one can go to see the government in total: government resides in many places. However, the varied perceptions of governing activity are likely to contain a common theme: we propose to define this common theme of **government** *as the institutional organization of political power within a given territory*.

THE MULTIPLE NATURE OF GOVERNMENT

A second characteristic of government is that it is multiple: each citizen is subject to a number of governments and governmental units. A common view of the uninformed is to perceive government as a cohesive organization, united in its goals, coherent in its programs, and consistent in the implementation of its policies. It is typical in political analysis to find phrases such as "the government decided." However, political reality suggests an alternative view: government is a plural, rather than a singular phenomenon. For example, all people in Canada are subject to at least two levels of government: the federal government in Ottawa and the government of the province in which they reside. Both levels have the power to tax and to otherwise regulate our behaviour. All citizens also confront local governments. Some citizens in the major metropolitan areas are faced with an additional layer of government and others are subject to various regional governmental units. Both metropolitan and regional governments interpose an additional layer of government between the local and provincial units of organization. An extreme example of the multiplicity of governments can be found in the array of governing authorities that control our nation's capital (Stevens, November 30, 1979). At least eight governments (the federal government in Ottawa, the Ontario provincial government, the National Capital Commission, the regional municipality of Ottawa-Carleton, the City of Ottawa, and the municipal, regional, and provincial administrations that govern Hull in Quebec) all vie for control of our nation's capital.

The complexity of government is further enhanced if we also remember that each governmental level (federal, provincial) is composed of numerous governmental units. Governmental units refer to such institutions and political structures as the executive, legislative, and judicial branches of government, as well as to various government departments and agencies. For example, there is a federal cabinet as well as 10 provincial cabinets, and a national Parliament as well as 10 legislative assemblies at the provincial level. One study of local government in the late 1960s in Metropolitan Toronto discovered a total of 101 governmental units (del Guidice and Zachs, 1976). The multiplication of governmental units within each governmental level has developed to such an extent that it would be difficult to make an accurate count of them. Thus, it is not surprising to find that one writer has insisted that "governments are like bees, birds, fish, cattle, or wolves; they come in swarms, flocks, schools, herds, or packs, but never alone" (Schattschneider, 1969: 12).

The number of governments imposed on the citizen by the state varies among political systems. In unitary political structures, such as Britain and France, the central government in the national capital governs, while local governmental structures are used primarily as a means for administering policies determined by that central government. In contrast, Canada, as a federal political structure, interposes an intermediate level of government (i.e., the provincial level) between the central government and the citizen, while local government is also more independent in Canada than it is in either Britain or France. Thus, the Canadian citizen deals with more governments than do citizens in unitary political systems.

The multiplication of governments has proceeded the furthest in the United States. As a federal political system, the United States has 50 state governments (compared to 10 provincial governments in Canada), in addition to the national government in Washington. However, it is at the local level where the multiplication of government occurs most dramatically: if one counts all units with the power to tax (federal, state, and local governments, as well as school districts and special districts), there are today nearly 80 000 governmental units in the United States, a reduction from the 155 000 such units that existed in the early 1940s.

Recognizing the multiplicity of governments helps us to understand how governments actually operate. If governments are multiple, then it stands to reason that each governmental level or unit may have different goals or purposes. As a result, governmental actions often appear contradictory or lacking in consistency for the rather simple reason that they are contradictory and inconsistent. Understanding the multiplicity of governing authorities allows us to see why such a pattern develops: different government levels and units with varying goals rarely act with unanimity in the making of public policy. For example, the Canadian federal political system, which divides political authority between a central government and various provincial governments, ensures conflict over major policy decisions. Setting the price of oil in Canada provides an illustration of this point: the federal government's usual goals (to achieve a rough equality of energy costs for all Canadians and to gain additional tax revenues for Ottawa) are at odds with the government of Alberta's typical goals (to move Canadian domestic oil prices to the world price for oil when the world price is high and to build up the Alberta Heritage

Trust Fund as a means of compensating future generations of Albertans when the province's natural resources are depleted).

The same type of conflict and contradictory policy occurs between governmental units within the same level of government. For example, within the federal government, one department, Health and Welfare, spends time and money trying to convince us of the harmful effects of alcohol, while other departments rely on the tax money raised by the sale of liquor to support their programs. The height of absurdity is probably reached in the Department of Consumer and Corporate Affairs: within a single department, two competing and often contradictory interests are joined in an uneasy marriage of convenience. Only through recognizing the multiplicity of governmental levels and units, and the political conflict that results from their contradictory policy objectives, can we understand the nature of the political process.

THE EXPANSIVE NATURE OF GOVERNMENT

A third characteristic of government is that it is expansive: the functions, costs, and personnel of government are constantly growing. Although conservatives argue for a slower expansion of government than do their opponents, they do not believe in, nor do they implement in office, an actual reduction in the absolute size of government.

> Government, it seems safe to say, is one thing that has been growing rapidly in the West. Wherever governments were once small they have become

big, and wherever they were big they have become bigger. Nothing is so rare as a shrinking government (Nutter, 1978: 1).

For example, during Ronald Reagan's terms of office (1981–1989), the number of government departments increased, while the size of the federal budget proposed for fiscal year 1990 ballooned to $1.06 trillion, with an expected deficit of $92.5 billion. For the fiscal year 1991, the proposed American budget reached $1.2 trillion. In contrast, in January of 1989 in Britain, a rather rare event occurred: for the first time in 300 years, the Bank of England retired (£500-million) part of the country's national debt.

Reasons for governmental growth

The growth of government in the 20th century, particularly evident in the rise of government expenditures in the decades since the Second World War, has occurred for a number of reasons. Perhaps most importantly in democratic political systems, people have simply demanded that their governments provide them with a greater range of benefits and services (e.g., medical care, pensions, unemployment insurance, consumer protection). Politicians and political parties have responded to these demands, which they have themselves helped to create, as a means of winning political power. Politicians prefer to run on platforms that offer more, not less to the average voter: the promise of mortgage interest deductibility by the federal Conservatives in the 1979 campaign in Canada exemplifies this point. Likewise, the defeat on December 13, 1979 of the Clark budget and his party's ensuing loss in the February 18, 1980 election can also be viewed in this light. The Conservative budget sought to slow the expansion of government expenditures and to substantially raise energy costs as a means of both forcing a conservation of scarce natural resources and of increasing government revenues. As then Finance Minister John Crosbie

> We are not promising things for everybody, and we are not seeing great visions. Government is no Santa Claus (Pierre Elliott Trudeau, 1968).

Source: Johnny Hart, *The Chronicle-Herald*, February 2, 1985. By permission of Johnny Hart and NAS, Inc.

phrased it, Canadians were being asked to bear "short-term pain for long-term gain." The short-term pain was borne, however, by the Conservatives rather than by the Canadian electorate. The Liberals returned to power after only nine months in opposition by promising not to impose the Tories' 18-cent-a-gallon excise tax on gasoline and by suggesting that their energy cost increases would be based on a "blended, Canadian-made price," far below those predicted by the Conservatives.

If a political party does advocate a withdrawal or tightening of government services, it does so in relation to those segments of the electorate that would not vote for the party anyway. The Conservative party's proposals in the 1979 campaign to make drastic cuts in the size of the Ottawa bureaucracy and to further tighten the eligibility rules for Canada's unemployment insurance program probably cost the party few votes, since the two groups affected by these changes were not likely supporters of the Conservatives anyway. Similarly, under then leader David Lewis, the 1972 NDP campaign theme of "corporate welfare bums" (i.e., the need to cut back government support for business) lost

the party little support, since it traditionally receives few votes from the corporate sector. These examples seem to confirm the view that in democracies "the bias in the electoral cycle favours increased spending. Rightly or wrongly, politicians consistently calculate that voters want more, and so, they promise more" (Rose and Peters, 1978: 112–113). Only an unwise politician campaigns on a platform to reduce government services or to raise taxes, or both. For example, in the 1984 American presidential election, Democratic party nominee Walter Mondale promised that "taxes must rise" in order to pay for the deficit. The ensuing and disastrous Democratic defeat could be attributed, at least in part, to his promise to raise taxes. The pattern was repeated in the 1988 presidential contest, as the Republican nominee, George Bush, promised not to raise taxes, if elected: "Read my lips—no new taxes!"

A second important cause for the expansion of government is simply increased population, also a significant factor in the initial development of government in society: "Governments were instituted among men not because men are bad but because there are too many of them"

Total Cost to Consumer—
$1.76 + $2.03 + $0.45 + $4.69 + $1.07
= $10.00

Provincial Sales Tax — $1.07

Liquor Control Board of Ontario Mark-up — $4.69

Federal Sales Tax — $0.45

Federal Excise Tax — $2.03

$4.24

Distiller Receives — $1.76

Source: Association of Canadian Distillers. Reprinted from Sally Pipes and Michael Walker (1984) *Tax Facts 4,* fourth edition, p. 12. By permission, The Fraser Institute, Vancouver.

(Schattschneider, 1969: 119). Government will cost more in absolute terms if the number of people governed increases: providing government for 27 million Canadians in the early 1990s will require larger expenditures than providing services for only 10 million people, as there were in 1930. More significant than their numbers is the age distribution of this increasing population. The baby boom of the postwar years meant that government expenditures on family allowances increased dramatically. Likewise, as the baby boom generation moved through the school system, governments were required to provide for the rapid expansion of educational facilities. When this generation reaches retirement age in the early 21st century, it will create

additional government expenditures on such items as old age pensions, medical care, and housing. Moreover, because people now live longer than in the past, governments are required to provide services to each individual for a greater number of years.

A third reason for governmental growth is that society itself, through such developments as urbanization and industrialization, has become more complex, necessitating a corresponding development of government services and regulations. The invention of the automobile at the beginning of the 20th century is one example of why government has expanded. With this new form of transportation, government has become involved in the building of highways and their maintenance (the cost of snow removal alone in Canada runs into millions of dollars each year); with regulations concerning the proper use of highways (speed limits, weight limits, traffic signals); with the regulation of the building of automobiles (including safety features, emission controls) and at times direct financial support for the automotive industry (aid to a nearly bankrupt Chrysler Corporation in 1980); and with the development of consumer protection (rust prevention, safety checks, licensing, seat-belt legislation, mandatory insurance requirements). In return, governments receive a considerable amount of tax revenue from the automotive industry through such mechanisms as a sales tax on the purchase of new cars, taxes on the sale of gasoline, and various required fees such as the issuance of individual drivers' licences.

Thus, governments have been drawn into new policy areas as a result of the nature of

In combating winter, Canadian governments utilize over 150 000 metric tonnes of salt on the roads each year. The annual cost, in terms of damage to roads and cars, was $240-million for the winter of 1988–1989.

modern society. Governments in earlier times did not have to deal with such problems as environmental protection (e.g., clean air and water), the regulation of air travel, new social diseases (AIDS) and the production, control, and sale of atomic power. Similarly, governments have become involved in such concerns as garbage. Major metropolitan areas in Canada have passed by-laws respecting the collection and disposal of solid wastes that specify in detail the amount and type of garbage a householder may leave for pickup, the time of day for placement and collection of garbage, the number of bags that can be disposed of at any one time, the type of containers that may be used, and the weights allowed for any single item of garbage. It is this area of regulation that "has emerged in recent years to rival taxing and spending as a primary means by which governments seek to influence, direct and control social and economic behaviour" (Schultz, 1984: 434).

A fourth reason for government expansion relates not to developments in society, but to the nature of bureaucratic institutions. For personal and organizational reasons, bureaucrats seek to increase their staffs, budgets, and functions.

> Internal influences and patterns of behaviour characteristic of bureaucratic organizations tend to promote a constant increase in the scope of activities undertaken by component agencies and, in doing so, expand the possibilities of greater monetary and non-monetary rewards for the bureaucrats themselves (Butler and Macnaughton, 1984: 19).

> The expansive nature of Canadian government can be seen in the spending to promote and support Canadian culture. By the late 1980s, all three levels of government were spending over $1-billion per year in support of the arts. The cost of the CBC alone would add another $1 billion to this total.

THE EXPANSIVE NATURE OF GOVERNMENT: BRITISH-STYLE

TAXPAYER REVOLT, ENGLISH STYLE

From How to Get Money from the GLC and Other Left-Wing Authorities, *a publication of Aims of Industry, a London group that was critical of the way taxes were spent in that city. According to the group, the following grants were made to "voluntary bodies" by the Greater London Council, the Labour-controlled authority that governed the city, from April 1983 to January 1984. The GLC was abolished in 1986.*

Organization	Amount £
Babies Against the Bomb	1,600
English Collective of Prostitutes	400
Camden Policing the Police	29,750
World Disarmament Campaign	3,000
Southall Black Sisters	25,338
Rastafarian Advisory Center	77,835
Marx Memorial Library	9,060
Chile Democratico	6,902
Liberation Movement for Colonial Freedom	9,170
London Gay Teenage Group	14,301
Public Accountability for Community Enlightenment	41,802
Abyssinian Society	16,508
See Red Women's Workshop	10,823
Gay Bereavement Project	375
Gay London Police Monitoring Project	17,616
Campaign to Curb Police Powers	8,637
Spare Rib	34,656

Source: Harper's Magazine (July, 1984), Volume 269, Number 1610, p. 28. By permission.

Once a program or agency is established, it usually expands (Wildavsky, 1984). Bureaucratic success is often measured in terms of budget appropriations. Those organizations that gain more one year are in a better position to acquire even greater rewards the following year. More government today leads inexorably

> While many political systems in the past must have starved to death for lack of revenue, there is also ample evidence of the adaptability and creativity of rulers in the face of new economic constraints. As one source of income ran dry, others were soon explored (Tarschys, 1988: 20).

to even more government tomorrow. This organizational explanation zeros "in on the motivational structure of the governmental bureaucracy as the primary source" for the expansive nature of government (Buchanan, 1977: 18).

The expansion of governmental activity in the 20th century is a reflection, then, of four primary causes: first, there are more people for which governments must provide basic services; second, citizens, particularly in democratic systems, have demanded more from government; third, the complexity of modern society has drawn government into an ever-increasing array of new policy areas; and fourth, once established, bureaucratic institutions have a tendency for growth. The result has been a tremendous expansion in the scope of governmental activity: governments today perform many functions that in the past have not concerned governing authorities. While there are some obvious differences between Western nations, it is generally true to say that in previous centuries government was perceived by most people, the public as well as leaders, as playing a limited role within a restricted political sphere. Today, government plays an expanding role within an expanded political sphere.

The growth of governmental activity is a trend as applicable to Canada as to other Western nations (Chandler and Chandler, 1979: 9–10). The data reveal a dramatic increase in total government expenditures and revenues during the last 70 years, especially noticeable in the past several decades. For

FIGURE 1.2 NATIONAL GOVERNMENT EXPENDITURES IN CANADA 1984–1985

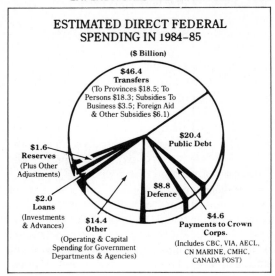

Source: Government of Canada Estimates 1984–85

example, between 1926 and 1950, total government expenditures, as a percentage of the Gross National Product, increased by only 6 percent (from 16 to 22 percent), but in the quarter-century between 1950 and 1976, they nearly doubled (from 22 to 42 percent). While government spent $4 billion in 1950, by 1976 all Canadian governments were spending nearly $55 billion or 51 percent of the country's National Income (Nutter, 1978: 36–37, 60–61). Indicative of this pattern of government expansion is the fact that total federal government expenditures in 1968, when Pierre Trudeau first became Prime Minister, were less than the federal government's deficit for the year he first left office a decade later in 1979. Estimates tabled in the House of Commons (February 1982) projected total federal government spending to be more than $76 billion in 1982–83. By the time the Liberal government's estimates for the 1984–85 fiscal year were given in February of 1984, the budget total had reached $98.2 billion, up from $88.9 billion in the previous year.

Growth of Canada's National Debt	
Period	*Amount ($ billion)*
1867–1981	$ 86
1981–1985	$114
1985–1989	$122
Total Debt	$322

Canadian Federal Government: Total Net Expenditures 1987–1988	
	($ Billion)
Agriculture	3.4
Communications	1.7
Consumer and Corporate Affairs	.6
Employment and Immigration	4.8
Energy, Mines and Resources	1.3
Environment	.8
External Affairs	3.2
Finance	38.1
Fisheries and Oceans	.6
Indian Affairs and Northern Development	2.8
Justice	.6
Labor	.2
National Defence	10.6
National Health and Welfare	29.0
National Revenue	1.3
Parliament	.2
Public Works	2.9
Regional Industrial Expansion	1.4
Science and Technology	.8
Secretary of State	3.4
Solicitor-General	1.9
Supply and Services	.8
Transport	4.8
Treasury Board	.4
Veterans Affairs	1.6
TOTAL	$115

In presenting its estimates for the fiscal year 1986–87, the Conservative government of Brian Mulroney projected a spending level of $106.5 billion. At the same time Canada's national debt would rise to $226 billion, with the result that each person in Canada would pay $999 in 1985–86 just to service that debt. By the 1989–90 fiscal year, the federal government's spending had risen to $142.9-billion, with the national debt standing at $320-billion. For the fiscal year ending in March 1991, the spending estimates announced in February 1990 called for expenditures of $147.6-billion by the federal government.

If more evidence is needed to support the claim about the expansive nature of government, then the burden of taxation would surely provide it. For example, by 1983, the average Canadian family was paying 51 percent of the family's total cash income in all kinds of taxes (Pipes and Walker, 1984: 36). In other words, the typical taxpayer works from January until Canada Day in order to pay for government largesse.

Although they are dramatic, the above figures underestimate the extent of government expansion in Canada: many actual costs of government are not included in government budgets. For example, since tax expenditures do not involve a direct outlay of public funds, they are not included as a government expenditure in Canada. **Tax expenditures** refer to the various deductions allowed by the government before arriving at a person's or corporation's taxable income: such items as the personal and married exemptions, registered retirement savings plan contributions, and the former employment expense deduction. A study by the federal finance department discovered 190 such tax exemptions, write-offs, and deductions in effect for the 1979 tax year. These tax expenditures amounted to $32 billion in "lost" revenue for the federal government. The difference between a budget expenditure and a tax expenditure sometimes helps to shape, as well as to explain, government policy. The move by the federal Liberal government in 1979 to shift from a focus on family allowances (a budget expenditure) to a child tax credit scheme (a tax expenditure) can be seen in this light: on paper the federal

Payment offered in 1988 by the provincial government of Quebec to families for their first two children: $500 each. For any additional children: $3000 each. The May 1989 budget proposals increased the amount for third and subsequent children to $4500, which was further augmented to $6000 in the April 1990 provincial budget.

government appears to be restraining its level of spending, while in fact it is spending more.

The pattern of government expansion seen for Canada is also evident in other Western nations. A study of 16 Western democracies over a 25-year period (1950–74) found a clear increase in the total amount of governmental expenditures (Nutter, 1978: 1–18). Government expenditures rose from a third of National Income in the early 1950s to more than one-half of a country's National Income by the early 1970s. More significant is the finding that the major cause of government expansion was domestic spending requirements (e.g., welfare programs, medical care) rather than external ones (e.g., defence and foreign affairs). This conclusion is consistent with our earlier discussion of why government has expanded: internal domestic pressures, rather than external international factors, are the primary cause of the extensive nature of government in modern society. These basic patterns are true for Canada, Great Britain, and the United States.

The expansive nature of government is perhaps best illustrated by the actions governments take to control their own size: more government is created in order to reduce the size of the present government. For example, in its attempt to convince the Canadian public that it seriously wanted to slow government's growth, the Trudeau administration in the late 1970s created the Office of Paperwork Burden. The task of this new bureaucracy was to reduce the duplication of forms and information requests that citizens and businesses were required to submit to various governmental authorities. A somewhat analogous process was set up in 1984 by the Mulroney government. A special committee of Cabinet, under Deputy Prime Minister Erik Nielsen, was created to search for waste and duplication in all government departments. The committee quickly generated a list of 1000 separate programs to be reviewed. When the Task Force on Program Review completed its work in March of 1986, it produced a 21-volume report which had cost the taxpayer $3.7-million. In a similar move in Britain (June 1985), Prime Minister Margaret Thatcher issued a four-volume Green Paper which suggested possible ways to check the growth of one of the world's most expensive social security systems. Thus, even the attempt to catalogue the extent of government expansion simply produces more government.

Even more revealing is the dramatic growth in the expenditures of the auditor general. The job of the auditor general is to examine or post-audit all government expenditures as one means of helping to keep government spending in check. The cost of this service rose from $4 million in the fiscal year 1972–73 to $26 million in 1978–79; a six-fold increase in just six years. By the time of the auditor general's report in late 1985, the cost of his office had soared to 43 million dollars. By the end of 1988, the cost had risen to over $48 million, with the auditor general's office employing more than 600 full-time members, plus many consultants hired on a contractual basis. Perhaps even more significant were some questionable expenditures that appeared in the accounts of the auditor general. For example, about $150 000 of taxpayers' money was used to produce six videos about the auditor general's office, indicating that self-promotion can be an expensive undertaking.

Similarly revealing was the expansion of the size of the first cabinet appointed by Prime Minister Mulroney in 1984. This cabinet of 40 members, the largest in Canadian history, was justified, in part, by the need to exert greater executive control over the bureaucracy. Moreover, the cost of the budget for ministers' staffs nearly doubled. As in other countries, the attempts in Canada to control government's size have simply produced more government.

In an attempt to control, or at least slow, the rate of government expansion, a worldwide trend of the 1980s was that of **privatization**. This new pattern, especially apparent in liberal democracies controlled by conservative leaders (Reagan, Thatcher, Mulroney), can be defined as "the deliberate effort by governments to increase reliance on market mechanisms as a means of pursuing public goals" (Henig, Hamnett and Feigenbaum, 1988: 442). In other words, the size of the state or government is to be curtailed by having government withdraw from areas that could now be handled (at least in the government's view) by private enterprise. Privatization could include a reduction in the extent of government regulation of the market, a contraction of support for existing government services, or an actual selling off of public enterprise to the private sector.

Although privatization was not a major plank in the Tory election platform in 1979, Margaret Thatcher put the policy forward, somewhat tentatively, after the election, showing the way for other countries in the 1980s. The first step in such a process is to sell profitable public enterprises to private industry, before trying to rid government of less financially stable ventures. For example, Thatcher first sold part of the government's shares in British Petroleum, receiving one-quarter billion pounds for the

> One of the "megatrends" in governance in the developed democracies since the mid-1970s is the attempt to restrain or cut back public sector spending or staffing. This is something embraced with enthusiasm by right-of-center governments and as a regrettable short term necessity by left-wing governments (Hood et al., 1988: 243).

> The business of government is to keep the government out of business—that is, unless business needs government aid (Will Rogers).

Treasury in 1979–1980. In 1987 alone, the Tories sold assets of 4.25-billion pounds.

The effect of Thatcher's privatization program on public enterprise in the United Kingdom has been dramatic: "Until 1979, the United Kingdom possessed one of the largest public enterprise sectors in Europe. By the end of three terms of Thatcher government (i.e., 1992), it is scheduled to be extinct" (Heald, 1988: 36). However, the total size of the British government has not been reduced: in real terms, public expenditure was 17 percent higher in 1986 than in 1979.

In the United States, where the extent of public enterprise was much smaller than in Britain, Ronald Reagan, in his two terms of office, focused on deregulation, less enforcement of the rules that remained, and, finally, the selling off of public enterprise. For example, the transportation industry was deregulated, the Environmental Protection Agency (EPA) barely enforced its pollution regulations against key industries, and such items as some federally owned lands were sold to private interests. On the whole, privatization has not been as important an issue in the United States as it has been in Britain.

Canadian governments initially proceeded rather cautiously on the issue of privatization, with the trend really gathering speed from 1984 onward. Between 1984–1989, federal and provincial governments sold Crown corporations and various assets worth $4.6-billion. For example, the federal government sold such manufacturing firms as de Havilland Aircraft of Canada and Canadair Limited, as well as an initial 45 per cent share of Air Canada (later, all shares were sold). In total, the federal government sold

$2.1-billion in assets. Several provincial governments also became heavily involved in privatizing public assets between 1984–1989: Quebec ($827-million), Saskatchewan ($430-million), and British Columbia ($1.1-billion). However, while the privatization trend will likely continue in the next few years, as in Britain, it has not reduced the size of government, but only slowed its rate of expansion.

THE NECESSARY NATURE OF GOVERNMENT

The fact that government is ubiquitous, multiple, and expansive creates the impression that government is also necessary: governments exist because of the functions they perform, that is, because of what they do for society.

Governments carry out many different tasks or jobs; that is, they have many consequences for and effects on society. Governments are required as the institutional means for controlling and regulating conflict within society. Any society is composed of many individuals, groups, classes, parties, interest groups, and regions, each of which typically desires a competitive advantage over the others. In Canada, with 27 million people, 10 provinces, many regions, and at least several social classes, to name only a few of the more obvious divisions in Canadian society, some mechanism is required to ensure social order. Government is just such a structure: it is a "central function of political processes to control conflict in organized society" (Pirages, 1976: 5).

Conflict develops in society primarily because of one fundamental fact of life: scarcity. Whether it is scarcity of wealth (gold, money, standard of living), natural resources (oil, natural gas, food), or status, the result is the same: conflict over who will control and benefit from the limited but highly valued goods and services. Given the scarcity of resources and the ensuing conflict over their distribution, government becomes the means for resolving these conflicts by certain agreed-upon rules of the political process. Political systems attempt to channel and transform conflict (including violence, coercion, and force) into peaceful competitive pursuits. For example, in liberal-democratic political systems, election campaigns between competing political parties are one way of arriving at decisions about the goals and purposes of the government. Elections determine which party will control the government, and thus, as a consequence, who will decide the allocation of scarce resources. Government budgets, for example, specify which groups, regions, or individuals receive the benefits of government, and which sectors of society bear the costs of these allocative decisions.

A second cause of social conflict is diversity. Linguistic, ethnic, economic, regional, and religious differences may all become linked to political concerns. In Canada, such sociopolitical cleavages have an important impact on the structure, operation, and future of the political system. Likewise, differences in values, that is, what people want and expect from government, may lead to conflict. In liberal-democratic political systems, governments seek to harmonize these divergent interests, not to eliminate them. Moreover, in most political systems, these two causes of conflict reinforce each other. For example, minority groups based on religious, regional, or ethnic differences are usually the same groups that receive the least in terms of the society's allocation of scarce

---

Edmund Burke (1790) on Government:
Government is a contrivance of human wisdom to provide for human wants.

The Golden Rule of Politics: He who has the gold, rules (Sabato, 1985: xii).

resources. The combination of scarcity and diversity produces difficult challenges to any polity. In Canada, it is just such a pattern that continually challenges the wisdom of our leaders, if not the very existence of our political system.

In viewing government as the institutional means for the settlement of conflict resulting from both scarcity and diversity, we have emphasized the negative side of government: its role in mediating, reducing, and avoiding conflict. However, government can also be creative, or at least attempt to be. Government's second major function is positive in the sense of being purposive, of wanting to achieve certain desired goals. For example, Pierre Trudeau's promise of a Just Society in the 1968 federal election, although it turned out to be just another example of campaign rhetoric, illustrates that politicians may often have goals or objectives other than simply winning power and maintaining themselves in office. Likewise, the Conservatives' 1979 election promise of mortgage interest deductibility could be seen, in its most favourable light, as an attempt to use government to achieve a desired end: namely, to encourage home ownership and family life in Canada. In the 1984 campaign, Conservative leader Brian Mulroney's promise of "jobs, jobs, jobs" was an obvious attempt to use the political process to promote a desired economic goal (i.e., employment). And finally, Liberal leader John Turner's crusade against free trade in the 1988 election, what he called the "fight of my life," was, from his point of view, a way of preserving Canada's political and cultural independence.

Governments seek to be creative mechanisms when they promote our health and welfare (e.g., medical care, dental care, consumer and environmental protection); when they attempt to alleviate the negative economic results of a capitalistic system (e.g., unemployment insurance, manpower retraining programs, disability and pension plans); when they

> However much the Canadian taxpayer may favour a policy of strict economy in government in the abstract, he likes nothing so little as its application (Sir Joseph Pope, 1894, quoted in Kirby, 1985: 6).

promote widespread educational opportunity through financial aid to education and vocational training programs; and when they seek to develop a sense of national unity (e.g., the adoption of "O Canada" as the official national anthem in time for the 1980 Dominion Day celebration).

The utilization of government as both a regulator of conflict and creator of values helps to explain the previously cited characteristics of government. The ubiquitous and multiple nature of government stems, in part, from its attempt to regulate an ever-increasing number of policy areas in an ever-expanding political sphere. The use of government as a creative instrument is directly linked to the expansive nature of government. If more and more individuals and groups seek to use government to achieve an increasing range of goals and purposes, then the size, cost, and scope of government is bound to grow. Finally, we should realize that the use of government as a creative mechanism leads to political conflict. Given the value differences among individuals, groups, or regions, it is not surprising that many political battles concern the goals and future direction of public policy.

THE VARIED NATURE OF GOVERNMENT

To utilize government in both its regulative and creative capacities, numerous types of governmental structures have been devised; in other words, government is varied. In some ways, of course, each government is unique: no two governments are identical in all respects. However, it would be an impossible task to describe in detail the historical and present array of governments if we assumed the absolute uniqueness of each political system. Instead, one of the significant tasks of political science and comparative political analysis is to look for patterns of similarities and differences among political systems so that various typologies or classifications of governments can be developed.

Classifying governments

Although political science has produced a prolific number of classifications, we should keep in mind that there is no right or wrong way of classifying governmental types. Classifications should be developed and used with a specific goal in mind, which thus allows for the selection of the appropriate criteria on which the typology is to be constructed. Since we are primarily concerned with comparing the political systems of Canada, the United States, and Britain, we have chosen for consideration several typologies that highlight their similarities and differences. In order to show the Canadian, American, and British pattern within the world context, we begin with a general classification of governments. The first typology emphasizes the similarities among the Canadian, American, and British forms of government. The second and third typologies to be discussed, namely the distinctions between federal or unitary and presidential or parliamentary forms of government, focus on the differences in governmental structure among these three liberal-democratic political systems.

Governmental types

After surveying the historical development of governmental types, British political scientist Bernard Crick (1973: 69–73) concluded that three basic forms could be identified: autocratic, republican, and totalitarian.

Autocracy . . . is the form of government which attempts to solve the basic problem of the adjustment of order to diversity by the authoritative enforcement of one of the diverse interests (whether seen as material or moral — almost always, in fact, both) as an officially sponsored and static ideology.

Republican government . . . is the attempt to solve the basic problem of the adjustment to diversity by conciliating different interests by letting them share in government or in the competitive choosing of the government.

Totalitarian government . . . is the attempt to solve the basic problem of the adjustment of order to diversity by creating a completely new society such that conflict would no longer arise: it attempts to do this by means of guidance and enforcement of a revolutionary ideology which claims to be scientific, thus comprehensive and necessary, both for knowledge and allegiance.

The advantage of Crick's classification is that the form of government (i.e., autocratic, republican, or totalitarian) is related to the functions of government (i.e., how government performs its regulative and creative tasks in reconciling diversity with political order). An autocratic system imposes one divergent interest over all others; a republican system conciliates competing interests; and a totalitarian system creates a new political society in which competing interests have been eliminated. Examples of autocratic governments would include the

---

Indeed, it is one of the attractions of a democratic society that it gives a place to the natural human emotion of critical resentment by the ruled of any pretension to infallibility in the rulers (Brogan, 1956: 138).

When communism destroys democracy, it does so because that is its intent. And when it fails to create democracy, that is because it is not its nature to do so (Revel, 1978: 54).

Jazz and Politics in Prague: In Czechoslovakia in March of 1987, five leaders of the Jazz Section, a cultural group that promotes jazz and art, were convicted of illegal economic activities (jazz concerts) and sentenced to prison terms of between 10 and 16 months.

monarchies in Europe through the 18th century, Czarist Russia, and Iran under both the Pahlavi dynasty and the Ayatollah Khomeini; republican governments would include the current liberal-democratic systems of Europe and North America, along with Israel and Japan; and totalitarian governments would be exemplified by Nazi Germany and Soviet Russia under Stalin and his successors through the early 1980s.

In addition to handling conflict and diversity by different means, these three basic forms of government also diverge on a number of more specific criteria. An autocratic government is characterized by an agrarian economy, a self-perpetuating elite group, a highly stratified social structure, an official doctrine typically based on religion, and a political system from which the ordinary citizen is normally excluded. A totalitarian government is characterized by an industrializing and planned economy, an elite group based on a single ideology, a social structure which in theory is based on equality but in practice is highly stratified around a sole political party, a revolutionary ideology, and a political structure based on mass participation but not mass control. Finally, a republican system centres on a capitalistic or market economy, an elite which is relatively open to new participants, a stratification system based on a large middle class, a mix of ideologies, and a political system based on competitive parties and elections.

Although the term republican has been utilized for several centuries within the field of comparative politics, in recent times the concept of liberal-democracy has become more

commonly used. In order to avoid any possible confusion, we will employ the term liberal-democracy — or just simply democracy — to refer to the type of government classified as republican by Crick. A liberal-democratic system "is one in which public policies are made, on a majority basis, by representatives subject to effective popular control at periodic elections which are conducted on the principle of political equality and under conditions of political freedom" (Mayo, 1960: 70).

The construction of any typology forces political analysts to specify the criteria which they feel are the most significant for investigating the similarities and differences among political systems. A classification scheme also produces an either/or decision by the political scientists; for example, Crick's classification results in the placement of any specific government in one of three possible categories. As a result, few political scientists would disagree that the Soviet Union under Stalin belonged in the totalitarian category. By contrast, under Nikita Khrushchev's leadership, the extent of state control and political repression in the Soviet Union receded, however modestly, while crackdowns on political dissent under Leonid Brezhnev and his immediate successors indicated a return to a more Stalinist approach by the leadership in Moscow. Such internal changes have led some observers to claim that the Soviet Union no longer exemplifies the characteristics of a totalitarian government. However, if one considers all of its governmental characteristics, the Soviet Union clearly belongs in the totalitarian category, both in the past and through the leadership of Konstantin Chernenko, who died in 1985. The rise to power of Mikhail Gorbachev and his dramatic reforms in the late 1980s, based on the ideas of *glasnost* (openness) and *perestroika* (restructuring), have certainly moved the Soviet Union away from some of the harsher characteristics of totalitarian government and toward the democratic model. Only time will tell how far this reform process will move the Soviet Union in the years ahead. Similarly, by 1990, the rapid changes in Eastern Europe, particularly in countries like Poland and Czechoslovakia, necessitate a re-evaluation of how these governments will be classified according to Crick's typology.

In addition to forcing either/or decisions on the political analyst, a second problem associated with the use of classifications is the assumption that a specific government exhibits all the characteristics of a particular category. For example, with respect to the control of property, the Soviet Union, as a pure totalitarian government, would not allow the existence of private property. In actual fact, however, private property has not only been allowed to exist, but at times has even been encouraged by the Soviet leadership, particularly with respect to private agricultural plots. Thus, no specific government exhibits, in all respects, every single characteristic of a particular classification scheme.

A good way of perceiving governmental types, therefore, is to see the classification as a continuum, with a specific government showing more or less of a particular characteristic. Such a procedure is especially useful when comparing governments within a particular category. For example, if we compare Canada, the United States, and Britain in terms of political participation with respect to the percentage of voting turnout in their national elections in the early 1980s, we would rank Canada first (76 percent in 1984), Britain a close second (73 percent in 1983), and the United States a distant third (53 percent in 1984). However, if we use criteria other than voting turnout — such as the number of opportunities for political participation offered the average citizen in each country — a very different ordering of these three countries emerges. The United States, given the number of political offices filled through elections, the frequency of elections, the openness of the political recruitment process through the use of direct primaries, and the opportunities for

utilizing the recall, initiative, and referendum techniques at the state and local levels, would be classified as the most participatory. Canada, which gives the average citizen the right to vote in national, provincial, and municipal elections and also allows for limited participation in the leadership selection process through the national party leadership convention, would rank second in terms of opportunities for political participation. In such a comparison Britain would rank third, because of its closed recruitment process, the traditional selection of the party leader by the party caucus, and the use of only national and local election campaigns. These examples demonstrate an important aspect of comparative political analysis: the conclusions reached in any comparison depend to a large extent on the aspect of the political process being considered.

Finally, with respect to classifications, we should remember that, since political systems change through time, so does their placement in any typology. For example, Germany has moved from autocracy in the 19th century to a democratic form of government during the Weimar Republic in the 1920s, to a totalitarian variety under Hitler and the Nazis, and back to a democratic form in West Germany and a totalitarian version in East Germany from the Second World War to 1989. Similarly, any particular government changes through time even within the same category: for example, Canada, Britain, and the United States are all more participatory today than they were 50 years ago. This problem of political change emphasizes an additional consideration in comparative political analysis: the conclusions reached depend on the historical period of the comparisons.

In addition to classifications that compare governments in total, more limited typologies, which focus on a particular aspect, may also prove useful, especially for comparing governments within a specific category. Two such limited typologies will be considered: first, the distinction between federal and unitary forms of government, and second, the differences between presidential and parliamentary governmental structures.

Federal, unitary, and confederal systems

The classification of governments into federal or unitary systems is based on the structure of the central or national government and the resulting way in which political power is shared with the constituent political units (i.e., provinces in Canada, states in the United States). A **federal** *form of government is constructed on the principle of the division of powers between levels of government*: in other words, in Canada, governmental power is shared between the national government in Ottawa and the 10 provincial governments, while in the United States governmental power is divided between the national government in Washington and the 50 state governments. The organization of the political units in a federal nation-state is on a geographical basis (i.e., provinces or states) and represents an attempt to incorporate diversity (economic, cultural, linguistic, ethnic, regional) within an overall unifying framework.

In such a system, each level of government can act directly on the citizen (e.g., taxation) and also independently exercise certain governmental powers, which are usually specified in the country's constitution. Generally, some responsibilities are shared between the levels of government. As a result, federalism creates a structure of government as well as a process of governing. After the initial design of a federal system, the continuing distribution and sharing of powers becomes a primary political issue. When jurisdictional disputes arise in a federal system, the judiciary is often called upon to act as an arbitrator of the precise role of each level of government. In other words, we can say that the essence of a federal system is the division of power between a national government and

various constituent units. Political systems which are federal in structure include Canada, the United States, Australia, and West Germany. In January of 1989, Belgium adopted constitutional changes which will transform it into a federal state in 10 years.

A **unitary government** *consists of a national or central government and local government units*; in other words, in contrast to a federal structure, the intermediate level of government (provinces or states) is missing. More importantly, the central government monopolizes political power and determines which powers it will allow the local government to use. For example, while politically British Prime Minister Margaret Thatcher found it difficult to control the spending of the local authorities, the national government was perfectly within its powers in its decision to try and abolish the Greater London Council in the early 1980s. In fact, the Greater London Council was officially abolished on April 1, 1986. Local government does not exercise power independently of the central government and the powers, structure, and boundaries of the local units can be changed by the central government acting on its own initiative. Examples of unitary systems include Great Britain, Sweden, and France.

A third alternative, although rarely tried in the 20th century, is that of a **confederal** structure. In such a system the constituent units create the national or central government, which then governs only with the consent of the constituent units. The central government's authority is not independent. It acts on behalf of its creators. Such a system was tried in the United States after the American Revolution with the Articles of Confederation. Its failure led to the adoption of a federal system under the present American Constitution. In Canada, some proponents of provincial rights come close to advocating a confederal form of government under a revised Canadian Constitution. The Premier of Newfoundland, Brian Peckford, asserted on the night of the Quebec referendum on independence (May 20, 1980) that the national government was a creation of the provinces. While such statements may be politically advantageous in Newfoundland, they are incorrect from both an historical and theoretical perspective. Although Canada is called a confederation, what was intended and created by the Constitution Act of 1867 was a federal political structure, and a highly centralized one at that.

Presidential and parliamentary systems

Our third classification, that of presidential or parliamentary systems, focuses on the structure of the executive (single or dual) and its relation (separation or fusion of powers) to the legislature within a single governmental level. A **parliamentary system** has a split executive: that is, a head of state or **formal executive** with relatively limited political power (e.g., the British monarch; in Canada, at the federal level the governor general, and in the provinces the lieutenant governors) and a **political executive**, which is the repository of extensive political power (e.g., the British and Canadian prime ministers, the premiers of the 10 Canadian provinces). The formal executive performs primarily symbolic and ceremonial functions, while the political executive exercises effective political power. A second characteristic of a parliamentary system is the executive's relation to the legislature: a parliamentary system is based on the principle of the fusion of executive and legislative power. Whichever party has a majority of seats in the legislature also controls the executive branch; in other words, the same group of political leaders operates both the executive and legislative institutions of government. This

> In favourable circumstances, any fool could govern a country—and some have (Rose, 1984: xxxii).

fusion of executive and legislative power is accomplished through the cabinet, described in the British context by Walter Bagehot (1867: 68) as a "a hyphen which joins, a buckle which fastens, the legislative part of the State to the executive part of the State." In turn, the cabinet is collectively responsible to the legislature for its actions and retains office only so long as it receives majority support in the legislature. A third characteristic of parliamentary government is that a maximum time limit, usually five years, is set for how long a government can stay in office without returning to the people through an election to renew its mandate. Within this maximum time limit, however, elections are held at varying intervals: for example, federal elections in Canada occurred in 1957, 1958, 1962, 1963, 1965, 1968, 1972, 1974, 1979, 1980, 1984, and 1988. The timing of elections is generally within the powers of the political executive to decide.

In contrast, each of these three characteristics of executive structure, executive-legislative relations, and the calling of elections operates differently in a presidential system. First, a **presidential system** operates with a unified or single executive. In the United States, the president performs both the formal and political executive functions of government. Second, the relation of the executive and legislature in a presidential system is based on the principle of the **separation of powers** (i.e., that each branch of government operates independently from the others). This separation of powers principle is maintained through a series of **checks and balances**, which are the specific constitutional powers granted each branch to control, in some respects, the operation of the other branches of government. For example, in the American system the legislature may pass a law, but the president may veto it. A countercheck is given to the legislature in that it may override a presidential veto by a two-thirds vote in both the House of Representatives and the Senate. A presidential system is also

TABLE 1.1 PARLIAMENTARY AND PRESIDENTIAL GOVERNMENTS

STRUCTURE OF GOVERNMENT

Characteristic	Parliamentary	Presidential
1. structure of the executive	*dual:* both a formal and a political executive	*singular:* formal and political executive combined in a single office
2. executive-legislative relationship	*fusion of powers:* achieved primarily through the cabinet and based on the principle of collective responsibility	*separation of powers:* based on independent branches of government, maintained by a system of checks and balances; no collective responsibility of the executive to the legislature
3. elections	*maximum time period* fixed, with varying election periods within the maximum determined primarily by the political executive	*set time period* for elections, with the political executive playing no role in determining when elections will be called

characterized by elections at set intervals: there is no leeway when an election will be held, because the dates are mandated by law. An American presidential election is held in November every four years: such elections are automatic and will be held in 1992, 1996, 2000, and 2004. The executive in the American presidential system has no power to determine when to seek a renewal of the mandate to govern. These various characteristics of parliamentary and presidential governments are summarized in Table 1.1.

In beginning our discussion of the presidential/parliamentary distinction, we indicated that these forms operated within a particular level of government. However, the presidential/parliamentary classification can be joined with the federal/unitary distinction to produce a combined classification of governmental forms. In Table 1.2 we present such a typology for various democratic governments. (A combination classification for other types of government could also be developed: for example, the Soviet Union, until Gorbachev, was a totalitarian government which in theory had a federal political structure, but in practice a unitary system of

TABLE 1.2 A COMBINED CLASSIFICATION OF DEMOCRATIC GOVERNMENTS

EXECUTIVE-LEGISLATIVE RELATIONSHIP	*LEVELS OF GOVERNMENT*	
	Federal	*Unitary*
Parliamentary	Canada	Britain
Presidential	United States	France

government). Canada is parliamentary and federal in structure, Britain is parliamentary and unitary, the United States is presidential and federal, and France is presidential and unitary. All of these designations are clear-cut except perhaps the case of France, which is usually labeled "quasi-presidential." The Fifth French Republic combines both parliamentary and presidential patterns, but since the presidential aspects tend to dominate, it is classified in the presidential category.

Our consideration of three basic classifications of government (autocratic, democratic, totalitarian; federal, unitary; presidential, parliamentary) demonstrates the useful nature of typologies in political analysis. Beginning with a criterion that appears to be an important point for comparing political systems (e.g., the structure of the executive-legislative relationships), a typology groups various systems in terms of their similarities within categories (e.g., all federal states share certain characteristics) and differences between categories (e.g., democratic governments vary from totalitarian governments in many ways). Thus, the classification of governments is a shorthand or summary method for describing their organizational structure and operating principles. For example, Canada's government is democratic, federal, and parliamentary in nature; Britain is democratic, unitary, and parliamentary; while the United States is democratic, federal, and presidential. To make such a description summarizes in three words a wealth of pertinent information concerning the operation and structure of these political systems. Therefore, classification is not merely an idle academic exercise—it is a particularly useful starting point for comparing political systems.

A Comparative Perspective on Canadian Government

In analyzing the nature of government as ubiquitous, multiple, expansive, necessary, and varied, we have suggested the need for viewing any particular political system from a comparative perspective. The importance of bringing just such a comparative focus to the study of Canadian government can be justified on several grounds. First, people's political experience, both historical and contemporary, has produced an array of possible political systems. Only a comparative approach can begin to introduce students to this diversity of political institutions and processes. Second, in learning about other

political systems, students can overcome the parochialism of their own limited political experience. Few people directly experience different forms of government. Knowledge of alternative political arrangements can thus broaden one's intellectual perspective. Third, the increasingly complex interdependence of nations means that it has become impossible to isolate domestic from foreign politics. Other political systems directly affect the internal politics of Canada. For example, the decision by OPEC in the mid-1970s to increase world oil prices underlay the recurring confrontations between Ottawa and the Western oil-producing provinces concerning the domestic price of oil and the distribution of the resulting tax revenues between the federal and provincial governments.

In addition to recognizing the diversity of political experience, overcoming the parochialism of a single system focus, and emphasizing the interdependence of political systems, a comparative approach to politics seeks to develop generalizations or hypotheses that explain the similarities and differences among political systems.

Comparative analysis is an integral part of the study of politics. The comparative study of politics suggests immediately the laboratory of the scientist. It provides us with the opportunity to discuss specific phenomena in the light of different historical and social backgrounds . . . More specifically, however, the function of comparative study is to identify uniformities and differences and to explain them (Macridis, 1955: 1).

It is this search for similarities and differences between political systems, and an explanation of such patterns, which has been described as the "highest objective of comparative analysis" (Scarrow, 1969: 8). However, before explanations can be developed, one must start with description, that is, a knowledge of what exists. After an understanding of the workings of several particular political systems has been developed, then the

THE SONG MY GOVERNMENT SINGS

My GOVERNMENT says
Yes,
...But not yes;
No,
...But not no;
We should, but we can't
We can, but we shouldn't.

Now, we might like to and we may want to –
Only, we might not be able to.
If we are not able to, then rest assured that we wanted to.
And if we are able to, well...you see, there are people who say we shouldn't.
Of course there are others who say we might not want to, but we must.
If this is the case, we certainly shall –
Unless it turns out that we can't.

So we will if we can't, we won't if we can; if we shouldn't we certainly wouldn't;
...although that might turn out to be wrong.
We are elected to lead. No one tells us what we should or shouldn't,
Would or wouldn't, could or couldn't do.
So we will!
...or we won't –
As the case may be.

In summary:
We have to if it's right and we shouldn't if it's wrong;
But dare we if it's wrong and must we if it's right?
Solutions? Please wait.
Someday –
We may or we may not
Reconsider our position
And call a general election.

We are the government, you know.

Allan Schwam
March 20, 1971.

---

student can begin to focus on the explanation of important patterns of political phenomena.

The reasons for utilizing a comparative approach in studying any particular political system are as applicable to Canada as to any other country. For example, the decade of the 1970s saw a much-needed focus among Canadian political scientists on an analysis of our own political system. However, as a consequence, an older tradition has been downplayed, if not entirely forgotten: that is, the explicit, comparative analysis of Canadian politics (Bryce, 1921; Corry, 1947; Brady, 1947). A comparative approach can widen our intellectual horizons and, at the same time, allow for a fuller understanding of our own political system. A comparative perspective is an aid, not a hindrance or substitute, for understanding the Canadian political experiment. Similarly, the interdependence of the modern world has particularly affected Canada. It is often forgotten that Canada is the only country in the world that borders on both superpowers.

Likewise, Canada's economic interdependence with other countries, particularly with the United States, is extensive.

A comparative approach is also useful because Canada's polity embodies an interesting combination of political principles. For example, Canada was the first political system to counterpose federal and parliamentary institutions within a single government.

> The Canadian constitution at the time of its creation presented to the world of political science a novel combination of constitutional principles. England's great contribution had been parliamentary and responsible government; the United States had shown that federalism was the system best adapted to a disunited people scattered over wide areas. Canada was the first nation to weld these conceptions into a new whole ... (Scott, 1977: 35).

As a result, Canada provides an interesting case study for comparing these principles with other possible variations. To date, however, the Canadian political system has often been neglected within the field of comparative politics.

Although we have argued for the need to compare Canada with other political systems, we have not yet justified the selection of countries to be used in our comparative analysis. While other political systems may be utilized on specific points, most comparisons will centre on Britain and the United States. Our choice is based on both historical and theoretical criteria. Historically, Britain and the United States have exercised the greatest impact on the evolution, development, and structure of the Canadian polity. In fact, Canada is often viewed as a mix of the political principles and practices of these two countries. Until World II, Britain was the dominant influence on Canada, a position since relinquished to the United States in both domestic and foreign affairs. Both political systems continue, however, to be an important influence on Canadian politics.

Summary

1. To understand Canadian politics properly requires a focus on two essentials: first, the importance of and difference between political structures and political processes and second, the significance of seeing the Canadian polity from a comparative point of view.
2. The nature of government can be described by five key attributes: government is ubiquitous, multiple, expansive, necessary, and varied. Each of these characteristics points to a significant element of government in the modern era.
3. Classifications of different types of government can focus on broad comparisons — such as the typology of autocratic, democratic, and totalitarian systems — or on a more limited criterion — such as the differences between federal and unitary or presidential and parliamentary systems.
4. The Canadian polity is democratic, federal, and parliamentary. Britain is democratic, unitary, and parliamentary. The United States is democratic, federal, and presidential. Such classifications are an important tool in comparing the various institutions and processes of a polity.

Recommended Readings

The Nature of Government

FINER, S.E. (1983) "Perspectives in the World History of Government — a Prolegomenon," *Government and Opposition* (Winter), Volume 18, Number 1, pp. 3–22.

HENIG, JEFFREY A., CHRIS HAMNETT, and HARVEY B. FEIGENBAUM (1988) "The Politics of Privatization: A Comparative Perspective," *Governance* (October), Volume 1, Number 4, pp. 442–468.

KATZENSTEIN, PETER (1985) *Small States in World Markets*. Ithaca, New York: Cornell University Press.

LAUX, JEANNE KIRK and MAUREEN APPLE MOLOT (1987) *State Capitalism: Public Enterprise in Canada*. Ithaca, New York: Cornell University Press.

MOYNIHAN, DANIEL PATRICK (1987) "The 'New Science of Politics' and the Old Art of Government," *The Public Interest* (Winter), Number 86, pp. 22–35.

NUTTER, G. WARREN (1978) *Growth of Government in the West*. Washington, D.C.: American Enterprise Institute for Public Policy Research.

ROSE, RICHARD (1978) *What is Governing? Purpose and Policy in Washington*, Englewood Cliffs, N.J.: Prentice-Hall.

_____ and GUY PETERS (1978) *Can Government Go Bankrupt?* New York: Basic Books.

SAVA, E.S. (1983) *Privatizing the Public Sector: How to Shrink Government*. Chatham, N.J.: Chatham House Publishers.

SHARKANSKY, IRA (1979) *Wither the State? Politics and Public Enterprise in Three Countries*. Chatham, N.J.: Chatham House Publishers.

TARSCHYS, DANIEL (1988) "Tributes, Tariffs, Taxes, and Trade: The Changing Sources of Government Revenue," *British Journal of Political Science* (January), Volume 18, Number 1, pp. 1–20.

TAYLOR, CHARLES LEWIS, ed. (1983) *Why Governments Grow*. Beverly Hills, California: Sage Publications.

TUCHMAN, BARBARA W. (1984) *The March of Folly: From Troy to Vietnam*. New York: Alfred A. Knopf.

WEAVER, R. KENT (1988) *Automatic Government: The Politics of Indexation*. Washington, D.C.: The Brookings Institution.

WILSON, GRAHAM K. (1985) *Business and Politics: A Comparative Introduction*, London: Macmillan.

Forms of Government

ARENDT, HANNAH (1958) *The Origins of Totalitarianism*. Cleveland: Meridian Books.

CRICK, BERNARD (1973) *Basic Forms of Government: A Sketch and a Model*. London: Macmillan Press.

DAHL, ROBERT A. (1982) *Dilemmas of Pluralist Democracy: Autonomy vs. Control*. New Haven: Yale University Press.

DELURY, GEORGE, ed. (1983) *World Encyclopedia of Political Systems: Volume I: Afghanistan-Mozambique; Volume II: Nepal-Zimbabwe*. Harlow: Longman.

FRIEDRICH, CARL J. and ZBIGNIEW K. BRZEZINSKI (1965) *Totalitarian Dictatorship and Autocracy*. New York: Praeger, 2nd ed.

HALPERN, SUE M. (1986) "The Disorderly Universe of Consociational Democracy," *West European Politics* (April), Volume 9, Number 2, pp. 181–197.

HARRINGTON, MICHAEL (1977) *Socialism*. New York: Bantam Books.

HIRST, PAUL (1988) "Representative Democracy and Its Limits," *The Political Quarterly* (April), Volume 59, Number 2, pp. 190–205.

HUNT, R.N.C. (1964) *The Theory and Practice of Communism*. Baltimore: Penguin Books.

HUNTINGTON, SAMUEL P. (1984) "Will More Countries Become Democratic?" *Political Science Quarterly* (Summer), Volume 99, Number 2, pp. 193–218.

IONESCU, GHITA (1984) *Politics and the Pursuit of Happiness: An Inquiry into the Involvement of Human Beings in the Politics of Industrial Society*. London: Longmans.

IRWIN, T.H. (1989) "Socrates and Athenian Democracy," *Philosophy and Public Affairs* (Spring), Volume 18, Number 2, pp. 184–205.

LEFORT, CLAUDE (1986) *The Political Forms of Modern Society: Bureaucracy, Democracy, Totalitarianism*. Cambridge, Mass.: MIT Press.

LIJPHART, AREND (1984) *Democracies: Patterns of Majoritarian and Consensus Government in Twenty-One Countries*. New Haven: Yale University Press.

MACPHERSON, C.B. (1977) *The Life and Times of Liberal Democracy*. Oxford: Oxford University Press.

MEYER, ALFRED G. (1984) *Communism*. New York: Random House, 4th ed.

PERLMUTTER, ARMOS (1984) *Modern Authoritarianism*. New Haven: Yale University Press.

REVEL, JEAN-FRANCOIS (1978) *The Totalitarian Temptation*. Middlesex, England: Penguin Press.

SARTORI, GIOVANNI (1987) *The Theory of Democracy Revisited, Part One: The Contemporary Debate*. Chatham, N.J.: Chatham House Publishers.

SHKLAR, JUDITH N. (1984) *Ordinary Vices*. Cambridge, Mass.: Harvard University Press.

SMITH, B.C. (1985) *Decentralization: The Territorial Dimension of the State*. London: Allen and Unwin.

TALMON, J.L. (1986) *The Origins of Totalitarian Democracy*. New York: Viking Penguin.

YUNKER, JAMES A. (1986) "Would Democracy Survive Under Market Socialism?" *Polity* (Summer), Volume 18, Number 4, pp. 678–695.

Canadian Government

CAMPBELL, ROBERT M. and LESLIE A. PAL (1989) *The Real World of Canadian Politics: Cases in Process and Policy*. Peterborough, Ontario: Broadview Press.

DICKERSON, MARK O. and THOMAS FLANAGAN (1986) *An Introduction to Government and Politics: A Conceptual Approach*. Toronto: Methuen, 2nd ed.

DYCK, RAND (1986) *Provincial Politics in Canada*. Scarborough, Ontario: Prentice-Hall Canada.

FOX, PAUL and GRAHAM WHITE (1987) *Politics: Canada*. Toronto: McGraw-Hill Ryerson, 6th ed.

GIBBINS, ROGER (1985) *Conflict and Unity: An Introduction to Canadian Political Life*. Toronto: Methuen.

JACEK, HENRY (1987) "Large state/small state Relations in the North American Political Economy: Are There Lessons from Europe?" *The American Review of Canadian Studies* (Winter), Volume 17, Number 4, pp. 419–438.

JACKSON, ROBERT J., DOREEN JACKSON, and NICOLAS BAXTER-MOORE (1986) *Politics in Canada: Culture, Institutions, Behaviour and Public Policy*. Scarborough, Ontario: Prentice-Hall Canada.

LANDES, RONALD G., ed. (1985) *Canadian Politics: A Comparative Reader*. Scarborough, Ontario: Prentice-Hall Canada.

MALLORY, J.R. (1984) *The Structure of Canadian Government*. Toronto: Gage, rev. ed.

STEWART, GORDON T. (1986) *The Origins of Canadian Politics: A Comparative Approach*. Vancouver, British Columbia: The University of British Columbia Press.

WARD, NORMAN (1987) *Dawson's Government of Canada*. Toronto: The University of Toronto Press, 6th ed.

WHITTINGTON, MICHAEL S. and GLEN WILLIAMS, ed. (1984) *Canadian Politics in the 1990s*. Toronto: Methuen, 3rd ed.

British Government

BEER, SAMUEL H. (1982) *Britain Against Itself: The Political Contradictions of Collectivism*. New York: W.W. Norton.

BIRCH, ANTHONY H. (1986) *The British System of Government*. London: Allen and Unwin, 7th ed.

BUDGE, IAN and DAVID MCKAY, eds. (1988) *The Changing British Political System: Into the 1990s*. London: Longmans, 2nd ed.

CHILDS, DAVID (1984) *Britain Since 1945: A Political History*. London: Methuen.

DEARLOVE, JOHN and PETER SAUNDERS (1984) *Introduction to British Politics: Analysing a Capitalist Democracy*. Oxford: Polity Press.

FORMAN, F.N. (1985) *Mastering British Politics*. London: Macmillan.

KAVANAGH, DENNIS (1985) *British Politics: Continuities and Change*. Oxford: Oxford University Press.

LEYS, COLIN (1983) *Politics in Britain: An Introduction*. Toronto: University of Toronto Press.

MILIBAND, RALPH (1984) *Capitalist Democracy in Britain*. Oxford: Oxford University Press.

MORAN, MICHAEL (1985) *Politics and Society in Britain: An Introduction*. London: Macmillan.

NORTON, PHILIP (1982) *The Constitution in Flux*. Oxford: Martin Robertson.

PUNNETT, R.M. (1988) *British Government and Politics*. London: Heinemann, 5th ed.

ROSE, RICHARD (1989) *Politics in England*. Boston: Little, Brown and Company, 5th ed.

American Government

BURNHAM, WALTER DEAN (1983) *Democracy in the Making: American Government and Politics*. Englewood Cliffs, N.J.: Prentice-Hall.

BURNS, JAMES MACGREGOR, J.W. PELTASON, and THOMAS E. CRONIN (1987) *Government By the People*. Englewood Cliffs, N.J.: Prentice-Hall, 13th ed.

CHASE, HAROLD W., ROBERT T. HOLT, and JOHN E. TURNER (1980) *American Government in Comparative Perspective*. New York: Franklin Watts.

LADD, EVERETT CARLL (1987) *The American Polity: The People and Their Government*. New York: W.W. Norton and Company, 2nd ed.

NICHOLAS, H.G. (1986) *The Nature of American Politics*. Oxford: Oxford University Press, 2nd ed.

PARENTI, MICHAEL (1988) *Democracy for the Few*. New York: St. Martin's Press, 5th ed.

VILE, M.J.C. (1983) *Politics in the USA*. London: Hutchinson, 3rd ed.

WILSON, JAMES Q. (1986) *American Government: Institutions and Policies*. Lexington, Mass.: D.C. Heath and Company, 3rd ed.

CHAPTER 2 Political Analysis: Concepts and Principles

You may not care about politics, but politics cares about you (Karp, 1988: 41).

The new, old, and constantly changing language of politics is a lexicon of conflict and drama, of ridicule and reproach, of pleading and persuasion. Color and bite permeate a language designed to rally many men, to destroy some, and to change the minds of others (Safire, 1978: ix).

The season on politicians runs from January to December every year. No license is required. Virtually any weapons are permissible, and no special clothing, equipment, training or knowledge is necessary. Restrictions on how, when and where politicians may be hunted are few. It is an ideal sport and therefore small wonder that so many enjoy it (Akerman, 1977: 7).

LIKE IT OR NOT, politics is a fact of human existence. One can detest it, ignore it, or attempt to change it, but the pervasiveness of politics remains. Human behaviour occurs in the context of political communities organized in modern times on the basis of nation-states. As with birth itself, initial membership in a political system gives one little freedom of choice—it is a nonvoluntary option. We are automatically members of a political system at birth and are subject to the consequences of such membership throughout our lives. If government is ubiquitous, then politics is more so, for government constitutes only a portion of the broader process of politics. If **government** *is the institutional organization of political power,* **politics** *can be defined as the exercise of power and influence on matters that affect the community.*

While pervasive, politics is not found in every facet of human existence, although many actions have potential political implications. For example, the alleged discovery of drugs in the suitcase of New Brunswick Premier Richard Hatfield during the Queen's visit in September of 1984 and the ensuing controversy illustrate this point. So does the late-1980s affair of Greek Prime Minister Andreas Papandreou (in his late 60s) with his mistress and future wife Dimitra Liani (in her mid-30s) and its impact on the fortunes of his Socialist government.

Matters which for the ordinary citizen may be considered private and nonpolitical can for a politician quickly generate potent political ramifications. For example, one's personal sexual behaviour and sexual preferences, including events that may have happened long before the individual entered the political arena, can have an impact on one's later political power and

> *Max Weber on Politics:* Politics is a strong and slow boring of hard boards. It takes both passion and perspective. Certainly all historical experience confirms the truth— that man would not have attained the possible unless time and again he had reached for the impossible . . . . Only he has the calling for politics who is sure that he shall not crumble when the world from his point of view is too stupid or too base for what he wants to offer. Only he who in the face of all this can say "In spite of all!" has the calling for politics (quoted in Gerth and Mills, 1958: 128).

influence. While it may be true, as Pierre Trudeau said in 1967 (Gwyn, 1980: 64), that in a liberal-democratic society "the state has no business in the bedrooms of the nation," the converse of that is not evident: the people often demand to know about the sexual behaviour and preferences of their leaders.

If politics is the exercise of power and influence on matters that affect the community, then **political analysis** *is the attempt to explain why a specific pattern of power and influence emerges, how power is gained and lost, and why certain political events occurred.* Thus, what we call political analysis is simply one approach used in answering that basic question of all the sciences, both natural and social: why? Political analysis is the exercise of imposing conceptual order on an apparently incoherent political process.

The political analyst assumes that things rarely happen by chance in politics. Even those events which appear at first glance to be part of a mysterious process are, upon closer inspection, understandable and explainable in light of certain regularities of human behaviour. For example, although it may be difficult to explain why a particular individual voted for a specific candidate in a single election campaign, the political analyst can make general explanations of

> Politics, n. A strife of interests masquerading as a contest of principles. The conduct of public affairs for private advantage (Bierce, 1911: 101).

> Politics is contingent; events that have every right to occur may be forestalled by others no one can predict (Polsby and Wildavsky, 1986: 281).

> *Sam Johnson instructing his 11-year-old son, Lyndon Baines Johnson, on the art of politics:* If you can't come into a roomful of people and tell right away who is for you and who is against you, you have no business in politics (quoted in Barber, 1972: 133).

Canadian voting behaviour based on socioeconomic factors such as class, occupation, region, religion, and ethnicity. One of the tasks of the political analyst is to search for such general patterns as a foundation for explaining what has happened.

In asserting that political life is founded on certain regularities of behaviour, such that we can describe and explain political events, we are not at the same time assuming that the political process is predestined to develop in a particular manner. One of the fascinating aspects of politics is the continuing occurrence of the unexpected. For example, Pierre Trudeau's announcement on November 21, 1979 that he intended to resign as leader of the Liberal party caught most people by surprise, including most members of his cabinet and party caucus. Such a move might appear to be logical in retrospect, but it certainly didn't seem so at the time. Since the political analyst is involved primarily in describing and explaining events after they have happened, there is a danger that such *ex post facto* explanations will impose a sense of inevitability on political events. While the defeat of the Joe Clark government in Parliament on December 13, 1979 can be described and explained, it was not a predestined development—it could have been avoided (Landes, 1981; Simpson, 1980).

The analyst is often called on to make predictions about future political events. Those who

> Predictions are usually ravaged by unforeseen events more brutally than beach houses by hurricanes (Sabato, 1985: 164).

pretend to know the future in politics, as in other areas, are usually very brave or very foolish, or both. The political landscape is littered with the decaying remains of political prophecies. For example, numerous pundits suggested that the Liberal party would not bring down the Clark government in December 1979. Even a person as close to Pierre Trudeau as Arnie Patterson, who had served as communications advisor for the 1979 federal Liberal campaign, predicted that the defeat of the Clark administration was highly unlikely—a prediction published two days after the event had actually occurred (Patterson, 1979). Such a well-known and respected political columnist as Peter C. Newman, then editor of *Maclean's*, can have his views falsified by events: in a November 26, 1979 editorial, Newman prophesied that the Liberal party could never again win with Pierre Trudeau as its leader. Less than three months later, in February 1980, Trudeau won a solid majority victory.

Political predictions are, at the best of times, risky, even though they are often politically necessary. Much of what occurs in the political process is based on the perception of future developments held by political leaders. For example, it is highly unlikely that the Liberal party would have defeated the Clark government (December, 1979) if they had not been working on the prediction, subsequently proven correct, that they could regain power in the next election (February, 1980). Often, however, politicians' predictions fare as badly as those of the political pundits; the defeat of the Parti

Québécois in the May 1980 referendum is a case in point. Similarly, Prime Minister John Turner's 1984 decision, after only a few weeks in office, to seek a mandate from the Canadian people was predicated on the perception, based on favourable public opinion polls, that he would win. Instead, John Turner suffered the greatest electoral defeat in Canadian history. Hindsight rarely overcomes such political miscalculations.

The political analyst frequently enters the treacherous arena of prediction when discussing the topics of political reform and change. The analyst is asked to predict the consequences of specific reforms. For example, what would be the impact of changing Canada's plurality electoral system to a proportional representation scheme? Political debate often centres on the expected consequences of proposed courses of action. For example, much of the response to Trudeau's patriation proposal in the fall of 1980 focused on just such a problem: how would the amendment formula and the Charter of Rights affect the power of the provincial governments in the years to come? Similarly, the free trade debate during the 1988 Canadian federal election concentrated on its long-term impact on the economy and the political culture of the country.

Once changes have been implemented, the political analyst is also concerned with evaluating such reforms. The question asked then is: Have the changes produced the desired effects and, if not, what effects have they brought about? For example, did the 1974 change in the financing of the federal political parties disturb the traditional pattern of Canadian party finance, or did this reform fail to produce the desired results?

The inability of politicians and political analysts alike to predict accurately events even in the immediate political future reveals a fundamental point about the nature of politics: that is, the human basis of the polity. As a result, politics itself is an art, a way of organizing varieties of individual uniqueness into patterns of

> Politics is a game of winners and losers, of ins and outs. The game is rough, unfair, and fickle, and the players take risks; you are a genius if you win and an incompetent if you lose (Sawatsky, 1989: 269).

collective purpose. The political analyst must thus accept the fact that the political process is not a mechanical one that can be dissected once and for all; if it were, a description of it would be as interesting as repeated explanations of the workings of the internal combustion engine. By contrast, the political process is a moveable feast rather than a sit-down dinner. A person who is trained in political analysis knows what to look for. For example, to learn the names, portfolios, and dates of appointment of current cabinet ministers is, quite likely, a meaningless exercise of one's memory. The political analyst will more properly ask: what are the functions or jobs of the cabinet, why have certain ministerial appointments been made, and how does the cabinet arrive at collective decisions under various prime ministers?

The Nature of Politics

Having lived in a political system for a number of years, most people, if they were asked to define what politics is all about, would likely respond with several basic ideas, which might include some of the following concepts: conflict, power, government, influence, the state, violence, decisions, patronage, laws, and corruption. Some people would see politics in a very favourable light, others might view it as a "dirty business." Some would perceive politics as involving almost all areas of social and economic life, while others would want to restrict the political sphere to rather narrow limits.

One would quickly realize that not only do definitions diverge widely among individuals,

HERMAN

"One day you'll realize that the people capable of running the country are too smart to get into politics."

Source: HERMAN COPYRIGHT 1979 Jim Unger. Reprinted with permission of Universal Press Syndicate.

they also differ extensively in various historical periods and between types of political systems. For example, people within a democratic system conceive of the political sphere in much different terms than those who live in an autocratic or totalitarian system. Although individuals and societies may differ in their definitions of politics, a common theme is a concern with order, or the lack thereof:

> I had learned the first real lesson of politics, government and history: governments are instituted among men in the first instance, and accepted by men gratefully, to protect them from random violence and killing. . . . They offered protection. Many other lessons in politics and government were to follow over the years, but none more important than that (White, 1978: 101).

The reason for the emphasis in various definitions of politics on the theme of order, which

can be labeled as the "godfather function" of politics, can only be appreciated in the context of how the political sphere initially developed as a distinct part of society in the Western world.

DEVELOPMENT OF THE POLITICAL SPHERE IN WESTERN SOCIETY

Early history was prepolitical; that is, the political system was not yet differentiated from other social systems. What we would now interpret as political power and influence were part of an integrated whole — human beings were a part of nature, not distinct from it. Speculative thought based on myth, rather than the rational and scientific approach of modern times, prevailed. However, such initial speculative thought served a similar function with later political thought: it sought to underpin "the chaos of experience" so that it might "reveal the features of a structure — order, coherence, and meaning" (Frankfurt et al., 1949: 11).

The development of a political sphere was a long and complex process, which involved the basic step of separating human beings from nature. Nature became an inanimate object to be understood, manipulated, and controlled. Divorcing humans from nature meant that they had to find a rationale for this separate organization — nature could no longer be depended on to provide it. As a result of this redefinition, which occurred during the 5th and 6th centuries B.C. in Greece, political thought replaced speculative thought and thus assumed the function of providing order, coherence and meaning. The task of the political philosopher was to "fashion a political cosmos out of political chaos" (Wolin, 1960: 8).

If the function of political thought is to develop a pattern from political chaos, then it is not surprising to find that most definitions of politics focus on the concept of order. Given this perspective, we can now expand our initial definition of politics to the following statement:

> Politics is about power. What democracy does is to change the context and conditions in which power and hierarchy operate. The decision-making process in a democratic regime bears only a faint resemblance to that of a non-democratic regime (Bealey, 1988: 260).

> Few issues have sparked more controversy or held more sway over the course of history than has equality. Ships have been launched, lives given, governments toppled — all in the name of this one ideal (Verba and Orren, 1985: 1).

politics *is the exercise of power and influence concerning the establishment, maintenance, and breakdown of order in the community.* The different types of political systems (autocratic, democratic, or totalitarian) establish different kinds of political institutions, with differing relationships between those institutions, in attempting to achieve order in the political community. One way of categorizing these numerous approaches to politics is to group them on the basis of whether or not they provide a normative or an empirical definition of the political sphere.

NORMATIVE VERSUS EMPIRICAL DEFINITIONS OF POLITICS

A comparison of normative and empirical interpretations reveals one basic difference: a **normative** view is concerned with "what ought to be," while an **empirical** definition is concerned with "what is." A normative conception of politics develops a desired or a preferred pattern of political organization, while an empirical approach is based on existing political reality. The perspective of this book is heavily cast in light of the second alternative; that is, an empirical assessment of the Canadian polity.

An example may help to explain the difference between the empirical and normative approaches. The statement that "All men are equal" may reflect a normative judgment that all men should be equal; as an empirical observation the assertion is simply false. An empirical approach would need to specify equal according

to which characteristics: sex, height, weight, intelligence, educational training, or social class? Does equality refer to *equality of condition* (i.e., money, economic rewards) or to *equality of opportunity* (i.e., the right to become unequal by earning more money or completing more education than other people)? Thus, the statement that "All men are equal" may be proposed or accepted as a normative view of how society should be structured; as an empirical statement it must be rejected. No political system, ancient or modern, of whatever type, has ever produced equality of social, economic, or political condition. No existing polity seems destined to change this historical assessment.

A normative statement cannot be disproven, while an empirical statement may be. A normative statement is neither true nor false, while an empirical statement may be either. A comparison of the view of politics held by Aristotle, one of the first practitioners of comparative political analysis, with that of Robert A. Dahl, a past-president of the American Political Science Association, should help to delineate the difference between a normative and an empirical approach to political experience.

The view of politics held by Aristotle is positive: politics is a worthwhile and noble activity — in fact, politics is the master science on which all else is founded. The **polis** or *political association* — in modern terminology, the political system — is the final and most perfect type of human association. In contrast to the lower forms of human organization — the household and the village — only the polis is a self-sufficient association and, thus, only it can provide justice

> Being in politics is like being a football coach; you have to be smart enough to understand the game, and dumb enough to think it's important (former American Senator and presidential candidate Eugene McCarthy).

> We don't need more, or less, politics. We need better politics, and citizens determined to make politics better, not by running away from it but by recognizing it as the essential activity it is (Bob Rae, leader of the Ontario New Democratic Party, 1987).

for its members. For Aristotle, man's full moral and psychological development can only be achieved by participation in the political community. Individual maturity requires participation in the polis: man, by definition, is a political being.

> The man who is isolated — who is unable to share in the benefits of political association, or has no need to share because he is already self-sufficient — is not part of the polis, and must therefore be either a beast or a god (Aristotle, trans. Barker, 1962: 6–7).

Thus, the polis existed for the moral development and perfection of the individual. Within the polis man was the best of animals; outside of it, he was the worst of all. Aristotle's normative conception of politics thus included a very positive view of political activity, of the polis and its benefits, and of the perfectibility of man in conjunction with a political association. Politics was a salient feature of the human condition. By contrast, recent empirical definitions of politics stand in stark disagreement on each of these major aspects.

In investigating how the American political system actually worked in New Haven, Connecticut, Robert Dahl (1961), in his now classic study *Who Governs?*, discovered that for most citizens politics was not a particularly salient activity. Politics was an area of limited concern and interest for the average individual.

> At the focus of most men's lives are primary activities involving food, sex, love, family, work, play, shelter, comfort, friendship, social esteem, and the

like. Activities like these — not politics — are the primary concerns of most men and women ... Since the primary activities are voracious in their demands for time, political activity must enter into competition with them. For most people it is evidently a weak competitor (Dahl, 1961: 279–280).

Politics is not a particularly salient focus for most individuals, and is seen by these same people as a "remote, alien, and unrewarding activity." By implication, the empirical approach also tends to view politics in a negative way: it may be important to some, but it is not a significant activity for most individuals. For Aristotle, political involvement was a precondition for individual fulfillment; for Dahl, political involvement rarely leads to such a result.

This brief comparison of the view of politics held by Aristotle and Dahl shows that they differ on a number of key features: what is meant by the word political; whether what is political is a positive or negative force in the community; and whether most people gain individual maturity and growth from political activity. It is on these kinds of indicators that most normative and empirical definitions of politics vary. Thus, the distinction between an empirical and normative definition of politics is not a trivial one, because each approach consequently differs on the subject matter to be studied, on how one should investigate the area, and on what one should do with the knowledge so gained. Given such profound differences, it is not surprising that there is sometimes considerable animosity between the practitioners of the normative and empirical approaches.

IDEOLOGICAL DEFINITIONS OF POLITICS

A second way of categorizing the multitude of possible definitions of politics is on an ideological basis. An **ideology** itself can be described as *"a set of ideas held by a number of people: it spells out what is valued and what is not; what must be maintained and what must be changed; it shapes accordingly the attitudes of those who share it"* (Macridis, 1980: 6). Different political ideologies project various conceptions of people's political experience.

> As collections of ideas informed by political perspectives they are, or they provide, ways of looking at the world, and interpreting specific issues: ideologies play like often-wandering searchlights on events (Duncan, 1987: 650).

To begin our discussion, we will analyze three basic ideological definitions of politics: conservative, liberal, and radical (Marxism). While no existing ideology is "pure," that is, unaffected by other ideologies or pragmatic considerations, these three form the basis, both theoretically and historically, for the development of other ideological alternatives. One such hybrid, democratic socialism, will also be presented. These four ideologies have had the greatest impact on the three countries that form the basis of our comparative approach.

Our initial ideological definitions of politics — conservative, liberal and radical (Marxism) — correspond to status quo, reformist, and revolutionary approaches. A **conservative** or status quo definition of politics is one that defends and rationalizes "the existing economic, social, and political order"; a radical or **revolutionary** approach, such as Marxism, advocates "far-reaching changes in the existing social, economic, and political order"; a **reformist** perspective, exemplified by liberal theorists, falls somewhere between these two extremes by favouring gradual or modest change in the exist-

ing system (Macridis, 1980: 9). These three political ideologies and their views of politics differ most significantly with respect to the idea of political change: for a conservative, change is always suspect, if not downright detrimental; for a revolutionary, change, including the use of violence, is mandatory and often a desired state of affairs; for a liberal, incremental change (slow, modest change) is preferred: change if necessary, but not necessarily change. The more hybrid ideology of **democratic socialism** seeks fundamental change in the social, economic, and political order, but through democratic means. Change will be implemented, not by revolution, but by the ballot box.

A conservative view of politics

Our example of a conservative view of politics will be the writings of Professor Michael Oakeshott of the London School of Economics and Political Science. Oakeshott (1962: 168) is explicitly conservative, defining it as a disposition to think and act in certain ways: "a propensity to use and enjoy what is available rather than to wish for or to look for something else; to delight in what is present rather than what was or what may be." Thus, a conservative favours tradition over innovation: the imperfections of the present are preferable to the unknown possibilities of the future. As a conservative, Oakeshott is opposed to many elements of modern political thought, which he labels as Rationalism. Rather than emerging from a people's tradition and accumulated experience, Rationalism, which he equates with modern political ideologies, attempts to structure the polity on the basis of preconceived principles. Oakeshott's (1962: 112) view of conservatism and his resulting critique of Rationalism is linked specifically to his definition of politics and political activity: "Politics I take to be the activity of attending to the general arrangements of a set of people whom chance or choice have brought together." Politics is not the pursuit of dreams or goals, but, instead, is a tradition of behaviour.

We have classified Oakeshott's view of politics as conservative because he prefers what exists to what might be: people are not only imperfect, but, quite likely, imperfectible. Politics and government are limited and specific types of activity that should not be confused with, or replaced by, rationalist thought. These themes are well expressed in the following metaphor:

> In political activity, then, men sail a boundless and bottomless sea; there is neither harbour for shelter nor floor for anchorage, neither starting place nor appointed destination. The enterprise is to keep afloat on an even keel; the sea is both friend and enemy; and the seamanship consists in using the resources of a traditional manner of behaviour in order to make a friend of every hostile occasion (Oakeshott, 1962: 127).

A liberal view of politics

If a conservative views politics as a tradition of behaviour, a liberal definition focuses instead on the individual's rights and responsibilities. A liberal philosophy argues for both the existence and expansion of basic human rights, such as the right to vote, and for the limitation of the state's role in interfering with these rights. Thus, liberalism has traditionally argued for limited government, with constitutional protection for fundamental political and civil liberties. The political system must be structured or organized in a manner that maximizes the rights and freedoms of the individual: the state exists to serve and to protect the individual. An interesting variation of what we would classify as a liberal view of politics can be found in British political scientist Bernard Crick's famous essay, *In Defence of Politics.*

Politics is defined by Crick (1964: 21) as the "activity by which differing interests within a given unit of rule are conciliated by giving them

a share in power in proportion to their importance to the welfare and survival of the whole community." This perspective sees "politics as conciliation," as a process for accommodating diversity within the political order. The unique aspect of Crick's analysis is that he argues that the acceptance of diversity is the basis of politics, and since the value of diversity is only accepted in free societies, then politics can only occur in such a context. For Crick (1964: 18, 20), "politics are the public actions of free men," and the "unique character of political activity lies, quite literally, in its publicity."

Several important implications flow from this particular definition of politics. First, politics is not a universal phenomenon that occurs in all societies. For example, politics and its corresponding pattern of governance, which is labeled political rule, does not exist in totalitarian systems. Since totalitarian governments seek to eliminate diversity, they also at the same time eradicate politics. Second, Crick's definition takes a narrow view of politics. Basic arenas of social interaction, such as art, education, and beliefs are not inherently political: the attempt to make them so results in the demise of politics. Third, politics is anti-ideological — politics cannot exist where one ideology becomes dominant and eliminates all of its competitors. The diversity of political ideologies helps to sustain political rule, while the dominance of a single political ideology results in the demise of politics. Fourth, politics is a valued activity because the conciliation of divergent interests is a better alternative than the use of violence and coercion in the making and implementation of public decisions. Finally, Crick explicitly rejects both the conservative and revolutionary approaches to politics.

Crick's analysis of politics as a worthwhile endeavour contrasts sharply with the negative view of politics and politicians currently dominant in many Western political systems. For Crick, politics is not only a virtuous activity, but the essence of freedom itself.

Politics, then, is civilizing. It rescues mankind from the morbid dilemmas in which the state is always seen as a ship threatened by a hostile environment of cruel seas, and enables us, instead, to see the state as a city settled on the firm and fertile ground of mother earth. It can offer us no guarantees against storms encroaching from the sea, but it can offer us something worth defending in times of emergency and amid threats of disaster (Crick, 1964: 140).

A revolutionary view of politics

Our third ideological definition of politics is an example of a revolutionary conception: namely, a Marxist look at the political sphere. Marx perceived politics in an extremely negative light: politics was a mechanism for the exploitation of people by people, the means by which the dominant class ruled over other classes. Since politics represented class domination, in the final stage of history, when class conflict was eliminated, politics would also disappear — there would be a "withering away of the state." In order to understand this perspective, a few essential aspects of Marxism must be discussed.

Three basic themes of Marxism can be identified: first, history operates through a recognizable series of economic laws, what is called dialectical materialism; second, history moves through various stages of development, culminating in a communist society; and third, the moving force of history is the class struggle or class conflict. Underlying these themes is a basic assumption that relates political development and organization to the economic sphere: for Marx, economics largely determines and controls politics. History evolves as people's relationship to the means of production shifts. The various stages of history (feudalism, capitalism, socialism) reflect differences in the basis and ownership of the means of production. For example, under capitalism, the capitalist class or bourgeoisie, operating under the principle of

> **On Revolution**
> We are usually told that revolutions are set in motion to realize radical changes. Actually, it is drastic change which sets the stage for revolution (Hoffer, 1964: 4–5).
>
> The saddest illusion of revolutionary socialists is that revolution itself will transform the nature of human beings (Shirley Williams, former British MP).
>
> I kept all my ideas. I have remained a Communist. I still believe nothing will change without violence. But, after you've said that, what then? (FLQ terrorist, Jacques Cossette-Trudel, on the 15th anniversary of the 1970 October Crisis, (*The Globe and Mail*, October 5, 1985, p. A–4).

private property, owns the means of production, while under communism, the proletariat or working class acquires such control. The dominant class in each historical period is the class that owns the productive capacity of society. As a result, the political system is one means of institutionalizing and perpetuating the dominance of the ruling class. Thus, at the base of all societal relationships lies economic reality (i.e., ownership of the means of production), which can be labeled the economic base or substructure; all else, including politics, art, law, and religion, are elements of the superstructure. If, for Marx, "politics is superstructure," then it is not surprising that he had a negative view of politics and felt that it would be and should be eliminated in the final stage of history.

Since the class structure at any given historical moment represents a pattern of domination by the ruling class and a pattern of subordination for those excluded from the ownership of productive forces, the classes of society find themselves in an antagonistic and possibly violent relationship with each other. This adversarial pattern is magnified as the substructure of economic relationships changes from one type of economic system of production to another (e.g., from a feudal pattern of production based on the landed aristocracy to a capitalist mode of production based on commerce and manufacturing). At some historical juncture the class struggle will reach a boiling point of frustration, the exploited class will rise up and in a revolution overthrow the previously dominant class, and a new pattern of dominance and subordination, based on a new series of economic relationships, will emerge. In the final stage of history, this class struggle will abate, because in a communist society, classes, and the dominance-subordination syndrome, will have disappeared.

The Marxist view of politics stands in sharp contrast to both the conservative and liberal definitions with respect to two essential aspects: the nature of political change and the relationship between the economic and political sectors of society. Given the nature of class conflict, the antagonistic relationship between social classes, and the use of the political system by the dominant class to ensure the continuation of the existing system of exploitation, political change can only be achieved through revolution. Revolution is a tidal wave of political change that crashes onto the shore of mother earth, sweeping it clean, and thus creating the conditions for the restructuring and rebuilding of economic and political relationships. This emphasis on revolutionary change in Marxism is diametrically opposed to the conservative's view of "politics as tradition" and the liberal's perspective of "politics as conciliation."

A second distinctive aspect of Marxism is its view of the relationship between economics and politics, with the former controlling the latter. The causal arrow runs from the economic structure to the political structure. By contrast, conservative and liberal theories reverse the Marxist pattern of causation; that is, politics determines economic relationships. In Marxism, economics is the substructure and politics the superstructure, while in conservative and liberal views, politics is the substructure and economics the superstructure. A liberal argues that "political life, then, is far more than an occasional random shock to a self-contained, isolated economic system; rather, economic life vibrates with the rhythms of politics" (Tufte, 1978: 173).

A democratic socialist view of politics

The reason we have classified democratic socialism as a hybrid ideology is apparent in the name itself: "socialism" is the noun which emphasizes economic equality, while "democratic" is the adjective which describes the political means for achieving such a goal. Democratic socialism excludes the revolutionary technique advocated by Marxism and replaces it with a reformed political process, which is an outgrowth of liberalism's emphasis on political rights and liberties. Economics prevails over or dominates politics, but the political process will be used to transform, peacefully, the distribution, control, and use of private property. Socialism will be achieved by evolution, not revolution.

Democratic socialists share with Marxists several key assumptions: first, the economic basis of society; second, the importance of economic equality as a goal; third, the need to prevent capitalists from controlling the economic system; and fourth, a utopian vision of an ideal society. Where democratic socialists and revolutionary socialists disagree is on the means for achieving their goal of equality. Democratic socialists are committed to political and civil liberties and to the existing constitutional system; revolutionary socialists are not. Democratic socialists want to revolutionize society by reforming it; revolutionary socialists want a revolution.

The alternative of democratic socialism developed in the European context in the late nineteenth and early twentieth centuries. A leading exponent was a German, Eduard Bernstein, whose book, *Evolutionary Socialism*, was first published in 1899. In it, Bernstein provided a definitive critique of Marxism and argued for democratic socialism as an alternative. A parallel development occurred in England, with the establishment of the Fabian Society in 1888. Among its members were Sidney and Beatrice Webb, George Bernard Shaw, and H.G. Wells. The Fabians argued that socialism could be achieved by democratic means through a gradual transformation of society.

In the political systems of England, Canada, and the United States, democratic socialism has had a far greater impact than revolutionary socialism. While revolutionary socialists have retained their ideological purity, they have had little impact on the game of power. In contrast, by accepting the legitimacy of the democratic and constitutional regime, democratic socialists have had a major impact on the political systems in Britain and Canada. In Britain democratic socialists helped to found and develop the Labour Party, one of the two main party rivals. In Canada, the New Democratic Party, while never winning power federally, has been responsible for much progressive social legislation and has been a major participant in the provincial political arena. In the United States, democratic socialists have been absorbed, for the most part, into the Democratic party, leaving the official socialist parties as the ineffectual depositories of revolutionary socialism.

The above consideration of four ideologically based views of politics (conservative, liberal, social democratic, and revolutionary) should amply demonstrate the array and complexity of such definitions. While numerous other perspectives are possible, these four illustrate that definitions of politics vary with respect to their images of politics (whether it is a positive or negative activity), to the scope of politics (conservative and liberal approaches define politics more narrowly than Marxism or democratic socialism), to the type of political change

allowed or desired (a conservative defends the existing order, a liberal favours change on an incremental basis, a revolutionary argues for radical change in the existing order, a democratic socialist argues for radical change by democratic means), and finally, to the relationship between the economic and political spheres (liberals and conservatives assert the dominance of politics over economics, while Marxists and democratic socialists argue the contrary position). Whatever their nature, however, all such definitions deal with the crucial problem of establishing order for the political community.

Basic Concepts of Political Analysis

POWER AND INFLUENCE

If politics is the exercise of power and influence concerning the establishment, maintenance, and breakdown of order in the community, then power and influence are two essential concepts that must be defined as precisely as possible. Power and influence share several common attributes. First, both concepts deal with human behaviour and human relationships. If a dog chased a cat up a tree, we would not say that the cat had been influenced by the dog (scared perhaps, but not influenced). However, if one person's behaviour is modified or changed as a result of another person's behaviour, then we can speak of influence or power.

Most Canadians have an ambivalent, perhaps even innocent, relationship with power. It is a subject that is not talked about very openly in our society, as if, with vestiges of Victorian prudery, it were somehow an unseemly topic—like sex (Flaherty, 1988: 99).

Not only do these important concepts concern people, but more significant is the point that they are the result of a relationship or pattern of behaviour. In other words, a power or influence relationship involves interaction between two or more people. If there is no such interaction, there is no relationship, and hence influence or power could not have been exercised. For example, if after attending a political rally and listening to a speech by a political candidate, a person decides to vote for that candidate, then we can say that the candidate has influenced how that person would vote. However, if another person attended the same rally and listened to the same candidate, but had already decided to vote for the candidate, then no influence was exercised. Although power and influence are based on human relationships between two or more people, such interaction need not be direct or on a face-to-face basis. A voter may watch a political advertisement on television for a particular candidate and decide to vote on that basis. In such a case, the interaction or relationship is indirect, but influence has still been exercised.

In emphasizing that power and influence are evident in the pattern of human interactions, we are also implying a second common attribute of both concepts; namely, the idea of causation. We cannot directly observe power and influence, but we can assess their presence in light of events. For example, we say a candidate influenced voters because they behaved in a different way than they would have otherwise. Likewise, politicians are judged to be powerful or not on the basis of their ability to influence or direct people's actions. A prime minister is seen as more powerful and influential than an ordinary citizen because a prime minister can make cabinet appointments, is a key participant in the legislative process, and can change the direction of public policy. In other words, power and influence are not directly observable, but the results of power and influence are. In saying that power and influence deal with causal relationships, we are also asserting that they are exercised before the change of behaviour is observed. For Factor A to cause Event B, it must occur prior to Event B: causation is thus antecedent to its behavioural result. In our previous illustration, a speech by a candidate was deemed to have influenced the behaviour of the voter because it occurred before the voter had decided how to vote; in the other example, the candidate's speech did not influence the individual's voting intention because it was presented after the voter had already made a decision on how to vote.

A third characteristic of power and influence is that, when we use these terms in political analysis, we are obviously speaking of political power and political influence. Power and influence are political when they affect the operation of the wider community or society, which thus distinguishes political power and influence from other forms, such as religious influence or economic power. For example, a clergyman who changes an atheist into a regular church attender may have exercised religious influence, but few would say he had also exercised political influence. However, if a preacher delivers a sermon on the evils of capital punishment to a congregation, which includes a politician, and that politician, because of that sermon, introduces a bill to outlaw capital punishment, then the preacher has exercised political influence. In this example, political influence has not been exercised simply because the person affected was a politician, but because the bill to abolish capital punishment is an action that affects the decision-making structure and concerns of society. For similar reasons, patterns of influence and power within the family are not normally considered political in form. Given these considerations, we can say that political power and influence are concepts that describe human relationships that are causal in nature and public in their import.

Although political power and influence share several attributes, these concepts describe

---

POWER IN OTTAWA

Ottawa is a city that talks incessantly about power: who has it, who wants it, who's misusing it, who's losing it. The talk starts first thing in the morning as soon as the buses begin to lumber around Confederation Square and the sun glances off the windows of the West Block. As the day wears on, the buzz becomes very nearly visible, blowing in the wind like the sulphur fumes that used to waft over the area from the paper company on the Ottawa River's farther shore.

Everybody talks about power. Secretaries talk in the corridors of the Commons at a quarter to ten on their way to the cafeteria for coffee; commissionaires gossip at the main door and the sound reverberates from the vaulted ceilings, rivalling the chatter of school-children lining up for official tours. MPs harangue each other while sprawling on leather sofas in each other's offices or hovering over the cold buffet in the parliamentary restaurant at noon. Deputies arrange to lunch late at Le Cercle Universitaire so they can sound out each other's weaknesses while glancing over their shoulders to see who else is talking there and to whom. Lobbyists reserve tables in the alcoves of the Chateau Grill and over underdone beef and overpriced Bordeaux float deals in voices that sound like chain saws. Ministers greet each other behind the gold curtains of the Commons chamber after Question Period, exchanging innuendos and anxieties. Diplomats display their volubility in Rockcliffe houses between six and eight, eating anchovies and uttering banalities with effortless sophistication in two languages and fifty-four accents. Hostesses call their best friends for advice while writing out place-cards for little dinners at eight, hopefully placing the assistant deputy minister's wife, who is famous for intelligently listening, between the privy councillor who is famous for continuously yapping and the ambassador who is famous for unstintingly imbibing. Late at night backroom boys and executive assistants of varying shapes and political hues meet in dark downtown bars to complain confidentially about the press, the Leader, the cabinet, and the drawbacks of their lives and wives. Everybody talks, talks about power all day long, spreading rumours, flying kites, seeking leaks, formulating strategies, and telling lies (McCall-Newman, 1982: 177–178).

---

somewhat different aspects of human interaction. Generally speaking, influence is the broader term, with power seen as a specific type of influence. *People exercise* **influence** *when they change another person's attitudes or behaviour*: "A influences B to the extent that he or she changes B's actions or predispositions in some way" (Dahl, 1984: 23). Individuals have been influenced when their attitudes and behaviour have been modified from what they would otherwise have been. In our previous examples, a candidate influenced a voter as a result of a speech because the voter's later behaviour was modified. **Power,** *likewise, represents a change in a person's behaviour, but for a different reason: namely, the use of sanctions.*

It is the threat of sanctions which differentiates power from influence in general. Power is a special case of the exercise of influence: it is the process of affecting policies of others with the help of (actual or threatened) severe deprivations for nonconformity with the policies intended (Lasswell and Kaplan, 1950: 76).

For example, if a candidate says to an elector, vote for me or you will lose your job, and the elector votes for the candidate because of the promised sanction, then the candidate has exercised power over the elector. Sanctions are usually more effective as threats rather than as actual behaviour. People over whom power is being exercised must, however, believe that the

Intellectuals and Politics

Knowledge may bring power, but, even so, men of knowledge have only rarely been men of power . . . . Power holders and intellectuals have traditionally looked upon each other with a measure of mistrust and mutual incomprehension. To be sure, there have been short periods of honeymoon, but no stable union has ever been achieved (Coser, 1970: 135–136).

. . . he [Trudeau] faced the insoluble dilemma of every professor who dares enter the political arena: the intellectual seeks truth, the politician power, and the twin quests operate in separate orbits (Newman, 1984: 74).

Norman Mailer (1972) on Political Resources: Politics is not an art of principles, but of timing. The principles are few and soft enough to curve to political winds. The fundamental action of politics is to gain the most one can from a favourable situation and pay off as little as possible whenever necessity forces an unpopular line.

Political resources therefore include money, information, food, the threat of force, jobs, friendship, social standing, the right to make laws, votes, as well as a great variety of other things (Dahl, 1984: 31).

The transformation of political resources into political influence is at least a two-stage process: first, a person must have control of resources, either directly, such as by being personally wealthy, or indirectly, such as by having wealthy political supporters; second, a person must have the willingness and ability to translate control of resources into actual influence. For example, wealth does not, in and of itself, generate political influence. A few people are able to translate wealth into power and influence, as the political success of Pierre Trudeau in Canada and John F. Kennedy in the United States demonstrates. But many wealthy individuals abstain from political activity or involvement. Other individuals may try to convert wealth into power and influence, but may lack the necessary skills and expertise to effect the transformation successfully. Wealth in no way guarantees political success, although it certainly can facilitate one's climb up the political opportunity structure.

threat will be subsequently carried out if their behaviour is not modified.

John Adams (1776) on Government: Fear is the foundation of most governments.

POLITICAL RESOURCES

Having delineated the basic meaning of influence and power, our next concern is with what makes an individual or group influential. People are influential to the extent that they both control political resources and are willing to exercise the control necessary to translate potential influence into actual influence. Although political resources may vary from one political system to another and from one historical period to the next, the following definition should adequately illustrate the nature of **political resources:**

A political resource is a means by which one person can influence the behaviour of other persons.

Winston Churchill on Political Skill: The ability to foretell what is going to happen tomorrow, next week, next month and next year. And to have the ability afterwards to explain why it didn't happen.

Another valuable political resource besides wealth is time. Some occupations are structured so that an employee may be able to take a leave of absence to run for political office, while in other occupations (e.g., self-employed and manual workers) no such possibility exists. For example, one reason the legal profession dominates the political process in North America (more so in the United States than in Canada) is the generous number of resources, such as time (i.e., the freedom to take a temporary leave of absence from their profession), which lawyers possess and ordinary citizens lack. By contrast to the legal profession, Canadian academics are discouraged from seeking political office: several recent contracts between university administrations and faculty unions have included provisions limiting a leave of absence to one term in office. With the vagaries of political life and the bleak prospects of university employment, few professors seem likely to trade economic security for possible political success. Thus, combined with political skills, political resources such as wealth and time are the tools needed for obtaining political influence.

POLITICAL AUTHORITY

Given the fact that in all political systems the control of political resources is unequally distributed and that various political actors differ in their willingness and ability to translate their potential for influence into actual influence, all political systems end up with some people and groups having more influence and power than others. If political influence is unequally allocated, the question becomes one of explaining why people accept such a pattern. A differential distribution of influence is permissible as long as it is seen as legitimate, as long as it is accepted by the people as a justifiable, if not a preferred, state of affairs. *When an individual's influence is perceived as legitimate, it is usually referred to as* **authority**.

Numerous ways of legitimating influence have been used historically, including racial, religious, and ethnic bases. Perhaps the best-known classification of the means for legitimating influence is Max Weber's typology of traditional, legal-rational, and charismatic modes of authority (Gerth and Mills, 1958: 294–301). The **traditional basis of authority** is a justification of influence which claims that the way things have been done in the past is the reason why they should be continued in the same manner in the future. An example of a traditional basis of authority is the existence of a monarch as head of state, typified by the Queen in Britain and Canada.

In contrast, the **legal-rational basis of authority** asserts that a distribution of influence is accepted because certain procedures or "rules of the game" have been followed in acquiring it. For example, if a political party wins an election by gaining a majority of seats in the legislature, it is accepted as the legitimate government with the right to run the country until the next election campaign. In a legal-rational system of authority, individuals do not necessarily like the result, in that they may have voted for a different party in the election. However, the results of the election are accepted as granting legitimacy to the winning party because certain well-established procedures were followed. One accepts the authority of Brian Mulroney because he occupies the office of Prime Minister of Canada. Authority resides with the office (i.e., prime minister, premier, mayor, president, senator) and not with the individual who happens to occupy that office at any particular time.

Weber's third basis of authority is what he labeled charisma or "gift of grace." **Charismatic authority** refers to rule over people in "which the governed submit because of their belief in the extraordinary quality of the specific person" (Gerth and Mills, 1958: 295). The

> **Political Authority:**
>
> In an age acutely conscious of scarcity, the resource which may be in shortest supply is authority (Rochan, 1984: 173).
>
> Mace, n. A staff of office signifying authority. Its form, that of a heavy club, indicates its original purpose and use in dissuading from dissent (Bierce, 1911: 82).
>
> A man's women folk, whatever their outward show of respect for his merit and authority, always regard him secretly as an ass, and with something akin to pity (Mencken, 1922: 3).
>
> ... the only acceptable justification of government, which also determines the limits to its legitimate authority, is its task of serving human needs — serving them better than would be done without any government. The only acceptable justification of a particular form of government, which again also determines the limits on its legitimate demands on the individual's obedience and loyalty, is that it serves to meet human needs better than other forms of government (Bay, 1968: 241).

individual leader is seen as being more than human, of having powers and capabilities well beyond those of most mortals. Historical examples would likely include Christ, Hitler, and Gandhi.

Unfortunately, the utility of the concept of charisma in political analysis has been greatly weakened in recent decades, since it has become a common theme of journalistic portrayals of the political process. Popularity, in terms of winning elections, is often equated with charisma; in political analysis, the two are not necessarily synonymous. Pierre Trudeau was not a charismatic figure on a national basis in Canada, although he may have been with respect to his standing in Quebec. An individual

who never won a majority of the popular vote in Canada in five election campaigns and who, in the so-called charismatic campaign of 1968, won only five percent more of the national vote than Lester Pearson had gained three years earlier, was a considerable distance from exemplifying the concept of charismatic authority as defined by Max Weber. In a similar vein, Brian Mulroney does not become a charismatic figure just because he won the largest federal electoral victory in Canadian history in September of 1984.

Although relatively infrequent, charismatic leaders have appeared in Canada, perhaps best illustrated by John Diefenbaker in the 1958 campaign or by Réal Caouette as leader of the Social Credit party in rural Quebec in the 1962 election. Typically, democratic political systems, such as Canada, the United States, and Britain, are more often characterized by leaders who lack, rather than exemplify, charismatic qualities.

Even if political systems vary in the emphasis given to each method of legitimating authority, these three bases are usually present, in differing degrees, in any particular political system. As a general comparison, legal-rational authority predominates as the basic mode of legitimation in Canada, Britain and the United States; charismatic authority is only rarely present; traditional authority is primarily used to reinforce legal-rational authority, especially in Britain and Canada. For example, although the prime minister of Canada prepares the Speech from the Throne, it is read and presented by the governor general. Similarly, although the governor general may have no alternative but to ask the leader of the party with a majority of seats in the legislature to form a government, no government is formed until the governor general so acts. Even though such actions are symbolic, they nevertheless reinforce the legitimacy of those who have acquired political influence on a legal-rational basis. An important form of traditional authority in Canada, which is often

---

Thoughts on Political Authority:

Core myths are central to the structure of all social belief and authority. For this reason they are normally appropriated by elites to reinforce claims to power and privilege (Walden, 1982: 12).

Numerous musings in Mr. King's diary notwithstanding, we can, I think, agree that none of our political leaders received his authority by divine right. Their pretensions to infallibility are another matter (Brown, 1980: 151)!

The Russian tactic is not to confront Authority, not to seek reform of the system, but to step back, endure, and look for a loophole or pray that someone else's inefficiency will somehow help you get by (Smith, 1977: 362).

Man, who prides himself on standing upright, can also, while remaining in the same place, sit, lie, squat or kneel. All these postures, and particularly the change from one to another, have their own special significance. Rank and power are traditionally connected with certain postures and from the way in which men group themselves we can deduce the amount of authority which each enjoys (Canetti, 1966: 387).

---

overlooked, is the role that custom and convention play in the operation of the political system (e.g., that a member of the Canadian cabinet is expected to also be a member of the House of Commons). Many key aspects of Canadian politics are based on "the practice," that is, on tradition. As a result, traditional authority is a significant, if secondary, base of political influence.

Even in the United States, where legal-rational authority prevails, there are elements of traditional authority. For example, the 150-year dominance of the Republican and Democratic parties has established a "tradition" against new parties or third parties in presidential election campaigns, illustrated by John Anderson's dismal failure in the 1980 contest. Traditional authority is probably the strongest among our three countries of comparison in Britain, best typified perhaps by the deference toward political authority and political institutions such as the monarchy. The outpouring of emotion over the marriage of Prince Charles and Lady Diana Spencer in July 1981 reveals much about the continuing importance of traditional authority in the British polity. Custom and convention play a significant role in the operation of the British political system,

because Britain lacks a comprehensive, written constitution, preferring instead to rely on traditional modes of behaviour. As these examples illustrate, each political system is first of all a mixture or combination of the various bases of authority and second, the strength of the differing bases of legitimation changes from one political system to the next.

If political systems seek to legitimate their distribution of influence through traditional, legal-rational, or charismatic means, then one can properly ask that basic question of political analysis: why? The answer is relatively straightforward:

> Authority is a highly efficient form of influence. It is not only more reliable and durable than naked coercion, but it also enables a ruler to govern with a minimum of political resources (Dahl, 1984: 54).

No political system which rested on the sole use of sanctions and coercion to maintain a particular pattern of influence could long endure. People are taught to obey, to accept the legitimacy of particular political institutions and political processes, thus making coercion unnecessary: the "vast majority of men have

Attacking Authority: British-style: In April of 1988, a left-wing member of the opposition Labour Party, Ron Brown, in protest against government cuts in welfare payments, picked up the seventeenth-century mace and allegedly threw it to the floor. The mace, part of the country's Crown Jewels, received $2000 (US) worth of damage. The militant Scottish MP was suspended from the British House of Commons for 20 sitting days.

Attacking Authority: Chinese-style: In May of 1989, Chinese students, protesting for more democracy in their political system, occupied Tiananmen Square in Beijing. Mass demonstrations, hunger strikes, and demands for the resignations of the political leaders of the Communist Party shook the regime. For several weeks martial law was unsuccessfully imposed. As an act of defiance, the students erected a replica (10 metres high) of the American Statue of Liberty in the centre of Tiananmen Square — daring the authorities to remove the "goddess of democracy."

the habit of law-abidingness" (MacIver, 1965: 58).

When a particular distribution of influence loses its legitimacy, assuming it was accepted as legitimate in the first place, and when a new distribution of influence is sought, then coercion and violence may become important aspects of the political process. Both those who wish to continue the existing arrangements and those seeking a new pattern of influence may turn to coercion and violence to accomplish their ends.

No political system is immune from such a development: "In politics we are always living on volcanic soil. We must be prepared for abrupt convulsions and eruptions" (Cassirer, 1946: 280). In Canada the willingness of the FLQ in the late 1960s to use violence (bombings, kidnappings, and murder) to overthrow the existing political system led to the use of coercion (the War Measures Act) by the political leadership. Similarly, Britain's continuing problem in dealing with the conflict in Northern Ireland shows that no system can entirely avoid such phenomena. For example, the IRA claimed responsibility for bombing the hotel in Brighton, England where the Conservatives were holding their annual meeting in October, 1984. Prime Minister Margaret Thatcher, as well as most of her cabinet, narrowly missed being killed. However, a legitimate distribution of influence reduces the likelihood of such conflicts.

POLITICAL LANGUAGE

Having defined the key concepts of political power, influence, and authority, we can now ask how it is that they are carried out. The answer is that if politics describes patterns of human interaction, then such relationships involve a process of communication, or as one writer described it, "politics is talk" (Bell, 1975: 10). Political communication, including the development of political concepts, their changes in meaning through time, and the control of political language by agencies of the political system, reveals a lot about the distribution and nature of political influence in any particular polity.

The importance of political language can be seen in the political controversies that have faced the Canadian system over the years. For example, the use of language and the language

A politician, in fact any public figure, learns by intuition and by observation what can and should be discussed as well as what cannot and should not be spoken. The issues that require silent accommodation, however, are often less clear than the fact of their existence (Bégin, 1988: 335).

Political Language:
Because much of what a politician does has to do with the art of putting people under an obligation to him, rhetoric must be recognized as a political instrument (Paine, 1981: 1).

Fuddle Duddle (Trudeau, February 16, 1971).

The critical element in political maneuver for advantage is the creation of meaning: the construction of beliefs about the significance of events, of problems, of crises, of policy changes, and of leaders (Edelman, 1985: 10).

In Canada, the politics of language is invariably divisive. This is not because the difference between "yes" and "oui" is worth dying for but because the language debate has always been the outer dress of the twin solitudes that identify the Canadian soul (Fraser, 1989: 13).

explicit meanings (i.e., their **denotative** aspects), but also with regard to what they imply (i.e., their **connotative** aspects). For example, René Lévesque as Parti Québécois leader insisted that the party use the term "independence" rather than "separation" to describe its political objectives. While the final products of independence and separation may be identical, the connotative aspects of both words are not: independence has positive connotations, while separation has negative connotations, conjuring up an image of secession and political strife, even violence. Similarly, during the 1976 American presidential election campaign, Gerald Ford announced that he would no longer use the word détente to describe Soviet-American relations. The reason for such a declaration was simply that détente was beginning to be critically viewed as an international balance-of-power system weighted in favour of the Soviet Union, and no president of the United States, especially

of use has been a key political issue in federal politics (bilingualism in the federal civil service) and Quebec provincial politics (Bill 101) (see Coleman, 1983; LaPonce, 1985). Moreover, concepts describing the federal structure of the country have included classical federalism, executive federalism, dual federalism, cooperative federalism, among a host of others. Perhaps more revealing about the significance of language than any other term is the concept of Confederation itself. If one assumes that Canada is a confederal system, then a totally incorrect view is the result: Canada may be a confederation, but it is not a confederal form of government. As well, a related battle over Quebec's role in the federal system has been in part a conflict over language and its meaning: will Quebec remain in the federal system as a result of a "renewed federalism," will it obtain greater autonomy under a "special status" option, or will it acquire "sovereignty-association"? The issue was further confused by the language of the now defeated Meech Lake accord. Quebec was designated "a distinct society," but the phrase was left undefined and thus open to various and conflicting interpretations.

Not only do political concepts differ in their

"When I use a word," Humpty Dumpty said in rather a scornful tone, "it means just what I choose it to mean — neither more nor less."

"The question is," said Alice, "whether you can make words mean so many different things."

"The question is," said Humpty Dumpty, "which is to be master — that's all."

Source: Lewis Carroll, *Through the Looking Glass.*

It is no exaggeration to describe plain English as a fundamental tool of good government (Prime Minister Margaret Thatcher, 1988).

a non-elected incumbent president in the midst of a primary election battle, could accept such a situation.

A further example of the connotative aspects of political communication was the assertion by then American Secretary of State Alexander Haig in March 1981, that those individuals and groups in the international system who used violence to achieve their ends were considered by the United States government to be "terrorists" backed by the Soviet Union, not "freedom fighters." The connotative difference between "terrorists" and "freedom fighters" is considerable. Such controversies as these over the denotative and connotative aspects of political language demonstrate that the political communication process is significant because it helps to structure how we perceive, think, and act politically.

The importance of political language is reflected in the extensive efforts political systems make to control or at least to regulate and influence various aspects of the political communication process. Generally speaking, the extent of control is greatest in totalitarian systems, least in democratic systems, and moderate to widespread in autocratic polities. One way of controlling language is to have a single, state-run communications network which can then be used to ensure conformity of political discourse, as in the Soviet Union. One of the most disturbing aspects of the growth of the Solidarity Union in Poland, from the Soviet Union's perspective, was the demand that this group be given access to and the right to appear on the state-run television system. The temporary acceptance of this demand, as a result of the strikes in the fall of 1980 and winter of 1981,

indicated to the Soviet Union that the Polish Communist Party was losing control of the overall political situation. State control of the political communication process can sometimes produce ludicrous results, as when Afghanistan's state radio announced that "President Noor Mohammed Taraki had resigned 'for reasons of ill health'; it turned out his health was affected by 12 bullet holes in his body" (Safire, 1980: 213).

Perhaps the most notorious use of political language in recent history was the direct control exercised by the state in Germany under Hitler (Mueller, 1973: 24–42). Through the Office of the Press, for example, Language Regulations were issued, as on December 13, 1937, when the order was given that the term "League of Nations" could no longer be used: "This word no longer exists." Under the Nazis new terms were created: for example, "Rassenschande," which meant marriage to or intimate relations with a non-Aryan, equivalent to "blemishing one's race." Old words acquired new meanings, as was the case for "Intellect," which in the Weimar Republic meant "creative capacity," but under Hitler was "a term denoting a critical, subversive, and destructive quality." The extent of state control over the political communication process in totalitarian systems is based on the explicit recognition of the fact that "language and political consciousness are elements that go hand in hand and that determine the way in which the individual relates to his environment" (Mueller, 1973: 19).

In democratic political systems like Canada, the United States, and Britain, such extensive control of the political communications network is limited. However, issues do arise on a fairly regular basis that provoke debate over the legitimate role of the state in the political discourse of the nation. For example, in the fall of 1980, the federal Liberal government ran a series of ads in support of its constitutional renewal efforts, ads that featured idyllic scenes of the Canadian landscape and talked generally of the

The State and Political Language:
Examples of attempts by the state to politically control language abound. For example, in Iran many Western clothes and names are outlawed. In 1986 government authorities indicated that "punk" and "Nike" were no longer acceptable terms in the Islamic Republic. In Israel, in the summer of 1988, a spokesman for the state-run Israel Broadcasting Authority announced that radio and television reporters could no longer use the word **intifada**, the Arabic term for the Palestinian uprising. In Argentina, since the late nineteenth century, the Argentine Civil Registry determines what names are permissible or not for your children. The names Ronald and Democracy are unacceptable.

Historically, one of the most famous examples is that of the French Academy, founded by Cardinal Richelieu in 1635 to protect the purity of the French language. A particular concern in recent decades has been the increasing use of English words incorporated into the French language.

While nothing approaching these systems exists in Canada, it would probably surprise most Canadians to discover that in 1890 an order-in-council was passed requiring the use of "our" in such words as labour or colour in all official documents and the *Canada Gazette*. Moreover, the Department of the Secretary of State in Canada publishes a separate style manual regarding the proper use of both the English and French languages.

Political Language and "The Oxford Dictionary": In preparing an edition of the *Shorter Oxford Dictionary* for sale in the Soviet Union in the mid-1980s, Oxford University Press was required to change the definitions of key political terms. For example, the definition of capitalism as the "condition of possessing capital or using it for production; a system of society based on this; dominance of private capitalists" was redefined in the Soviet edition as an "economic and social system based on private ownership of the means of production operated for private profit, and on the exploitation of man by man" (Pincher, 1986: 106).

need for political change. Opposition parties rightly attacked such advertising as an example of how the Liberal party was using public money to build support for its own purposes. After viewing the constitutional ads, which featured Canadian wildlife, then NDP finance critic Bob Rae asserted, "I'll never look at a beaver or a Canada goose in the same way again. I'll see them as Liberals in disguise."

The significant issue raised by government advertising is the proper role of government agencies in controlling the nature of and access to the political communication process. Democratic political systems have tended to refrain from state control, and if state-supported communications systems are created, such as the CBC in Canada or the BBC in Britain, then provisions are made to try to ensure the political neutrality or nonpartisanship of such an effort. The recurring charges of a supposedly "separatist" bias in the French CBC network are a case in point. So also is the BBC incident in July, 1985 concerning the airing of a one-hour documentary entitled "At the Edge of the Union" in the BBC's "Real Lives" series, which included an interview with the reputed chief of staff of the Provisional IRA. As a result of unprecedented pressure from officials in the Thatcher government, the BBC's board of governors decided not to show the interview. Other cases of alleged interference by the British Tories in the affairs of the BBC were evident throughout the 1980s. The blatant use in the 1970s of the state-run network in France by the political executive also illustrates the danger, even in a democratic

---

**Political Language:
The Style of George Bush**

"I will never apologize for the United States of America—I don't care what the facts are."

On the drug problem: "I'm going to be coming out with my own drug problem."

On Ronald Reagan: "We have had triumphs, we have made mistakes, we have had sex . . . We have had setbacks."

On himself: "I feel like a javelin thrower who won the coin toss and elected to receive."

---

language election debate all illustrate such a conclusion.

Basic Principles of Political Analysis

The concepts of political influence, power, authority, resources, and language are the basic building blocks of political analysis. However, they only provide a starting place, not our final destination. In using these basic concepts, we must also be familiar with a number of more general items, what we have called basic principles of political analysis. Each of these five basic principles focuses on how we study and analyze political phenomena.

Principle one—political theory versus political practice

In the sphere of politics, considerable distance separates the practices or reality of the political process from the way that process was designed to operate. The political analyst is particularly concerned with the discrepancy between intent and practice.

A classic example of the difference between theory and practice concerns the respective roles of the governor general and prime minister in the Canadian system. While the Constitution Act of 1867 contains an extensive description of the duties of the governor general, no mention is made of the prime minister. However, no political analyst would seriously argue, as a result, that the governor general is more influential and powerful than the prime minister. To assume that the governor general's role is the same as that described in the 1867 Constitution Act would give one a totally fallacious perspective of the political influence of Canada's formal executive (Dawson, 1970: 59).

An analogous argument could be made about the respective powers of the monarch and prime

political system, of involving the state directly in the political communication process.

The ability to use language has had an impact on the success of various political leaders in Canada. The dominance of Pierre Trudeau over both Robert Stanfield and Joe Clark was due in no small measure to his greater effectiveness as a political communicator. Inability to communicate is seen by the Canadian voter, rightly or wrongly, as reflecting an inability to lead the country, or as Allan Fotheringham (1981: 60) wrote, "the real reason why Joe Clark has trouble grasping the nerve ends of the nation is that he does not talk like a normal 41-year-old male North American." For example, I have often suggested that Joe Clark might define an examination as the students' opportunity to explicate the totality of the specificity of their ignorance. Effectiveness of political communication and the ability to use political language are an important political resource, therefore, in gaining influence in the political system. John Crosbie's inability to speak French and his ensuing loss in the 1983 Conservative leadership convention, Brian Mulroney's fluency in both official languages, as demonstrated in the leaders' debates during the 1984 federal election, and Ed Broadbent's poor showing in the 1988 French-

> The gap between political ideal and political reality is a continuing central phenomenon of American politics in a way that is not true of any other major state (Huntington, 1981: 3).

minister in British politics: the monarch reigns, the prime minister governs. What has happened is that the political executive in both Canada and Britain has followed "the technique of the hermit crab, the crustacean that destroys a mollusk in order to set up housekeeping in its shell. The outer appearance is scarcely altered but the interior is completely changed" (Duverger, 1974: 51–52). In other words, the governor general has retained some of the trappings of power in the Canadian system, while the prime minister has acquired its substance.

Any political system provides numerous instances of the differences between theory and practice. In the United States, for example, the Vietnam war created a major constitutional debate over which branch of government (executive or legislative) had the right to commit American power and prestige to a foreign conflict. Although the United States Constitution is explicit in granting Congress the power to "declare war" (Article 1, Section 8), in practice the president has acquired, particularly in the 20th century, the power to "make war." The president, as Commander-in-Chief of the Armed Forces, can commit troops or take other actions to involve the United States in a war. As a result, although the legislative prerogative to declare war remains, in current circumstances it is largely a formality.

Similar examples of the differences between theory and practice are evident in other countries as well. For example, in France, the Constitution of the Fifth Republic (1958 to the present) envisages the role of the president as an arbitrator of the constitutional system: however, under Charles de Gaulle, the president

quickly became the chief politician and policy-maker. In theory, the Soviet Union is a federal political structure; in practice it is more unitary than federal. However, the nationalist aspirations of the Baltic states and various ethnic groups in the Soviet Union may alter this assessment in the 1990s. What these examples show is the importance of recognizing in political analysis the difference between how a political system was theoretically designed to operate and how it works in fact. The political analyst usually begins with a consideration of intent and concludes with a focus on actual political practice.

Principle two — political custom and convention

The emphasis on actual political practices brings us to our second principle of political analysis, which stresses the role of custom in any political system. In many respects this principle is an outgrowth of Oakeshott's argument that politics in any country represents a "tradition of behaviour." Some of that tradition may be embodied in law; much of it, however, reposes in the custom of the polity. Political custom and convention fill in the interstices of the political structure, turning abstract principles into working institutions. For example, if a constitution provides a structural skeleton for the political system, custom and convention flesh out the body politic.

In Canada, the role of custom and convention is particularly significant. Many of the most important aspects of the Canadian political system are nowhere written down. For example, the notion of responsible government, that a government must have the support and confidence of the House of Commons in order to remain in power, is based on political tradition, not law. The need for a cabinet minister either to have a seat in the House of Commons or to be appointed to the Senate is similarly undefined. Custom requires ministers to seek a seat at the earliest reasonable opportunity, but if they lose in the first election bid, they can remain in the cabinet and try again later. The composition of the cabinet is likewise based on custom. The working of the representation principle, that all provinces and major groups, whenever possible, be given cabinet portfolios, which has been the basis of cabinet selection since John A. Macdonald, has become a "rigid convention" of the Canadian political process (Matheson, 1976: 27).

Custom and convention may even modify those aspects of the political process which have been defined in law. For example, the legal right of the federal government to disallow any piece of provincial legislation within one year of its passage has been greatly restricted in actual practice. The last time a provincial act was disallowed was 1943. The federal government, because of the convention of only considering disallowance if the provincial legislation usurps federal jurisdiction or powers, has allowed its legal power to fall into nonuse. The legal basis for disallowance remains; the political will to exercise it has been circumscribed by custom.

In some cases, a specific custom or convention may be recognized as so important that it is later incorporated into law. For example, until 1940 in the United States, no individual had ever served for more than two terms as president of the United States. However, when Democrat Franklin Roosevelt broke this tradition with his four presidential victories (1932, 1936, 1940, 1944), the Republicans, when they won office, secured the Twenty-Second Amendment to the American Constitution, which limited all future presidents to two terms. Thus did a 150-year-old custom become law in 1951.

Although custom and convention fill in the details of a political structure, too heavy a reliance on tradition can create some difficult political conflicts. If everyone, or at least all major political actors, are agreed on what the convention is and how it operates, few problems arise. However, when there are differing interpretations of a political custom, controversy may

result. A good example of this point is the Canadian constitutional crisis of 1968: a Liberal government, defeated on a tax measure, refused to resign, claiming that its defeat did not constitute a motion of non-confidence. So much for the convention that a defeat of a government's legislation constitutes a defeat of the government itself.

Custom and convention pervade all aspects of the political process, as the polity accommodates itself to its political environment. Custom and convention, then, flesh out the workings of the body politic. In particular, custom and convention are adaptive mechanisms for reconciling the political structure to evolving circumstances. As such, they point to the importance of our third principle of political analysis — namely, the significance of political change.

Principle three—time and political change

Time is probably the most overlooked element in political analysis. More often than not political analysis has ignored the historical dimension, concentrating instead on the problems of the present. However, "without knowledge of the details and patterns of the past, a student of politics is like a man without a memory" (McNaught, 1983: 89). The political patterns of the present are the children and grandchildren of the political battles of the past. One cannot adequately understand the present polity without some understanding of how we got here.

Every major issue facing the Canadian system has been influenced by how that issue was dealt with previously. For example, the desire by the new Mulroney government in 1984 to move towards freer trade with the United States reflected past historical battles. Previously, the support of free trade, then known as reciprocity, had led to the defeat of governments in general elections (e.g., the Liberals in the 1911 federal election). Thus, the Conservatives in 1984–1985 initially spoke not of reciprocity nor of free

Time and Politics:

A week is a long time in politics (former British Prime Minister Harold Wilson).

No political structure of any size can dispense with order, and one of the fundamental applications of order is to time, for no communal human activity can take place without it. Indeed one might say that the regulation of time is the primary attribute of all government (Canetti, 1966: 397).

. . . politicians, like hockey players, seem destined to push back the day of reckoning. In sports, as in politics, rare are the players who know when their time has come (Simpson, 1984).

trade, but instead chose the term freer trade, hoping to rid themselves of some of the historical legacies of the other concepts.

The move by Pierre Trudeau to patriate the Constitution unilaterally in the fall of 1980 was justified, in part, by the federal government for historical reasons: half a century of attempts to acquire unanimous provincial consent for such a move was seen as sufficient provocation to act alone. Likewise, Canadian-American relations must be seen in an historical context, otherwise more current problems, such as the failure of the United States senate to ratify the fishing treaty in the fall of 1980, the dispute between North Dakota and Manitoba over the Garrison Dam Project, or differing interpretations of the importance of acid rain appear to be unintelligible. Similarly, the way particular political institutions, such as Parliament, have evolved can only be appreciated in their historical context.

Time, then, is the context of history, which provides the setting for the drama of politics. Time is also involved in the process of political change for the simple reason that birth is highly correlated with death: no political leader can last forever (even those, like Mackenzie King, with extensive contacts in the spirit world). When Pierre Trudeau became Prime Minister in 1968, he was the youngest member at any First Ministers' Conference; at the point of the 1979 election, he was the oldest. Trudeau's reincarnation less than a year later as Prime Minister, and his subsequent move to patriate the British North America Act of 1867, were greatly influenced by historical considerations: he viewed giving Canada a new Constitution as possibly his last political contribution before retirement.

Time is also a direct influence on the polity because many basic political events are conditioned by when they occur. For example, the timing of a budget, a cabinet shuffle, or an election call can have an important bearing on the distribution of influence in a political system. While our analysis will centre on present political practices in Canada, Britain, and the United States, we will attempt to show how these current patterns have evolved historically.

Principle four — legal versus political decisions

Our fourth principle of political analysis focuses on the differences between a legal decision or action and a political decision or action. We use legal in the sense of pertaining to the law: a legal decision is based on the law and constitution, or one that is assumed to be consistent with the law, even though it may not be specifically dealt with in a particular statute. A political decision is one based on considerations of influence and power. While we would expect that political decisions would also be legal ones, especially in democratic systems, such a congruence need not be the case. The legitimacy of government is certainly enhanced when legal and political decisions mesh, and undercut when they do not.

The difference between a legal and a political decision is well illustrated by the federal government's reaction to the introduction of Bill 101 by the Parti Québécois and its passage by the National Assembly after the PQ's 1976 provincial election victory. There was no doubt that certain aspects of Bill 101, which moved Quebec towards being a unilingual province, infringed on the language rights guaranteed by the British North America Act of 1867 (now the Constitution Act of 1867). In particular, Section 133 of the Constitution, which gave protection to both the English and French languages in the Quebec provincial legislature and the federal and provincial courts in Quebec, was explicitly disregarded by Bill 101, as subsequent court rulings made clear. Why then did the Quebec government pass the legislation in the first place and why did the federal government, in response, not disallow such a measure? The answer to both questions should be obvious: the provincial and federal governments were making political, not legal, decisions.

Having won their first provincial victory on a "nationalist" program designed to protect the French language and culture in Quebec, the Parti Québécois had little to lose and much to gain by being seen as the only political party with the will to take strong action to protect French interests in the province. With 80 percent of the population French-speaking, being in favour of the linguistic rights for that sector could only be politically rewarding, particularly in light of the party's 41 percent popular vote in the recent provincial election. An emotive issue like language rights was being used to appeal to those members of the public who had not voted for the party in 1976. Moreover, vigorous action in promotion of the French language undercut the political base of the opposition parties, particularly the Liberals, who were labeled by the government as the party defending English interests in Quebec. No party could survive such an image, since it would be impossible to win power in any future election on the basis of the English sector alone. Thus, certain provisions of Bill 101 were known in advance to be contrary to Section 133 of the British North America Act—a fact that did nothing to deter

the provincial government's passage of the legislation. The possibility of Bill 101 being disallowed by the federal government was also a political plus for the Parti Québécois: such a move by Ottawa could then be seen as further proof that the French culture would survive only through independence.

The federal government's response to Bill 101 was political, rather than legal, in form. Even though Prime Minister Trudeau repeatedly condemned the legislation, Ottawa decided not to use its power of disallowance against Bill 101, because of the political repercussions such an action might precipitate in Quebec. The federal Liberals took a legal hands-off attitude, while at the same time they encouraged private groups and individuals to challenge the legislation in the courts. It must also be remembered that the Liberal party was in a majority position in the national legislature in 1976, making it most unlikely that their stance on this issue could bring about their defeat and, second, that the Liberal party's dominance in national politics resided in their Quebec stronghold. No federal party based in Quebec could use the power of disallowance against their "home" province on a piece of legislation designed to protect the French language and culture in Quebec. Hence, for political reasons, the federal Liberal party did not invoke the disallowance power against Bill 101: legally it could have done so, but the political judgment was contrary, and it prevailed.

Many events in the political process can be understood only if the distinction between legal and political actions is kept in mind. For example, the formal executive in Canada, the governor general, has the legal basis for refusing a request coming from the prime minister for a dissolution of Parliament. Politically, however, such an action by the governor general is unlikely, except in the most extreme circumstances. Such an argument could be made about other aspects of the formal executive's role in Canada as well: as one writer asserted, the governor general is "a legal survivor who has contrived to remain a political necessity" (Dawson, 1970: 143).

While the governor general's role illustrates the pattern of having a legal basis for decisions, even though such action is rarely taken for political reasons, governments also find that political decisions are made without having a legal foundation for them. For example, considerable evidence presented to the McDonald Royal Commission on RCMP Activities showed political actions being taken that were clearly illegal. The most notorious situation involved the burning down of a barn in Quebec so that a group of political radicals could not hold their meeting. One wonders whether the Forum in Montreal might also have been torched if the radicals had decided to meet at a hockey game. Other actions were also clearly illegal, but seen as politically necessary, as when the computer tapes containing the membership files of the Parti Québécois were stolen, copied, and then returned.

If too many such examples come to light, they might undercut the legitimacy of the government. As a result, governments may make legal actions they consider to be politically necessary. The federal government's move in the mid-1970s to provide a legal basis for wiretapping is a case in point. Similarly, in response to the RCMP wrongdoings revealed before the McDonald Royal Commission in the late 1970s, both major parties, when in office, took the view that the way to handle the situation was to make whatever the RCMP was doing legal in the future.

Even if political actions are challenged in court and ruled illegal, the government can always call the legislature into session and, in most cases, pass what is known as **retroactive legislation**. Such legislation changes the law so that previously illegal actions are declared legal after they have occurred — a convenient weapon in the arsenal of government power. A citizen may also find that a previously legal action can be declared illegal by the government, with pen-alties imposed retroactively. For example, with the imposition of the War Measures Act in 1970, it became a crime, retroactively, to have ever been a member of the FLQ, even though being an FLQ member in the 1960s was not illegal (Stewart, 1971: 59)! Such examples demonstrate the importance of our fourth principle of political analysis.

Principle five — political structures and political functions

Our final principle of political analysis looks at the difference between political structures and political functions. A **political structure**, such as the House of Commons or the cabinet, *is composed of a set of political roles or expected patterns of behaviour.* No matter which party or individual happens to fill these roles, certain behavioural patterns can be discerned. For example, the House of Commons will be presided over by the speaker or deputy speaker, the government will sit on the speaker's right-hand side and the opposition on his or her left, and legislation will be passed after proceeding through First, Second, and Third Readings. In other words, the House of Commons is a structure composed of regular and recurrent patterns of action. Political analysis usually begins with a look at political structures, presenting a description of the framework or institutional context of the political process.

Political functions *refer to the consequences or results of the various political structures: the jobs or tasks the structures perform for the political system.* To describe the structure of the Canadian cabinet, a political analyst would discuss its size, how its members are selected, how it arrives at decisions, and how it is internally composed of various cabinet committees. In describing the function of the Canadian cabinet, the political analyst would look at its effects on the political process in terms of a policy-making function (i.e., it is the primary policy-making institution) and possibly a representation-symbolic function (i.e., it represents the various groups in the Canadian parliamentary system).

Any political structure can perform one or more political functions and any political function can be carried out by one or more political structures. A structure such as a political party provides several functions, including the recruitment of candidates to run for office, the organization of the electorate around certain policies and programs, and, if it wins the election, the provision of people to occupy the top political positions in the country. An example of a function being performed by several structures would be the policy-making function, exercised by the cabinet, the prime minister's office, and the civil service. Thus, in political analysis we must distinguish between structures and functions and deal with both topics in examining any particular political system.

The above five principles of political analysis, as well as the basic concepts, will serve as our guide in investigating the political process in Canada, Britain, and the United States. These principles and concepts reflect a combination of the basic ways through which we study political phenomena.

Comparative Political Analysis

Several basic approaches can be used to make a comparative analysis of the political process. After discussing these approaches, we will consider the goals and purposes of comparative political analysis.

Approaches to political analysis

There are three basic approaches to political analysis: historical, institutional, and behavioural. Each approach focuses on somewhat different aspects of the political process, but each adds to our understanding of the polity.

The **historical approach** stresses the development and evolution of the political system, rightly arguing that in order to understand the present and future, we must know something about our past. Every political institution and political practice has been molded and refined by history and each political system has had a different history. For example, to speak of the monarchy in Canada is to discuss a very different institution from the monarchy in Britain. History has given each polity certain unique characteristics and practices.

The second approach to political analysis focuses on political institutions and political structures. The **institutional approach** describes and explains the basic political structures and how they were designed to operate. Political institutions and structures reflect and create a distribution of power and influence in any political system, for "government institutions consist of those structures whose incumbents actually or potentially regulate all other power centers or institutions . . . within that country" (Redekop, 1983: 149). Thus, political institutions provide the framework within which the struggle for power and influence takes place. An institutional approach will therefore discuss such factors as a country's constitution and the structure of the various branches of government (legislative, executive, and judicial). Since politics occurs within a particular institutional context, the student of politics must have a firm grasp of political structures in order to achieve an understanding of politics in a specific country.

Although the historical and institutional approaches contribute valuable insights into the political process, an additional perspective is also needed. The **behavioural approach** focuses specifically on how individuals, groups, and institutions actually behave and operate in the political process. For example, knowing the institutional structure of the polity will not tell us how that institution operates in practice. As James Bryce (1888: 159) observed,

> The great tragedy of science—the slaying of a beautiful hypothesis by an ugly fact (T.H. Huxley).

"Institutions are said to form men, but it is no less true that men give to institutions their colour and tendency." The presidency of the United States was a very different institution under John F. Kennedy than under any of his successors. The office of prime minister in Britain operates differently with Margaret Thatcher as its occupant than with James Callaghan or Edward Heath. The impact of the behavioural approach has been to expand our attention from institutions and their development to a concern with actual behaviour. The result has been a focus on such topics as voting and political parties. The behavioural persuasion in politics has as its goal the "explanation of why people behave politically as they do, and why, as a result, political processes and systems function as they do" (Eulau, 1963: 24).

An **approach to political analysis**, then, is a "way of looking at and explaining politics" (Redekop, 1983: ix). The historical, institutional, and behavioural perspectives each provide insight into different aspects of the political process. No single approach can adequately describe and explain the workings of the polity. Our five principles of political analysis reflect the wisdom of integrating the historical, institutional, and behavioural perspectives.

Comparing political systems

To this point, we have dealt with the nature of politics, the basic concepts of political analysis, the key principles of political analysis, and the various approaches to political phenomena. However, we have also indicated that the overall goal of our study is to make a comparative analysis of the political process in Canada, Britain, and the United States. Such a view implies that there is something distinctive about both the subfield of comparative politics and its method of analysis.

At its most basic level comparative politics is focused, obviously, on politics in two or more countries.

> Comparative politics is concerned with behaviour, institutions, processes, ideas, and values present in more than one country. It searches for those regularities and patterns, those similarities and differences between more than one nation-state that help to clarify the basic nature, working, and beliefs of regimes (Curtis, 1978: 1).

Comparative politics, then, analyzes political phenomena in several countries as a way of describing and explaining the nature of the political process. Hence, **comparative political analysis** refers to the method used in making such comparative descriptions and explanations.

Comparative political analysis is significant because of the understanding of politics it can provide. It not only overcomes the parochialism of simply dealing with one's own country, but it also allows us to develop a better appreciation of that system, including both its strengths and weaknesses. For example, the immediate reaction to the victory of the Parti Québécois in the 1976 provincial election was one of disbelief, bordering on panic, among some English-Canadians. However, a comparative perspective on Canadian politics might suggest that the opposite response would have been more appropriate. Few countries in the world would even permit a separatist party to develop in the first place, let alone allow it to contest for office through the electoral process. Such parties are regularly banned, even in democratic systems, and if they are not made illegal, they are discriminated against directly or indirectly. The Canadian polity not only allowed a separatist party to peacefully win power in a major province, but further allowed it to later hold a referendum on its platform of independence. A comparative assessment of the Canadian polity leads this author to contend that the political system is much stronger and more vibrant than most gloom-and-doom pundits and politicians can bring themselves to admit.

A comparative analysis of Canadian politics greatly enhances our knowledge of how the political process operates and pinpoints needed areas of reform. The expansion of the political executive's role in Canada, for example, is not an isolated development—similar trends have occurred in Britain and the United States. Only a comparative approach can make such a Canadian development explicable in terms of similar processes elsewhere. Likewise, political reform in Canada has often been inspired by events abroad. The Watergate scandal in the United States in the early 1970s helped to create a climate favourable for the adoption in 1974 of public financing of federal election campaigns in Canada. The existence of a freedom of information law in the United States helped to spur the demand for such legislation in Canada. Viewing a country's political system from a comparative perspective thus expands our knowledge of our own and other systems, and produces explanations for the patterns of politics that are discovered. Comparing political systems, however, creates a number of problems for the political analyst.

Problems of comparing political systems

While the following concerns are relevant to any political analysis, their importance is enhanced when we compare political systems with each other. The first problem is the selection of countries to be compared. The subject of comparison should be chosen to increase the likelihood of being able to identify similarities and differences between them. For that reason, since we seek to understand Canadian politics from a comparative perspective, we will primarily compare it with British and American politics, the two systems that have had the greatest historical impact on the development of the Canadian system. Moreover, these two systems, given their particular composition of various types of political structures, should highlight key aspects of the political process in Canada.

The second problem concerns which aspects of those systems to compare. At the most general level, we are interested in cross-national comparisons, that is, comparing Canadian politics with the British and American patterns. However, in order to make our comparisons more manageable, we will most often compare various subunits of each system. For example, in Chapter 11 we compare the electoral systems used in the three countries, investigating both the types utilized and their effects. Comparisons of electoral systems, legislatures, or parties are examples of structural or institutional comparisons. However, we will also consider functional comparisons, that is, how the tasks carried out by an institution, such as the legislature, vary between political systems.

A third problem relates to the question of time: which historical periods should serve as the basis for the comparison? The use of different historical periods would greatly change the nature and conclusions of our comparisons. For example, a comparison of Canadian and American politics in the 1890s would produce very different results than such a study a century later, because both systems have changed drastically in the past 100 years. The time frame for our comparison will thus be the current political practices in Canada, Britain, and the United States.

While problems such as these increase the difficulty of comparing political systems, if they can be overcome the results can be most rewarding, for comparisons help us answer that basic question of political analysis: why? In this sense, political analysis has an objective analogous to that of political philosophy, namely, the search for order.

Summary

1. Politics can be defined as the exercise of power and influence on matters that affect the community, while political analysis is the attempt to explain why a specific pattern of power and influence emerges, how power is gained and lost, and why certain political events occur.

2. Politics can be defined in numerous ways, with normative approaches stressing "what ought to be" and empirical ones focusing on "what is." Politics can also be defined in ideological terms, with a conservative definition seeing "politics as tradition," a liberal one viewing "politics as conciliation," and a revolutionary perspective, such as Marxism, perceiving "politics as superstructure."

3. Political power and influence are concepts that describe human relationships that are causal in nature and public in their import. People exercise influence when they change other people's attitudes or behaviour and they exercise power when such changes are accomplished by the use of sanctions, real or apprehended. Authority is legitimate influence and can be based on tradition, charisma, or legal-rational norms. Political communication is the means of carrying out influence and power relationships, with political language structuring how we perceive, think, and feel about politics.

4. In analyzing politics, five principles should be kept in mind: first, the difference between political theory and political practice; second, the importance of political custom and convention; third, the historical dimension and political change; fourth, the difference between legal and political decisions; and fifth, the difference between political structures and political functions.

5. Approaches to political analysis include the historical (a focus on the development and evolution of political institutions and processes), the institutional (a look at political structures and how they were designed to operate), and the behavioural (a focus on how individuals, groups, and institutions actually operate).

6. Comparative political analysis, which is based on a consideration of politics in two or more countries, helps to overcome the parochialism of only dealing with one's own country, while at the same time it aids in a recognition of the strengths and weaknesses of various kinds of political institutions and political systems.

Recommended Readings

The Nature of Politics

AKERMAN, JEREMY (1977) *What Have You Done For Me Lately? A Politician Explains*. Windsor, Nova Scotia: Lancelot Press.

BARADAT, LEON P. (1988) *Political Ideologies: Their Origins and Impact*. Englewood Cliffs, N.J.: Prentice Hall, 3rd ed.

BARKER, ERNEST, ed. (1962) *The Politics of Aristotle*. New York: Oxford University Press.

BÉGIN, MONIQUE (1988) "Debates and Silences — Reflections of a Politician," *Daedalus* (Fall), Volume 117, Number 4, pp. 335–362.

EBENSTEIN, WILLIAM and EDWIN FOGELMAN (1985) *Today's Isms: Communism, Fascism, Capitalism, Socialism*. Englewood Cliffs, N.J.: Prentice-Hall, 9th ed.

ELLUL, JACQUES (1972) *The Political Illusion*. New York: Vintage.

KARP, WALTER (1988) "In Defense of Politics," *Harper's* (May), Volume 226, Number 1656, pp. 41–49.

LEFTWICH, ADRIAN, ed. (1984) *What is Politics: The Activity and Its Study*. Oxford: Basil Blackwell.

MACIVER, R.M. (1965) *The Web of Government*. New York: The Free Press, rev. ed.

MCLELLAN, DAVID (1986) *Ideology*. Minneapolis: University of Minnesota Press.

RAHE, PAUL A. (1984) "The Primacy of Politics in Classical Greece," *The American Historical Review*, Volume 89, Number 2, pp. 265–293.

SARTORI, GIOVANNI (1987) *The Theory of Democracy Revisited. Part Two: The Classical Issues*. Chatham, N.J.: Chatham House Publishers.

WOLIN, SHELDON S. (1960) *Politics and Vision: Continuity and Innovation in Western Political Thought*. Boston: Little, Brown and Co.

Basic Concepts of Political Analysis

BELL, DAVID V.J. (1975) *Power, Influence, and Authority: An Essay in Political Linguistics*. New York: Oxford University Press.

CAMERON, STEVIE (1989) *Ottawa Inside Out: Power, Prestige and Scandal in the Nation's Capital*. Toronto: Key Porter Books.

CANETTI, ELIAS (1966) *Crowds and Power*. New York: Viking Press.

DAHL, ROBERT A. (1970) *After the Revolution? Authority in a Good Society*. New Haven: Yale University Press.

DE JOUVENEL, BERTRAND (1962) *On Power: Its Nature and the History of Its Growth*. Boston: Beacon Press.

GRAHAM, ROGER (1970) "Charisma and Canadian Politics," pp. 100–121 in John S. Muir, ed., *Character and Circumstance: Essays in Honour of Donald Grant Creighton*. Toronto: University of Toronto Press.

HWANG, KWANG-KUO (1987) "Face and Favor: The Chinese Power Game," *American Journal of Sociology* (January), Volume 92, Number 4, pp. 944–974.

KERTZER, DAVID I. (1988) *Ritual, Politics, and Power*. New Haven: Yale University Press.

LANE, CHRISTEL (1984) "Legitimacy and Power in the Soviet Union Through Socialist Ritual," *British Journal of Political Science* (April), Volume 14, Part 2, pp. 207–217.

LASSWELL, HAROLD D. and ABRAHAM KAPLAN (1950) *Power and Society: A Framework for Political Inquiry*. New Haven: Yale University Press.

MERRIAM, CHARLES E. (1964) *Political Power*. New York: Collier Books.

OLIVER, DAWN (1989) "Law, Convention and Abuse of Power," *The Political Quarterly* (January), Volume 60, Number 1, pp. 38–49.

PLANO, JACK C., ROBERT E. RIGGS, and HELENAN S. ROBIN (1982) *The Dictionary of Political Analysis*. Santa Barbara, California: ABC-CLIO Information Services, 2nd ed.

RUDOLPH, SUSANNE HOEBER and LLOYD I. RUDOLPH (1984) *Ghandi: The Traditional Roots of Charisma*. Chicago: University of Chicago Press.

SABETTI, FILIPPO (1984) *Political Authority in a Sicilian Village*. New Brunswick, N.J.: Rutgers University Press.

SMITH, HEDRICK (1988) *The Power Game: How Washington Works*. New York: Random House.

WILLNER, ANN RUTH (1984) *The Spellbinders: Charismatic Political Leadership*. New Haven: Yale University Press.

Political Language

BARBER, BENJAMIN (1986) "A New Language for the Left: Translating the Conservative Discourse," *Harper's* (November), Volume 273, Number 1638, pp. 47–52.

BOTTOMORE, TOM, ed. (1983) *A Dictionary of Marxist Thought*. Cambridge, Mass.: Harvard University.

EDELMAN, MURRAY (1977) *Political Language: Words that Succeed and Policies that Fail*. New York: Academic Press.

ELDER, CHARLES D. and ROGER W. COBB (1983) *The Political Uses of Symbols*. New York: Longman.

ELSHTAIN, JEAN BETHKE (1985) "The Relationship Between Political Language and Political Reality," *PS* (Winter), Volume 18, Number 1, pp. 20–26.

HIRSCHMAN, ALBERT O. (1989) "Reactionary Rhetoric," *The Atlantic Monthly* (May), Volume 263, Number 5, pp. 63–70.

LARUE, L.H. (1988) *Political Discourse: A Case Study of the Watergate Affair*. Athens, Georgia: The University of Georgia Press.

LEWIS, BERNARD (1988) *The Political Language of Islam*. Chicago: The University of Chicago Press.

MUELLER, CLAUS (1973) *The Politics of Communication: A Study in the Political Sociology of Language, Socialization, and Legitimation*. New York: Oxford University Press.

PAINE, ROBERT (1981) *Ayatollahs and Turkey Trots: Political Rhetoric in the New Newfoundland — Crosbie, Jamieson and Peckford*. St. John's: Breakwater.

SAFIRE, WILLIAM (1978) *Safire's Political Dictionary*. New York: Ballantine Books.

SCHATTSCHNEIDER, E.E. (1969) "Some Political Words," Chapter 6, pp. 97–112 in *Two Hundred Million Americans in Search of a Government*. New York: Holt, Rinehart and Winston.

Basic Principles of Political Analysis

DAHL, ROBERT A. (1956) *A Preface to Democratic Theory*. Chicago: University of Chicago Press.

_____ (1984) *Modern Political Analysis*. Englewood Cliffs, N.J.: Prentice-Hall, 4th ed.

EDELMAN, MURRAY (1988) *Constructing the Political Spectacle*. Chicago: The University of Chicago Press.

EULAU, HEINZ (1963) *The Behavioral Persuasion in Politics*. New York: Random House.

REDEKOP, JOHN H., ed. (1983) *Approaches to Canadian Politics*. Scarborough, Ontario: Prentice-Hall Canada, 2nd ed.

RIKER, WILLIAM H. (1986) *The Art of Political Manipulation*. New Haven: Yale University Press.

SCHATTSCHNEIDER, E.E. (1975) *The Semisovereign People*. New York: Holt, Rinehart and Winston.

WILSON, JEREMY (1988) *Analyzing Politics: An Introduction to Empirical Methods*. Scarborough, Ontario: Prentice-Hall Canada.

Comparative Political Analysis

ALMOND, GABRIEL A. and G. BINGHAM POWELL (1988) *Comparative Politics: System, Process, and Policy*. Boston: Little, Brown and Co., 4th ed.

CHARLTON, ROGER (1986) *Comparative Government*. London: Longman.

DOGAN, MATTEI and DOMINIQUE PELASSY (1984) *How to Compare Nations: Strategies in Comparative Politics*. Chatham, N.J.: Chatham House Publishers.

MACRIDIS, ROY C. (1955) *The Study of Comparative Government*. New York: Random House.

ROBERTS, GEOFFREY K. (1972) *What is Comparative Politics?* London: Macmillan.

_____ (1986) *An Introduction to Comparative Politics*. London: Edward Arnold.

SCARROW, HOWARD A. (1969) *Comparative Political Analysis: An Introduction*. New York: Harper and Row.

WALLES, MALCOLM (1988) *British and American Systems of Government*. Oxford: Philip Allan.

PART TWO

The Political Structure of the Canadian Polity

Institutions are living things, and they do not easily yield their secrets to the printed word. Predominately, that is not because they are in themselves mysterious. It is rather because they change with changes in the environment within which they operate, and partly because they differ, from one moment to the other, in terms of the men who operate them (Laski, 1940: 1).

Institutions are like fortresses. They must be well-designed and properly manned (Popper, quoted in Johnson, 1983: 91).

I am not an advocate for frequent changes in laws and constitutions, but laws and institutions must go hand in hand with the progress of the human mind. As that becomes more developed, more enlightened, as new discoveries are made, new truths discovered and manners and opinions change, with the change of circumstances, institutions must advance also to keep pace with the times (Thomas Jefferson, 1816).

3 The Constitution and Federalism: Operation and Reform

For a Constitution does not merely provide the means of settling present disputes, it is a legal garment that reveals the values that we hold. It is a document expressing that decent respect which the present owes the past; it is, at the same time, a document addressed to future generations (Berger, 1982: xiv).

Every constitutional question concerns the allocation and exercise of governmental power. No constitutional question, therefore, fails to be "political" (Black, 1963: 1).

. . . the most ancient, the most persistent, and the most lasting of the essentials of true constitutionalism still remains what it is has been almost from the beginning, the limitation of government by law (McIlwain, 1947: 22).

SOMEWHERE IN THE WORLD TODAY there is bound to be a busy group of constitution writers scribbling out their design for either a new or a reformed political system. Although we live in an era of constitution-making, we do not, at the same time, exist in an age of constitutional government. Constitutionalism is an unrealized ideal for the vast majority of nation-states in the international system, while in others it is no longer even a goal to be sought. For example, in its annual report issued in October, 1988, Amnesty International accused 135 countries (out of 159 in the United Nations) of serious human rights abuses. Nonetheless, political systems continue to produce constitutions, even when they may not be operative for any great length of time, because constitutions render important political functions.

Constitutions structure the polity by establishing the boundaries of political action; that is, they outline the basic rules of the political game. For example, when a new political system is being established, such as after a revolution, the first task to be faced is the form the desired polity will be given. Constitutional design, therefore, is an act of political creation, an attempt to translate political principles into actual institutions of government.

The daily workings of the political process take place within these rules of the game, with constitutional matters usually becoming salient only during times of crisis. For example, the federal government's imposition of the War Measures Act in Canada during the October Crisis of 1970 sent concerned members of the public and constitutional scholars scurrying to the textbooks to brush up on the Act's provisions, since the last time it had been imposed was in 1939.

By establishing some of the key rules of the

Having a constitution seems to be a matter of self-respect: no state is properly dressed without (Ridley, 1988: 340).

political game, constitutions not only structure power, but they do so in a way that helps some groups gain power and influence, while limiting the political significance of others. The rules of the political system are never neutral in their effects, although their legitimacy is certainly enhanced when they are so perceived by the public. Constitutional rules protect the interests of the people who write them: the "final, finely chiseled product then reflects the way in which the ruling elite desires its national community to be governed for its own good—and for the elite's good" (Duchacek, 1973: 9). By bestowing political advantages to some groups and disadvantages to others, constitutional rules not only structure the polity, but determine the kinds of issues and concerns likely to be dealt with in the political process. As James Mill put it in 1824, the "favorite opinions of people in power are the opinions which favour their own power." Although all kinds of systems typically utilize constitutions as a way of outlining the key features of the political regime, only in a small group of political systems does having a constitution also mean having a constitutional form of government.

Characteristics of Constitutional Government

In the current international system, there is not a strong correlation between having a piece of paper called a constitution and actually running the polity on constitutional principles. A constitution may aid in the creation of a constitutional government, but it certainly does not guarantee it. Almost all countries have constitutions, but few embody the principle of constitutionalism. A **constitutional government** *is one wherein the constitution effectively limits the power of the political elite*. Thus, in a constitutional polity

Experience has further established that institutions useful at the outset because they were appropriate to the state of society into which they were introduced, will end by becoming intolerable abuses, owing to the fact that everything around them will change (Sir Wilfrid Laurier, quoted in Forbes, 1985: 140).

Constitutions are themselves political devices. They may be viewed as self-sufficient truths in the short run; but in the long run it is political activity itself which gives—

and changes—the meaning of any constitution (Crick, 1964: 147).

. . . in so far as there is any general protection in human society against the deprivation by one group of the freedom desired by another, it is probably not to be found in constitutional forms. It is to be discovered, if at all, in extra-constitutional factors (Dahl, 1956: 134).

Political liberty is a difficult food to digest. It is only extremely robust constitutions that can take it (de Tocqueville, quoted in Commager, 1984: 71).

the "constitution organizes, but also restrains" (Friedrich, 1968: 133).

The key idea of constitutional government is the effective restraint of power, not simply whether such theoretical limitations are specified in a constitutional document. Although constitutions in the Soviet Union (e.g., the Stalinist Constitution of 1936 and the revised Constitution or fundamental law of 1977) granted each Union Republic the "right freely to secede from the USSR," no such right existed in fact, as illustrated by the denial of nationalist aspirations in the Baltic republics. While other examples could be cited, the Soviet Union's use of a constitution illustrates that constitutional government is ultimately dependent on political restraints and political forces, not constitutional niceties. A constitutional format does not lead inexorably to constitutional substance. Constitutionalism is dependent on appropriate belief and behaviour patterns to buttress an initial constitutional structure. Such a pattern of constitutional forms, reinforced by appropriate beliefs and political activity, is found in democratic systems, while autocratic and totalitarian polities may have constitutions, but not systems of constitutional government.

CONSTITUTIONAL ELEMENTS

Particularly in those countries with constitutional government, the constitution usually contains four basic elements: a preamble, an organizational chart, an amending clause, and a bill of rights (Duchacek, 1973: 25–38). The preamble serves as a political manifesto, setting out the goals and priorities of the polity. Most manifestoes are nationalistic in outlook and emotional in content, a summary statement of political idealism. Once the broad goals are defined, the rest of the constitution usually outlines the basic structures of government.

Constitutions provide an organizational chart or power map of the polity. In so doing, the constitution delineates whether the political institutions are to be federal or unitary, presidential or parliamentary in nature. For example, if a federal structure is created, then the constitution attempts to specify which level of government can exercise which political functions, which tasks are exclusive to a single level, and which functions can be performed by both levels.

Since political goals and functions change over time, constitutions may also incorporate a procedure for their own future revision, that is, an amending clause. Amending clauses are often made difficult to use, on the assumption that the "supreme law of the land" should not be routinely changed or manipulated. An amending clause attempts to specify who is involved, the nature and kinds of amendments allowed, and the procedures to be utilized.

> The language of rights has become part of the common currency of modern political life. Asserting a right has become the orthodox way in which to make a case or to formulate a demand (Jones, 1989: 69).

> What it adds up to is that a constitution, any constitution, is not a panacea but an experimental attempt of arriving at a viable and legitimate government (Friedrich, 1974: 11).

Finally, constitutions are likely to incorporate a bill of rights, based on the assumption that individuals need extra protection from their own government, as well as from the actions of their fellow citizens. Certain liberties, such as freedom of speech and freedom of assembly, are so fundamental to a democratic polity that they must be made immune to attack, no matter what the size of the government's majority or the state of public opinion. Unfortunately, it is often forgotten that popularity has nothing necessarily to do with constitutionality. In fact, it is when what is constitutional is also unpopular that the real mettle of constitutional government becomes apparent.

If constitutions outline the ingredients of the political structure and the basic rules of the political game, then they are inherently political by their very nature, for they help to determine the distribution of influence and power in the polity. The notion of constitutional impartiality is a myth, because constitutions are political documents with significant political consequences. Although constitutions are often valued as somehow being "above mere politics," such a belief has to be interpreted as a means of legitimating the constitution, rather than a description of its role in the political process.

Constitutions are political mechanisms of considerable import because they deal "with the hard core of all politics, namely who leads whom, with what intent, for what purpose, by what means, and with what restraints" (Duchacek, 1973: 9). Constitutions are also political in the sense that they may become symbols of national unity or disunity. In many countries, especially in those which have thrown off a colonial power, a constitution is an initial symbol of sovereignty, of political independence in the international arena. Constitution-making is, therefore, an ingredient of nation-building, of creating a national identity where none may have existed before.

Reforming a constitution or writing a new one is a reflection of a changing distribution of influence and power. For example, after the death of Mao Zedong in China, the constitution was revised to reflect the evolving patterns of influence and power within both the state and party structures. However, because the process of constitutional reform is often difficult, political practices may simply evolve. Thus, there is often a considerable discrepancy between the political process envisaged in the constitution and the realities of current practice. Political systems modify constitutional intent through such devices as judicial interpretation, custom and convention, and changing public beliefs. As a result, a constitution must be interpreted not only with respect to its initial design, but also in light of its adaptation to present circumstances.

The Canadian Constitution

While the Canadian polity is an example of constitutional government, the nature and specifics of that constitutional system are complex. Much of its intricacy stems from the difficulty of delineating exactly what is included in Canada's Constitution. For example, while the Constitution Act of 1867 (formerly the British North America Act of 1867) is certainly the basic constitutional document, it is not the only one. Other

> Of all constitutions based on a parliamentary framework, Canada's Constitution surely offers the richest mine of materials for the political scientist and the constitution maker. It teaches a number of lessons about the mechanics of constitution making and it raises questions about almost every major problem of constitutional government . . . (Marshall, 1988: 156).

documents of constitutional consequence would include the Bill of Rights, the War Measures Act and the 1988 Emergencies Act, the Statute of Westminster, the Supreme Court Act, and the various acts which have added new provinces since 1867. If the rejected 1987 Meech Lake accord had been ratified, it would have become an important part of Canada's constitutional system. Thus, while Canada is usually classified as having a written constitution (i.e., the Constitution Act of 1867), it has more than one written constitutional document.

Canada has had, in fact, a series of Constitution Acts. The major revisions to the initial act are entitled Constitution Acts as well. For example, the Constitution Act (Number Two) of 1949 empowered the federal government to amend its own structure and operation without resort to the British Parliament. Thus, the Canadian constitutional system includes all Constitution Acts from 1867 to the present (minus those that have been repealed, such as the Constitution Act Number Two of 1949), plus the various constitutional documents such as the 1988 Emergencies Act. The addition to this series, the Constitution Act of 1982, has brought the amending power to Canada from Britain, as well as adding a Charter of Rights and Freedoms, which applies to both the federal and provincial governments.

The complexity of constitutional government is further enhanced by the importance of custom and convention in the Canadian context. Some of the most essential aspects of the polity are nowhere written down. For example, the two key ingredients of the political process, the prime minister and the cabinet, are not mentioned in the Constitution Act of 1867. The principle of the collective responsibility of the cabinet to the House of Commons, the necessity for a cabinet minister to hold a seat in the Commons, the relationship between the formal and political executives, and the practice that a defeat on a major piece of government legislation is also a defeat of the government are all examples of crucial customs of parliamentary government that are constitutional in import but unspecified in law. Thus, when we speak of constitutional government in Canada, we include such constitutional practices, in addition to the series of constitutional documents.

CONSTITUTIONAL STRUCTURE

The Constitution Act of 1867 created a political structure based on the principles of parliamentary sovereignty and federalism. As set forth in the Preamble, the provinces of Canada, Nova Scotia, and New Brunswick desired to be "federally united" in a new political structure, "with a Constitution similar in Principle to that of the United Kingdom." The "similar in principle" phrase, in effect, designated a parliamentary structure for Canada; at the same time, it enshrined an important role for custom and convention in the Canadian polity. Unfortunately, the principles of parliamentary sovereignty and federalism are potentially contradictory in operation, especially in a decentralized federal system. However, the highly centralized federation outlined in 1867 did not bring the potential discrepancies between federalism and parliamentary sovereignty immediately into the open.

The initial structure of power provided for in the Constitution Act of 1867 strongly favoured the federal government over the provinces. This highly centralized federalism, which seemed almost unitary in design, is well-illustrated with respect to the following areas: the initial allocation of federal and provincial powers outlined, for the most part, in Sections 91 and 92; the residual power clause; the declaratory power; and the powers of disallowance and reservation.

The federal division of power

The principle of **federalism**, *that is, the division of powers between levels of government*, created two layers of government in Canada: the national or federal government in Ottawa and the various provincial governments. The allocation of powers to these respective levels could theoretically range from a highly centralized federal system (i.e., most of the power retained by Ottawa) to a highly decentralized one (i.e., most of the power retained by the constituent units or provinces), with numerous variations between them. The intent of the Fathers of Confederation clearly placed Canada in the first category, as witnessed by the political functions assigned to each level.

In Section 91, the federal government was granted a list of 29 classes of subjects, ranging from several minor functions (Section 9: Beacons, Buoys, Lighthouses, and Sable Island; Section 11: establishment and maintenance of Marine Hospitals) to major ones (Section 2: Regulation of Trade and Commerce; Section 3: any Mode or System of Taxation; Section 7: Militia, Military and Naval Service, and Defence; Section 14: Currency and Coinage). It must be remembered that government itself in the mid-19th century was limited, but of the political functions performed at the time, the federal government received the vast majority.

> Federalism has been to us what football is to Britain. It is our blood sport (former Prime Minister Joe Clark).

In addition to the powers already mentioned, the federal government was given control over the public debt and property, public credit, the postal service, navigation and shipping, banking, Indians and their lands, marriage and divorce, and criminal law.

In contrast, the remaining political functions allocated to the provinces were mostly minor ones, perhaps best stated in Section 92(16) as "Generally all Matters of a merely local or private Nature in the Province." Such powers included prisons in and for the province, the borrowing of money on the sole credit of the province, licences for the raising of provincial revenue, and the administration of justice in the province. While limited in their initial effect, several classes of subjects in Section 92 would later become significant, particularly the control of public lands, property and civil rights, and municipal institutions. Moreover, Section 92(7) laid the basis for provincial control over health and welfare, although such powers did not emerge as major ones until well into the 20th century.

Provincial control of municipal institutions in Section 92(8) means that the federal system created in 1867 was composed of two levels of government, not three as popularly perceived. The constitutional position of local government is subservient to the provincial level, and no relationship at all is established by the Constitution Act of 1867 between local government and the national government in Ottawa. For example, a provincial government can legally rearrange local government, setting up regional or metropolitan governments as it desires. A provincial government can cause two towns or cities to merge or it can impose spending restrictions on the municipal units. Local governments are typically forced by their provinces to balance their budgets, a restriction which is obviously inapplicable to the provinces themselves.

In addition, the power of the provinces over local government is seen with respect to the

> In the particular chemistry of provincial-
> local relations, the style of the game has
> much more in common with poker than do
> provincial-federal relations: for the latter,
> skills are based in the simulated warfare of
> chess, for the former in the cut, thrust and
> bluff of poker (Lightbody, 1989: 42).

process of constitutional reform and federal-provincial agreements. Local government representatives may be included for political reasons as part of a province's delegation, but they have no legal right to participate or even to have their views presented. In recent years, the Canadian Federation of Municipalities has several times requested that all the municipalities be recognized as a separate level of government within a revised constitutional structure, and just as regularly have the provinces ignored their pleas.

While the provinces demand more power from the federal government, they have obstinately refused to give up any of their own power to local government. In an attempt to make an end run around provincial control of the municipalities, the federal government created the Ministry of State for Urban Affairs in 1971. However, the outcry from the provinces was such that this experiment was largely unsuccessful and the ministry was disbanded in 1978. The result is that when the federal government deals with the municipalities, it does so through their respective provincial governments. For example, in the early 1970s, the federal government sought to reduce the tax strain on municipal budgets by granting the provinces money for their urban areas. However, several provincial governments siphoned off part of this money for their own purposes and legally the municipalities could do nothing to stop it.

In addition to the powers already mentioned with respect to Sections 91 and 92, another important one is the area of taxation. The federal level was given the superior taxing power in Section 91(3), since it could raise "Money by any Mode or System of Taxation," while the provinces were limited by Section 92(2) to "Direct Taxation within the Province in order to the raising of a Revenue for Provincial Purposes." The consequence of this inequity has meant that throughout Canadian history the federal level has more easily raised revenue than the provinces. As a result, the provinces have legally given up a portion of their power by agreeing to an amendment to the Constitution Act of 1867 that has allowed the federal government to pay for a social program technically within an area of provincial jurisdiction. For example, the 1940 amendment added Section 91(2a) to the list of federal powers, giving Ottawa the legal basis for providing unemployment insurance. The superiority of the federal taxing power is one reason why the initial expansion of government in Canada was an expansion of the national government.

The allocation of powers and functions between the two levels of government in Sections 91 and 92 was predicated on the assumption that the tasks of government could be neatly delineated and given to one or the other level. This pattern of federalism has often been labeled as **classical federalism** (Smiley, 1976: 54). For example, if the provinces were given control of municipal institutions, then the federal government was excluded from that area of activity. Similarly, federal jurisdiction over defence, the money supply, and the post office meant lack of provincial participation in such concerns. Thus, by and large, Sections 91 and 92 delineate areas of **exclusive jurisdiction**. Another example can be found in Section 93, which gives the provinces control over education, although the federal government was granted the task of protecting religious minority educational rights. Thus, even from the beginning in some areas, exclusive control was limited by exceptions to exclusivity.

A second type of jurisdiction is also apparent

in federal constitutions, namely, the idea of shared or **concurrent jurisdiction**. In these areas of activity, both levels of government may legislate: for example, in Section 95, both the national and provincial governments may regulate with respect to agriculture and immigration.

Since both levels may legislate in these areas, there is a need for negotiation and cooperation between the federal and provincial governments. For example, in February of 1978 the federal government and Quebec signed an agreement over what powers Quebec was to exercise with respect to immigration. In particular, Quebec was given the power to define the type of immigrant it desired to reside in the province. The ideal candidate was seen as married, French-speaking, with several children under the age of 12, and predisposed to living and participating within a Francophone society.

If both levels can legislate in areas of concurrent jurisdiction, then a means must be established for deciding questions of precedence when federal and provincial laws conflict. Such a provision in a federal constitution is known as the **supremacy clause**. In Canada, supremacy in areas of concurrent jurisdiction, such as agriculture and immigration, is given to the Parliament of Canada. However, the supremacy clause does not apply to the division of powers in Sections 91 and 92, because that allocation was seen as exclusive in nature, and hence no supremacy clause was logically needed.

Once matters of exclusive and concurrent jurisdiction are designated, the drafters of a federal constitution face an additional problem: which level of government is given control over the present or future activities of government not explicitly dealt with in the allocation of the exclusive and concurrent powers? Not everything can be specified in the constitution, so a **residual power clause** is included, which allocates those powers not dealt with to one or the other levels of government. Typically, the residual power clause is given to that level of government that the constitution writers want

to be paramount. In Canada, the residual power was granted to the federal government in the opening sentence of Section 91, which empowers Parliament to make laws for the "Peace, Order, and Good Government of Canada" (or, as a student once put it, "Peace, Order, and Good Times").

The residual power or POGG clause is a potentially sweeping grant of power to the national government. It takes little mental agility to be able to justify any government action under it, for what Peace, Order, and Good Government means is defined by the federal government itself. For example, the POGG clause served as the justification for the federal government to pass and use the War Measures Act. In addition, the residual power clause was the cornerstone for legitimating the imposition of wage-and-price controls in 1975. A 1976 court challenge to the anti-inflation program was rejected by the Supreme Court on the grounds that, if the federal government perceived an economic emergency, then such a situation existed in fact and could thus be dealt with under the residual power clause. While such powers are not invoked frequently, the POGG clause is an important reserve power retained by the federal government that allows it to become involved within areas of provincial jurisdiction.

In addition to the centralized allocation of governmental responsibilities and the residual power clause, a third aspect that sought to buttress the federal government's dominance over the provinces in 1867 was the declaratory power given the national government. The **declaratory power** contained in Section 92(10c) allows the federal government to usurp provincial powers if the federal Parliament asserts that such an action is "for the general Advantage of Canada or for the Advantage of Two or more of the Provinces." Significant is the placement of the declaratory power phrase in the 1867 Constitution Act: within the list of powers given the provinces in Section 92 is a means by which any of them may be taken over by the federal government acting on its own initiative. It is difficult to conceive of a power or activity that could not be justified or rationalized as to the benefit of at least two provinces. Interestingly, Canada is the only federal system in the world with such a power given to the national government. This declaratory power has been used to bring such diverse works as atomic energy and grain elevators under federal jurisdiction (Romanow et al., 1984: 47–48).

Although the declaratory power has been rarely used, it is not a dead issue in Canadian politics. In the constitutional bargaining of the mid-1970s, Premier Lougheed of Alberta asked for the dropping of the federal government's declaratory power as the price to be paid by Ottawa for a constitutional agreement. Alberta and the Western provinces were fearful that the declaratory power might be used to give Ottawa control over natural resources, such as oil and natural gas. As might be suspected, the federal government refused to give serious consideration to the suggestion. The potential use of the declaratory power remains, however, as an important bargaining chip for the federal government. For example, during the summer of 1981, when the energy-pricing talks between Ottawa and Alberta were deadlocked, Minister of Energy Marc Lalonde had his office issue a statement denying rumours that the federal government was contemplating breaking the impasse by invoking its declaratory power. It is highly unlikely that such a move was in fact being contemplated, but the rumoured possibility (probably started deliberately by Ottawa) of invoking Section 92(10c) served to remind Alberta of the need to reach an accord with Ottawa. Currently, the declaratory power remains in place. The federal government last used the declaratory power in 1961.

A fourth set of techniques through which the federal government could exert control over the provincial units in the Constitution Act of 1867 concerns the national government's powers of disallowance and reservation. Although they dif-

> **Disallowance is one of several constitutional methods of defending the central citadel of federal power against invasion by provincial governments (Mallory, 1954: 169).**

fer in the details of their application, the effect of disallowance and reservation is to give the federal government a potential veto power over the provincial legislatures.

Disallowance is the procedure by which the federal government rules a provincial law null and void within one year of its passage. In other words, a provincial legislature passes a law, it receives royal assent from the lieutenant-governor, and it is enforced as a provincial law until the federal government decides otherwise. Provincial laws are sent to the minister of justice and, if he or she recommends, within one year from the date of receiving a copy of the legislation from the province, that the bill be rejected, then an order-in-council (i.e., a decision of the cabinet) is so issued.

The grounds for disallowance need to be neither explained nor specific: they can be as vague as claiming that the provincial law runs counter to "sound principles of legislation." Under disallowance, the federal government can observe the implementation of a law before it decides whether or not to veto it. The last time the disallowance power was used was 1943. In total, slightly over 110 acts since Confederation have been disallowed.

Reservation is a procedure by which a provincial law is not applicable until the federal government reviews it. **Reservation** means that the bill has passed the provincial legislature, has been sent to the lieutenant-governor for royal assent, but the lieutenant-governor reserves the bill by neither granting assent nor refusing it. Such a bill is then sent to the federal government for a decision, wherein the governor-in-council (i.e., the cabinet) may or may not decide to allow the bill to become law.

In the case of reservation, a provincial bill, in effect, is held in abeyance until the federal government has a chance to consider it. Over 70 bills have been reserved since 1867, with about a dozen eventually allowed to become law. The last time reservation was used was in Saskatchewan in 1961. Thus, the national government's powers of disallowance and reservation placed the provinces in 1867 in a situation of colonial subordination to the federal government, just as the federal government, itself, was so positioned with respect to Britain.

Given the original distribution of powers between the national and provincial governments, the granting of both the residual and declaratory powers to the federal level, and the national government's right to disallow or reserve provincial legislation, the intent of the Fathers of Confederation was clearly to establish a highly centralized federal system. The primary functions of government in 1867 went to the federal government, with those designated for provincial control able to be usurped by the national government acting on its own initiative. For such reasons, the Constitution Act of 1867 has been classified as containing important "quasi-unitary" attributes (Smiley, 1980: 22–27).

Umpiring the federal system

Although the Fathers of Confederation felt that the allocation of powers in the new federal structure was clear-cut, a federal political system inherently produces disputes and conflicts between the various levels of government over their respective powers. One way of settling such disputes is through a process of judicial review. On a general level, **judicial review** *is the right of the courts to make judgments respecting the constitutionality of executive and legislative actions*.

In Canada, a restricted view of such a process has traditionally been used to settle jurisdictional disputes between the federal and pro-

vincial governments. In such a federal polity, the courts may be used in a pattern of **limited judicial review**, *whereby they rule on which level of government can exercise what powers*. In that sense, then, the courts are used as the referees of federalism: their task is not to stop the game by declaring an action unconstitutional, but to decide which team (the federal or provincial government) has control of the ball so that the game can continue. For example, on November 30, 1978, the Supreme Court ruled that the federal government had exclusive jurisdiction over cable television, thus ending provincial hopes of controlling that new area of activity. Similarly, in August 1989, the Supreme Court ruled that the federal government has the necessary constitutional power to regulate all domestic telephone companies, including those that are provincially owned. Moreover, the practice of limited judicial review has meant that, as long as the federal and provincial governments legislate within their powers as allocated in the 1867 Constitution Act, the courts will take a hands-off attitude toward the content of such legislation. By implication, such an approach favours the national government, since the courts are interpreting a document that created a highly centralized federal system.

The use in pre-Charter Canada of a pattern of limited rather than full judicial review is a reflection of the principle of parliamentary sovereignty. If the courts were to exercise full judicial review, the result would be that a supposedly supreme legislature was subject to the interpretations of an outside body. However, a pattern of limited judicial review is consistent with a federal and parliamentary system, because the courts are merely interpreting which legislature has the right to exercise supremacy with respect to which powers. A movement in Canada from a pattern of limited to full judicial review would likely produce a clash between these two political principles. A key ingredient of the debate about the impact of the Canadian Charter of Rights and Freedoms

We are the umpire of the Canadian constitutional system, the only umpire; and in enforcing the rules under which the system operates, rules which we did not formulate but which we are sworn to apply, we are getting an occasional sting from some of the players and even from some of those on the sidelines, much like the soccer referee sometimes [receives] from the frenzy that in some places seizes both players and spectators at a soccer final (Chief Justice Bora Laskin, public speech, 1978).

Unlike the American Supreme Court, some of whose more momentous decisions can be chronicled by schoolchildren, Canada's top court labours silently in the shadows of Parliament Hill (Sheppard and Valpy, 1982: 234).

(1982) centred on whether or not, or by how much, it would extend the exercise of full judicial review in the Canadian context. In fact, the application of the Charter since 1982 has greatly enhanced the role of full judicial review.

Additions to the initial constitutional structure

In addition to the matters dealt with in the 1867 Constitution Act, three major enactments since then have grafted important elements onto the initial constitutional structure: the War Measures Act from 1914–1988 and its replacement, the 1988 Emergencies Act; the Bill of Rights in 1960; and the Constitution Act of 1982. It is important to look at each of these modifications and refinements in the Canadian pattern of constitutional government. Since the now rejected Meech Lake accord (Constitution Amendment, 1987) was a natural outgrowth of the 1982 Canada Act, it will be discussed in detail in Chapter fourteen.

Although highly centralized in design, the Constitution Act of 1867 did not specifically deal with the means by which the federal government could act to meet either domestic or international crises. For 50 years it was assumed that the federal government's residual and declaratory powers were sufficient to counter any such threats. However, by the early 20th century the growing pattern of decentralization and the judicial restriction of the POGG clause, in conjunction with a world crisis, prompted the federal government to give itself emergency powers. Passed in 1914 as a federal statute, the **War Measures Act** set up a system of "constitutional dictatorship" under the direction of the prime minister and cabinet.

In effect, the federal government could rule by decree, usurping not only Parliament's powers, but those of the provinces as well. Moreover, penalties for failure to observe the new regulations could be imposed, with a fine of $5 000 and/or five years in jail for each offence. A person could also be detained for a maximum period of 21 days, without being charged for a specific violation. Such regulations could also be made retroactive: in the 1970 October Crisis it became illegal to ever have been a member of the FLQ! Under the War Measures Act, basic civil and political liberties were suspended on the grounds that such actions were necessary to preserve the body politic. For example, at the height of the 1970 crisis, Prime Minister Trudeau was asked by a reporter how far he would go in suspending basic liberties in order to defeat the FLQ. The Prime Minister's response was blunt and vintage Trudeau: "Just watch me!"

The bringing into force of the War Measures Act was accomplished by a proclamation of the governor-in-council (i.e., the prime minister and cabinet) that there existed a situation of "war, invasion, or insurrection, real or apprehended." Of interest is the phrase "real or apprehended," which meant that if the federal government perceived a crisis involving war, invasion, or insurrection, then a crisis existed. No evidence to support such a view needed to be presented.

Once the Act was in place, it was a prerogative of the federal government to decide how long it remained—there was no legal time limit on its application. The War Measures Act could last several months, as in 1970, or several years, as during the Second World War, from 1939 to 1945. The government could also relax the extent of its control, once the immediate crisis had passed, but not to the position of returning to its normal powers. In this situation, it could impose a Public Order Temporary Measures Act, which limited some of its own arbitrary authority. This procedure was used in both the 1970 crisis, when a public order temporary measures act was in place from December to April 1971, and after World War II from 1945 to 1954. The decisions about whether to use this procedure, the extent of the powers retained by the federal government, and the length of the application of a Public Order Act were all taken by the federal government itself.

Although there was no legal restriction on how often such emergency powers could have been used, for political reasons it was not likely to be resorted to too often. Since its passage, the War Measures Act was utilized on three occasions: during both world wars and the October Crisis in 1970. Even though it was a federal statute like any other law, the War Measures Act was a constitutional document with respect to both its content and its consequences for the political system.

The rather extreme power given to the federal government under the War Measures Act led to suggestions for its reform or replacement. After the 1970 October Crisis, the Trudeau Government promised new emergency powers legislation, but none was ever passed. In January of 1985, Defence Minister Robert Coates indicated that the Mulroney Government would be bringing forward new legislation to replace the War Measures Act. After several delays, in June of 1987 the federal government finally introduced its replacement for the War Measures Act, with royal assent granted on July 21, 1988.

The 1988 Emergencies Act defines four broad classes of emergencies. Unlike the draconian War Measures Act, which, from 1914–88, was either imposed in total or not at all, the Emergencies Act allows for a graduated response to different types of crises:

1. *Public welfare emergencies*: floods, accidents, pollution or diseases. Under this provision, authorities can requisition property, order the evacuation of areas, or restrict travel.

2. *Public order emergencies*: threats to Canada's security that are so serious that they cannot be handled by a province. The October Crisis of 1970 would now fall into this category.

3. *International emergencies*: acts of violence which threaten Canada or its allies. Under this provision, the government could prevent citizens from leaving the country, seize property, and authorize searches and seizures without warrants.

4. *War emergencies*: a war or imminent conflict for Canada or one of its allies that is so "serious as to be a national emergency." Powers under this provision are similar to those of the original War Measures Act.

In addition to defining different types of crises and possible responses, the Emergencies Act allows for compensation to individuals who may be harmed by its application, allows a review by Parliament of its necessity, and is subject to the limitations of both the Bill of Rights and the Canadian Charter of Rights and Freedoms. As such, the Emergencies Act is a much needed improvement upon the War Measures Act.

The second major addition to Canada's constitutional structure came in 1960, with the passage of the **Bill of Rights**, although most of its provisions have now been superseded by the Charter of Rights contained in the 1982 Constitution Act. It is well to remember, however, that the Bill of Rights is still operative, even after the adoption of the new Charter of Rights. For example, in July of 1988, the Bill of Rights, not the Charter of Rights, was the basis for a ruling by the Federal Court of Canada against the Immigration Department.

The basic assumption of a bill of rights or charter of rights is that the people need protection from their government, a view that challenges a core belief of parliamentary government. Historically, Parliament has been seen as the guarantor of people's freedoms, but a bill of rights asserts, in effect, that Parliament is not only incapable of continuing to protect the public, but also that the public needs a means of defence from its protector.

A bill of rights is designed to establish a series of civil and political liberties, which no government can ignore or abuse. One way such protection is enhanced is to place the bill of rights explicitly in the constitution, a process known as **entrenchment**. Since constitutions are usually made difficult to change, having a bill of rights entrenched means it is less likely to be done away with or changed by the government of the day. An effective bill of rights stands, therefore, as a limit on parliamentary supremacy.

The late arrival of the Canadian Bill of Rights was a reflection of Parliament's belief that no such rights were needed as a protection against itself. However, public pressure and opinion was such that Parliament finally acquiesced and passed the legislation that created a potential check on its own power. The Bill of Rights was a normal piece of federal legislation that was not entrenched in the Constitution Act of 1867. The Bill of Rights also reflected the impact of federalism, because it applied only to the federal level of government. However, by the mid-1970s, all provinces had enacted some type of "human rights" legislation, although most of these bills were not as comprehensive as their federal counterpart.

The result of its lack of entrenchment and its applicability to only the federal level left the constitutional position of the Bill of Rights open to question. These concerns were reflected in the fact that it was nine years before the Supreme Court, in the *Drybones* decision of 1969, used the Bill of Rights to invalidate a section of federal law. However, in later decisions in the mid-1970s, the Supreme Court backed off from the full implications of such a stand and seemed reluctant to consider the Bill of Rights as a basis for challenging the legislative or executive actions of the federal government.

The provisions of the Bill of Rights were fairly typical in content, in that they protected a series of civil and political liberties. Unfortunately, these protections were not as effective as they appeared to be, because they could be bypassed by the federal government. By inserting the phrase "notwithstanding the Canadian Bill of Rights," any act of Parliament could be made immune from the application of these basic freedoms. Fundamental freedoms were simply not as fundamental as the principle of parliamentary supremacy.

A second limitation concerned the relationship between the Bill of Rights and the War Measures Act, with the latter taking precedence over the former. In times of crisis, when protection of basic civil and political liberties was most needed, fundamental human rights were held in abeyance. For example, the Bill of Rights in Part Two, Section 6(5), with reference to the War Measures Act, asserts that any action taken under the emergency powers provision "shall be deemed not to be an abrogation, abridgement or infringement of any right or freedom recognized by the Canadian Bill of Rights."

Although the War Measures Act took precedence over the Bill of Rights, nevertheless, the Bill of Rights did modify the procedure for imposing emergency powers. After 1960, any use of the War Measures Act had to be accompanied by a notice to Parliament that a crisis existed. If Parliament was sitting, notification had to be done "forthwith," that is, without undue delay. In a situation where Parliament was not in session when the emergency was declared, then it had to be informed within the first 15 days of its next sitting. Within 10 days of Parliament's notification, any 10 members in either House could have forced a debate on the proclamation of the War Measures Act. If, at the conclusion of this debate, both Houses of Parliament resolved "that the proclamation be revoked, it shall cease to have effect." However, the government, if it felt it necessary, because of a continuing crisis or because of a new one, could have legally invoked the War Measures Act a second time.

The lack of entrenchment, its application to only the federal level of government, the ability of the federal government to bypass it, and its inapplicability with respect to the imposition of the War Measures Act, were some of the major deficiencies of the Bill of Rights that led to a search for a more comprehensive and effective document. The result, in part, was the adoption of the **Constitution Act of 1982**, the third major addition to Canada's constitutional structure since 1867. While a detailed consideration will be given to the Constitution Act in Chapter 14, here we must indicate its two major modifications to the constitutional system: a Charter of Rights and amending formulas for future constitutional change.

The Charter of Rights supplants the previous Bill of Rights, is more comprehensive in its powers, is entrenched, and applies to both levels of government. However, an override provision allows certain fundamental freedoms to be bypassed by the federal or provincial legislatures, although an override resolution would have to be renewed every five years. The second major change brought about by the Constitution Act concerns the amending formulas. Until 1982, the power to amend parts of the Constitution Act of 1867 remained with the British Parliament. The new amending formulas allow revisions to the Constitution as a result

of agreements between the federal government and the provinces. As a consequence, Canada now has the power to amend all aspects of its own Constitution.

This brief review of the key elements of Canada's constitutional structure of 1867 and the major additions since that time has stressed the idea of the almost unlimited power and influence of the national government in the affairs of the country. However, as in most countries, the intended constitutional structure may not be reflected in actual constitutional practice. The present Canadian Constitution operates very differently than the above description would seem to indicate, a reflection, perhaps, of the view that a "constitution that did not change would, by definition be nominal and not normative—an exercise in logic and not in life" (McWhinney, 1979: 9).

THE EVOLVING CONSTITUTIONAL MILIEU

Before analyzing the major causes for its evolution, we must first begin with a description of how Canada's constitutional system has developed since the Confederation agreement. The general pattern of change can be summarized as follows: Canada has moved from the highly centralized political structure of 1867 to one of the most decentralized federal systems in the world. However, within this broad trend there have been alternating periods of centralization and decentralization.

Canada was a centralized polity during both world wars, when the political system was run under the emergency powers legislation. Moreover, it is often forgotten that for 15 years, from 1939 to 1954, the polity was overwhelmingly Ottawa-directed. From this highly centralized system of the mid-1950s emerged a new round of provincial demands for greater autonomy, best symbolized by the Quiet Revolution in Quebec in the early 1960s. By the 1970s the provinces had gained a rough equality of power with the federal government, reflected in the Alberta-Ottawa battles over energy-pricing.

This growing trend of decentralization was a prime motivation for Pierre Trudeau's entry into federal politics. One of the tenets of Trudeau's political philosophy was that the decentralization of the early 1960s had gone too far and too fast and, as leader of the Liberal party and Prime Minister, he tried to reverse that pattern. Changes sought by Pierre Trudeau in the early 1980s with respect to limiting Ottawa's financial role in areas of provincial jurisdiction, a refusal to allow a further decline in Ottawa's constitutional powers in relation to the provinces (especially concerning Quebec), and the passage of the 1982 Constitution Act have all reflected a reassertion of the national government's role in the Canadian federal system. The basic equality of power established between the two levels by the early 1980s means that any conflict is likely to resemble a 15-round, heavyweight championship match that ends in a draw. Neither level of government can govern effectively, for any extended period, without the cooperation of the other.

The causes of constitutional evolution

While the reasons for the change to a decentralized political system are complex, five interdependent causes seem to be important. First, the provinces quickly became dissatisfied with the highly centralized structure created in 1867 and began, by the last decades of the 19th century, to demand greater powers. One of the results of a federal system is to create a perception on the part of politicians in both levels of government that their level should be preeminent. Thus, the actual powers of each level of government in a federal system are always in a constant state of change.

A second cause of decentralization should perhaps be seen as a corollary of the first: as the provinces gained power, several of the key powers of the federal government became restricted. The legal basis for the exercise of these powers remained, but the federal government's political will to use them did not. Three important powers would fall into this category, namely, the declaratory power, disallowance, and reservation.

Based on custom and convention, these powers of the federal government had become largely inoperative by the 1940s. For example, the declaratory power was last exercised in 1961 on a relatively minor matter, disallowance last occurred in 1943, and the power of reservation was last exercised by a lieutenant governor in 1961. However, these dates tend to hide the fact that the pattern had already been well-established. For example, while reservation occurred in 1961, it did so without the direction of the federal government, which then quickly moved to allow that piece of legislation to become law. Thus, the powers of disallowance, reservation, and declaration remain legally available to the federal government, but their exercise has been severely restricted by custom and convention. The use of these powers is still possible in a crisis situation, but their exercise is dependent on a political judgment by the federal government that they can get away with their implementation.

A third reason for enhanced provincial powers relates to a series of judicial decisions which began in the 1880s and continued into the early decades of the 20th century. Until the establishment of the Supreme Court of Canada in 1949 as the final court of appeal for Canadian cases, the highest court of appeal was the Judicial Committee of the British Privy Council (JCPC). Composed mainly of members of the British House of Lords, the JCPC rendered a series of decisions that had the effect of restricting federal powers and enhancing those of the provinces. For example, the broad grant of power to the federal government in the residual power clause was interpreted restrictively, that is, it was seen as only applying under special circumstances. In contrast, some of the powers of the provincial units, such as their control of property and civil rights, were generously applied by the JCPC. The result of such judicial decisions was to reinforce the evolving pattern of decentralization characteristic of the Canadian federal system in the 20th century.

A fourth contributing factor reflects the effect of the changing nature of society on the respective powers of the federal and provincial governments. Some of the activities granted the provinces in 1867, which were minor governmental functions in the 19th century, have since become major ones. For example, while the provinces obtained exclusive control of education in Section 93, few people received any schooling, despite the existence of a public school system. The acceptance of the notion of universal, public education through the high school years caused a massive expansion of this provincial government responsibility. A similar pattern has occurred with respect to the health and welfare functions. The result has been that provincial governments now spend about one-half of their entire budgets on these three concerns. Thus, minor provincial powers in 1867 have become major ones, and with that change has come more influence for the provincial units in the federal system.

A final reason for Canada's decentralized federalism is, perhaps, an outgrowth of the first four causes, that is, the emergence of a pattern of **province-building**. This concept stresses the development and significant role of the provincial governments in the federal structure (Hockin, 1976: 31). The growth of the provincial governments with respect to their size and areas of responsibility is both a cause and consequence of the enhanced power of the Canadian provinces. The trend of recent decades for the provinces to establish their own departments of intergovernmental affairs or, at least, to have a provincial minister given responsibility for handling relations with the national government is

an indication of this change. In the past, the size and expertise of the Ottawa bureaucracy, in comparison to its provincial counterparts, were a means of federal government control of the provinces. How much this pattern has changed was revealed in December 1981, when a meeting of federal-provincial finance ministers ended in confusion because Ottawa and the provinces could not agree on which set of financial figures (Ottawa's or the provinces) was correct. The expertise of the provincial bureaucracies allows for such challenges to federal government dominance. Even in the area of foreign policy, the provinces increasingly insist on a greater role. At the First Ministers' Conference in Halifax in November 1985, the premiers demanded and received assurances from the Mulroney government that they would have a major role to play in the "free trade" negotiations with the United States.

The evolution of the Canadian system from a pattern of centralized to decentralized federalism has occurred, for the most part, as the result of custom and convention rather than formal constitutional amendment. The lack of an explicit amending clause in the 1867 Constitution Act made the amending procedure difficult to use. In order to adapt to a changing environment, the Canadian polity simply altered the way it operated, without formally changing the rules of the game. This pattern is one basic reason why custom and convention play such a significant role in the Canadian political experience. Although explicit amending formulas are now included in the 1982 Constitution Act, it is still important to understand the amending dilemma that confronted the political system from 1867 to 1982.

Constitutional amendment 1867–1982

Two factors seem to account for the initial absence of an amending clause in the original Constitution: first, because Canada was a colony, there was no need for a specific amending procedure since any changes would be made by the British Parliament and second, the allocation of powers was seen as comprehensive by the Fathers of Confederation and, thus, no changes appeared to be needed in the immediate future (Stevenson, 1979: 207–208). Such an optimistic view appears shortsighted in retrospect. The lack of a specific amending procedure created two obstacles which had to be overcome whenever a change in the Constitution was proposed: agreement had to be reached on the amendment procedure and on the content of the reform. However, questions of process and substance could not be easily divorced.

Before delving into these intricacies further we must first qualify our assertion that Canada lacked an amending formula. In fact, between 1867 and 1982, three different ways of formally changing the constitutional structure existed (Mallory, 1971: 375–378). First, from the very beginning, the provinces have been empowered to change their own structure and operation. The 1867 Constitution Act sets forth the structure of government for the four initial provinces, with the stipulation that such institutions would exist "until the provinces otherwise provide." For example, acting on this amending power, the provinces of Quebec (1968), Nova Scotia (1928), and New Brunswick (1892) all abolished their upper chambers or legislative councils.

The second way of amending the Constitution was for the federal government to claim the same power for changing its own structure and operation as that given the provinces. The Constitution Act (Number Two) of 1949 formally established the federal government's legitimacy in this regard. For example, changes in the size of the House of Commons are made possible without a formal amendment, as long as the rules for the allocation of seats between the provinces specified in the 1867 Constitution Act (as amended) are not violated.

The real amending problem developed with respect to the third area, that is, the "safe-guarded" portions of the Constitution Act of 1867 (i.e., federal and provincial powers in Sections 91 and 92, minority religious educational rights in Section 93, language protection in Section 133). These responsibilities could only be altered by an amendment passed through the British Parliament at the request of the Canadian government. Several facets of Britain's power to amend the Canadian Constitution must be kept in mind: first, no amendment was ever made except at the request of the Canadian government; second, no request from the Canadian government was ever refused; and third, the amending power remained in Britain because of the lack of an agreement within Canada itself on an amending formula. If points one and two, in particular, are kept in mind, then Canada has always had the *de facto* power to amend even the safeguarded portions of the Constitution, if agreement on the content of such an amendment could be achieved in Canada.

Disputes about the content of such amendments to the safeguarded portions invariably raised concerns about procedure as well. Such amendments usually resulted after the federal Parliament passed a resolution outlining the contents of the changes proposed to Britain for implementation. The key procedural problem occurred prior to this resolution: if and when were the provinces to be consulted and, if consulted, the kind of consensus required before the federal government could proceed. From a narrow legal point of view, the federal government could act unilaterally. However, the custom and convention soon developed that the provinces should be consulted, or, at least, those provinces that were directly affected by the proposed amendments. If consultation did not lead to agreement between the federal government and the provinces, then the federal government, on political grounds, would usually not proceed with the reforms. Thus, the content of the proposed amendment affected the procedure for its adoption, and both content and procedure limited the frequency of altering the Constitution from 1867 to 1982.

OPERATING THE FEDERAL SYSTEM

Difficulties of making formal amendments, a changing distribution of power between the federal and provincial levels, the impact of judicial decisions, and a changing political environment have all contributed to the complexity of the Canadian federal system. One result has been that both levels of government are involved in almost every major policy area. The exclusive powers of Sections 91 and 92 have, in many instances, become concurrent powers in practice. For example, the federal level's exclusive control of foreign affairs has been directly challenged since the 1960s by Quebec's insistence on its right to attend international conferences among French-speaking nations. Most other provinces now have the same kind of representation abroad, with Ontario having more than a dozen such offices. Similarly, the exclusive control of education given the provinces has not prevented the federal government's extensive participation in university and vocational education programs. Such complexity requires a constant process of negotiation between the two levels of government in order to keep the federal system functioning. This bargaining pattern between the elected and appointed officials of the two levels of government has been labeled **executive federalism** (Smiley, 1980: 91). For example, it was announced in March of 1987 that the federal and British Columbia governments

For a country as regionally diverse as Canada, intergovernmental negotiation leading to specific agreements may reflect more suitable compromise than constitutional amendment (Romanow et al., 1984: 275).

would form a special council of ministers to oversee their relationship. In the Throne Speech of May 18, 1989, the Manitoba government indicated that it would be opening an office in Ottawa, in an attempt to improve their federal-provincial relationship. In October 1989, Manitoba appointed its first envoy to Ottawa, Mr. John Blackwood, a former career diplomat.

The pattern of negotiations is best symbolized by the Conference of First Ministers, which usually meets once a year, or sometimes more often, to handle special concerns such as economic problems or constitutional reform. Attended by the prime minister and the 10 premiers, plus a retinue of other elected and appointed officials, these conferences resemble meetings between heads of state. This pattern is a reflection, perhaps, of the current powers of the provincial units, as well as the fact that the first such conference, held in 1927, was organized along the lines of the Imperial Conference (i.e., an international meeting of nation-states in the British Commonwealth). The typical pattern of such meetings is for the first day of discussions to be held in public, before the full glare of the television cameras. The speeches by the prime minister and premiers are aimed at the folks back home, not towards each other. As in international diplomacy, the real bargaining goes on behind closed doors, away from the press and public, during the second or subsequent days of the conference.

In addition to the First Ministers' Conference, the premiers, themselves, hold an annual meeting to discuss their common concerns. For example, at their August 1989 meeting, the provincial premiers unanimously rejected as unacceptable the proposed new 9 percent federal sales tax (known as the GST for Goods and Services Tax), which was scheduled to be implemented in January 1991. As well, the Western premiers meet annually, as do the Maritime premiers. Bilateral talks between two premiers are common, and Alberta and British Columbia even held a joint cabinet meeting in the summer

> Bill Vander Zalm plays a national role in these locked-door conferences in Ottawa: he explains the complicated parts to Don Getty (Canadian columnist Marjorie Nichols, 1987).

of 1981. More important, perhaps, are the almost daily contacts and discussions behind the scenes by various interprovincial and federal-provincial committees. Such constant contact, interaction, and bargaining have been important mechanisms for adapting an inflexible written constitution to a changing environment.

Financing Federalism

One of the key areas in the Canadian federal system is finance, probably the most complex aspect of federal-provincial relations. The basic conflict stems from the fact that each level of government wants credit for beneficial programs, yet at the same time it seeks to get the other level to pay the expenses. While the trend in recent decades has been for the provincial governments to seek financial aid from Ottawa, the pattern began to change in the 1980s. Provincial reliance on federal largesse is well-illustrated by the equalization grants the poorer provinces receive from Ottawa, which mushroomed from $136 million in 1958 to $2.5 billion by the mid-1970s. By the mid-1980s, as much as 45 to 55 percent of some provincial budgets were federal dollars. By the time of the 1989–1990 fiscal year, equalization payments

> To provide a measure of balance and fairness to all Canadians, the concept of equalization was devised, and is now an integral part of our concept of Canada as a single, undivided social and political structure (Liberal Premier of Prince Edward Island, Joe Ghiz, June 1989).

were more than $7-billion. Total federal transfers to the provinces (including equalization payments as well as specific purpose transfers for such items as medicare and education) reached $18.5 billion in 1984–1985. In 1989 the three Maritime provinces received $1.7 billion in equalization payments. Because of the economic boom in central Canada in the mid-1980s, this figure was $186-million more than expected. By the 1989-1990 fiscal year, total federal transfers to the provinces were $24-billion.

Because the provinces spend the money, they receive credit for such programs as health, education, and medical care, while the federal government pays the bills. In renegotiating these financial arrangements for the 1982 fiscal year, the federal government insisted that it be given political credit for its good deeds — earthly rewards now, rather than heavenly ones later. A good example of the federal government's attitude took place in the summer of 1981, when Pierre De Bane, Minister of Regional Economic Expansion, publicly refused to continue the financing of a joint Manitoba-Ottawa program because Ottawa was not gaining enough favourable publicity from its expenditures. Another example can be seen in the November 1981 budget, which sought to limit future federal government support in areas such as equalization payments and established program financing (EPF).

By limiting its rate of growth in these areas, the federal government not only appears to be holding its expenditures in line, but also forces the provinces to assume more of the financial costs of these popular programs. Although the Mulroney Conservatives promised better federal-provincial relations during the 1984 campaign, by the end of their first year in office, they too — like the Trudeau Liberals before them — found the provinces opposed to any reductions in their transfer payments from the federal government. In September 1985, Finance Minister Michael Wilson announced

ONLY TORIES CAN PROVIDE
RESPECT QUE. DESERVES

EDWARDS. *The Whig-Standard*, Kingston

Source: Reprinted from *The Whig-Standard* (Kingston, Ontario). By permission.

that the cutbacks in EPF funding would begin a year earlier than previously indicated (i.e., the increase would be only 5 percent, not the anticipated 7 percent). These reductions in the rate of growth of transfer payments saved the federal government $6 billion by 1991. Such conflicts over federal-provincial financial arrangements are inherent in the Canadian federal system, regardless of who is prime minister or which parties are in power.

Conflicts between the federal and provincial governments over money are a result, in part, of their differential taxing powers. With the superior taxing power, the national government quickly became the financier of federalism, a source of revenue for tax-hungry, some would

> Federalism has many virtues, but maximum economic or operational efficiency is not one of them (Robertson, 1989: 124).

say greedy, provinces. The provinces have even been willing to give to Ottawa areas of provincial jurisdiction, such as old-age pensions, because the federal level has the tax sources to pay for such new activities.

Against provincial opposition, the federal government has utilized its superior taxing power to become involved in other areas of provincial jurisdiction. For example, **conditional grants**, that is, federal money with strings attached, can be given to the provinces if they agree to spend it as the federal government desires. Provinces are often forced into cooperating because not to do so means the loss of millions of dollars for their citizens. Once such a program is established, the federal government may have second thoughts about it and later withdraw its funding, leaving the provinces either to pick up the tab or to face the political consequences of dismantling the program. For example, in October 1981, Prince Edward Island had to eliminate 161 civil

> There was a woman member of the British Columbia Legislature back in the 1950s who embarked upon a campaign to change the name of sex. She wanted it called BOLT, an acronym for Biology of Living Today. Perhaps federal-provincial fiscal arrangements could be called LOVE, for Lots of Veryimportant Expenditures (Valpy, 1981: 6).

service jobs because of federal government cutbacks in the province's economic development program. A further example of federal-provincial financial conflict was clearly evident in the 1981 Ottawa-Alberta energy-pricing dispute: the long delay was primarily the result of both levels wanting as large a share as possible of the increased tax revenues that would result from expected higher energy costs.

Although the traditional dispute in matters of finance has involved federal-provincial conflicts over who pays the costs and who receives the benefits from the federal system, a new financial concern came up in the early 1980s. This problem was a reflection of interprovincial financial arrangements, rather than a federal-provincial one, and was based on the Alberta Heritage Trust Fund. With its extensive revenues from oil and natural gas, Alberta decided to save a portion of these funds to use for long-term provincial undertakings. By 1987, the revenues had reached over $15 billion and the trust fund was projected to climb to $20 billion in the next decade. Thus, Alberta remained financially solvent, while the other provinces and the federal government faced problems of deficit financing in the 1980s.

Alberta undertook to lend money at preferred interest rates to the other provinces, such as Quebec and Nova Scotia. These loans totaled nearly $1.8 billion by 1987. The potential implications of such interprovincial loans are clear: one excessively wealthy province, which has loaned money to other provinces, might control

or influence their policy stands at a First Ministers' Conference or in particular areas of federal-provincial conflict. While there is no clear evidence that such a tactic has been utilized so far by Alberta, the potential exists, even though the Alberta government announced in May 1982 that it intended to curtail future loans to the other provinces because of its own declining financial position.

Our survey of the constitutional structure of the Canadian polity has emphasized that there is considerably more to it than simply the Constitution Act of 1867. Beginning with a highly centralized federal structure, the Canadian political system has evolved into a decentralized one, characterized by an intermingling of federal-provincial responsibilities and finance. This pattern reflects the needs of a changing society, as well as the impact of judicial decisions and evolving public beliefs about the role of the federal and provincial levels. Moreover, major additions to the initial constitutional structure, including the 1988 Emergencies Act and the 1982 Constitution Act, have been effected. This combination of reforms has filled in some of the interstices of constitutional government, so that Canada has not only a series of written constitutional documents, but significant constitutional customs and conventions as well, both of which combine to produce a particular version of constitutional government.

British Constitutional Practice

In describing the British system, one is faced with a problem: the British pattern of constitutional government is not outlined in a written constitution. Instead, as former Prime Minister Harold Wilson (1977: 208) put it, the British Constitution is "based on seven hundred years of mainly pragmatic experience." As a result, constitutional traditions are significantly embodied in the customs and conventions of the political process, although disagreements do exist over some of the specific ingredients of British constitutionalism.

> Thus, England . . . has not felt the need to spell out for all time the principles of government in a single constitutional document. England's Constitution is not primarily a document distilling the abundant . . . wisdom of an oppressed people, the inspired vision of revolutionaries and the common sense of contemporary politicians anxious to limit the sphere of government. It is a somewhat abstract and foggy notion which few people fully comprehend, but which most people dimly understand because of custom and convention (Verney, 1976: 37–38).

Although Britain is characteristically classified as lacking a written constitution, such a view must be modified, because Britain does have a series of written constitutional documents. Such constitutional statutes would surely include the following: the Magna Carta (1215); the Petition of Rights (1628); the Habeas Corpus Act (1701); the Act of Union with Scotland (1706); the Parliament Acts of 1911 and 1949; the Government of Ireland Act (1920); and the Representation of the People Acts (1948 and 1949). Also of constitutional import are the Reform Acts (1832, 1867, 1884), the Statute of Westminster (1931), the emergency powers legislation (1914, 1939), the Peerage Act (1963), and the 1972 European Communities Act. Each of these constitutional documents helps to delineate the workings and structure of major segments of the British constitutional system. However, what is missing in Britain is a single, written, and comprehensive constitutional statement.

In addition to its series of constitutional documents, the second significant element of constitutionalism in Britain is custom and convention. Tradition, for example, established the relationship between the various governmental institutions that is indicated in the concept of the dual

> For the British Constitution is essentially a *political* constitution, one whose operation depends upon the strength of political factors and whose interpretation depends upon the will of its political leaders (Bogdanor, 1988: 71).

executive. The evolution of power from the formal to the political executive, and the present pattern of their interaction, is unspecified in any constitutional document. Similarly, notions of the collective responsibility of the government to the House of Commons, as well as the evolution of a system of party discipline and party government, both reflect custom rather than law. The lack of any comprehensive constitution has made the role of custom and convention even more significant in British politics than in the Canadian system.

A third aspect of constitutionalism concerns the role of the courts and the common law in Britain. Although the judiciary interprets the law in Britain, it in no sense takes an activist role in challenging Parliament's authority to define the law. Moreover, the concept of the common law, that is, the law based on custom and convention, has been an important ingredient of constitutionalism by establishing basic civil and political liberties, such as freedom of speech. Britain, for example, does not have a specific bill of rights to protect individual freedoms: instead, the Bill of Rights of 1689 established parliamentary control over the monarch. These ideas concerning judicial decisions and the common law are, perhaps, best summarized by the concept of the rule of law: "everybody, from the highest rank to the lowest, is subject to the overriding claims of the law" (Wright, 1973: 10).

The various elements of British constitutionalism (i.e., the series of constitutional documents, customs and conventions, and the rule of law) are reflected in the major institutions and principles of government. Of paramount importance is the principle of parliamentary sovereignty, which is unlimited in Britain. The law is what Parliament says it is and there is no legal basis for challenging its authority, since Britain has never accepted the American principle of full judicial review or the need for a bill of rights to protect human liberties. Second, the structure of the polity is unitary in form, and, thus, the national government does not share power with other political units. Local government exists at the prerogative of the national government—it is not a separate level of government with independent authority. Third, Britain is a constitutional monarchy, that is, the Queen reigns, but the political executive, working through Parliament, governs. A monarchical form does not produce monarchical power, with the modern British monarch fulfilling primarily the symbolic and ceremonial tasks of the state. Fourth, cabinet government, centred around its collective responsibility to the House of Commons, has been combined with party discipline and unity to produce a pattern of governance classified as party government. Party government is the motor of the modern British parliamentary system, the key technique for the fusion of executive and legislative powers. Finally, explicit protection of civil and political liberties is not provided, nor thought to be needed, since Parliament itself will seek to guarantee their existence.

These five factors have created a political system strongly centralized in both theory and practice. From a legal point of view, there is very little that the government of the day could not achieve, including doing away with basic civil and political liberties. For example, in the Fall of 1988, in an attempt to combat the continuing problem of IRA terrorist activities, the Thatcher government introduced legislation taking away the centuries-old right of British jurisprudence of a suspect (in Northern Ireland) to remain silent. Usually, the customs and conventions of the polity limit the potential abuse

> A striking feature of constitutional law in Britain has been the minimal level of legal regulation of political institutions (Oliver, 1989: 38).

of such a system of concentrated power, even if they do not eliminate such a possibility altogether. A political system of concentrated power is not inconsistent with constitutional government, as long as that power is constrained in use and effectively circumscribed by the customs and conventions of the polity.

The major advantage of the British constitutional system is its flexibility in reacting to changing public beliefs and circumstances. Since the basic constitutional documents are simply acts of Parliament like any other, they can be readily modified or replaced. Thus, there is no need for a specific amending procedure or a long, drawn-out debate about the content of the reforms, as there is in Canada. Moreover, since so much of British constitutionalism is dependent on custom and convention, its flexibility is further enhanced because the practices of politics are modified in the daily workings of the political institutions and processes of government. A final advantage of a British-style system is its ability to act, to get its legislative program passed, and to meet both domestic and international crises. Concentration of power has never been seen as automatically deleterious to constitutional government, but often in the modern era, as a prerequisite for its continuation. In contrast, the philosphical assumptions of constitutional government in the United States are based on the desire to limit any such concentrations of political authority:

> Lord Acton's famous phrase that "power tends to corrupt and absolute power corrupts absolutely," while that of an Englishman, has nevertheless found greater acceptance in the United States than in Great Britain itself (Mitchell, 1970: 109).

Percentage of Americans who say "of the people, by the people, and for the people" is in the Constitution: 82. Who say "from each according to his ability, to each according to his need" is in the Constitution: 45 (*Harper's Magazine* [May, 1987], Volume 274, Number 1644, p. 13).

The American Constitutional Experience

The nature of constitutional government in the United States has to be understood in the context of the American Revolution and its consequences. First, by achieving independence through the force of arms, the colonial leaders were confronted with the need to specify in a written, comprehensive document the structure of a new system of government. However, their initial attempt in the Articles of Confederation failed, which led ultimately to the present American Constitution. Second, the revolutionary context resulted in a revised philosophy of democratic government, which, in contrast to the British pattern of concentrated authority, emphasized the need to limit government. The Fathers of the American Constitution "did not believe in man, but they did believe in the power of a good political constitution to control him" (Hofstadter, 1948: 3). Finally, the people were made the basis of political authority: power flowed from the public to the government, the idea of popular sovereignty. This outlook was summarized best in the words of the Declaration of Independence, which asserted that men were "endowed by their Creator with certain unalienable rights, that among these are life, liberty, and the pursuit of happiness," and that to secure such rights, "governments are instituted among men, deriving their just powers from the consent of the governed." The con-

trast of the liberal-based American perspective of "life, liberty, and the pursuit of happiness" with the British-based, conservative Canadian view of government's role as "peace, order and good government" reflects an important difference in the constitutional perspectives of these two political systems.

The essence of American constitutionalism, therefore, reflects the view that the people must be protected from government. To achieve limited government, any undue concentration of political authority must be prevented. Such a philosophy of democratic government was explicitly argued in *The Federalist Papers*, a series of newspaper editorials written to convince the people of the need to adopt the new system of government. The best summary of the American political philosophy remains Federalist Paper Number 51, written by James Madison, who is often referred to as the Father of the American Constitution.

But the great security against a gradual concentration of the several powers in the same department consists in giving to those who administer each department the necessary constitutional means and personal motives to resist encroachments of the others. The provision for defence must in this, as in all other cases, be made commensurate to the danger of attack. Ambition must be made to counteract ambition. The interest of the man must be connected with the constitutional rights of the place. It may be a reflection on human nature that such devices should be necessary to control the abuses of government. But what is government itself but the greatest of all reflections on human nature? If men were angels, no government would be necessary. If angels were to govern men, neither external nor internal controls on government would be necessary. In framing a government which is to be administered by men over men, the great difficulty lies in this: you must first enable the government to control the governed; and in the next place oblige it to control itself. A dependence on the people is, no doubt, the primary control on the government; but experience has taught mankind the necessity of auxiliary precautions.

In addition to being the closest thing to poetry in the conversation of political analysts, this quotation stresses the need to limit government through the use of certain "auxiliary precautions," that is, those principles of government upon which the American system is founded. These auxiliary precautions are fourfold: separation of powers, checks and balances, federalism, and a bill of rights. The heart of American constitutionalism is reflected in the way the political structures embody these four principles, all of which seek to fragment and restrain the use and concentration of influence and power by the political elites.

SEPARATION OF POWERS

The adoption and implementation of the separation of powers doctrine represents one of the unique contributions of American politics to the art of democratic government. **Separation of powers** *refers to the establishment of several branches of government (executive, legislative, and judicial), the allocation of governmental powers among these three branches, and a pattern of political and constitutional independence of each branch of government from the other.* The separation of powers principle is a reflection of the view that "ambition must be made to counteract ambition." Each branch of government is inherently in conflict with the others, as it jealously guards its own prerogatives and seeks to carry out the tasks assigned to it. Moreover, each branch must have the cooperation of the others in order to carry out these activities. Such cooperation among branches is essential in order for the American system to work, while such a pattern is made difficult by the structure of government so created. By fragmenting power among the several branches, cooperation among all three institutions was made improba-

"If you are ever again taking an exam on American government," the professor scolded his students, "and come up against a question you can't figure out, for heaven's sake just put down 'separation of powers.' It explains roughly half of everything that happens" (Ladd, 1986: 3).

ble. In that sense, the American polity was created to prevent government activity – a goal that has, more often than not, been admirably achieved.

The political and constitutional independence of the three branches of government is explicitly provided for in the Constitution. For example, the officers in each institution are kept distinct, since no individual can serve in two branches of government at the same time. Thus, a separation of powers doctrine is implemented, in part, by a separation of personnel, in sharp contrast to the Canadian and British parliamentary systems. A further means of creating political independence for each branch is to have the executive, legislature, and judiciary responsive to varying political constituencies. Thus, the president and vice-president have a national constituency, members of the Senate a statewide electorate, members in the House of Representatives a locally-based constituency, and judicial appointees a combination of such bases, depending on which court an individual serves. Moreover, members of each branch remain in office for differing time periods: the president serves a four-year term, with the possibility of being reelected once; senators are chosen for a six-year period, with one-third elected every two years; all representatives are voted on every two years; and judicial appointees generally serve for life. With each branch of government composed of different personnel, responsive to different constituencies, and staying in office for different time periods, individuals' outlooks and political interests rarely coalesce. The result is the prevention of any undue concentration of political power.

CHECKS AND BALANCES

In order to guarantee the continuation of the separation of powers principle once the political structure began operating, the second auxiliary precaution — namely, a series of checks and balances — was included in the Constitution. In other words, **checks and balances** *are the constitutionally-specified mechanisms and powers designed to preserve the political independence of each branch of government.* For example, the right of the executive branch not to turn over information to either the legislature or judiciary, what is known as **executive privilege**, is a major means for protecting its independence. Such a procedure is also a key defence against legislative supremacy, that is, the development of a parliamentary-style system.

Numerous other such checks and balances could be cited. For example, Supreme Court appointments are recommended by the executive, but must be approved by the Senate. A treaty negotiated and signed by the president must be approved by a two-thirds vote in the Senate before becoming law. Any piece of legislation must be approved by both the executive and legislative branches of government, except when the legislature overrides a presidential veto. Even when approval by both branches is gained, the Supreme Court may rule such legislation null and void.

The result of the separation of powers princi-

There are two fundamental arguments for a constitutional system of separate institutions sharing powers: It helps preserve liberty and it slows the pace of political change. These arguments are as valid today as they were in 1787 (Wilson: 1987: 49).

It was too much to expect that vice could be checked by virtue; the Fathers relied instead upon checking vice with vice (Hofstadter, 1948: 7).

This is not powdered wigs and pewter mugs; this is street fighting (Congresswoman Barbara Mikulski on the separation of powers principle, quoted in Friendly and Elliot, 1984: 283).

---

ple and the series of checks and balances has been to create a governmental system "of separated institutions sharing power," a pattern of "mutually dependent relationships" (Neustadt, 1980: 26, 28). In such a system, every branch of government is given a certain portion of executive, legislative, and judicial power. For example, while the executive branch exercises most of the executive authority, both the legislature and judiciary are also given executive powers. The same argument holds true for the other branches (see Figure 3.1). Thus, each "department is given a voice in the business of the others, and each is made dependent on the cooperation of the others in order to accomplish its own business" (Peltason, 1979: 24).

FEDERALISM

The third major restriction on the concentration of power is the principle of **federalism**, previously defined as *the division of powers between levels of government.* The division of powers and the separation of powers are principles that are not interchangeable in political analysis. In the American system, each level of government (i.e., national and state) is structured internally on the separation of powers principle. For example, the national government is composed of three branches of government, as are each of the 50 state governments. Thus, a federal structure is consistent with either a presidential

FIGURE 3.1 SCHEMATIC PORTRAYAL OF SEPARATE INSTITUTIONS SHARING POWER

EXECUTIVE AUTHORITY	LEGISLATIVE AUTHORITY	JUDICIAL AUTHORITY
Exercised by	*Exercised by*	*Exercised by*
Judicial Branch	Judicial Branch	Executive Branch
Legislative Branch	Executive Branch	Legislative Branch
Executive Branch	Legislative Branch	Judicial Branch

system based on the separation of powers principle or a parliamentary system founded on a fusion of powers doctrine.

Although both Canada and the United States are federal political systems, the federal principle was adopted for very different reasons in each country. Canadian federalism was a means primarily of handling ethnic diversity, while American federalism was designed to fragment and mitigate the concentration of political power. To enhance that fragmentation, the American federal system was initially decentralized. Although for generally similar reasons as in Canada, the evolution of American federalism runs counter to the Canadian experience: beginning with a largely decentralized federal structure, American federalism has become highly centralized, especially during the past 60 years.

The American Constitution allocated a series of explicit powers to the national government in Article One, Section 8, which included the right to collect taxes, provide for the common defence and general welfare, coin money, declare war, establish post offices, regulate commerce, and borrow money. Such functions are referred to as **enumerated powers** with the national government also given the **implied powers** that might be needed to carry out the enumerated ones. Of interest is the fact that, after the list of powers given to the federal government, there followed a list of powers

> Our federalism is much like a piece of earth that is subject to constant redevelopment. It can be bulldozed and built up, flattened and regraded, virtually beyond recognition. Yet certain elemental properties of it, the bedrock and the composition of the soil, endure (Derthick, 1989: 35).

denied to Congress (Section 9) and a list of powers denied to the states (Section 10). No specific allocation of powers was made to the states, because it was assumed that all powers not specifically granted the national government were retained by the states. A specific **residual power clause** was later added as the Tenth Amendment, to confirm the reserve power of the several states. However, within those powers granted to the national government, its laws would be supreme over those of the states (Article Six).

Local government was not recognized as a separate level, but was assumed to be under the powers retained by the states. Although local government was, therefore, in a unitary relationship with its respective state, over the years the municipalities have gained a good measure of independence. Despite considerable objections from the states, the national government has been able to deal directly with local governments, thus bypassing the intermediate state level. Such a development runs counter to the Canadian experience.

The American Constitution initially did not contain any provisions for emergency powers for the national government, nor have any such powers been added by the amendment process. However, the implied powers of the national government, with respect to defence and the general warfare functions, have been a sufficient basis for strong governmental action, when required. In addition, the prerogative powers of the president, especially those growing out of his role as Commander in Chief, combined with special emergency powers granted to him by Congress, have been sufficient to meet any crisis situation. As a result, the United States has no specific counterpart to the Canadian War Measures Act, or its successor, the 1988 Emergencies Act.

Finally, the American Constitution, unlike the Canadian, contained a specific amending clause (Article Five). Two ways of proposing amendments and two methods for ratifying such changes were outlined, thus producing four possible amending procedures. The usual method has been for an amendment to be proposed by a two-thirds vote in both Houses of Congress, followed by ratification by three-fourths of the state legislatures. Neither the president at the national level nor the governors at the state level have any veto power with respect to the amendment resolutions. However, such procedures are difficult to use, with the result that in almost 200 years, with over 10 000 proposed amendments, only 26 formal amendments have been made to the American Constitution.

Although the initial federal structure was decentralized, currently the United States is an example of a strongly centralized federal system. Changes in society, governmental functions, and court interpretations have all contributed to such a pattern. For example, decisions of the American Supreme Court enhanced the powers of the national government with respect to three key areas: trade and commerce, taxation, and the war power (Burns et al., 1984: 53–54). Remember that in Canada, court decisions restricted the powers of the national government.

Another cause of a centralized federalism in the United States can be seen in the responses to both domestic and international crises. Until the 1930s, American government remained decentralized, but in order to respond to the Great Depression, the national government assumed many of the previous functions of the state and local units with respect to welfare, unemployment, and economic development. As in Canada, for example, the superior taxing power of the American national government eventually led to its participation in matters originally under state and local control. Through a series of financial mechanisms, such as the recent program of revenue-sharing, the federal government has become extensively involved in the financing of state and local government (Burns et al., 1984: 56–59).

In addition, the Second World War and the emergence of the United States as a superpower in international affairs have greatly expanded the powers of the American presidency and, by implication, those of the national government. Such changes, more often than not, have been based on developing beliefs and conventions, rather than on explicit constitutional amendments. Finally, social changes, such as the civil rights movement of the 1960s and the urban crisis of the 1970s, have drawn governments, especially the national government, into new areas of activity. For these reasons, the national government has become the dominant level in the American federal system.

BILL OF RIGHTS

The final auxiliary precaution, a bill of rights, was not included in the original Constitution. However, in order to gain public support for its ratification, the backers of the Constitution promised that a bill of rights would be a priority of the new government. Thus, the first 10 amendments to the Constitution were adopted in 1791 and they comprise the American Bill of Rights.

Protections are given to basic civil and political liberties, including freedom of speech, religion, and assembly. Citizens are guarded against unreasonable searches and seizures by the government, granted the right of reasonable bail and the due process of law, prevented from self-incrimination and guaranteed a trial by jury in common law cases. Although it was entrenched, the American Bill of Rights only applied initially to the national government. Beginning in the 1920s and continuing through the 1960s, a series of court decisions effectively "nationalized" the Bill of Rights, making it applicable to the states as well as to the federal government. This development was accomplished by judicial interpretation rather than by formal constitutional amendment.

The four auxiliary precautions of the separation of powers, checks and balances, federalism, and a bill of rights are the centrepieces of American constitutional practice. Based on the assumption of the inherently evil nature of political power, all four principles were designed to prevent its accumulation in the polity. Concentration of power and by implication its misuse were made improbable by dividing political power between two levels of government (federalism); by splitting power within each level into executive, legislative, and judicial arenas (separation of powers); by structuring each department of government so that it would jealously guard its own powers and prerogatives (checks and balances); and by limiting the powers of any government through a series of civil and political liberties (a bill of rights). According to the American perspective, the way to create constitutional government is to structure a government of limited and circumscribed powers.

Comparing Constitutions

The most significant element in any political analysis of constitutions is determining whether or not they effectively restrain governmental power, that is, whether they produce, in fact, a pattern of constitutional government. Distinctions such as that between written and unwritten constitutions are secondary to questions of constitutionalism. However, to classify a polity as constitutional government, one has to go beyond the literal constitution to consider such things as whether or not a political system allows political dissent and political opposition. If a pattern of constitutional government does exist, then the way in which it is produced in different political systems becomes a significant basis for comparing political systems.

The structure of government itself may contribute to a system of constitutionalism. For example, some constitutional polities are presidential in format, while others are parliamentary. A presidential system, based on a separation of powers doctrine, seeks to constrain executive authority, while a parliamentary system concentrates power through the fusion of the executive and legislative branches of government. Some political systems are unitary in structure, while others are federal. If a polity is federal, then questions of how many levels of government have been created and their respective powers become significant. In analyzing federal systems, an important consideration is not only the initial distribution of powers outlined in the constitution, but the way in which those powers may have changed in practice. If there have been changes, then one must investigate how they have occurred and how the initial allocation of powers has been modified. The causes for the evolution and development of the pattern of power in a federal system are complex, but usually include a changing environment, the impact of judicial decisions, and modified public beliefs about the proper political role of each level of government.

Changes in constitutional systems may be accomplished by a formal amending process, but, more often than not, are more typically produced by the evolving customs and conventions of the polity. These customs and conventions have a significant bearing on the existence and operation of constitutional government. The nature of these conventions, their strength, and the result of any non-observance of them are all significant indicators for comparing the varieties of constitutional government.

A final point for the comparison of constitutions concerns their protection of civil and political liberties. A political analyst must consider what human freedoms are protected and how. The typical pattern in the modern era is to have some sort of bill of rights, which can be either entrenched in the constitution or passed in its own right. In federal systems, a key question is the application of such guarantees to each level of government: do human rights exist in relation to one or both levels of government? Moreover, in times of crisis, can a bill of rights be bypassed through the application of emergency powers and, if so, how long do such actions hold human freedom in limbo?

Three main areas, therefore, form the basis for any comparative analysis of constitutions: first, whether a constitution has helped to produce a constitutional government in practice; second, the kind of political structure that is outlined in the constitution (e.g., presidential or parliamentary, federal or unitary); and third, the mechanism, if any, that is used to protect basic human freedoms.

Summary

1. A constitution is a political mechanism that structures the institutions of government; it is a power map of the polity. However, no such outline of the basic rules of the political game is ever neutral in its effects: constitution writers defend their own interests above all others. A country's constitution usually includes not only a written part, but significant political customs and conventions as well.

2. Having a piece of paper called a constitution and having a system of constitutional government are not necessarily synonymous developments. Few constitutions produce constitutional government, that is, a polity that places effective limits on the powers and actions of its rulers.

3. The Canadian Constitution includes not only the Constitution Act of 1867, but a series of constitutional documents as well. Moreover, political customs and conventions are significant elements in Canada's federal and parliamentary constitutional matrix. Beginning with a highly centralized federal structure, Canada has evolved to a decentralized federal pattern, with a rough equality between the provinces and Ottawa. Three major additions to the constitutional pattern have been added since Confederation: the War Measures Act and its successor, the 1988 Emergencies Act, the Bill of Rights, and the Constitution Act of 1982. Although the 1867 Constitution Act initially lacked an amending clause and a bill of rights, because of the 1982 Constitution Act, such discrepancies have now been rectified.

4. The British Constitution is unwritten in the sense of having a comprehensive constitutional statement. However, Britain does have a series of constitutional documents, plus an array of political customs and conventions, all of which produce a pattern of constitutionalism. Although political power is concentrated, as a result of its unitary and parliamentary structure, it is restricted in use, thus producing a unique example of constitutional government.

5. American constitutionalism is predicated on the view of the evil nature of political power

and the need to restrict its concentration in the polity. Four basic techniques are used to achieve such a result: separation of powers, checks and balances, federalism, and protection for civil and political liberties. In contrast to the Canadian pattern, the United States has evolved from a decentralized to a centralized federal system. As a result of its revolutionary origins, the American Constitution was initially more comprehensive than the Canadian one, since it contained an amending formula, with an entrenched bill of rights soon added. Probably the unique contribution of the American example to the art of constitutional government is the principle of the separation of powers and its implementation through the various checks and balances. From the American perspective, the way to create constitutional government is to fragment and decentralize political power.

Recommended Readings

Constitutional Government: General

BANTING, KEITH G. and RICHARD SIMEON, eds. (1985) *Redesigning the State: The Politics of Constitutional Change in Industrial Nations*. Toronto: University of Toronto Press.

BOGDANOR, VERNON, ed. (1988) *Constitutions in Democratic Politics*. Aldershot, England: Gower.

CARALEY, DEMETRIOS (1986) "Changing Conceptions of Federalism," *Political Science Quarterly*, Volume 101, Number 2, pp. 289–306.

COHLER, ANNE M. (1988) *Montesquieu's Comparative Politics and the Spirit of American Constitutionalism*. Lawrence, Kansas: University Press of Kansas.

DAVIS, S. RUFUS (1978) *The Federal Principle*. Berkeley: University of California Press.

DUCHACEK, IVO D. (1973) *Power Maps: Comparative Politics of Constitutions*. Santa Barbara, California: ABC-CLIO Press.

DWORKIN, RONALD (1977) *Taking Rights Seriously*. Cambridge: Harvard University Press.

FRIEDRICH, CARL J. (1968) *Constitutional Government and Democracy: Theory and Practice in Europe and America*. Waltham, Mass.: Blaisdell Publishing Co., 4th ed.

HAHN, RANDOLPH K. (1988) "The British Influence on the Initiation and Introduction of Commonwealth Bills of Rights," *The Journal of Commonwealth and Comparative Politics* (March), Volume 26, Number 1, pp. 54–71.

HEARD, ANDREW D. (1989) "Recognizing the Variety Among Constitutional Conventions," *Canadian Journal of Political Science* (March), Volume 22, Number 1, pp. 63–81.

HICKS, URSULA K. (1979) *Federalism: Failure and Success — A Comparative Study*. Oxford: Oxford University Press.

LANE, DAVID (1984) "Human Rights under State Socialism," *Political Studies* (September), Volume 32, Number 3, pp. 349–368.

MARSHALL, GEOFFREY (1971) *Constitutional Theory*. Oxford: Oxford University Press.

MCILWAIN, CHARLES HOWARD (1947) *Constitutionalism: Ancient and Modern*. Ithaca, New York: Great Seal Books, Cornell University Press, rev. ed.

MCWHINNEY, EDWARD (1981) *Constitution-Making: Principles, Process, Practice*. Toronto: University of Toronto Press.

RIKER, WILLIAM H. (1964) *Federalism: Origin, Operation, Significance*. Boston: Little, Brown.

ROSSITER, CLINTON (1963) *Constitutional Dictatorship: Crisis Government in the Modern Democracies*. New York: Harcourt, Brace and World.

VIPOND, ROBERT C. (1989) "1787 and 1867: The Federal Principle and Canadian Confederation Reconsidered," *Canadian Journal of Political Science* (March), Volume 22, Number 1, pp. 3–25.

WATTS, RONALD L. (1987) "The American Constitution in Comparative Perspective: A Comparison of Federalism in the United States and Canada," *The Journal of American History* (December), Volume 74, Number 3, pp. 769–791.

The Canadian Constitution

BERGER, THOMAS R. (1982) *Fragile Freedoms: Human Rights and Dissent in Canada*. Toronto: Clarke, Irwin and Company.

BOROVOY, A. ALAN (1988) *When Freedoms Collide: The Case for Our Civil Liberties*. Toronto: Lester and Orpen Dennys.

FORSEY, EUGENE (1974) *Freedom and Order: Collected Essays*. Toronto: McClelland and Stewart.

FRANKS, C.E.S. (1987) "Aboriginal Self-Government in Canada," *Queen's Quarterly* (Autumn), Volume 94, Number 3, pp. 666–679.

HEINRICHS, TERRY (1988) "Free Speech and the Zundel Trial," *Queen's Quarterly* (Winter), Volume 95, Number 4, pp. 837–854.

MAGNUSSON, WARREN (1985) "The Local State in Canada: Theoretical Perspectives," *Canadian Public Administration* (Winter), Volume 28, Number 4, pp. 575–599.

MAHLER, GREGORY S. (1987) "Canadian Federalism and Constitutional Reform," *The Journal of Commonwealth and Comparative Politics* (July), Volume 25, Number 2, pp. 107–125.

MALLORY, J.R. (1954) *Social Credit and the Federal Power in Canada*. Toronto: University of Toronto Press.

MCWHINNEY, EDWARD (1979) *Quebec and the Constitution 1960–1978*. Toronto: University of Toronto Press.

MILNE, DAVID (1986) *Tug of War: Ottawa and the Provinces Under Trudeau and Mulroney*. Toronto: James Lorimer.

RUSSELL, PETER H., ed. (1984) *Leading Constitutional Decisions*. Ottawa: Carleton University Press, 3rd ed.

SCOTT, FRANK R. (1977) *Essays on the Constitution: Aspects of Canadian Law and Politics*. Toronto: University of Toronto Press.

SHEPPARD, ROBERT and MICHAEL VALPY (1982) *The National Deal: The Fight for a Canadian Constitution*. Toronto: Macmillan of Canada.

SMILEY, D.V. (1987) *The Federal Condition in Canada*. Toronto: McGraw-Hill Ryerson.

STEVENSON, GARTH (1989) *Unfulfilled Union: Canadian Federalism and National Unity*. Toronto: Macmillan of Canada, 3rd ed.

TARNOPOLSKY, WALTER SURMA (1975) *The Canadian Bill of Rights*. Toronto: McClelland and Stewart, 2nd rev. ed.

TRUDEAU, PIERRE ELLIOTT (1968) *Federalism and the French Canadians*. Toronto: Macmillan of Canada.

WALSH, BREN (1985) *More Than a Poor Majority: The Story of Newfoundland's Confederation with Canada*. St. John's: Breakwater Books.

The British Constitution

BAGEHOT, WALTER (1867, 1963) *The English Constitution*. London: Collins, The Fontana Library.

BARNUM, DAVID G. and JOHN L. SULLIVAN (1989) "Attitudinal Tolerance and Political Freedom in Britain," *British Journal of Political Science* (January), Volume 19, Number 1, pp. 136–146.

HOOPER, DAVID (1987) *Official Secrets: The Use and Abuse of the Act*. London: Secker and Warburg.

JOWELL, J. and D. OLIVER, eds. (1985) *The Changing Constitution*. Oxford: Clarendon Press.

MADDEN, A.F. (1988) "Constitution-Making and Nationhood: The British Experience — An Overview," *The Journal of Commonwealth and Comparative Politics* (July), Volume 26, Number 2, pp. 123–134.

MARSHALL, GEOFFREY (1984) *Constitutional Conventions: The Rules and Forms of Political Accountability*. Oxford: Oxford University Press.

NORTON, PHILIP (1982) *The Constitution in Flux*. Oxford: Martin Robertson.

RIDLEY, F.F. (1988) "There Is No British Constitution: A Dangerous Case of the Emperor's Clothes," *Parliamentary Affairs* (July), Volume 41, Number 3, pp. 340–361.

ROSE, RICHARD (1982) *The Territorial Dimension in Government: Understanding the United Kingdom*. Chatham, N.J.: Chatham House Publishers.

SHARPE, L.J. (1985) "Devolution and Celtic Nationalism in the UK," *West European Politics*, Volume 8, Number 3, pp. 82–100.

SMITH, B.C. (1985) *Decentralization: The Territorial Dimension of the State*. London: Allen and Unwin.

STALLWORTHY, MARK (1989) "Central Government and Local Government: The Uses and Abuses of Constitutional Hegemony," *The Political Quarterly* (January), Volume 60, Number 1, pp. 22–37.

VERNEY, DOUGLAS V. (1976) *British Government and Politics: Life Without a Declaration of Independence*. New York: Harper and Row.

WILLIAMS, SHIRLEY (1989) "The New Authoritarianism," *The Political Quarterly* (January), Volume 60, Number 1, pp. 4–9.

The American Constitution

BELZ, HERMAN (1988) "Abraham Lincoln and American Constitutionalism," *The Review of Politics* (Spring), Volume 50, Number 2, pp. 169–197.

BERGER, RAOUL (1973) *Impeachment: The Constitutional Problems*. New York: Bantam Books.

BRENNAN, WILLIAM J., JR. (1987) "Interpreting the Constitution," *Social Policy* (Summer), Volume 18, Number 1, pp. 24–28.

CARTER, LIEF H. (1985) *Contemporary Constitutional Lawmaking: The Supreme Court and the Art of Politics*. New York: Pergamon Press.

ELAZAR, DANIEL J. (1984) *American Federalism: A View from the States*. New York: Harper and Row, 3rd ed.

FISCHER, LOUIS (1987) *The Politics of Shared Power: Congress and the Executive*. Washington, D.C.: CQ Press, 2nd ed.

HAMILTON, ALEXANDER, JAMES MADISON, and JOHN JAY (1788) *The Federalist Papers*.

JILLSON, CALVIN C. (1988) *Constitution Making: Conflict and Consensus in the Federal Convention of 1787*. New York: Agathon Press.

KOBYLKA, JOSEPH F. and BRADLEY KENT CARTER (1987) "Madison, 'The Federalist,' and the Constitutional Order: Human Nature and Institutional Structure," *Polity* (Winter), Volume 20, Number 2, pp. 190–208.

LEVINSON, SANFORD (1988) *Constitutional Faith*. Princeton, N.J.: Princeton University Press.

MCCLOSKY, HERBERT and ALIDA BRILL (1983) *Dimensions of Tolerance: What Americans Believe About Civil Liberties*. New York: Russell Sage Foundation.

PELTASON, J.W. (1979) *Corwin and Peltason's Understanding the Constitution*. New York: Holt, Rinehart and Winston, 8th ed.

SUNDQUIST, JAMES L. (1988) "Needed: A Political Theory for the New Era of Coalition Government in the United States," *Political Science Quarterly* (Winter), Volume 103, Number 4, pp. 613–635.

WILSON, JAMES Q. (1987) "Does the Separation of Powers Still Work?" *The Public Interest* (Winter), Number 86, pp. 36–52.

4 The Executive Branch of Government: The Facade and Reality of Political Power

Like other tourists, we went to watch the Changing of the Guard, a ceremony of which I disapproved vigorously. Much as I was intrigued by the uncanny precision of the performance, I could not accept the sight of healthy men in uniform putting on a show of marching like robots, turning like puppets, and standing immobile like inanimate wax figures, all for the glory of royal and military symbols of authority and subservience. It took me years to learn to appreciate the power of symbolism in the behaviour of individuals and groups in society (Lewis, 1981: 61).

For political theorists, conceptions of the ideal polity presuppose that certain types of leaders are optimal, if one is to maximize fairness, democracy, political stability, or government efficiency . . . . Who rules does indeed make a difference (Bunce, 1981: 3, 256).

If one reduces politics to its bare bones, to what is most visible to most citizens, it is the national political leaders, both at home and abroad, that remain once everything else has been erased; they are the most universal, the most recognized, the most talked about elements of political life (Blondel, 1987: 1).

THE CENTREPIECE of all forms of modern government — autocratic, democratic, or totalitarian — is the executive branch. The expansive nature of government in the 20th century has been both a cause and consequence of executive dominance. A combination of several factors has made the executive branch the engine of the political process, not the least of which has been the willingness of the political executives to provide leadership for the polity and to adapt themselves to a changing environment: "the birth of power presumes not merely a situation in which a form of arrangement and understanding is ripe for development, but likewise individuals or groups of individuals who are ready to utilize the opportunity afforded by the conjunction of circumstances" (Merriam, 1964: 45). Paralleling the growth of executive-centred government has been the phenomenal rise of the bureaucracy, the primary mechanism for implementing executive decisions.

The Nature and Growth of Executive Power

The frequent assertion of many analyses of the rise of executive government in the modern era is that executive power is a new trend. Unfortunately, the historical accuracy of such a conclusion is suspect, for few governments have ever been anything but executive-centred. The rise of executive government in the 20th century is a reassertion of the executive's traditional role which was only temporarily lost to the legislature in democratic polities and never lost in autocratic and totalitarian systems. However, the reappearance of executive power has been accompanied by a change in the executor of that leadership in parliamentary systems from the formal to the political executive. The historical development of executive power has been from the king, to the king in Parliament, to a pattern of the prime minister in Parliament.

PARLIAMENTARY EXECUTIVES

The characteristics of a parliamentary executive include its dual structure (i.e., both a formal and a political executive), its relationship with the legislature, which is based on the fusion of powers principle, and its term in office, which is variable within a maximum time limit. The **formal executive**, that is, the monarchical element, such as the queen or governor general, performs primarily symbolic and ceremonial functions for the polity. While an organizational chart of the executive branch would place the formal executive at its pinnacle, such a positioning represents the facade rather than the reality of political influence and power.

The **political executive**, which includes the prime minister, cabinet, and bureaucracy, is the real locus of influence in modern parliamentary systems. Theoretically subservient to the formal executive, the political executive in fact controls the monarchical element. The formal executive reigns but does not govern, while the political executive governs but does not reign. This symbiotic relationship has always been an unequal one, with the formal executive initially controlling the political executive, while the reverse of this pattern is true in the reassertion of executive power in the modern age.

The connection between the political executive and the legislature in a parliamentary system is based on two principles: collective responsibility and ministerial responsibility. The concept of **collective responsibility** emphasizes the group basis of parliamentary government: as a team, the cabinet, that is, the government of the day, is sustained or defeated in Parliament. Individual government ministers

> A constitutional monarch protects democracy from the results of the bends at the heights of political power (MacKinnon, 1973: 61).

One of Parkinson's Laws holds that the ideal government cabinet contains just five members. One of them knows the law, one knows finance, one knows foreign policy, and one knows defense. The fifth member, the one who has failed to master any of these subjects, usually becomes the Prime Minister (Roberts, 1986: 22).

cannot be rejected by a vote in Parliament. Moreover, unity of purpose is a necessary outgrowth of collective responsibility: the cabinet sings a common song, although some of its members may not always be in tune. Public disagreement with cabinet policy by a minister is rare. Typically, a cabinet minister who openly disagrees with government policy resigns, as did Suzanne Blais-Grenier who quit the Mulroney cabinet in December, 1985 over the closing of an oil refinery in Montreal. While initially developed as a means of legislative control over the executive, the combination of party discipline with collective responsibility has produced, in practice, executive control of the legislature.

In contrast to collective responsibility, the principle of **ministerial responsibility** emphasizes the individual responsibility of each cabinet member to Parliament. Individual ministers are responsible to the cabinet and the Commons for the conduct of their departments, including its finances, programs, and policies. Ministers must explain to the House any wrongdoing of officials under their jurisdiction, as well as justify to the public the direction of their department's major public policy decisions. Ministerial responsibility does not necessarily mean that ministers are personally responsible for wrongdoings in their department, but it does mean they must answer questions and explain to Parliament what has happened, as well as be responsible for correcting present abuses and trying to prevent their reoccurrence. Failure to guide their department adequately or to live up

to their party's or public's expectation may lead to ministerial resignations, such as that of Fisheries Minister John Fraser in the "tunagate affair" in the fall of 1985. In modern parliamentary systems, the practice of ministerial responsibility can be circumvented (e.g., ministers refusing to take responsibility for wrongdoings in their department), while that of collective responsibility remains largely, if not totally, in place (e.g., the Canadian Constitutional Crisis of 1968).

PRESIDENTIAL EXECUTIVES

A presidential executive is characterized by the singular office of president, which combines the formal and political executive roles of a parliamentary system; by its relationship with the legislature, which is based on the separation of powers principle; and by its election periods, which are fixed by law. Because it has been rarely imitated, the American system remains the primary example of a presidential structure. As both the ceremonial and political leader, the American president has become the symbol of the nation. What has been created in the American presidential system is an executive office with the potential for leadership which, when combined with political skill and ambition, can make it the prime mover in the political process.

One of the most important distinctions between presidential and parliamentary government concerns the means of selecting the political executive. In a parliamentary system, the

There is no foreign institution with which, in any basic sense, it can be compared, because, basically, there is no comparable foreign institution. The president of the United States is both more and less than a king; he is, also , both more and less than a prime minister (Laski, 1940: 11).

leader of the majority party is asked to form a government by the monarch. The prime minister is thus not technically elected by either the whole country (but is elected to the Commons from a single constituency, as is any other MP) or by Parliament. In contrast, presidential systems are based on a national constituency, which may select the president directly through popular election or indirectly through some sort of electoral college mechanism.

This more direct relationship with the mass public has been an important reason for the enhancement of American presidential leadership in both domestic and international affairs. The dominance of the presidential office over the other political institutions is the basis for the idea of the **imperial presidency**, that is, a dominant office that directs the course of events in the political process. Transferring this idea to a parliamentary context has resulted in the concept of **prime ministerial government**, where one individual, the prime minister, becomes the key actor in the parliamentary system. In such a system, cabinet government is superseded: the prime minister is no longer *primus inter pares* (first among equals) for the simple reason that he has no equals. As former British Prime Minister Winston Churchill (1949: 14) put it: "In any sphere of action there can be no comparison between the positions of number one and numbers two, three and four." The growth of prime ministerial power has often been labeled as the "presidentializing" of parliamentary government.

EXECUTIVE BRANCH FUNCTIONS

Whether of the presidential or parliamentary variety, the functions of the executive branch of government are similar in most political systems. There are three basic executive functions: leadership, policy-making, and the implementation of public policy.

The leadership role focuses on the executive

> The essentials of political leadership . . . transcend particular cultures and particular societies. What are these essentials? A summary descriptive answer is: malefaction. Everywhere leaders, on pain of failure, must break out of the morality they recommend to other people (Bailey: 1988: x).

as the initiator of public policy, the branch of government given the responsibility for providing overall direction for the polity. In many cases, the leadership role of the executive branch is not constitutionally prescribed, but is based on custom and convention. A combination of circumstances, including the increasingly complex nature of both domestic society and the international system, the political will of the executive to exercise its powers, and the expansive nature of government in the modern era, has contributed to the leadership dominance of the executive branch of government. If the executive does not lead, then stalemate and confusion may characterize the polity. Neither constitutional prescription nor political custom can force or guarantee executive direction. However, one result is apparent: if the executive fails to lead, no other political institution appears, on a continuing basis, to be either adequately equipped or politically willing to assume the leadership function.

Executive direction is provided through the development of public policy. A **policy** is *"an explicit set of preferences and plans drawn up in order to make the outcomes of a series of future decisions more nearly predictable and consistent"* (Deutsch, 1968: 77). A **public policy** is *a set of such preferences that has consequences for the community.* Public policies would include examples such as a government's budget, taxation rules, or specific content areas such as economic development, immigration, culture, education, and foreign affairs. For example, a budget can "be characterized as a series of goals with price tags attached" (Wildavsky, quoted in Bunce, 1981: 39).

The initiation, development, and passage of public policy differs among political systems. The traditional makers of public policy in a parliamentary system have been the cabinet and the civil service, while prime ministerial government has shifted such power to appointed advisors. In a presidential system, the cabinet is rarely the centre of policy decisions; while individual cabinet members may play a significant role, the key decision-making power lies with the president and his advisors. On occasion, the legislature may assume the initiative for policy formulation. More often than not, the legislature's role is to legitimate the policy decisions of the executive branch of government.

Once a policy has been decided, the third function of the executive is to implement its provisions. The application and enforcement of public policy is the designated task of the bureaucracy, that portion of the executive branch referred to as the civil service. It is in the size of the bureaucracy that the real expansion of government has occurred in the 20th century.

In addition to the factors that have contributed to the general growth of executive power, several others have enhanced bureaucratic powers. Most legislation is general in its provisions, leaving it up to the civil servants to fill in the details of how a policy will work in practice. The way a policy or law is implemented and applied may be more significant than the generalized wording as approved by the legislature. In this sense, applying a general law to specific cases gives the bureaucracy the power to make policy. Moreover, the bureaucratic role has been magnified by the expertise of its members. Knowledge and information are important political resources that the bureaucracy has often skillfully utilized to increase its own significance in the decision-making process. Modern government would quickly become inoperative

without its bureaucratic component (or so the bureaucrats would like us to believe).

A **bureaucracy** *is a hierarchically structured organization, which implements public policy on the basis of impartially applied rules*. Comprised of appointed officials or civil servants who have been trained in the art of public administration, the bureaucracy is the major point of contact between the individual and the political regime. In theory, the bureaucracy is designed to be free of political interference, applying set procedures to specific cases.

However, the view of the bureaucracy as impartial and outside of direct political involvement is wrong. Despite civil service examinations and appointments supposedly on the basis of merit, the bureaucracy remains a major bastion of partisanship and political patronage. Civil service regulations can often be circumvented. A party in power for any length of time can fashion the bureaucracy in its own image. Moreover, upon assuming office, parties usually demand the right to restructure at least the very top of the bureaucracy, that segment that plays a significant role in the policy-making process (Michelman and Steeves, 1985).

The roles of the bureaucracy in implementing public policy and of the political executive in its initiation and development have made the executive branch of government the dominant force in the political process of autocratic, democratic, and totalitarian systems. The factors that have produced this pattern seem unlikely to recede in the decades ahead—if anything, these trends will become more pronounced. However, what is open to change is the evolving relationship between the various segments of the executive branch of government.

The Formal Executive in Canada

It would probably surprise many people to discover that executive authority is legally granted

"Once," said the Mock Turtle at last with a deep sigh, "I was a real turtle" (from *Alice in Wonderland*, quoted in Forsey, 1985: 55).

to the formal executive or head of state in the Canadian political system (Constitution Act of 1867, Section 9). Moreover, that executive authority is vested in the Queen of Canada and exercised by her representatives (governor general and lieutenant governors) on a daily basis, a situation that has not been altered by the 1982 Constitution Act. The formal executive is surrounded and aided by a group of advisors known as the Queen's Privy Council for Canada (Section 11). Neither the prime minister nor the cabinet, the two key operative elements of the modern executive, are mentioned in the delineation of executive authority in the 1867 Constitution Act. On the surface, therefore, the formal executive would appear to be preeminent. Consideration of the appointment of the formal executive and of the structure of the Privy Council should quickly dispel such an interpretation.

SELECTING THE FORMAL EXECUTIVE

Since the day-to-day functions of the formal executive are performed by the governor general, that person will be treated as Canada's head of state in the ensuing analysis. Although the governor general was initially selected by the British monarch, since 1926, the Canadian prime minister has recommended to the Queen the individual desired by the Canadian government. While still technically appointed by the Queen, for all practical purposes such a procedure puts the appointment power in the hands of the Canadian political executive. Although it has never happened, it would also appear that the governor general could be removed on the

advice of the prime minister to the Queen. Thus, while an organizational chart places the formal executive over the political executive, the appointment process demonstrates the contrary.

The governor general's term of office is five years, although extensions of several months to several years have been granted. For example, because of the illness of his successor (Jeanne Sauvé), Governor General Edward Schreyer remained on the job until May, 1984, even though his five-year term was completed in January. Likewise, Jeanne Sauvé agreed to extend her term from May, 1989 to January, 1990, so as to allow Prime Minister Mulroney more time to name her replacement. The Honourable Ramon Hnatyshyn was installed as Canada's twenty-fourth Governor General on January 29, 1990. Since 1952, Canadians have been appointed, with the first seven governors general being Vincent Massey, Georges Vanier, Roland Michener, Jules Léger, Edward Schreyer, Jeanne Sauvé, and Ramon Hnatyshyn. The appointment of Edward Schreyer as Governor General in 1978 produced a number of "firsts," probably the most significant being his youth and his Western Canadian background. The selection of Jeanne Sauvé as the 23rd Governor General in December of 1983 produced Canada's first woman occupant of that post.

At the provincial level the formal executive is appointed by the governor general, to whom the lieutenant governors are responsible. This selection procedure puts the effective appointment power for the provincial formal executives in the hands of the federal political executive, since the Prime Minister recommends to the Governor General who is to be appointed. Usually, the provincial political executives are consulted, at least informally, by their federal counterpart before any appointment is made. The term of office for the lieutenant governors is five years, with their salaries determined and paid for by the federal government.

Lieutenant governors have more often been

selected on the basis of patronage and political considerations than has the governor general. For example, Pauline McGibbon of Ontario was the country's first woman lieutenant governor, while her successor, John Aird, was a former Liberal Senator and party fundraiser. In turn, Aird's replacement was former Conservative MP and federal cabinet minister, Lincoln Alexander, the first black to hold the position of lieutenant governor. Similar political factors seem to have influenced the selection of various vice-regal occupants in other provinces as well: Al Abraham in Nova Scotia (past president of the province's Liberal party); Gilles Lamontagne in Quebec (formal Liberal federal defence minister); Frederick W. Johnson in Saskatchewan (former unsuccessful Liberal candidate in both federal and provincial elections); and James McGrath in Newfoundland (former federal Tory cabinet minister and 30-year veteran of the House of Commons). In 1989 Prime Minister Mulroney appointed David See-Chai Lam as lieutenant governor of British Columbia, the first Chinese-Canadian to fill a vice-regal office.

THE ADMINISTRATOR OF CANADA

If for some reason formal executives are unable to perform their duties (e.g., illness, travel outside the country), the 1867 Constitution Act makes provision for their replacement (Sections 10 and 67). At the federal level, the governor general can be replaced by a person appointed as the **Administrator of Canada**, who can exercise all of the formal executive's traditional powers and who serves until the governor general reassumes the duties of the position. In such a situation, the Chief Justice of the Canadian Supreme Court becomes the Administrator of Canada, as happened following Jules Léger's stroke in the mid-1970s and his temporary replacement by Chief Justice Bora Laskin. A

similar procedure is followed for the replacement of a lieutenant governor at the provincial level.

THE PRIVY COUNCIL

The structure and workings of the **Privy Council** are a second clear indicator of the dominance of the political executive over the formal executive in Canada. The advisors to the governor general are selected by the prime minister and, in fact, advise the prime minister rather than the formal head of state. The operative or working part of the Privy Council is the cabinet. However, since the cabinet is not mentioned in the 1867 Constitution Act, to acquire the right to exercise executive authority, its members are sworn into office as members of the Privy Council. Decisions of the cabinet are issued as decisions of the Privy Council (i.e., orders-in-council or minutes-in-council).

While individuals are federal cabinet members only for the duration of their postings as determined by the prime minister, they continue as members of the Privy Council for life. Thus, in the late 1970s there were over 100 members of the Privy Council, but the typical cabinet had only 30 to 35 people. By the mid-1980s that number had grown to over 200, given the turnover of governments in 1979, 1980, and 1984, as well as the increasing size of recent cabinets. By 1988 there were 218 living members in the Privy Council. Since Confederation, close to 600 privy councillors have been appointed. The first case of a person resigning from the Privy Council occurred in 1987, when former federal Liberal Cabinet Minister Jacques Olivier did so in order to run in a municipal election in Quebec.

Although former cabinet ministers remain privy councillors for life, they do not retain the right to advise the current government of the day. Pierre Trudeau had no right to sit in the cabinet discussions of either John Turner's or

Brian Mulroney's government. The cabinet meets frequently, but the full Privy Council rarely does so — only three times between 1945 and 1970 and nine times between 1900 and 1970. A Privy Council meeting is usually held when the Queen visits or on other special occasions (e.g., to receive the announcement from the Queen concerning the marriage of Prince Charles and Lady Diana).

While most members of the Privy Council are there as the result of once being in the cabinet, other individuals may be appointed as well. In honour of the centennial celebration in 1967, the provincial premiers were named to the Privy Council. In January of 1982, Gordon Robertson, former Clerk of the Privy Council and senior cabinet advisor, was named by Prime Minister Trudeau to the body he had long served. In honour of the 1982 Constitution Act, all premiers were invited to join, with only Quebec Premier René Lévesque turning down the appointment. In 1984 former clerks of the Privy Council, Robert Bryce and Michael Pitfield, were added, as was former NDP leader Tommy Douglas. As opposition leader, Brian Mulroney was named to the Privy Council in April, 1984 by Prime Minister Pierre Trudeau, so as to allow him to be briefed on matters of national security. In June of 1985, constitutional expert Eugene Forsey and Conservative MP Lloyd Crouse, the longest-serving member of the House of Commons, were selected as members of the Privy Council.

These considerations on the structure of the Privy Council emphasize that while the formal executive was granted executive authority, it is exercised in fact by the political executive. The formal executive retains the facade of power, while its substance has been coopted by the prime minister and cabinet.

FUNCTIONS OF THE FORMAL EXECUTIVE

The functions of the formal executive reflect this pattern as well. Two basic roles can be identified: a symbolic-ceremonial one and a political one. Most of a governor general's daily tasks fall into the symbolic-ceremonial category, which includes such duties as attending state dinners, receiving ambassadors, and officially granting memberships in the Order of Canada. For example, during his term of office (1979–1984), Governor General Edward Schreyer made more than 300 speeches, spent half his time travelling the equivalent of 12 trips around the world, handed out 1200 medals in the Order of Canada, and hosted countless receptions, dinners, and other functions at Rideau Hall. During her 5 1/2 year term of office (1984–1990), Jeanne Sauvé presented 1921 medals, gave 427 speeches, and travelled 573 000 kilometres. The cost of the office is about $10 million per year.

As a symbol of national unity, the Office of Governor General has been used to stress the bilingual and diverse aspects of the Canadian nation. For example, the first four Canadian governors general were from Ontario and Quebec, with an alternation between those who claimed English or French as their mother tongue. The fifth Canadian Governor General, Edward Schreyer, broke this tradition by being of non-French and non-British origin and by coming from Western Canada. The sixth Canadian Governor General, Jeanne Sauvé, was born in Saskatchewan, while Ramon Hnatyshyn, the first Governor General of Ukrainian descent, was not bilingual at the time of his appointment. Although often viewed as a unifying office, critics are apt to point out that, with its ties to the British Crown, the Canadian monarchy may be a symbol of subjugation for French Canadians. Moreover, more recent immigrant groups than either the French or English may feel no emotional ties to the Canadian Crown at all.

In its symbolic-ceremonial tasks, the formal executive exemplifies what Walter Bagehot described as the dignified elements of the constitution: "The duties of the Queen, Governor General, and Lieutenant Governors include the decorative functions to facilitate the conduct of

> What I do reject, but I mean entirely, is the suggestion that Rideau Hall has — what is the expression — lost its glitter . . . . There's as much glitter as ever (Governor General Edward Schreyer, April 19, 1984).

public business" (MacKinnon, 1976: 136). However, such dignity can be expensive, since the gold-braided uniforms for a lieutenant governor now cost close to $40 000 each. Since the lieutenant governors have to pay this expense themselves, most current provincial formal executives do without the traditional attire. At the federal level under Governor General Edward Schreyer, such formality was generally not invoked.

These ceremonial or decorative tasks may not always be appreciated by either the public or the government of the day. For example, when the CCF (Cooperative Commonwealth Federation) became the government in Saskatchewan in 1944, the symbolic role of the lieutenant governor was greatly diminished, even to the extent of not providing him with an official residence, except for a three-room hotel suite. The initial Government House had its goods auctioned off and even though it had undergone a $4-million refurbishing in 1981, it remained a museum rather than the formal executive's residence. Such conditions must reduce the dignified and decorative tasks of the monarchy in Saskatchewan.

In Quebec, the position and financing of the lieutenant governor was diminished by the PQ government of René Lévesque. This behaviour showed the PQ's view of the office as a reflection of both British and federal government influence in the province. For example, during his six years in office between 1978 and 1983, Lieutenant Governor Jean-Pierre Cote was basically ignored by the Lévesque government, with personal contact with the Premier limited to half-a-dozen occasions in as many years. In 1984, the budget for the office was cut by 37 percent, 10 people were cut from the staff, and one limousine was done away with — actions designed to clearly indicate to the new Lieutenant Governor Gilles Lamontagne (a former federal Liberal cabinet minister) the attitude of the PQ government toward the monarch's representative in Quebec.

While the formal executive carries out a number of political tasks, most of these take place only under highly unusual circumstances. The key remaining political role of the formal executive is to select a prime minister or premier, thus ensuring that there is always a government in office. However, even in this function, the governor general's leeway is greatly circumscribed by various political customs.

If, after an election, an opposition party has obtained a majority of seats in the House of Commons, then the governor general has no choice but to ask the leader of that party to form a government. (This assumes, of course, that the current Prime Minister has resigned, since he can remain in office until being defeated in the House of Commons.) Another party leader asked to form a government would surely be unable and, quite likely, unwilling to do so, since it would be an impossible undertaking to gain the confidence of the Commons. No party leader except Brian Mulroney could possibly have formed a government after the landslide election of 1984. Since he won reelection in 1988, Brian Mulroney simply retained his position as Prime Minister, without having to be selected again by the Governor General. In a minority election result, the theoretical discretion of the formal executive is enhanced in choosing a prime minister, once a vacancy exists, but in practice such discretion is rarely maximized. Since minority governments in Canada have usually been close to an actual majority of seats or for other reasons have been relatively stable, the governor general's leeway in naming a prime minister is limited. For example, while a coalition of the Liberal, NDP, and Social Credit parties could have governed after the 1979 federal election, its stability in office would have been weak. Moreover, since the Conservatives had a 22-seat margin over the Liberals, custom required that they be given the first chance to govern, once Prime Minister Trudeau had resigned.

In a minority election result, the parties sometimes act on their own to limit the formal executive's potential discretion. For example, after the Liberal minority victory in 1972, Liberal leader and Prime Minister Pierre Trudeau called a press conference to announce that his government would unofficially have the backing of the New Democratic Party. Trudeau was immediately followed to the microphone by NDP leader David Lewis, who confirmed the "working majority" between their two parties. Although either the Conservatives or Liberals could have governed with NDP support, the Liberal-NDP arrangement precluded a Conservative government. Thus, after the 1972 election, Pierre Trudeau simply continued on as Prime Minister. During his career, Trudeau was appointed as Prime Minister only twice: in 1967 and in 1980.

In addition to majority or minority election results, other scenarios are conceivable that might increase the discretion of the formal executive in naming a prime minister. For example, if a prime minister were to suddenly die in office and if there was either no obvious successor or if the governing party was divided on its choice, the governor general could name a prime minister until the governing party could hold a national party leadership convention or use some other mechanism to decide upon a new leader. However, it is unlikely that the governing party would not agree on a successor, thereby eliminating any discretion by the formal executive.

Another possible scenario would be a major political scandal involving the prime minister and key cabinet members. If those individuals resigned, the formal executive might be forced to ask another member of the cabinet or of the full House of Commons to form a new government. Such a case is possible, but not very probable; for all practical purposes, the formal executive has very minimal discretionary powers in naming the person who will become the prime minister.

The remaining political tasks of the formal executive are theoretically important and legally possible, but even more than with respect to selecting the prime minister, they rarely involve any real exercise of power. The various legislative tasks of the formal executive clearly demonstrate such a pattern. For example, while the governor general officially summons, prorogues, or dissolves Parliament, this is done on the initiative of the political executive. For example, in Manitoba in 1984, with the provincial legislature in the middle of a bell-ringing episode over the NDP government's legislation on French language guarantees, the government of Howard Pawley advised the lieutenant governor to prorogue the House (Mackintosh, 1985: 60–66).

Similarly, the governor general delivers the Speech from the Throne to open Parliament but does not write it, even though phrases such as "my government will recommend" are liberally distributed throughout the address. The prime minister, in consultation with advisors and ministers, determines the content of the throne speech. The formal executive may be consulted or the broad outline of government policy may be discussed between the formal and the political executive, but there is no legal requirement for this. A formal executive does not have the right, based on custom and convention, to make changes or additions to the throne speech.

A second legislative task, which has become a formality, is the granting of assent. When a bill has passed both the Commons and the Senate, the assent procedure is held in the upper chamber. In some provinces, the entire work of a legislative session is presented in total to the formal executive for approval at the end of a session. Such a process certainly eliminates any chance for the formal executive to give detailed thought to each item before granting assent.

The formality of the assent procedure is illustrated by the fact that assent has never been refused a federal piece of legislation in Canada. The granting of assent by the formal executive is such a foregone conclusion that people rarely check to see if it has been carried out. For example, the passage of the language legislation (Bill 101) by the Quebec National Assembly in August 1977 only received assent in its French version. Lieutenant Governor Hugues Lapointe apparently refused to sign the English version into law, a fact that was not revealed until January 1978. At that point, the Lieutenant Governor was presented with another English copy of the law, which he signed in early February. The reason for Lapointe's refusal to sign the English version of Bill 101 the first time remains unexplained, but this incident illustrates the view that assent by the formal executive is assumed to be automatic. This example also reveals the irony that Bill 101, which was designed to make Quebec a unilingual French province, had to be passed in a bilingual format.

A final duty of the formal executive, which illustrates the difference between legal niceties and political reality, concerns the granting of dissolution when requested by the prime minister (Forsey, 1974). If the political executive has been defeated on a non-confidence motion or if it desires a new election without having suffered such a defeat, it must obtain a dissolution of Parliament from the governor general. If the government has a majority or if it is the only party capable of forming a "working majority" even though it has only a minority of seats, the governor general has no leeway for refusing a dissolution request. However, if another party could form a government, then legally the governor general might not grant a dissolution, but instead ask another party leader to form a government.

Such a situation did develop in the 1920s during the King-Byng Affair, when Governor General Lord Byng refused a dissolution request from Prime Minister Mackenzie King. Unfortunately for monarchists, this controversy ended up as an issue in the ensuing 1926 election campaign, with Mackenzie King vowing to prevent any future governor general from saying no to a dissolution request. When King won the election, he proceeded to undermine the power of the governor general, so that, since that time, the formal executive has, for all practical purposes, lost the ability to deny the political executive a dissolution of Parliament.

A more recent example came to light in December 1979, with the defeat of the Joe Clark government. After his Thursday night defeat, Prime Minister Clark met with Governor General Schreyer on Friday morning to ask for a dissolution of Parliament. After nearly an hour's meeting, no dissolution was forthcoming; the Governor General made the Prime Minister return to his office before he was given his requested dissolution (Simpson, 1980: 38). In a later interview, Governor General Schreyer maintained that he had the right to consider the dissolution request without being simply a rubber stamp for the Prime Minister (Valpy, 1981: 10). However, such reflection lasted only an hour, demonstrating a more acute political judgment by Governor General Schreyer than by Lord Byng a half a century earlier. A political realist would seriously doubt whether the formal executive could have said no to Prime Minister Clark and gotten away with it. Governor General Schreyer was probably asserting his political independence in his recently acquired job, rather than attempting to enhance the formal executive's power in the Canadian polity of the 1980s. In contrast to the 1979 example, on October 1, 1988 Prime Minister Brian Mulroney received his requested dissolution 13 minutes after visiting Governor General Jeanne Sauvé.

In considering both the structure and functions of the formal executive in Canada, we have emphasized that the head of state embodies the facade, rather than the substance, of political

> Over the past two decades, the decline in the significance and prestige of the office of governor general of Canada has been gathering its own quiet momentum with little evidence of any wide public or political concern (Fraser, 1988: 9).

influence and power. Most of the governor general's legal duties, such as opening Parliament or granting a dissolution, are exercised on the initiative of the political executive. Even those tasks in which some theoretical power remains, as in selecting a prime minister, are tightly circumscribed by custom and tradition. The formal executive's daily impact on the political system is thus modest, because the possible exercise of the position's potential powers becomes tenable only during the gravest of constitutional emergencies. As then Governor General Schreyer put it in 1981, "Understanding this office in the full has to include some contemplation of worst-case scenarios and what is to be done" (Valpy, 1981: 10). Fortunately, such worst-case scenarios rarely develop, so that the potential influence of the formal executive is infrequently tested in the heat of political battle.

The Political Executive in Canada

In contrast to the office of the formal executive, that of the political executive occupies centre stage in the struggle for policy, power, and patronage. The public visibility of the formal and political executives reveals much about their relative influence in the Canadian political process. While the role of the formal executive is poorly understood or, for that matter, scarcely recognized, that of the political executive is the focus of public attention. For example, while the Queen is recognized by most Canadians, her representatives seem not to have made much of an impression on the ordinary citizen. One study of high school seniors found that 68 percent could not name the Governor General (Hurtig, 1975). In December of 1989, one month before his installation, only one in five Canadians were able to identify Ray Hnatyshyn as the new Governor General (*The Mail-Star*, December 11, 1989). If one proceeds past simple recognition of these leaders, the level of ignorance becomes overwhelming: considerable confusion surrounds their particular roles. For example, a national poll in 1977 discovered that more people chose the Prime Minister as Canada's head of state (42 percent) than those who named the Queen (37 percent) as the formal executive (*Weekend Magazine*, October 22, 1977). As Governor General Edward Schreyer pointed out, "It would be totally unrealistic to argue there is a keen awareness of this office" (*The Globe and Mail*, February 7, 1983, p.2). Such findings reveal much about the substance of influence in the Canadian polity, as does the fact that the first press conference ever held by a governor general took place on December 15, 1981.

This dominant role of the political executive is primarily a consequence of custom and convention, rather than a result of legal prescription. The prime minister and cabinet are not mentioned in the 1867 Constitution Act, although the prime minister is named in other statutes. The evolution and development of the prime minister's tasks reflect an important mechanism of adaptation by the political system to a changing environment. Moreover, to a considerable extent, the role of the prime minister depends on the individual who occupies that office.

Although Canada's political system culminates in this one man, and the arsenal of his authority is indeed huge, both the basis and the boundaries of that authority are ill-defined . . . . What the Prime Minister of Canada is not is established by legislative checks and the circumscribing realities of

It's not a perfect job, but it sure beats working (Pierre Trudeau, October 8, 1975).

The Canadian Government has become an elected monarchy with Pierre Trudeau as the ruling king (Gordon Gibson, former national director of the Liberal party, February 27, 1983).

Canadian Prime Ministers survive and enjoy power only so long as they succeed in accommodating those with whom they are obliged to deal (Punnett, 1977: 160).

Jean Chrétien (1984), on cabinet loyalty: You know, Trudeau would give me the ball and sometimes he'd say, "Jean go to the right" and sometimes he'd say "Jean go to the left." And I'd put my head down and push forward. I'd get hit and tackled but when they unpiled after the play, I'd always have the ball. I never fumbled.

Canadian politics. What he is depends on him. The office is reconfigured by its occupant (Newman, 1973: 80–81).

BASES OF PRIME MINISTERIAL PREEMINENCE

Given such a context, the prime minister has come to be the key political actor of Canadian politics by combining political resources and skills with a political will so as to provide leadership on major questions of public policy. The preeminence of the prime minister is an outgrowth of the incumbent's relationship with the public, the formal executive, the party, and the cabinet.

With respect to the ordinary citizen, the prime minister is the most visible and salient symbol of political leadership in the country. Rarely will a prime minister escape or seek to escape the limelight—for visibility can be an important political resource of the office. It is not entirely coincidental that the growth of prime ministerial influence in the past few decades has occurred at the same time that television has become the essential political medium. The impact of television and its intimate relationship with the enhancement of the prime minister's role is clearly evident in recent election campaigns, which have become partisan-based media contests. Moreover, between election campaigns, the prime minister can clearly dominate the other party leaders with respect to news coverage: when the prime minister speaks, people listen, even if not always attentively or reverently.

The second basis of prime ministerial preeminence is the relationship between the formal and political executives. Once the governor general has named a prime minister by asking that individual to form a government, the prime minister is the sole link between these two parts of the executive. As the head of the political executive, the prime minister alone deals with the governor general. For example, only the prime minister—not the cabinet, personal aides, opposition parties, or even Parliament as a whole—can request a dissolution of Parliament from the formal executive. Although others may be consulted, it is the prime minister who recommends to the governor general those individuals who are to be named to the Privy Council, Senate, and other governmental institutions. Since much of the formal executive's role is only carried out on the initiative of the political executive and since the prime minister determines when those powers will be exercised, the prime minister's indirect control over the formal executive also enhances the direct control over the other elements of the political executive, such as the cabinet.

A third element of prime ministerial influence

Sir John A. Macdonald had been absent from his office for a few days when the Governor-General sent out a search party, in the person of his aide-de-camp, to find him. He was located in bed enjoying a sherry and reading a book. The aide-de-camp bluntly told him to sober up and get back to work. Macdonald demanded to know whether he spoke in an official or private capacity, and the aide asked: "What difference does that make?" Macdonald thundered: "Just this! If you're here in your official capacity, you can return to the Governor-General, give him my compliments, and tell him to go to hell. But if you're simply a private individual, you can go there yourself" (Dunn, 1989: 11).

THE PARTY CAUCUS IN CANADA

Source: Andy Donato, *The Agony and the Exit: Donato's Political Cartoons, 1984.* By permission of Canada Wide Feature Service and Andy Donato.

reflects the political executive's role as a party leader: control of the party organization, when combined with the principle of party discipline within Parliament, gives the prime minister control of the legislative branch of government. Failure by the party leader to control the party makes it difficult to be elected prime minister, since the public probably perceives such an individual to be lacking in the necessary leadership qualities required by the job. Such a fate was that of Conservative leader Robert Stanfield. And those who gain the office of prime minister may lose it, at least in part, because of their difficulty in controlling their party caucus or organization (e.g., John Diefenbaker and Joe Clark). While the cabinet may help to impose a fusion of powers between the executive and legislature, it is embodied to an ever greater extent in the role of the prime minister. Because the prime minister stands "at the apex of the party both within Parliament and outside," he is "by far the most powerful man in the Canadian system" (Matheson, 1976: 214).

The combination of these first three factors creates a fourth basis of prime ministerial leadership, namely, the prime minister's supremacy over the cabinet. Similarly, a premier dominates his provincial cabinet, as Colin Thatcher discovered in January of 1983, when he was unexpectedly eliminated as the Energy Minister in the cabinet of Saskatchewan Premier Grant Devine. Control over cabinet selection gives the prime minister the power to make or break the political careers of others. Talent, in and of itself, is not necessarily enough for cabinet promotion— that talent must be recognized by the prime minister. However, prime ministerial perception of talent is not always omniscient, as the 1983 case of federal cabinet minister Roger Simmons illustrates. The Newfoundland MP lasted only 10 days in the Trudeau government, the shortest duration of any cabinet minister in

TABLE 4.1 THE CANADIAN FEDERAL CABINET (June 1989) (in order of precedence)

The Right Hon. Martin Brian Mulroney	Prime Minister
The Right Hon. Charles Joseph Clark	Secretary of State for External Affairs
The Hon. John Carnell Crosbie	Minister for International Trade
The Hon. Donald Frank Mazankowski	Deputy Prime Minister, President of the Queen's Privy Council for Canada and Minister of Agriculture
The Hon. Elmer MacIntosh MacKay	Minister of Public Works and Minister for the purposes of the Atlantic Canada Opportunities Agency Act
The Hon. Arthur Jacob Epp	Minister of Energy, Mines and Resources
The Hon. Robert R. de Cotret	President of the Treasury Board
The Hon. Henry Perrin Beatty	Minister of National Health and Welfare
The Hon. Michael Holcombe Wilson	Minister of Finance
The Hon. Harvie Andre	Minister of Regional Industrial Expansion and Minister of State for Science and Technology
The Hon. Otto John Jelinek	Minister of National Revenue
The Hon. Thomas Edward Siddon	Minister of Fisheries and Oceans
The Hon. Charles James Mayer	Minister of Western Economic Diversification and Minister of State (Grains and Oilseeds)
The Hon. William Hunter McKnight	Minister of National Defence
The Hon. Benoît Bouchard	Minister of Transport
The Hon. Marcel Masse	Minister of Communications
The Hon. Barbara Jean McDougall	Minister of Employment and Immigration
The Hon. Gerald Stairs Merrithew	Minister of Veterans Affairs
The Hon. Monique Vézina	Minister of State (Employment and Immigration) and Minister of State (Seniors)
The Hon. Frank Oberle	Minister of State (Forestry)
The Hon. Lowell Murray	Leader of the Government in the Senate and Minister of State (Federal-Provincial Relations)
The Hon. Paul Wyatt Dick	Minister of Supply and Services
The Hon. Pierre H. Cadieux	Minister of Indian Affairs and Northern Development
The Hon. Jean J. Charest	Minister of State (Youth) and Minister of State (Fitness and Amateur Sport) and Deputy Leader of the Government in the House of Commons
The Hon. Thomas Hockin	Minister of State (Small Businesses and Tourism)
The Hon. Monique Landry	Minister for External Relations
The Hon. Bernard Valcourt	Minister of Consumer and Corporate Affairs
The Hon. Gerry Weiner	Secretary of State of Canada and Minister of State (Multiculturalism and Citizenship)
The Hon. Douglas Grinslade Lewis	Minister of Justice and Attorney General of Canada and Leader of the Government in the House of Commons
The Hon. Pierre Blais	Solicitor General of Canada and Minister of State (Agriculture)
The Hon. Lucien Bouchard	Minister of the Environment
The Hon. John Horton McDermid	Minister of State (Privatization and Regulatory Affairs)
The Hon. Shirley Martin	Minister of State (Transport)
The Hon. Mary Collins	Associate Minister of National Defence
The Hon. Alan Redway	Minister of State (Housing)
The Hon. William Charles Winegard	Minister of State (Science and Technology)
The Hon. Kim Campbell	Minister of State (Indian Affairs and Northern Development)
The Hon. Jean Corbeil	Minister of Labour
The Hon. Gilles Loiselle	Minister of State (Finance)

Canadian history, before he was forced to resign as a result of charges of income tax evasion.

THE PRIME MINISTER AND THE CABINET

Once a person has gained a cabinet nomination, a further prime ministerial prerogative becomes significant. Remember that elevation to the cabinet increases a backbencher's salary by about $50 000 per year. The prime minister not only determines the number of cabinet members and the structure of departmental responsibilities, but the portfolios assigned to individual ministers. Federal cabinets under Pierre Trudeau were unusually large — about 35 members in his later years. The first cabinet of Brian Mulroney set a size record for federal cabinets at 40 members; after his victory in 1988, his first new cabinet, at 39 (January, 1989) was only slightly smaller. The smallest cabinet of recent times was that of the initial group selected by the new NDP Premier of Manitoba, Howard Pawley, in December 1981 — it contained only 13 members. Perhaps more typical is the intermediate size of the Ontario cabinet (27 members) formed by Premier David Peterson in August of 1989, or the November, 1989 cabinet in British Columbia which contained 23 members.

Once the question of size is determined, which itself sets limits on the allocation of departmental duties (and *vice versa*), then specific ministers for each department must be named. Political careers can be crushed or enhanced at this point, with probably more devastating effect than even with respect to cabinet elevation in the first place. It is difficult to become a national political figure when one is made Minister of State for Fitness and Amateur Sport. However, a high-profile ministry, such as Justice, External Affairs, or Finance, need not be a political advantage. Much depends on what the individual makes of the assignment. The visit of Defence Minister Robert Coates to

a West German striptease bar, and his subsequent resignation from the Mulroney government in early 1985, is a case in point.

Some portfolios are seen more as liabilities than as steppingstones to higher political office. In the last several decades, the position of Minister of Finance has often been the suicide portfolio of Canadian politics, as the subsequent career patterns of former finance ministers Walter Gordon and Edgar Benson illustrate. Moreover, even though former Finance Minister John Turner ended up becoming Prime Minister, his stay in that portfolio lead to his resignation from the Trudeau government and put off for nearly a decade his "race for the rose" and the leadership mantle of the Liberal party.

Once in the cabinet, a minister must also be concerned about **cabinet shuffles**, that is, a reallocation of ministerial responsibilities. Since the status or prestige of each portfolio is well-known, cabinet shuffles reveal who is on the "up" or "down" side of the political escalator, as well as the minister's current influence in Ottawa's political pecking order. Cabinet shuffles are a convenient means for the prime minister to help out ministers who are in political trouble in their current portfolios by moving them to a different posting. For example, in his first cabinet shuffle (August, 1985), Prime Minister Brian Mulroney moved Suzanne Blais-Grenier from her position as Minister of the Environment, in which she had been in constant political battles with environmentalists over budget cuts, to the much less visible portfolio of Minister of State for Transportation.

Sometimes the prime minister does not want to salvage a minister in trouble, as Lloyd Axworthy found out in 1981. As minister responsible for the Status of Women, Mr. Axworthy became involved in a highly publicized dispute with the Advisory Council on the Status of Women. At one point the minister sought to have then Prime Minister Trudeau relieve him of his responsibility for this area of public policy, but the Prime Minister and his cabinet colleagues refused, until severe damage had already been done to his political career (i.e., his presumed plans to follow Pierre Trudeau as leader of the Liberal party).

One of the strangest cases of cabinet selection procedure occurred in an Ontario cabinet shuffle in December of 1983. Premier Bill Davis interviewed prospective cabinet members at his home, so as to keep the press, as well as other cabinet possibilities, from knowing who might be annointed. However, as interviews ran long, a backlog of individuals developed. At that point, a Tory backbencher, Susan Fish, ended up waiting under the bushes outside Premier Davis's home, so as not to be spotted by the press or colleagues. The ignominy of such a procedure was likely worthwhile — Susan Fish became the new Ontario Minister of Citizenship and Culture.

The extent of a prime minister's influence over the cabinet is also clear from the way ministers depart from the inner sanctum of power. For those loyal allies who have retained the prime minister's support, leaving the cabinet is made easier by appointment to the Senate or some other government institution. For those who have alienated their leader, a return to the backbenches may be their only reward for past service. There are few instances in which a minister who has been demoted from the cabinet has ever returned to it. A rare exception was the situation of Liberal Herb Gray, who asked so many questions of his own government from the backbenches that, in order to silence him, then Prime Minister Trudeau brought him back into the cabinet. However, when ministers who are liked by the prime minister have been forced to leave the cabinet, the prime minister may resurrect their political careers by reappointing them. The careers of Liberal cabinet ministers Francis Fox, John Munro and André Ouellet under Pierre Trudeau are instructive on this point — a prime minister has the ability to breathe life back into apparently dead political careers.

In addition to being ousted by the prime minister, cabinet members may leave of their own accord, although not necessarily willingly. Sometimes resignations reflect personal problems, as when the Alberta Solicitor General Graham Harle resigned (November, 1983) after being found by police in a government car with a prostitute. Another example would be that of Newfoundland's Minister of Fisheries, Jim Morgan, who resigned from the provincial cabinet in October, 1984, after he was found guilty of illegal salmon fishing. Resignations can be a symbol of protest against the prime minister's policies, but they also demonstrate that the minister who has resigned is an outcast in the cabinet and the governing party. For example, in December of 1988, three anglophone members of Quebec Premier Bourassa's cabinet resigned in protest against the government's language policy. Even when ministers have quit the cabinet, they have no right to explain in detail why they resigned, unless the prime minister releases them from the oath of secrecy they take upon being sworn into the cabinet. Ministers who have resigned rarely remain in the public eye for long — former Liberal Defence Minister James Richardson is a classic example of this point, as is the demise of Suzanne Blais-Grenier (resignation from the cabinet followed by electoral defeat in 1988).

CABINET COMPOSITION

While it is a prime minister's prerogative to decide the size of the cabinet, its departmental structure, the frequency of cabinet shuffles, and the individuals to be named to this key decision-making body, some of the prime minister's leeway in these matters is circumscribed by political tradition. For example, each of the parties contains various ideological strands that insist on having representatives in the cabinet. Likewise, a prominent party figure with a significant base of support in the country usually

> Give me better wood and I'll make you a better cabinet (Canadian Prime Minister John A. Macdonald).

cannot be overlooked in the process of cabinet construction. At times, dissidents within the party are promoted to the cabinet to silence them by their cooptation into the party and governmental hierarchy; the selection of Liberal MP Serge Joyal to the Trudeau cabinet in the fall of 1981 could be seen in this perspective. Probably the most important restriction on cabinet composition, however, is the representation principle, a crucial convention of the Canadian political process.

The **representation principle** refers to the practice of naming representatives of the various regions, provinces, and major social and economic interests of Canadian society to the cabinet (Matheson, 1976: 22–46). This practice was instituted with respect to the composition of Canada's first federal cabinet by John A. Macdonald and has been followed ever since. The workings of the representation principle are embodied in a series of informal rules.

Where possible, each province should receive at least one cabinet appointment. However, having elected all Liberals in the 1988 contest, Prince Edward Island received no cabinet representation in the Tory cabinet of January, 1989. In those cases where a province has not elected anyone to the governing party's caucus, then a prime minister may appoint a senator from that province to the cabinet. It would run counter to

> The continuation of the regional minister system under Mulroney testifies to its durability in Canadian political life. It represents a constant that can be traced through the cabinets of Mackenzie King and Wilfrid Laurier back to Sir John A. Macdonald's first ministry (Bakvis, 1989: 130).

political custom to use senators from a province in the cabinet if the government had seats in the Commons from the same province. Minimal representation in Quebec for the Conservatives in the 1979 election and no representation in the Commons at all from British Columbia, Alberta, and Saskatchewan for the Liberals in the 1980 election forced both Joe Clark and Pierre Trudeau, respectively, to use several senators in putting together a cabinet. Such a practice diminishes to the extent that the winning party in the general election gains seats from each province. The massive Tory victory in 1984 and the solid win in 1988 allowed Brian Mulroney to choose only one member from the Senate (the Government's Senate Leader) for his cabinet — a return to the traditional practice in this regard. This minimal rule of one cabinet position for each province means that the prime minister's leeway in choosing that representative may be narrow, especially for the smaller provinces, when only one or two government members are elected to the Commons.

More than one seat in the cabinet is allocated for the larger provinces. Under Pierre Trudeau, Ontario and Quebec were typically granted about 10 seats each in a 30-seat cabinet, with British Columbia receiving from two to four positions. The exact number of such portfolios for each province varies from one government to the next, but the general pattern remains: Ontario and Quebec, which have a majority of the population and a majority of seats in the Commons, also receive a majority (from one-half to two-thirds) of the cabinet postings. In Brian Mulroney's first cabinet of 40 members, Ontario and Quebec received 22 positions, the four Western provinces got 13, and Atlantic Canada obtained five portfolios. After the second Tory electoral victory in 1988, the 39-member cabinet of January, 1989 was regionally composed as follows: Central Canada 25 positions (13 from Quebec, 12 from Ontario); Western Canada 10 positions (British Columbia 4, Alberta 3, Manitoba 2, Saskatchewan 1); and

> Westerners have more power in Ottawa today than at any other time in our history . . . . Central Canadians may be in charge of economic policy, but it's westerners who decide where nearly all the federal dollars go (Gray, 1989: 15,17).

Atlantic Canada 4 (New Brunswick 2, Nova Scotia 1, Newfoundland 1, PEI 0).

The number of posts for the more populous provinces are distributed throughout that province, a pattern of regionalism within regionalism. For example, Northern Ontario usually receives one cabinet post, as do the major metropolitan areas. Major cities like Toronto and Montreal have often had more cabinet positions each than the Atlantic provinces in total.

Once the regional allocation has been made, other factors such as race, ethnicity, sex, and religion are considered. For example, Quebec's cabinet representatives include French-speaking Catholics (a majority of posts) and English-speaking Protestants (usually several portfolios). On an ethnic basis, those of non-English or non-French origin have traditionally been underrepresented, although since the Second World War other ethnic groups are receiving greater attention (e.g., John Diefenbaker appointed the first minister of Ukrainian descent). Women are the most underrepresented group in the cabinet, a reflection of the fact that few women are candidates for office. The first women appointed to the federal cabinet was Ellen Fairclough, selected as Secretary of State by John Diefenbaker in 1957. In comparison to the "average Canadian," the cabinet, on factors such as age, sex, education, and occupation, is quite unrepresentative. In this regard it is well to keep in mind that the representation principle refers primarily to provincial and regional concerns, rather than to ethnic and religious ones, and only coincidentally to such factors as sex, age, and occupation.

Whatever the reasons for their selection to the cabinet, once there, MPs are expected to speak for their province or region, irrespective of their specific portfolio. A Minister of External Affairs from Alberta is Alberta's cabinet representative. A Minister of Public Works from Ontario is expected to be a representative for Ontario in the cabinet's policy-making process. Ministers' portfolios may change, but their role as defenders of provincial interests does not.

Based again on custom, certain portfolios have come to be associated with particular provinces. For example, Public Works, which is a key patronage department because of the number of jobs and contracts that it controls, is usually given to a minister from the governing party's "home" province or provinces. In the Mulroney cabinet, this portfolio initially went to Roch LaSalle from Quebec. Responsibility for the Wheat Board is allocated to a minister from the West or perhaps rural Ontario, while Fisheries goes to a minister from the Atlantic Provinces (Romeo LeBlanc) or British Columbia (Jack Davis, John Fraser). Finance is typically granted to an English-Canadian, usually from Ontario, who has strong ties with the business community. Jean Chrétien's brief stint as Minister of Finance in the mid-1970s was the first time a French-Canadian had ever served in that post. The prime minister may assume the role of a minister with departmental responsibilities, such as that of External Affairs. However, the custom in recent decades has been not to do so, a pattern continued by Trudeau, Clark, Turner, and Mulroney. At the provincial level, premiers more often assign themselves a specific portfolio: Premier Grant Devine of Saskatchewan became his own Minister of Agriculture in 1986, and Ontario Premier David Peterson designated himself as Minister of Intergovernmental Affairs in 1989.

These traditional assignments of particular portfolios being granted to specific regions or interests is a reflection of the impact of the representation principle. Nothing legally prevents a Minister of Fisheries coming from a Metropolitan Toronto constituency; however, the political absurdity of such a move renders it highly unlikely. Along these lines of thought, a somewhat strange appointment in Mulroney's first cabinet needs explanation: the appointment of David Crombie—the former Mayor of Toronto, the country's largest metropolitan area—as Minister of Indian Affairs and Northern Development. It is likely that Crombie's ideological background as a "red Tory," rather than geography, accounts for this particular appointment.

In addition to circumscribing the leeway of the prime minister in forming a cabinet, the representation principle has other significant effects on the political process. First, because it is designed to protect regional and provincial concerns, the cabinet has become the key decision-making body, as well as the primary defender of provincial interests, effectively usurping, in the process, the designated role of the Senate. Second, the size of the cabinet keeps increasing as more and more sectors of society demand representation. One internal cabinet result of this increasing size is a specialization of function, which has resulted in turning over a considerable amount of the effective decision-making power to a series of cabinet committees. Third, the cabinet is not necessarily composed of the most talented individuals available, for the most talented rarely have had the foresight to be elected to the Commons on a regional basis. As Conservative Senator Jacques Flynn put it, in commenting on the Trudeau cabinet of 1981, in "a cabinet of pygmies, a midget can be king." Fourth, the cabinet, in its attempt to accommodate the various regions and interests, is not very efficient in its operation.

While the representation principle affects the allocation of the departmental portfolios, some cabinet members are also named as political ministers. **Political ministers**, sometimes referred to now as **regional ministers** (Bakvis, 1989), are cabinet members who are given the additional party responsibilities of party organization and patronage for the governing party within their province. These positions are allocated by the prime minister and reflect the political influence of the individual so named. To assess a minister's overall role in the cabinet, one needs to know his or her official responsibility and his or her party responsibility, if any. To be the political minister for a province is often more significant for one's political influence and power than an individual's departmental responsibilities. For example, even though many expected Lucien Bouchard to be named as the political minister for Quebec after the 1988 election, Marcel Masse (Minister of Communications) was retained in that position in the cabinet shuffle of January, 1989. For the larger provinces several political ministers may be named (e.g., one for Northern Ontario, Southern Ontario, Metropolitan Toronto), while only one is typically selected for the smaller provinces.

CABINET ORGANIZATION

Once the composition of the cabinet has been finalized, it is up to the prime minister to determine its uses and internal organization. Under the guidance of the prime minister, the cabinet determines its own structure and operation. The frequency of its meetings, the kinds of questions or issues it deals with, the decision-making procedure that it follows (i.e., majority vote or consensus) all emerge from the prime minister's intent, as well as from the evolving practice of the cabinet itself. Since the internal structure of the cabinet is undefined in law, its organization and role tend to reflect the prime minister's leadership qualities. Diefenbaker's demise as Prime Minister reflected the disintegration of his cabinet, while Trudeau's longevity was attributable, in part, to the restructuring of the cabinet decision-making process instituted on his becoming Prime Minister in 1968.

The Trudeau cabinet

The revisions made in the cabinet decision-making process by Trudeau reflected two fundamental assumptions: first, decision-making needed to be more rational, and second, the cabinet, rather than the traditional bureaucracy, had to become the effective decision-making centre. Two major structural innovations of the cabinet corresponded to these two goals: first, the cabinet, in order to become more efficient in its handling of issues and problems, greatly revised its committee structure and second, in order to gain independent advice, the cabinet developed its own bureaucracy, which resulted in a significant expansion of its support staff in the Privy Council Office (PCO).

The use of cabinet committees reveals a specialization of function caused by the increasing size of the total cabinet and the complexity of modern legislation. Eight cabinet committees were set up, four dealing with broad policy areas and four others concerned with coordination of policy and purposes among the various departments and agencies. Each minister typically served on two committees, although under Trudeau the composition of these committees was not made public. It is doubtful that such secrecy kept the major interest groups or Ottawa's insiders from knowing their composition, but it did keep the public in the dark on this vital element of the political executive.

As an issue was brought to the cabinet by a minister, the bureaucracy, or public protest, it would be referred to the appropriate cabinet committee for detailed consideration. After studying the problem and deciding how to act, the cabinet committee would report back to the full cabinet. Except on highly controversial issues, the cabinet usually accepted the decision of the cabinet committee. For this reason, on many matters, real decision-making power had evolved to the cabinet committees acting in the name of the larger cabinet. Votes were rarely taken; instead, a consensus was sought, with the prime minister playing a critical role in its formation. Once the cabinet had settled on policy, it was communicated to the departments and bureaucracy for implementation.

The second major change instituted by Trudeau concerned the size and functions of the Prime Minister's Office (PMO) and the PCO, both of which were greatly enhanced. The PMO is composed of the PM's immediate aides and advisors, whose tasks range from the mundane ones, such as typing and airline scheduling, to policy-making ones, such as recommendations on the major political issues of the day (Radwanski, 1978: 133). The PCO is the support staff to the cabinet and its various committees and, as such, has become a most important actor in the political process (Campbell and Szablowski, 1979: 69). Even during the years when government restraint put a "freeze" on hiring personnel for government departments, the PMO and PCO were exempted.

Together, the task of the PMO and PCO is to give the political executive advice and policy recommendations independent from that of the civil service. This counter-bureaucracy had the expertise and political clout to free the cabinet from its former dependence on the advice coming from the policy advisors at the departmental level. Some of the fiercest battles of the Trudeau years concerned the organization and the role of the PMO and PCO structures. With the backing of Prime Minister Trudeau, the PMO and PCO, especially the latter, won a leading role in the policy-making process. Enhancement of the PMO and PCO and a revised cabinet committee structure were the major organizational changes implemented by Prime Minister Trudeau (1968–1979) in order to make the decision-making role of the political executive more rational and efficient. The same basic pattern was reasserted on his return to power during the 1980–1984 period.

The Clark cabinet

The flexibility of cabinet organization is illustrated by the fact that each new prime minister reorganizes it in some manner. The major innovation of the short-lived Clark government in 1979–80 concerned the first formal use of an inner and outer cabinet in Canadian history. Based on the British practice of making a distinction between all departmental ministers (the ministry) and the major departmental ministers (the cabinet), the inner-outer cabinet model sought to overcome the problem of the excessive size of federal cabinets; at the same time, it rationalized and made more efficient the decision-making process.

From a cabinet of 29 members, 10 were chosen for the inner cabinet. Although decisions from the inner cabinet could be appealed to the full cabinet, this was rarely the case in the Clark government. Besides setting up a highly visible caste system within the cabinet, the major flaw of the inner-outer cabinet structure in the Canadian context was its rigidity and inability to implement the representation principle. For example, the initial Clark inner cabinet contained no representation from British Columbia, so John Fraser (MP—Vancouver South) was added, while an individual as prominent as David Crombie, former Mayor of Toronto, was excluded (Simpson, 1980: 94–95). While all prime ministers have had an informal inner cabinet or "kitchen cabinet" composed of their most influential aides and ministers, to formally structure the cabinet along the same lines meant that the primary cabinet function of regional and provincial representation could not be sustained. An inner-outer cabinet structure can be justified by the need to make the decision-making process more efficient, but it failed in the Canadian context because it ignored the representation principle of cabinet composition.

The Turner cabinet

Although the government of John Turner may go down as simply an asterisk in Canadian political history, in the sense that it only lasted about three months before facing the largest defeat in the country's electoral history, it produced some interesting variations on the cabinet structure of both of his predecessors. Basically, the cabinet of John Turner rejected the patterns of decision-making of Joe Clark and Pierre Trudeau.

With respect to Clark's formal inner-outer cabinet structure, Turner rejected it. Second, the size of the cabinet was reduced to 29, considerably smaller than the 36 or 37 members of the last years of Pierre Trudeau. Prime Minister Turner also indicated that the cabinet might be reduced further, if he won a mandate from the people. Third, Trudeau's cabinet committee system was streamlined and simplified: Turner specifically sought to dismantle much of the bureaucracy which had come to surround the process of cabinet decision-making. Fourth, Turner desired to increase the power of departmental ministers, a move which would have been at the expense of both the PMO and PCO.

These alterations in the structure of the cabinet and its decision-making process indicated that the new Liberal leader was rejecting many of the significant changes instituted during the 15-year reign of Pierre Trudeau. The Turner cabinet was reminiscent of previous Liberal leaders such as Lester Pearson. Since most of the time Turner's government was in office was taken up by the 1984 election campaign, it remains a matter of speculation whether or not such a traditional cabinet structure would have worked in the late-1980s.

The Mulroney cabinet

Their many years in opposition, during which they strongly criticized the Trudeau-Pitfield pattern of cabinet decision-making, combined with Clark's failure in instituting an inner-outer cabinet structure, led the Mulroney government to try what they thought would be an innovative cabinet structure. The Mulroney Tories instituted a system which, while reforming some of the minor aspects of the Trudeau years, had more in common with them than most Conservatives would probably want to admit.

In their first two terms in office, the Mulroney government and cabinet could be characterized by one broad theme: an increasing centralization of power and influence in the position of the Prime Minister and his staff in the Prime Minister's Office (PMO). This centralization proceeded further and faster under Brian Mulroney than under Pierre Trudeau. For example, in 1983–1984 under Trudeau, the PMO had been authorized a staff equivalent of 90 person-years, a figure that was expected to rise to 104 person-years in 1984–1985. Under Mulroney, that figure rose to 120 person-years, and by the end of his first year in office, the new Prime Minister had even surpassed that figure. In fact, in 1984–1985 the PMO was over budget by 72 percent.

More important than the size of the PMO were the additional political functions granted to it — the PMO became the locus of policy, patronage, and power. As a result, the Privy Council Office (PCO), which had become the key player under Trudeau, suffered a decline in significance. The PCO or cabinet secratariat played background music for the lead singer and his immediate advisors in the PMO. For example, in the summer of 1986, longtime Tory stalwart Dalton Camp was appointed as a senior policy advisor to the government, but attached to the "nonpartisan" PCO. What this represented, in fact, was a politicization of the PCO and an increase in the power of the PMO, where Dalton Camp actually did most of his work. By the time of his resignation in 1989, the PMO was clearly the locus of power in Ottawa.

> I wouldn't say it [the Prime Minister's Office] is staffed by dolts, but perhaps they're not as politically intuitive as they should be and there is something lacking in the system there, smelling out political dangers (Justice Minister John Crosbie commenting on the tuna scandal, October 7, 1985).

One result of this shifting balance between the PMO and PCO was a decline in the power of the cabinet and of the traditional departments. Key policy decisions were made in the PMO, not around the cabinet table. As a corollary of this new pattern, the power of the civil service, particularly of its senior mandarins, was reduced as well: "Under the Tories, power has shifted radically away from the senior bureaucrats and to the politicians, away from departments and to the Prime Minister's Office" (Little, 1985: 32).

A centralized decision-making structure quickly demonstrated some disadvantages, perhaps best illustrated by the "tunagate" affair in 1985. Fisheries Minister John Fraser had overruled his own departmental officials, and had allowed tunafish of questionable quality to be sold in Canada. The CBC program, the *Fifth Estate*, was doing an investigation of the matter and the PMO had been "warned" of the impending exposé. However, nothing was done before the CBC aired the story and the PMO, Prime Minister, and Tory party received a shellacking in the press, in Parliament and in the country at large. The result of such problems led to a restructuring of the PMO in 1986 and to a temporary shift of power back to the PCO under its new clerk, Paul Tellier.

However, the most significant trend of the early years of the Mulroney government was its centralization of power in the Prime Minister and his staff in the PMO. The charges of "presidentializing" the Canadian parliamentary system that were made so often against Pierre

FIGURE 4.1 CANADA'S EXECUTIVE BRANCH OF GOVERNMENT

Trudeau would be heard about Brian Mulroney as well, particularly after the changes in the cabinet's structure announced with the cabinet shuffle of January, 1989,

The size of the cabinet remained large, dropping only marginally, from 40 to 39. The most significant changes occurred internally, shifting power away from the full cabinet to several of its component parts.

First, the growth in the importance of the Priorities and Planning Committee (P&P) that was started under former Prime Minister Pierre Trudeau was enhanced by the 1989 cabinet modifications of Prime Minister Brian Mulroney. P&P, which increased in size to include the Prime Minister and 18 ministers, became an unofficial inner cabinet consisting of the key ministers in the most significant areas of public policy. The P&P committee was made responsible for all new government spending.

The second cabinet change was the addition of a new cabinet committee called the Operations Committee. Informally started in the spring of 1987, this new committee is primarily concerned with short-term political planning. Composed of the Prime Minister and 8 key ministers, the Operations Committee serves as a kind of "executive committee" of P&P. Nothing goes to P&P that does not first pass through the Operations Committee. Thus, we now have an inner cabinet (the Operations Committee) within an inner cabinet (P&P).

A third modification of the cabinet structure concerned its committees, which increased from 10 to 14. However, the membership on the policy committees was reduced, from a previous high of 25, down to between 7 and 12 members. Most importantly, the standing committees of cabinet no longer decide, or even really have a role in, allocating government expenditures.

Combined with the centralization of decision-making in the hands of the Prime Minister and the PMO, what these 1989 cabinet changes signify is that the cabinet, as a whole, represents the facade, rather than the foundation, of political power in Canada in the 1990s.

Conclusion on cabinet structure

Our brief look at the cabinet structures and decision-making patterns of the governments of Prime Ministers Trudeau, Clark, Turner, and Mulroney seem to support the conclusion that "all cabinet systems are designed by prime ministers to suit their own personal styles and the particular circumstances of the time" (Clark, 1985: 191). Moreover, whatever its internal structure and operation, the key political functions of the cabinet are the initiation, development, and implementation of public policy under the direction of the prime minister. If the prime minister and cabinet fail to lead, there is little that can be done, except elect a new prime minister at the next election. Matters such as the representation principle are significant because they help to determine the quality of that leadership and the content and effectiveness of public policy.

The complex nature of the executive branch of government in Canada reflects, in part, its political role as the core or centre of the political system. The basic features of the executive branch are outlined in Figure 4.1. The growth and expansive nature of government in the modern era has been primarily the growth of the executive branch. Through constitutional evolution and political tradition, the formal executive has become a bit player in the drama of Canadian politics, while the political executive, especially the prime minister, has assumed the leading role.

The British Parliamentary Executive

In broad outline, the structure and operation of the British executive parallels that of the Canadian. On a number of specific points, however, British and Canadian practices diverge with respect to both the formal and political executives.

The formal executive in Britain—what has been referred to as "the Rolls Royce of Monarchies"—is hereditary in terms of succession and constitutional with respect to its role in the polity. Tracing its origins back 10 centuries, the slow evolution and public acceptance of the British monarchy has placed it in a far more secure position than its Canadian counterpart. Popular support for the monarchy and Royal Family is extensive, although some members may be held in less than high regard. The legitimacy of the monarchy is rarely challenged and, when it is, the result is usually an overwhelmingly positive response from the public in defence of the formal executive. The hereditary nature of the office and its public support has effectively allowed the British monarchy to become a unifying symbol of the nation, in sharp contrast to the Canadian experience.

Britain is also an example of a constitutional monarchy, where the head of state or monarch exercises his or her powers on the advice of the political executive. Historically, monarchs governed as they desired, with few limitations on their roles or powers, a situation sometimes classified as absolute monarchy. However, as Parliament and, much later, the political executive emerged to challenge the monarch, the latter became more and more a figurehead, serving primarily symbolic and ceremonial roles. Thus, the monarch was once dominant over the political executive in Britain. This relationship between the formal and political executives is clearly demonstrated with respect to the Royal Prerogative, that is, the authority that rests with the Crown as the embodiment of executive influence.

> The extent of the Royal Prerogative has not diminished appreciably during the last 200 years. What has happened is that, whereas 200 years ago the reigning monarch performed many or most of these acts at his own discretion, today the monarch performs the acts on the advice of ministers or other persons. The acts are performed in the name of the Crown, but except in a few special cases *the decision is no longer taken by the monarch* (Birch, 1983: 44, *emphasis added*).

Although the British monarch acts on the advice of the government, a procedure that strongly circumscribes his or her political role, some political functions remain. For example, as in Canada, the formal executive is not to become involved in partisan politics or to make statements of a political nature. However, in October 1985, the heir to the realm, Prince Charles, criticized Margaret Thatcher's Tory government with respect to her inner-city and housing policies. Prince Charles summarized his view of the matter as follows: "I think it is

> One of the drawbacks of having an unwritten constitution is that no one is certain what the rules are. Current political conditions in Britain have made the uncertainty especially acute concerning the "prerogative" powers of the monarch (Rasmussen, 1987: 139).

part of my job to stir controversy as long as it is not party political controversy." However, the line between "controversy" and "party political controversy" is not always an easy one to make. Given the legitimacy of the monarchy in Britain, the king or queen has more leeway and thus more influence in such matters than the governor general in Canada. As British Labour Party leader Neil Kinnock put it in July of 1986, the "Queen enjoys enormous respect in Britain. She could make herself heard without moving her lips. That is the essence of her greatness."

On several occasions in the 20th century, the British monarch has been called upon to take an active role in naming a prime minister. For example, in 1957, there was no clear successor within the Conservative caucus to Prime Minister Anthony Eden. Two people were possible successors—Harold Macmillan and R.A. Butler—and after it was clear that the Conservative party could not quickly settle the question among themselves (a specific leadership election mechanism was not used until 1965), the Queen asked Macmillan to form a government, thus making him Prime Minister. A more complex situation occurred in 1931 when no party had a majority of seats in the House of Commons. The King took the initiative to bring the various party leaders together for consultation, but, rightly, he did not advocate which of them he preferred as prime minister. What these examples indicate is that the monarch infrequently acts on his or her own initiative and, on those rare occasions, proceeds in an impartial and nonpartisan manner. While in theory the monarch can dismiss ministers, deny a dissolution request from the prime minister, or refuse assent to a piece of legislation, in practice a much more modest constitutional role has evolved for the formal executive in Britain: the "monarchy survives because it is politically weak" (Rose, 1982: 50).

The real power of the executive branch is granted to the occupant of Number 10 Downing Street, the British prime minister's official residence. The prime minister in Britain is preeminent with respect to public policy, party, and Parliament to an even greater degree than the Canadian prime minister. Since the political structure is unitary, the prime minister does not share either power or the political limelight with the leaders of an intermediate level of government. Thus, the British prime minister's policy-making role is greater than in Canada, where it is limited by the federalization of responsibility between the national and provincial governments. Moreover, British parties have traditionally been highly centralized in structure and operation, as well as disciplined within Parliament itself. British party leaders, especially Conservative ones, have usually exerted strong control over their party's parliamentary wing. These considerations reveal that a British prime minister is not constrained by some of the typical limitations imposed on any prime minister in Canada.

Cabinet composition is also based on different premises in Britain than in Canada, because the rigid representation principle regarding regional and provincial interests does not apply. For example, the cabinets of Margaret Thatcher in the late 1980s witnessed few positions for MPs from Scotland because the Tories won few seats there in 1983 and 1987. Moreover, the major parties have usually received some Commons' seats from all areas within Britain, so regionalism need not be the major factor for cabinet selection or promotion. Instead, ideology plays a significant role in a cabinet's compo-

sition, with all major factions traditionally included. Margaret Thatcher's emphasis on "ideological purity" in cabinet composition is something of an exception in modern British politics. For example, in the cabinet shuffle of June 1983, she dropped her foreign secretary, Francis Pym, from the cabinet and promoted several right-wing Conservatives to important portfolios. Moreover, a resignation from cabinet by a major political figure, such as that by Nigel Lawson in October of 1989, can seriously erode the political base of the Prime Minister. However, party figures with strong support in the party or the electorate are usually ignored at the leader's peril. Ministers may be appointed from either House of Parliament, although the vast majority are from the Commons. Members from the House of Lords are more frequently used in British cabinets than are senators in Canadian ones, a reflection of the greater status and prestige of the upper House in Britain.

On the surface, the size of the British cabinet is small, averaging about 20 members in recent years. The lack of applying the representation principle in cabinet composition has helped to keep the size of this key decision-making body limited (20 out of 650 members in the British House, compared to about 40 out of 295 in Canada). However, the importance of the cabinet can only be appreciated by distinguishing it from the ministry. In Canada, the cabinet and ministry are identical, while in Britain the cabinet is the smaller operative part of the ministry. A British ministry includes all cabinet officers, plus the parliamentary secretaries and parliamentary under-secretaries. The ministry may number over 100 members, while only the key portfolios are designated as cabinet ones. The positions included as part of the cabinet are based on tradition and on the desires of the prime minister with respect to how the government should be organized. Thus, the British cabinet is small, while the ministry is large. Appointments to the ministry often provide a means of recruitment and socialization for

A British government may retreat or reverse itself under a threat of future political disaster, but as long as it is in office, it has the Roman mandate to see that no harm befall the commonwealth and a practically completely free choice of means to carry out the mandate (Brogan, 1960: 227).

British Prime Minister Margaret Thatcher on the Cabinet(1979): There are two ways of making a Cabinet. One way is to have in it people representing the different points of view within the party, within the broad philosophy. The other way is to have in it only the people who want to go in the direction which

every instinct tells me we have to go: clearly, steadily, firmly, with resolution. As Prime Minister, I could not waste any time having internal arguments.

Jeremy Thorpe, future British Liberal Leader, on a Conservative Cabinet Shuffle in 1962: Greater love hath no man than this, that he lay down his friends for his life.

. . . the present centralization of power into the hands of one person has gone too far and amounts to a system of personal rule in the very heart of our parliamentary democracy (Benn, 1980: 7)

future cabinet appointees. In Britain, the ministry rarely, if ever, meets, while the cabinet does so on a regular basis. Decisions of the cabinet are based on a consensus approach, with only rare challenges to its authority emanating from the ministry, party caucus, or Parliament.

The power of the prime minister with respect to the cabinet has resulted in the thesis that the prime minister, not the cabinet, is the centre of influence and power in modern British politics. This thesis has been forcefully stated by former professor and Labour party minister Richard Crossman. Because a skillful prime minster can control the party, the Parliament, and the bureaucracy, the concept of cabinet government has become a myth: "the best description of the present system of control is that it is not Cabinet Government any more but Prime Ministerial Government" (Crossman, 1972: 29–30). In effect, then, the concept of collective responsibility has been replaced by prime ministerial responsibility to party and nation, bypassing or at least manipulating Parliament in the process. The facade of power has expanded from the formal executive to elements of the political executive as well: the cabinet reigns, the prime minister governs.

While the thesis of prime ministerial govern-

The doctrine of parliamentary sovereignty has become the doctrine of the sovereignty of the executive in Parliament, no longer effectively modified by convention and practice . . . (Williams, 1989: 4).

ment is becoming a common one in assessments of British politics, it is premature to accept it uncritically. Much depends on the political skills and the political will of the occupant of Number 10 Downing Street. The position of prime minister creates the potential for prime ministerial government, it does not guarantee it. Moreover, the cabinet, if pushed too far, can make life very unpleasant for the prime minister, even to the extent of forcing him or her to resign (e.g., the resignation in 1917 of Prime Minister Asquith). Finally, the prime ministerial thesis ignores the constraints of custom and convention that have limited the prime minister's actual role in cabinet composition, direction, and control (Wilson, 1977). A prime minister must "carry his colleagues" with him (or her) on major policies and programs. To the extent that the prime ministerial thesis emphasizes the key role of the prime minister in

> The Thatcher years as Prime Minister are . . . not only an example of prime-ministerial rather than Cabinet government, but also a period in which aspects of the doctrine of individual and collective responsibility have been considerably undermined (Doherty, 1988: 67).

modern British politics, it is correct; to the extent that it ignores the collegial nature of that leadership, it is wrong: "In this, as in many other areas, it is necessary to draw a distinction between the inherent powers of the Prime Ministership and an individual Prime Minister's ability or willingness to wield them" (Alderman and Cross, 1985: 387).

As our discussion shows, the nature of executive power in Britain is divided between an hereditary and constitutional monarch and an elected and temporary political executive. The formal executive retains primarily symbolic and ceremonial tasks, while the prime minister and cabinet have become the engine of the political process. Thus, in broad outline, the tasks of the Canadian and British executives are similar, although they vary in the manner and context of how these functions are carried out. In contrast to these two parliamentary systems, the American presidential executive is based on a single executive office and the separation of powers principle.

The American Presidential Executive

The Office of the President of the United States, often described as the most powerful elective office in any democratic system, has become the focal point of the American political process. This central leadership role of the president has clearly emerged in the past 50 years, a develop-

ment based primarily on political convention rather than any explicit constitutional enhancement of presidential powers.

As the national government became the key player in the American federal system, American presidents often seized the opportunity to exert their influence in both domestic and foreign affairs. In the process, the presidency became the symbol of the American nation, embodying high principles of political virtue backed by popular support. American citizens believe "that no matter how the faith may be destroyed elsewhere, at one particular point— the Presidency—justice will be done beyond prejudice, beyond rancor, beyond the possibility of a fix" (White, 1975: 332). This democratization of the presidency allowed for the further growth of presidential power to such an extent that by the early 1970s the office was increasingly referred to as the imperial presidency.

> . . . in our own time it has produced a conception of presidential power so spacious and preemptory as to imply a radical transformation of the traditional polity. In the last years presidential primacy, so indispensable to the political order, has turned into presidential supremacy (Schlesinger, 1974: 10).

The public reaction, however, to such misuses of presidential power as Watergate and Vietnam provided for at least a temporary retrenchment of the imperial presidency. The inability of Republican President Gerald Ford (1974–1977) and Democrat Jimmy Carter (1977–1981) to provide successful leadership in either domestic or foreign affairs reflected the decline of presidential power in the 1970s. In contrast, Republican Ronald Reagan's landslide electoral victory in the 1980 presidential contest allowed him to reassert the powers of the presidency upon taking office in January 1981, best illustrated by his initial budget-cutting successes against a Democratically-controlled House of Representatives. Moreover, Reagan's

> When passions cool and the dust raised by current contentions settles, judicious historians are apt to place Reagan in the front rank of the second rank of American presidents (Will, 1989: 17).

> The Presidency is the focus for the most intense and persistent emotions in the American polity. The President is a symbolic leader, the one figure who draws together the people's hopes and fears for the political future. On top of all of his routine duties, he has to carry that off—or fail (Barber, 1985: 2).

overwhelming reelection in 1984 further consolidated his preeminent position in American politics, as did his continuing dominance of Congress. President Reagan's popularity declined in 1987–1988, however, as the Iran-Contra Affair battered the last two years of his administration. It seems unlikely that George Bush will be able to match the long-term popularity of his predecessor—especially with Dan Quayle as his vice-president. This ebb and flow of presidential power illustrates the ambivalent attitude most Americans feel about the presidency itself: they are "excited by its potential for good, yet fearful of the abuse of power" (Pious, 1979: 10).

The creation of the presidency provides for an understanding of such a paradox. The American presidency was designed to be a revised combination of the British formal and political executives of the mid-18th century; as Theodore Roosevelt described it, a position "almost that of a king and a prime minister rolled into one." Thus, the tasks or functions of an American president are extensive, because they include the symbolic and ceremonial duties of a formal executive and the political functions of a prime minister. This fusion of roles is an important basis of presidential power in the American system and illustrates why Duverger (1974: 52) classified the American president as a "democratic transplant of the king of England."

PRESIDENTIAL ROLES

The importance of the presidency in the American political process is clearly revealed in the various jobs the president is called upon to play.

First, the president is Head of State, that is, the symbolic and ceremonial leader of the nation. In this capacity, the president carries out the duties of a formal executive in a parliamentary system. A considerable portion of a president's time is spent in greeting foreign leaders, attending social functions such as state dinners, or meeting representatives of various social and economic sectors of society. Under President Richard Nixon, this aspect of the job was so time-consuming and troubling that it was turned over, in part, to Vice-President Spiro Agnew. The attempted delegation of these ceremonial duties to a vice-president was unsuccessful because the vice-president does not hold the same prestige and status as the president. These monarchical tasks have sometimes led presidents to absurd undertakings, as when Richard Nixon dressed up the White House Guard in new uniforms patterned on European lines. The din of the ensuing national laughter was so great that the "tin soldier" look was quickly removed from public view. What President Nixon failed to comprehend was the democratized nature of the monarchical element contained in the American presidency. President Reagan appeared to appreciate the subtlety of this point, so that he reasserted more of the monarchical side of the presidential office than his predecessor, Jimmy Carter.

An important ingredient of the president's role as Head of State is the ability to veto legislation, a power similar to the formal executive's granting of assent to a piece of legislation in a parliamentary system. However, unlike the assent procedure, which has become a formality in Canadian and British politics, the veto power is real, effective, and frequently utilized in American politics. Between 1789–1988, the presidential veto was utilized a total of 2 467 times.

A presidential veto usually acts to defeat a bill, although it is possible for Congress to override a presidential veto with a two-thirds vote in both the House of Representatives and the Senate. For example, in his two terms of office, President Ronald Reagan vetoed 76 items, but only 8 were overridden by Congress. In total, from 1789–1988, only 102 vetoes have been overridden. An important limitation on the veto power results from the fact that the president must accept or reject a bill in total. This procedure means that a president will often compromise and accept a bill because it has at least some favourable provisions. A president can, however, sometimes get the contents of a bill changed prior to its submission for executive approval by threatening to use the veto unless Congress changes some of the bill's provisions, at which point the legislature may compromise. Unlike assent, which is automatic, in American politics presidential approval of a bill need not be: the monarchical element or royal prerogative remains an important weapon in the arsenal of presidential power.

The second major role of the president is that of Chief Executive, that is, the head of the government. This job is equivalent to the prime minister's role in a parliamentary system, sometimes referred to as the Chief of State's role. As the Chief Executive, the president plays the leading role in the domestic policy-making process and supervises the administration of all federal government departments and personnel (approximately three million civilian employees). The president is a significant actor, as well, in the legislative process, since most major bills are in fact proposed and drafted by presidential advisors. Although the president is not formally involved in passing legislation until the very end

of the process (when a bill is either signed or vetoed), political tradition permits the president to take an active role by using the influence of the executive position to persuade the legislature to pass a given bill. Once passed, it is the duty of the Chief Executive to see that the laws are implemented, or, as the Constitution puts it (Article Two, Section Three), "he shall take Care that the laws be faithfully executed." The vast size of the executive structure creates advantages and disadvantages for any president, although typically more of the latter than the former. If a president can exert control over the executive branch, it can become an important resource for and basis of national leadership — if not, the executive structure will frustrate the incumbent's leadership potential.

A third significant job of the American president is the role of Chief Foreign Policy Maker. Subsumed under this heading are the president's tasks of Chief Diplomat and Commander-in-Chief of the Armed Forces. For example, in this diplomatic capacity, the president sends and receives ambassadors, recognizes foreign governments, and negotiates treaties or executive agreements with other countries. In recent decades, presidents have taken on explicit diplomatic tasks. A good example of this diplomatic function was the November 1985 summit between President Reagan and Soviet leader Mikhail Gorbachev. Similarly, in May of 1988, during their Moscow summit, President Reagan and Soviet leader Mikhail Gorbachev exchanged ratified copies of the INF Treaty (intermediate-range nuclear forces). Moreover, the direction and content of American foreign policy can be changed solely by the president, as Richard Nixon's rapprochement with Communist China in the early 1970s clearly demonstrates.

Backing up the diplomatic role is the constitutionally-designated position as Commander-in-Chief: the president can make war by committing American troops to battle. Once the armed forces have become involved, public opinion will rally round, making it most unlikely that

Congress will challenge presidential authority. For example, no official declaration of war was ever made by the United States during its long involvement in the Vietnam conflict. The significance of the president's role as Chief Foreign Policy Maker has been a major factor in the expansion of presidential power since the Second World War. The emergence of the United States as a superpower in world affairs automatically thrusts any American president into a leadership position in the international arena, which reinforces the president's domestic preeminence as well.

A final role, and one that is often overlooked, is the president as party leader. Although the president is deemed to be a unifying symbol and national leader, an individual obtains that exalted position as head of a political party. Moreover, if the president wishes to be reelected for a second term, and most do, then party support is likely to be an important ingredient in that campaign. Between elections, the president may find it helpful to be nonpartisan, but the historical record clearly demonstrates that the most successful presidents have been the most party-based presidents. The reason for such a pattern is clear: party support and organization make the president's other roles easier to accomplish, whether it be in terms of passing legislation, having a treaty approved by the Senate, gaining congressional approval of appropriations to be used by the military in foreign affairs, or in asserting control over the vast reaches of the federal bureaucracy.

As the discussion of the role of the president as party leader indicated, the various tasks of the American presidency need not be harmonious. For example, a president often has to choose between foreign policy priorities and domestic ones — usually described as the choice between guns and butter. The success of any American president depends both on an ability to fulfill each role separately and on a political judgment of how to combine the multiple roles when they are in conflict.

> The seeds of both successful and failed presidential leadership can be found in the complex, contradictory role requirements of the presidency itself (Greenstein, 1988: 2).

While the American presidency combines the typical roles of both the formal and political executives of a parliamentary system, it would be incorrect to conclude that the president of the United States is more powerful than a prime minister in Canada or Britain. Much of a president's power stems from the superpower position of the United States in the international arena. An American president may be the most powerful elected official with respect to world affairs, but in domestic affairs this is not the case, given the separation of powers principle. Since the executive does not control the legislature, no American president can guarantee the passage of a legislative program. In contrast, prime ministers, especially in majority government situations, usually have a success ratio of nearly 100 percent in passing their major policies. For this reason, we can conclude that a Canadian or British prime minister has considerably more power in domestic affairs than any American president. Prime ministers have even more power to control the foreign policy of their countries than do American presidents. For example, a prime minister can conclude a treaty with a foreign country and, unlike an American treaty, it does not need the approval of the legislature before it becomes binding. What makes the American presidency such an important political office is the role of the United States in world affairs, not the president's constitutionally-prescribed duties in the domestic political process.

THE VICE-PRESIDENCY

A final element of the American executive is the position of vice-president of the United States.

Elected in conjunction with the president, the vice-president has two main constitutionally-defined roles. First, the vice-president, in the event of the death or disability of a president, becomes the new president. For example, the assassination of John F. Kennedy on November 22, 1963 led to the immediate swearing-in of Lyndon Baines Johnson as President of the United States. In the event of a temporary disability, the vice-president becomes acting president under section three of the 25th amendment. The first time this provision was used occurred in July of 1985, when Ronald Reagan was hospitalized for a cancer operation. While the President was being operated on, George Bush served as acting president for eight hours.

Moreover, holding the office gives a vice-president a head start over party rivals when seeking the presidency at a later date. Since the Second World War, former Presidents Truman, Johnson, Nixon, and Ford had all served as vice-presidents before assuming the mantle of the American presidency, as did the current President, George Bush.

The second designated task of the vice-president is to serve as President of the Senate, the upper house of the legislature. This position is one of very little influence or power and is primarily ceremonial in nature. However, on the rare occasion when there is a tie on the Senate floor, the vice-president can cast the deciding vote, as then Vice-President George Bush did in July of 1983 (the first such deciding vote since 1969) when he voted in favour of new United States production of nerve-gas weaponry.

Outside of these two tasks, the daily functions of the vice-president are determined by the president. Historically, once in office most vice-presidents have been ignored, although recent presidents have attempted to upgrade the vice-presidential role by allocating to it an effective part in the decision-making process. Walter Mondale was a very active Vice-President for

> Percentage of Americans who don't recognize Mr. Clean: 7. Percentage who don't recognize Vice-President George Bush: 44 (*Harper's Magazine*, July, 1985, p. 9).
>
> *Daniel Webster (1848) on why he declined to run for vice-president*: "I do not choose to be buried until I am really dead."

Jimmy Carter, as was George Bush for President Reagan. However, vice-presidents still suffer 'the slings and arrows of outrageous fortune," as George Bush discovered when star Washington Redskins running back John Riggins snored through his speech to the Washington Press Club (Janaury 1985). Early indications from the Bush administration in 1989–1990 are that Vice-President Dan Quayle will return us to the previous pattern of vice-presidents being ignored.

However, while the vice-president is only a heartbeat away from the presidency, this individual's day-to-day involvement in the direction of the executive branch remains minimal. The key player in American politics is the president; the vice-president rarely grabs either the political limelight or much influence in the American political process.

Comparing Executives

Of the various institutions of government, the executive branch was created first, remains the most complex, and has reemerged as the core of modern government. The political process is executive-centred and controlled, even though the specific structures and contexts of the executive branch differ from one polity to the next.

The executive branch is the centre of modern government because it both makes and implements policy with the help of the civil service. Executives have the potential for leadership and typically the will and resources to turn that

> Put simply, the president, elected directly and separately, is virtually secure from all possible removal . . . . The prime minister, however, lives far more dangerously in that he can be ousted from office at very short notice if he loses control of Parliament (Wilson, 1977: 206).

potential into action and decisions on major matters of public policy: "the nature of our political institutions in both the broad and narrow sense places them at the centre of political consciousness" (Young, 1978: 282). If executives do not lead, then it is most unlikely that any other branch or institution of government will do so — the polity will drift without a rudder. Of course, this should not be taken to mean that a political system will not drift, even with executive direction.

In seeking to provide leadership, the executive branch in democratic systems is typically structured along either parliamentary or presidential lines, with different functions for their component parts. A parliamentary executive is a dual one, with the formal executive performing primarily symbolic and ceremonial duties, while the political executive (prime minister, cabinet, and bureaucracy) governs. The fusion of powers in a parliamentary system guarantees the success of the government's program, at least in a majority situation. In contrast, the separation of powers principle of the American presidential system tends to limit the power of the executive branch, although it remains the centre of the political process in the United States.

In comparing executives, therefore, we must identify the location of executive power, on whose initiative or prerogative that power is exercised, and in what contexts. Such considerations would lead us to the following conclusions in comparing the parliamentary executives of Canada and Britain with each other and with the American presidential executive.

While similar in broad powers, the formal executive in Britain has more influence and plays a somewhat more active political role than its Canadian counterpart. Moreover, because the British political executive is not constrained by the factors of federalism or the representation principle of cabinet composition, prime ministerial government is a more correct description of British than of Canadian politics. In both systems, the cabinet is a crucial mechanism of executive power, second only to that of the prime minister.

By contrast to these two parliamentary systems, the American presidency finds itself constrained, particularly with respect to the legislature, given the separation of powers principle. Moreover, other factors such as a two-term limit, the need to gain legislative approval for treaties, and the public reaction to such fiascoes as Vietnam have further limited presidential prerogatives in recent decades. In both domestic and foreign affairs — especially in the former — no American president ever approaches the power of a Canadian or British prime minister. Thus, the power of the American president stems, in large measure, from the role of the United States in world affairs, rather than from presidential power over the other branches of government.

Given this comparison, it should be obvious that the idea of "presidentializing" the Canadian parliamentary system would mean a considerable decrease in prime ministerial power. From a comparative perspective one would have to ask why any prime minister would want to be a president and thereby give up this grip on the polity. The expansion of the PMO and PCO has not caused prime ministerial preeminence, for the prime minister has always dominated Canadian politics. What the recent trends in the executive branch have done is to strengthen the prime minister's already firm grasp on and leading role in the Canadian polity, thereby helping to transform cabinet government into prime ministerial government.

Summary

1. The executive branch is the engine of the modern political process, performing the tasks of leadership, policy-making, and policy implementation. A parliamentary executive is dual, dividing the executive functions between a formal and a political executive. Founded on the fusion of powers concept, a parliamentary executive operates under the principles of both collective and ministerial responsibility. In contrast, a presidential executive is based on the separation of powers principle, with neither collective nor ministerial responsibility.

2. The formal executive (governor general) in Canada is an appointed, nonhereditary position of limited duration that performs primarily symbolic and ceremonial tasks for the polity. The most significant political function retained by the formal executive is to see that there is always a government in office. In practice, however, the governor general's choice of the prime minister is greatly limited by political traditions. Most of the formal executive's remaining powers are exercised on the initiative of the political executive. The formal executive represents the facade, rather than the substance of power.

3. The political executive dominates the Canadian political scene, a role based on custom rather than on the Constitution. The prime minister is preeminent within the political executive; this leading position is an outgrowth of the prime minister's relationship with the public, formal executive, party, and cabinet. In spite of extensive powers over the structure, composition, and function of the cabinet, the prime minister is constrained by the workings of the representation principle. Public policy is under the direction of the prime minister and cabinet, although aided by the bureaucracy.

4. The formal executive in Britain is hereditary, a prime symbol of national unity, constitutional with respect to its powers, and, at times, an important participant in the political process. The centre of executive power is the British prime minister and the cabinet. In contrast to the Canadian political executive, the British prime minister is not circumscribed by the application of the representation principle, but political tradition does limit the full development of prime ministerial government.

5. The American president performs the combined duties associated with the dual executives in Canada and Britain. The president of the United States is Head of State, Chief Executive, Chief Foreign Policy Maker, and Party Leader. The ability to fulfill these various roles, and the conflicts between them, largely determines a president's success. The president plays a leading role in the initiation, development, and implementation of public policy. Vice-presidents have frequently been elevated to the presidency by death, assassination, resignation, or election, but the vice-presidency remains an office of little power in the normal workings of the polity.

Recommended Readings

Executive Power: General

BLONDEL, JEAN (1987) *Political Leadership: Towards A General Analysis*. London: Sage.

BUNCE, VALERIE (1981) *Do New Leaders Make a Difference? Executive Succession and Public Policy under Capitalism and Socialism*. Princeton, N.J.: Princeton University Press.

CAMPBELL, COLIN (1983) *Governments Under Stress: Political Executives and Key Bureaucrats in Washington, London, and Ottawa*. Toronto: University of Toronto Press.

CLARKE, HAROLD D. and MOSHE M. CZUDNOWSKI, eds. (1987) *Political Elites in Anglo-American Democra-*

cies. DeKalb, Illinois: Northern Illinois University Press.

DUVERGER, MAURICE (1974) *Modern Democracies: Economic Power versus Political Power*. Hinsdale, Ill.: The Dryden Press.

IONESCU, GHITA (1986) "On the Present and Future Uses of Constitutional Monarchy," *Government and Opposition* (Summer), Volume 21, Number 3, pp. 362–366.

MACKIE, THOMAS T. and BRIAN W. HOGWOOD (1984) "Decision Arena in Executive Decision Making: Cabinet Committees in Comparative Perspective," *British Journal of Political Science* (July), Volume 14, Part 3, pp. 285–312.

PUTNAM, ROBERT (1976) *The Comparative Study of Political Elites*. Englewood Cliffs, N.J.: Prentice-Hall.

ROSE, RICHARD and EZRA N. SULIEMAN, eds. (1981) *Presidents and Prime Ministers*. Washington, D.C.: American Enterprise Institute for Public Policy Research.

WELLER, PATRICK (1985) *First Among Equals: Prime Ministers in Westminster Systems*. London: Allen and Unwin.

The Canadian Parliamentary Executive

AVIO, KENNETH L. (1987) "The Quality of Mercy: Exercise of the Royal Prerogative in Canada," *Canadian Public Policy* (September), Volume 8, Number 3, pp. 366–379.

BAKVIS, HERMAN (1988) "Regional Ministers, National Policies and the Administrative State in Canada: The Regional Dimension in Cabinet Decision-Making, 1980–1984," *Canadian Journal of Political Science* (September), Volume 21, Number 3, pp. 539–567.

_____ (1989) "Regional Politics and Policy in the Mulroney Cabinet, 1984–88: Toward Theory of the Regional Minister System in Canada," *Canadian Public Policy* (January), Volume 15, Number 2, pp. 121–134.

CAMPBELL, COLIN (1980) "Political Leadership in Canada: Pierre Trudeau and the Ottawa Model." pp. 50–93 in Richard Rose and Ezra N. Suleiman, eds., *Presidents and Prime Ministers*. Washington, D.C.: American Enterprise Institute.

_____ and GEORGE J. SZABLOWSKI (1979) *The Superbureaucrats: Structure and Behaviour in Central Agencies*. Toronto: Macmillan of Canada.

CLARK, IAN D. (1985) "Recent Changes in the Cabinet Decision-Making System in Ottawa," *Canadian Public Administration*, Volume 28, Number 2, pp. 185–200.

GRAHAM, RON (1986) *One-Eyed Kings: Promise and Illusion in Canadian Politics*. Toronto: Collins.

GWYN, RICHARD (1980) *The Northern Magus: Pierre Trudeau and Canadians*. Toronto: McClelland and Stewart.

JACEK, HENRY (1979) "John Munro and the Hamilton East Liberals: Anatomy of a Modern Political Machine," pp. 62–73 in Bill Freeman and Marsha Hewitt, eds. *Their Town: The Mafia, The Media and the Party Machine*. Toronto: James Lorimer and Company.

MACKINNON, FRANK (1976) *The Crown in Canada*. Calgary, Alta.: McClelland and Stewart West, Glenbow-Alberta Institute.

MACKINTOSH, GORDON H.A. (1985) "The Fateful Prorogation: The Death of Constitutional Proposals in Manitoba," *The Parliamentarian* (April), Volume 66, Number 2, pp. 61–66.

MALLORY, J.R. (1985) "An Affair of Discretion," *Queen's Quarterly* (Winter), Volume 92, Number 4, pp. 758–764.

MATHESON, W.A. (1976) *The Prime Minister and the Cabinet*. Toronto: Methuen.

NEWMAN, PETER C. (1973) *Renegade in Power: The Diefenbaker Years*. Toronto: McClelland and Stewart.

_____ (1978) *The Distemper of Our Times*. Toronto: McClelland and Stewart, 2nd ed.

PAL, LESLIE A. and DAVID TARAS, eds. (1988) *Prime Ministers and Premiers: Political Leadership and Public Policy in Canada*. Scarborough, Ontario: Prentice-Hall Canada.

PUNNETT, R.M. (1977) *The Prime Minister in Canadian Government and Politics*. Toronto: Macmillan of Canada.

RADWANSKI, GEORGE (1978) *Trudeau*. Scarborough, Ontario: Macmillan-NAL.

SAYWELL, JOHN T. (1986) *The Office of Lieutenant-Governor*. Toronto: Copp Clark Pitman.

SIMPSON, JEFFREY (1980) *Discipline of Power: The Conservative Interlude and the Liberal Restoration*. Toronto: Personal Library.

The British Parliamentary Executive

ALDERMAN, R.K. and J.A CROSS (1985) "The Reluctant Knife: Reflections on the Prime Minister's Powers of Dismissal," *Parliamentary Affairs* (Fall), Volume 38, Number 4, pp. 387–408.

_____ (1987) "The Timing of Cabinet Reshuffles," *Parliamentary Affairs* (January), Volume 40, Number 1, pp. 1–19.

BENN, TONY (1980) "The Case for a Constitutional Premiership," *Parliamentary Affairs* (Winter), Volume 33, Number 1, pp. 7–22.

BURCH, MARTIN (1988) "The British Cabinet: A Residual Executive," *Parliamentary Affairs* (January), Volume 41, Number 1, pp. 34–48.

CROSSMAN, RICHARD H. (1972) *The Myths of Cabinet Government*. Cambridge, Mass.: Harvard University Press.

_____ (1976) *Diaries of a Cabinet Minister*. London: Hamilton.

DOHERTY, MICHAEL (1988) "Prime-Ministerial Power and Ministerial Responsibility in the Thatcher Era," *Parliamentary Affairs* (January), Volume 41, Number 1, pp. 49–67.

HAMILTON, WILLIE (1975) *My Queen and I*. Don Mills, Ontario: Paperjacks, General Publishing Co.

HAYDEN, ILSE (1987) *Symbol and Privilege: The Ritual Context of British Royalty*. Tucson: The University of Arizona Press.

HENNESSY, PETER (1986) *Cabinet*. Oxford: Basil Blackwell.

JENKINS, PETER (1989) *Mrs. Thatcher's Revolution: The Ending of the Socialist Era*. London: Pan.

KING, ANTHONY, ed. (1985) *The British Prime Ministers*. London: Macmillan, 2nd ed.

RASMUSSEN, JORGEN (1987) "Constitutional Aspects of Government Formation in a Hung Parliament," *Parliamentary Affairs* (April), Volume 40, Number 2, pp. 139–153.

ROSE, RICHARD (1980) "British Government: the Job at the Top," pp. 1–49 in Rose and Ezra N. Suleiman, eds., *Presidents and Prime Ministers*. Washington D.C.: American Enterprise Institute.

_____ (1987) "Steering the Ship of State: One Tiller but Two Pairs of Hands," *British Journal of Political Science* (October), Volume 17, Number 4, pp. 409–433.

WILSON, HAROLD (1977) *The Governance of Britain*. London: Sphere Books.

YOUNG, HUGO (1989) *One of Us: A Biography of Margaret Thatcher*. London: Macmillan.

The American Presidential Executive

BARBER, JAMES DAVID (1985) *The Presidential Character: Predicting Performance in the White House*. Englewood Cliffs, N.J.: Prentice-Hall, 3rd ed.

BERMAN, LARRY (1987) *The New American Presidency*. Boston: Little, Brown.

CEASER, JAMES W. (1979) *Presidential Selection: Theory and Development*. Princeton, N.J.: Princeton University Press.

CRONIN, THOMAS E. (1986) "The Origins of the American Presidency," *This Constitution* (Fall), Number 12, p. 11–18.

GOLDSTEIN, JOEL K. (1982) *The Modern American Vice-Presidency: The Transformation of a Political Institution*. Princeton, N.J.: Princeton University Press.

GREENSTEIN, FRED I. (1982) *The Hidden-Hand Presidency: Eisenhower as Leader*. New York: Basic Books.

_____ ed. (1988) *Leadership in the Modern Presidency*. Cambridge, Mass.: Harvard University Press.

HERSH, SEYMOUR M. (1983) "The Pardon: Nixon, Ford, Haig, and the Transfer of Power," *The Atlantic* (August), Volume 252, Number 2, pp. 55–78.

HINCKLEY, BARBARA (1988) *The Symbolic Presidency: How Presidents Present Themselves to the Nation*. Chatham, N.J.: Chatham House Publishers.

JONES, CHARLES O. (1988) *The Reagan Legacy: Promise and Performance*. Chatham, N.J.: Chatham House Publishers.

KELLERMAN, BARBARA (1986) *The Political Presidency: Practice of Leadership from Kennedy Through Reagan*. New York: Oxford University Press.

KERNELL, SAMUEL (1985) *Going Public: New Strategies of Presidential Leadership*. Washington, D.C.: Congressional Quarterly Press.

LOWI, THEODORE J. (1985) *The Personal President: Power Invested, Promise Unfulfilled*. Ithaca, New York: Cornell University Press.

MCKAY, DAVID (1989) "Presidential Strategy and the Veto Power: A Reappraisal," *Political Science Quarterly* (Fall), Volume 104, Number 3, pp. 447–461.

NELSON, MICHAEL (1988) "Choosing the Vice President," *PS* (Fall), Volume 21, Number 4, pp. 858–868.

NEUSTADT, RICHARD E.(1980) *Presidential Power: The Politics of Leadership from FDR to Carter*. New York: John Wiley and Sons.

PIOUS, RICHARD M. (1979) *The American Presidency.* New York: Basic Books.

ROSE, RICHARD (1988) *The Post-Modern Presidency.* Chatham, N.J.: Chatham House Publishers.

SCHLESINGER, ARTHUR M., JR. (1974) *The Imperial Presidency.* Toronto: Popular Library.

WHITE, THEODORE H. (1976) *Breach of Faith: The Fall of Richard Nixon.* New York: Dell.

WILLIAMS, ROBERT (1989) "Presidential Power and the Abuse of Office: The Case of the Iran-Contra Affair," *Corruption and Reform*, Volume 3, Number 2, pp. 171–183.

CHAPTER 5

The Bureaucracy and Policy-Making

In a well-ordered polity, politicians and bureaucrats each can do what they are best able to do: politicians articulate society's dreams, and bureaucrats help bring them gingerly to earth (Aberbach et al., 1981: 262).

For forms of government let fools contest, whate'er is best administered is best (Pope, Essay on Man, *Espistle Three, lines 303–304).*

Bureaucracies are things we may dislike but nevertheless always seem to have with us. On all sides—even in our political rhetoric—we constantly adopt the refrain: "Resolved: that government structures loom large, are growing, and should be curtailed" (Krislov, 1974: 8).

ONE OF THE MOST IMPORTANT characteristics of government is the bureaucracy — "the armature of the modern state" (Finer, 1980: 353).

> Every political system must include some patterned means whereby wishes or statements of public policy are transformed into action affecting those within the system over whom political power is exercised (LaPalombara, 1963: 34).

Such is the task of the public bureaucracy or civil service, or, to put it another way, the bureaucracy administers the public's business. The growth of government and of the bureaucracy are coeval: as governments assumed more powers and functions, the mechanism for carrying out those duties (i.e., the **bureaucracy**) multiplied as well.

The history of the development of the bureaucracy is a lengthy one, when we consider that the "Chinese invented the bureaucracy over two thousand years ago . . ." (Fraser, 1980: 86). Yet, in Western Europe, modern administration dates from approximately the year 1660 (Barker, 1944: 1), with the term bureaucracy itself first used by the French philosopher, the Baron de Grimm, on July 1, 1764 (Albrow, 1970: 16). Whatever its exact origin, this facet of modern life is clear: "in the contemporary world, man is organized into bureaucracy as never before" (Lindblom, 1977: 28). Thus, a comparative analysis of political systems must consider the bureaucratic connection.

The Nature of Bureaucracy

If bureaucracy developed as an outgrowth of government, then it is evident in all kinds of political systems. The need to implement public policy is a requirement of democratic, authoritarian, and totalitarian systems. However much bureaucracy has grown in democratic systems,

> "Whoever says state, says bureaucracy" (Finer, 1980: 372).
>
> *Political Leadership and the Bureaucracy:* The art of modern political leadership consists not only in the prudent search for appropriate goals and policies, but also in an attempt to learn how to interact with the massive and complex bureaucracy — how and when to press and coerce it, reshuffle it, terminate its redundant and obsolete parts, flatter and reward it, teach it, and be taught by it (Almond and Powell, 1978: 279).

it has expanded even more rapidly in totalitarian ones (Lindblom, 1977: 239). The reason is quite straightforward: bureaucratic structures are used in totalitarian systems not only as a means of applying public policy but also as fundamental mechanisms of social control (Djilas, 1957: 37–69). The red tape evident in countries such as Russia and China is legendary. As one observer of China put it: "The vastness of a bureaucracy that orders the lives of a billion people can scarcely be imagined" (Fraser, 1980: 86).

In democratic systems, the public's perception of the bureaucracy has often been ambivalent, if not downright hostile. As Weber (Gerth and Mills, 1958: 228) pointed out in his classic analysis of bureaucracy, the basis for such a perspective is likely that, because bureaucracy "has been and is a power instrument of the first order," people naturally fear the abuse of such power. As a result, the "identification of bureaucracies with red tape and antagonism to the public is so ingrained that it is hard to think of their positive functions" (Krislov, 1974: 7). However, at the same time, the bureaucracy is often ridiculed as lazy, incompetent, and unable to carry out the day-to-day functions of government. Civil servants become silly servants, defined as those people who will not work but can not be fired. Thus, bureaucracy as an institution of government is a monster with two heads — one of which is perceived as a Leviathan, the other as a Court Jester (Peters, 1981: 57).

BUREAUCRATIC FUNCTIONS

A common and, at the same time, an incorrect view of the role of the bureaucracy is that it simply implements public policy decided by other institutions; in other words, that politics and administration are divorced in theory and in practice. From this perspective, policy is decided by the executive, approved by the legislature, and implemented by the bureaucracy. Unfortunately, life is rarely so clear-cut and simple. In the modern era, politics and administration are intertwined like Siamese, not fraternal, twins. As one writer put it, the political process is now based on "the bureaucratization of politics and the politicization of bureaucracy" (Aberbach et al., 1981: 19).

Recognizing the interconnections between politics and administration helps us to define the functions of the bureaucracy. Two basic roles can be identified: first, a policy-making function and second, an implementation function. In the first function, the bureaucracy is seen as a key player in the initiation, proposal, and development of public policy. In the second function, the bureaucracy implements that policy, after it has been approved by the executive and legislature. The bureaucracy not only helps to make public policy, but then administers that same policy as well. As a result, the potential for bureaucratic importance and power is self-evident. The significant power and role of the bureaucracy is recognized in the concept of the **administrative state**, that is, a political system in which the state and government dominate the political process through bureaucratic structures. In that sense, all major polities, whatever

> Policy making is not as easy as slurping down cabbage soup. Caution should be combined with decisiveness. As the saying goes, before going into the room, make sure you can get out again (Yegor Ligachev, addressing the Soviet Communist Party conference, July, 1988).

their type, are now administrative states, with some systems more so than others.

BUREAUCRATIC CHARACTERISTICS

In carrying out its policy-making and implementation functions, the bureaucracy has developed some particular characteristics. The most famous description of such traits is Max Weber's ideal-type of bureaucratic attributes (Gerth and Mills, 1958: 196–204; Presthus, 1962: 27–58).

The major bureaucratic characteristics would include the following patterns. First, bureaucratic organizations are hierarchically structured on the basis of graded authority roles. Second, officials are assigned fixed responsibilities and act only on the basis of specific regulations. Third, the officials are trained for their tasks, thereby bringing expertise to the organization. Fourth, the officials are appointed, usually for long periods, and paid compensation from public funds. Fifth, being an official is a career, not a hobby, so that outside ties which might produce any conflicts of interest are discouraged, if not banned outright. Sixth, the organization of officials in a bureaucracy provides a rational method of administration based on specialization, efficiency, and equality.

These typical characteristics of the bureaucracy have traditionally meant the exclusion of civil servants from direct involvement in the political process. To become political is to put

> All traditional public services at their highest levels operate in extremely political — though mostly covert and reactive — ways (Campbell, 1988: 271).

one's job on the line. For example, in Canada, Neil Fraser, an auditor in the Department of National Revenue and later a leadership candidate for the Tories in 1983, was fired from his job in 1982 because of his public criticism of the government's metric conversion policy. Moreover, even leaking government information to the press or public can be dangerous to one's bureaucratic survival. For example, Richard Price, a senior official in Canada's Department of Indian Affairs and Northern Development, was fired in 1985 for leaking a secret cabinet document. Likewise, in Britain, Clive Ponting of the Defence Ministry, who gave a Member of Parliament secret documents relating to the Falkland's War, was not only fired but also prosecuted (but later acquitted) by the Thatcher government. A wise civil servant refrains from open political involvement, especially that of a directly partisan nature.

Because Weber's model of bureaucracy is an ideal type, it does not exist in reality. As with most ideals, human nature keeps getting in the way. For example, bureaucratic recruitment may be based on patronage or nepotism instead of on expertise. Party and family connections, however, do not guarantee bureaucratic competence. Thus, civil service examinations were introduced, in theory at least, to recruit on the basis of expertise, not expediency. Moreover, although bureaucracy is designed to deal with problems rationally, in actual practice the opposite may occur. Fervent attachment to rules and procedures may produce patterns of behaviour or responses which are not adapted to the unique characteristics of a particular case. For example, in the international arena, containment worked as an appropriate response by the Western powers in regard to Europe, but it turned out to have rather disastrous consequences in Vietnam. All bureaucratic systems depart from Weber's ideal, although obviously some do so more than others. The extent of that distance between ideal and reality can be determined in relation to a series of questions regarding bureaucratic structures and functions.

QUESTIONS FOR ANALYZING BUREAUCRACIES

Numerous issues are raised by the significant role of bureaucracies in the political process. These can be summarized under questions relating to composition, control, and neutrality.

Questions concerning the composition of the bureaucracy would include the following: How large with respect to the number of personnel is the bureaucracy by comparison to private enterprise? How is the bureaucracy selected or recruited? Is selection based on competitive examination or on the individual's connections with the powers that be (i.e., patronage)? Is the bureaucracy representative of the composition of the larger society or is it narrowly based on a segment of society (e.g., particular classes or ethnic groups)?

Questions of control focus on the relationship of the bureaucracy with the other institutions of government, such as the executive or legislature. To which institutions, if any, is the bureaucracy accountable? Does the bureaucracy operate in a system based on ministerial responsibility? How responsive is the bureaucracy to public needs and demands? How is control over budgets and policy exercised? What penalties or sanctions, if any, exist for bureaucratic noncompliance? How, under what conditions, and under which procedures can officeholders be dismissed? Basically, matters of control centre on the old question of "Who's in charge?" At times, the answer may be, nobody.

The final set of questions concentrates on a complex and difficult problem; namely, is the bureaucracy politically neutral (some might say neutered) or as it partisan-based? In theory the civil service in democratic systems stays out of politics and serves whichever party happens to form the government. In reality, depending on recruitment practices and the length of a party's stay in power, bureaucracy and party may become intertwined in a web of political relationships. Bureaucrats may become politicians and politicians, in a Kafka-like metamorphosis, sometimes emerge as bureaucrats.

Matters of composition, control, and neutrality all affect each other, as well as the way the bureaucracy carries out its functions of policy-making and implementation. Few would deny that the bureaucracy plays, along with the other parts of the executive, a key role in decision-making. As a result, a look at the decision-making process, and the role of the bureaucracy in it, is appropriate.

Models of Decision-Making

In trying to understand how political decisions are made, numerous models have been developed (Allison, 1971; Halperin, 1974). For our purposes, we will consider two basic approaches: the rational-actor model and the organizational-politics model. Each one makes different assumptions about human nature, about the factors which influence decisions, and the way in which decisions are implemented.

THE RATIONAL-ACTOR MODEL

The basic assumption of our first model is that events, actions, or decisions happen for a reason, that is, they are caused by something. Life is not random, but planned. To understand why

> *John F. Kennedy on Decision-making:* **The essence of ultimate decision remains impenetrable to the observer—often, indeed, to the decider himself . . . . There will always be the dark and tangled stretches in the decision-making process—mysterious even to those who may be most intimately involved (quoted in Allison, 1971: i).**

something happened, it is necessary to discover the relationship between means and ends. In the rational-actor model that relationship is specific: the particular means chosen to achieve certain ends are those which maximize such a relationship. In the words of cost-benefit analysis, the means chosen is the one with the least cost that will produce the greatest benefit in achieving one's goal.

With the rational-actor model, five steps are involved in decision-making. First, the goals and objectives that are sought must be specified. Second, in seeking to achieve a particular goal, several options or alternative courses of action may be possible. Each option needs to be clearly stated and considered. The third step is to project what consequences will follow from each possible option. Fourth, the decision involves selecting that option which has as its consequence the achievement of the desired goal, that is, the option which maximizes the means-end relationship. A decision which maximizes one's goals in this manner is a rational one. (We should point out that rationalizing a decision and making a rational decision are opposites of each other!) Fifth, and finally, once a decision has been taken, it is quickly and efficiently implemented.

While many of us would like to believe that we act in such a manner, a rational consideration of mankind would quickly produce the conclusion that, while he may be a political animal, man is rarely, if ever, a rational one. For example, the rational-actor model makes the following assumptions: first, that one has goals and that

---

STANDARD OPERATING PROCEDURE

BIGFOOT COULD BE SUCH A BIG FUSS

WASHINGTON (AP) — What would happen if you stumbled across the legendary Bigfoot monster while walking in the woods, managed to capture it and reported your catch to the U.S. Fish and Wildlife Service? Would the agency know what to do?

Yes, says the agency, and to prove its readiness to handle the purported 8-foot, 900-pound Pacific Northwest humanoid, it has written a lengthy news release describing just what would happen when you called.

"Word of its discovery would be flashed around the world within hours. Hysteria, fear or panic might accompany the news in the area where the creature was located. The throngs of curiosity seekers, would-be captors and others wanting to find Bigfoot would not only create a serious threat to the animal itself, but to public safety as well. . . ."

After receiving 120-day temporary protection under the Endangered Species Act, Bigfoot would undergo processing for long-term safe-guarding. The following would be considered:

How big is the Bigfoot population? Do Bigfeet occur any-where else? Is the Bigfoot population in danger of decline? Is Bigfoot's habitat secure? Is the Bigfoot species being exploited? And what is Bigfoot's reproductive rate?

"But for the record," said Keith Schreiner, associate director, "I doubt we'll ever have to do anything, because I don't believe there are any of the things around to be discovered in the first place."

Source: The Globe and Mail, January 25, 1978. By permission of The Associated Press.

---

these goals are clearly defined; second, that one considers all options and can even identify all possible courses of action; third, that the consequences of each action can be accurately foretold (without recourse to soothsayers reading the entrails of a sheep) and finally, that one wants to maximize the means-ends relationship. Human experience would seem to indicate a low probability that each of these assumptions will be met in the course of any particular decision. For example, the revelation in 1988 that President Ronald Reagan and his wife Nancy — the latter in particular — were guided in some of their decisions by the advice of astrologers is evidence of other-than-rational bases of action. As a result, alternative models of human behaviour have been developed to explain the decision-making process.

THE ORGANIZATIONAL-POLITICS MODEL

From the perspective of our second model of decision-making, people do not maximize, but, instead, they "satisfice" or act on what is sometimes called "bounded or limited" rationality. To **satisfice** is to choose a course of action that is good enough, given such constraints as time, money, information, and effort. The difference between maximizing and satisficing can be illustrated as follows. A student, to maximize his chance for employment after university, should try to achieve the highest possible score on every assignment in every class every year of his college career. To satisfice is to accept a "gentleman's C" as good enough. Most students, as most people, are satisficers.

The organizational politics model also views decisions as the outputs of large organizations externally battling with other organizations and internally facing conflict among their subunits. To understand decision-making, one must know something about the mores of organizational behaviour.

Organizations and their subunits view a problem from their own perspective, that is, a pattern of **parochial priorities**. For example, a minister of external affairs is likely to see an

---

THE PROBLEM OF IMPLEMENTATION

CHIEF EXECUTIVE VERSUS THE WHITE HOUSE MOUSE

Students sometimes see presidents as sitting high atop the executive branch pyramid, barking out commands. Occasionally this is the case, but the degree to which a president can win cooperation or compliance varies enormously. And presidents can often be just as frustrated as parents are with their teenage offspring. Listen to the sad story of the White House Mouse. He or she had climbed inside a wall of the Oval Office and died there. The odor became offensive just as President Carter was about to greet a visiting diplomat.

An emergency call went out to the General Service Administration (the agency that maintains and oversees federal property), but the GSA refused to respond. The dead mouse, GSA officials said, had obviously come in from outside the building and was therefore the responsibility of the Department of the Interior. Interior officials, however, objected; they contended the mouse was not their concern because it was now inside the White House and their jurisdiction was merely the outside grounds.

Well, an exasperated Carter finally ordered officials from both agencies to his office where he angrily told them, "I can't even get a damn mouse out of my office . . . ." So how was the problem solved? By a two-agency White House supervised task force, of course.

Source: James MacGregor Burns et al., *Government by the People.* Englewood Cliffs, New Jersey: Prentice-Hall, 1984, national edition, 12th edition, p. 428. By permission of Prentice-Hall.

---

international problem as an exercise in diplomacy, while a minister of defence may propose a military solution. Similarly, a provincial premier will usually assess the worth of a federal government budget in terms of how it affects his province, while the federal minister of finance has to act on what he considers to be good for the entire country. The parochial priorities of organizational behaviour affect the subunits of an organization as well. For example, in the defence department, those in the navy will likely recommend a solution involving the navy, the army the army, and the air force the air force. Parochial priorities give support to the idea that "where you stand depends on where you sit."

Just as each unit or subunit perceives a problem from its own perspective, so also is it likely that each organization will have its own goals, which may or may not be compatible with those of the other organizational units. Thus, unlike the rational-actor model, the organizational-politics model has multiple goals, sometimes in conflict with each other.

In trying to deal with reality, organizations develop what are known as **standard operating procedures** (SOPs). In other words, given situation A, the organization will automatically react with response B. This pattern is one of the chief characteristics of bureaucracies: rules try to govern every eventuality. Nothing creates so much bureaucratic confusion as a situation which has not been anticipated; therefore, possible scenarios, no matter how improbable, are dreamed up, with the appropriate response "ready and waiting." While standard operating procedures may typically help to make organizations more efficient, applying them uncritically or never reassessing their appropriateness may be counterproductive.

In our second model, a decision is a result of the organizational battle and, thus, will likely not maximize anything. A decision depends on who the players are, the rules of the game, and the interagency bargaining which takes place. From this perspective, a decision is the end result of a series of compromises by the organizational units in the political process. Rational calculations of advantage give way to bureaucratic outputs of necessity and self-interest.

Finally, the organizational-politics model differs from the one based on rationality in relation to the problem of implementation. From the organizational perspective, implementation is never assured. To implement a decision is often as difficult as it is to arrive at a decision in the first place. In fact, many analysts would argue, with more than a little justification, that how a decision is effected is usually more significant than the wording of the decision itself. For example, it is easy to declare in a Charter of Rights and Freedoms that discrimination is illegal; it is quite another matter to have such values observed and respected in the discourse of daily life on the streets of Toronto or Vancouver or any other city. Obtaining a favourable decision is only half of the battle; getting it implemented is often the more difficult half.

The Bureaucracy-Policy Nexus in Canada

To investigate who makes policy in Canada is quickly to discover the importance of the bureaucracy. For example, the size of the bureaucracy indicates its potential for influence: over half-a-million civil servants work for the federal government (Brown, 1985). To that number must be added thousands of provincial and municipal government officials as well. While not all members of the bureaucracy, such as secretaries and support staff, are policy-makers, others, such as the top officials in each government agency, most certainly may be. Moreover, the long tenure of a dominant party in office (e.g., the federal Liberals from 1921–1984) has often led to an intimate party-

bureaucratic connection: "the chief function of the party is to stay in power by defining and refining bureaucratic initiatives" (Newman, 1984: 74). This important role of the bureaucracy can be quickly ascertained by analyzing the key participants in the decision-making process.

THE PROCESS OF PUBLIC DECISION-MAKING — AN OVERVIEW

Before a government is faced with making a decision on a matter of public policy, somebody or some part of the political system must want or must demand some action to be taken. These demands can emanate from any segment of the political process—from individuals, political parties, interest groups, parliament, or the government itself. Specific calls for action by the public are rare, although they do occur, as in the request from several municipalities in 1984 and 1985 that the federal government act with respect to the problem of prostitution in urban areas. Peace demonstrations, rallies for or against capital punishment, and the controversies surrounding the abortion issue are examples of how the public can demand that their government deal with specific concerns on the policy agenda. However, most of the time, the general public is not intimately involved with policy concerns, nor are the public's representatives (i.e., the parties). The political executive, in conjunction with the bureaucracy, monitors and largely determines the nation's political agenda. Much of this process is controlled, at the federal level, by the Priorities and Planning Committee of the cabinet. A key player in deciding which issues must be dealt with, of course, is the prime minister federally and a premier provincially.

Once a policy area is identified for action, the bureaucracy is called upon to develop specific proposals for consideration. In addition, sometimes parliamentary committees may hold special hearings; task forces (such as the Pepin-Robarts Task Force on National Unity) may be utilized; or Royal Commissions may be announced. Particularly in controversial policy areas, a preliminary statement about what public policy should be (e.g., a Green Paper) is sometimes presented in order to test the political waters. In their own areas of concern, interest groups may develop quite detailed recommendations for action. However, for most issues most of the time the bureaucracy dominates.

With specific proposals identified, major policies are brought before cabinet for debate and action. The cabinet itself is composed of a series of cabinet committees, which in most cases are used to consider the details of any potential changes in public policy. After considering the item, the cabinet committee will send the matter on for full cabinet consultation. Discussions with the governing party's caucus may also occur during this time period, or after the cabinet has decided to act on the matter, but before the policy is sent to the legislature. Once cabinet has decided the issue at hand, it may be implemented by an order-in-council or by preparing legislation for Parliament to consider. Parliament's role is not to develop the specifics of policy, but to approve and refine policy presented to it. Once approved by the cabinet and/or Parliament, policy is implemented on a day-to-day basis by the bureaucracy.

While no overview of the policy process can handle all possible variations, the above pattern of decision-making would seem to be the "normal" one. Policy is controlled and directed by the political executive and the bureaucracy, with the public, Parliament, and other actors typically assigned to minor roles.

Royal commissions and policy-making

A favourite technique of governments in the making of public policy is the utilization of royal commissions, task forces, or special study groups of one kind or another. The usually declared intent of such commissions is to help the government formulate relevant policy options. The royal commission may hold public hearings, call for expert testimony, or undertake special studies on a particular problem. The royal commission, at the end of such a consultative process, will then issue a report, with its recommendations for action, to the government of the day. For example, the Macdonald Commission on the economy lasted three years, issued a three-volume report plus 72 research reports, and cost the taxpayers $20 million dollars. However, what may happen is that a royal commission becomes a mechanism for avoiding hard policy decisions, rather than a means for taking action. A brief look at the structure and procedure of a typical royal commission will help to explain why and how such bodies sometimes avoid policy.

The decision to form a royal commission, along with its terms of reference (i.e., structure, duration, funds, and powers), is the prerogative of the government of the day (i.e., the political executive). At times a royal commission may be appointed not to consider all policy alternatives, but instead to build support for a policy option the government already has decided to undertake. One significant way of controlling such a royal commission is through the power to make appointments. Only those people already in agreement with government intent may be appointed. For example, one would expect no separatists to be appointed to a royal commission on national unity. Moreover, when a royal commission issues its report and recommendations, its views are advisory, not mandatory, for the government of the day. Thus, a finding not in line with government policy can easily be rejected.

Appointing a royal commission, which may last for several years, is often a way of avoiding policy. During the sitting of a royal commission, the government can deflect action or comment,

A CANADIAN ROYAL COMMISSION

"... way deep down I think what would make me deliriously optimistic about Canada is, like if we could somehow clean out all the politicians and the entire civil service we are blessed with today and start all over again..."

Source: Sid Barron, *The Toronto Star*, May 13, 1984. Reprinted with permission—The Toronto Star Syndicate.

until the commission reports. Such a stance is particularly useful to a government during question period in the House of Commons. A change in government may even occur during the stay of a particular royal commission. In such instances, of course, the new government may not feel bound, for a variety of reasons, to give much credence to the policy views of a commission appointed by its political opposition. An interesting reversal of this general pattern occurred in 1985 with the release of the report of the Macdonald Commission (Royal Commission on the Economic Union and Development Prospects for Canada). While in opposi-

tion, the Tories had bitterly attacked the creation of this Royal Commission. However, on coming to power, the Mulroney government allowed the Macdonald Commission to finish its work and issue its findings, primarily because the Macdonald Commission favoured free trade with the United States, a policy initiative which the Tories liked.

These reflections on some of the limitations of royal commissions and policy-making in Canada should not automatically be taken to mean that such bodies have no positive consequences. Current or future policy may be influenced by the work of royal commissions. Moreover, royal commissions may be more important as consultative rather than as policy-making mechanisms. However, the political uses of royal commissions, task forces, and study groups need to be recognized, along with their more beneficial results (Courtney, 1969).

While practices such as appointing royal commissions may help to set the content of public policy, other considerations influence the political agenda as well. Given the nature of modern government, especially its expensive and expansive attributes, money is a central concern of the policy process. It would be difficult to conceive of a policy that had no financial implications. Thus, decision-making must focus on not only what public policy should be, but how much it will cost. Monetary considerations more often determine the content of policy than do moral concerns. Two important aspects of spending practices in Canada are the role of the Treasury Board and the introduction in 1979 of expenditure envelopes in determining how much money would be provided for implementing public policy.

The Treasury Board

The president of the Treasury Board is a cabinet-level position. The composition of the Treasury Board, which is a statutory committee of the Privy Council, includes the ministers of the various financial departments, such as National Revenue, with the Minister of Finance serving in an *ex officio* capacity. In other words, the Treasury Board is a special committee of cabinet composed of cabinet members, in a hierarchical position over the specific governmental departments. Its significance is further enhanced because it plays (or can play) a key role in the budgetary process, for which it has general responsibility. Moreover, the Treasury Board is the manager of the public service and in this capacity can control spending and employee levels of the particular government departments.

While the detailed budget process is indeed complex, the general position of the Treasury Board, and its potential importance, can be seen as follows. In the budget cycle, the Treasury Board has to match departmental requests for funds to overall expenditure projections. With the backing of the prime minister and cabinet, the Treasury Board can be the mechanism for imposing spending controls or other limits on the various departments. For example, when former Prime Minister Trudeau sought to control the work of the then Auditor-General Maxwell Henderson, he did so to a considerable extent through the Treasury Board, which would not hire the staff needed by the Auditor-General to carry out his post-audit of government expenditures. The attempts in the late-1970s and early-1980s to control government spending centred on the ability and willingness of the Treasury Board to control departmental expenditures. The success or failure of such Treasury Board efforts depended on the political will of the government, for it ultimately controlled not only the composition, but also the credibility of its own cabinet committee. Typically, the political will to control government spending has lasted about as long as springtime in the Maritimes. As a result, a new way of controlling expenditures, known as the envelope budgeting system, was introduced into the workings of the Canadian budgetary process in 1979 (McCaffrey, 1984).

The envelope budgeting system: 1979–1989

The traditional budgetary process has been one based on each department or agency, acting through its minister, fighting to get as much of the expenditure pie as possible on a short-term, year-to-year basis. The envelope budgeting system transformed this process with respect to several crucial assumptions. First, long-term projections of five years served as the basis for deciding policy priorities. Second, these priorities were supposedly determined by the elected politicians in the cabinet, rather than by anonymous civil servants. Third, broad policy areas known as envelopes (e.g., social affairs, economic development, public debt) formed the basis for departmental allocations. Fourth, general government policy was intended to be more rational, because the overall priorities in the expenditure envelopes were set by the cabinet in the Priorities and Planning Committee. Each department had to contest with all other departments whose expenditures fell within the confines of a given envelope.

While this system developed gradually during the 1970s, an obvious precursor was the emphasis by Pierre Trudeau that "government policy-making should not be haphazard; it should be planned" (McCall-Newman, 1982: 209). The short-lived Clark government specifically introduced the envelope budgeting system in 1979, a process that was maintained by more recent governments, until the Mulroney cabinet shuffle of January, 1989. Probably the most significant impact of the envelope budgeting process was that the "system tied *policy* and *spending* together" (McCaffrey, 1984: 58) and thus marked a major reorientation of the traditional Canadian budgetary process.

The 1989 structural changes (see Figure 5.1) to the cabinet decision-making process which marked the end of the envelope budgeting system are another attempt to impose effective spending restraints on the budgeting process. The expansion of the Priorities and Planning Committee, along with the formalization of the Operations Committee (see Chapter four), were designed to increase the ability of the government to control expenditures. P&P, for example, has been given the task of specifically approving all new government programs, as well as the responsibility for approving any significant government expenditures, including those for existing programs. Thus, P&P, along with the Treasury Board, which now controls all routine government expenditures, has a

potential veto on any financial expenditures of government. Moreover, the standing committees of cabinet (e.g., those dealing with major policy areas) are now relieved of any role in determining spending priorities. Thus, the policy role of the standing cabinet committees has been reduced, since they play no part in budgeting decisions, while the policy roles of P&P and the Operations Committee have become crucial.

A special standing committee of cabinet, known as the Expenditure Review Committee, was created by the 1989 reforms. Chaired by the Prime Minister, this new committee is responsible for an ongoing review of all government expenditures. A new coordinating committee, entitled the Communications Committee, has been set up to provide information (some might say, propaganda) to the public; in other words, to sell the government's decisions and programs to the Canadian voter. Finally, the changes outlined above will lead, over the next several years, to a significant reorganization of federal government departments.

While it will take a few years to consolidate all of these changes and to see how they actually mesh, three things are clearly evident: first, the power of the total cabinet has been reduced, while that of the P&P and the Operations Committee has been greatly enhanced; second, these reforms are congruent with the increasing centralization of decision-making in the PMO; and third, these modifications are the latest in a series of pragmatic responses to ongoing budgetary problems, such as the deficit.

Ideology and public policy

So far in our discussion of decision-making, we have focused on the process of policy-making, with an emphasis on the budget. We have not discussed in detail the factors which might influence policy content in specific areas. However, one element stands out as having relatively little influence, namely, ideology. One

FIGURE 5.1   FEDERAL CABINET STRUCTURE (January 1989)

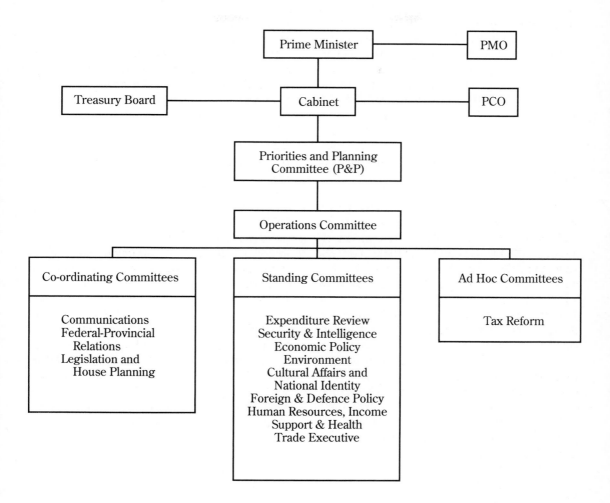

recent study concluded that the analysis "clearly speaks against exaggerating the influence of ideological debate on the public policy process" (Ornstein and Stevenson, 1984: 338).

A number of factors contribute to this pattern. First, all governments at the federal level have either been Conservative or Liberal, thus based on parties famous for their pragmatism and non-ideological nature. Second, many elements of the Canadian political culture (e.g., deference,

elite accommodation) enhance a pragmatic pattern of government decision-making. Third, federal-provincial conflict has rarely been ideologically based. Fourth, factors such as region and religion, which are not necessarily tied to ideological concerns, have formed the basis of much of the political agenda since Confederation.

The result of these attributes is a decision-making process which minimizes political ideology. Instead, public priorities are dependent on political considerations of party, personnel, and patronage.

> Undoubtedly the strongest incentive against the rational setting of, and adherence to, priorities is found in the inexorable ticking of the electoral clock. A political party without power cannot make policy (Doern, 1985: 106).

CHARACTERISTICS OF CANADIAN DECISION-MAKING

In addition to its nonideological nature, several aspects of the decision-making process characterize the nature of public policy in Canada. First, most policy is **incremental** in design, implementation, and effect; that is, change is slow, modest, and usually inefficient. Incrementalism means building on existing policy and practices, rather than starting over in a wholesale fashion. For example, tax reform in Canada involves tinkering with the existing structure, such as raising tax on some items, lowering it on others, or adding or deleting specific tax loopholes. A pattern of incremental decision-making reflects not only general bureaucratic tendencies, but certain elements of Canada's political culture (e.g., deference, elitism, and conservatism).

A second characteristic of decision-making concerns the particular role of cabinet ministers as **generalists**, rather than as specialists. One of the assumptions of cabinet government, one that is probably incorrect, is that a minister can adequately direct and control any department, irrespective of the content of that department's responsibilities. Cabinet shuffles specifically reflect such a view, since a minister can be in charge of Finance one day and External Affairs the next. If one is a competent administrator, then supposedly one can administer any department.

Canadian cabinets are overwhelmingly composed of generalists—there are few specialists in the inner sanctum of power. In fact, sometimes competence in a particular policy area keeps a minister from being named to the most relevant cabinet post. Eric Kierans, with extensive business and financial expertise, became Postmaster General, instead of receiving a portfolio that dealt with economic matters. Mark MacGuigan's background as a constitutional lawyer reputedly kept him out of the cabinet for many years, until he ended up in the External Affairs portfolio. A more relevant initial post for Mark MacGuigan might have been as Minister of Justice, which he subsequently became in the September 1982 cabinet shuffle. Incremental public policy developed and administered by generalists is the context of the bureaucratic function and the most important source of the power of the civil service in the Canadian political process.

The theoretical or designed role of the bureaucracy is to implement the decisions regarding public policy that have been made by the political executive and authorized by the legislature. However, direction concerning the course of public policy may be vague, so that the act of implementation puts the bureaucracy in a policy-making role. To apply general policy to specific situations is neither easy nor neutral; it necessitates a decision-making function for the civil service.

Considerable bureaucratic influence flows from its role as the interpreter of the meaning of the general law or what is called **delegated power**. For example, delegated legislative power means that the legislature has passed a bill that authorizes the executive and bureaucracy to flesh out the details of the bill's general provisions. A classic illustration of this pattern is demonstrated by the wage-and-price control legislation (Bill C-73), which passed the House of Commons on December 3, 1975. Section 3 of the Anti-Inflation Act provided the authority for detailed specification by the civil service of how the wage-and-price restraint plan would work:

"The Governor in Council may from time to time cause to be published and made known guidelines for the guidance of all Canadians in restraining profit margins, prices, dividends and compensation." The initial bureaucratic guidelines (many more were to follow later), known as the Anti-Inflation Act Regulations, were 60 pages long—four times the size of Bill C-73 itself!

A second basis of bureaucratic influence is the reputed expertise of the civil service with respect to the nature and content of public policy and of the government regulations based thereon. For example, there are probably very few politicians or civil servants in the entire country who can explain in detail the provisions of Canada's equalization formula. Moreover, because civil servants have long tenure in office (generally they can be removed only for "cause"), they have become significant participants in the decision-making process. Cabinet ministers come and go, while the bureaucracy remains in place. In a spirit of derision, bureaucrats often refer to their cabinet bosses as "our political masters." Often in Canadian history, the so-called political masters have been controlled by their servants, and not always in a civil fashion.

The bureaucracy is intimately involved not only in the implementation of public policy, but also in its initiation and formulation. The structure of the departments of government reflects this pattern (see Figure 4.1 in Chapter Four). At the head of each department is a cabinet minister, surrounded by various aides and executive assistants who are directly responsible to him or her. The purpose of these ministerial assistants is to help the cabinet minister establish control over the bureaucracy. In October 1984, the new Conservative government doubled the budget for ministers' staffs (to $15 million dollars) and created a chief of staff position in each office.

Also included in this entourage are the **parliamentary secretaries**, who are MPs

> ... changes in political parties have little effect on the tenure of deputy ministers in the Canadian federal government. Deputy ministers have been surviving the hazards of politics since the beginning of Confederation (Bourgault and Dion, 1989: 145).

assigned to help the cabinet minister. Parliamentary secretaries are allocated to the major portfolios (ministers of state usually receive no such help) on a regional basis according to the representation principle. Parliamentary secretaries are not members of the cabinet, but the position has been used as a training and testing ground to spot future cabinet material. These backbench MPs of the governing party often serve as standins for the minister with respect to speaking engagements and as a "lightning rod" to attract any political flak away from the minister. The involvement of parliamentary secretaries in the decision-making process is usually very modest.

In terms of authority in and direction over a government department, the second in command to the cabinet minister is the **deputy minister**. As administrative head of a department, the deputy minister is responsible for the overall direction and day-to-day operation of the bureaucracy. A deputy minister is not an MP, but is, in effect, the top civil servant assigned to each department. Even though deputy ministers are appointed by the prime minister and are removable by the PM, as career public servants, such a change costs them power, but not job security.

Deputy ministers are more directly involved in the political process than most civil servants and, therefore, occupy a rather distinctive position in the bureaucracy. As the "permanent" department head, the deputy minister fulfills not only an administrative role, but a political one as well (Hodgetts, 1985). Deputy ministers are usually important participants in the

The Ottawa bureaucracy's reaction to the 1984 Tory victory: Some top bureaucrats ducked and prayed that the barbarians would go away. Some tried ingratiation, saying whatever they thought their new political masters wanted to hear. Some pitied themselves as misunderstood martyrs to the public good. Most simply hunkered down, willing to serve but reluctant to change (Gray, 1988: 11).

policy-making process. As a result, a shuffle of deputy ministers may be more significant as an indicator of changing government priorities than a shift of cabinet portfolios would be. Because a shuffle of deputy ministers is usually less frequent than one of cabinet ministers, and given their expertise and knowledge, deputy ministers often control the cabinet ministers who in theory direct the department. Some departments have been particularly affected by frequent cabinet shuffles. Under Pierre Trudeau, the defence portfolio was changed eight times and that of national revenue 11 times. In such a situation, deputy ministers often acquire and exercise power at the expense of their minister. Arrayed beneath the deputy ministers are the component units of each government department, a structure that varies from one department to the next.

The important political role of the bureaucracy in the decision-making process means that, despite the civil service's supposed impartiality, all governments seek to control its composition and influence. A government that has been in power for any length of time can fashion the bureaucracy in its own political image. At the top of the bureaucracy (i.e., deputy minister level), the government party has the prerogative to appoint and remove civil servants as it desires, while at the intermediate levels, civil-service hiring guidelines are flexible enough to allow the government to shape its structures and hiring procedures.

The political nature and importance of the bureaucracy is clearly evident when an opposition party, especially one that has been out of office for a long time, wins an election and forms a government. At least some highly visible public servants lose their jobs, if for no other reason than as a symbol of the changing of the political guard—such an interpretation can account for the departure of Privy Council Clerk Michael Pitfield, Trudeau's longtime friend and confidant, shortly after the Clark government took office in 1979. Sometimes the leaving of imbedded allies of the former government can be a messy business, as illustrated by the forced departure of Bryce Mackasey as chairman of Air Canada, a federal crown corporation. Mackasey was a veteran cabinet member and Liberal MP whose appointment to head Air Canada before the 1979 election was widely interpreted as a fairly blatant patronage appointment. Because Mackasey refused to leave of his own volition, he was fired by Prime Minister Clark.

Such problems between a new government and the bureaucracy are common at the provincial level as well, where the bureaucratic turnover after an election is apparently more extensive. For example, upon assuming office in January 1982, NDP Leader Howard Pawley removed 10 top bureaucrats in the Manitoba civil service, replacing most of them with individuals who had ties with the New Democratic Party (i.e., former candidates or party officials). One woman who had been in the civil service, but had temporarily left to run as a Progressive Conservative candidate in the 1981 Manitoba election, was laid off when she sought to return to her job. A similar, but even more widespread, replacement of public service personnel occurred after the Conservatives won power from the NDP in Saskatchewan in the 1982 provincial election (Michelmann and Steeves, 1985).

Once the initial turnover of key positions in the civil service has been accomplished, the government has considerable leeway in establishing and extending its influence throughout

HOW A TORY MINISTRY IS SET UP....

Source: Portfolio 85: The Year in Canadian Caricature, CROC Publishing, 1985.
Reproduced by permission of Adrian Raeside, *Victoria Times-Colonist*.

the bureaucracy during its stay in office. Parties in opposition are usually in favour of rather drastic civil service reform. For example, in February 1985, the provincial Liberal party in Quebec called for a major transformation of the civil service. The concern of all governments to control the structure, operation, and composition of the civil service is a reflection of the political nature of the bureaucracy and its significant role in the policy-making process.

Which decision-making model applies to Canada?

Reforms incorporated into the Canadian policy process during the past several decades appear to conform to the rational-actor model. Certainly the cabinet procedures introduced by Pierre Trudeau and followed by his successors were attempts to take a rational view of decision-making, as were the improvements in the budgetary process, such as the expenditure envelopes. However, such changes have been at the top of the decision-making structure and appear to have been followed less closely as one moves away from the centre of authority.

The organizational-politics model, in all likelihood, holds sway in most areas, on most decisions, on a day-to-day basis. Standard operating procedures, departmental conflict, and the typical array of bureaucratic games are renowned throughout Canada's governmental structure, both federally and provincially. What has happened has been the addition of a rational-actor model on top of the existing traditional pattern of decision-making (i.e., the organizational-politics approach). Governmental policy-makers want to appear rational, even when they are not. However, if our characterization of the decision-making process as incremental, nonideological, and carried out by generalists is correct, then the organizational-politics model tells us more about public decision-making in Canada than do considerations of rationality.

The British Bureaucracy: The Role of Whitehall

In the comparative study of bureaucracies and as an example for other countries, the British civil service has long been seen, historically at least, as an institution to be emulated, because of its professionalism, competence, and efficiency. Although these traits have been challenged and questioned since at least the 1960s, by and large they remain in place. The British public service was composed in the mid-1980s of approximately three-quarters of a million individuals, a 15-fold expansion since the turn of the century. Reductions by the Thatcher government had lowered this number to 600 000 by the 1990s. This size of bureaucratic personnel is one basic reason why increasingly politicians and the public view Britain as an "overgoverned country" (Williams, 1981: 187). Moreover, the importance of the civil service in running the country was demonstrated by their 1981 strike against Margaret Thatcher's government.

Descriptions of the British bureaucracy frequently use two terms, that of Whitehall and of the mandarins. Whitehall is in fact a street on which many of the major departments of the British government are located. As a result, **Whitehall** is used as a term to describe the political executive and bureaucratic components of government. (The Prime Minister lives at Number 10 Downing Street, a small avenue off Whitehall, with Parliament itself located at the end of Whitehall). The senior officials and administrators of the approximately 30 government departments are often called **mandarins**, after the Chinese term for a high-ranking official. The term mandarin would certainly include the top 6 000 people in the administrative class,

> *The Impact of British Mandarins:* The mandarins in modern Britain work as closely with the Emperor or Empress who governs from Downing Street as can ever have occurred in Ancient China. Together they control the real levers of state power, many of which are so secret that most Cabinet ministers do not even know of their existence, let alone how they are being operated (Benn, 1982: 48).

individuals likely to play some significant role in the policy process.

The role of the bureaucracy has been a significant one in the policy-making process, because in Britain the relationship between the civil service and the government of the day has usually been an intimate one. It appears that the Canadian practice of bypassing the traditional bureaucracy by setting up a counter-bureaucracy around the office of the prime minister has not been a major development in British politics. Instead, a counter-bureaucratic structure has been created, which parallels the structure and political functions of the civil service. These organizations, estimated to total in the range of 2 000 (500 with executive functions and 1 500 with advisory powers), have been labelled as **quangos** (quasi-autonomous non-governmental organizations). Since members of the quangos are appointed by the ministers, they are usually patronage-based because normal civil service hiring rules do not apply. Quangos can be used to bypass the traditional influence of Whitehall in the policy-making process. In most cases, however, the quangos accommodate themselves to the existing system: "their basic rationale is representation and advice to government and the permanent bureaucracy" (Presthus, 1981: 313). The quangos are an interesting and unique example of the expansive nature of government in general and of the importance of the bureaucracy in particular in the political process of the modern era.

MINISTERIAL-DEPARTMENTAL RELATIONS

In Britain the old adage that a minister proposes while a bureaucrat disposes no longer is entirely correct. The tradition of generalist ministers has certainly enhanced the power of the bureaucratic specialists. Moreover, some ministers may be temporary birds of passage of one or two years duration, while members of the administrative class may spend decades, if not their entire adult life, within the confines of a single department. For example, "between 1944 and 1976, there were nineteen Ministers of Education" (Norton, 1982: 84). Rapid turnover of ministers increases the potential of civil service influence. Moreover, the growth of government departments and services has rendered the day-to-day supervision of the civil service nearly impossible. In the 1990s a ministry of about 100 people oversees a civil service of 600 000, compared to a ministry of about 60 persons in charge of a civil service of 50 000 in 1900.

Rapid turnover of generalist ministers is exacerbated by the techniques the bureaucracy can use to frustrate the will of a new minister. These bureaucratic games have been analyzed by former Labour Minister Tony Benn (1982: 53–61). Techniques which enhance civil service power include secrecy, ministerial briefings, control of information, setting the broad framework of policy, expertise, patronage, and bargaining within Whitehall. The problem for the minister is to control his department without being controlled by it. The necessary balance is often a difficult one to achieve: the "effective Minister is the man who wins the support of his Department without becoming its cherished mascot" (Crossman, 1972: 65).

> A study of Greek philosophy is an almost perfect training for a Mandarin. It means you know nothing in particular about what you are actually doing but you have a "perfectly trained mind" . . . . Nonexpertise is the mark of a man who is going to get on in the British Civil Service (Crossman, 1972: 55–56).

THE CIVIL SERVICE AND POLICY-MAKING

One of the long-held views of the British bureaucracy is its vaunted political neutrality — no matter which party or individual assumes office, the civil service will carry out its functions and specifically assigned tasks. A good example of this nonpartisan outlook occurs during an election campaign: the bureaucracy prepares, based on the parties' platforms, a Throne Speech for each party. As former Prime Minister Harold Wilson (1977: 60) put it: the "Civil Service is extremely agile and politically, almost cynically, dispassionate in reading the electoral portants."

The supposed neutrality of the civil service is surely tested when a switch occurs between Labour and Conservative governments. Because British parties are ideological, class-based, with specific party manifestos, a change in party can lead to a major reorientation of government policy. Few would mistake Margaret Thatcher's policies (the Mrs. T. of British politics) with those of her predecessor James ("Sunny Jim") Callaghan. Historically, the gaining of power by the Labour party after the Second World War and the rather enthusiastic implementation of its policy of nationalizing certain key industries by the civil service is often cited as a demonstration of Whitehall's nonpolitical stance to new governments. Moreover, when an opposition party gains power, few top-level bureaucrats lose their jobs — certainly far fewer on a percentage basis than in Canada and the United States.

Recruitment to the civil service has traditionally been narrowly conceived, with most recruits — certainly for the senior levels — coming from those who have attended Oxford or Cambridge. However, in terms of more general population characteristics, this has meant that the civil service was almost a distinct caste in British society. Reforms of the last two decades have opened up the recruitment basis for the civil service, thereby producing a more representative bureaucracy in Britain.

In addition to factors of expertise, education, and political neutrality, the civil service plays a significant policy-making role in the political process because of the structure of the political system. The parliamentary system, with its fusion of powers between the executive and legislature, has enhanced the power of not only the political executive, but of its handmaiden, the civil service, as well. Moreover, the unitary nature of the institutional structure means that when something is decided as policy in Whitehall, it becomes policy without the need to negotiate compromises with other levels of government as in Canada and the United States. While political leaders may come and go, while parties may change course or direction over the specifics of the political agenda, the bureaucracy remains in place, exercising considerable influence in the political process.

> The total effect is like that of a ship with its existing course and momentum and a crew with established practices which can easily tire out a new or unconventional officer at the helm (Mackintosh, 1982: 89).

Policy-Making in the American Presidential System

Unlike the parliamentary systems of Canada and Britain, wherein government and, by implica-

tion, the bureaucracy have been a legitimate part of the political landscape, the American presidential system has been inimical, if not down-right hostile, to the growth of the public service. From the days of the American Revolution, which included the tarring and feathering of tax collectors, to the presidential campaigns of both Jimmy Carter (1976) and Ronald Reagan (1980, 1984), a successful political strategy has often been based on anti-government, anti-bureaucracy, and anti-Washington themes. This American antipathy to government and bureaucracy is a reflection of both political structure and political culture. In turn, the decision-making process is heavily influenced by the nature of the political institutions and the political values of the American polity.

THE IMPACT OF POLITICAL CULTURE

The view that "that government which governs least, governs best" has meant a more limited role for the bureaucracy in the United States than in other comparable countries. Government functions and services have been slower to expand than in Canada and Britain. A good example of this restricted use of government in the United States would be the lack of a publicly funded health care system for the average person. Private enterprise, not government, is seen as the proper institution to provide needed social and economic services. Government and the bureaucracy are the last resort, usually after the private sector has either failed or refused to respond to public wants. As a result, the percentage of GNP spent by American governments is still lower than in other liberal democracies.

The emphasis in the American value system on individualism and self-reliance has also contributed to suspicion of the bureaucracy. Having outsiders — particularly government personnel — tell someone what to do is a sure way to create political antagonism, whether it concerns taxes, busing, or economic planning. For example, revenue sharing, whereby the federal government turns money back to the states and localities to use as they see fit, is a reflection, at least in part, of the American notion of self-reliance and the importance of local government.

The ideal of "government by the people" has also affected the structure of the American bureaucracy, perhaps best reflected in the concept of representative bureaucracy (Krislov, 1974). Unlike in many other countries such as Britain, where the bureaucracy has been rather explicitly class-based, the American public service has more often faced the problem of not being able to recruit the needed and talented individuals to make the system effective. In recent decades the representation of minority groups, especially blacks, has been a point of contention in American politics. With the growth of government services and the important role of the bureaucracy in policy-making, the representative nature of the public service has become an important focal point of the political agenda.

THE IMPACT OF POLITICAL STRUCTURE

The presidential system, based on the separation of powers principle, has given the American decision-making process a number of important attributes. First, numerous actors are involved in any decision, including the president, White House staff, the legislature, interest groups, the public, and even, at times, the judiciary. Multiplicity of policy actors increases the complexity, as well as the length, of the political process.

Second, the general fragmentation and decentralization of power is reflected in the process of policy-making. Very rarely can even the president commit the government to a specific policy priority. As a general rule, the more precise the proposal, the less likely that it will be passed or accepted in its original format. Policy

> There is nothing quite like the ease with which officials of a newly elected administration take over the departments and agencies of government. Only later do the difficulties emerge. In the beginning a sense of immense power is conveyed. For a short time anything seems possible (Moynihan, quoted in Bunce, 1981: 59).

is the result of numerous compromises, trade-offs, and logrolling, such that the details of policy may change considerably as coalitions are formed and held together. Moreover, this fragmentation of power in the policy process often leads to an obvious lack of coordination, as well as to contradictory policies being adopted by the government.

Third, because parties are themselves non-ideological and pragmatic and because different parties may control different sectors of the government, they rarely serve as guides to government intent. A Republican president may or may not be supported by a Democratically-controlled legislature or an independently-minded judiciary. Moreover, at state and local levels, the use of initiatives and referendums may be a way for the attentive public to force certain policy decisions on a reluctant government. Limitations on tax rates in California (Proposition 13) in the 1970s or votes on a nuclear freeze in the early 1980s are two examples of the general public's attempting to take key policy decisions away from elected officials.

Fourth, the fragmentation of power, the nature of the parties, and the multiplicity of actors all contribute to the important role of the bureaucracy in making policy. Not only are the details of legislation often filled in by the civil service, but its continuity is an important political resource which the bureaucracy can use to advantage in the struggle over the political agenda. Moreover, the bureaucracy, because of the separation of powers principle, can often circumvent the policy direction and decisions of the president, by making alliances with the legislature and the public. (For a further discussion of this process, see the comments on iron triangles in Chapter 13). Thus, in a presidential system, the bureaucracy is often an important policy player, even able to counter the power of the president, the chief executive officer under the American Constitution. A brief look at the policy process will illustrate some of these conclusions.

THE POLICY PROCESS — AN OVERVIEW

In our discussion of the American presidency, we stressed the policy-making role of the chief executive. While the president is the chief policy-maker, he is not, by any means, the only one.

In addition to the presidency, several other components of the executive branch are worthy of mention. First, surrounding the American leader is the Executive Office of the President, which includes a retinue of personal aides, policy advisors, bodies such as the Council of Economic Advisors, and technical support staff. The president's staff has assumed a major policy-making role in the political arena in the last 50 years. In American politics, an important political resource is proximity to the president, a fact that gives advisors an often critical role in the decision-making process. Thus Donald Regan, who served as Ronald Reagan's chief of staff during his second term, was likely the second-most powerful man in Washington, D.C. Such an assessment would also be valid for most individuals who have served as the president's chief of staff in the modern era. In Canada, the growth of the staff of the PMO and PCO parallels this American development and is one reason for the argument that the Canadian polity has become "presidentialized."

Unlike the various members of the White House staff, the American cabinet has almost no influence or even an accepted group role in policy-making. The cabinet is made up of about 20 individuals, including the president, vice-president, the heads of the executive departments and others — such as the CIA Director and the UN Ambassador. Technically, under the Constitution, a president is not required to even form a cabinet or to meet with it. Since there is no collective responsibility in a system based on the separation of powers principle and because its use and functions depend on the desires of the incumbent president, the American cabinet usually meets infrequently, carries little weight as a group in the policy-making process, and performs primarily administrative tasks. Individual members of the cabinet may have considerable influence, but, if they do, it is because of their relationship with the president and not because of their cabinet title. For example, Henry Kissinger's role as probably the most significant member of Richard Nixon's administration stemmed from his personal relationship with the president, not from his cabinet portfolio as Secretary of State. A similar argument could be made about James Baker, the Secretary of State (1989) for President George Bush, who was often described as the President's best friend. In the American context, elevation to the cabinet is not usually a political promotion or a steppingstone to higher office (i.e., the presidency itself).

The public bureaucracy plays a vital role in policy-making, by serving as the support staff to the President and cabinet officers. Moreover, as in Canada, the bureaucracy may often be the initiator of new policy proposals. This potential impact of the civil service can be seen in terms of its size. By the early 1990s, the federal government employed nearly three million civilian employees, with state and local governments adding another 12 million to the total. There are 14 cabinet-level departments (e.g., Education, Defence, Agriculture) headed by a cabinet member, under which are arrayed various agencies and subunits of government. The problem of presidential and executive control of this vast bureaucracy is perhaps best exemplified by the fact that the president has the power to hire and fire only about 5 000 of the top bureaucratic positions.

At times, the legislature may play an important policy-making role, as does the judiciary. However, on most occasions the executive, led by the president, is the key policy-maker, even if he shares that responsibility with the bureaucracy. A brief look at the American budgetary process will confirm this view.

The American budgetary process

Under presidential direction, the Office of Management and Budget (OMB), which is one part of the Executive Office, sets overall spending targets for the total budget and each department. Then each department develops its own specific budget and submits it to the OMB for approval. Once the executive has reconciled existing demands with general spending targets, the president's budget is submitted to Congress for approval. However, by the time the House and Senate have considered the budget, it may be in a very different shape from its initial outline. Once the budget has received legislative and presidential approval, the OMB is responsible for seeing that the money is spent as it has been authorized.

Unfortunately, what appears at first glance to be a neat, orderly process turns out on closer inspection to be messy, haphazard, and inefficient. In fact, in the American system a series of budgets may actually be considered. For example, the budget proposed by President Reagan in February 1985 was met by overwhelming apathy from the American Congress. Then the Republicans in the Senate wrote their own budget, with the Democrats in the House doing the same. However, since any measure must be identical in content from both the House and the Senate, a further compromise version was finally produced. This conflict between the President, House, and Senate in

> The victories and defeats, the compromises and the bargains, the realms of agreement and the spheres of conflict in regard to the role of national government in our society all appear in the budget. In the most integral sense the budget lies at the heart of the political process (Wildavsky, 1984: 5).

1985 over the new budget demonstrated that "the classic sign of political dissensus is inability to agree on the budget" (Wildavsky, 1984: 252).

The budgetary process, as well as the general policy process in the American system, clearly conform more to the organizational-politics model than to the rational-actor model. In fact, the House, Senate, and presidential battles of recent years have made rationality less of an element of decision-making in the American political arena.

Comparing Bureaucracies

All modern governments rely on an extensive bureaucracy in the initiation, development, and implementation of public policy. What differs from one polity to the next are matters of composition, control, and neutrality of the public service. Moreover, no current political system has been able to successfully divorce politics from administration, for the two are inextricably intertwined. Thus, a comparative analysis of bureaucracies reveals an important actor in the political process.

While historically public services have often been narrowly based on particular ethnic or class interests, the general pattern in liberal democracies has been to move towards more representative bureaucracies. Political issues such as bilingualism in Canada and ethnic/racial representation in government in Britain and the United States have centred on the question of

> *A Burmese Proverb about Bureaucracy:*
> Three major calamities: fire, flood and officials (quoted in Wilson, 1981: 345).
>
> *Parkinson's Law and the Bureaucracy:* Work expands so as to fill the time available for its completion . . . . The fact is that the number of the officials and the quantity of the work are not related to each other at all (Parkinson, 1957: 2, 4).

> The metaphorical ship of state has one tiller but two pairs of hands that can give it direction, one belonging to party politicians and the other to higher civil servants (Rose, 1987: 408).

the composition of the bureaucracy. The assumption of an ideal of representative bureaucracy is that such a public service will produce a better public policy than a civil service narrowly-based on class or ethnicity.

A second general trend for bureaucracies has been a shift in recruitment patterns from those based on patronage to those based on merit, usually meaning that positions are filled on the basis of competitive examinations. Most positions in the civil service in Canada, Great Britain, and the United States are now based on merit, with the political executive able to fill only a small percentage of positions on party and political considerations. While this trend has clearly reduced some of the abuses of corruption and nepotism, it has also meant that the government of the day — especially a new one — may be faced with a hostile or uncooperative public service about which it can do little.

Questions of composition and control lead inevitably to concerns of impartiality: Does the public service favour one party over another? Does the public service get itself involved in election campaigns? In theory, the bureaucracy should impartially serve any government. Whether that practice happens in fact remains open to various interpretations.

In explaining different bureaucratic patterns, two key factors seem preeminent: namely, attributes of political structure and political culture. Particularly crucial in comparing the public services in Canada, Britain and the United States

is the institutional structure of presidential and parliamentary systems. Moreover, political values help to explain the functions of the bureaucracy and the way in which the public expects those functions to be carried out. However, regardless of the type of system or of the political culture, one pattern seems dominant, namely, the importance of the bureaucracy in the making of public policy.

Summary

1. The public service or bureaucracy plays a key role in the initiation, development, and implementation of public policy. A bureaucracy is a hierarchically-organized institution based on written rules and staffed by officials paid from public funds. In analyzing bureaucracies from a comparative perspective, three basic problems must be looked at: first, how is the bureaucracy structured; second, how is the public service controlled and by whom; and third, is the public service neutral or nonpartisan?

2. Policy-making and the role of the bureaucracy in that process can be investigated by using two models: the rational-actor model and the organizational-politics model. The rational-actor model focuses on the maximization of the means-ends relationship, while the organizational-politics model stresses the concept of satisficing. The organizational-politics model emphasizes the importance of parochial priorities and standard operating procedures in analyzing the decision-making process.

3. In Canada, the political executive, aided and abetted by the bureaucracy, dominates the policy process. Royal commissions and related bodies may be used to avoid policy rather than to create it. Generally, public policy is little affected by ideology. Instead, policy is incremental in nature and administered by generalists. While recent reforms have sought to move Canada towards a rational-actor model of decision-making, few observers would conclude that the trend has been overwhelmingly successful.

4. In Britain, the bureaucracy, or Whitehall, given the unitary and parliamentary political structure, has always been a preeminent feature of modern government. In conjunction with the political executive, Whitehall is a crucial participant in the policy process. Professional civil servants with a generalist education dominate the bureaucracy, although efforts have been made to make the public service more representative in recent years.

5. The American bureaucracy is the least professionally-trained and most partisan-based among our three countries of comparison. A political structure based on the separation of powers principle encourages bureaucratic power. At the same time, elements of the political culture have expressed an anti-bureaucratic theme among American political values. Although the president dominates the policy process, numerous actors are involved in setting the political agenda.

6. In liberal democracies, the public service has expanded its size and functions, has become increasingly selected on the basis of merit, and has evolved, usually grudgingly, towards a more representative composition.

Recommended Readings

Bureaucracy and Policy-making: General and Comparative

ABERBACH, JOEL D., ROBERT D. PUTNAM, and BRET A. ROCKMAN (1981) *Bureaucrats and Politicians in Western Democracies*. Cambridge, Mass.: Harvard University Press.

BARKER, ERNEST (1944) *The Development of Public Services in Western Europe: 1660–1930*. Oxford: Oxford University Press.

CROZIER, MICHEL (1964) *The Bureaucratic Phenomenon*. Chicago: University of Chicago Press.

DJILAS, MILOVAN (1957) *The New Class: An Analysis of the Communist System*. New York: Praeger.

DOGAN, MATTEI (1975) *The Mandarins of Western Europe: The Political Role of Top Civil Servants*. New York: John Wiley and Sons.

GERTH, H.H. and C. WRIGHT MILLS, eds. (1958) *From Max Weber: Essays in Sociology*. New York: Oxford University Press.

GOODSELL, CHARLES T. (1983) *The Case for Bureaucracy*. Chatham, N.J.: Chatham House Publishers.

GRUBER, JUDITH E. (1987) *Controlling Bureaucracies: Dilemmas in Democratic Governance*. Berkeley: University of California Press.

KEMP, D.A. (1986) "The Recent Evolution of Central Policy Control Mechanisms in Parliamentary Systems," *International Political Science Review* (January), Volume 7, Number 1, pp. 56–66.

PARKINSON, C. NORTHCOTE (1957) *Parkinson's Law*. Boston: Houghton Mifflin.

PETERS, B. GUY (1978) *The Politics of Bureaucracy: A Comparative Perspective*. New York: Longmans.

PRESTHUS, ROBERT (1962) *The Organizational Society: An Analysis and a Theory*. New York: Vintage Books.

_____ (1974) *Elites in the Policy Process*. London: Cambridge University Press.

SARANGI, PRAKASH (1986) "Determinants of Policy Change: A Cross-National Analysis," *European Journal of Political Research*, Volume 14, Numbers 1–2, pp. 23–44.

SULIEMAN, EZRA N., ed. (1984) *Bureaucrats and Policy Making*. New York: Holmes and Meir.

The Canadian Bureaucracy

ATKINSON, MICHAEL M. and WILLIAM D. COLEMAN (1985) "Bureaucrats and Politicians in Canada: An Examination of the Political Administration Model," *Comparative Political Studies* (April), Volume 18, Number 1, pp. 37–57.

BASHEVKIN, SYLVIA (1988) "Does Public Opinion Matter? The Adoption of Federal Royal Commission and Task Force Recommendations on the National Question, 1951–1987," *Canadian Public Administration* (Fall), Volume 31, Number 1, pp. 390–407.

BEATTIE, CHRISTOPHER (1975) *Minority Men in a Majority Setting: Middle-Level Francophones in the Canadian Public Service*. Toronto: McClelland and Stewart, Carleton Library.

D'AQUINO, THOMAS (1984) "The Public Service of Canada: The Case for Political Neutrality," *Canadian Public Administration* (Spring), Volume 27, Number 1, pp. 14–23.

HODGETTS, J.E. (1973) *The Canadian Public Service: A Physiology of Government, 1867–1970*. Toronto: University of Toronto Press.

JOHNSON, ANDREW F. and JEAN DAIGNEAULT (1988) "Liberal 'chefs de cabinets ministeriels' in Quebec: Keeping Politics in Policy-making," *Canadian Public Administration* (Winter), Volume 31, Number 4, pp. 501–516.

JOHNSTON, RICHARD (1986) *Public Opinion and Public Policy in Canada: Questions of Confidence*. Toronto: University of Toronto Press.

KERNAGHAN, KENNETH (1979) "Power, Parliament and Public Servants in Canada: Ministerial Responsibilities Reexamined," *Canadian Public Policy* (Summer), Volume 5, Number 3, pp. 383–396.

MALLORY, J.R. (1986) "Review Article: The Macdonald Commission," *Canadian Journal of Political Science* (September), Volume 19, Number 3, pp. 597–613.

MANZER, RONALD (1985) *Public Policies and Political Development in Canada*. Toronto: University of Toronto Press.

MCCAFFREY, JERRY (1984) "Canada's Envelope Budgeting System," *The American Review of Canadian Studies* (Spring), Volume 14, Number 1, pp. 45–62.

MICHELMANN, HANS J. and JEFFREY S. STEEVES (1985) "The 1982 Transition in Power in Saskatchewan: the Progressive Conservatives and the Public Service," *Canadian Public Administration* (Spring), Volume 28, Number 1, pp. 1–23.

MUNRO, GARY (1987) "Changing the Crow's Nest Freight Rate," *Journal of Canadian Studies* (Winter), Volume 22, Number 4, pp. 93–114.

OSBALDESTON, GORDON F. (1989) *Keeping Deputy Ministers Accountable*. Scarborough, Ontario: McGraw-Hill Ryerson.

PLUMPTRE, TIMOTHY (1987) "New Perspectives on the Role of the Deputy Minister," *Canadian Public Administration* (Fall), Volume 30, Number 3, pp. 376–398.

VEILLEUX, GERARD and DONALD J. SAVOIE (1988) "Kafka's Castle: The Treasury Board of Canada Revisited," *Canadian Public Administration* (Winter), Volume 31, Number 4, pp. 517–538.

WILSON, V. SEYMOUR (1981) *Canadian Public Policy and Administration: Theory and Environment*. Toronto: McGraw-Hill Ryerson.

The British Bureaucracy

BENN, TONY (1982) *Arguments for Democracy*. Middlesex, England: Penguin Books, see especially pp. 44–67, Chapter 3, "The Case for a Constitutional Civil Service."

CHRISTOPH, JAMES B. (1984) "Rubbing Up or Running Down? Dilemmas of Civil Service Reform in Britain," pp. 48–68 in Donley T. Studlar and Jerold L. Waltman, eds. *Dilemmas of Change in British Politics*. London: Macmillan Press.

CROSSMAN, RICHARD H.S. (1972) *The Myths of Cabinet Government*. Cambridge, Mass.: Harvard University Press.

FRY, GEOFFREY K. (1984) "The Attack on the Civil Service and the Response of the Insiders," *Parliamentary Affairs* (Autumn), Volume 37, Number 4, pp. 353–363.

_____ (1985) *The Changing Civil Service*. London: Allen and Unwin.

_____ (1986) "The British Career Civil Service under Challenge," *Political Studies* (December), Volume 34, Number 4, pp. 533–555.

JAMES, SIMEON (1986) "The Central Policy Review Staff, 1970–1983," *Political Studies* (September), Volume 34, Number 3, pp. 423–440.

JONES, G.W. (1989) "A Revolution in Whitehall? Changes in British Central Government since 1979," *West European Politics* (July), Volume 12, Number 3, pp. 238–261.

JORDAN, A.G. and J.J. RICHARDSON (1987) *British Politics and the Policy Process: An Arena Approach*. London: Allen and Unwin.

KELLNER, PETER and LORD CROWTHER-HUNT (1980) *The Civil Servants: An Inquiry into Britain's Ruling Class*. London: Raven Books.

LYNN, JONATHAN and ANTHONY JAY (1984) *The Complete Yes Minister*. London: BBC Books.

PONTING, C. (1986) *Whitehall: Tragedy and Farce*. London: Hamish Hamilton.

RIDLEY, F.F. (1983) "The British Civil Service and Politics: Principles in Question and Traditions in Flux," *Parliamentary Affairs* (Winter), Volume 36, Number 1, pp. 28–48.

SUMMERTON, NEIL (1980) "A Mandarin's Duty," *Parliamentary Affairs* (Autumn), Volume 33, Number 4, pp. 400–421.

The American Bureaucracy

ARNOLD, R. DOUGLAS (1979) *Congress and the Bureaucracy: A Theory of Influence*. New Haven: Yale University Press.

BARDACH, EUGENE (1977) *The Implementation Game: What Happens After a Bill Becomes a Law*. Cambridge, Mass.: MIT Press.

CAMPBELL, COLIN (1986) *Managing the Presidency: Carter, Reagan, and the Search for Executive Harmony*. Pittsburgh: University of Pittsburgh Press.

HECLO, HUGH (1977) *A Government of Strangers*. Washington, D.C.: Brookings Institute.

KRISLOV, SAMUEL (1974) *Representative Bureaucracy*. Englewood Cliffs, N.J.: Prentice-Hall.

NAKUMURA, ROBERT T. and FRANK SMALLWOOD (1980) *The Politics of Policy Implementation*. New York: St. Martin's Press.

PRESSMAN, JEFFREY and AARON WILDAVSKY (1973) *Implementation*. Berkeley: University of California Press.

RIGGS, FRED W. (1988) "Bureaucratic Politics in the U.S.: Benchmarks for Comparison," *Governance* (October), Volume 1, Number 4, pp. 343–379.

ROURKE, FRANCIS E., ed. (1978) *Bureaucratic Power in National Politics*. Boston: Little, Brown, 3rd ed.

—— (1987) "Bureaucracy in the American Constitutional Order," *Political Science Quarterly* (Summer), Volume 102, Number 2, pp. 217–232.

SCHWARTZ, JOHN E. (1988) *America's Hidden Success: A Reassessment of Public Policy from Kennedy to Reagan*. New York: W.W. Norton and Company, rev. ed.

SHUMAN, HOWARD (1984) *Politics and the Budget*. Englewood Cliffs, N.J.: Prentice-Hall.

WILDAVSKY, AARON (1979) *Speaking Truth to Power: The Art and Craft of Policy Analysis*. Boston: Little, Brown.

—— (1988) *The New Politics of the Budgetary Process*. Glenview, Illinois: Scott, Foresman.

6 The Legislative Branch of Government: Representation and Legitimation

Legislative assemblies have long been experiencing difficult days. Where totalitarian movements have been successful in gaining power, the independence and autonomy of legislatures have been diminished or lost altogether. Elsewhere, under democratic conditions, legislatures have declined in popular esteem, at times to the point of disrepute (Keefe and Ogul, 1985: 3).

In most nations, legislators do not legislate. Executives legislate. True, many legislators have a formal role in lawmaking and many continue to debate, review, delay, and legitimize policies. But when it comes to initiating and enacting policies that regulate public behavior and allocate scarce resources, few legislators have much independent authority (Obler, 1981: 127).

The history of parliamentary reform is littered with good intentions left unfulfilled, democratic arguments conceded on undemocratic grounds, and undemocratic practices justified by recourse to democratic principles (Judge, 1983: 9).

TO THE ORDINARY CITIZEN, the legislative branch of government is mysterious and confusing, a little-understood institution, a jumble of rules and procedures with passing relevance to one's daily concerns. For example, a Gallup poll in August 1983 found that two-thirds of the Canadian public had little or no interest in Parliament (Landes, 1985). Outside of the pageantry of an opening of Parliament, a particularly rancorous Question Period, or the controversy usually accompanying an increase in the members' salaries, few citizens pay much attention to their legislators. As a member of the French National Assembly put it, one reason for the public's indifference, perhaps, is that the legislature is a "theatre of illusions" (Servan-Schreiber, quoted in Smith, 1980: 152).

The most basic of these illusions, which we are taught from childhood, is that the legislature is sovereign, that it makes the laws. Historically, however, legislative dominance has been restricted to the last decades of the 19th and the early decades of the 20th century: the golden age of legislatures was one of limited duration. Declining decision-making power of legislative institutions has led some observers to question their continuing relevance. The decline of the lawmaking function, however, has not meant the imminent demise of the legislative branch of government: "while parliament may never have been the sovereign, basic entity described by theoreticians, while it is no longer the majestic law-giver of liberal-democracy, it is still irreplaceable and important" (Duverger, 1974: 150). The continuing legislative functions of legitimating executive actions and representing the public in the governing process remain important duties. While the notion of parliamentary sovereignty may indeed be a myth, so also is the view of legislative nonimportance.

The Development of Legislatures

The significance of legislatures is reflected in the fact that they were the first political institutions designed to give the public a role in the political process, even though initially that public was only a tiny fragment of the total population. Legislatures were developed as representative institutions in the struggle with the king. As the mass public became incorporated into the body politic, the legislature became the symbol of liberal-democracy. Reflective, perhaps, of the public's power through the legislature is the prominence given to it in the American Constitution: Article One deals with the legislature and is twice as long as Article Two, which delineates executive power and structure.

The public's role in the political process through the legislature, however, is once removed: representative government is an example of **indirect democracy**. The people do not rule directly on a day-to-day basis; instead, the people select representatives to govern. In an attempt to guarantee the public's role through the legislature, democratic systems constitutionally require a yearly meeting of the legislature. The origin of legislative institutions suggests, therefore, two key questions for evaluating their current status: first, what is the nature of the legislative-executive relationship and second, what is their role as representative agencies in the political process?

PARLIAMENTARY SOVEREIGNTY

The importance of the legislature as the public's representative is embodied in the principle of **parliamentary supremacy or parliamentary sovereignty,** *which asserts the fundamental right of the legislature to make any law whatsoever.* As British political leader Disraeli once phrased it, "we are governed not by logic but by Parliament." Those who defy parliamentary authority discover their mistake in short order: for example, Jean-Claude Parrot, head of the Canadian Union of Postal Workers, spent time in jail for his failure to heed Parliament's back-to-work legislation to end a postal strike

> *Walter Bagehot (1867) on Parliament:* A parliament is nothing less than a big meeting of more or less idle people.
>
> There is a myth of a golden age of legislatures when wisdom and oratory and gentlemanly behaviour and public spirit all seemed somehow to flourish and to flourish together (Wheare, 1963: 232).
>
> The institution of Parliament is the heart of our system of parliamentary democracy. Increasingly, it is coming under fire for its seeming ineffectiveness and lack of relevance (D'Acquino et al., 1983: ix).
>
> The first thing I'd do would be to pass less laws (Alberta Conservative leadership candidate Donald Getty, October 9, 1985).

in the late 1970s. Moreover, parliamentary sovereignty is the basis for what is known as **retroactive legislation**, that is, legislation which is passed after-the-fact to change the previously existing law. For example, the provincial government in Newfoundland passed an amendment to its Labor Standards Act in 1984 regarding the time required for giving workers notice of layoff and made the amendment retroactive to 1978, thereby saving employers $27 million dollars in potential claims.

As developed in Britain, parliamentary supremacy includes four essential features: "There is no higher legislative authority; no court can declare Acts of Parliament to be invalid; there is no limit to Parliament's sphere of legislation; and no Parliament can legally bind its successor, or be bound by its predecessor" (Punnett, 1980: 173). In the Canadian context, however, parliamentary sovereignty is circumscribed by the political principles of federalism and judicial review.

PARLIAMENTARY PRIVILEGE

An important mechanism for maintaining the supremacy of Parliament is **parliamentary privilege**, *a series of rights given to the legislature and to nobody else, in order to ensure that Parliament and its members are collectively and individually free of any outside control.* Historically, parliamentary privilege was an outgrowth of the early battles between king and Parliament for

control of the political system, with the privileges preventing the detention or arrest of any member during a legislative session. The right of members to carry on the public's business was not to be interfered with. For example, in November 1985 three MPs (Sheila Copps, Ian Deans and Lorne Nystrom) were served with subpoenas in relation to a trial in Hamilton, Ontario. However, because of parliamentary privilege, they did not have to respond while the House of Commons was sitting. In addition, parliamentary privilege gives the legislature the power to determine its own procedure. For example, the use of legislative committees, rather than the full legislature, to consider bills is a decision for the legislature alone to take.

Parliamentary privilege also enables the legislature to discipline its own members and to determine its own membership. A member may be expelled from a day's sitting or for longer periods of time, with the legislature having the ultimate right to prevent a duly elected candidate from taking his or her place (e.g., a seat may be declared vacant, with a new election called). For instance, historically two important examples come to mind: both Louis Riel and Fred Rose (the only Communist ever elected to the Canadian House of Commons) were prevented from sitting in Parliament. More recently, Colin Thatcher, after his conviction for the first degree murder of his wife, was expelled from the Saskatchewan Legislature in November 1984.

A rather extreme example of the power of

a legislature to discipline its own members occurred in British Columbia in 1983. The ideological division and extreme animosity between the Social Credit government of Bill Bennett and the NDP opposition led by former Premier Dave Barrett reached its height in October as the government sought to force its economic restraint package through the provincial legislature. Charges of "lying" (definitely unparliamentary language) were bandied back-and-forth between the government and opposition. When the Speaker refused to accept a motion of adjournment, opposition Leader Dave Barrett challenged his decision and refused to withdraw his challenge. After 45 minutes, the Speaker ordered Barrett expelled and the sergeant-at-arms literally dumped him out of his chair and dragged him by his feet down the centre-aisle and out of the chamber. Thus, Dave Barrett became the only member of the British Columbia Legislature ever to be physically removed from the House. As a result, the Speaker then banned Barrett from the rest of the legislative session.

In addition to handling its own affairs, parliamentary privilege guarantees the right of free speech to members carrying out the public's business within Parliament itself. For example, an individual member cannot be sued for libel for remarks made in the legislature; however, if those same statements are repeated outside the legislature, libel suits are a possibility. While such rights can be abused, free speech is considered essential for the conduct of the public's business.

A final, and often overlooked, example of parliamentary privilege is the right of the legislature to determine its own worth, that is, to set its own salary. For example, in August 1989, the Alberta provincial legislature gave themselves a 30 percent pay raise, doubling their salary levels from only 8 years earlier. There is no legal limit on what the legislators could decide to pay themselves, although there are some real political constraints, in particular, the fear of electoral reprisal. In February of 1989, for example, the United States House of Representatives voted against a 51 percent pay raise because of public outrage over the proposed salary hike. If any outside body determined salary levels, then control of the legislature would be possible, since the legislators might be bribed by extravagant salaries or forced into submission by reducing their pay to minimal levels. In 1990 the basic salary for MPs was $62 100, plus a tax-free expense allowance of $20 600, bringing the total to $82 700 a year.

LEGISLATIVE STRUCTURE

Although legislatures developed as a means of public representation in the political process, the public's influence was not only indirect but further restrained by the original design of legislative institutions. The first legislatures were **bicameral** rather than **unicameral** in structure. A bicameral legislature is composed of two parts, a lower house (e.g., the House of Commons in Canada and Britain, the House of Representatives in the United States) and an upper house (e.g., the Senate in Canada, the House of Lords in Britain and the Senate in the United States). The lower houses are designed to be the closest to the people—hence they are based on popular election with relatively frequent elections (two years in the United States, with a maximum of five years in Canada and Britain). The upper houses are designed to check the power of popular passion as contained in the lower house by allowing for a "sober, second thought" on all legislation.

In order to provide the political basis for resisting the lower house, the upper legislative chambers were insulated from mass pressure by having their members appointed for long terms (e.g., Canada) or by using an indirect method of selection (e.g., senators in the United States were initially chosen by the state legislatures). By contrast, in a unicameral system, where there is only one legislative chamber, there is no mechanism within the legislature itself for checking the decision it has taken. The national legislatures in Canada, Britain, and the United States are bicameral; all of the American state legislatures are bicameral except for Nebraska; and all of the Canadian provincial legislatures are now unicameral in structure.

A federal political structure and a bicameral national legislature work together in an interesting way: the upper house of the national legislature is used to give representation to the constituent units of the federal system. For example, Senate representation is based on the provinces in Canada and on the states in the American system. The diversity that encourages the adoption of federalism also promotes use of the upper legislative chamber as a means of guaranteeing representation in the national government of various regional, religious, cultural, and ethnic groups. Thus, bicameral legislative structures function both as a safeguard against popular passion and as a tool for representing various interests within the national government.

Exercising Legislative Power: The Role of the Canadian House of Commons

By the time the Canadian Confederation was established in 1867, the role of the legislature had been well developed, with the basic principles of parliamentary supremacy and parliamentary privilege accepted as fundamental. However, in contrast to the British pattern, the adoption of federalism and the resulting use of the courts to settle jurisdictional disputes between the two levels of government limited the supremacy of the Canadian Parliament. The federal and provincial legislatures were

> It was like looking at Westminster through the wrong end of the telescope. The Governor delivered the Speech from the Throne. The military band outside struck up God Save The Queen with great vigour; the people shouted; the Ins rubbed their hands; the Outs shook their heads; the Government party said there never was such a good speech; the Opposition declared there never was such a bad one; and in short everything went on and promised to go on just as it does at home (Charles Dickens on observing the opening of the Nova Scotia Legislature in 1842).

supreme, but only within their own areas of competence. From the beginning, Canadian federalism has made parliamentary sovereignty something of an illusion.

Likewise, the notion of the legislature making the laws has been a mirage. While in the early years of Confederation governments had their legislation rejected in Parliament (Forsey, 1974: 123–138), defeating a piece of legislation is reactive, and not the same thing as writing legislation. Moreover, it is often forgotten that the so-called golden age of legislatures occurred at a time of extremely limited government: governments passed little legislation in few substantive areas in the late 19th century.

The expansion of government in the 20th century is the fundamental reason why executives have become the key actors in the political process. Power between institutions, as with individuals, is relative: executives and legislatures have both gained power in the 20th century, but executives have done so at a much faster rate. Canadian legislatures currently deal with more topics in a greater number of areas in more detail than ever before; in that sense legislators in the modern era have little in common with their 19th century counterparts. Moreover, although the national legislature in Canada is bicameral, the two parts have never

> The Canadian Parliament is a good source of examples for anyone who wants to demonstrate the decline of parliaments (Kornberg and Mishler, 1976: x).

been equal. The House of Commons has always been preeminent and has become more so in recent decades: rarely does the Canadian Senate awake from its institutional slumber to take an active, if fleeting, role in the political process.

STRUCTURE OF THE HOUSE OF COMMONS

The institutional and physical structure of the House of Commons influences the way it performs its various political functions. After the 1981 census the size of the House of Commons was raised to 295 seats from its previous number of 282, with further increases projected after each decennial census. Seats are allocated among the geographical units (provinces) primarily on the basis of population: the largest province, Ontario, has 99 seats, while the smallest province, Prince Edward Island, has four.

Other criteria (Sections 51 and 51A of the 1867 Constitution Act, as amended) than population are also included in the seat allocation process. For example, no province can have fewer seats in the House than members in the Senate, which means that the small provinces are over-represented in the Commons. In order to protect the French-Canadian minority, Quebec is assigned a given number of seats and the other provincial seat allocations are then computed from that starting point. Thus, the membership structure of the House is territorially-based around the provincial units, with population the main basis in assigning provincial seat totals.

The physical structure of the Commons is divided between government and opposition

members, with the speaker of the House presiding over both. The government sits on the speaker's right and the opposition on his or her left, a seating arrangement with perhaps Biblical connotations. However, in Prince Edward Island the seating arrangement is reversed, due apparently to the historical anomaly that the heater in the legislature was so positioned. Perhaps this fact is indicative of the opposition's legislative power.

Each member is assigned a particular seat, with government and opposition members facing each other across the centre aisle, symbolic of the antagonistic relationship between them. The prime minister and cabinet occupy the first two rows centre on the government side, with the official opposition leader and his or her shadow cabinet facing them. Those MPs not in the cabinet or shadow cabinet fill in the remaining rows on each side of the aisle; hence, they are called backbenchers. If more than two parties are in opposition, the minor parties sit on the opposition benches farthest removed from the speaker, with any independents on the far side of them.

THE SPEAKER OF THE HOUSE

The most important position in the House of Commons is that of the speaker. The speaker was, until 1986, nominated by the prime minister but elected by the House. As the presiding officer it is the speaker's job to ensure the smooth and fair functioning of the lower House. In so doing, he or she recognizes those members who wish to participate in the debate, attempts to be impartial in the business of the House, and rules on disputed questions of procedure.

Decisions of the speaker should be nonpartisan and fair to all participants: if they are not seen as impartial, then the ability of the legislature to carry out its political tasks becomes seriously impaired. For example, although he

Source: Reprinted from *The Leader-Post* (Regina, Saskatchewan). By permission of the paper and Brian Gable.

initially received good reviews of his work after his appointment in 1984, by early 1986 Speaker John Bosley was being widely criticized for his "partisan" rulings. Opposition members openly challenged his authority, leading one observer to describe Speaker Bosley's position as follows: "Few Speakers have been so abused in recent years—they laugh at him and repeatedly ignore his plaintive calls to order. Sometimes they tell him in the plainest language what they think of his decisions" (Cleroux, 1986: A1).

The speaker is expected to be bilingual; by tradition, the choice of speaker alternates between members with English or French as their mother tongue. A deputy speaker, whose primary task is to replace the speaker when the speaker is unable to carry out the job, is selected as well. The deputy speaker needs to be bilingual, although his or her mother tongue is usually opposite to that of the speaker. For example, after the 1988 election, John Fraser from British Columbia was elected as speaker,

with Marcel Danis from Quebec selected as deputy speaker.

The importance of the speaker's role can be seen in the kinds of decisions he or she is called upon to make. For example, the speaker decides who is recognized to talk, and if the speaker chooses not "to see" a member, that member is excluded from the debate. Failure to get Speaker John Bosley to recognize him led Tory MP Jack Shields to complain in 1986 that the only way to get on national television was to "moon the Speaker." The speaker likewise rules on whether a member has exceeded the time limit for discussion, whether a member's parliamentary privileges have been violated, and resolves disputes about parliamentary procedure, ranging from motions of adjournment to those of closure to acceptable amendments. In a majority government situation, the speaker must pay particular attention to ensure that the government does not trample on the rights of the opposition or of Parliament as a whole (Newman, 1973: 88).

The speaker is also faced at times with opposing the government of the day, as in the summer of 1981, when then Speaker Jeanne Sauvé ruled out of order a series of government spending estimates, forcing the government to pass each item separately before the House could adjourn. Similarly, in October of 1989, Speaker John Fraser strongly criticized Conservative government ads regarding the proposed goods and services tax (GST), because the legislation had not yet been approved by Parliament. An even more dramatic confrontation between the speaker and government occurred in the Manitoba legislature in 1984. At the height of the debate on Franco-Manitoban rights, the Conservative opposition members walked out, producing a bell-ringing incident. The frustrated NDP Premier Howard Pawley ordered the speaker, James Walding, to call a vote on the matter, even if the opposition parties did not return to participate. Speaker Walding, however, refused to do so. Interestingly, he was widely criticized by his party and faced two challengers for his party's nomination in January 1986. Despite rhetoric to the contrary, even the NDP, at times, trespasses on the speaker's supposed nonpartisanship. Although Walding won re-election in the 1986 provincial election, he was not reappointed as speaker or named to the cabinet. On March 8, 1988, NDP backbencher James Walding voted with the opposition parties and brought down the minority NDP government of Howard Pawley.

The speaker is called upon to supervise the running of the House of Commons itself, a not insignificant task, given its yearly budget in 1989 of nearly $191 million dollars. For example, in November 1980, former Auditor General J.J. MacDonnell submitted a report to then Speaker Jeanne Sauvé that indicated poor management of the Commons' budget. Indicative of that claim was the discovery in December 1979 that an exclusive restaurant for the senior staff had been opened without either the speaker's knowledge or approval. In July 1981, Speaker Sauvé ruled that the restaurant, which served full-course dinners for $2.75, be closed.

In carrying out such tasks, the speaker is expected to be nonpartisan, which, in many ways, is another illusion of the legislative system. For example, the Conservative speaker (John Turner) of the Ontario Legislature was rightly criticized for participating in a Tory party meeting in 1984 during the leadership selection process to replace Conservative Premier Bill Davis. Since the speaker was, until 1986, nominated by the prime minister, but technically elected by the Commons, the position has always been a partisan one, even though the person chosen need not be a member of the government party. Most often the speaker is a government party member who has been bypassed for the cabinet, as illustrated by the selection of John Bosley in 1984 after the Conservative election victory in September.

In an attempt to undercut the partisan basis of appointment, recent practice has been for the opposition parties to second the nomination of the speaker. Other steps were also taken in the late 1960s to make the speaker more nonpartisan: in the 1968 election, Speaker Lucien Lamoureux ran as an independent, won reelection, and was reappointed as speaker. However, the conclusion (Mallory, 1971: 248) that such events demonstrated that the office of the speaker was "in the process of evolving from a major political office to one . . . essentially above politics" has proven premature, given the developments of the 1970s and the early 1980s.

With a minority government situation in 1972, the Liberals chose Robert McCleave, Conservative MP from Halifax, as deputy speaker, supposedly with an agreement that he would be elevated to speaker when Lucien Lamoureux retired. However, after gaining a majority in the 1974 election, this deal became inoperative: Liberal MP James Jerome from Sudbury, Ontario was selected, with the Conservatives refusing to second his nomination. As a consolation prize, Robert McCleave later received a judicial appointment in his native Nova Scotia.

Even when a government party member is not picked, the speaker may still have been chosen on political grounds. For example, a common practice of both federal and provincial minority administrations has been to appoint an opposition member as a speaker, thus reducing the opposition caucus by one vote and redressing slightly the government's chance of defeat in the legislature. Although the speaker votes only in case of a tie, it would be most unlikely, based on convention, for him or her to vote against the government. For such political considerations, Joe Clark renominated James Jerome as speaker following the 1979 election, even though the Conservatives had refused to second Jerome's nomination in 1974. With the demise of the Clark government, Jerome did not run as a candidate in the 1980 election, but, interestingly enough, during the campaign he was appointed by Clark as an associate chief justice of the Federal Court of Canada. Thus, in the experience of one individual we see examples of both the partisan nature of the office of speaker of the House and of judicial appointments as well.

A classic example of picking a speaker on political grounds occurred after the 1978 New Brunswick election, which saw a narrow Conservative majority of 30 to 28 over the Liberals. Premier Hatfield nominated Liberal Robert McCready as speaker. The McCready selection created internal problems for the Liberal party caucus, since McCready had contested against leader Joe Daigle in the 1978 Liberal leadership race. In anger over his acceptance of the speakership, the Liberals expelled McCready from their party caucus.

Although a minority government may choose an opposition member as speaker, the political nature of the position is clearly evident if that minority government gains a majority position. The opposition member speaker is usually dumped in favour of a government backbencher,

as illustrated by the selection of John Turner (no relation to the then federal Liberal party leader) as speaker of the Ontario Legislature following the 1981 Conservative majority victory.

In addition to the political considerations evident in the selection process, the speaker's role is also political in another sense; that is, the speaker's rulings help to determine the influence of individual members and parties within the House, and, on occasion, in the country as a whole. Rulings on procedural disputes, on matters of privilege, on Question Period, influence individual and party standings in the eyes of the electorate, as illustrated in the famous Pipeline Debate in 1956 (Newman, 1973: 37–43). Thus, although the speaker has been selected historically on partisan grounds and even though the speaker's rulings have the potential to greatly affect individual and party influence both inside and outside of the legislature, one of the sustaining myths of parliamentary government is the speaker's impartiality.

> Myths are the grease that make the machine work, for if the MPs are allowed to call each other cheats and liars, Parliament will break down; if there is no chairman who can rule impartially over the savage debates that shake the chamber, democratic government, with its open, sometimes brutal questioning of the ruling powers, will become impossible (Stewart, 1971: 147).

While the above pattern of speaker selection remains in place at the provincial level, a rather dramatic political reform has taken place in the federal House of Commons. Following the September 5, 1986 resignation of Speaker John Bosley, which was alleged to be the result of political pressure from the prime minister's office, the new speaker-selection process was utilized for the first time. In a free vote on October 1, 1986, the House of Commons named Speaker John Fraser to replace John Bosley. The significant aspect of this reform, which took

11 hours and 11 secret ballots under the new rules, was that the House of Commons itself, and not the prime minister, determined its own presiding officer. In the 1988 election, although he ran as a Conservative candidate, John Fraser attempted to run a largely nonpartisan election campaign. On December 12, 1988, John Fraser was reelected speaker on the first ballot. Given the success of the reformed selection process at the federal level, Ontario (July 1989) became the first province to adopt it; the change became effective after the September, 1990 provincial election.

PARTY ORGANIZATION

The work of the House is facilitated by the political party organizations. Each party selects a House leader and party whips, who help to ensure an orderly flow of business. The party's House leader is usually different from the national party leader, so that the party leader is able to be absent from the Commons without disrupting the public's business. The House leader is chosen by the party leader, usually in consultation with the major figures in the party caucus. The government House leader is a cabinet level position, with the person so selected sometimes being named in recent years as president of the Privy Council.

Party whips help to "whip," at least symbolically, the party members into cohesive groups in the legislature. The job of the party whips is to make sure their caucus members know the party's stand on a given issue, know when the vote is taken, and have their members on the floor of the House to support the party's leadership. An extreme example of a party whip's job was apparent in the events leading to the Constitutional Crisis of 1968: as the division bells were kept ringing for over an hour, the Liberal whips searched the bars of Ottawa, bringing several members back to the party fold, but not enough were rounded up to prevent

> The party machine now interposes its own special will between the MP, his conscience, and his constituents. The machine warps the will of the public for its own purposes—electoral victory and the spoils of and the thirst for power (March, 1974: 136).
>
> Presently, MPs have little role except as party adherents—the more unquestionably loyal the better, if they are ambitious (Bain, 1985: 24).

defeat (Stewart, 1971: 196–198). The usual business of the party whips is more mundane, since most members are more than willing to follow the decisions of the party leadership.

The importance of the political parties in organizing the work of the legislature is probably best demonstrated in the **principle of party discipline**; that is, the parties work as cohesive groups rather than as an array of disparate (a cynic might say desperate) individuals. Party discipline is so pervasive and accepted that it is rarely challenged; most party members never vote against their party during the course of their entire political life. Those members who do openly challenge party unity may find their party careers to be of short duration. Most members accept "the whip" or party discipline because they want to, because they know that future party and governmental promotions are dependent on it. Party discipline, which has been firmly established throughout the 20th century, is the key to understanding both party control and executive dominance of the legislative branch of government.

Party discipline is strongest in the governing party, where a break in party ranks might cost the party control of office. Opposition parties are somewhat more lenient in demanding party unity, because it makes little difference in their current position. For example, when former Conservative party leader John Diefenbaker voted against his party and successor Robert

Stanfield, the party was in opposition and thus a breakdown in party discipline could be tolerated. Retribution for such behaviour when the party is in power is more severe, with the possibility of being refused the party's nomination in your own riding in the next election. For example, Halifax Conservative MP Edmund Morris, who abstained on two want-of-confidence motions against the Diefenbaker government, was denied his party's nomination in the 1963 election (March, 1974: 87).

COMMITTEE STRUCTURE

In addition to party organization in the house, the Commons is also structured into a series of small committees, where much of the intensive work of the legislative branch takes place. The use of legislative committees, however, is a recent development in Canada, with the standing committee structure blossoming in the 1965 and 1968 parliamentary reforms. The late adoption of small legislative committees is a reflection of the principle of parliamentary supremacy; Parliament as a whole was very reluctant to give up any of its functions and powers. The reforms were finally adopted in the mid-1960s as a result of the pressures, of time: Parliament was becoming so bogged down in the details of bills that little government legislation was being passed.

There are numerous kinds of legislative committees. The two most important types are the striking or selection committee and the standing committees. The function of the **striking committee** is to decide on the membership of all the other committees in the legislature. It meets in the first few days of a session and is composed of seven members, including the party whips. In practice, the striking committee accepts the committee assignments decided on by the parties themselves, rather than getting into the contentious practice of assigning individual members to specific committees. Each

party caucus, in consultation with its party and House leaders, decides which of its members will sit on which committees. The party whips then take these committee assignments to the striking committee, which approves them. Such a process avoids the possibility that the government party could use its majority to assign the least able opposition members to the most important committees, thereby undercutting the effectiveness of the opposition in the legislature.

The second and most important committee type is the **standing committee**, which gives clause-by-clause consideration to each piece of legislation between its second and third readings. It is at the standing committee stage where much of the real work of the legislature occurs, in that detailed consideration, sometimes including witnesses both for and against the legislation, is given.

The structure of the standing committees is roughly parallel to that of the executive departments, with each committee considering the legislation related to one or more departments. For example, while the executive has a Department of Veterans Affairs and a Department of National Defence, the Commons has a single standing committee called National Defence and Veterans Affairs, which oversees the legislation for both departments. Membership on each standing committee, given recent rule changes, is now set at a minimum of 10 and a maximum of 15; cabinet members are not assigned to them but a cabinet minister's parliamentary secretary may be; and the committees have the legal power to call witnesses, with testimony given under oath. Each committee selects a chairman and vice-chairman to preside over its meetings.

The composition of the standing committees, as well as of all other types, is party-based. The basic principle is that a party's strength in the full House is reflected within each committee. For example, if a party has 60 percent of the seats in the Commons, it will gain approximately 60 percent of the positions on each committee. Since the committees select their own chairman and vice-chairman, these positions are typically allocated to the governing party as well. Based on custom only, the **Public Accounts Committee**, which oversees government expenditures, is chaired by an opposition member. Not even that small token of influence has been granted the opposition in some provinces: in Nova Scotia, for example, during the 1970s, the Liberal Minister of Finance was also chairman of the Public Accounts Committee, which produced a fairly blatant conflict of interest between his executive and legislative roles.

The party-basis of the standing committees means that party discipline ensures executive-dominance of the legislative process. In a majority government situation, the standing committees will often refuse to investigate matters that might be embarrassing to their own party. For example, in Ontario in January of 1983, the Tory members refused to allow opposition committee members the right to call witnesses regarding the collapse of several trust companies. At the federal level, for example, former Prime Minister Pierre Trudeau always refused to allow his top aides, in particular Michael Pitfield, to testify before parliamentary committees. Only once in his career, on November 4, 1980, did Trudeau condescendingly appear before a Commons' committee.

In a majority situation, the standing committees, given this party base, are not in a position to change government legislation against the wishes of the government. Even if they do revise a bill, such alterations can be reversed when the bill reappears at third reading before the full House. If a committee does object to a government bill, recalcitrant government committee members can always be removed. In 1976, Liberal MP Simma Holt complained that she had been prevented from attending a meeting of the Broadcasting Committee, which was considering legislation on ending tax conces-

sions to both *Time* and *Reader's Digest*, by then Secretary of State Hugh Faulkner, the minister responsible for the legislation (*The Globe and Mail*, February 5, 1976). Four Liberal MPs had already been removed from that committee in December 1975, so as to ensure that the government's bill would emerge in the form desired (Campbell, 1977: 127). Similarly, in April of 1989, Tory MP Alex Kindy from Alberta claimed that he had been removed from the Commons Health and Welfare Committee by Conservative Whip James Hawkes because he had failed to vote along party lines.

In a minority government, the influence of the committees is temporarily enhanced if the opposition parties can overcome their differences and work together to amend the government's legislation. For example, in 1973, the Conservative and New Democratic parties combined at the committee stage to amend the minority Liberal government's wiretap legislation. The opposition parties inserted a notice provision in the bill, which required the government to inform people that they had been under surveillance, if after 90 days no wrongdoing had been discovered. When the bill came back to the full House the government tried to have the notice amendment deleted, but was unsuccessful. However, even in a minority government situation, the opposition parties usually do not cooperate, since they are usually more opposed to each other than to the government of the day. Minority governments create the potential for increased standing committee influence in the legislative process, but they certainly do not guarantee it.

THE PASSAGE OF LEGISLATION

Having considered the institutional structure and context of the House, we can now proceed to a discussion of how legislation is passed. The rites of passage that turn a bill into a law are extremely complex: it may take a neophyte MP

> Legislation is never quite right. It arrives on the parliamentary order paper full of backroom compromises that will weaken its effectiveness and spoil its aim, but it will be passed (Callwood, 1985: 11).

several sessions before even the basic intricacies are mastered. The fundamentals, however, centre around three topics: first, the different types of bills; second, the stages of legislation; and third, legislative procedures such as closure and Question Period.

Types of bills

Any member of Parliament can introduce legislation, but the kind of legislation proposed and its chance of passage varies depending on whether it is a government bill or a private member's bill. A **government bill** is part of the ruling party's legislative program, is introduced by a minister, and backed by the full weight of the government party caucus. Government bills are given priority and are usually passed, especially under majority governments.

Private member's bills are those bills introduced by an MP that do not have government support. They are most often introduced by opposition members, but may be introduced by a government backbencher as well. Private member's bills are given little time for consideration in the Commons, have been traditionally dealt with in the order in which they were introduced (which means that many are not even debated), and are almost never passed. A rare exception appeared in the spring of 1984, when Liberal backbencher John Reid successfully managed to get his private member's bill passed, which allowed for the release of secret Second World War documents. A second exception occurred in June 1988, when NDP MP Lynn McDonald's bill to ban smoking in workplaces and public transportation was approved by the

House of Commons. The most common use of private member's bills is to influence public opinion, with the intent of changing future government policy. Reform proposals have often appeared first as a private member's bill, only to be coopted as a government bill in a later Parliament, as public support and acceptance of the idea becomes apparent.

Legislative stages

Although specific details may vary from one type of bill to the next, all legislation goes through six stages: first reading; second reading; committee stage; third reading; consideration by the other House; and royal assent. Even this six-stage process greatly simplifies the actual passage of a bill by Parliament. In most cases, first reading, third reading, and royal assent have become mere formalities; the crucial steps are the second reading and committee stages.

At first reading, the bill is introduced into the legislature by indicating the title of the bill and perhaps giving a very brief statement about the bill's subject matter. The legislation at this point is not open to amendment or debate, although in extremely rare cases it may be rejected. For example, in an almost unprecedented move, the Conservatives in the Ontario legislature denied a member the right to introduce a bill at first reading in May 1981.

The initial debate on a bill takes place at second reading, which is known as "approval in principle." The bill cannot be amended, but must be accepted or rejected in total. Second reading usually involves the major debate on a bill, for once it has been "approved in principle" it becomes difficult, although not impossible, to defeat it at a later stage.

In contrast to steps one and two, the committee stage does not usually involve the full House, but only a part of it. In most instances, a bill is sent to one of the standing committees for detailed, clause-by-clause review. It is at this step that the bill can be amended for the first time, in addition to being debated. Witnesses, both pro and con, may be called to testify, and the process may take a number of weeks.

Once the committee is finished with a bill, it is sent back to the full House for third reading. It is possible for the committee to have made changes in the legislation, but the full House has the right to accept or reject such revisions when it receives the bill back from the Committee. Having given approval in principle to a bill at second reading, plus a detailed look at its contents during the committee stage, means there is little work to be accomplished at third reading. Usually, by this time, it is a foregone conclusion that the bill will pass, although the opposition parties may debate a controversial bill at some length at third reading. Government defeats, however, can happen at this stage, as with the rejection of a tax bill that provoked the Constitutional Crisis of 1968.

Once the bill is passed by one of the Houses of the legislature, the same basic steps are repeated by the other House in Canada's bicameral legislature. Although either House may initially consider any bill — except for money bills, which have to originate in the Commons — usual practice is for government legislation to be presented first to the Commons and then to the Senate. Although the Senate may traditionally make minor changes in a piece of legislation, for all intents and purposes its approval has become perfunctory. However, in a bicameral legislature, the bill as passed by both Houses must be identical, so that if the Senate amends legislation coming from the Commons, the revisions must be sent back to the lower House for its approval. Rarely is there any dispute between the two Houses over the content of a piece of legislation; if there is conflict, the lower House usually asserts its power and carries the day.

The sixth and final stage concerns approval by the formal executive through the royal assent procedure, which takes place in the Senate chamber. Royal assent has never been refused a federal piece of legislation, and the bill usually becomes the law of the land as soon as royal assent has been granted. In some instances, a section or the entire bill itself may not become operative until it is proclaimed. For example, the Canada Act received royal assent in Britain on March 29, 1982, but it did not become effective until it was proclaimed on April 17, 1982.

Legislative procedure

Given this process for the passage of legislation, it should not be surprising to discover that legislative approval is often a long drawn-out affair consuming many weeks, months, or even years. If the opposition parties make full use of their rights to talk and debate, as well as to propose amendments, then the government may be delayed, but not defeated, in obtaining legislative enactment of its policy proposals. Each step of the legislative process normally occurs on a different day, with several days required between some steps, as between the committee stage and third reading. If the opposition desires it, the legislative process can become very time-consuming. However, if the parties in the House are in agreement, a piece of legislation can literally breeze through: in July 1981, the bill to increase legislative salaries passed all of the stages in the Commons in five hours. There is nothing like self-interest to make short work of the legislative obstacle course.

Such consensus in the legislature is rare, however; typically, the parties confront each

> Obstruction is as old as Parliament itself. It is perhaps a regrettable part of parliamentary activity because it tends to discredit the institution, but it has been argued that under certain circumstances it is an appropriate tool in the public interest (MacKintosh, 1985: 64).

other over almost every piece of legislation. If the government has a majority mandate, there is usually no way that the opposition parties can stop the ruling party's legislative program from becoming law. For example, in March 1982, the opposition Conservatives walked out of the Commons, leaving the division bells ringing for two weeks, in order to force the Liberals to compromise on the structure of the energy security bill. The compromise that was finally reached broke the large omnibus bill into eight separate bills, with the Conservatives promising that all eight would be allowed passage by the end of June. This procedural dispute forced a delay in the government getting its legislation approved, but it did not change the content of the legislation. This incident and other bell-ringing episodes did, however, result in a change in procedure. Beginning in January 1986, the bells were replaced by chimes.

If the opposition parties utilize their delaying tactics and if the government is adamant about the need for a particular measure, then the government can always force it through the legislature by invoking closure. **Closure** is the cutting off of debate by the government, and it is a powerful tool for ensuring the passage of government legislation. Historically, it has been only occasionally used in the Canadian House, although the frequency of its usage has increased in recent years. For example, the Mulroney government, despite its huge legislative majority, resorted to closure seven times between October and December 1985. Similarly, in February of 1990, the Mulroney government moved closure to end the debate at the second reading of its controversial legislation to implement the goods and services tax (GST).

At the provincial level, closure has been more rarely used than at the federal level. For example, the use of closure in the Manitoba Legislature in January, 1984 was the first time it had been used since 1929. However, in British Columbia in the fall of 1983, the Social Credit government, in forcing its restraint package

through the legislature, invoked closure extensively (i.e., 20 times between September 19 and October 13, 1983). Previous to this brutal use of majority power, closure had only been invoked once, in 1957, in British Columbia's entire history (*The Globe and Mail*, October 14, 1983). The first use of closure in the history of Saskatchewan occurred in August 1989.

The threat of closure is often sufficient to bring the opposition into line, unless the opposition is attempting to force the government to use closure, so it can then claim that the government is "abusing Parliament." Closure, combined with party discipline, ensures the passage of the government's legislation, especially in a majority context. Using closure, it would take approximately 10 sitting days of Parliament for any bill to become law. Thus, if a majority government is not successful in enacting a bill, it is for the quite simple reason that it does not really want it passed (e.g., the failure of freedom of information legislation throughout the late 1970s and early 1980s).

With this process of legislative approval, it is apparent that much of the work of the legislature involves disputes about procedure rather than about content or subject matter. The reason for a procedural emphasis is quite clear: with a government that has a majority mandate, the substance of legislation cannot be altered without that government's concurrence. Hence, if the opposition wants to delay a bill, it will try and tie it up in a series of procedural disputes and points of privilege. While such tactics may not defeat a government, they may embarrass it, as in December 1974, when the NDP pointed out to the speaker that a quorum of MPs was not present to vote themselves a 47 percent increase in their own salary.

In minority government situations, the opposition may be more successful, for the government may agree to substantive changes rather than risk defeat in the House. However, minority governments have rarely feared legislative rejection: several examples, such as Trudeau's

Opposition, *n*. In politics the party that prevents the Government from running amuck by hamstringing it.

The King of Ghargaroo, who had been abroad to study the science of government, appointed one hundred of his fattest subjects as members of a parliament to make laws for the collection of revenue. Forty of these he named the Party of Opposition and had his Prime Minister carefully instruct them in their duty of opposing every royal measure. Nevertheless, the first one that was submitted passed unanimously. Greatly displeased, the King vetoed it, informing the Opposition that if they did that again, they would pay for their obstinacy with their heads. The entire forty promptly disembowelled themselves.

"What shall we do now?" the King asked. "Liberal institutions cannot be maintained without a party of Opposition."

"Splendor of the universe," replied the Prime Minister, "it is true these dogs of darkness have no longer their credentials, but all is not lost. Leave the matter to this worm of the dust."

So the Minister had the bodies of his Majesty's Opposition embalmed and stuffed with straw, put back into the seats of power and nailed there. Forty votes were recorded against every bill and the nation prospered. But one day a bill imposing a tax on warts was defeated—the members of the Government party had not been nailed to their seats! This so enraged the King that the Prime Minister was put to death, the parliament was dissolved with a battery of artillery, and government of the people, by the people, for the people perished from Ghargaroo (Bierce, 1911: 94).

---

defeat in 1974 or Clark's defeat in December 1979, probably indicate that the executive wanted to be brought down in each case so as to force an election. It would be hard to demonstrate in either situation that the legislature was exercising effective control over the executive.

Although the government is rarely defeated in the legislature, it is, nonetheless, kept from doing everything its little heart desires. Probably the best check against government pigheadedness, incompetence, or downright malfeasance is the **oral question period** in the Commons. When the House is in session, the opposition members, or once in a while a brave government backbencher, can challenge the government over its past, present, or projected behaviour. Since the government ministers do not know what the questions will be, the opposition attempts to embarrass them over policy, patronage, or corruption.

While the opposition cannot force ministers to answer, their failure to do so, or their seeming unwillingness to do so, influences their own and their party's image among the electors. It is

quickly apparent whether a minister has control over or an understanding of his or her department. Yet ministers with political savvy can answer a question without really being specific, thereby frustrating the opposition. Another possibility is to take the particular question "on notice," that is, to say that one does not have the answer on hand, but will, of course, search diligently for it and report back. On highly controversial matters, a court case may have started or a royal commission may have been appointed to look into the matter. In these situations, the minister refuses to answer the questions on the grounds that he or she does not want to prejudice the court case now underway or refuses to respond since a royal commission is investigating the problem. In the late 1970s, anyone appointed solicitor general had to learn two things: first, the oath of office and second, a statement indicating an inability to answer any questions about RCMP activities and wrongdoings because the McDonald Royal Commission was currently investigating the matter.

Such techniques of avoidance have done

> Pierre Trudeau's longevity as Prime Minister . . . was in no small measure due to his ability to dominate question period and debate through the force of his intelligence and personality (Franks, 1985: 14).

much to undercut the effectiveness of the question period, but it remains one of the few ways the legislature, and particularly the opposition, can bring the government to task. The fact that the question period is significant in its impact is demonstrated by the lengths governments sometimes go to try to undercut it. For example, the Liberal minority government in January 1974 attacked the opposition's use of oral and written questions on the grounds that it was delaying the House from considering important legislation and that it had cost the taxpayer $9 million in 1973 to answer all of the inquiries (Halifax, *Mail-Star*, January 19, 1974). Another undermining of the question period is evident in the practice of not allowing past ministers to answer questions, even if they are still members of the House. A new minister can feign ignorance of past events, and the former minister, sitting only a few feet away, is not forced to respond.

The most serious attack on question period occurred between 1968 and 1972, after former Prime Minister Trudeau's first election victory. Arguing that it was inefficient to have all ministers present every single day (an outside observer might assume that it was part of their job), Trudeau introduced the infamous **roster system**, whereby only a given number of ministers would be present (say one-half) on any specific day. Amazingly, a number of ministers who would be absent from question period would appear on the floor once the routine business of the House began. The roster system was rightly attacked by the press and opposition parties as a blatant attempt to muzzle question

period. After the Liberals won only a minority government in 1972, the roster system was dropped at the insistence of the opposition members. Although it has not been formally reintroduced, many governments unofficially follow it: a common complaint of federal and provincial opposition members is the poor turnout of government ministers during question period.

FUNCTIONS OF THE HOUSE OF COMMONS

It should be clear from our discussion of both the structure and procedure in the House of Commons that its role is heavily influenced by the nature of the executive-legislative relationship. In the Canadian parliamentary system, the fusion of executive and legislative power, based on party cohesion and cabinet direction, has meant that the notion of parliamentary supremacy is a myth. Parliament does not write the legislation, revise it to any great extent, or defeat the government's program. Control of the legislature by the executive has, however, produced a system wherein the government of the day has the capacity, if not always the will, to act decisively. Given such a pattern, these questions might rightfully be asked: why is the concept of parliamentary supremacy maintained? If Parliament does not in any real sense make the laws, what functions does the legislature perform?

The principle of parliamentary sovereignty is retained because it is useful for the legislature in carrying out its two most important remaining and interdependent political functions of legitimation and representation. In approving executive decisions, the legislature legitimates the exercise of influence and power by the prime minister and cabinet; that is, it makes the government's actions acceptable to the public. Because it is a representative institution, the

Source: Reprinted from the *Times-Colonist* (Victoria, British Columbia).
By permission of Adrian Raeside.

House of Commons can continue to serve as a repository of public authority, even if that authority is effectively exercised by the political executive. People may not like increases in their taxes, but if approved by Parliament, then they will most likely accept them. In many respects, Parliament is based on both traditional and legal-rational bases of authority. If the traditional basis is not sufficient, then the fact that the proper procedure has been followed can be used to justify obedience.

A good example of the legitimation function of the legislature can be seen with respect to a government's budget. Probably no piece of legislation is more fundamental than a budget, for it sets the priorities of the polity. The typical procedure in a budget's preparation, which is done in secret, is for the Minister of Finance, in consultation with the prime minister and perhaps several other cabinet ministers, to set the broad outlines of policy, which are then specified in detail by the bureaucracy. The budget is written and printed before the full cabinet sees it or before the government party caucus is informed of its content. It is then presented by the Minister of Finance in the Commons and becomes the subject of a special debate.

However, while the budget debate rarely changes the content of the document, it gives the opposition a chance to air public grievances about the decisions already taken. Such a procedure allows the legislature to legitimate decisions that have already been taken by the political executive. If any further evidence of this point is required, then the implementation of wage-and-price controls in the mid-1970s would provide it. Although Pierre Trudeau went on national television in early October 1975 to announce the immediate imposition of wage-and-price controls, the bill authorizing such a move was not passed by Parliament until several months later. The extent to which Parliament can effectively legitimate such actions is based in part on the public's perception of it as a representative institution.

The House of Commons is representative in the obvious sense that the people, through the election process, select its members. However, the representative function usually includes more than simply the process of selection, comprising in most cases the implication that once the members are chosen they will make known the concerns of their constituents and reflect the socioeconomic attributes of the electorate. With respect to the latter point, it is clear that Canadian legislators have never been a mirror image of the general public. Lawyers have traditionally dominated the membership in the House (usually about 30 percent of MPs are lawyers), with business and the professions running a close second. However, legislators attempt to represent their constituents by their activities in the House, including the debates, committee hearings, and question period. Through such mechanisms, individual MPs, particularly opposition members, make their constituents' views known and publicize government wrongdoing or incompetence in handling the affairs of the nation. In that sense, then, the "essential day-to-day business of the Canadian House of Commons is not decision-making but representation" (Hockin, 1973: 361).

Although the current legislative functions of representation and legitimation are not as grand as the principle of parliamentary sovereignty, they are important tasks. The House of Commons has adapted to changing circumstances and thereby has maintained a significant place for itself in the political system. In the process, some of the initial patterns of Canadian politics have been altered, such as the lack of party unity in the Commons. Moreover, parliamentary privilege, which emerged historically in the battles between the king and Parliament, is now used to buttress the representational tasks of the legislators, guaranteeing their right to question the government, as well as to raise issues of concern to their constituents. The 20th century has also witnessed changes in the structure of the House (e.g., number of members and number of provinces) and in its procedures (e.g., closure, standing committees). Such changes reflect the evolution of the House of Commons from a law-making institution (if it ever truly was) to one concerned with the remaining functions of representation and legitimation.

REFORMING THE HOUSE OF COMMONS

Because the House of Commons is the font of legislative authority and because through it is exercised the fusion-of-powers principle by the prime minister and cabinet, proposed changes to its structure and functions are often the centre of political reform efforts. Over the past quarter century, major changes have been made in the powers of the speaker, in the use of standing committees, and in rules of procedure and debate. The latest reform effort, and the one that might prove to be the most significant of all, culminated in a series of recommendations in June of 1985 (*Report of the Special Committee on Reform of the House of Commons*). Headed by longtime Conservative MP James McGrath, the special committee recommended major changes in both the structure and, in particular, the functions of the House of Commons.

In general, the role of the individual legislator would be greatly magnified, as a result of variations in the nature of the confidence convention and party discipline. MPs would actively participate in the policy process, scrutinize order-in-council appointments, and review the details of delegated legislation. The enhancement of MPs' roles and participation would have the ultimate result of returning Parliament itself to centre stage in the political process. Such a

> What will come out of the reform process is a Parliament that follows neither the traditional model of Westminster nor the Congressional system, but one that is uniquely Canadian (McGrath, 1985: 59).

perspective is explicitly stated in the *Report* (page one, emphasis added):

> The purpose of reform of the House of Commons in 1985 is to *restore* to private members an effective legislative function, to give them a *meaningful role* in the formation of public policy and, in so doing, to *restore* the House of Commons to its *rightful place* in the Canadian political process.

Out of its approximately 60 specific recommendations for parliamentary reform, several are particularly worthy of attention. First, the use of the confidence convention on nearly every matter that comes before the House is seen as both unnecessary and unwarranted. The confidence designation for government legislation should be relaxed, freeing the individual MP and the House from some of the more severe constraints of party discipline: "the judgment of this committee . . . is that Canadian politics has become too dominated by the ethic of party solidarity" (*Report*, page 60). A relaxation of party discipline is seen as a prerequisite to increased participation and power of backbenchers in general and of the full House in particular.

A second significant reform idea concerns the structure and powers of the standing committees in the legislative process. The size of the standing committees would be reduced to a minimum of seven members each, with parliamentary secretaries unable to serve on them. A reorganized committee system would provide added expertise for use in scrutinizing government legislation. Most importantly, the powers and functions of the standing committees would be enhanced, so that a vigorous committee sys-

tem could oppose the government of the day: "No longer dominated solely by the government's agenda, and led by strong chairmen and active private members, committees will become influential and important in their own right" (*Report*, page 27).

Certain procedural reforms form a third focus for future parliamentary change. Not only should the speaker be chosen by a secret ballot, but the disciplinary powers of the chair should be greatly enhanced. The way in which private member's bills are dealt with would be altered, as would the use of emergency debates, petitions from the public, and the administration of vacant constituencies.

While the above proposed reforms received generally favourable reviews when the *Report* was presented, several crucial questions need to be examined. First, what is the attitude of the present government, or any government, towards these proposed changes? The real crux of parliamentary reform is how to convince the government of the day to give up some of its own powers. Finding itself as the government has created a problem for the Tories. Is the political will really there to enhance the powers of the Commons and that of the political opposition? One suspects that the longer the Conservatives are in power, the less likely the chance that a political will in favour of significant parliamentary reform will be continued.

A second basic question in evaluating the various reforms is whether or not they will produce the expected result. The *Report* relies heavily on attitudinal change among the backbenchers, as well as the government, in order to overcome such things as the stricture of party discipline. However, it seems that good intentions and more active backbenchers may be insufficient medicine to save the parliamentary patient.

A final criticism of the *Report* would be that it has probably misread the nature of parliamentary sovereignty in Canada. This point is crucial, for the *Report* seems to be predicated on the assumption that something that has been lost

> Reforms are for Oppositions. It is the business of governments to stay in office (Sir Wilfrid Laurier).

(possibly our political innocence?) can be regained through internal reforms of the House of Commons. The lower House is seen as potentially a key player in the policy process. However, it seems suspect to conclude that the Canadian Parliament has played such a role in the past or that it might in the immediate future.

As an outgrowth of the 1985 *Report*, the House of Commons, in February 1986, adopted, on a provisional basis, some of the *Report's* recommendations. Among the major changes accepted were the following: the speaker of the House would be elected by a free vote of the House; the standing committees were reorganized with respect to their membership and functions; and private member's bills were given enhanced status and consideration. Most importantly, the ideas of reducing the use of the confidence convention or of increasing the role and power of the typical backbencher were not adopted.

The most spectacular success centred on the election of the speaker, already utilized twice (1986 and 1988). Moreover, the speaker's authority has also been enhanced as he seeks to preside over the Commons. The changes in the standing committee system have only been partly successful. The committees have not yet emerged as strong power bases from which to challenge the party leadership in the House. The only strong committee chairman to emerge on the national public scene is Don Blenkarn, Chairman of the Finance Committee. It seems unlikely, at least on the basis of the current reforms, that we will see Canadian standing committees approach the power of their American counterparts. A third change, making private member's bills somewhat easier to pass,

has been mildly successful, as evident in the passage of Lynn McDonald's anti-smoking bill. Overall, however, the political impact of the 1986 reforms has been modest; the House of Commons is still dominated by the principle of party discipline and controlled by the political executive.

The Decline of Legislative Power: The Role of the Canadian Senate

Unfortunately for Senate admirers (one assumes there are a few, at least, outside of current, former, or prospective aspirants), the upper House of Canada's legislature has neither performed as expected nor adapted to the changing circumstances of the 20th century. As a result, the Senate, although never the equal of the House of Commons, has witnessed a steady erosion of its legislative role. For example, one study of the Canadian Parliament uses the "terms parliament and House of Commons interchangeably," because of the minimal legislative power retained by the Senate (Kornberg and Mishler, 1976: 17–18). Technically, however, Parliament includes the Senate, the House of Commons, and the formal executive. While the imminent demise of the Senate is not apparent, neither is its rejuvenation, even given its temporary resurgence in the late 1980s. After a brief look at the structure of the Senate, we will consider its current functions in the political process, particularly its relationship with the House of Commons. (The changes regarding the Senate contained in the rejected Meech Lake accord will be considered later, in Chapter 14.)

STRUCTURE OF THE SENATE

The basic institutional composition of the Senate is outlined in Sections 21–36 of the 1867 Constitution Act. In contrast to the Commons, which is directly elected, the Senate is an appointed body. Although formally chosen by the governor-in-council, Senate selection, for all practical purposes, has become a prerogative of the prime minister, even though others may be consulted in the process.

Legal qualifications are fairly straightforward: an individual must be 30 years of age, a resident of the province for which he or she is appointed, a natural born or naturalized subject of the Queen, and have real property, over and above all debts, of $4000. For Quebec senators, the province is broken down into 24 districts, with the person appointed either a resident of that district or meeting the property qualifications therein. Based on custom, Senate appointments are spread throughout a province, with senators being designated for particular areas. For example, legally all of Ontario's representatives could be appointed from Toronto, but such a pattern would be bad politics and, hence, has never happened. Revealing is the monetary requirement of $4000, which has remained constant, despite inflation. A barrier to most people in 1867, the $4000 figure disqualifies few people in the 1990s.

The allocation of Senate seats is based on the provinces and regions, with a current maximum total, if all the positions were filled, of 104 members: Quebec 24, Ontario 24, Maritimes 24 (Nova Scotia 10, New Brunswick 10, Prince Edward Island four), the West 24 (six for each province), Newfoundland six, Yukon one, Northwest Territories one. Initially senators held office for life, but any senator appointed from 1965 onward must retire at the age of 75. However, a number of quite elderly Senators have remained in the Red Chamber, despite the 1965 reform. For example, 87-year-old Senator Salter Hayden, the last surviving appointee of Mackenzie King, resigned from the Red Chamber in 1983, after serving for 43 years. In 1986, the oldest Senator was Elsie Inman from Prince Edward Island; when she died in that year at the age of 95, she had been a Senator for 31 years. A senator may be removed from office (Constitution Act of 1867, Section 31) for failing to attend two consecutive sessions, by ceasing to be a citizen, or by failing to meet the requirements of residency or financial solvency.

THE SELECTION PROCESS

The main criterion for Senate appointment is based on custom and convention: the upper House is selected on the basis of patronage or party service. The combination of patronage and being an appointed body in a democratic age has seriously eroded the legitimacy of the Senate and has helped to reduce its legislative powers to minimal levels. To classify a practice as one of **patronage** means that the controlling factor in appointment is past party work and loyalty, although that does not necessarily mean that people of talent will not be chosen. Because of patronage, the Senate has become a base for national party organization: the work is not too taxing or time-consuming and the pay is good and from public, not party, funds. Those who raise the party finances and those who organize election campaigns are often made senators. Senator Keith Davey, often dubbed "the rainmaker," because of his influence in the Liberal party organization, is one example.

The patronage base of appointment has also meant a severe party imbalance in the upper House, since one party (the Liberals) has controlled national office for most of the last half century. The Liberals, in the 1960s and 1970s, held a four-to-one ratio over the Conservatives in the upper chamber, with minor parties or independents usually excluded from service.

> Because senators do not have to worry about getting re-elected and because their position makes them financially secure, they can become the focus for essential heresy (Gigantes, 1985: 7).
>
> We have a body of men and women technically responsible to no one, certainly not the electorate, who are frustrating the will of the elected people of Canada and that no other democracy at this point in our history would tolerate (NDP Leader Ed Broadbent, February 24, 1985).

The imbalance was becoming so acute in the late 1970s that then Prime Minister Trudeau adopted a policy of appointing Conservatives to fill vacancies caused by Conservative deaths or retirements. However, because of the appointments made by Joe Clark in 1979 and Brian Mulroney after 1984, the overwhelming Liberal dominance of the Senate has been somewhat reduced in recent years (approximately a two-to-one advantage by the late 1980s). In September of 1988, for example, the Liberals held 59 seats, the Conservatives 35, Independents five, Independent Conservatives one and four vacancies.

While the final selection is a prime ministerial prerogative, considerable jockeying and infighting occurs within the party organization over who should be called to the Senate. The interests of the provincial and national party organizations must be reconciled, as well as other competing interests (ethnic, religious, and racial). For example, in early 1986 the one vacant Senate seat in Ontario produced party infighting between the provincial and federal wings of the Conservative party as four candidates lobbied for support (Frank Miller, Norman Atkins, Hal Jackman, and John Bassett). It is not unknown for an individual to campaign extensively behind the scenes for a Senate appointment, as Sam Bronfman did in seeking to become the first Jewish member in the Red Chamber (Newman, 1979: 47–60).

A number of vacancies are usually kept open until shortly before an election, in order to exact as much work or money as possible out of Senate aspirants. A good indicator of a forthcoming election, therefore, is a series of Senate appointments, as the governing party tries to use up all of its patronage powers before calling an election that might result in the loss of office. Few parties are willing to gamble that they will win. In contrast, the Liberals were so confident of victory in 1957 (they had, after all, been the government since 1935) that 16 positions were not utilized, which allowed the Conservatives a chance to appoint a large number of new senators after winning power.

Given the party basis of the appointment process, there are many political uses to which the Senate can be put. Before the adoption of a pension plan and the large salary increases of recent years for members of the House of Commons, the Senate was often utilized as a retirement pension for loyal MPs. Senate appointments have also been used to ease members out of the cabinet gracefully, without forcing a longtime minister to return to the backbenches (e.g., Paul Martin's appointment to the Senate).

The prime minister may also manipulate the Senate selection process to open up a safe seat in the House. What seems destined to become a classic example of this practice occurred in July 1981, when 45-year-old Peter Stollery, MP for the Spadina riding in Toronto, was appointed to the Senate to make room for Jim Coutts, who had been principal secretary to the prime minister for many years. The Spadina constituency, which was heavily populated with ethnic members who had strong ties to the Liberal party, was touted to be the "safest" Liberal seat outside of Quebec. Stollery, who had spent a decade as a Liberal backbencher and had never been selected for the cabinet, had no immediate prospects for such a development. With the pay increase of 1981, Stollery's Senate appointment, given his mandatory retirement age of 75, was worth over $1 million in salary alone. Unfortunately for Jim Coutts' electoral career pattern, which was rumoured to include a cabinet position as well as a try for the Liberal party leadership upon Trudeau's departure, the voters of Spadina rejected him in the August 17, 1981 by-election.

Senate appointments may also have an impact on general election results. Knowing that defeat was possible, in preparing for the 1979 election, Trudeau appointed Bob Muir, longtime Conservative MP from Cape Breton, to the Senate in the hopes of winning that riding in the forthcoming contest, which the Liberals did. Senate appointments can also help to sow dissension within an opposition party. In the early 1960s, Hazen Argue, House leader and briefly national leader of the CCF, was defeated by Tommy Douglas for the leadership of the just-formed New Democratic Party. Argue subsequently became a Liberal, but upon losing his seat was appointed to the Senate in 1966 (Young, 1969: 235–238). An even more blatant attempt to produce internal disunity within an opposition party was revealed in Trudeau's appointment of Claude Wagner to the Senate, again as a prelude to the 1979 contest. Wagner had been Joe Clark's primary rival for the party leadership in 1976, losing by only a handful of votes on the fourth ballot. Moreover, Wagner was one of the few Conservative MPs from Quebec, around whom the party had hoped to rebuild. Although they had tried strenuously to beat him in the previous elections, the Liberals selected Wagner for the Senate because it would hurt the Tory rebuilding effort in Quebec, as well as producing disunity within the Conservative party organization there. Such continuing machinations regarding Senate appointments is a major reason why senators have "on the whole . . . turned in what must be considered an undistinguished performance" (Dawson, 1970: 283). Moreover, the patronage and party

organization uses to which the Senate has been put have undercut its legislative role and its relationship with the House of Commons.

FUNCTIONS OF THE SENATE

The initial design of Canada's upper House reflected two main purposes: first, to serve as a check on the lower House and second, to represent the provinces and regions within the national government. Neither function remains very viable currently.

The Senate has never been equal to the House. For example, all money bills must be introduced in the Commons first, and the government is responsible for retaining legislative support there. While the Senate can theoretically defeat a bill, such a defeat would not bring the government down. The Canadian Senate is not a confidence chamber. Thus, the power of the Senate in the bicameral federal legislature was designed to be inferior to that of the Commons in 1867 and has become more so since then.

A good indicator of the Senate's power is its typical work week — and it should not be forgotten that it sits only about half of any year. The average Senate week is nine hours long, divided down among Tuesday evening, Wednesday afternoon, and Thursday afternoon. Even with such a schedule, the Senate can still run out of something to do, as when it took an extra week of vacation in November, 1985. A legislative body that had any real power would meet more frequently. As Senator Heath McQuarrie (PEI) once put it, the "way the Senate keeps its power is by not using it." In 1987, for example, the Senate sat for only 91 days, but one-fifth of the membership attended less than one-half of these meetings.

Considerable debate surrounds the extent of the Senate's current legislative role. In theory, the Senate retains the right to reject legislation coming from the Commons; in practice, it

The Canadian Senate: A Day's Work
5:15 p.m. Senate begins its sitting for the day.
5:20 p.m. Senators and members of the Commons hear Mr. Justice Brian Dickson of the Supreme Court give royal assent to two bills.
5:25 p.m. The MPs withdraw from the Senate Chamber.
5:30 p.m. Senate adjourns until Thursday, April 28, at 2 p.m.
   Salary cost for the 88 existing senators: $14,304.38 for the day, or $953.63 per minute of the sitting.
Source: The Globe and Mail (April 30, 1983), p. 4.

We will make sure that once an agreement is struck in the House of Commons, that it is not, in a vexatious and clearly frivolous way,

held up by a bunch of unelected and highly paid rejects of the Liberal Party (Prime Minister Brian Mulroney, February 28, 1985).

Senate: It has two functions. One is to give an opinion on certain bills being suggested by the House. The other is to say yes or yes as to whether the bill should be allowed to pass (Wicks, 1984: 107).

The Canadian Senate is like a punching bag: insensate, impervious and irrepressible. No amount of editorial or political fury, it seems, will ever change the Senate. It has absorbed more blows than any institution in Canada without changing its shape (Simpson, 1983: 5).

almost never happens nor, for that matter, is the issue of rejection scarcely even contemplated. An important distinction must be made between vetoing legislation in total or making significant amendments to it, and the more limited approach of revising the work of the Commons. The Senate often revises legislation coming from the Commons by making many technical or housekeeping amendments to a piece of legislation. These revisions can be quite numerous on a complicated bill and are usually accepted by the Commons without any controversy. Moreover, the Senate can make major changes, but only if the Commons does not see them as a challenge to its own dominance in the legislative process. If the House perceives the Senate's actions as a challenge, then a major confrontation between the two Houses occurs, and the House of Commons carries the day.

An example of this took place in late 1973 and early 1974 over the Liberal minority government's wiretap legislation. As discussed earlier, the NDP and Conservative parties had combined forces at both the committee stage and in the House to insert a notice provision to persons under surveillance for 90 days. When the

bill reached the upper House, the Liberal-dominated Senate removed the notice provision and sent the bill back to the Commons for approval. Justice Minister Otto Lang recommended to the Commons that the Senate revisions be accepted. In the House, the opposition Conservative and New Democratic parties were outraged, rightly perceiving that the Liberal minority in the House was attempting to use the Liberal majority in the Senate to circumvent the power of the Commons. Press and public reaction were scornful of the Senate, pointing to its patronage and nonelected base—in other words, questioning the legitimacy of its actions. John Diefenbaker, who had once gone so far as not to include any senators in his cabinet, declared that if the Senate wanted "a free-for-all, let's let them have it." Blunt talk of Senate abolition began to be heard. The Commons proceeded to reinsert the notice provision into the wiretap legislation and sent it back to the Senate, daring them, in effect, to have the guts to reject it or to revise it again. The second time the Senate acquiesced and the legislation was passed in the form preferred by the Commons.

The fact that these confrontations are rare in

AN AFTERNOON IN THE CANADIAN SENATE

Source: Andy Donato, *Donato's 1981 Political Cartoons*. By permission of Canada Wide Feature Service and Andy Donato.

recent decades is indicative of the dominance of the Commons over the Senate. Such battles are more likely, however, when the Commons and Senate are controlled by different parties, thus giving the Senate-House confrontations a partisan basis (Newman, 1973: 295–321). Just such a situation developed in 1985, when a Liberal-dominated Senate delayed the passage of a borrowing bill required by the new Mulroney government. Interestingly, the Commons had unanimously passed the bill, so that the Liberals in the Senate, including many new senators appointed by former Prime Minister Trudeau, were in opposition to their leader (John Turner) and their House colleagues. This battle, from

which the Senate backed off, produced yet another round of Senate reform speculation. An analogous situation developed in 1988, when the Liberal-dominated Senate threatened, with the agreement of the Liberal opposition in the House of Commons, to stop the Conservative government's free trade legislation. Although it could not legally force the government to the polls, this Senate threat was certainly one factor in the government's decision to call an election. Temporary injections of geritol rarely save a dying patient, however.

While it rarely challenges the lower House directly, the Senate not only influences the Commons, but sometimes has been able to convince the lower House to accept revisions to its legislation. While most changes are minor, one investigation has argued that many of the so-called technical changes made by the Senate are in fact significant because they provide a means for business and corporate influence in the legislative process (Campbell, 1978: 10–19). It is in this role of a minor revising chamber that the Senate retains a modicum of influence in the Canadian legislative process.

The second intended function of the Senate in 1867 was to serve as an institution that would provide regional and provincial representation within the national government. The regional allocation of Senate seats prescribed in the 1867 Constitution Act was designed to guarantee such a result: thus, in a technical sense, the Senate continues to be based on regional and provincial interests. However, as a regional voice within the national government, particularly as an effective one, the role of the Senate has been disappointing.

From the time of Macdonald's first cabinet, in which he allocated portfolios on a provincial and regional basis, the lower House, through the cabinet, has usurped the Senate's role as the defender of provincial interests. Moreover, the inability of the Senate to defend provincial and regional interests is directly linked to its declining role in the legislative process: minimal legislative influence exacerbates the Senate's failure to be the defender of the provinces, even when it tries to undertake such a task. The patronage base of Senate selection has also meant that many members are not particularly concerned either with checking the work of the Commons or of being effective regional defenders. Few party warhorses at career's end are likely to be political activists, no matter what the intent of the body to which they have been appointed.

If the Canadian Senate does not serve as a restraint on the Commons or as an effective voice of regional and provincial concerns within the national government, what are its current functions? First and foremost, the upper House is a tool for party organization and development: declining legislative functions have been replaced by party tasks, especially for the governing party. Second, the Senate plays a minor revising role in the legislative process. Third, the Senate provides at least symbolic representation for the regions in the affairs of the national government, although the provinces seem less than satisfied with such a continuing role for the Senate.

Fourth, occasionally the Senate contributes to the political process over and above its minimal legislative tasks. Several senators have been active in investigating areas of social concern — Senator David Croll's committee's look at poverty in Canada is an example. Other significant committee reports from the Senate have included a look at the Canadian Security and Intelligence Service, at human rights, and at the problem of delegated legislation. Such useful tasks, however, seem more dependent on the interests and concerns of an individual senator than a necessary outgrowth of the Senate's overall political role. Additionally, the Senate-sponsored hearings on Senate reform proposals in the late 1970s led to an advisory opinion from the Supreme Court of Canada in December 1979 that the federal government did not have the power unilaterally to alter the composition of the Senate.

Fifth, relatively infrequently, the Senate is called upon to provide regional representatives for the cabinet. Such a use is a result, however, of inadequate provincial representation within the governing party in the House of Commons itself. For example, both Joe Clark in 1979 (for Quebec) and Pierre Trudeau in 1980 (for three Western provinces) made use of the Senate to bolster provincial representation in their cabinets. The appointment of Senator Robert de Cotret as Minister of Industry, Trade and Commerce by Joe Clark in 1979 was the first major portfolio given to a Senator since 1935. However, once a party has gained seats in the House from a province, it would be contrary to custom to select senators rather than members of the House for ministerial positions. For example, after winning seats in all provinces in his landslide victory of 1984, Prime Minister Mulroney only included one senator (the government's senate leader) in his initial cabinet. Given these reflections, the Senate's present role could be summarized as follows: an upper House with minor revising powers in the legislative process and a base for party organization and development, which rarely emerges as a significant actor in the political process.

REFORMING THE SENATE

One thing is clear: the Canadian public increasingly supports the necessity of Senate reform. A poll released in December of 1984 and conducted for the Canada West Foundation discovered that 34 percent favour Senate reform, 20 percent want it abolished, 18 percent have no opinion, and 28 percent feel it is fine the way it is (*The Globe and Mail*, December 14, 1984). The Senate seems to lack a large reservoir of public support.

As a result, numerous reform proposals regarding the appointment and structure of the

Source: Reprinted from the *Times-Colonist* (Victoria, British Columbia).
By permission of Adrian Raeside.

Canadian Senate have been advanced in recent years. One incentive for reform, in addition to the problems of patronage and minimal legislative duties, is simply cost. With the pay increases of recent years, the price tag of the Senate, for salaries alone, is about $7 million yearly. For many young recent appointees, who can serve 30 to 35 years before they reach mandatory retirement at age 75, these salary figures, along with projected increases over the years, will give them each a total guaranteed income of over $6 million dollars. (It might also be kept in mind that senators are not prevented

> In America, we are told, every native son has the opportunity to grow up and become president. In Canada, opportunity exists for anyone to grow up and reform the Senate (Camp, 1984: B3).

from holding other jobs. For example, Senator Edward Larson, Canada's top Teamster official, was reported to have received a union salary of $300 000 in 1984, in addition to his senate salary. Similarly, after his appointment to the upper House, Senator Michael Pitfield served on the Boards of Directors of the following corporations: Power Corporation, Cadillac Fairview Corporation, The Great-West-life Assurance Company, and Montreal Trustco.) Other costs include the parliamentary restaurant and library, printing, upkeep, pensions, and a host of ancillary services, which would likely bring the direct Senate burden to many more millions a year (about $34 million in 1989). Rather than attempting to reduce its direct costs, the reform proposals have sought to change the Senate's patronage base or to enhance its role in the legislative process.

Reforms dealing with the age and patronage

factors are generally modest in their contemplated changes to the Senate, while a greater legislative role would bring into question the current imbalance of power between the Commons and the Senate. Although the reform of 1965 requires any senator appointed since that date to retire at the age of 75, which has led to a 20-year reduction in the average age of senators, nevertheless an age problem remains. It is not so much a problem of mandatory retirement deadlines, as it is of the trend toward appointing senators who are in middle age. While youth may help to rejuvenate the Red Chamber, a person appointed at age 45 has a possible 30 years of service, with no performance review. For example, these Senators, at the time of their appointment, had about three decades of possible service in the upper House: Peter Stollery, Anne Cools, Jerry Grafstein, Michael Kirby, Lowell Murray, Michael Pitfield, Lorna Marsden, Michel Cogger, and Jean Bazin. Particularly, if the appointment of younger persons is the trend, then Senate appointments should be for a fixed term (e.g., five years or 10 years), with the possibility of one reappointment. Such a tenure might encourage senators to be active and would not create the problem of a member being a possible nonparticipant for several decades.

A second often-suggested reform is to make Senate selections from a wider range of people, especially to include individuals for other than patronage considerations. While such appointments would create a Senate of greater diversity in its social and economic makeup, it is not apparent that such a change is in the self-interest of the major parties, particularly the governing party. For example, the first woman was only appointed to the Senate in 1930 (Cairine Wilson) and the first black in 1984 (Anne Cools).

A third proposed change is to alter the dominance of the federal level in the selection process by giving the provinces control of half of the Senate seats. Such a change would prevent large imbalances, at least, in the upper House

between the two major parties (Liberals and Conservatives) and would provide for some third party representation (Social Credit, NDP) as well. Although this reform would alter the party balance, it would not change the patronage base of selection: half of its appointees would be provincial patronage appointments instead of federal ones. A variant of this change was contained in the rejected Meech Lake accord (see Chapter 14).

A final set of reforms aim at altering the Senate's role in the legislative process. For example, the Alberta government's proposal for a Triple E (Elected, Equal, Effective) Senate would illustrate such a reform. Alternately, the Senate may be renamed the House of the Provinces or the House of Confederation, a change that would coincide with the initial intent that the Senate represent regional and provincial interests within the national government. However, to be effective, such a change would necessitate an increase in the Senate's current legislative powers. If the Senate cannot alter legislation, it cannot protect provincial concerns. If Senators are rarely included in the cabinet, how can Senators be effective defenders of provincial interests? Unfortunately, this question is not always asked by those making reform proposals.

Changes in the selection process, the age of those chosen, or the tenure of the appointment will do little to alter the current overall position of the Senate: it will remain a minor revising body, patronage-based. Only such changes, in combination with additional powers, will do much to alter the Senate's political role in the current system. To grant the Senate more power would mean a reduction in the current status of the House and, by implication, the cabinet. Senate reform has been inhibited by the self-interest of other political institutions: the major stumbling block to a rejuvenation of the Senate is the House of Commons.

One proposal by Trudeau in 1978 would have given the Senate a "suspensive veto" power for

> It is most likely that in spite of the many calls for reform, few changes of substance will actually be implemented. Reforming the Senate would mean challenging the authority of the Prime Minister, Cabinet and others in a position of power (Lemco, 1986: 277).

> Because government, as well as Opposition, accept the principle of accountability, continual effort is put into explaining and justifying what is done, in the name of the nation, by our leaders. And continual effort is made by Parliament to put this explanation under scrutiny (Jack, 1985: 306).

six months. A **suspensive veto** *is the ability to delay legislation for a given period of time, rather than rejecting it outright.* In other words, the theoretical total veto would have been replaced by an actual veto of half a year. Many critics wrongly perceived this as a further reduction of the Senate's power. In fact, in our view, a six-month suspensive veto would mean an increase in the traditional power of the Senate, and as such would be unacceptable to the Commons. Another example of a change that would not be tolerated by the lower House would be the consistent use of Senators in ministerial positions. However, such a reform would be necessary to make the Senate an effective defender of regional concerns, since the cabinet is the key decision-making body in the Canadian polity.

These examples indicate that the likelihood of Senate reform is related to the prospects such a change would make in the overall balance of power between the two parts of Canada's bicameral legislature. The greater the proposed change in the Senate's role and powers, the greater will be the opposition to it coming from the Commons. The Senate thus finds itself between a rock and a hard place: even if it wanted to, which it probably does not, it could do little to reform itself. It is not in the political self-interest of the institutions that control its fate—the House of Commons and cabinet—to see a revived and effectively-functioning Senate. Any reform is likely to be illusory, leaving the basic role of the Senate intact, with its legitimacy further eroded in the years ahead.

The Legislature in Great Britain

While the "mother of Parliaments" is a venerated institution, as most mothers are, and while the years have not been totally unkind to her, they have, nevertheless, taken their toll: the British "Parliament does not and cannot" govern (Bradshaw and Pring, 1972: 9). The basic trends regarding the role of legislatures in the political process, or the balance of power between the constituent parts of bicameral institutions, have not bypassed "this sceptered Isle." In the nation of its birth, the principle of parliamentary supremacy has become a myth (Crossman, 1972). The House of Commons dominates the legislature, with the House of Lords generally continuing to recede in political significance. While in broad outline the British Parliament resembles its Canadian counterpart, both in structure and function, it differs on a number of important specific points.

THE HOUSE OF COMMONS

The predominant lower House is composed of 650 members elected in single-member plurality districts. Based on the latest redistribution, England has a total of 523 seats, with Scotland receiving 72, Wales 38, and Northern Ireland 17. Unlike the Canadian House, the physical structure of the British Commons is composed of benches that provide seats for only about

> There are three golden rules for parliamentary speakers: stand up, speak up and shut up (J.W. Lowther, Speaker [1919], British House of Commons).

65 percent of its members. The result of such seating arrangements is an intimacy in the British House of Commons that is lacking in the Canadian and American legislatures, because of individual desks or seats in both. Interestingly, when the Commons was destroyed by fire during the Second World War, no increase in the physical size or seating arrangement of the legislature was approved.

Internally, the Commons is under the direction of the speaker of the House, who is expected to be nonpartisan. British speakers are traditionally more independent than their Canadian counterparts in terms of both selection and tenure. For example, upon selection, the speaker ends previous political connections and ceases to be a member of any political party. Upon retirement, custom prevents a former speaker from taking up the partisan battle again. Thus, considerable controversy arose in early 1985 when former Speaker George Thomas, now known as Lord Tonypandy, published his autobiography, which was quite critical of many politicians still in the House of Commons. Once selected, the speaker may run in the next general election as an independent and, if returned to the House, is usually reelected to the speaker's post. These conventions have made a British speaker more independent, with greater status, than the more partisan-based Canadian office.

The more independent status of the British speaker is clearly revealed by the details of the selection procedure. The speaker's selection requires the approval, not only of the Commons, but of the Queen as well. Moreover, the British Prime Minister does not name the speaker, even though he or she is likely to play a major role in the behind-the-scenes negotiations. In fact, in 1983, in selecting the successor to George Thomas, the House of Commons chose Bernard Weatheril, in part, because he was known not to be the choice of Margaret Thatcher. In British politics, not even the Iron Maiden has enough clout to force her choice of speaker on a reluctant House of Commons.

The committee structure in the British Commons is not as well developed as in Canada (Rush, 1982). The mother of Parliaments has been less than enthusiastic in delegating some of its authority to its constituent parts. The result has been the rather late and limited development of a standing committee system. The basic function of the standing committee is the detailed consideration of legislation between second and third readings, although their structure and membership limit their power in this task.

Usually a number of standing committees are appointed during a session, with a core membership of 20 MPs each. In addition, as many as 30 additional MPs may be appointed to a committee when it considers a particular bill. The additional membership on these committees is not stable—the composition of the standing committees is altered for each bill that it considers. The rationale for this approach is to have as much expertise as possible on the standing committee for each item it reviews. Typically, those members who have shown an interest in a bill during the second reading are appointed to the committee that will consider the legislation. Membership is allocated according to party strength in the full House by the committee of selection. British standing committees are not broken down along departmental lines as in Canada (they are named as Standing Committee A, etc.); however, recommendations for parliamentary reform may move Britain along more Canadian lines in the years ahead.

As in Canada, the organization of the British House revolves around the political parties, in particular the principle of party discipline. The cohesive behaviour of the political parties within the legislature has long been cited as one of the distinguishing hallmarks of the British party system. For example, in eight sessions since the Second World War, governments have successfully passed 100 percent of their legislative program, with the average success rate since 1945 standing at 97 percent (Rose, 1986: 90). Such results indicate that most members of Parliament willingly accept "the whip" and thus support their leader and party, both inside and outside the legislature. Interestingly, the whip received its name in typical British fashion from "the hunt": the concept "derives from the whippers-in of the hunting field who keep the hounds working as a pack and prevent them wandering" (Bradshaw and Pring, 1972: 30).

The strength of party discipline is distinguished between one-line, two-line, and three-line whips, which refers to the number of times an upcoming vote is underlined on the outline of the week's expected activities prepared for party members by the party whips. The greater the number of underlinings, the greater is the expected loyalty of party members: rarely will a member vote against the party if a three-line whip has been called. For example, a three-line whip was called in the passage of the Canada Act through the British House of Commons. Because the national parties play an extensive and direct role in the recruitment of candidates for office, party leaders may deny a straying member renomination in the next election. The 1970s and 1980s provided examples of members increasingly defying their party whip, but the principle of party discipline remains as a basic operating rule of the British House in the 1990s. The example of a number of Conservatives voting against their government's budget in June 1981 is still rather exceptional behaviour in the House of Commons. More typical is the view of a member of Parliament as "a G.I. in a political army, whose rifle is his vote" (Crossman, 1972: 100).

The passage of legislation follows the usual pattern of three readings, with the committee stage occurring between the second and third readings. While the House of Lords repeats the process, for all practical purposes, the legislative function resides with the House of Commons, which in turn is controlled by the political executive. The government determines the priorities to be dealt with by the Commons and can ensure the passage of its legislation through use of closure. In contrast to the Canadian system, closure is frequently used. For example, between 1950 and 1970, closure was invoked 525 times in the British House (Bradshaw and Pring, 1972: 152), while in Canada closure was used only seven times between 1913 and 1957 (Newman, 1973: 39).

While the British House of Commons does not share legislative power with provincial or state governments and while its laws cannot be overturned by the judiciary, since judicial review is not part of the political process, it is nonetheless true that the notion of parliamentary supremacy is illusory. More so than in Canada, given the absence of federalism and judicial review, the British political executive is not constrained by the legislature: the political process is executive-centred and executive-dominated.

However, the Commons is still involved in an important way in the representation and legitimation functions. The Commons is representative not only in terms of its geographical constituencies, but also as a mechanism for registering individual and group concerns with the government of the day. Moreover, in its consideration of legislation, in its review and debate of a government's program, the House of Commons helps to legitimate executive actions. In other words, the task of the British House of Commons is "not that of initiating legislation but of authorizing and approving proposals for law formulated outside the legislature proper, most often by the executive" (Loewenberg and Patterson, 1979: 197). In this regard, the British and Canadian Houses of Commons reflect a distinct familial resemblance.

THE HOUSE OF LORDS

On a day-to-day basis, the upper House of the British Parliament typically plays a very minor legislative role. The dominance of the House of Commons has long been established in British politics, beginning with the Reform Act of 1832 and consolidated by the Parliament Acts of 1911 and 1949. In many respects, the House of Lords is a monarchical, rather than a legislative institution, given its membership and overall role in the political process (Punnett, 1980: 279–291; Birch, 1983: 51–60).

The composition of the House of Lords is based on appointment, most of which is hereditary in nature. The total number is about 1200 members, although most of these never actively participate in the legislative process; only about 300 members make an effort at regular participation in the business of the Lords. Approximately two-thirds of the Lords are **hereditary peers**: that is, they either inherited their titles or they were given a peerage themselves as a reward for public service. The remaining members are what are known as **life peers**, those whose appointment to the upper House ends with their own death.

Selection to the Lords is a prime ministerial prerogative, although technically the appointments are made by the sovereign. The result is that the composition of the Lords reflects, in part, partisan control of the Commons. Since the Conservative party has dominated British politics over the past century, the Lords is heavily weighted in favour of that party. Moreover, the preponderance of Conservative peers in the Lords reflects their traditional and appointive tie to the nobility. One reason for allowing life peers, beginning in 1958, was to correct this

> The House of Lords is an anachronism which works (Lord Ponsonby of Shulbrede, Chief Whip for the Labour Party, April 1988).

imbalance by giving the government greater flexibility in the appointment process. Most new peers in recent decades have been life peers and these members, as a group, are more active in the Lords than their hereditary counterparts. Since the prime minister has the right to create new peers, he or she can do so to break a deadlock between the Commons and the Lords: usually the threat of such action is enough to bring the upper House into line. Historically, the major confrontations between the Commons and the Lords have occurred when the lower House is controlled by a party other than the Conservatives.

The hereditary and appointed composition of the House of Lords has led some critics to refer to it as "a political geriatric unit" with few remaining significant functions in the political process: "a harmless political eunuch, possessing no power and little influence" (Hamilton, 1975: 9, 136). While such an assessment is perhaps extreme, most observers of the Lords would agree that in terms of legislation its major powers "have been reduced almost to nil" (Beer, 1973: 239). The Lords does retain, however, a role as a revising and debating chamber, in addition to its ability to deal with the private member's bills and to consider certain kinds of legislation ahead of the Commons. In these respects, the House of Lords relieves the Commons of some of its heavy workload. Perhaps the most revealing indicator of the remaining power of the House of Lords concerns its ability to veto legislation passed by the Commons, in particular the adoption and use of the suspensive veto.

As in most bicameral legislatures, either House traditionally shared the right to reject or veto legislation passed by the other chamber.

> In a nation that calls itself democratic, an unelected House of Lords is, of course, a splendid impertinence (Shenker, 1988: 34).

> *Anthony Wedgewood Benn on the British House of Lords:* The British House of Lords is the British Outer Mongolia for retired politicians.
>
> On summer evenings and winter afternoons, when they have nothing else to do, people discuss how to reform the House of Lords. Schemes are taken out of cupboards and drawers and dusted off: speeches are composed, pamphlets written, letters sent to the newspapers. From time to time, the whole country becomes excited (Morgan, 1981: 18).
>
> This is the fundamental dilemma of change of British political institutions—reform can occur only by the support of that institution, the Cabinet, that has no motivations to want reform. There is little point in expecting that the barons of Parliament can stage a Runnymede (Rasmussen, 1984: 41).

The ability to veto measures passed by the Commons was first lost in 1911, when the Lords' total veto was replaced by a suspensive veto of two years' duration. For example, if the Lords rejected a bill and the Commons still wanted it, then the Commons could pass the legislation in three successive sessions (i.e., a minimum period of two years) and it would become law whether the Lords liked it or not.

The suspensive veto was further reduced from two years to 12 months in 1949. As might be suspected, the change to a suspensive veto and its decline to a period of one year were both opposed by the House of Lords. However, the Parliament Act of 1911 was passed after two general elections had been held on the issue and after the sovereign threatened, at the request of the government, to appoint enough new peers to the Lords to ensure the bill's passage. Rather than see their beloved chamber inundated by new and non-Conservative members, the Lords finally acquiesced and accepted the suspensive veto. The change in 1949 to reduce the suspensive veto to one year was passed after the Lords had delayed it for two years. More than anything else, the suspensive veto symbolizes the current role of the House of Lords in British politics: "If we cannot speak of the decline of Parliament, we surely can speak of the decline of the House of Lords" (Beer, 1973: 240).

While historically the Lords has lost power in its battles with the Commons, in recent years, and particularly under the terms of office of Margaret Thatcher, it has surprisingly reasserted its legislative role in relation to the government. Perhaps indicative of this changing mood was the 1985 decision of the Lords to televise their debates, in contrast to the policy of the Commons, which only accepted TV in October of 1989. More importantly, during Thatcher's first term in office between 1979–1983, the Lords made 45 major amendments to government legislation. After Thatcher's huge reelection in 1983, the Lords continued to oppose important parts of her legislative package. For example, between 1979 and 1988, the House of Lords defeated the Government 112 times on specific clauses and amendments. However, despite this evidence of at least a temporary renewed legislative interest of the Lords, the historical assessment that the House of Commons is the preeminent legislative chamber still rings true, even though it may now be slightly off-pitch.

Thus, the legislature in Great Britain can be described as bicameral in structure, with the elected House of Commons dominating the appointed and largely hereditary House of Lords. Increasingly peripheral to the political process, the upper House has steadily lost power to the Commons in the present century, despite some temporary reversals of this trend. While the Commons performs important representation and legitimation functions, it does not govern. Parliamentary sovereignty is illusory, with the Commons itself controlled by the political executive working through the party system.

The American Legislature

If any legislature in the world could be cited as an example that would belie the "decline of Parliament" thesis, it would be the American Congress. As a result of the separation of powers principle, which provides the potential for an assertive legislative branch, the continuing role of Congress in the lawmaking process runs counter to the trend in most countries. Moreover, the American experience also differs with respect to the relationship between the two legislative chambers: the House of Representatives and the Senate were designed to be coequal in theory and, for the most part, have remained so. In contrast to the Canadian Senate or the British House of Lords, the American upper House has successfully adapted to the demands of the democratic era. In so doing, the American Senate has preserved a vital role for itself in the political process. Since the House and Senate are coequal partners, we will consider them together with respect to three areas: legislative organization, procedures, and functions.

LEGISLATIVE ORGANIZATION

The physical structure of the Capitol places the House of Representatives and Senate at opposite ends, symbolizing, perhaps, their distinct role, as well as their often adversary relationship. However, unlike the seating arrangements in most British parliamentary systems, the parties in the American House and Senate do not face each other, but are instead arrayed

> Anyone who is unfamiliar with what Congress actually does and how it does it, with all its duties and all its occupations, with all its devices of management and resources of power, is very far from a knowledge of the constitutional system under which we live; and to everyone who knows these things that knowledge is very near (Wilson, 1885: 57).

in a semicircle around their presiding officers. This seating arrangement helps to mitigate antagonism between the parties within each House. Moreover, the concepts of government and opposition found in a parliamentary system would be hard to achieve in a polity based on the separation of powers, because the government, the party in control of the presidency and White House, is not necessarily the majority party within either legislative chamber.

Membership in both the House of Representatives and the Senate is based on direct, popular election, although the constitutional requirements for service and length of tenure vary in each. For the House of Representatives an individual must be 25 years old, a citizen for seven years, and a resident of the state in which his or her legislative district is based. The term of office is two years, with the number of congressional districts allocated to each state based on population. For example, the House of Representatives has a total of 435 members, with the largest state, California, assigned 45 districts and the smallest states, such as Vermont and Wyoming, receiving only one.

For the Senate a member must be 30 years old, a citizen for nine years, and a resident of the state that he or she represents in the upper House. The allocation of Senate seats is on a geographical or territorial basis: each state, no matter its size, receives two Senate seats. Thus, with 50 states, the Senate is composed of 100 members. Initially senators were selected by their respective state legislatures: for example,

> It could probably be shown by facts and figures that there is no distinctly American criminal class except Congress (Mark Twain).

the New York state legislature would select that state's representatives to the upper House of the national legislature in Washington. However, since the adoption in 1913 of the Seventeenth Amendment to the American Constitution, senators are popularly elected. This reform is a major reason why the Senate has remained an important element in the American governmental system. Senators serve a six-year term, with one-third of the membership elected every two years. For example, one-third of the Senate will be elected in 1992, one-third in 1994, and one-third in 1996; they will all serve a six-year tenure before facing reelection in 1998, 2000, and 2002, respectively.

Both the House and Senate generally organize themselves internally along similar lines. The House of Representatives is presided over by the speaker of the House, who is chosen by the majority party. The person selected has usually been a senior member who has built up a power base within the legislature itself. The job of the speaker of the House is not usually a stepping stone to higher office in the American political system. In addition, each party elects a floor leader, whose function is similar to the Canadian House leader, as well as several party whips. The speaker, majority and minority floor leaders, and party whips are responsible for organizing the day-to-day business and operation of the House of Representatives.

The Senate's structure varies slightly from this pattern: its presiding office is the President of the Senate, who is the vice-president of the United States. As Senate president, the vice-president is not an integral part of the legislature: the position is largely routine, with the incumbent casting a vote only in the case of a

tie. Often the vice-president does not preside, at which point the presiding officer of the Senate is the **president pro tempore**, typically a junior member of the majority party. Effective power lies not with the office of the President of the Senate, but with the majority and minority leaders selected by each party. These positions are often ones of national prominence and can sometimes be used as springboards to national office. For example, Lyndon Johnson's mastery of the Senate as majority leader during the 1950s was one reason John F. Kennedy selected him as his running mate in the 1960 presidential election.

While the presiding officers and party leaders are influential positions within the legislature, their power is constrained by the nature of party discipline and the committee system. Although the leadership usually gets its way, it may be forced to compromise or even be defeated outright on a particular vote. The reason for this is that, while the political parties work as groups within the legislature, their degree of cohesion and unity is considerably lower than in a British parliamentary system.

The legislative parties are neither controlled nor directed by the executive, a reflection of the separation of powers doctrine. Moreover, the use of the primaries for political recruitment and the local power base of both House and Senate members has meant that the party leadership has few resources or sanctions with which to ensure strong party cohesion. As a result, party discipline in the American legislative chambers rarely approaches 100 percent: "Almost every vote in both houses shows a minority of each party voting against the majority of their party" (Hilsman, 1979: 116–117). Although party discipline is weaker than in Canada and Britain, it is still the most important factor in determining how individual members of Congress will cast their ballots. As a general rule most Congressmen vote with their party about two-thirds of the time. The nature of party discipline in the American Congress was a key reason for the ability of Ronald Reagan to push his controversial programs through the legislature. During both of his terms of office, President Reagan forged a "conservative" coalition across party-lines, allowing him to get around the numerical majority of Democrats in the House of Representatives.

The second constraint on the party leadership is the committee system in each House. Unlike the committees in a parliamentary system, which are tightly controlled by the government, American committees have an independent power base, which results in considerable clout in the legislative process. While these committees have as their main function the detailed clause-by-clause analysis of a piece of legislation, there is little else about them similar to their Canadian counterparts. Significantly, American committees have the effective power to delay, to amend, or to defeat a bill outright. As such they are a further example of the decentralization and fragmentation of power so typical of the American political process. Moreover, it is in the committees or "little legislatures" that most of the real work of Congress is accomplished.

Each chamber is divided into a series of standing committees: 16 in the Senate and 22 in the House, organized around substantive concerns such as agriculture, justice, and foreign affairs. Individual senators and members of Congress serve on several committees, move from one committee to another on a voluntary basis, and typically remain for many years on the same committees, thus building up considerable expertise in several policy areas. Party strength on the committees reflects the party's overall standing in each chamber, with the parties determining which of its members serve on the specific committees. In addition, each of the standing committees usually creates several subcommittees, so that the 22 standing committees in the House of Representatives have generated about 140 subcommittees. Generally speaking, the standing committees in the House have more power than their Senate counterparts.

Each committee is directed by a chairman, individuals who have traditionally been extremely powerful in the legislative process. Until the reforms of the mid-1970s, an individual committee chairman could quite literally tie up the entire legislative process: today they remain key actors in the House and the Senate. For example, Wilbur Mills, from a rural congressional district in Arkansas, for many years chaired the House Ways and Means Committee, one of the most important committees in the House of Representatives. During those years, the Democratic members on his committee served as that party's committee of selection, thus choosing all other committee assignments for the Democratic party. As a result, Wilbur Mills was the most influential and powerful member in the legislature. When he briefly entered the presidential race in 1971, one of his colleagues asked him, "Wilbur, why do you want to run for president and give up your grip on the country?" (Green et al., 1972: 71). A few years later, Wilbur Mills was involved in a Washington sex scandal and lost his party and House positions.

These positions of chairman of the standing committees are usually determined by the **seniority principle**, or, as critics have called it, the senility system. Based on custom, the chairmanships are usually given to the senior member of the majority party on each committee with the longest continuous service. The result of this practice is to reward members from safe districts, since it is necessary to win continuous reelection for many years in order to qualify to be chairman of one of the key committees. Moreover, many of these districts have traditionally been rural in nature and based in the South. These powerful positions have often been filled, therefore, by elderly men from rural and mainly conservative constituencies, at a time when the American population was becoming young, urban, and based in the big-city states of the North. The South may have lost the Civil War, but for a century it controlled Congress and was able to prevent effective civil rights legislation from being passed until the mid-1960s. However, scandals such as those involving Wilbur Mills, as well as the autocratic power of many chairmen, led to a revolt in the 1970s against this longstanding custom. For example, in 1975 the Democrats in the House of Representatives ousted three committee chairmen. Reforms adopted in the mid-1970s have both given members of the party caucuses more say in the choice of committee chairmen and have curtailed some of the more blatant misuses of power. However, the seniority principle remains as the most important factor in selecting committee chairmen, whose powers are still considerable.

LEGISLATIVE PROCEDURES

A number of points should be kept in mind when trying to understand the passage of legislation in the American system. First, the already discussed rites of passage of a parliamentary system scarcely apply to the approval of a bill in a presidential-style process. Second, the American system was designed to make the enactment of legislation exceedingly difficult and it has succeeded admirably. Third, legislative politics are extremely complex because of both the coequal status of the House and Senate and the general fragmentation of power within each legislative chamber. Fourth, this decentralization of power has produced a series of multiple veto points in the legislative process, so that a single member or a small group of legislators can stop the passage of a particular bill. These veto points and the access that they provide are a key reason for and explanation of the important role of lobbies in the American legislative process.

As a result, it is much easier to defeat a bill than it is to pass it. Simple majority support

(more than 50 percent) in the full legislature is not enough to win: against determined opposition one must have overwhelming support (two-thirds of those present and voting). In such a system, reform legislation is not necessarily prevented from gaining approval, but the process for such legislation is difficult without strong public and congressional support. As an old adage on the American legislative process puts it, "those who care for the law and sausage should not watch either being made."

The passage of legislation can be broken down into four major stages: first, introduction of the bill in both Houses; second, committee action; third, consideration by the full House and Senate, sometimes called floor action; and finally, enactment into law upon presidential approval (Oleszek, 1978: 15). Each stage involves a number of steps, with defeat of the bill possible at any single one. Except for money bills, legislation may be introduced in either House, although it is usually introduced simultaneously in both chambers. A bill must be passed by both Houses in an identical format before being sent on for presidential action.

Submission of a bill is normally routine, with only members having the right to introduce a piece of legislation. For example, the president cannot formally introduce a bill, but can and does get supporters to do so in both the House and Senate. Once introduced, a bill is sent to one of the standing committees.

It is at the committee stage that close scrutiny is given to a bill, the so-called clause-by-clause review. A committee may hold public hearings, ask for expert testimony, or have the committee's staff prepare reports on the expected consequences of the bill. Committees may allocate this responsibility to subcommittees, which then hold hearings and consider the bill as well. Once the full committee has reviewed the legislation, it votes either to send it on to the next stage or not. A committee can also "sit" on a piece of legislation; that is, it does not consider the bill and therefore it cannot proceed any further. This is a fate that awaits most bills. Of the approximately 15 000 bills introduced during a two-year legislative session, approximately 95 percent are killed at the committee or subcommittee stage. In the 97th Congress (1981–1983), only 210 public laws were eventually passed. By the 1990s, between 900 and 1000 bills were being passed each year by the American national legislature.

From committee the bill moves on to stage three, discussion and debate by the full House and Senate. In most cases, there remains the right to amend the legislation at this juncture. However, except on highly controversial bills, legislators usually accept the recommendation of the committee that has considered the bill in detail. To this point, then, the House and Senate have each considered the bill in committee and have each granted approval to it by their total membership. Floor action is not complete, however, until the versions of the bill passed by the two chambers are identical. As the bill has proceeded through each chamber separately, it is quite likely that it has been revised and amended differently. If the versions passed by the full House and Senate are not identical, the bill is sent to the Joint Conference Committee to work out the differences. The Joint Conference Committee is composed of members from both the House and Senate Committees that considered the bill at the initial committee stage. If a compromise is reached, the bill goes back to the full House and Senate for final approval, after which it is sent to the White House for presidential approval.

In the fourth stage, the president has several options: to sign the bill; to let it sit for 10 days, after which it becomes law in any case; or to veto it and send it back to Congress. If both Houses pass the bill a second time with a two-thirds majority—what is called **overriding** a presidential veto—the bill becomes law without the president's signature. For example, in March 1988, after a civil rights bill had been vetoed by President Ronald Reagan, the House

of Representatives (292–133) and the Senate (73–24) overrode his veto—the ninth time they had done so during his presidency. When the vetoed bill is returned to Congress, it goes back to the full House and Senate and does not have to go through the committee stage again. If Congress overrides a presidential veto, the bill is not sent back to the president for approval: the president cannot veto the bill the second time around. As this simplified outline should demonstrate, the passage of legislation is extremely complex and difficult in the American system. Moreover, at each juncture a bill can be defeated, while approval only comes after all the possible veto points have been successfully passed.

Although legislative procedures in the House and Senate are very similar, there are several important differences which not only distinguish each chamber but demonstrate the extreme decentralization of power in the American Congress. For example, between the committee stage and floor action, the House of Representatives uses a special committee known as the House Rules Committee, through which most legislation must pass before reaching the full membership. This committee determines when a piece of legislation will be considered, how much debate will be allowed, and whether or not amendments to a bill can be made by the full House. If the Rules Committee refuses to pass "a rule" on a bill, then it has effectively defeated the legislation, because the bill cannot move forward without it.

Distinctive to the Senate is the **filibuster**, the right of individual senators to talk for as long as they want on a piece of legislation. This practice of unlimited debate can be used by an individual or small group of senators to bring the work of the upper House to a halt, thereby either preventing the passage of a bill or forcing the proponents of the legislation to compromise on specific points. Often the threat of a filibuster is sufficient to bring about such changes by the backers of a bill. One of the most successful uses of the filibuster was by former Senator Wayne Morse of Oregon, who used to pin a fresh rose on his lapel and threaten to talk until it wilted. The record for the longest single speech in trying to stop a bill is held by Senator Strom Thurmond (now a Republican but then a Democrat). In 1957, in an attempt to stop a civil rights bill, Senator Thurmond spoke for 24 hours and 18 minutes.

A filibuster can be limited by the use of **cloture**, which cuts off debate and allows a vote on the bill. However, a cloture vote is rarely won in the Senate, because most senators do not want to set a precedent for the device to be used against themselves at some future date. Moreover, until 1975, a cloture vote required a two-thirds majority of those present for passage; since then, a three-fifths vote of the elected membership is needed. As a result of this modification, filibusters have lost some of their power, but they still remain an important avenue for possible legislative obstruction.

LEGISLATIVE FUNCTIONS

While similar to other democratic legislatures in its representation and legitimation functions, the American Congress is unique in terms of its lawmaking tasks: "the constitutional separation of powers has preserved for Congress an independent role that distinguishes it from legislative bodies in most western democracies" (Oleszek, 1978: 215). Moreover, in carrying out its law-making function, Congress is further distinctive because of the coequal status of its chambers, which means that the House of Representatives and the Senate each have the power to oppose the wishes of the other. As a result, the American legislature is a major participant in the political process, perhaps best symbolized by its independent power of the purse.

The basis of legislative significance is the principle of separation of powers, which creates the possibility of legislative independence from executive control. Although at times the American Congress has been seen as an ineffective body controlled by a strong presidency (e.g., in the 1960s and early 1970s, there was the notion of an "imperial presidency"), the legislature reasserted its power in the late 1970s. More often than not, the American legislature can prevent executive action by vetoing, revising, or delaying a measure, although it is much less likely to take major policy initiatives on its own.

The separation of powers doctrine forces a mutual dependence on both the executive and legislative branches: the ability to withdraw its cooperation is often the key to legislative power in the American political process. Moreover, if the executive does not cooperate with the legislature's priorities, then Congress may override a presidential veto to force particular policy upon a reluctant executive. The basis for such a legislative role lies, of course, in the broad power allocated to Congress by Article One of the Constitution. While some of the specified tasks given to the Congress (e.g., the power to declare war) have been modified by events and custom, they remain the foundation for an assertive legislative branch. The result is that "contrary to some popular opinion, Congress plays a major role in national policy-making—both in foreign and domestic spheres" (Hinckley, 1979: 138).

Comparing Legislatures

While the structures, functions, and procedures of legislatures may vary widely among different types of political systems and historical periods, the view of these institutions as lawmakers is as widespread as it is illusory. Even in democratic systems, where there is the best chance for legislative importance, parliamentary supremacy is clearly a myth in the last decade of the 20th century. Only regarding the American system can one make a strong argument for legislative significance in the policy-making process. This conclusion reflects the basic differences between legislatures in parliamentary and presidential systems.

Central to an understanding of the role of the legislature in a parliamentary or presidential system is the nature of the relationship between the executive and legislative branches of government. The fusion of powers in a British parliamentary-style system between the executive and legislative institutions has reduced the legislature's role from one of policy-making to one of representation and legitimation. Parliament remains a symbol of authority, but effective decision-making power lies with the executive. By contrast, in the American presidential system, the separation of powers principle divorces executive and legislative institutions, thereby creating the potential for an assertive legislature. This potential, when combined with competent legislators and public support, can be translated into an effective policy-making role by the American Congress. Separate institutions sharing the power to pass bills give Congress a major bargaining chip with which to force compromises and concessions from the executive branch. Thus, the variation in executive-legislative relationships between parliamentary and presidential systems creates a somewhat different role for the legislature in each: in the American presidential system there is a policy-making function, in addition to the functions of representation and legitimation.

Presidential-parliamentary differences are also apparent with respect to the passage of legislation. In a parliamentary system, the government (especially a majority one) clearly controls the ebb and flow of legislation, determining when it will be considered, whether it will be labeled a government bill or not, and whether closure or other techniques will be used. As long as party discipline holds, the legislative proposals of the government are assured of passage. By contrast, in the American presidential system, committees and committee chairmen

are independent bases of influence and power. An individual member of Congress can effectively bring the entire legislative process to a halt. Moreover, there is a series of multiple veto points, which makes it easy to defeat a bill.

A good example of the differences between parliamentary and presidential systems can be seen in the techniques of closure in the Canadian House of Commons and cloture in the American Senate. Closure is imposed by a majority vote and is applied against the opposition parties, while cloture requires a three-fifths vote and is applied against groups and individuals, not parties. In Canada, the use of closure is controlled by the government, while in the United States the imposition of cloture is not, thus symbolizing the difference between the fusion of powers and separation of powers doctrines.

In addition to the executive-legislative nexus, an important concern in analyzing bicameral legislatures is the relationship between the upper and lower chambers. The general pattern of the 20th century has been for a decline in the power and importance of the second chambers, again with the exception of the American Senate. What is often overlooked in assessing such a pattern is the fact that in most parliamentary systems, the executive is responsible only to the lower House, which is one reason why upper chambers have receded in significance. Control of the legislature by the executive, or more precisely, by the political executive, is based on executive-dominance in the lower House. As a result, the second chambers have become increasingly superfluous in the legislative process. By contrast, the American Senate remains an integral part of the polity, a result due in no small measure to its coequal relationship with the House of Representatives within the legislature. And, unlike the Canadian Senate or the British House of Lords, the American Senate has adapted, or been forced to adapt, to the demands of a democratic age. While the upper Houses do not necessarily have to be popularly elected to survive, what they do need is a method of selection or appointment that is seen as legitimate by the public. Until such changes are accomplished, the Canadian Senate and British House of Lords will never have the potential for regaining a significant and continuing role in the legislative process.

The initial legislative institutions were designed to give the public a voice in government and, although they rarely make the laws in fact, that first function remains a viable one for democratic legislatures in the decades ahead.

> The function of the legislature is to provide a means of ensuring that there are channels of communication between the people and the executive, as a result of which it is possible for demands to be injected into the decision-making machinery whenever they exist and for the executive decisions to be checked if they raise difficulties, problems, and injustices (Blondel, 1973: 135).

Summary

1. While the concept of parliamentary sovereignty may be a myth, so is the view of legislative irrelevance. Legislatures in democratic systems serve both representation and legitimation functions, while in the United States a policy-making role has also been retained. Structurally, legislatures may have either one (unicameral) or two (bicameral) chambers, with federal systems usually adopting a bicameral legislature so as to guarantee regional or cultural representation in the upper House. Typically, bicameral legislatures are now controlled by the lower House, which is selected by direct popular election. Upper Houses based on heredity or appointment have seen a major decline in their legislative role.

2. Canada's bicameral national legislature is dominated by the House of Commons, while the Senate's legislative power is severely constrained. Based on representation by population and selected by direct popular election, the Commons is organized on the basis of party discipline and protected by the principle of parliamentary privilege. While designed as a means for ensuring regional and provincial representation, the appointive nature of the Senate has instead resulted in its use as a patronage-related institution, undercutting its legitimacy and power in the political process. In the Canadian context, the notion of parliamentary sovereignty is constrained not only by executive-dominance, but by the principles of federalism and judicial review.

3. In Britain's bicameral legislature, the upper chamber or House of Lords is composed of appointed members who hold office either as hereditary or life peers. The power of the House of Lords has been greatly diminished, but it does retain a suspensive veto over the lower House. The Commons contains 650 members selected by direct popular election, is organized along party lines, and is the pre-eminent legislative chamber. However, even in the nation of its birth, parliamentary supremacy has become a myth.

4. Unlike its Canadian or British counterparts, the American legislature has retained for itself a significant role in the policy-making process, a result of the separation of powers principle. Again in contrast to the Canadian and British pattern, the American bicameral legislature was designed to be composed of two equal chambers and has, for the most part, remained so in practice. The House of Representatives and Senate are both chosen by direct popular election, with the House seats based on population and the Senate seats based on geography (e.g., the states). Passage of legislation in the American system is not only extremely complex, but difficult, given the multiplicity of veto points in the process. Influence and power

are decentralized within each chamber, symbolized by the filibuster in the Senate and the traditional role of committee chairmen in both Houses.

5. In understanding the role of legislatures, a key concern must be the nature of the executive-legislative nexus. In bicameral systems, an additional focus must be the kind of relationship that exists between the two chambers. Does one chamber dominate, or are the two houses roughly equivalent in power? While they are rarely lawmaking institutions, legislatures remain an important mechanism of communication between the governed and their governors.

Recommended Readings

Comparing Legislatures

BLONDEL, J. (1973) *Comparative Legislatures*. Englewood Cliffs, N.J.: Prentice-Hall.

BRADSHAW, KENNETH and DAVID PRING (1972) *Parliament and Congress*. London: Quartet Books.

GRUMM, JOHN G. (1973) *A Paradigm for the Comparative Analysis of Legislative Systems*. Beverly Hills: Sage Publications.

KORNBERG, ALLAN, ed. (1973) *Legislatures in Comparative Perspective*. New York: McKay.

LOEWENBERG, G., ed. (1971) *Modern Parliaments: Change or Decline?* Chicago: Atherton.

_____ and C. PATTERSON (1979) *Comparing Legislatures*. Boston: Little, Brown.

OLSON, DAVID M. (1980) *The Legislative Process: A Comparative Approach*. New York: Harper and Row.

ORNSTEIN, NORMAN J., ed. (1981) *The Role of the Legislature in Western Democracies*. Washington, D.C.: American Enterprise Institute for Public Policy Research.

SHEPSLE, KENNETH A. (1988) "Representation and Governance: The Great Legislative Trade-off," *Political Science Quarterly* (Fall), Volume 103, Number 3, pp. 461–484.

SULIEMAN, EZRA N., ed. (1986) *Parliaments and Parliamentarians in Democratic Politics*. New York: Holmes and Meier.

WHEARE, K.C. (1963) *Legislatures*. London: Oxford University Press.

The Canadian Legislature

BARRIE, DOREEN and ROGER GIBBINS (1989) "Parliamentary Careers in the Canadian Federal State," *Canadian Journal of Political Science* (March), Volume 22, Number 1, pp. 137–145.

BOYER, J. PATRICK (1982) *Law-making by the People: Referendums and Plebiscites in Canada*. Toronto: Butterworths.

CAMPBELL, COLIN (1978) *The Canadian Senate: A Lobby From Within*. Toronto: Macmillan of Canada.

CLARKE, HAROLD D., COLIN CAMPBELL, F.Q. QUO, and ARTHUR GODDARD, eds. (1980) *Parliament, Policy and Representation*. Toronto: Methuen.

COURTNEY, JOHN C., ed. (1985) *The Canadian House of Commons: Essays in Honour of Norman Ward*. Calgary: The University of Calgary Press.

FEEHAN, JOHN and RONALD G. LANDES (1984) "The Parliamentary Tradition in Nova Scotia," *Canadian Parliamentary Review* (Summer), Volume 7, Number 2, pp. 2–6.

FRANKS, C.E.S. (1985) "Debates and Question Period in the Canadian House of Commons: What Purpose Do They Serve?" *American Review of Canadian Studies* (Spring), Volume 15, Number 1, pp. 1–15.

_____ (1986) "Reform of the Canadian House of Commons," *American Review of Canadian Studies* (Winter), Volume 16, Number 4, pp. 399–412.

_____ (1987) *The Parliament of Canada*. Toronto: University of Toronto Press.

_____ (1988) "The Canadian Senate in an Age of Reform," *Queen's Quarterly* (Autumn), Volume 95, Number 3, pp. 663–681.

JACKSON, ROBERT J. and MICHAEL M. ATKINSON (1980) *The Canadian Legislative System*. Toronto: Macmillan of Canada, 2nd rev. ed.

JEROME, JAMES (1986) *Mr. Speaker*. Toronto: McClelland and Stewart.

KOHN, WALTER S.G. (1984) "Women in the Canadian House of Commons," *American Review of Canadian Studies* (Fall), Volume 14, Number 3, pp. 298–311.

KORNBERG, ALLEN and WILLIAM MISHLER (1976)

Influence in Parliament: Canada. Durham, N.C.: Duke University Press.

LANDES, RONALD G. (1985) "Public Perceptions of the Canadian Parliament," pp. 206–210 in Landes, ed., *Canadian Politics: A Comparative Reader*. Scarborough, Ontario: Prentice-Hall Canada.

LEMCO, JONATHAN (1986) "Senate Reform: A Fruitless Endeavor," *The Journal of Commonwealth and Comparative Politics* (November), Volume 24, Number 3, pp. 269–277.

MAINGOT, J.P. JOSEPH (1982) *Parliamentary Privilege in Canada*. Toronto: Butterworths.

MARCH, ROMAN R. (1974) *The Myth of Parliament*. Scarborough, Ontario: Prentice-Hall Canada.

MCCONNELL, HOWARD (1988) "The Case of a 'Triple E' Senate," *Queen's Quarterly* (Autumn), Volume 95, Number 3, pp. 683–698.

MCGRATH, JAMES (1985) *Report of the Special Committee on Reform of the House of Commons*. Ottawa: Queen's Printer.

SUTHERLAND, SHARON L. (1986) "The Politics of Audit: the Federal Office of the Auditor General in Comparative Perspective," *Canadian Public Administration* (Spring), Volume 29, Number 1, pp. 118–148.

ZOLF, LARRY (1984) *Survival of the Fattest: An Irreverent View of the Senate*. Toronto: Key Porter Books.

The British Legislature

ADONIS, ANDREW (1988) "The House of Lords in the 1980s," *Parliamentary Affairs* (July), Volume 41, Number 3, pp. 380–401.

BLACKBURN, R.W. (1985) "Unparliamentary Language," *The Political Quarterly* (October-December), Volume 56, Number 4, pp. 396–402.

BRAND, JACK (1989) "Faction As Its Own Reward: Groups in the British Parliament 1945 to 1986," *Parliamentary Affairs* (April), Volume 42, Number 2, pp. 148–164.

CRICK, BERNARD (1964) *The Reform of Parliament*. London: Weidenfield and Nicholson.

DREWRY, GAVIN, ed. (1985) *The New Select Committees: A Study of the 1979 Reforms*. Oxford: Oxford University Press.

JACK, MALCOLM (1985) "Parliament's Role as a Check on Government," *Parliamentary Affairs* (Summer), Volume 38, Number 3, pp. 296–306.

JENNINGS, W.I. (1969) *Parliament*. Cambridge: Cambridge University Press, 2nd ed.

JUDGE, DAVID, ed. (1983) *The Politics of Parliamentary Reform*. London: Heinemann Educational Books.

—— (1989) "Parliament in the 1980s," *Political Quarterly* (October-December), Volume 60, Number 4, pp. 400–412.

MACLENNAN, ROBERT (1987) "Parliamentary Representation: What Is Wrong with the British Model?" *Parliamentary Affairs* (July), Volume 40, Number 3, pp. 325–332.

MARSH, IAN (1988) "Interest Groups and Policy Making: A New Role for Select Committees?" *Parliamentary Affairs* (October), Volume 41, Number 4, pp. 469–489.

NORTON, PHILIP (1986) "Britain's Reform Parliament," *The Parliamentarian* (April), Volume 67, Number 2, pp. 59–65.

PATTERSON, SAMUEL C. (1989) "Understanding the British Parliament," *Political Studies* (September), Volume 37, Number 3, pp. 449–462.

SHELL, DONALD R. (1985) "The House of Lords and the Thatcher Government," *Parliamentary Affairs* (Winter), Volume 38, Number 1, pp. 16–32.

The American Legislature

FENNO, RICHARD E. (1973) *Congressmen in Committees: A Comparative View*. Boston: Little, Brown and Company.

—— (1978) *Home Style*. Boston: Little, Brown and Company.

FIORINA, MORRIS (1977) *Congress: The Keystone of the American Establishment*. New Haven: Yale University.

FISHER, LOUIS (1985) *Constitutional Conflicts Between Congress and the President*. Princeton, N.J.: Princeton University Press.

KEEFE, WILLIAM J. and MORRIS S. OGUL (1985) *The American Legislative Process: Congress and the States*. Englewood Cliffs, N.J.: Prentice-Hall.

OLESZEK, WALTER J. (1989) *Congressional Procedures and the Policy Process*. Washington, D.C.: Congressional Quarterly Press, 3rd ed.

SCHWARTZ, JOHN E. and EARL SHAW (1976) *The United States Congress in Comparative Perspective*. Hinsdale, Ill.: The Dryden Press.

WAYNE, STEPHEN J. (1978) *The Legislative Presidency*. New York: Harper and Row.

WHALEN, CHARLES and BARBARA WHALEN (1985) *The Longest Debate: A Legislative History of the 1964 Civil Rights Act*. New York: New American Library.

WILSON, WOODROW (1885, 1956) *Congressional Government: A Study in American Politics*. New York: Meridian.

The Judicial Branch of Government: The Reluctant Exercise of Power

The duty of the court, as I envisage it, is to proceed in the discharge of its adjudicative function in a reasoned way from principled decision and established concepts. I do not for a moment doubt the power of the court to act creatively — it has done so on countless occasions; but manifestly one must ask — what are the limits of the judicial function (Dickson, 1985: 213)?

When a priest enters a monastery, he must leave — or ought to leave — all sorts of worldly desires behind him. And this court has no excuse for being unless it's a monastery (Felix Frankfurter, 1943, quoted in Murphy, 1983: xii).

When justices interpret the Constitution they speak for their community, not for themselves alone. The act of interpretation must be undertaken with full consciousness that it is, in a very real sense, the community's interpretation that is sought (Brennan, 1987: 24).

IN DEMOCRATIC SYSTEMS the political process, and the public's perception of it, is dominated by the elected politicians of the executive and legislative branches of government. In most of these polities the third branch of government, the judiciary, rarely comes into public focus and, when it does so, its actions are little understood by the ordinary citizen. Such a lack of attention once led former Chief Justice Bora Laskin to call a news conference at which he complained of the media's minimal coverage of the Canadian Supreme Court. Characteristically, the news conference was sparsely attended and its contents only briefly reported.

This pattern of low political visibility is a reflection of the judiciary's typical guardianship role in the polity: its legitimacy depends, in large measure, on the public's perception of its neutrality and nonpartisanship. To stay above mere politics necessitates that the court system abstain from active and direct involvement in the daily workings of the political process. However, low visibility does not necessarily translate into little political power and influence, for, despite the public perception of their nonpolitical status, the courts are political institutions that render political judgments with, at least occasionally, far-reaching political consequences.

The Nature of Judicial Power

As with many aspects of the political process, the often significant political role of the judiciary emerged from practice rather than from theory. Of the three branches of government, least attention is typically paid to the judiciary in most constitutions. Moreover, in the American system, the principle of full judicial review was asserted by the judiciary itself, rather than being prescribed in the Constitution.

Although the court system was often viewed

> The problem of the guardianship of a constitution is the touchstone of its efficacy as the basic law of the land. While in a sense all authorities are called upon to protect the constitution, as expressed in their oaths of office, there needs to be an individual or body which has the "last word." Constitutional experience points to the judiciary, and more specifically, its apex, as the least objectionable choice for such guardianship (Friedrich, 1968: 265).

initially as a kind of disinterested referee of the political process (e.g., in federal systems deciding which level of government could constitutionally exercise which powers), it was also conceived as a potential means for counteracting the effects of popular sentiment on the executive and legislature. In contrast to its conservative intent, however, the expansion of judicial power has coincided with the democratization of the political process. Paradoxically, an appointed branch of government in a democratic age has had the potential for increasing and protecting human rights against encroachments by the elected political institutions.

JUDICIAL INDEPENDENCE

The court system's ability in Anglo-American democratic systems to counteract executive and legislative abuses of power reflects the principle of judicial independence. In broad terms, **judicial independence** *means the lack of political direction and control over the courts by any outside body*, including the executive and legislative branches of government. The fusion of powers between the executive and legislature in a parliamentary system does not extend to the judiciary, while the separation of powers principle in a presidential polity is a major reinforcement of judicial independence. Judicial independence is designed to prevent any person or institution from dictating to the courts the content of their rulings, a reflection of the view that the courts should be nonpolitical. Sometimes, however, certain groups seek to use extra-legal means to influence the court system (e.g., attempts by organized crime and others to intimidate or to bribe a judge or juror).

The independence of the judiciary in democratic systems is protected by giving the judges legal immunity from the consequences of their decisions. If judges, in carrying out their official duties make an incorrect ruling, they cannot be sued as individuals. A redress of grievances can usually be sought, however, by suing the government. Technically speaking, an individual would sue the Crown, the embodiment of executive authority. Thus, the courts are protected by a legal immunity, as well as a political immunity, from outside intervention in their affairs. For example, in 1988, when a Nova Scotia Royal Commission (known as the Marshall Inquiry) sought to subpoena five appeal court justices to testify, the Chief Justice of Nova Scotia, Constance Glube, quashed the subpoenas on the grounds that they violated the independence of the judiciary.

Judicial independence is further enhanced by the nature of judicial tenure. Judges are either appointed for long terms of office or for life, although some systems have imposed a mandatory retirement age. Once appointed, a judge can be removed only for "cause," that is, some sort of improper behaviour (e.g., a criminal conviction). For example, in Australia in 1985 a member of the High Court (the equivalent of the Canadian Supreme Court) was charged with involvement in the drug trade, while another judge was sentenced to four years in jail for his manipulation of the judicial process in favour of certain interests. However, removal for cause does not mean that people simply disagree with a judge's rulings. Such removal is often made difficult, so as to reduce any chance of government manipulation of judicial personnel. Moreover, salaries of judges cannot be individually

tampered with, either up or down, thus preventing political pressure from being applied monetarily.

The principle of judicial independence has often been misinterpreted to mean that somehow the courts are above or outside of the political arena. Nothing could be further from the truth. The myth of judicial impartiality is an important basis for legitimating the political effects of court decisions, even as it provides an incorrect description of the role of the judiciary in the political process.

Courts are inherently political by reason of their composition, the content of their rulings, and the consequences of their decisions. For example, patronage has often been the leading criterion of court appointments in democratic systems, especially at the lower levels of the judicial structure. Even when explicit partisanship is not the prevailing basis of selection, the appointment of court members, so as to reflect particular ideological views or to represent various interests of society (racial, regional, ethnic, linguistic), is often done for political considerations. The contents of judicial decisions are political because they involve the allocation of power and influence within the polity. For example, in a federal structure, court rulings have been a means of settling questions of jurisdiction between the levels of government.

Finally, the consequences of judicial decisions are political, for they may alter the existing distribution of power and influence or raise new issues, which must be handled by the other branches of government. For example, court decisions have had the political consequence of helping to alter the initial allocation of powers in both the Canadian and American federal systems. Thus, the principle of judicial independence does not exclude the court system from the political arena, but, instead, creates the potential for its political involvement by keeping the judiciary free from executive or legislative tutelage.

JUDICIAL REVIEW

An important means of judicial participation in the political process is what is known as judicial review. Two basic types exist, what we have labelled as **full judicial review** (interpretations of constitutionality) and **limited judicial review** (decisions regarding the allocation of powers in a federal polity). The concept of full judicial review includes the narrower idea of limited judicial review. For example, in the United States — which operates under full judicial review — the judiciary is still called upon to make decisions about which level of government can exercise what powers. However, the more important task of the American judiciary regards rulings about whether or not any government can exercise certain powers (e.g., freedom of speech controversies).

The political consequences of full judicial review are potentially of far greater significance than those of limited judicial review. For example, a basic reason for the extensive political impact of the American judiciary stems from its application of full judicial review, while the historically more modest Canadian judicial result is congruent with a limited judicial review process. In Britain, judicial review does not exist, since its application would be in direct opposition to the principle of parliamentary sovereignty. The greater the extent of judicial review, the greater the likelihood of the court system's involvement in politics, because court cases based on full judicial review often thrust the judiciary into a policy-making role.

Judicial review has been criticized as undemocratic, since it allows a small group of appointed officials to overturn the actions or legislation of elected ones. However, full judicial review has, at times, expanded civil and political liberties against the conservative interests that controlled the other two branches of government. A good illustration of this point is the civil rights rulings that began in the mid-1950s in the American system. However, the impact of full judicial review on the polity will depend, to a considerable extent, on the composition of the courts. The principle of judicial review supplies the legal basis for the assertion of judicial power. If such a pattern results, it depends, in large measure, on the individuals appointed to the judiciary.

Whether the judiciary operates under either full or limited judicial review, the interpretation of a constitution and its application in specific contexts is often a tricky business. Two broad approaches to constitutional interpretation can be identified: judicial activism and judicial restraint. In a pattern of **judicial restraint**, the courts take a very narrow view of their own powers of interpretation. In fact, the judges seek to divine the literal and intended meaning of the initial constitution. This approach implies that it is not the role of the courts to adapt the law to changing circumstances, but to apply the law as it was written. If changes in the law are needed, then it is up to the executive and legislature to respond accordingly. In contrast, the second pattern, that of **judicial activism**, reflects a willingness on the part of the judges to use their powers vigorously, to take a broad view of any powers delineated in the constitution, and, if necessary, to adapt the law to changing circumstances, especially if the other two branches are reluctant to do so.

While patterns of judicial restraint or judicial activism depend, in part, on the individuals appointed to the courts, there is an important relationship between trends of judicial interpretation and the two basic kinds of judicial review. Full judicial review creates the potential for an activist judiciary, while limited judicial review makes more likely a pattern of judicial restraint.

> The popularity of judicial review as a constitutional institution is a post-World War II phenomenon, in Canada not less than in other countries (McWhinney, 1987: 63).

> Rulings on the Constitution are not babies brought by judicial storks; they are politics of the highest order (Burnham, 1983: 134).
>
> We [the justices] are not final because we are right; we are right because we are final (former American Supreme Court Justice Robert Jackson, quoted in Burnham, 1983: 97).

> We are under a Constitution but the Constitution is what the judges say it is (Charles Evans Hughes, 1907).
>
> Percentage of Americans who believe that the accused are guilty until proven innocent: 50 (*Harper's Magazine*, July, 1984, p.9).

A pattern of judicial activism or restraint reflects a country's political culture and the prevailing attitudes about the proper role of the judiciary. Moreover, no judicial system is able to decide cases on its own initiative. Conflicts must be brought to the courts before the judicial branch can get involved. Like a car that only starts on a cold winter morning with the help of booster cables, the court system must be continually jump-started before it can render any decision.

OPERATING PRINCIPLES

The actual operation of the judiciary in Anglo-American democratic systems embodies several key features. First, in most instances, an individual is presumed innocent in criminal proceedings until proven guilty during the course of a judicial hearing. This assumption is a direct result of the principle of judicial independence: the judicial system, not the executive or legislature, decides the questions of guilt or innocence. In contrast, totalitarian systems reverse this view, assuming that a person charged by the state is guilty until the individual proves otherwise. In such a system, the judicial structure is not independent, but is seen as a political extension of the state. The role of the courts in a totalitarian polity is to enforce the political decisions of the ruling party, with accusation of wrongdoing being tantamount to conviction. However, even in some democratic systems, such as France, which use the inquisitorial method, the individual is basically presumed to be guilty until the facts show otherwise (Abraham, 1986: 101).

The second tenet of a democratic judiciary concerns the process for arriving at decisions of guilt or innocence, that is, the **adversary or fight system of justice**. Both the prosecution, those trying to show that the individual is guilty, and the defence, those attempting to prove the individual's innocence, are given the opportunity to bring the facts of the case, as they see them, before the court. Then, the judge or jury acts as an impartial arbitrator, deciding guilt or innocence on the basis of the testimony presented. Assumptions of innocence and an adversary system of court procedure help to produce what is known as the **due process of law** in democratic polities.

A final significant aspect of court procedure is the principle of **stare decisis** or *the rule of precedent*. Once a court has ruled on a particular question or type of case, that ruling stands as a guide or precedent for similar cases in the future. Thus, the principle of *stare decisis* provides for some continuity of judicial interpretation, as well as limiting the number of cases the court system must handle. However, precedents may not be definitive, since they are often multiple, as well as

> . . . judicial decisions give a three-dimensional picture of the constitution. They set down for all time a record of how a complex arrangement of bodies in space looks from one particular point within it (Mallory, 1954: 181).

contradictory. One can always argue that the facts of a particular case are different enough from previous similar cases as to require a further elaboration of the law. In addition, precedents change. Judicial rulings can be applied in new contexts or simply reversed, thereby creating a new precedent for further court decisions.

Once a court has issued a decision, the question of its implementation comes to the forefront. In democratic systems, the executive branch of government, either by constitutional prescription or custom, is typically required to enforce the decisions of the judiciary. Thus, a possible conflict of interest might arise when a judicial decision goes against the executive, for the executive is supposed to enforce such a decision against itself. These cases, however, are infrequent because of the prevalent belief in democratic systems that judicial decisions should be obeyed. Force is rarely needed to gain acquiescence with judicial intent.

The legitimacy of the judiciary, based on the belief of its impartiality, is usually sufficient so that court orders are self-enforcing. If they are not, a court can take several actions, in addition to notifying the executive of any nonobservance. For example, an **injunction** may be issued by the judiciary, which may either command that some action be taken or order that certain actions be stopped. Failure to comply with judicial decisions may also result in an individual or group being held in contempt of court, an offence that carries penalties meted out by the judiciary itself. Thus, the court system is not only lacking a self-starting mechanism, but it is given no direct means for implementing the decisions it has taken. As a result, the judiciary in most democratic systems has often been a reluctant participant in the political process.

The Canadian Judicial System

In analyzing the nature of judicial power in any specific polity, four broad areas must be considered: the structure, composition, operation, and consequences of the court system. Comparing judiciaries on the basis of these criteria reveals more variation among Canada, Britain, and the United States than with respect to the other two branches of government.

JUDICIAL STRUCTURE

The structure of the Canadian judiciary is complex, with responsibilities and functions shared between the federal and provincial governments. Moreover, each province has the power to determine the organization of its own court system, thus producing considerable variation of detail. Overall, the Canadian court system is hierarchically structured and composed of three court levels: federal courts (Supreme Court and Federal Court of Canada); provincial courts (a provincial Supreme Court and superior, county, and district courts); and lesser provincial courts (such as family courts).

Responsibilities for the structure of the courts is federalized, with the national government controlling the federal courts, the provinces in charge of the minor courts, and federal and provincial governments sharing jurisdiction over the intermediate level. For example, while the provinces determine the number and structure of the major provincial courts, the federal government was given the power of appointment, tenure, and salary of these same courts. In total the federal government appoints about 800 judges. Thus, as an area of shared control, the intermediate court level can only function effectively on the basis of federal-provincial cooperation with regard to its structure.

Defining the law's content was also federalized, with the national government granted the right to define the criminal code and procedure and the provinces allocated powers over civil procedure. Thus, an area such as the decriminalization of marijuana is a federal responsibility, while the "solemnization of marriage" is provincially determined.

The federalization of jurisdiction in defining criminal and civil law and of control over the intermediate court level has been incorporated, nevertheless, into an overall hierarchical court structure, now presided over by the Supreme Court of Canada. Although it was first created in 1875 under the authority granted the national government in Section 101 of the 1867 Constitution Act to provide a "General Court of Appeal" for the Canadian system, the Supreme Court only became the highest court of appeal in 1949. Prior to this change (e.g., the abolition of appeals to the JCPC), the ultimate court of appeal for Canadian cases resided in Britain with the **Judicial Committee of the Privy Council** (JCPC). Moreover, even after its creation in 1875, many cases were never considered by the Supreme Court, since "it was possible for appeals to go directly from a court of appeal within a province to the Judicial Committee" (Cheffins and Tucker, 1976: 95).

The result of such a judicial structure was not only to make explicit the nature of Canada's colonial position, but to give the JCPC the role of being "the major interpreter of the Canadian constitution and the major expander of explicit views on the nature of Canadian federalism" (Stevenson, 1979: 55). Thus, Canada faced the anomaly of having judges trained in British law and its role in a unitary state trying to comprehend and interpret the nature of Canadian conditions and the evolving pattern of Canadian federalism.

While considerable controversy surrounds the overall impact of the JCPC on the Canadian polity, there is little question that its decisions at the end of the 19th century were an important contributing factor to the initial decentralizing trend within the federal system. Since any case that was before the courts at the time of the abolition of appeals in 1949 retained the right to appeal to the JCPC, a number of years passed before the Supreme Court of Canada became, in fact, the final court of appeal. Canada was thus in a colonial judicial relationship with Britain until the mid-20th century. With its elevation to the position of the highest court of appeal, the composition, operation, and consequences of the Supreme Court became crucial for understanding the nature of judicial power in the Canadian context.

JUDICIAL COMPOSITION

There is strong reason to suspect that the composition of the Canadian judiciary is patronage-based, particularly at the lower levels of the court system. From this view it makes little difference which level of government has the appointment power: the party in office at either level rewards its own members more often than not. While judicial patronage is pervasive, it rarely becomes a matter of public attention, as it did in Nova Scotia in 1981, when several lawyers openly questioned their ability to have their clients receive a fair hearing. Moreover, although opposition parties traditionally criticize such practices, they are usually quick to adopt them when the gain power. For example, one study by Professors Peter Russell and Jacob Ziegal asserted that, in 50 percent of the judicial appointments made by the Mulroney government in its first term of office, patronage was the dominating factor in the selection process (Makin, 1989: A1).

Any listing of patronage-inspired judicial appointments would be lengthy, so a few examples should be sufficient. The appointment in 1979 of former Conservative candidate for the Commons, Julien Chouinard, to the Quebec Superior Court by the Joe Clark government and of Joe Daigle, former provincial Liberal leader in New Brunswick, to the bench in early 1982 by the federal Liberal government, are both illustrative. Before leaving office in 1984, Prime Minister Trudeau made a rash of patronage appointments, including a number (five former MPs) to the bench. For example, three former Liberal cabinet ministers (Yvon Pinard, Mark MacGuigan, and Bud Cullen) were appointed to the Federal Court of Canada. The

Pinard appointment was the most controversial, because the government had not sought the advice of the Canadian Bar Association before announcing the decison — thereby breaking the government's 17-year-old agreement with that legal group. In a report published in 1985, the Canadian Bar Association demanded that the appointment of judges be less political in the future, with Chief Justice Brian Dickson indicating that judges should be selected on the basis of ability, rather than partisanship. However, an immediate change in the basic patronage pattern of judicial appointments appears unlikely. For example, in December of 1986, Prime Minister Mulroney appointed the former Tory Premier of Manitoba, Sterling Lyon, to the Manitoba Court of Appeal.

To overcome the image of a patronage-based selection process, a revised procedure was put into effect in January of 1989. All persons considered for a judgeship are now assessed by a provincial committee made up of "nonpartisan" members representing the Canadian Bar Association, the provincial law society, and the federal and provincial governments. This new process will likely reduce the most blatant examples of judicial patronage.

While such partisan abuses are infrequently associated with the Supreme Court of Canada itself, the selection of its members is still political in the sense of the ideological views the appointees bring to the Court. The selection of Bora Laskin as Chief Justice of the Supreme Court by former Prime Minister Trudeau was political because of Laskin's publicly expressed views on the Canadian judiciary. In a similar vein, Prime Minister John Diefenbaker had earlier refrained from appointing Laskin to the Supreme Court because of a critical assessment by then Professor Laskin (1959) of Diefenbaker's proposed Bill of Rights (MacKay, 1981).

In addition to the patronage factor, other considerations influence court appointments. Since judges are selected from among members of the legal profession, the court members are typically unrepresentative of the total population in terms of such basic sociopolitical factors as race, ethnicity, education, and social class. For example, while the two charter groups of Canadian society are well-represented, those of neither British nor French origin have received few judicial appointments to date. Particularly evident has been the lack of women in the Canadian judiciary. Perhaps that is not as surprising as it might seem, given the fact that in the late 1920s the Canadian Supreme Court, which was composed of all males, unanimously agreed that women were not "persons" as defined in the BNA Act of 1867 (Section 24). Because traditionally few women have become lawyers or politicians, few have been appointed to the bench. For example, Madam Justice Constance Glube became, in 1977, the first woman ever appointed to the Supreme Court in Nova Scotia.

To help ensure French-Canadian representation on the national courts, Quebec is guaranteed three positions on the Supreme Court and, since 1985, eight of the 25 positions on the Federal Court, although no such guarantees exist for other groups. The main reason for Quebec's representation is to ensure that judges familiar with the civil law tradition of Quebec sit on cases that deal with such matters. Although some effort is made to distribute judicial appointments among the various socioeconomic interests of society, the composition of the judiciary is more immune to the democratic ethos than either the executive or legislature.

The tenure of judges in Canada is indeterminate, extending from their appointment to their mandatory retirement, usually at age 75. Within this period judges are typically not subjected to any formal review or reappointment process. However, judges can be removed for "cause." For example, Section 98 of the 1867 Constitution Act empowers the federal government to remove any judge of the superior courts after an address by the governor general to both Houses of Parliament. The exercise of this legal power is rare, for a judge in trouble because of personal problems or alleged wrongdoing will usually resign before being removed from office.

Several such incidents came to the public's attention in the early 1980s, including one case where a judge was alleged to have regularly consorted with a prostitute in his chambers. Since judicial independence was never designed to protect such antics and because of the media attention the case received, the judge in question was forced to resign. A more tragic case developed with British Columbian Supreme Court Judge Davie Fulton. A former federal justice minister and leader of the provincial Conservative party, Judge Fulton developed a serious drinking problem. After his second conviction for driving while intoxicated, Judge Fulton resigned from the court. Such incidents, while rare, demonstrate that judges, like any other group, are human. On the whole, however, the quality of Canadian judicial personnel is good, even with its patronage-base and sometimes human failings.

The Supreme Court of Canada is composed of nine justices, one of whom is named the chief justice and presides over and directs the work of the court (Table 7.1). In recent years the workload of the Supreme Court has involved about 100 appeals per year — a schedule that will likely increase as the numerous Charter-related cases make their way through the judicial hierarchy. The position of Canadian Chief Justice is one of influence rather than one of power, for there is nothing that guarantees support from the other justices. On several significant occasions in the 1970s, former Chief Justice Bora Laskin found himself in the minority, exemplified by his dissent in 1975 on the power of parole boards to change the conditions of a person's parole without any apparent reasonable justification. The Supreme Court must contain three members from Quebec, with a quorum consisting of five of the nine justices (on any appeal from Quebec, two members of the quorum must be from that province). Those appointed must have considerable legal experience (i.e., 10

years of practice as a barrister) or be members of a provincial superior court. These requirements have usually prevented blatant patronage appointments to the highest court.

However, political considerations do intrude even at the Supreme Court level. For example, based on custom, Supreme Court justices are selected on a regional basis. When Mr. Justice Roland Ritchie resigned in 1984, it was necessary, based on custom, to replace him with a judge from the Atlantic provinces. Even though Justice Minister John Crosbie was from Newfoundland, a province which has never been represented on the highest Canadian court, the appointment went to New Brunswick — Mr. Justice Gérard LaForest of the province's Court of Appeal.

JUDICIAL OPERATION

In addition to the structure and composition of the judiciary, a third important attribute of the court system is its method of operation. The broad functioning of the judicial system in Canada can be described by the concepts of judicial independence, limited judicial review, and judicial restraint.

Although the principle of judicial independence has sometimes been violated, its acceptance has never been open to serious attack. The judiciary is designed to be free of executive or legislative control and when violations of such a principle become known, the political consequences can be severe. For example, in Ontario in the late 1970s, one minister resigned because of his alleged intercession with a judge on behalf of a constituent with respect to a pending court case. Similarly, in the famous Judges Affair in 1977, two federal cabinet ministers resigned or lost their portfolios because of reported interventions with a judge with respect to a contempt of court citation against one of their fellow cabinet officers. In January 1990, Fitness and Amateur Sport Minister Jean

Charest resigned from the cabinet after phoning the office of a Quebec superior judge regarding the case of a coach who was seeking to be reinstated to the Canadian team for the Commonwealth Games.

Sometimes judicial independence is challenged by the reverse of this process, that is, when a judge intervenes openly in current partisan controversy. Such a case occurred when then Justice Thomas Berger of the British Columbia Supreme Court wrote a lengthy critique about the dropping of native rights from the patriation accord, a critique that was published in *The Globe and Mail* on December 10, 1981. Prime Minister Pierre Trudeau, who had appointed Mr. Berger to the judiciary, reacted bitterly to the critique, openly attacking Justice Berger for his views. In April 1982 a complaint against Justice Berger's intervention into the patriation controversy was brought before the Canadian Judicial Council.

The Canadian Judicial Council, created in 1971, is composed of the various chief justices of the Canadian court system. Its purpose is to investigate complaints about judges and may, if the facts warrant, recommend to the federal minister of justice an individual's removal from office. Judicial councils have also been created at the provincial level. In the Berger case, the Council decided that his conduct had been indiscreet, but did not recommend removal from office. Justice Berger responded by saying that he would continue to speak out on minority rights in the future. However, mainly as a result of this controversy, Judge Berger resigned from the bench in 1983. Although such incidents concerning the principle of judicial independence occur, they are relatively infrequent in Canada.

The second operating principle of the Canadian judiciary is that of limited judicial review. This practice of delineating the respective powers of the federal and provincial governments is not directly contradictory to the principle of parliamentary sovereignty, since the judiciary determines only which level of government is supreme with respect to which powers. As

already mentioned, such rulings can, however, have considerable impact on the balance of power between the two levels of government in a federal polity. An example of the exercise of limited judicial review is the Supreme Court ruling on the wage-and-price control legislation of the mid-1970s. The anti-inflation program was held to be within the federal government's powers because of the residual power clause in the 1867 Constitution Act. Similarly, attempts by the provinces to deal with the problem of prostitution were ruled unconstitutional because prostitution is a criminal matter that falls within the jurisdiction of the federal government. Thus, a Calgary bylaw was struck down by the Supreme Court in 1983, as was Nova Scotia's attempted use of an injunction in 1984 as a means of dealing with the prostitution matter. Such decisions are classified as examples of limited judicial review because they deal with the kinds of powers and functions that the federal and provincial governments may exercise.

The third operating principle of the Canadian courts is the traditional practice of judicial restraint, that is, the limited exercise of the limited powers given to them. In part, the pattern of restraint reflects the attitudes of the judges themselves (what could be called, perhaps, judicial self-restraint), as well as the overall constitutional position of the judiciary in Canada. Quite frankly, the other two branches of government, usually under some version or variation of the parliamentary supremacy doctrine, have sought to limit any expansion of judicial power. As a result, the umpire of the Canadian federal system has traditionally been called upon to make very few close calls at home plate.

A good example of the impact of limited judicial review and judicial self-restraint occurred during the internment and evacuation of Japanese Canadians during the Second World War. By the powers of the War Measures Act, implemented through orders-in-council, the Canadian government, under Liberal Prime Minister

TABLE 7.1   THE CANADIAN SUPREME COURT 1990

Justices	Appointed by	Date	Province
Antonio Lamer	Trudeau	1980	Quebec
Chief Justice	Mulroney	1990	
Bertha Wilson	Trudeau	1982	Ontario
Gérard LaForest	Mulroney	1985	New Brunswick
Claire L'Heureux-Dube	Mulroney	1987	Quebec
John Sopinka	Mulroney	1988	Ontario
Charles Gonthier	Mulroney	1989	Quebec
Peter Cory	Mulroney	1989	Ontario
Beverly McLachlin	Mulroney	1989	British Columbia
William A. Stevenson	Mulroney	1990	Alberta

> Judges, however bright, however knowledgeable on public affairs, cannot bring their judicial office into a public forum by participating in public affairs. Their choice of a vocation has meant, in my view, a deliberate choice to leave public affairs alone and let others — and there are many others — deal with them (Chief Justice Bora Laskin, public speech, 1983).

Mackenzie King, attacked the fundamental liberties and rights of Japanese Canadians. Appeals to the Supreme Court of Canada and to the Judicial Committee of the Privy Council proved to be of no avail: "The issue was regarded as one for political judgment, in no way subject to the jurisdiction of the courts" (Berger, 1981: 118).

JUDICIAL CONSEQUENCES

Given the workings of limited judicial review and a pattern of judicial restraint, the political impact of the Canadian judiciary might be expected to be extremely modest. In fact, however, the Canadian courts have played a fairly significant political role, particularly considering the context within which they have traditionally operated. Such a conclusion is supported by a political analysis of the Supreme Court of Canada, a body that has not been immune to political controversies.

Since the Supreme Court is the final body to hear matters of federal-provincial conflict and because its members are appointed by the federal government, the provinces have always harboured the suspicion that the Supreme Court is biased in favour of the national government. This view is reinforced by the legal requirement that Supreme Court justices, after their appointments, must "reside in the national capital region" (Supreme Court of Canada Act, Section 8), thus supposedly helping to overcome any regional or provincial bias they may have had. Premier Peter Lougheed of Alberta put it bluntly in 1978 when he said that it didn't matter where the Supreme Court justices were born, because after 20 years in Ottawa, they all thought alike anyway. In a similar vein, in its constitutional reform proposals of 1978, the province of British Columbia questioned the impartiality of the Supreme Court, because of

SUPREME COURT DECISION-MAKING

"WE'RE STARTING TO LOSE THEM ... GET INTO THE NATIVE RIGHTS STUFF AND WE'LL BRING ON THE INDIAN DANCERS"

Source: Andy Donato, *Donato's 1981 Political Cartoons*. By permission of Canada Wide Feature Service and Andy Donato.

Ottawa's supposed control over the Court's jurisdiction and composition.

However, a perusal of Supreme Court decisions from 1949 onward reveals a mixed pattern, with the Court sometimes ruling in favour of

I have long been fascinated with the phenomenon of judicial power in different societies, but especially in our own. It is (or has been) such quiet power, so unacclaimed, so often denied! It is precisely the subtle, ironic strength which our judiciary derives from its hidden nature that so fascinates me (Russell, 1975: 75.)

the provinces and sometimes in favour of the federal government. The decisions of the Laskin Court of the 1970s often upheld federal government powers, as in the wage-and-price control decision, but it also ruled in favour of the provinces (e.g., the December 1979 decision regarding Senate reform). Contrary to provincial perceptions, it would be difficult to make a strong case for inherent Ottawa bias in the decisions of the Supreme Court of Canada or to argue that judges are primarily appointed because they appear to be centralist or nationalist in their judicial outlook.

Instead of an explicit bias in favour of Ottawa, what seems more realistic as the cause of provincial concerns is the following pattern. The typically narrow or legalistic interpretation of the 1867 Constitution Act by judges operating under a pattern of judicial restraint and limited judicial review has been seen to support the national government because the 1867 Constitution Act itself remains, in theory, a highly centralized document, unreflective of the decentralized pattern of modern Canadian federalism. Perhaps revealing is a study of the Supreme Court undertaken by the Quebec government following the Parti Québécois victory in 1976. Released in 1978, the report claimed that there was no specific bias on the part of the Supreme Court simply because it was appointed by Ottawa. Any bias resulted instead from the Supreme Court's literal interpretation of a near-unitary document (*The Globe and Mail*, October 18, 1978).

Provincial suspicions remain, however, and help to determine some aspects of federal-provincial relations. For example, the provinces are reluctant to settle federal-provincial disputes in the courts if negotiations can possibly resolve the matter. Fear of federal bias has restricted the judicial alternative, as in the case of the Atlantic provinces' refusal in the 1970s to take questions of jurisdiction over offshore oil and natural gas to the Supreme Court for resolution. In the fall of 1981, federal Energy Minister Marc

The Supreme Court of Canada is not a federal institution. It is a national institution and its members are under no federal allegiance, there is no regional allegiance and no political allegiance (Chief Justice Bora Laskin, public speech, 1971).

Lalonde openly dared Nova Scotia and Newfoundland to seek a court ruling, which they declined to do. However, failure to reach a negotiated settlement led the federal government to take the question of the ownership of resources off Newfoundland into the court system. In February 1983, the Supreme Court of Newfoundland ruled that Ottawa, not the province, owned offshore resources, a view that was later upheld by the Supreme Court of Canada (March 1984). By refusing a negotiated settlement and forcing the federal government to turn to the judicial option, Premier Brian Peckford of Newfoundland lost it all. Interestingly, Nova Scotia, during this same time period, negotiated the issue with Ottawa. Thus, one reason for modest judicial involvement in political disputes has been a provincial fear of a federalist bias on the part of the Supreme Court of Canada.

In addition to the perceived centralist bias of the Supreme Court, a second important political element of judicial operation concerns the use of **advisory or reference decisions**. Unlike some court systems where only actual cases are heard, the Supreme Court of Canada can be asked to rule on matters of legislation before they are implemented. At the request of the governor-in-council (for all practical purposes, the prime minister and cabinet), the Supreme Court will issue an advisory opinion as to the constitutionality of a proposed course of action. Some of the most significant Supreme Court decisions of recent years fall into this category, including the rulings on Senate reform in 1979, the patriation proposal in 1981, and offshore jurisdiction in 1967. Although actual cases

might lead to a challenge of an advisory opinion at a later date, the court is unlikely to change its opinion in the near future.

An advisory opinion in its favour is an important political resource for either level of government. However, since the provinces cannot ask for advisory opinions from the Supreme Court, but must work their cases up through the hierarchical court system to the final court of appeal, the federal government has a decided advantage in this regard. Moreover, the federal government is unlikely to ask for such Supreme Court advice unless it feels that the court is likely to rule in its favour. If a negative advisory opinion results, the proposed legislation or government action can be modified to take account of the court's objections. If a positive decision is forthcoming for either level of government, then future court action will be unlikey, since the side which has lost will seek a negotiated settlement with the other level of government rather than risking a future anticipated loss before the Supreme Court.

A third political effect of judicial decisions has been to make the court system one element among many in Canadian political conflicts: "The court's declarations are often viewed as a factor in political bargaining, rather than as decisive statements" (McMenemy, 1980: 146). The determination to take a conflict or dispute into the court system is a political, rather than primarily a legal decision: "One of the most obvious consequences of judicial review is that political questions often come to the courts clothed as legal, constitutional questions" (Fletcher, 1977: 100).

A good example of this political use of the judiciary can be seen with respect to Quebec's Keable Commission's powers in the late 1970s. Under the direction of Commissioner Jean Keable, the province of Quebec sought to investigate alleged RCMP wrongdoing in the province. In order to do so, the Keable Commission subpoenaed extensive information from the RCMP's secret files. As a federal body, the

> Supreme Court of Canada justices have become our new philosopher-monarchs. These black-robed, secluded figures hand down solutions to society's problems from the Olympian detachment of the highest court in the land . . . . By the judge's own admission, politics and law are now inextricably linked and their fates joined (Hutchinson, 1987: A7).

RCMP resisted, with the full backing of the Liberal government in Ottawa. The federal government proceeded to take the issue to the judiciary, arguing that no province had the right to investigate police matters, especially those which clearly fell under federal jurisdiction. Moreover, since criminal law was a federal responsibility, if the police had broken any such laws, it was a matter for federal prosecution and, thus, not of concern to the provinces. The province of Quebec, with the support of four other provinces, argued that, since the administration of justice was a provincial concern, the province had a constitutional right to investigate even a federal police agency. The eventual outcome of this dispute was a court ruling that backed the federal position and effectively shut down the Keable Commission.

While it was shrouded in legal principles, what was really taking place was a political battle between the Parti Québécois government in Quebec and the federal Liberals in Ottawa, with each side seeking political support within the province. The clear intent of the provincial Keable Commission was to embarrass the federal government and to thus increase backing for the independence option, while the purpose of the federal government was to prevent such an investigation so as to protect its own political flank. However, not all judicial decisions are as definitive as the one on the Keable Commission, so that a court ruling may not settle the conflict at all. The ruling of the Supreme Court on the Canada Act in September 1981 is a case in point:

both the federal and provincial governments claimed victory, with the battle continuing until a politically negotiated resolution finally settled the matter.

A further aspect concerning the political consequences of court actions can be seen with respect to judicial protection of the broad areas of civil and political liberties. As with a constitution, so also with a bill of rights: the effectiveness of each depends more on their implementation than on their wording. Key to the maintenance of human freedoms is the willingness of the court system to use judicial power to make them effective in practice. A bill of rights or charter of rights depends, to a considerable extent, on the willingness of citizens to challenge arbitrary governmental actions and on the political will of the judiciary to prevent political abuses when they are given the opportunity to do so.

Unfortunately, the record of the Canadian courts in this area is not as encouraging as it might be. For example, the judiciary has typically backed the powers of the state and has resisted any effort to make themselves the agents of social change (McNaught, 1976: 160). Moreover, during the 1970s, the Supreme Court made several significant decisions. The judiciary ruled that illegally obtained evidence was admissible in court, with the only recourse left to the citizen a suit against the individual police officer involved in the alleged wrongdoing. Of course, a person could be in jail a long time before such a suit was resolved. In a similar vein, the Supreme Court upheld the need to have a public permit for demonstrations in the city of Montreal, under the suspect view that such an assembly of citizens might lead to a breakdown of public order and safety. As a result, any group wishing to protest against local politicians, such as then Mayor Jean Drapeau, had to gain a permit from the city to do so. Needless to say, such permits were often difficult to obtain.

Even after the passage of the Constitution

The stegosaurus, we are told, was a dino-saur so big and so slow that its brain took an hour to notice that something had hit its tail. Six years after the Charter of Rights was attached to the constitution of Canada, the Canadian public is a last sluggishly perceiving the immense power that the constitutional reforms of 1982 entrusted to the Supreme Court (Frum, 1988: 58).

Act of 1982, with its Charter of Rights and Free-doms, the Supreme Court made rulings which give civil libertarians cause for concern. In December 1984, for example, the Supreme Court ruled that police officers who have received judicial approval to place wiretaps also have the power to secretly enter premises with-out the owner's consent in order to install those same listening devices. Such a ruling is particu-larly ominous in light of a study released in January 1986 which showed that, by comparison to the United States, Canada, on a proportionate basis, has 20 times the number of wiretaps of its southern neighbor. It is one thing to have a Charter of Rights and Freedoms; it is quite another matter to implement it on a day-to-day basis.

However, judicial protection of civil and politi-cal liberties has certainly been enhanced by the Constitution Act of 1982 (see Chapter 14). The major advantage of the 1982 Constitution Act is that it applies to both levels of government, rather than to just the federal one. Thus, the basis for greater judicial activism has been laid; whether such activism becomes an integral part of the judicial process remains to be seen in the next several decades. We must remember that it took nearly a decade before the Supreme Court used the previous Bill of Rights to invali-date a federal piece of legislation. Moreover, the 1982 Constitution Act contains several mecha-nisms, such as the override provision in Section 33, by which basic liberties can be circum-vented. Those who seek a fervently activist

Canadian judiciary will find some solace, and likely increasingly so, from the 1982 Constitu-tion Act. Already, the Charter, in its first decade of existence, has had a major impact in a number of key areas (see Chapter 14). However, the traditional reluctant exercise of judicial power will also remain an important, even if diminish-ing, element of the Canadian political process.

The Court System in Britain

The most important fact about the British judi-ciary is its lack of direct involvement in the political process. The practice of judicial review as utilized in Canada and the United States is unknown in the current British polity: "no court of law can override the British Parliament, which is supreme" (Verney, 1976: 35). Parlia-mentary supremacy has rendered unacceptable any exercise of full judicial review concerning the constitutionality of government actions. As long as the government is exercising the pow-ers granted to it, no court will intervene. If a person or group does not like the law, then the opportunity exists to change the law or to replace the lawmakers with new ones through the electoral mechanism.

In addition to the impact of parliamentary supremacy, the unitary structure of the political system has also eliminated the need for the exercise of a pattern of limited judicial review, as used historically in Canada. Since there is no division of powers between levels of govern-ment, there is obviously no logical or practical basis for delineating their respective powers.

Instead of settling questions of constitutional-ity, British courts are involved in interpreting executive or legislative actions in light of their statutory or legal basis. If the executive or legis-lature has overstepped the authority granted to it (i.e., its statutory power), the judiciary may order a halt to such behaviour. For example, in October 1975, the High Court in London rejected a request from the government for an injunction to stop the publication of the diaries of former Labour Minister Richard Crossman. In a similar vein, if proper administrative procedures have not been followed, the courts may nullify government actions. However, as long as government behaviour has a statutory basis, the courts will not become involved. Even if executive or legislative actions are overturned, the government may simply pass retroactive legislation, giving itself authority for its previous behaviour and thus bypassing the court ruling. The consequence of a pattern of neither limited nor full judicial review has kept the political role of Britain's third branch of government modest indeed.

The judicial structure is complex in Britain, divided down into both civil and criminal courts. Included in the civil court wing are the county courts and family courts, while at the bottom of the criminal court structure are the justices of the peace and the juvenile courts. Although there is no supreme court in Britain, appeals from the top civil and criminal courts may be sent to the House of Lords, if they involve a matter of general public importance. Technically the appeal is to Parliament, but the House of Lords has been given the specific judicial function of interpreting the laws of Parliament. However, the Lords in general do not hear such appeals; they are heard by only the Lord Chancellor and the 10 Law Lords (technically, the Lords of Appeal in Ordinary). The Lord Chancellor is a member of the government and thus changes when there is a government turnover. The Lord Chancellor and prime minister together share the responsibility for selecting members from the legal profession for judicial posts. The British court system operates under the principle of judicial independence; the judges are selected by the executive, and they may be removed for cause. For example, in 1983 a High Court judge, who had been caught smuggling whisky and cigarettes into Britain,

was dismissed from office — the first British judge to be so treated in more than a century.

Given the pattern of no judicial review of government actions and neither a written constitution nor a specific charter of rights, the British polity utilizes a very different mechanism than either Canada or the United States to protect basic civil and political liberties. Instead of delineating citizens' rights in a bill of rights or a charter of rights, individuals in Britain are given all rights not denied them by law. Fundamental freedoms "rest simply on the age-old assumption by British courts that a citizen is free to do as he likes provided he does not commit any specific breach of the law" (Birch, 1983: 236). Thus, British citizens enjoy such basic rights as freedom of speech and assembly, even though they are unspecified in law.

The American Judiciary

In no other political system does the judicial branch of government play as significant or controversial a role as it does in the American. The basic reason for such a pattern is the exercise of full judicial review by the American court system: "Judicial review is the power of the judges, ultimately those of the Supreme Court, to interpret the Constitution and to refuse to enforce those measures that in their opinion are in conflict with the Constitution" (Peltason, 1979: 27). This tremendous power of full judicial review was not contained in Article Three of the American Constitution, but developed from the initial assertion of judicial power by Chief Justice John Marshall in the famous case of *Marbury v. Madison* in 1803. While the details of the case are complex, the result was the acceptance of the view that the courts were the official interpreters of constitutional matters in the American system. The political consequences of this development have been extremely significant, for they have made the court system in the United States more politically oriented

> Where, ladies and gentlemen . . . do you think these great constitutional rights . . . came from? The stork didn't bring them. These came from the judges of this country . . . (Justice Potter Stewart, March 9, 1975, quoted in Friendly and Elliott, 1984: 1).
>
> The Court does not operate in a vacuum, nor is it composed of Olympians. It functions as a legal, governmental, *and* political institution under a basic document that stands in constant need of interpretation . . . (Abraham, 1985: 340).
>
> The very political setting in which American judges toil places powerful constraints upon their conduct (Silverstein, 1984: 208).

and more powerful than the judiciary in any other democratic polity.

JUDICIAL STRUCTURE

The structure of the American court system is federalized in the extreme. Unlike the Canadian court system, which creates a hierarchical and unified structure of federal and provincial courts, the American court system has a complete set of both federal and state courts. Moreover, the large municipalities may have their own court system, thus further decentralizing the judicial structure. The jurisdiction of these court systems stems from the powers granted each level of government by the Constitution: federal courts hear cases involving the powers of the national government, while state courts generally consider all other matters. Some areas of jurisdiction may be shared, thus allowing the accused to be tried in either the state or federal courts, but not in both for the same wrongdoing. At the apex of the judiciary stands the American Supreme Court, which under Article Three (Section 2) hears cases involving the national government or matters of dispute between citizens and governments in two or more states. Cases tried in the state courts can only be appealed from the state supreme courts to the national Supreme Court if they involve important matters of constitutional law under federal jurisdiction.

JUDICIAL COMPOSITION

Composition of both the American federal and state court systems is patronage-based and politically motivated to an even greater extent than in Canada. For example, the creation of federal judgeships is a legislative prerogative, although the president nominates, with the advice and consent of the Senate, the individuals to fill the federal judicial positions. If Congress and the presidency are controlled by different parties, then a stalemate over new positions is likely. Moreover, if a presidential election is on the horizon, the party in control of Congress may wait to see if it is also able to win control of the executive branch, thus enhancing its patronage powers. For example, the Democratically-controlled Congress refused to authorize any new judgeships for Republican President Gerald Ford, but was willing to create 152 new federal posts for his successor, Democratic President Jimmy Carter.

Once the judgeships have been established, the composition of the courts is further politically influenced because of the party basis of judicial selection. The overwhelming percentage of federal judicial appointments are from the same party as the president, with the rate of partisan selection around 90 percent. For Ronald Reagan's two terms, 97 percent of the judges appointed were Republican; in total, he appointed 379 federal judges. Moreover, since federal judicial appointments are held for life, judges often retire early or stay on the job, despite ill-health, in an attempt to get a successor to their position modelled on their own image. Thus, a Democratic judge will seek to retire when a Democratic president is in office or will hold onto the judgeship in the hopes that the next president is a Democrat. For example, Supreme Court Justice William O. Douglas, a liberal-Democrat who had been appointed by Franklin D. Roosevelt, tried to stay on the bench, despite grave health problems, so as to let a Democrat appoint his successor. However, Justice Douglas was unsuccessful and resigned in 1975, thus allowing Republican President Gerald Ford to name John Paul Stevens to the Supreme Court.

Federal judicial appointments are highly political because of the practice of **senatorial courtesy**. Based on custom rather than on law, senatorial courtesy gives the senator from the state where the judge will serve a "veto" power over who is selected. This customary veto power is especially strong when the senator has the same political affiliation as the president. Moreover, senatorial courtesy is a good example of the political interdependence created by the separation of powers principle: the executive recommends the nominee that the Senate accepts or rejects to fill a vacancy in the judicial structure. The practice of senatorial courtesy can be used to deny a judicial posting not just on partisan grounds, but on ideological and sociopolitical factors as well. Those of liberal or conservative persuasions tend to have an abiding affinity for their own kind; in patronage-inspired appointments, opposites repel.

While federal judges are appointed, many judicial posts are filled by election (nonpartisan) at the state and local levels. The most significant aspect of electing judges relates to its impact on the principle of judicial independence. Most court systems assume that an appointed judiciary will be insulated from political pressure. However, the various reform movements in American politics, such as Jacksonian democracy of the 1830s, viewed an appointed judiciary as a bastion of elite influence that had to be brought under public control. Electing judges would free the courts from elite manipulation and possible corruption, increasing their independence from big business interests. Judicial election was designed to enhance judicial independence from the special interest groups in society; at the same time, the judiciary was to be made more responsible to the people. If citizens do not like a judge's rulings, then they can try and beat him electorally the next time he seeks office. For example, in Ohio in July 1985, a judge ruled that an eight-year old girl had consented to sexual acts. Outraged individuals and parent groups sought his resignation and started to work against his reelection plans. In California senior judges face a periodic referendum in order to stay in office. In 1986, after nine years on the judiciary, the voters threw the Chief Justice of the state Supreme Court, Rose Bird, out of office by a 2 to 1 vote, mainly because of her consistent rulings against capital punishment. However, in practice, judicial election has rarely interfered with the principle of judicial independence.

For those judges who are appointed, removal from office can occur through two processes: death or impeachment. In the latter and, some would say, more difficult method, the legislature may remove a judge (or any other civil officer of the United States) for improper conduct. Impeachment, however, is not used to make the judiciary politically accountable for its decisions. Technically, impeachment means bringing charges of wrongdoing against an official before the House of Representatives. If the impeachment resolution passes, then the Senate sits as a court to hear evidence and to possibly convict the accused. If convicted by the Senate, individuals are removed from office, at which point they may be prosecuted as any other citizens would be. For example, in August of 1985, the House of Representatives voted 17 articles of impeachment against U.S. District Judge Alcee

> . . . the Supreme Court, always an institution of political judgment masquerading as a council of priests (White, 1982: 345).

> I sometimes wonder whether Republican Supreme Court choices are dictated by the same mischievous gremlin who controls Democratic conventions (Bryden, 1988: 201).

Hastings of Miami by a vote of 413 to 3. Judge Hastings thus became the twelfth judge, and the first black, in American history to be impeached.

The structure and composition of the American Supreme Court can be described with respect to its size and method of appointment. The size of the Supreme Court is currently nine, a number determined by the legislature. There have been politically motivated attempts to change this number, the most famous being Franklin Roosevelt's court-packing plan of the late 1930s. In responding to the exigencies of the Great Depression, the federal government sought to lead in the revitalization of the American economy. However, a number of laws giving the national government the power to act were held to be unconstitutional by the Supreme Court. By enlarging the size of the Supreme Court, President Roosevelt felt that he could tip the balance of judicial opinion in his favour. The court-packing plan failed to gain approval, but shortly thereafter, the Supreme Court started upholding the constitutionality of Roosevelt's key economic programs. The Supreme Court usually follows the election returns, even if somewhat belatedly.

Appointments to the Supreme Court are less blatantly partisan than those to the federal courts in general, although political considerations are not entirely removed (Table 7.2). Rather than partisanship, ideology is a leading criterion in nominees to the highest court, as well as ethnic, racial, and other sociopolitical attributes. These factors are not legally required, but based on custom and convention. For example, the major religious groups often receive appointments, with an attempt made to select at least one Catholic and one Jewish justice. Justice Thurgood Marshall was the first

black elected to the Supreme Court, and President Reagan placed the first woman, Sandra Day O'Connor, on the Supreme Court in 1981.

During the 1984 presidential campaign, the nature of future Supreme Court appointments became an issue. Because several justices were ill and approaching possible retirement, the person winning the 1984 race might be able to appoint three to four justices to the Supreme Court. President Reagan favoured strict constructionists who conceived a narrow role for the courts. From Reagan's perspective, the judiciary should not "pre-empt legislative prerogatives or become vehicles for political action or social experimentation." The contrary point of view was expressed by Justice William Brennan, who stated that so-called conservative or strict constructionists "have no familiarity with the historical record." However, President Reagan's reelection meant that he was able to appoint two additional justices (Antonin Scalila in 1986 and Anthony M. Kennedy in 1988) to the Supreme Court, as well as elevating William Rehnquist to the position of Chief Justice in 1986. Thus, by 1989 only two of the nine justices (White and Marshall) had been appointed by Democrats, and both were clearly reaching the end of their judicial careers.

Although presidential nominees to the Supreme Court must receive Senate approval, the custom of senatorial courtesy does not apply. The Senate will typically approve the presidential recommendation, as long as the individual is deemed qualified. Presidents Nixon and Reagan both had two nominees rejected by the Senate, not because they were conservative and the Senate was liberal, but because they

TABLE 7.2   THE AMERICAN SUPREME COURT 1990

Justices	Appointed by	Year
Byron R. White	Kennedy	1962
Thurgood Marshall	Johnson	1967
Harry Blackmun	Nixon	1970
William H. Rehnquist	Nixon	1971
Chief Justice	Reagan	1986
John Paul Stevens	Ford	1975
Sandra Day O'Connor	Reagan	1981
Antonin Scalila	Reagan	1986
Anthony M. Kennedy	Reagan	1988
David Souter	Bush	1990

were deemed not to be among the best-qualified conservatives available. Once appointed, Supreme Court justices may be removed by impeachment and conviction, but no justice has ever been so treated and removed from office (one justice was impeached, but not convicted).

JUDICIAL OPERATION

The operation of the American court system is based on the principles of judicial independence and *stare decisis*, with the Supreme Court standing as the highest court of appeal. Judicial independence is sometimes challenged, particularly when individuals or groups disagree with the content of court rulings. A movement may be undertaken to remove a particular judge, such as the attempt to impeach Chief Justice Earl Warren in the 1960s, or to overturn a court decision by passing new legislation to make a judicial interpretation inapplicable. The most blatant attempts in judicial memory to threaten judicial independence were evident in the Watergate episode, particularly the suggestion by the Nixon White House that they might

ignore adverse court rulings, even those coming from the Supreme Court itself. The second operating principle, that of *stare decisis* (rule of precedent), helps to provide a degree of continuity in a judicial system with over 10 000 federal and state judges.

Several unique aspects of judicial operation are characteristic of the American court system. First, before a case can be taken to court the individual or group must be recognized as having "standing to sue," that is, the right to utilize the judicial alternative. In the American legal system only those who are directly affected by a law or government action have the right to challenge it in court. Trumped up cases or those designed simply to allow judicial involvement do not have "standing to sue" and are rejected by the courts. A second unique aspect relates to the nature of the cases presented: a law or government action can only be challenged after it has been implemented. The American judiciary does not give advisory or reference opinions on hypothetical cases. If the executive or legislature is unsure of the constitutionality of a proposed bill, the only thing they can do is to pass it into law and be prepared for possible judicial intervention at a later date. Third, the Supreme Court itself decides which cases it will hear from the thousands presented to it annually for possible consideration. Usually, only several hundred are selected (typically less than 200) and these are the cases the justices feel have broad public and constitutional significance.

JUDICIAL IMPACT

The crucial element in the operation of the American judiciary is the previously explained principle of full judicial review, the basic reason for the often extensive political impact of court decisions. The pattern of full judicial review has given to the Supreme Court an inherent policy-making role, so that major areas of political conflict become matters for judicial, rather than executive or legislative, resolution.

> In recent years the federal courts have taken the lead in eliminating segregation in public life, ensuring the separation of church and state, defining relationships between individuals and law enforcers, guaranteeing individual voters an equal voice in government, and establishing the right of women to obtain abortions (Dye, 1977: 186).

For example, in a dispute over racial equality in the city schools and the related issue of busing to achieve racial balance, the city of Boston literally had its school system supervised for 11 years (1975–1985) by Federal Judge W. Arthur Garrity. Such day-to-day judicial policy-making is unique to the American system. In total, from 1798 to 1989, 135 federal pieces of legislation passed by Congress have been declared unconstitutional, as well as nearly 1000 pieces of state legislation.

The exercise of full judicial review is particularly crucial in defence of the civil and political liberties established by the American Bill of Rights. Initially, the Bill of Rights applied only to the national government — no protection was given the citizen from the state governments. This pattern began to change significantly in the 1920s, when the Supreme Court, in an exercise of judicial power perhaps only surpassed by the *Marbury v. Madison* decision of 1803, asserted the applicability of fundamental freedoms to all levels of government. This use of the power of judicial review had the effect of nationalizing the American Bill of Rights, thus providing the political basis for an even more activist Supreme Court in American politics in later decades.

The American judiciary, backed by the various checks and balances, operating under the principle of full judicial review, composed of judges often willing to exercise their potential for power, and repeatedly jump-started into action by a litigious citizenry, has played a significant and, at times, crucial part in the political

> The American ideal of democracy lives in constant tension with the American ideal of judicial review in the service of individual liberties. It is a tension that sometimes erupts in crisis (Bork, 1986: 5).

process. This combination of factors has given the American Supreme Court a powerful and "often decisive role" in the polity, while at the same time making it the most "unique judicial body in the world" (Oddo, 1979: v).

Comparing Judiciaries

In considering the nature of the judicial branch of government in the democratic polities of Canada, Britain, and the United States, four factors have been analyzed as the bases of comparison: the structure, composition, operation, and consequences of the court systems. Such comparisons stress the role of the judiciary in the political process with respect to three areas: politics, patronage, and policy. Contrary to the legitimating myth of their noninvolvement in the political arena, the judiciaries in democratic polities are intimately involved in political conflicts and the struggle for power and influence. The principle of judicial independence has not transformed the third branch of government into a political eunuch, impotent in its relationship with the executive and legislature.

The political nature of the judiciary is clearly evident with respect to the process of judicial selection: in most cases, the court system remains a bastion of political patronage in a democratic era. Judges are often created from among those individuals with past or present partisan ties. Such a criterion does not automatically produce either good or bad judges, for partisan affiliation is not necessarily a causal factor of judicial competence. Probably the most debilitating effect of a patronage-based selection process for judicial appointments is its impact on the legitimacy of judicial power in the eyes of the public. Since the effectiveness of a court ruling is heavily dependent on the public's acceptance of the judicial decision, any factor that undercuts the legitimacy of the judiciary should be a prime area for political reform.

Judges and their actions are also political because of the ideological views brought by them to the bench, beliefs which serve as an important factor in the process and content of judicial interpretation. Since judges typically serve long terms of office, these views may continue to have a political impact long after the politicians who appointed the judges have disappeared from the political landscape. Moreover, individual judicial temperament is also an ingredient in producing a pattern of judicial activism or judicial restraint. Some judges are willing to exercise their constitutional powers to the fullest, at times even expanding them, while other judges are content to take a narrow view of their own political role.

Finally, judges are political with respect to their constitutionally-defined roles, which can range from no judicial review to limited judicial review to full judicial review. The particular type of judicial review helps to create a specific style of judicial activism or judicial restraint: the greater the powers of judicial review, the greater is the potential for an activist judiciary. Whatever the type of judicial review, the court system is a political player that is sometimes given a bit part and on other occasions a leading role in the polity.

Summary

1. The judicial branch of government is a significant political actor, especially in Anglo-American democratic polities. Basic operating principles of a democratic judiciary include the concept of judicial independence and the interpretive guideline of *stare decisis*.

Configurations of judicial review range from its absence in Britain to a limited judicial review process in Canada to full judicial review in the United States. The type of constitutionally-prescribed judicial review is an important ingredient in creating a pattern of either judicial activism or judicial restraint.

2. The Canadian court system is patronage-based and hierarchically organized, even though responsibility for it is shared by the federal and provincial governments. Since 1949, the Supreme Court of Canada has become the highest appeals court, replacing the Judicial Committee of the Privy Council in Britain. Appointed by the federal government, the Supreme Court is viewed with suspicion by the provinces who are reluctant to take federal-provincial disputes into the court system. Operating historically under the principles of limited judicial review and judicial self-restraint, the judicial branch has, nevertheless, had significant political consequences for the Canadian polity. Judicial interpretations, for example, have been an important ingredient in the evolving pattern of federal-provincial power. However, with respect to judicial protection of civil and political liberties, the Canadian historical pattern leaves much to be desired. If past performance is any guide to the future, then the Constitution Act of 1982, which has increased the potential for an activist judiciary, might have modest overall long-term impact on the traditionally reluctant exercise of power by the Canadian courts. The bright spot for judicial activists is the increasing impact of the Canadian Charter of Rights and Freedoms in the late 1980s and early 1990s.

3. Given the principle of parliamentary sovereignty, judicial review is unknown in the British context. While courts will rule on whether executive or legislative actions are within the statutory powers of these two branches of government, a redress of

grievances in Britain must be politically, rather than judicially, obtained.

4. The most powerful judiciary in any democratic system is the American, which is also the one most widely selected on the basis of patronage. The custom of senatorial courtesy gives the national legislature control of most federal court appointments, while at the state and local levels a majority of states now elect their judges. The structure of the American court system is federalized, with a complete set of both state and federal courts. The highest court of appeal is the United States Supreme Court, which has often played a significant political role, given the principle of full judicial review. As a consequence, the American judiciary is activist in outlook and intimately involved in the political process, often taking the lead in new areas of public concern, especially when the executive or legislature is reluctant to do so.

Recommended Readings

The Nature of Judicial Power

ABRAHAM, HENRY J. (1986) "Contemporary Judicial Processes and a Democratic Society," *Political Science Quarterly*, Volume 101, Number 2, pp. 277–288.

——— (1986) *The Judicial Process: An Introductory Analysis of the Courts of the United States, England, and France*. Oxford: Oxford University Press, 5th ed.

BLOM-COOPER, LOUIS (1986) "The Role of the Judge in Modern Society," *The Political Quarterly* (April-June), Volume 57, Number 2, pp. 144–155.

CARDOZO, BENJAMIN (1921) *The Nature of the Judicial Process*. New Haven: Yale University Press.

ELY, JOHN HART (1980) *Democracy and Distrust: A Theory of Judicial Review*. Cambridge, Mass.: Harvard University Press.

GOLDMAN, SHELDON (1982) "Qualities that Make a Good Judge," *Annals*, Volume 462, pp. 112–126.

GOLDSTEIN, LESLIE F. (1987) "Judicial Review and Democratic Theory: Guardian Democracy vs. Representative Democracy," *The Western Political Quarterly* (September), Volume 40, Number 3, pp. 391–412.

JONES, PETER (1989) "Review Article: Re-examining Rights," *British Journal of Political Science* (January), Volume 19, Number 1, pp. 69–96.

LANE, ROBERT E. (1986) "Market Justice, Political Justice," *American Political Science Review* (June), Volume 80, Number 2, pp. 383–402.

MCWHINNEY, EDWARD (1969) *Judicial Review in the English-Speaking World*. Toronto: University of Toronto Press, 4th ed.

SHAPIRO, MARTIN (1986) *Courts: A Comparative and Political Analysis*. Chicago: The University of Chicago Press, rev. ed.

WOLFE, CHRISTOPHER (1985) *The Rise of Modern Judicial Review: From Constitutional Interpretation to Judge-Made Law*. New York: Basic Books.

The Canadian Judicial System

BERGER, THOMAS R. (1982) *Fragile Freedoms: Human Rights and Dissent in Canada*. Toronto: Clarke, Irwin and Co.

BOLDT, MENNO and J. ANTHONY LONG, eds. (1985) *The Quest for Justice: Aboriginal Peoples and Aboriginal Rights*. Toronto: University of Toronto Press.

FRUM, DAVID (1988) "Who's Running This Country, Anyway?" *Saturday Night* (October), Volume 103, Number 10, pp. 57–66.

MACKINNON, FRANK (1946) "The Establishment of the Supreme Court of Canada," *Canadian Historical Review* (September), Volume 27, Number 3, pp. 258–274.

MORTON, F.L., ed. (1985) *Law, Politics and the Judicial Process in Canada*. Calgary: The University of Calgary Press.

RUSSELL, PETER (1975) "The Political Role of the Supreme Court of Canada in its First Century," *Canadian Bar Review*, Volume 53, pp. 584–595.

——— (1987) *The Judiciary in Canada: The Third Branch of Government*. Scarborough, Ontario: McGraw-Hill Ryerson.

SNELL, JAMES G. and FREDERICK A. VAUGHAN (1985) *The Supreme Court of Canada: History of the Institution*. Toronto: University of Toronto Press.

STRAYER, B.L. (1968) *Judicial Review of Legislation in Canada*. Toronto: University of Toronto Press.

VERNEY, DOUGLAS V. (1989) "Parliamentary Supremacy versus Judicial Review: Is A Compromise Possible?" *The Journal of Commonwealth and Comparative Politics* (July), Volume 27, Number 2, pp. 185–200.

WILSON, BERTHA (1986) "Decision-making in the Supreme Court," *University of Toronto Law Journal* (Summer), Volume 36, Number 3, pp. 227–248.

The Court System in Britain

DREWRY, GAVIN (1985) "The GCHQ Case — A Failure of Government Communications," *Parliamentary Affairs* (Fall), Volume 38, Number 4, pp. 371–386.

GRIFFITH, J.A.G. (1981) *The Politics of the Judiciary*. London: Fontana, 2nd ed.

NORTON, PHILIP (1982) *The Constitution in Flux*. Oxford: Martin Robertson.

OLIVER, DAWN (1988) "Politicians and the Courts," *Parliamentary Affairs* (January), Volume 41, Number 1, pp. 13–33.

RIDLEY, F.F. (1984) "The Citizen Against Authority: British Approaches to the Redress of Grievances," *Parliamentary Affairs* (Winter), Volume 37, Number 1, pp. 1–32.

SMITH, DAVID G. (1986) "British Civil Liberties and the Law," *Political Science Quarterly*, Volume 101, Number 4, pp. 637–660.

WALTMAN, JEROLD L. (1984) "Change and the Rumours of Change: Courts and the Rule of Law," pp. 210–230 in Donley T. Studler and Jerold L. Waltman, eds., *Dilemmas of Change in British Politics*. London: Macmillan Press.

The American Judiciary

ABRAHAM, HENRY J. (1983) *The Judiciary: The Supreme Court in the Governmental Process*. New York: Allyn and Bacon, 6th ed.

_____ (1985) *Justices and Presidents: A Political History of Appointments to the Supreme Court*. New York: Oxford University Press, 2nd ed.

BAUM, LAWRENCE (1985) *The Supreme Court*. Washington, D.C.: Congressional Quarterly Press, 2nd ed.

BERGER, RAOUL (1977) *Government by Judiciary: The Transformation of the Fourteenth Amendment*. Cambridge, Mass: Harvard University Press.

BORK, ROBERT H. (1986) "Judicial Review and Democracy," *Society* (November/December), Volume 24, Number 1, pp. 5–8.

CORSI, JEROME R. (1984) *Judicial Politics: An Introduction*. Englewood Cliffs, N.J.: Prentice-Hall.

COX, ARCHIBALD (1976) *The Role of the Supreme Court in American Government*. New York: Oxford University Press.

_____ (1987) *The Court and the Constitution*. Boston: Houghton Mifflin.

DERSHOWITZ, ALAN M. (1989) "Shouting 'Fire'!" *The Atlantic Monthly* (January), Volume 263, Number 1, pp. 72–74.

HODDER-WILLIAMS, RICHARD (1980) *The Politics of the US Supreme Court*. London: George Allen and Unwin.

_____ (1988) "The Strange Story of Judge Robert Bork and a Vacancy on the United States Supreme Court," *Political Studies* (December), Volume 36, Number 4, pp. 613–637.

MURPHY, WALTER E. (1986) "Who Shall Interpret? The Quest for the Ultimate Constitutional Intepreter," *The Review of Politics* (Summer), Volume 48, Number 3, pp. 401–423.

O'BRIEN, DAVID M. (1986) *Storm Center: The Supreme Court in American Politics*. New York: W.W. Norton and Company.

RAKOVE, JACK N. (1986) "Mr. Meese, Meet Mr. Madison," *The Atlantic Monthly* (December), Volume 258, Number 6, pp. 77–86.

SILVERSTEIN, MARK (1984) *Constitutional Faiths: Felix Frankfurter, Hugo Black, and the Process of Judicial Decision Making*. Ithaca: Cornell University Press.

_____ and BENJAMIN GINSBERG (1987) "The Supreme Court and the New Politics of Judicial Power," *Political Science Quarterly* (Fall), Volume 102, Number 3, pp. 371–388.

STUMPF, HARRY P. (1988) *American Judicial Politics*. Chicago: Harcourt Brace Jovanovich.

WALD, MICHAEL S. (1986) "Judging the Judges: What Standards Should Voters Use?" *Criminal Justice*, Number 25, pp. 70–77.

WITT, ELDER (1986) *A Different Justice: Reagan and the Supreme Court*. Washington, D.C.: Congressional Quarterly Press.

WOODWARD, BOB and SCOTT ARMSTRONG (1979) *The Brethren: Inside the Supreme Court*. New York: Simon and Schuster.

PART THREE
Political Processes and Political Behaviour

It is not on political forms, it is on political forces that I dwell . . . . To really understand the character of social action, its modes of procedure must be studied in light of the character of those who apply them, and of the social and political conditions in which their wills are formed and manifested (Ostrogorski, 1902).

The formal structures of government are only the scaffolding of power. They do not account for its human chemistry (Smith, 1988: 42).

CHAPTER 8

Political Culture: The Beliefs and Values of the Polity

National contexts greatly influence the practical significance of political universals (Rose and Suleiman, 1981: preface).

I am convinced that the most advantageous situation and the best possible laws cannot maintain a constitution in spite of the customs of a country; while the latter may turn to some advantage the most unfavourable positions and the worst laws (de Tocqueville, 1835).

Ultimately, we are governed by what we think . . . . Governing has much less to do with control of the bodies of people than it has with what is going on in their minds (Schattschneider, 1969: 99).

THE FOCUS OF OSTROGORSKI on political forces rather than political forms and of de Tocqueville on customs rather than on laws both stress the importance of political values and beliefs in comprehending and analyzing the political process. Each polity attaches a particular combination of meanings to its political structures and political practices. An understanding of this subjective aspect of political action is necessary, for it provides the context within which the political system operates: "politics makes sense only when we know the political culture, the pattern of thinking and meaning, that participants share" (Bell and Tepperman, 1979: 1).

Political Culture Definition and Types

As a concept that stresses the meaning of politics for the individual participants, as well as for the wider political community, **political culture** can be defined as *the attitudes and beliefs people have about the political system*: it is a "shorthand expression to denote the emotional and attitudinal environment within which the political system operates" (Kavanagh, 1972: 10). A political culture defines both the nature and scope of legitimate political activity and the individual's role in the polity. From the individual's perspective, his or her political self or political identity is a specific combination of the major themes of a country's political culture, while from the viewpoint of the political system, the political culture of a country is the total combination or mixture of political attitudes

held by its members. A country's political culture reflects its history and shapes its future, while it influences the present operation of the polity.

TYPES OF POLITICAL CULTURE

Numerous ways of classifying political cultures have been developed. For our purposes, the most useful typologies are those that relate political culture to the role of the individual in the political process, focus on the degree of consensus in political values, or link political cultures to their ideological composition.

The role of the individual in the polity can be used as the basis for classifying political cultures as parochial, subject, or participant (Almond and Verba, 1965: 11–26). A **parochial political culture** is one in which a specific political system has not developed and hence no particular political role has been assumed for the individual. In a sense, then, these systems are prepolitical. While no pure parochial cultures remain in the modern era, pockets of parochialism may exist within other systems. For example, a so-called national government in a capital city, headed by an autocrat, may have no relevance to isolated rural groups, which may remain either apolitical or parochial in outlook. In a **subject political culture**, the individual is aware of the specialized political structure, is affected by its decisions, such as paying taxes or serving in the army, and may accept the legitimacy of the system. The role of the individual is a passive one, however, confined to obeying the decisions of the state. A **participant political culture** is

Both social analysis and social policy would be much simpler if people from different societies were interchangeable robots. But a large body of evidence indicates that they are not (Inglehart, 1988: 1228).

Because it filters perceptions, determines attitudes, and influences modalities of participation, culture is a major component of the political game (Dogan and Pelassy, 1984: 67).

> **The Great Canadian National Prayer:**
> "Oh God, give me a mediocre life. Do not let me be disturbed by any great thing" (Robertson Davies, *The Lyre of Orpheus*).

> The history of the modern nation-state is littered with examples of partitioned political systems in which intense sectional conflict preceded national disintegration: outside the United States, one must look no further than Canada or the United Kingdom for examples of sectional stress in the modern world (Bensel, 1984: 3).

one in which the person is given an explicit political role, with various opportunities provided for participation.

All political cultures represent a mixture of parochial, subject, and participant orientations. For example, at the individual level, each person reflects a unique combination of political values as part of his or her political self, values that likely include subject ones (e.g., a willingness to obey laws) as well as participant ones (e.g., a desire to vote or to influence political leaders). At the system level, each political culture is mixed in the sense that different regions, classes, and ethnic groups may have varying conceptions of politics. Thus, one region might be classified as more participant or more subject in outlook than other regions in the same system. Generally speaking, democratic systems have participant political cultures, autocratic systems usually have a combination of subject and parochial values, while totalitarian systems stress subject orientations with participant values grafted on.

A second way of classifying political cultures is dependent on their degree of unity with respect to fundamental political values. On this basis, two types of political culture can be identified, with many possible variations between these extremes. A **fragmented political culture** is "one whose population lacks broad agreement upon the way in which political life should be conducted," while an **integrated political culture** has developed a consensus

about a core set of political beliefs (Rosenbaum, 1975: 37–57).

In a fragmented political culture, many people identify with governmental units other than the national government; patriotism and national identity are weak; distrust between the major sociopolitical groups is evident and often widespread; and the legitimacy of the existing political regime may be in question, as various sectors of the polity demand major changes in the social, economic, and political structure. Fragmentation may be based on factors of race, religion, class, ethnicity, region, or language. When these various bases of fragmentation coalesce, conflict and violence may erupt, which further decreases the level of unity in the polity. Highly fragmented political cultures may spawn movements or parties that demand separation or independence from the larger political system. In contrast, an integrated political culture is characterized by identification with the national government; strong patriotic sentiments; a moderate to high level of social trust; acceptance of the existing social, political, and economic arrangement; and rare occurrences of open conflict and secessionist threats.

Fragmented political cultures are often associated with unstable political systems, for the bases of such fragmentation may be unresolvable through normal political processes. For example, questions of language, culture, and religion are often so intense that the political system may be torn asunder. Integrated political cultures have either dealt successfully with such issues in the past or they have managed

> Americans want to be loved; the English want to be obeyed (Quentin Crisp).

> Talking about Canadian patriotism is like talking about the virtue of one's wife—one doesn't say very much about it as a rule (former Senator Eugene Forsey, 1984).

> Political practitioners in Canada have never been anxious to entrust their fate to anything as ethereal as ideas (Laxer, 1985: 17).

to keep such issues from becoming focal points of contention. For example, the doctrine of the separation of church and state in Western society is one way of keeping religious issues from becoming politicized. The fragmented or integrated nature of a country's political culture influences the way in which the political institutions are structured initially, as well as how they continue to function.

Our third way of analyzing political cultures focuses on their attitudinal and ideological composition: what are the specific beliefs that comprise their core elements? For example, such values as nationalism and social trust have often been seen as key elements of political culture. From a somewhat broader perspective, we might focus on a political culture's ideological mixture in terms of the major political ideas of the modern era: conservatism, liberalism, and socialism. The ideological approach to political culture emphasizes the content of beliefs, while the fragmented-integrated distinction focuses on the degree of consensus evident with respect to these fundamental political values.

Each of the three approaches to political culture suggests that a specific political culture will not only be complex, but also mixed, comprising a variety of values and beliefs not necessarily consistent with each other. What often happens is that certain segments of a polity acquire a set of beliefs that distinguishes them from the dominant pattern. We refer to such a pattern as a **political subculture**. These subcultures may be based on any of the major socioeconomic cleavages such as class, religion, race, and ethnicity, as well as around a particular ideology. When such factors not only distinguish a group from the dominant pattern, but also place the group in a specific geographical location, then we refer to the subculture as a **regional political culture** (Landes, 1979). Some political cultures lack any subcultures, while others have many. Generally, we would expect, for example, that integrated political cultures based on one dominant ideology would be unlikely to produce subcultures, while fragmented political cultures with a mixture of ideological beliefs might contain several distinctive subcultures.

The Canadian Political Culture

The pattern of core political beliefs in Canada can be summarized with respect to four major themes: elitism, regionalism, dualism, and continentalism. Each one has had a significant impact on the structure and operation of the political system. After analyzing these themes, we will discuss their interaction by taking a look at the nature of consociational politics in Canada.

ELITISM

Our first major theme is that of **elitism**, which can be defined as *a pattern of decision-making in which "small groups of people . . . exercise considerable power"* (McMenemy, 1980: 95). While it is difficult to put an exact figure on the size of the elite, it is quite likely a very small group, based on any kind of percentage figure in comparison with the total population. A figure of 1 percent, for example, would produce an elite of 270 000 members, given the 1989 population

" WHEN YOU THINK ABOUT IT... I'VE BEEN WORKING ON THIS IDENTITY PROBLEM A LONG **LONG** TIME, EH DOC?... DOC?

Source: Reprinted from *The Leader-Post* (Regina, Saskatchewan). By permission of the paper and Brian Gable.

figure of 27 000 000 Canadians. Some, including this author, would argue that such an estimate is much too large. But for our purposes, an elite is a small group with both control over the crucial political resources and a willingness and ability to use such resources to determine the outcome of the decision-making process. Moreover, the elite is not a unified grouping, but, as our definition indicates, is composed of a series of subgroupings. For example, democratic polities are usually seen as having a plurality of elites, which would, at least, include political, economic and bureaucratic components. The exact nature of the Canadian elites — with respect to their structure, composition, and influence — is a controversial topic. However, observers agree on one conclusion: the various elites are seen as exercising considerable clout in the Canadian context (Panitch, 1981; Forcese, 1978; Presthus, 1973).

Evidence of elitism is pervasive in the Canadian system. For example, the Official Secrets Act prohibits disclosure of government information, even if that information has nothing to do with national security, although it might have something to do with the governing party's political security. When the Trudeau government introduced the Access to Information Act, which came into force on July 1, 1983, the government, while taking credit for more openness in government, privately distributed among top bureaucrats a memo about how to avoid implementing the Act. Moreover, the federal government could, between 1914 and 1988, impose, on its own initiative and authority, the War Measures Act, which in effect placed the entire polity under martial law. Canada was governed by such means during the October Crisis of 1970 and throughout both world wars. The longest imposition of the War Measures Act occurred

> You can always tell a Canadian by the fact that when he walks into a room, he automatically chooses to sit in the most uncomfortable chair. It's part of our genetic affinity for discomfort and self-denial, which has formed the Canadian character as clearly as our geography (Newman, 1985: 7).

> Ideas are not a phenomenon which one rediscovers every decade or so when tired leaders are replaced by fresh faces. Ideas are inherent in Canadian political life (Doern, 1983: 1)

> Popular sovereignty receives here, as in every democracy, all the lip service it can desire. But it is not a self-assertive, obtrusive, gesticulative part of the national consciousness (Bryce, 1921: 42).

> In order that institutions may be stable and work harmoniously, there must be a power of resistance to the democratic element (George Etienne Cartier).

between 1939 and 1954, although the period from 1945 to 1954 was less restrictive than a full imposition of governmental control would have allowed. During this 15-year period Canada was governed by what can be described as a constitutional dictatorship—a not so inaccurate description of politics in Canada even when the War Measures Act was not in place.

The elitist pattern of Canadian politics is also evident in numerous actions by which governments can exempt themselves from the existing rules of the game. For example, cutbacks in Via Rail service during 1981 were done on the authority of an order-in-council (i.e., a cabinet decision), rather than by legislation, wherein the government exempted itself from the authority of the Canadian Transport Commission to rule on such matters. An order-in-council was also used to implement the "gag law" with respect to Canada's alleged participation in an international uranium cartel. When accusations of wrongdoing began to be heard in the mid-1970s, primarily as a result of the release of information and the findings of several investigations in the United States, the Canadian cabinet issued a regulation in 1976 that prohibited the release or disclosure of any documents relating to "production, import, export, transportation, refining, possession, ownership, use or sale of uranium or its derivatives or com-

pounds" between 1972 and 1975. Even the 1960 Bill of Rights could have been bypassed if the government so wished, simply by the government declaring that a specific law was exempted from its protection (Bill of Rights, Part I, Section 2). The ability of the government to override certain protections in the Charter of Rights (Section 33) and to circumvent existing laws or to pass new regulations to protect its own possible wrongdoing can occur only in a political system in which influence is centralized and accepted as legitimate by most people—in other words, in a polity characterized by elitism.

Consistent with an elitist pattern of control are deferential attitudes towards authority, limited means for citizen participation, and political structures that embody such values. Deferential views of authority can be seen in Canada's continuing ties to the monarchy and traditional forms of authority; after all, monarchical institutions are historically based on the assumption that a small group has a right to rule. It must also be remembered that the Fathers of Confederation were not fervent believers in democracy. Confederation itself was more of an attempt to stop democratic ideas from crossing the Canadian border than it was a means for the extension of the democratic ideal. The political system constructed in 1867 was federal, but it was a highly centralized structure in which few

> The beaver today is rightly a national Canadian symbol, but perhaps the beaver hat would have been quite as symbolic. At any rate, to a great extent Canada was built on the back of the beaver (Careless, 1970: 28).

citizens participated. Indicative perhaps of what lay ahead were the methods used to create the new system: the "procedures restricted effective participation to a very small number of persons, and even symbolic participation by the voters was virtually excluded" (Stevenson, 1979: 45).

Although the polity has become democratized during the past century, reflected best by the extension of the suffrage, few direct avenues for political participation are provided. Other than voting in federal, provincial, or local contests, most citizens rarely seek to influence their leaders between elections—an attitude and behaviour pattern encouraged by the political elite itself. Typical of the elite view of the public's participatory task is that expressed many times by former Prime Minister Pierre Trudeau: "he says that the role of the government is to govern, and the role of the public is to judge him on the quality of his performance when he chooses to call an election" (Stewart, 1971: 103).

Such a pattern of limited mass participation has been classified as "quasi-participative politics" (Presthus, 1973: 38). A good example of quasi-participative politics can be seen in the rare use of the referendum: the public is only asked to decide on an issue when the elite chooses, but even when a referendum is held, the results do not bind a government to any specific policy. The last time a referendum was

> Our true symbol is not the beaver but the carp (Mavor Moore, 1986).

held in national politics was in 1942 over the conscription issue during the Second World War. The vote (80 percent in favour in the English-speaking provinces and 72 percent against in Quebec) only served, if it was necessary, to release Mackenzie King from his no-conscription promise.

A number of historical developments have contributed to the strength of elitist values in Canada. In addition to the monarchical ties, Canada has not experienced a revolution, but has evolved slowly towards nationhood. The political culture of an evolutionary pattern of development is more conservative and traditional than a revolutionary society, perhaps best symbolized by the phrase in the 1867 Constitution Act that describes its purpose as "Peace, Order, and Good Government." Confederation was an act of counterrevolution, which sought to preserve the power of the elite. Moreover, such factors as the hierarchical class system (e.g., the Family Compacts); the non-egalitarian school system, dominated by the private schools such as Upper Canada College; religious groups, such as the Anglicans and Roman Catholics, which are hierarchically organized; and a weak sense of national identity have all helped to produce and to preserve elitist values in the Canadian context (Lipset, 1970). In particular, the government's parliamentary structure embodies and perpetuates the significance of elitism.

> What insulates the elites in the British Commonwealth countries is the political system. The cabinet-parliamentary system with its disciplined legislative parties, which fuse executive and legislative powers in the cabinet, make for a governmental system strong enough to withstand very great public pressure . . . . The effect of the British parliamentary system is to damp down the waves of public agitation (Truman, 1971: 511–512.)

REGIONALISM

The second major theme of the political culture is that of **regionalism**, a reflection of the fact

I began to think during my years in Canada, chatting, overhearing, and reading, that for many Canadians perhaps their unfortunate identity was to search forever for an identity, a Sisyphean task guaranteed to ensure eternal angst (Malcolm, 1985: 56).

Regional identity is at the heart of Western political consciousness. For many Westerners, as for many francophone Quebecers, the significant public realm is not Canada but the region or province. Canada, for them, is first and perhaps last, a legal structure that performs certain administrative functions (Cooper, 1984: 213).

We are not seen as a country of sophisticated cities with nightlife—just the great outdoors with no place to boogie (Canadian Tourism Minister Thomas McMillan, February 19, 1985).

that "nature and history have conspired to make geography central to the Canadian existence" (Schwartz, 1974: 1). Regionalism is both a cause and consequence of the regional political cultures, producing different patterns of politics across the country. As an old saying about Canadian politics puts it, in the Atlantic area politics is patronage, in Quebec a religion, in Ontario a business, in the Prairies a protest and in British Columbia entertainment.

Regionalism is so pervasive that it is rarely overlooked, although once in the late 1970s the Canada Day celebrations in Ottawa forgot to include representatives from New Brunswick as participants. Similarly, in 1977, an individual from Newfoundland who applied for a job in a Toronto hospital was told that foreigners were not hired and that before his request could be seriously considered he would have to seek landed immigrant status (*The Globe and Mail*, September 16, 1977). In a more serious vein, regionalism is a continuing political issue with respect to constitutional reform, as well as in relation to everyday political decisions. For example, in 1978, the British Columbia government asserted that, in any revised constitution, the province must receive official recognition as a distinct region, rather than being grouped as simply a part of Western Canada. With respect to policy-making, almost every major decision, whether it concerns unemployment insurance benefits or Via Rail cutbacks, has differing consequences for the various regions of Canada.

Regionalism reflects diversity of geographic factors and economic concerns that are politically important and are perceived as such by members of the political system. However, it is difficult to specify precisely the nature of the regional units in the Canadian system. With few exceptions, most writers have assumed that the provinces, or some combination thereof, adequately delineate regional boundaries.

The first technique is to equate provincial boundaries with regional units. For example, John Wilson (1974: 440) argues that there "must be at least one political culture for every independent political system." Since the provinces are such independent units, they each have a separate political culture. The second way of defining regions is to group various provinces together to form larger political units. The most typical way is to combine the eastern provinces together as either the Maritime or Atlantic provinces and the Western provinces together as either the Prairies and British Columbia or as simply the West. The usual rationale for such groupings is that the various provinces within each region are seen as relatively homogeneous in nature.

The grouping of several provinces together to form a single region, however, has been questioned in several investigations of the Canadian political culture. For example, The Maritime/ Atlantic region is dismissed by those most familiar with the area as a reflection of the "annoying tendency of Canadians west of New Brunswick to assume the existence of an integrated Atlantic region" (Cameron, 1971: 25). The further one is removed from the area, the greater is the commonality perceived. Such a conclusion is demonstrated, perhaps, by British Columbia's constitutional reform proposals of 1978, which called for the formal union of the Atlantic provinces into a single political entity. Within the Eastern provinces the notion of a Maritime Union has no appeal, while outside of the area it is still seen, at times, as a viable option. In analyzing the supposed commonality among the Eastern provinces, one researcher came to the conclusion that "the familiar entity, the Maritime Provinces . . . has no existence" (Beck, 1977: 16). In the following analysis, we will assume that regional boundaries, more often than not, coalesce around the provincial units.

While such considerations should caution us against grouping various provinces together to form larger regions, we should also be aware that equating provinces and regions may lead us to neglect the extent of diversity within each provincial unit. The provinces themselves are not necessarily homogeneous in either socioeconomic structure or in political attitudes. For example, considerable differences in quality of life and political values are evident between northern and southern Ontario, between northwestern and southeastern New Brunswick, between Cape Breton Island and mainland Nova Scotia, and between northeasten British Columbia and the crowded southern mainland. Such internal differences are true of every province, although they are minimal in the smallest province of Prince Edward Island.

Having discussed the nature of regionalism and the ways in which regional units have typically been classified, we can now deal specifically with the content of the regional political cultures in Canada. The regional political cultures are, in effect, a series of political subcultures based around the territorially-defined provincial units. These political subcultures reflect differences in the economic base of each region, their access to and abundance of natural resources, their rate of economic development and modernization, and the varying effects of urbanization and industrialization. The result of such factors has been to produce a series of regional economies. As one study by the Economic Council of Canada (1977: 212) put it, "no amount of juggling with statistics can lead any reasonable person to deny that economic well-being is sharply affected by the region in which one happens to be born or brought up. In short, disparities are real."

In addition to economic indicators, the various regions of Canada differ with respect to their cultural, linguistic, and ethnic composition. English-French differences are important to Quebec, Ontario, and New Brunswick, but less so in the remaining provinces. The idea of bilingualism in these regions may be popular and refer to the English and French languages, while in Cape Breton, English and Gaelic, and in Saskatchewan, English and Ukrainian would be the two most useful languages to know. The various regions also differ with respect to their religious composition and class structures.

The consequences of the regional economies and of the varying social and cultural makeup of each province have been the production of differences in political values and behaviour, that is, the creation of a series of regional political cultures. These regional cultures are distinctive in terms of their core beliefs, reflected in individual attitudes toward and active participation in the political process (Schwartz, 1974). For example, a study by Simeon and Elkins (1974) found significant variations among the regional political cultures in terms of political efficacy and political trust. Based on answers to a series of questions from national political surveys, the Simeon and Elkins' analysis discovered that individuals in the Atlantic

Most Newfoundlanders believe that trying to understand Canadians has been found to cause tumors in rats (Ray Guy, Newfoundland journalist, 1981).

There was acre upon acre of farmland, and all we could see—thought I pressed my forehead against the cold window—all we could see were little lights here and there. And I was wondering: What kind of people live in those houses? And what kind of people worked in this part of Canada? And lived and loved here? (Pierre Trudeau, on a trip to Strathroy, Ontario, October 13, 1983).

Canada, we must first recognize, is a geographically illogical nation—the British leftovers of the American Revolution (Webster, 1986: A7).

provinces ranked low on the efficacy indicators, while persons in Ontario and British Columbia reflected high efficacy ratings. With respect to political trust, individuals in Ontario, British Columbia, Manitoba, and Saskatchewan ranked high, while those persons in Eastern provinces, especially in New Brunswick, ranked low. Overall, they concluded that "there are strong differences among the citizens of Canadian provinces . . . in some basic orientations to politics" (Simeon and Elkins, 1974: 432).

In addition to variations in efficacy and trust, the regional political cultures are distinctive with respect to attitudes towards specific aspects of the political process. For example, although patronage occurs in all of the provinces, it is seen as a legitimate activity in some (the Atlantic provinces and until the mid-1970s in Quebec), an unsavoury practice in others (Saskatchewan), and a tolerated activity, as long as it remains limited and out of public view, in provinces like Ontario. Moreover, the regional political cultures often exhibit different types of parties and party systems (Wilson, 1974). In British Columbia, the two main provincial competitors are the Social Credit and New Democratic parties, although in other provinces, like New Brunswick, neither party has had much success. Parties in Quebec are nationalist in orientation, a rare concern for parties in the other provinces. Such difference in parties and party systems, attitudes toward patronage and the political process, and feelings of efficacy and

trust are some of the core values that distinguish the regional political cultures in the Canadian system.

Paralleling the variations in basic political orientations, the regional political cultures are also seen as composed of individuals with regional loyalties and identities. Regionalism implies a perceived commonality, that is, a regional consciousness among the individuals within each of the political units. On a general level people do recognize regional divisions and they do express an identity along regional lines (Clark et al., 1979: 41–66). However, these regional identities are both very general and unsophisticated among many individuals. Given the significance of regionalism in the Canadian polity, the level of regional consciousness among the mass public is lower than might be expected. We would suggest that regional consciousness may be strongly felt by the political elites in a country, while it is only weakly or modestly perceived by the mass public. This elite-mass distinction could account for a pattern whereby relatively low regional consciousness exists among the Canadian public, while at the same time regionalism remains a vital element affecting the operation of the polity (Landes, 1979).

Such an interpretation reveals that regionalism, in addition to being a major characteristic of the Canadian political culture, is also a valuable political resource, which the federal and provincial political elites seek to manipulate in order to enhance their own influence and power. For example, federal political leaders can argue that a strong central government in Ottawa is needed so that they can preserve national unity by overcoming the deleterious effects of regionalism. In contrast, provincial political leaders demand greater powers from the federal government so that they can fulfill the regional aspirations of their constituents. Conveniently, such a demand also helps to insulate the provincial political elites from their own people. As long as a province is fighting with Ottawa or the other provinces over regional interests, then political support at home is increased, since it is difficult to attack a government that is seen as the defender of provincial interests in the larger political system. As a result, the typical procedure has been for those parties in control of the provincial governments to run against Ottawa in provincial election campaigns, instead of against the provincial opposition parties. Such a pattern is particularly evident when different parties are in power in Ottawa and the provinces. These ideas suggest that, once the pattern of regionalism became established in Canada, it has been maintained more as a result of elite perceptions and behaviour than because of the attitudes held by the mass public (Gibbins, 1982: 188).

The presence of regionalism and the regional political cultures has significantly affected the structure, operation, and customs of the Canadian political system. For example, with respect to the political structure, Canada was made a federal system in order to preserve the various regions in existence at the time of Confederation. Explicit recognition of Canada's regional nature is reflected in the structure of the Senate and the House of Commons, as well as in relation to many other institutions of government. Moreover, the decision-making process, both federal or provincial, must continuously deal with the regional implications and possible consequences of any issue, whether it is one of constitutional reform, economic development, or social policy. Finally, the customs and conventions of the Canadian polity are rife with regional practices, perhaps best exemplified by the representation of the provinces within the federal cabinet.

DUALISM

The third major theme of political culture is **dualism**, that is, the impact of and relationship between Canada's major cultural groups, what Canadian historian Arthur Lower has called "Canada's tragic leitmotif." While Canada has become a multicultural society, especially since the Second World War, the political system has been slow to accommodate such changes. Instead, the political structure reflects and the major concern of domestic politics focuses on the continuing problems between the two "charter groups." In addition, the pattern of dualism has combined with regionalism to produce Canada's most distinctive political subculture in Quebec.

As the largest minority group in the political system, which has continually feared for its fate at the hands of the English-speaking majority, French Canada has developed several unique political values. First and foremost, French Canada, which in recent decades has become increasingly concentrated within the province of Quebec, has used the political process as a means of cultural defence. The key concern of French Canada has always been a preservation of its language and culture. As a result, the relationship between Quebec and the other provinces and Ottawa, as well as the nature of politics within Quebec itself, has focused on the values of nationalism. It is not by chance that the provincial legislature in Quebec is named the National Assembly. Indeed, during the nine years of Parti Québécois government, the Canadian flag was not displayed in Quebec's legislative council room. Moreover, all parties in Quebec, whether at the federal or provincial levels, are nationalist in orientation. It is ironic,

Whatever the future may hold for relations between the two nationalities that form present-day Canada, the reality of the one can never be expunged from the collective consciousness of the other (Monière, 1981: vii).

No political leader in Quebec would dare voice a doubt about the sacrosanct objective of "la survivance française en Amérique." Survival of the French-Canadian people is an obligation, an article of faith. It has been so for 200 years (Bernard, 1978: 24).

Weary of forever asking themselves the question: "What does it mean to be a French Canadian?" to which no satisfactory answer has ever yet been given, Quebec Francophones, in growing numbers since 1961, have begun to ask themselves instead: "What does it mean to be a Québécois?" (Dion, 1976: 31).

The examination of Canadian language politics can be compared to opening a carved set of Russian dolls; within the first doll is another, and within that another, and so forth until one is left with a table covered in doll parts but no doll. Like the set of dolls, the components of language politics are nested within one another (Gibbins, 1985: 39).

perhaps, that within the provincial party system there has not been a serious "federalist" party competing for at least several decades, while the party that represents Quebec in the national legislature in Ottawa is the one perceived to be the best defender of French-Canadian interests in the federal system.

The necessity for cultural defence, combined with an agrarian society and hierarchical church structure, helped to produce an adherence to the values of centralized authority and elitism within the traditional political culture in Quebec (McRoberts and Posgate, 1980). As a result, historically the political orientations in French Canada have usually been classified as parochial and subject in nature, at least in comparison to the more participant values of English Canada. A reflection of such beliefs, perhaps, was the late extension of the suffrage to women in Quebec, an enfranchisement that was about two decades later than in other provinces. The lack of participant values was typified by French Canada's attitude toward democracy: "French Canadians have not really believed in democracy for themselves . . ." (Trudeau, 1968: 103). Parliamentary democracy was foreign in origin and design and, instead of being used as a mechanism for the democratization of Quebec society, it became a means for the defence of

French-Canadian interests in the larger federal system.

A third attribute of Quebec's traditional political values is revealed in attitudes toward the proper role of the state in the Quebec polity. Historically, the role of the state has been limited in Quebec, with the scope of governmental activity and purpose narrowly conceived. This core value of "anti-statism" is illustrated by the pattern of economic development under Maurice Duplessis: " . . . it was assumed that economic processes should remain in the hands of private interests; the economic responsibility of the provincial government was to facilitate the pursuit by private interests of their own objectives" (McRoberts and Posgate, 1980: 61). What was true of the economy was applicable to other sectors as well, including the areas of both social and political reform. Quebec was a late entrant into the era of the expansive welfare state.

The characteristics of the traditional political culture in Quebec thus included a defence of the French language and culture and a resulting emphasis on nationalist values, acceptance of centralized authority and a pattern of elite decision-making, and a negative view of the role of the state in the political process. Such attributes were dominant through the 1950s,

> We are Québecois. What that means first and foremost—and if need be, all that it means—is that we are attached to this one corner of the earth where we can be completely ourselves: this Quebec, the only place where we have the unmistakable feeling that "here we can be really at home" (Lévesque, 1968: 1).

but beginning with the Quiet Revolution in the 1960s, several of these core values were fundamentally altered. While the defence of the French-Canadian community remained fundamental, the method of survival was changed.

Rather than defending the status quo, Quebec began demanding greater powers from the federal government so that the provincial unit could more adequately preserve French Canada's language and culture. Paralleling these new powers was a change in attitude towards the role of the state. Government acquired positive functions, with a corresponding increase in the scope and extent of state activity. Two prime examples are the creation of Hydro-Quebec in the early 1960s and the James Bay project in the 1970s.

Greater powers for defence led inexorably to an increased role for government in matters of social, economic, and political reform. Moreover, such changes modified the participatory elements of the political culture, moving Quebec into the forefront of democratic sentiments. For example, the use of the referendum in May 1980 is revealing in that the public was seen as a necessary source of legitimacy for any move towards the independence option, a view uncharacteristic of the previous elitist pattern of decision-making. Legislation regarding the public funding of election campaigns and the control of political party finance has helped to make Quebec a leader in democratic reforms in recent years. Thus, several of Quebec's traditional core political values have been modified, but constant throughout has been a concern for

defending the language and culture of French Canada.

Much of the continuing conflict between English and French Canada is reflected in concerns over language, perhaps best summarized in Richard Joy's (1972) **bilingual belt thesis**, which argues that a bilingual zone around Quebec increasingly isolates an English unilingual population from a French one. This buffer zone extends roughly from Sault Ste. Marie, Ontario, to Moncton, New Brunswick. While the Canada of the 19th century was a linguistic checkerboard of many languages, in the 20th century, English and French have become dominant. Moreover, these two preeminent languages have been increasingly separated on both a geographical and a practical basis. Within the territorial boundaries of the bilingual belt live over 90 percent of those claiming French as their mother tongue. In terms of language use, bilingualism is most often found among those with French as their initial language, although a very small and growing percentage of the total population is bilingual. The result of such a configuration is that, while Canada may be officially a bilingual country, it is overwhelmingly composed of unilingual citizens (Joy, 1972: 3–15).

A number of historical factors help to explain the development of such a pattern. Within the bilingual belt, the French language has been preserved because it is used in daily discourse, while outside it is dying the slow death of assimilation from nonuse and from the preference for English in terms of the economic system. Moreover, those pockets of French culture in English Canada have lost more than the battle of language use: in recent decades, additional French-speaking immigration into those areas has dwindled to negligible levels, while young people who want to live in a French milieu are increasingly returning to Quebec. Inside Quebec, the birth rate has changed from the highest in Canada to the lowest, while the large waves of non-English and non-French immigration into Quebec have overwhelmingly chosen

English as their new language. Moreover, French-Canadian emigration from Quebec has historically gone to the United States rather than to other areas of Canada. On the basis of these historical trends, Joy (1972: 135) concluded that "two languages of unequal strength cannot co-exist in intimate contact and that the weaker must, inevitably, disappear."

In an attempt to prevent such a development, both the federal government in Ottawa and the provincial governments in Quebec have passed legislation designed to protect the French language. At the federal level, the 1969 Official Languages Act declared both French and English to be the official languages of Canada, set up bilingual districts — where numbers warranted — so that citizens could deal with their federal government in the language of their choice and sought to make the status of French equal to that of English throughout the country. The reaction of Quebec — one that was largely correct — was that the Official Languages Act was too little and too late, since, as the bilingual belt thesis argues, the French language outside of Quebec had already been lost.

Instead, the Quebec provincial governments of the past three decades, whether they have been formed by Liberal, Union Nationale, or Parti Québécois members, have all sought to use the powers of the provincial government to promote and defend the French language within Quebec itself. In that sense, the genesis of Bill 101 passed in 1977 by the Parti Québécois is the relationship between English and French in the rest of the country: accepting the defeat of French outside of its borders, the party was determined to prevent such a pattern within Quebec itself. Generally Bill 101 moved Quebec toward being, for all practical purposes, a unilingual French province, thereby seeking to emulate the pattern of English dominance in all the other provinces.

The reaction to Bill 101 inside Quebec was enthusiastic from the French-speaking segment, while English-Canadians and recent immigrant groups were strongly opposed. Those individuals most upset, in fact, emigrated from Quebec, a trend which in the long run will help to further consolidate the growing unilingual nature of the province. For example, between 1976 and 1981, a total of 154 000 Anglophones emigrated from Quebec to other parts of Canada, a total equal to about one-fifth of the English-speaking population remaining in that province (Joy, 1985: 94). Even the provincial Liberal election victory of Robert Bourassa in 1985 and his return to power, which initially softened some of the harsher aspects of Bill 101, did not change this overall trend. Moreover, Premier Bourassa's use of the notwithstanding clause (Section 33 of the Charter) and the Quebec Charter to protect the dominance of the French language in Quebec by overturning the Supreme Court decision in December of 1988 on two sections of Bill 101 clearly rejuvenated the language issue, moving it up, once again, to near the top of the nation's political agenda.

While the dualism is perhaps best symbolized by current disputes over language, its impact is also clearly evident with respect to the structure and operation of the polity. For example, the federal principle was adopted as a means of guaranteeing the existence of both the English and French cultures, with the provinces given control of "those matters where the traditions of the English- and French-speaking communities of the former province of Canada differed significantly" (Smiley, 1980: 20). Moreover, within the federal government itself, English-French duality is indirectly recognized, as in the allocation of provincial seat totals in the House of Commons. The customs and conventions of Canadian politics also reflect the theme, exemplified by the selection of the speaker and deputy speaker of the House of Commons, cabinet representation for Quebec as well as for francophone areas in New Brunswick and Northern Ontario, and the typical alternation of French and English leaders within the Liberal party. Thus, through both institutional structures and political customs has the theme of dualism remained a significant influence on the Canadian political process.

CONTINENTALISM

In contrast to the themes of regionalism and dualism, which are based on internal realities and problems, our fourth theme of **continentalism** reflects the importance of external factors, namely, the impact of the United States on Canadian politics. American influence runs the gamut from basic principles of government, such as federalism, to political practices, such as the use of national party leadership conventions. In some cases we have imitated American practices, while in others we have resisted their encroachments. However, overall, the impact of the United States on Canadian politics has been extensive.

One of the reasons, of course, for the movement towards Confederation in the 1860s was the fear of American expansionism and the attempt to prevent the absorption of the English colonies into the American orbit. While the results of the War of 1812 prevented a military conquest, Canada remained apprehensive about possible American intervention until the early decades of the 20th century. For example, until the 1920s, Canada maintained a secret contingency plan of how to respond to an American invasion, even though such a threat had not been very likely for some time. The result has been an element of anti-Americanism among basic Canadian political values—as Frank

> ... the worst way to look at North America is in a rearview mirror. Here, as the place where the future always happens first, two nations have evolved that are utterly alike in almost all of their externals and yet are utterly unlike in their political cultures ... (Gwyn, 1985: 11).

Underhill once described us, Canadians are the "world's oldest and continuing anti-Americans." One consequence of the American impact has been a low sense of national identity, which in itself is defined in negative terms: we know what we are not (i.e., Americans), but we do not know what we are (i.e., the essential attributes of being a Canadian).

The desire to contain and possibly reduce American influence in Canada led to a growing movement of nationalism, particularly economic nationalism, during the 1960s and 1970s. For example, the preferential tax position for *Time* and *Reader's Digest* was removed, Canadian content regulations were established and implemented for the mass media, and the National Energy Program of 1980 sought to make the energy sector "Canadianized." In response to the impact of multinational corporations in Canada, a Foreign Investment Review Agency (FIRA) was established to screen all takeover bids; however, the subsequent success of takeover applications was high, usually in the neighbourhood of 80 percent or more. In foreign affairs, former Prime Minister Trudeau's policy review and his later actions during the 1970s and early-1980s were based on an attempt to reduce Canadian dependence on the American superpower and to give Canada a more independent position in the international arena.

However, partly as a reaction to the Trudeau years, the conservative election victory of 1984 was based on the promise of improving Canadian-American relations. Brian Mulroney

> The noses of a great many Canadians resemble Porky Pig's. This comes from spending so much time pressing them against the longest undefended one-way mirror in the world (Margaret Atwood, 1986).

"IT ALL STARTED THE MORNING AFTER THE ELECTION... I WOKE UP SINGING THE AMERICAN ANTHEM... I BEGAN TO REPEAT THE PLEDGE OF ALLEGIANCE AND THEN I STARTED HAVING THIS INCREDIBLE URGE TO PURCHASE A HANDGUN..."

Source: Reprinted from *The Leader-Post* (Regina, Saskatchewan). By permission.

declared that Canada was "open for business" and he negotiated a "free trade" deal with the United States. Such a pro-American stance stands at odds with much of Canadian history and seems likely to produce yet another swing of the political pendulum, with Canadian nationalism becoming, once again, a key political issue, as it temporarily did during the 1988 election.

Policies aimed at limiting the extent of American influence in Canada are a reflection of the kind of control exercised by the United States, particularly in relation to the economic sector. During the 19th and early 20th centuries, when Britain was the dominant foreign power in Canada, a pattern of *indirect investment* allowed control to remain in Canadian hands. In contrast, American investment has been *direct*, with control shifting to the multinational corporations.

The distinction between the two types of investment is significant because "indirect investment is basically a financial transaction that can be paid off, while direct investment involves at least partial ownership and control" (Redekop, 1978: 38). Because of the pattern of direct investment, economic decision-making

power has shifted to the American system. For example, during the 1970s, several instances occurred of the application of American law on Canadian territory. The Canadian branch plants of the American multinationals were prevented from dealing with a country such as Cuba, even though Canadian law did not prevent such business transactions. What is true of the economic sector is also found in other areas such as culture, defence, and politics.

Having discussed the four main themes of elitism, regionalism, dualism, and continentalism, we can now classify the Canadian pattern of core political beliefs in terms of the basic types of political culture. Overall, Canada has a fragmented political culture composed of a series of regional political orientations. The most distinctive political subculture is that of French Canada, which is increasingly centred in the province of Quebec. By comparison to most countries, Canada's political culture is participant, but the strength of elitism indicates pockets of subject and parochial values that limit extensive participation in the political process. Moreover, the elements of regionalism, dualism, and continentalism have all contributed to a lack of national identity and unity, that is, to a pattern of attenuated nationalism. From an ideological perspective, liberalism has been dominant, although it must compete with both conservatism and socialism to retain such a position (Horowitz, 1968: 3–57). Canadian conservatism is unique in its collectivist emphasis and willingness to use the power of government for national objectives (e.g., John A. Macdonald's National Policy). Similarly, Canadian socialism is characterized by its British heritage and its belief in democratic socialism rather than Marxist socialism. This particular mixture of ideologies has helped to solidify the unique characteristics of the Canadian political culture.

CANADA AS A CONSOCIATIONAL DEMOCRACY

Given the ideological, regional, and cultural fragmentation of basic political values, the next concern might be with trying to explain how the overall system manages to stay together. The answer that has often been given is that Canada exemplifies a political system that can be classified as a **consociational democracy**, sometimes referred to as a pattern of elite accommodation (Presthus, 1973; McRae, 1974).

Based on the experience of how the smaller European democracies have been able to function successfully despite linguistic, cultural, and ethnic differences, the theory of consociational democracy indicates that a system's survival is heavily dependent on the intention and ability of the political elite to make it work. Effective decision-making power is given to the elite so that it can successfully accommodate and mediate among the various social, economic, and political interests. In addition, there is often the fear of an external threat, which reinforces the need of the elite to control the system. The policies adopted by the elite are pragmatic rather than ideological in scope, thus allowing

> Canadians have long looked at themselves and their country with an ambivalence verging on the schizophrenic. The Canadian identity—the phrase is both a chimera and an oxymoron—is full of odd conjunctions, split visions, and unresloved tensions (Kilbourn, 1988: 1).

for conciliation between the political subcultures. In such a system the masses must be willing to delegate political authority to the elite, refrain from interference in the conciliation process, and accept the bargains struck by the political leadership. Mass participation is limited and is generally confined to voting in elections.

These characteristics of a typical consociational democracy are consistent with the four major themes of the Canadian political culture. The elitist nature of the British parliamentary structure allows for the exercise of considerable power in the accommodation process, while the deferential attitudes toward authority make such a pattern legitimate. A limited degree of nationalism among the masses, along with a pattern of quasi-participation, restricts their ability to upset the bargains made by the elite. Fear of an external threat is symbolized by the American presence in Canada; that is, continentalism has been historically a major incentive to keep the present system going. The themes of regionalism and dualism reveal two of the fundamental policy areas that must be continually accommodated by the elite. Such conciliation is more effective when the elites themselves are representative of the various political subcultures.

The future of this pattern of elite accommodation was obviously thrown into question by the election of the Parti Québécois in the Quebec provincial contests of 1976 and 1981. The assumption that the key actors of the political elite wanted to make the system work was no longer tenable. It is in the long-term interests

FEDERALISM   SOVEREIGNTY-ASSOCIATIONISM

QUÉBEC SEPARATISM   CANADIAN SEPARATISM

BALKANISM   REALISM

Source: Montreal Gazette. Reprinted with permission — The Toronto Star Syndicate.

of a separatist party to show that the existing system does not and cannot be made to work, thereby providing justification for independence. No amount of political reform or constitutional tinkering can accommodate or satisfy the national aspirations of the Parti Québécois. The defeat of the Parti Québécois in the 1985 provincial election and the return to power of Robert Bourassa has brought back a bargaining style of leadership to Quebec-Ottawa relations. However, the negative political reaction to the negotiations that produced both the 1982 Can-

> The central symbol for Canada — and this is based on numerous instances of its occurrence in both English- and French-Canadian literature — is undoubtedly survival, *la Survivance* (Atwood, 1972: 32).

ada Act and the rejected 1987 Meech Lake accord indicates a decline in the public's acceptance of the results, as well as the process, of elite accommodation.

The British Political Culture

Because Britain lacks a comprehensive written constitution, political custom and convention play a vital role in the political process. These conventions embody the core values of the British political culture, which include the importance of tradition, deferential attitudes toward political authority, and a consensus regarding key political norms and practices. In many respects, especially in its elitist and quasi-participative tendencies, the pattern of British political beliefs resembles the Canadian one.

The first characteristic of British political culture is the significance of **tradition**, a reflection of the evolutionary nature of the polity over the course of many centuries. The weight of history is heavy, as new beliefs and practices merge with existing ones. Two institutional survivors are the monarchy and the House of Lords. For example, while the substance of monarchical power is no longer exercised by the monarch, the institution remains in place: "The British monarch is a powerful living symbol linking the British of today with a rich past and a royal future" (Roth and Wilson, 1980: 11). The role of tradition is emphasized by the symbols and ceremonies of the polity, what Walter Bagehot called the "theatrical show of society," such as the opening of Parliament or the pageantry of a royal marriage. One major result of the evolution of tradition has been to give a pragmatic thrust to British politics, which in most instances has taken precedence over ideological concerns.

The role of tradition is reinforced by the second characteristic of British political culture,

> In any country, the story of modernization is in great part simply the displacement of the old by the new in outlook and institutions. On the other hand, in Britain, . . . much of the traditional world survived, sometimes alongside, sometimes fused with the modern (Beer, 1982: 56).
>
> It is evident that no difficulty can be greater than that of founding a deferential nation. Respect is traditional; it is given not to what is proved to be good, but what is known to be old (Bagehot, 1867: 250).

namely, **deferential** attitudes toward political authority. Deference or respect for authority can be seen in the support of traditional political institutions, as well as in the acceptance of a class-based society and an elitist pattern of decision-making. The "dignified" parts of the system—"those which excite and preserve the reverence of the population" (Bagehot, 1867: 61)—are a means of legitimating the power of the political elite to rule between elections. A further indicator of deferential beliefs is the acceptance of the "rule of law" and the notion that violence is not a legitimate means for achieving political goals.

This deferential nature of political values parallels the structure of the British polity. A system that is unitary in form, based on the principle of parliamentary supremacy, and without a pattern of judicial review is inherently elitist in style and operation. Such a pattern may be democratic in form, but the overall result is a system "of government of the people, for the people, with, but not by, the people" (Amery, quoted in Beer, 1973: 140).

The third attribute of the British political culture is its **consensual** nature: that is, there is widespread agreement on political fundamentals. The rules of the political game have not been seriously challenged for several centuries: "Since the end of the seventeenth century, the

British constitution and the government have been generally accepted" (Finer and Steed, 1978: 35). One reason why a political consensus has long dominated British politics is the ability of the political system to adapt to changing circumstances. No major group has been excluded outright from the political system, although several have "peacefully" forced their entry into the political game. Gradual adaptation rather than a politics of confrontation has successfully coopted the major socioeconomic interests into accepting the legitimacy of the political structure.

In addition to its adaptability, a second factor contributing to consensus has been the relatively homogeneous nature of British society. There have been few sharp cleavages, such as language or ethnicity, which might tear the political fabric asunder. Finally, the geographical compactness of Britain has helped to minimize the development of regional differences, which often characterize larger systems like Canada and the United States.

The traditional, deferential, and consensual characteristics of the British political culture all support the view that it is an integrated political culture, with a high sense of national identity and purpose. While generally participant in outlook, the deferential attitudes toward political authority reveal strong subject orientations as well. Few political subcultures can be identified and regionalism is minimal, with the major ideological differences revealed in the class-based structure of the polity.

While this interpretation of the British political culture is a fairly typical one, it can be challenged on several grounds. First, the characteristics apply better to England than to the United Kingdom (England, plus Wales, Scotland, and Northern Ireland). The inclusion of these areas greatly increases the diversity of core political values, reduces the homogeneity of the overall political culture, and recognizes the crucial factor of regionalism. Second, while violence may have been excluded from the normal political process, it most certainly is an important ingredient in the internal politics of Northern Ireland, as well as in the conflict between that area and the British government in London. Third, the pervasive nature of deference as a distinguishing characteristic of British values has been questioned in recent years (Kavanagh, 1980). Fourth, the social homogeneity of Great Britain has also changed, given the large increase in non-white immigration in the past several decades, as well as the resurgence of nationalism in the mid-1970s in both Scotland and Wales. Finally, class-based tensions can, at times, become magnified, symbolized by the Conservative government's confrontation with the coal miners in the early 1970s and the radicalization (i.e., leftward movement) of the Labour party in the early 1980s. Certainly in the 1990s, after three terms in office by Margaret Thatcher, the class antagonisms, particularly over economic policy, increased in the British polity. While these developments may have begun to limit some of the traditional, deferential, and consensual aspects of the polity, by comparison to most systems, the British political culture remains a highly integrated one.

The impact of the core political values can be seen in many aspects of the political process. For example, with respect to voting behaviour, the Conservative party, which represents the middle and upper classes, receives about one-third of its total vote from members of the working class. A partial explanation for such a pattern is the deferential attitudes toward authority, whereby some groups see others as having a "right to govern." Continued support for the monarchy, with high levels of political affect for that institution, reveal the elitist tendencies of the British polity. The nature of particular institutions and their role in the political process is, more often than not, based on a "tradition of behaviour" rather than statutory requirements. The relationship between institutions (e.g., House of Commons and House of Lords) is a reflection of the historical evolution of the vari-

ous structures of government. These examples illustrate the significant nature of the core political beliefs in analyzing the structure and operation of the British polity.

In comparison to the fragmented Canadian pattern, the British political culture is an integrated one. The set of Canadian political beliefs reflects a diversity of cultures and regions, two factors of modest historical importance in a more homogeneous Britain. Both systems are elitist, quasi-participative, and deferential in outlook, but because of Britain's unitary and centralized political and parliamentary structure, these attributes are more significant than in Canada.

The American Political Culture

The core values of the American polity differ in certain key areas from the beliefs of both the Canadian and British political cultures. Overall, the American pattern is an integrated one, although for different reasons than in Britain. Born out of a revolution, the United States was forced to define the nature of its core political values from the outset, in contrast to the evolution of political ideas in Canada and Britain. This delineation of goals was embodied in the writings of the English political theorist John Locke, as interpreted by the American founding fathers in such writings as *The Federalist Papers*.

Essentially the core political values embraced the doctrines of liberalism, which came to be seen as synonymous with the "American way of life." The dominance of liberalism was so pervasive that ideological diversity was discouraged, with the result that a consensus on political fundamentals quickly congealed. Symbolized by the Declaration of Independence and the American Constitution, this consensus has remained in place for 200 years.

The manner in which diversity has been

> The structural picture of American politics is not so much Hamlet without the Prince of Denmark as it is Deuteronomy without the vision of the promised land (Huntington, 1981: 10).
>
> Politics in America is the binding secular religion; and that religion begins with the founding faith of the Declaration of Independence . . . (White, 1976: 410).

> As a national symbol, the American Pledge of Allegiance is of recent vintage. Written in 1892 by an editor of *The Youth's Companion* magazine to celebrate the anniversary of Columbus's discovery of America, it was made an official oath only in 1942.

handled in the United States has served to reinforce this liberal preeminence. While socially complex and composed of immigrant groups from many lands, the melting pot emphasis of the school system and of society has helped to produce a unity of political outlook and sense of national identity that few other political cultures can match. As a result, the American political culture is a highly integrated one. The most significant regional political culture in American history has been the South, but the last three decades have witnessed its incorporation into the mainstream of American politics, best symbolized by the election of Jimmy Carter from Georgia as President in 1976.

To define the nature of the American political culture, therefore, is to describe the main tenets of liberalism, as they have been adapted in the American context (Mitchell, 1970: 105–121). First, Americans are inherently suspicious of political power and its uses, seeing it, at best, as a necessary evil that must be circumscribed in practice. If political power is evil, then the institutional organization of power, that is, government, is likely to be seen in a similar light. One result of such a view is a rather negative

> The number of American states that have passed English-only laws: 17.
>
> *Source: Report on Business Magazine* (June, 1989), Volume 5, Number 12, p. 96.

perception of politicians. Another consequence has been the desire to limit government's role and effectiveness, summarized in the view that "the government which governs least governs best." To minimize the possible abuse of power, government is structured in such a way as to make difficult its accumulation in any single institution or individual. Such an outlook is the basis for the separation of powers principle and a Bill Rights as elements of the American Constitution.

Even though government was to be limited in both scope and purpose, the government that was created was to be controlled by the people. Lincoln's phrase that American government was a "government of the people, by the people, and for the people" symbolizes the importance of popular, not parliamentary, sovereignty in the United States. Participation was to be encouraged, with public officials elected rather than appointed and serving relatively short terms of office. State judges, county officials, and special tax districts of one kind or another are electorally-based. The ballot is extensive, often containing numerous tax proposals, constitutional amendments and referendum questions. Thus, the belief in popular sovereignty led to the adoption of a political structure designed to promote public participation in and control over the elected political elite.

A third theme of American liberalism concerns the importance of individualism and its emphasis on the values of liberty and equality. Self-reliance is necessary in a system of limited government where liberty is defined typically as freedom from state intervention. Moreover, self-reliance or individualism parallels the American conception of equality as an "equality of opportunity" rather than an "equality of condition." An equality of opportunity philosophy puts the burden for one's own success, or lack thereof, on the individual. While liberty and equality are goals and are accepted by most Americans as admirable political values, their application in practice often leaves much to be desired, as the battle over civil rights illustrates.

A fourth theme of the American political culture can be called political moralism: "The moralistic fervor of many Americans has long been a source of both amusement and confusion to perceptive foreigners" (Mitchell, 1970: 118). One result of this moralistic outlook is that politicians, because they deal with power that is evil, must try to be better than an ordinary citizen, to set an example of proper or exemplary behaviour. Corruption, dishonesty, or other lapses of morality can cost one political office, as the Watergate scandal of the early 1970s illustrates with respect to Richard Nixon. More recently, Gary Hart's meetings with model Donna Rice and questions about his "womanizing" effectively ended his bid for the 1988 Democratic presidential nomination. An emphasis on political morality has also led, through the course of American history, to

> The American people tend to take themselves with the utmost seriousness, to assume that they and their achievements and hopes are in some way unique, and harbour a special meaning both for themselves and for all peoples everywhere. The nation was a gauntlet thrown down to time (Roelofs, 1986: 324).

alternating periods of political reform (i.e., John F. Kennedy's "New Frontier") and political conservatism (i.e., Ronald Reagan's two terms as President). Another outgrowth of political moralism concerns the typical and traditional American view of their own political system as not only unique, but superior to that of all other countries.

These themes of the American political culture, an outgrowth of liberalism, have been challenged in recent decades in terms of both foreign and domestic crises. They are goals of the polity that most people would agree with on a general level, but that become points of political conflict when applied in specific contexts or with regard to particular issues; for example, equality as a goal, but not necessarily busing as a means to achieve equality of educational opportunity. Such conflicts become

> *Lyndon Baines Johnson:* I bridle at the question, what is your political philosophy? I am a free man, an American, a United States Senator, and a Democrat, in that order. I am also a liberal, a conservative, a Texan, a taxpayer, a rancher, a businesssman, a consumer, a parent, a voter . . . . At the heart of my own beliefs is a rebellion against this very process of classifying, labeling, and filing Americans under headings.
>
> The political principles of the [American] Revolution were so unsophisticated in expression and inclusive in appeal as to seem a declaration of faith rather than a body of theory (Rossiter, 1963: 5).
>
> The antinomy of power and liberty was accepted as the central fact of politics, and with it the belief that power was aggressive, liberty passive, and that the duty of free men was to protect the latter and constrain the former (Bailyn, 1968:56).
>
> . . . a consensual political culture has existed in the United States, essentially unchanged during its entire history (Devine, 1972: 47).

frequent when the goals of a polity are seen as possibly unattainable by major sectors of the political system. However, the dominance of liberalism remains largely intact; from a comparative perspective, the American pattern is a highly integrated and ideologically-unified political culture.

Comparing Political Cultures

In describing the major themes and patterns of the Canadian, British, and American political cultures, we have focused on three ways of comparing their core political values: the role of the individual in the political process (parochial, subject, participant political cultures); the degree of consensus on political fundamentals (integrated or fragmented political cultures); and the ideological mix of political ideas (the content of the core political values). While other ways of classifying political cultures could be considered, these three approaches all emphasize the influence of political beliefs on the structure and operation of the polity.

With respect to the political structure, the core political values translate statutory requirements into working institutions of government. For example, while the 1867 Constitution Act details many of the considerations that must be taken into account in making Senate appointments, the most important factor, that of patronage, is based on beliefs and customs rather than law. In the American system, constitutional

> The Canadian is often a baffled man because he feels different from his British kindred and his American neighbors, sharply refuses to be lumped together with either of them, yet cannot make plain this difference (J.B. Priestley).

duties set the parameters of the presidential office, but the dominant place of the president in recent decades stems from public beliefs about the proper presidential role, not from constitutional prescriptions. In all three of the systems considered, support for and protection of civil and political liberties are more heavily dependent on popular and elite beliefs that these rights should be protected than on their specification in law. Thus do political beliefs transform legal structures into operating institutions of government.

A second manner in which beliefs influence the polity can be seen in the various functions of particular institutions and the way these change over time. When first created, a political structure might be designed with a specific task or function in mind. However, as beliefs change, so do the functions of particular institutions. For example, one of the initial functions of the Canadian Senate was to be the voice of provincial and regional concerns within the national government. However, from the time of Macdonald's first government, the cabinet has performed this task. The initial delineation of Senate functions has not been changed, nor has such a task been assigned to the cabinet in law; however, the practice of Canadian politics has been so modified. Likewise, the evolution of the relationship between the formal and political executives in Canada represents primarily changing public expectations about the proper role of each structure in the political system, rather than legally-defined modifications. Thus, beliefs can alter the functions of various political institutions, while the political structures themselves remain in place.

If the core political values help to transform political structures into working institutions and if they help to modify the functions of these institutions over time, then political beliefs are an important mechanism for adapting the polity to changing circumstances. Beliefs are more readily transformed than are political structures. By modifying both the structures and

> The United States and Canada remain two nations formed around sharply different organizing principles. As various novelists and literary critics have emphasized, their basic myths vary considerably, and national ethoses and structures too are determined in large part by such myths (Lipset, 1986: 147).

functions of government, the core political values are an important mechanism of political change. Generally speaking, the beliefs and structures of the political system should reinforce each other. When they do not, then demands for political reform begin to be heard, with the aim being a reintegration of structures, functions, and beliefs.

Summary

1. The political culture of a system refers to the attitudes and beliefs people hold about the polity and their role in it. Some political cultures have developed a consensus around key political values and hence are integrated, while others are internally divided along the lines of the basic sociopolitical cleavages and therefore are fragmented. Each political culture is a particular mix of ideological elements, illustrated by their various political values. Political cultures also differ with respect to the role of the individual in the political process (parochial, subject, or participant).
2. The Canadian political culture is characterized by the themes of elitism, regionalism, dualism, and continentalism. As a result, Canada has a fragmented political culture composed of an important series of political subcultures. The most distinctive of these regional political cultures is centred in Quebec, whose main political preoccupation is a defence of the French language and culture.

Despite its fragmented nature, the Canadian system has managed to survive by operating a consociational style of political management.
3. The British political culture centres around the political values of tradition, deference, and consensus. The lack of a comprehensive written constitution enhances the importance of political beliefs and customs in the British context. Although increasingly challenged in recent decades, the integrated nature of the British political culture is high in comparison to most political systems.
4. The overwhelming dominance of liberalism in the United States means that the American political culture is, for all practical purposes, defined in terms of its characteristics. Attributes of American liberalism include a negative view of political power and government, an emphasis on popular sovereignty, a stress on individualism, and a strong strain of political moralism. The political culture is an integrated one, although the application of the tenets of liberalism in specific contexts may lead to political conflict.
5. Political beliefs are an important factor in comparing political systems, because they shape both the structures and functions of government. Moreover, the influence of beliefs on both the structures and functions of the political system is a significant mechanism for adapting the polity to changed circumstances.

Recommended Readings

Political Culture: General

ALMOND, GABRIEL A. and SIDNEY VERBA (1965) *The Civic Culture: Political Attitudes and Democracy in Five Nations*. Boston: Little, Brown and Co.
_____ eds. (1980) *The Civic Culture Revisited*. Boston: Little, Brown and Co.
CHILTON, STEPHEN (1988) "Defining Political

Culture," *The Western Political Quarterly* (September), Volume 41, Number 3, pp. 415–445.

FORBES, H.D. (1987) "Hartz-Horowitz at Twenty: Nationalism, Toryism and Socialism in Canada and the United States," *Canadian Journal of Political Science* (June), Volume 20, Number 2, pp. 287–315.

GIBBINS, ROGER (1982) *Regionalism: Territorial Politics in Canada and the United States*. Toronto: Butterworths.

GOODSELL, CHARLES T. (1988) "The Architecture of Parliaments: Legislative Houses and Political Culture," *British Journal of Political Science* (July), Volume 18, Number 3, pp. 287–302.

HARTZ, LOUIS, ed. (1964) *The Founding of New Societies*. New York: Harcourt, Brace and World.

HUEGLIN, THOMAS O. (1986) "Regionalism in Western Europe: Conceptual Problems of a New Political Perspective," *Comparative Politics* (July), Volume 18, Number 4, pp. 439–458.

INGLEHART, RONALD (1988) "The Renaissance of Political Culture," *American Political Science Review* (December), Volume 82, Number 4, pp. 1203–1230.

KAVANAGH, DENNIS (1972) *Political Culture*. London: Macmillan.

KELLEY, ROBERT (1984) "Comparing the Incomparable: Politics and Ideas in the United States and the Soviet Union," *Comparative Studies in Society and History* (October), Volume 26, Number 4, pp. 672–708.

LIPSET, SEYMOUR MARTIN (1970) *Revolution and Counterrevolution: Change and Persistence in Social Structures*. New York: Anchor Books.

——— (1986) "Historical Traditions and National Characteristics: A Comparative Analysis of Canada and the United States," *The Canadian Journal of Sociology* (Summer), Volume 11, Number 2, pp. 113–155.

MORGAN, EDMUND S. (1988) *Inventing the People: The Rise of Popular Sovereignty in England and America*. New York: W.W. Norton and Company.

O'BRIEN, CONOR CRUISE (1988) *God Land: Reflections on Religion and Nationalism*. Cambridge, Mass.: Harvard University Press.

PUTNAM, ROBERT D. et al. (1988) "Institutional Performance and Political Culture: Some Puzzles about the Power of the Past," *Governance* (July), Volume 1, Number 3, pp. 221–242.

ROSENBAUM, WALTER A. (1975) *Political Culture*. New York: Praeger Publishers.

ROUSSEAU, MARK O. and RAPHAEL ZARISKI (1987) *Regionalism and Regional Devolution in Comparative Perspective*. New York: Praeger.

SEE, KATHERINE O'SULLIVAN (1986) *First World Nationalisms: Class and Ethnic Politics in Northern Ireland and Quebec*. Chicago: The University of Chicago Press.

THOMPSON, KENNETH W. (1988) "The Religious Transformation of Politics and the Political Transformation of Religion," *The Review of Politics* (Fall), Volume 50, Number 4, pp. 545–560.

TUCKER, ROBERT C. (1971) *The Soviet Political Mind: Stalinism and Post-Stalin Change*. New York: W.W. Norton, rev. ed.

Canadian Political Culture

ASHAN, SYED AZIZ-AL (1984) "School Texts and the Political Culture of British Columbia, 1880–1980," *BC Studies* (Autumn), Number 63, pp. 55–72.

BAER, DOUGLAS E. and JAMES E. CURTIS (1984) "French Canadian-English Canadian Differences in Values: National Survey Findings," *The Canadian Journal of Sociology* (Fall), Volume 9, Number 4, pp. 405–427.

BEHIELS, MICHAEL D. (1985) *Prelude to Quebec's Quiet Revolution: Liberalism versus Neo-Nationalism, 1945–1960*. Montreal: McGill-Queen's University Press.

BELL, DAVID and LORNE TEPPERMAN (1979) *The Roots of Disunity: A Look at the Canadian Political Culture*. Toronto: McCelland and Stewart.

BERNARD, ANDRÉ (1978) *What Does Quebec Want?* Toronto: James Lorimer and Company.

BERTON, PIERRE (1987) *Why We Act Like Canadians*. Toronto: Penguin Books, rev. ed.

DION, LEON (1976) *Quebec: The Unfinished Revolution*. Montreal: McGill-Queen's University Press.

FORBES, H.D., ed. (1985) *Canadian Political Thought*. Toronto: Oxford University Press.

GAGNON, ALAIN and MARY BETH MONTCALM (1989) *Quebec: Beyond the Quiet Revolution*. Scarborough, Ontario: Nelson Canada.

GIBBINS, ROGER (1980) *Prairie Politics and Society: Regionalism in Decline*. Toronto: Butterworths.

GWYN, RICHARD (1985) *The 49th Paradox: Canada in North America*. McClelland and Stewart.

HOROWITZ, GAD (1968) *Canadian Labour in Politics*. Toronto: University of Toronto Press.

MALCOLM, ANDREW H. (1985) *The Canadians*. Toronto: Fitzhenry and Whiteside.

MCRAE, KENNETH, ed. (1974) *Consociational Democracy: Political Accommodation in Segmented Societies*. Toronto: McCelland and Stewart.

MONIERE, DENIS (1981) *Ideologies in Quebec: The Historical Development*. Toronto: University of Toronto Press.

ORNSTEIN, MICHAEL (1986) "The Political Ideology of the Canadian Capitalist Class," *The Canadian Review of Sociology and Anthropology* (May), Volume 23, Number 2, pp. 182–209.

PRESTHUS, ROBERT (1973) *Elite Accommodation in Canadian Politics*. Toronto: Macmillan of Canada.

PROSS, A. PAUL (1989) "Mobilizing Regional Concern: Freight Rates and Political Learning in the Canadian Maritimes," pp. 173–200 in William D. Coleman and Henry J. Jacek, eds., *Regionalism, Business Interests and Public Policy*. London: Sage.

RESNICK, PHILIP (1984) *Parliament vs. People: An Essay on Democracy and Canadian Political Culture*. Vancouver, B.C.: New Star Books.

STEWART, WALTER (1985) *True Blue: The Loyalist Legend*. Toronto: Collins.

TAYLOR, CHARLES (1984) *Radical Tories: The Conservative Tradition in Canada*. Halifax, Nova Scotia: Formac Publishing.

TORRANCE, JUDY (1986) *Public Violence in Canada*. Montreal: McGill-Queen's University Press.

TRUMAN, TOM (1971) "A Critique of Seymour M. Lipset's Article, 'Value Differences, Absolute or Relative: The English-Speaking Democracies'," *Canadian Journal of Political Science* (December), Volume 4, Number 4, pp. 497–525.

VERNEY, DOUGLAS V. (1986) *Three Civilizations, Two Cultures, One State: Canada's Political Traditions*. Durham, North Carolina: Duke University Press.

British Political Culture

BAGEHOT, WALTER (1867, 1963) *The English Constitution*. London: Collins, The Fontana Library.

DOIG, ALAN (1984) *Corruption and Misconduct in Contemporary British Politics*. London: Penguin.

HILL, CHRISTOPHER (1975) *The World Turned Upside Down: Radical Ideas During the English Revolution*. Middlesex: Penguin Books.

KAVANAGH, DENNIS (1980) "Political Culture in Great Britain: The Decline of the Civic Culture," pp. 124–176 in Gabriel A. Almond and Sidney Verba, eds., *The Civic Culture Revisited*. Boston: Little, Brown and Co.

——— (1985) "Whatever Happened to Consensus Politics?," *Political Studies* (December), Volume 33, Number 4, pp. 529–546.

LEYS, COLIN (1980) "Neo-Conservatism and the Organic Crisis in Britain," *Studies in Political Economy* (Autumn), Number 4, pp. 41–63.

MORGAN, KEVIN (1985) "Regional Regeneration in Britain: The Territorial Imperative and the Conservative State," *Political Studies* (December), Volume 33, Number 4, pp. 560–577.

RHODES, R.A.W. (1987) "Territorial Politics in the United Kingdom: The Politics of Change, Conflict and Contradiction," *West European Politics* (October), Volume 10, Number 4, pp. 21–51.

ROSE, RICHARD (1982) *The Territorial Dimension in Government: Understanding the United Kingdom*. Chatham N.J.: Chatham House Publishers.

American Political Culture

BAILYN, BERNARD (1967) *The Ideological Origins of the American Revolution*. Cambridge, Mass.: Belknap Press of Harvard University Press.

——— (1973) "The Central Themes of the Revolution," pp. 3–31 in Stephen G. Kurtz and James H. Hutson, eds., *Essays on the American Revolution*. Chapel Hill, North Carolina: University of North Carolina Press.

BECKER, CARL L. (1956) *The Declaration of Independence: A Study in the History of Political Ideas*. New York: Alfred A. Knopf.

BENSEL, RICHARD (1984) *Sectionalism and American Political Development 1880–1980*. Madison, Wisconsin: University of Wisconsin Press.

BOORSTIN, DANIEL (1959) *The Genius of American Politics*. Chicago: University of Chicago Press.

BROGAN, D.W. (1956) *The American Character*. New York: Time Incorporated.

CROZIER, MICHEL (1984) *The Trouble With America*. Berkeley: University of California Press.

DE TOCQUEVILLE, ALEXIS (1835, 1945) *Democracy in America*. Phillips Bradley, ed. New York: Vintage Books.

DEVINE, DONALD J. (1972) *The Political Culture of the*

United States: *The Influence of Member Values on Regime Maintenance*. Boston: Little, Brown and Company.

HARTZ, LOUIS (1955) *The Liberal Tradition in America*. New York: Harcourt Brace Jovanovich.

HOFSTADTER, RICHARD (1948) *The American Political Tradition*. New York: Vintage Books.

HUNTINGTON, SAMUEL P. (1981) *American Politics: The Promise of Disharmony*. Cambridge, Mass.: Harvard University Press.

KIRK, RUSSELL (1961) *The Conservative Mind*. Chicago: Regnary.

LAPHAM, LEWIS H. (1988) *Money and Class in America: Notes and Observations on Our Civil Religion*. New York: Weidenfeld and Nicolson.

LIPSET, SEYMOUR MARTIN (1967) *The First New Nation: The United States in Historical and Comparative Perspective*. New York: Anchor Books.

MCCLOSKY, HERBERT and ALIDA BRILL (1983) *Dimensions of Tolerance: What Americans Believe About Civil Liberties*. New York: Basic Books.

—— and JOHN ZALLER (1985) *The American Ethos: Public Attitudes toward Capitalism and Democracy*. Cambridge, Mass: Harvard University Press.

MERELMAN, RICHARD M. (1984) *Making Something of Ourselves: On Culture and Politics in the United States*. Berkeley: University of California Press.

NORTON, ANNE (1986) *Alternative Americas: A Reading of Antebellum Political Culture*. Chicago: The University of Chicago Press.

RODGERS, DANIEL T. (1987) *Contested Truths: Keywords in American Politics Since Independence*. New York: Basic Books.

ROGIN, MICHAEL PAUL (1986) "The Countersubversive Tradition in American Politics," *Berkeley Journal of Sociology*, Volume 31, pp. 1–33.

ROSSITER, CLINTON (1963) *The Political Thought of the American Revolution*. New York: Harcourt, Brace and World.

SHARKANSKY, IRA (1970) *Regionalism in American Politics*. Indianapolis: Bobbs-Merrill.

SUSSMAN, BARRY (1988) *What Americans Really Think and Why Our Politicians Pay No Attention*. New York: Pantheon Books.

VERBA, SIDNEY and GARY ORREN (1985) *Equality in America: The View from the Top*. Cambridge, Mass.: Harvard University Press.

WALD, KENNETH D. (1986) *Religion and Politics in the United States*. New York: St. Martin's Press.

WALZER, MICHAEL (1965) *The Revolution of the Saints*. Cambridge, Mass.: Harvard University Press.

9 Political Parties: The Acquisition and Retention of Political Power

Parties were created out of a blend of public and private interests. They are agencies for the acquisition of power, not selfless political versions of the Red Cross, to whom citizens may go crying in time of need (Lawson, 1980: 23).

The deathbed watch for the party system must rank as one of the longest in Canadian political history. The most severe critics are sure that rigor mortis will set in any day now; the least severe have accepted the view that the patient is dying and have begun organizing the wake (Landes, 1984: 4).

So great are the political advantages of a party that in a representative democracy a politician without a party is a politician without power (Dahl, 1970: 74).

WHILE IT WOULD BE DIFFICULT to imagine how the Canadian political system could operate without political parties, it is also true that most political systems have only recently discovered their usefulness in organizing and operating the political process. On the whole, national political parties are predominantly products of the past century, with the first major theoretical analyses of parties written in the early decades of the 20th century. The recognition of their important role in modern politics was undefined in the works of the classical democratic theorists, so much so, that parties have been referred to as "the orphans of political philosophy" (Schattschneider, 1942: 10). Born of circumstance rather than by design, political parties represent an organizational means for governing the political system.

The Nature of Political Parties

Most definitions of political parties exhibit a common theme, namely, that **parties** *are organizations that seek to physically control the government by nominating candidates for office and winning power through the election process*. A typical view is that of Sartori (1976: 64), who defines a party as "any group that presents at elections, and is capable of placing through elections, candidates for public office." Thus, parties aim to acquire power and to retain such power once it has been won, organizing both the electorate and the government in the process.

THE ORIGIN OF PARTIES

The historical development crucial in the origin of political parties was the acceptance of the idea that the mass of people had to be taken into account in the organization of the polity. Throughout the 18th century and well into the 19th, a very small segment of the population was eligible for political participation. For example, in addition to such items as property qualifications, until the early decades of the 20th century, over 50 percent of the population was prevented from participation by the disenfranchisement of women, a restriction which was not lifted until the 1940s in Quebec, France, and Italy. It is not merely coincidental that the expansion of the **suffrage** (i.e., the right to vote and to participate in politics) paralleled the development of political parties in countries such as Britain, the United States, and Canada. As the number of potential participants in the political process expanded, a mechanism was needed to organize the mass of people now legally qualified to vote. Such a structure was the political party.

While one can find historical antecedents that trace back many centuries, the origin of the modern political party dates from approximately the mid-19th century. In the United States, the experience of Jacksonian democracy in the 1830s, in Britain, the series of Reform Acts in the 19th century, and in Canada, the achievement of representative and responsible government by the beginning of Confederation, all laid the basis and necessity for party organizations.

The historical development of a political party is a reflection, therefore, of the acceptance within a country's political culture of the legitimacy of mass participation: "the emergence of a political party clearly implies that the masses must be taken into account by the political elite" (LaPalombara and Weiner, 1966: 4). However, it is important to realize that being taken account of can mean either mass participation and control over the elite, as in democratic systems, or elite control over the masses, as in totalitarian systems. In either case, the political party serves in an intermediate position between the individual and the government. In carrying out such a role, political parties connect individual preferences with public policy,

> The rise of political parties is indubitably one of the principal distinguishing marks of modern government. The parties, in fact, have played a major role as makers of governments, more especially, they have been makers of democratic government (Schattschneider, 1942: 1).

> Parties are the link between existing political structures and the processes which lead to new political institutions (von Beyme, 1985: 70).

> Whatever else it might be, whatever its other functions or activities in modern democratic societies, a political party is first and foremost an organization that seeks control of government through the electoral process (Wald, 1988: 283).

linking the governors with the governed in the process.

PARTY FUNCTIONS

Although the tasks, jobs, or functions that political parties carry out vary from one political system to the next, two basic functions of parties can be identified: organizing the electorate and organizing the government.

The **electoral function** of parties can be seen in the way in which they recruit candidates to run for political office, dominate the election process, and serve as focal points for individual and group attachments. In a Canadian federal election, literally hundreds of people must be found to compete in the election process. Most of these individuals are recruited to run for office by the political parties—there are few self-starters in Canadian politics. While parties are crucial mechanisms in the recruitment of individuals for electoral competition, it should not be forgotten that parties are also key recruitment agencies for numerous nonelective positions. Electoral success provides the party with the opportunity to place party members within the bureaucracy and the various agencies, boards, and commissions of government. The surest route to a political sinecure is to

be a defeated candidate of the winning political party.

Parties also serve an electoral function by organizing campaigns and simplifying the choices presented the individual citizen. With about 13 million people voting in recent Canadian federal elections, some way is needed to sort out, from among all the theoretically possible courses of action, a limited set of alternatives for public judgment. Moreover, the party campaigns help to stimulate public interest in the issues of the day, aid in the registration or enumeration of voters, and promote more widespread participation in the political process. Citizens may also identify with a particular party by developing an emotional tie with it, what is known as a partisan attachment. While not the only factor, such partisan attachments help to influence how the citizen will vote in a specific election campaign.

The second major task of parties can be called a **governing function**. As an electoral organization that seeks to gain control of the government, the winning party serves as an integrating mechanism for getting the various branches and agencies to work together across institutional boundaries. For example, in Canada, a party with a majority mandate gains sole control of both the legislative and executive branches of government and thereby acquires the effective political power to implement its party's platform and policies. However, as electoral organizations, parties are self-interested structures that seek power: "parties formulate policies in order to win elections, rather than win elections in order to formulate policies" (Downs, 1957: 28).

Good examples of this assertion include the Liberals' stand against wage-and-price controls in the 1974 campaign, a program they later implemented in the fall of 1975, or their promise in the 1980 election, later forgotten, not to raise the price of energy by as much as proposed in the Conservative budget. Similarly, in the 1988 federal election, the Conservatives' support for free trade and the Liberals' opposition to it — positions contradictory by both parties of their historical views on the issue — illustrate the Downsian proposition as well. In other words, parties propose policies in order to win votes, thereby linking their electoral and governing functions.

Parties serve a governing function not only by integrating the various institutions of government and providing policy direction, but also by determining the leadership options presented to the voter. The Canadian citizen indirectly chooses the prime minister from among those individuals who lead a recognized political party. Parties put forth the pool of available talent from which the electorate picks its leaders: in 1980, the Canadian voter could have selected either Pierre Trudeau, Joe Clark, Ed Broadbent, or Fabien Roy by casting a ballot for that leader's representative in his or her particular constituency. By 1984 the choices had changed to a selection among John Turner, Brian Mulroney, and Ed Broadbent, a pattern that was repeated in 1988. Thus, the process of national party leadership selection is significant because it sets the outer boundaries of electoral choice. By organizing the electorate and the government, parties provide a linkage mechanism between the citizen and the political structure.

PARTY TYPES

While innumerable classifications of party types have been developed, the most useful are those which relate party type to both the party's origin and the manner in which the electoral and governing functions are carried out. Three basic classifications will be considered: first, with respect to a party's origin, the difference between internally and externally created parties; second, in relation to party structure, the variation between cadre and mass parties; and third, in light of ideological concerns, the difference between programmatic and pragmatic parties.

Circumstances of party origin influence both a party's structure and ideology. The parties that emerged from within the legislative branch of government are referred to as **internally created or parliamentary parties**. Developing out of the various factions contending for control of the legislature, internally created parties were the first to appear historically. These parties have been primarily electorally-oriented organizations intent on winning power rather than on implementing programs of reform. Loosely structured, except during elections, such parties have accepted the legitimacy of existing political arrangements, have rarely been ideologically inclined, and have dominated the party politics in most democratic political systems. Examples of internally created or parliamentary parties include the Liberal and Conservative parties in Canada, the Republican and Democratic parties in the United States, and the Conservative and Liberal parties in Britain.

In contrast, **externally created or extra-parliamentary parties** are of more recent historical vintage, with origins outside of the legislature. These parties have usually challenged key aspects of the existing social, economic, and political structure, have been more intent on implementing programs than on winning power, have usually been better organized and ideologically articulate than their internally created counterparts, but have generally been electorally frustrated (Duverger, 1964: xxiv-xxxvii; LaPalombara and Weiner, 1966: 7–14). Examples of externally created parties include the Communist, Socialist, and States Rights parties

> Our task is not merely to listen but to lead, not simply to manage but to change. Utopia, realizable or not, must be our guide. Political power must be our means (NDP leader Ed Broadbent, announcing his retirement, March 1989).

> A political party is not a thinking organization (Rose, 1984: 44).

in the United States, the Labour party and nationalist parties (Scottish Nationalist Party and Plaid Cymru) in Britain, and the Parti Québécois, Social Credit, Reform and New Democratic parties in Canada.

A second classification of party types focuses on variations in party structure and membership. A basic structural distinction is that between cadre and mass parties. In a cadre party, the organization exists primarily for electoral purposes, with little formal activity undertaken between elections. A **cadre party** is a "grouping of notables" whose primary goal is attaining office. Membership is loosely defined, with no formal admission procedures or registration forms. The party's ideology is general rather than specific, if it is defined at all. Party finance is dependent on large individual and corporate donations. The major North American parties, the British Liberal and Conservative parties, and most moderate European parties exemplify this type of party structure.

In contrast, the **mass party** is characterized by permanent organization and effort even between election campaigns, by formal membership requirements, and by an emphasis on ideology and platform rather than simply electoral success. Mass parties have based their party finances on individual membership dues, trade union support and, in recent years, the public financing of election campaigns. The closest examples to mass parties in Canada are the Parti Québécois and the New Democrats, while in Britain the Labour party is a prime example.

Our final look at party types centres on the nature of a party's ideology. The parties that

have long-term goals and platforms can be called **programmatic parties**, while parties with little ideology and short-term goals (usually meaning winning the next election) can be classified as **pragmatic parties** (Epstein, 1967: 261–272). A programmatic party would rather educate the public on the need for reform than win power, if electoral success means giving up the party's reform ideals. In a pragmatic party, policy is a matter of electoral convenience, a tool for gaining power. In Western democratic systems, pragmatic parties have generally prevailed over programmatic ones.

Although presented separately, these three classifications of party types based on origin, structure, and ideology are interdependent. Parliamentary parties are usually cadre structures with pragmatic policies, while extra-parliamentary parties are typically mass structures with specifically delineated programs. These three typologies have for the most part dealt with the nature of individual parties. However, a party's origin, structure, and ideology also influence how it interacts with other parties, thus leading us to a discussion of the nature of party systems.

PARTY SYSTEMS

A **party system** refers to *the competitive relationship between two or more political parties* (Rae, 1971: 47). If only one party exists, then a party system is logically impossible. However, simply because a party exists does not mean that it is a relevant member of the party system. To say that a party is relevant implies that its presence more than marginally affects the behaviour of other parties; that is, it has an impact on the network of competitive relationships

"... Harold can't stand the Liberals, Conservatives and NDP anymore, so he's been busy this past week checking out the alternatives...."

Source: Reprinted from the *Toronto Star*, by permission of the Toronto Star Syndicate.

(Sartori, 1976: 121–125). For example, in recent Canadian federal elections the Libertarian Party of Canada has been an officially registered political party (Table 9.1). However, because its presence has not visibly affected the campaign strategies of the other parties, because it wins only a minute percentage of the popular vote, and because it wins no legislative representation, the Libertarian Party of Canada is irrelevant in discussions of the current Canadian party system.

On such criteria, the Canadian federal party system contained four relevant parties in the 1960s and 1970s—the Liberal, Conservative, New Democratic, and Social Credit parties. With the elimination of the Social Credit party after the 1980 federal election, the Canadian federal party system has been reduced to three relevant groups. However, the support for the new Reform Party in the 1988 election, and its victory in a federal by-election shortly thereafter, may alter this assessment during the 1990s. The United States usually has only two parties (Republicans and Democrats) that affect the competitive relationship, although once in a while a minor party must be included (e.g., John Anderson's effort in 1980 or George Wallace's group in 1968). The growth of small parties

TABLE 9.1 OFFICIALLY REGISTERED POLITICAL
PARTIES—CANADIAN ELECTION 1988

Political Party	Number of Candidates Nominated
1. Liberal Party of Canada	295
2. Progressive Conservative Party of Canada	295
3. New Democratic Party	295
4. Libertarian Party of Canada	88
5. Rhinoceros Party	74
6. Reform Party of Canada	72
7. Green Party	68
8. Christian Heritage Party	63
9. Party for the Commonwealth of Canada	60
10. Communist Party of Canada	52
11. Confederation of Regions Western Party	52
12. Social Credit	9

in the 1970s greatly increased the number of significant parties in Britain; the relevant groups included the Conservative, Liberal, Labour, Scottish Nationalist, Plaid Cymru, and National Front parties, as well as the newly formed Social Democratic party in the mid-1980s. However, the decline of support for the various nationalist parties in the 1979 and 1983 elections and the decline of the Social Democratic Party after the 1987 election has meant that, for the 1990s, the party system will be dominated by the Conservative and Labour parties, even though the various minor parties continue to exist.

If a party system concerns the interaction between two or more parties, then different types of party systems are possible. Two basic patterns are evident: competitive and non-competitive party systems (LaPalombara and

Weiner, 1966: 33–41; Sartori, 1976: 131–243). A **competitive party system** exists when the government of the day can be replaced through an election by an opposition party; in other words, the government must compete with and be challenged by another party that is capable of forming a new government. The struggle for power between two or more parties that have a chance of winning an election is the primary condition for calling a party system a competitive one. By such a criterion, the Canadian, British, and American party systems are competitive.

A **non-competitive party system** exists when one party dominates governmental office, is not effectively challenged for power through the electoral process, and, as a result, always forms the government of the day. Opposition parties exist, but they pose no real threat to the governing party. What often happens is that the dominant governing party openly and aggressively discriminates against its political opposition. A classic example of a non-competitive party system is Mexico, where the PRI (Partido Revolucionario Institucional) has totally dominated the party battle. Many of the party systems in the developing countries are examples of the non-competitive pattern. The Philippines under Ferdinand Marcos, until his overthrow in 1986, exemplified this pattern. Interestingly, Marcos had the 1986 election process rigged, so that he was declared the winner—despite the fact that he obviously did not have the votes to remain in power.

Our typology of competitive and non-competitive party systems does not, however, cover all of the possible configurations of party politics, because in some political systems only one political party is allowed to exist. However, we can classify these one-party polities as party-state systems, rather than simply party systems (Sartori, 1976: 42–47). In a **party-state system**, a single party exists, no organized political opposition challenges it for power, and control of the party gives the party leaders control of

Source: Adrian Raeside, *Fireside Raeside*. Toronto: Stoddart Publishing Company, 1985. By permission of Adrian Raeside.

the state. Party-state systems are usually associated with totalitarian political systems, such as Nazi Germany and the Soviet Union (at least through the late 1980s). The essential assumption of a party-state system is the necessary congruence of interests between the sole political party and the governmental apparatus. As described by Yugoslav dissident Milovan Djilas (1957: 70), the party-state system "originates from the fact that one party alone . . . is the backbone of the entire political, economic, and ideological activity." Party-state systems are usually based on a comprehensive ideology or revolutionary doctrine, with the single party

perceived as the mechanism for transforming society. In Marxism-Leninism the single party is perceived as necessary so that the working class can overthrow the existing political arrangements. The single party is seen as the organizational weapon of the working class.

The competitive, non-competitive, and party-state systems reflect the origins, structures, and ideologies of the individual parties. For example, the Communist Party of the Soviet Union, which originated under Czarist autocracy as a means of overthrowing the existing political system, adopted a cohesive structure and an all-encompassing ideology and thus rejected the need for or the possibility of establishing a competitive party framework. The result was a party-state system rather than a party system. Non-competitive party systems that originated in the struggle to throw off colonial rule and to set up new nations have not yet fully accepted the legitimacy of political opposition, arguing instead that nation-building is a higher priority than party competition. In democratic systems, the initial origin of parties within the legislature, the gradual extension of the suffrage, the pragmatic concerns of the major parties, and the acceptance of the legitimacy of political dissent and political opposition have created the conditions for competitive party politics.

The Canadian Party System

As with any particular aspect of a political system, the political analyst must be concerned not only with general patterns, as exemplified by the above classifications of party types and party functions, but also with how these patterns have developed within specific historical contexts. The interplay between general patterns and the specific Canadian milieu can be seen with respect to both the characteristics of the individual parties and the attributes of the party system.

CHARACTERISTICS OF CANADIAN PARTIES

While the emergence of political party organizations can be traced to pre-Confederation Canada, the birth process was an arduous one, consuming nearly half a century in an extended gestation period. As a consequence, modern political parties were not developed until the end of the 19th century (Thorburn, 1979: 2). In the initial decades of Confederation the nascent parties were very loose coalitions of various factions within the legislature, poorly organized, and lacking party discipline. For example, Macdonald's "party" was composed of those interests favouring Confederation and his National Policy, while the opposition factions were, in the beginning, opposed to Confederation and its implications. Several characteristics of the election process helped to produce such a pattern.

Following Confederation, the federal electorate voted in a system of **non-simultaneous elections**, in which the federal vote was taken on different days in different constituencies. The government would call the election first in those constituencies that supported it and then work outward to the remaining areas, attempting to build up a bandwagon effect as it went. Such non-simultaneous elections might occur over an extended period, as in the 1867 election, which stretched over six weeks. Combined with the lack of a secret ballot, which meant that the government knew how one voted, non-simultaneous elections produced legislative factions of **ministerialists**, members whose primary political aim was to be on the winning side in order to reap the rewards of office.

As elected Members of Parliament who were uncommitted to any particular coalition, these ministerialists would support the government of the day on the basis of what they or their constituency might receive from that government. Such ministerialists constituted a significant element in "all of the early parliaments: Macdonald called them 'loose fish,' George Brown, 'the shaky fellows,' and Cartwright, 'waiters on Providence' " (Reid, 1979: 13). While the elimination of non-simultaneous elections and the introduction of the secret ballot for most electoral areas in 1878 gradually helped to solidify party organization and cohesion by the 1896 election, the effect of such initial election practices was to keep the emerging parties poorly organized, while at the same time emphasizing the rewards of a pragmatic style of party politics.

The success of the Liberal and Conservative parties is directly linked to their parliamentary origins and the attributes thus acquired. Born in the struggle for power in the legislature and for control of the new political structure after 1867, the Liberal and Conservative parties have been electorally-focused organizations whose primary goal has been winning power and the spoils of office. With such an aim the major parties have been "practical, flexible, and manipulative" (Winn and McMenemy, 1976: 11). As Pierre Trudeau said of the Liberal party in the 1960s, a statement often true of the Conservatives as well, the party will say anything and do anything to win power. An NDP supporter in 1963, Trudeau viciously attacked Prime Minister Pearson for his decision to accept nuclear weapons on Canadian soil:

> I would have to point out in strongest terms the autocracy of the Liberal structure and the coward-ice of its members. I have never seen in all my examinations of politics so degrading a spectacle as that of all those Liberals turning their coats in unison with their Chief, when they saw a chance to take power . . . . The head of the troupe having shown the way, the rest followed with the elegance of animals heading for the trough (Trudeau, quoted in Stewart, 1971: 11).

However, practical politics resulted in similar behaviour after Pierre Trudeau became leader of the Liberal party in 1968 (e.g., the wage-and-price control reversal in 1974–1975). Such actions would seem to confirm the view that "politicians are hardly notable for their consis-tency—and the sweet fruits of office can lead men through strange manoeuvrings of con-science and conviction" (Hamilton, 1975: 109).

This pragmatic style of the two dominant par-ties is clearly illustrated with respect to party platforms, principles, and policy positions. Rarely do either the Liberal or Conservative

EYE-TWISTER

SEE HOW MANY DIFFERENCES YOU CAN SPOT IN THE DRAWINGS ABOVE.

Source: Alan King, *Portfolio 85: The Year in Canadian Caricature,* CROC Publishing, 1985. By permission of Alan King.

parties take a stand that clearly differentiates it from the other. Specificity of purpose limits a party's electoral appeal. As a result, party plat-forms are general in nature, or, at least, open to multiple interpretations, especially after the campaign is over. For example, the Liberal party was unwilling or unable in the 1980 contest to explain the meaning of a "blended, made in Canada" price for oil, even though Pierre Tru-deau made numerous general statements about the need for such a policy. Perhaps even more revealing was the decision of the Liberal party to keep its total platform secret during the 1980 contest, a decision subsequently maintained even after victory had been achieved. One can assume, perhaps, that this approach to policy had the interest of the voters at heart—there is no point in confusing people with facts, espe-cially in the midst of an electoral contest.

The Conservative party's failures until 1984 are attributable, at least in part, to its explicit policy positions, such as its budget, which became the central issue in the 1980 contest, its stand in favour of wage-and-price controls in 1974, or its views on conscription in earlier times. In that sense, the Conservatives have often not been as pragmatic as their Liberal counterparts, sometimes forgetting that the "fortunate parties are those whose names no longer carry meaning to the electorate" (Mallory, 1954: 168). This basic political lesson had been learned by the Conservatives by the time of the 1984 campaign. As John Crosbie stated on the election trail, the Conservatives would only specify the details of their programs after winning power. Generalized Tory promises were many (e.g., "Jobs, Jobs, Jobs"), but specifics were few. Thus, the 1988 federal election stands out as a significant exception to the general pattern of Canadian party politics: not only did one issue dominate (free trade), but the parties took clearly defined positions on it.

The pragmatic nature of the Liberal and Conservative parties is clearly evident in relation to the question of party membership. At the mass level, a person is usually considered to be a party member simply by claiming such an affiliation. Offer your services at election time and you will, in all likelihood, be welcomed with open arms; background checks on previous partisan ties are not a precondition of current partisan loyalty. At the elite level, numerous examples abound concerning the flexible nature of party membership. An outstanding historical example would be that of Joseph Howe. Although initially opposed to Confederation, and elected to the House of Commons on that basis in 1867, Howe joined Macdonald's cabinet only two years later, after renegotiation of Nova Scotia's annual subsidy from the federal government (Winn and McMenemy, 1976: 11). More recently, Paul Hellyer's switch from the Liberals to the Conservatives and back to the Liberals shows the continuing presence of the flexible nature of partisan loyalty. An added example is that of John Turner. After his resignation from the Liberal party, a faction in the Conservative party tried unsuccessfully to get him to run in the 1976 Tory leadership race.

With respect to party organization, the Liberal and Conservative parties are weak. Since they are electoral organizations, the party struc-

ture is only fleshed out prior to and during an electoral engagement—between elections, the party organization remains a paper tiger. Most elements of the party structure, such as the constituency organizations or the provincial parties, hold an annual meeting of little consequence. Even when an election is expected or called, most party units are unprepared for the electoral battle. A considerable portion of the early weeks of the campaign is simply spent in nominating candidates in each of the constituencies.

A corresponding aspect of party organization concerns the component units of the federal Liberal and Conservative parties. While the federal Liberal and Conservative parties appear to be hierarchically organized, in fact, much of their real power lies in their provincial units: in other words, the party organizations are decentralized. As with constitutions in general, party constitutions are rarely accurate descriptions of the internal power relationships within either of the old-time parties.

The characteristics of Canada's major parties, the Liberals and Conservatives, therefore, include the following: their parliamentary origin; their pragmatic style of party politics with respect to platform, ideology, and membership; and their weak and essentially decentralized party structures. Electorally-based organizations, the Liberal and Conservative parties are coalitions of individuals, groups, and regions intent on winning for themselves the spoils of office.

In addition to the two dominant parties of parliamentary origin, since the 1920s, Canada has seen the rise and development of a series of minor parties. These newer parties typically illustrate opposite attributes from those identified for the Liberals and Conservatives, for the simple reason that their origins, structures, and functions are different. Parties such as the Progressives, the Cooperative Commonwealth Federation—which later became the New Democratic Party—and Social Credit

> . . . political parties in this country are not ideological armies but temporary collections of disparate men and women, in it not for glory but for fun (Newman, in Peterson, 1984: 10).
>
> If we see politics as a morality play with integrity constantly at war with political success, we have created for ourselves a political life doomed to unhappiness (Ontario NDP leader Bob Rae, October 19, 1985).
>
> Here is the dilemma of the NDP in Canada: to remain true to its principles at the probable expense of permanently eschewing political power, or to move further to the centre where it risks losing its soul and becoming indistinguishable from other "liberal" opposition parties (Gerald Caplan, former NDP federal secretary, *The Globe and Mail*, September 3, 1983, p. 7).
>
> In a sense, there are only two party labels that really count in Canadian politics — the Ins and the Outs (Little, 1985: B8).

are extra-parliamentary in origin and ideologically-based. The latest entrant into this category — the Western-based Reform Party — was founded in late 1987 and won its first seat in the House of Commons in March of 1989.

These externally created parties have often been outgrowths from social movements that have sought extensive changes in the economic and political structures of Canada. Since they have a need to justify such proposed changes, these extra-parliamentary parties have usually propounded an ideology that both attacks the existing order and suggests the outlines of a new pattern of power relationships. Membership in such an organization entails acceptance of the party's ideology and platform, with enduring organization between election campaigns. These characteristics are exemplified by the New Democratic Party of Canada.

Although officially formed in 1961, the New Democratic Party's predecessor, the Cooperative Commonwealth Federation (CCF), began in 1933, itself the outgrowth of some remnants of the Progressives of the 1920s. The CCF, as an externally created party, clearly attacked the existing economic and political structures of capitalism. The ideological commitment of the CCF was enunciated in the Regina Manifesto, the party's initial declaration of principles. Membership obligated one to support the par-

ty's principles and to help in party finance through annual membership fees.

The CCF was both a social movement and a party, with inevitable strains between these varying conceptions of its role in the political system (Young, 1969: 286–302). The evolution of the CCF from 1933 onward demonstrated this basic conflict between the demands of a political movement and those of a political party. Gradually the CCF became more electorally-focused, with an increasing concern for electoral results, symbolized by the role of David Lewis as national party secretary from 1936 to 1950.

The radical thrust of the Regina Manifesto became blunted and was eventually replaced in 1956 by a more moderate statement of party aims known as the Winnipeg Declaration. However, the attempt to refurbish the party's image failed, and combined with the Diefenbaker sweep of 1958, encouraged the CCF moderates to seek the establishment of a new party aimed at implementing social democracy in Canada. The result was the creation of the New Democratic Party in 1961, a party more power-oriented than the CCF, which sought to establish a union of farmer and labour groups within the party, and predicated on a strategy of appealing more to urban than to rural voters. Thus, the formation of the New Democratic Party is itself a reflection of the pervasive nature of the pragmatic style of Canadian politics.

Many of the initial patterns of party structure, organization, and membership used by the CCF were continued by the NDP after 1961. As well, the inherent tension between reform and electoral victory persisted: "the NDP is both an electoral organization and a political movement, pledged to the eventual transformation of society" (Morton, 1974: 3). Within the NDP, the moderate wing, which focuses more on power than on principle, has carried the organization behind it in terms of leadership selection, party policy, campaign tactics, and parliamentary behaviour. The pragmatic nature of the current NDP is perhaps best exemplified by its support of Pierre Trudeau's Liberal minority government between 1972 and 1974. Although more moderate than the CCF, the NDP still stands apart from the Liberal and Conservative parties with respect to its emphasis on platforms and ideology, internal party democracy, mass party membership, and reform of the social, economic, and political institutions of Canada.

Canadian parties, therefore, are not created from a uniform mold. The two major and long-dominant parties are parliamentary in origin, pragmatic in style, nonideological in philosophy, and electorally-centred coalitions whose primary goal is winning power. The series of minor parties since the 1920s have been, by contrast, extra-parliamentary in origin, programmatic in style, ideological in appeal, and both political movements and partisan organizations. This combination of cadre and mass parties has helped to produce a unique party system in the Canadian context.

CHARACTERISTICS OF THE PARTY SYSTEM

The most important attribute of the Canadian party system is the fact that it is a **competitive** one, although it is not an equally-balanced pattern of interaction. Historically, one party has tended to dominate national politics, with the Conservatives monopolizing that role from Confederation until 1896 and the Liberals bearing the mantle of power for most years between 1921 and 1984 (approximately 80 percent of the time). This pattern led one author (Thorburn, 1979: 45) to suggest that during this period the national party system contained the normal government party (the Liberals), the normal opposition party (the Conservatives), and the normal minor party (the New Democratic Party). Such a system rarely produced party turnover in government; instead, the important alternation was "not between different parties in office but between majority and minority Liberal governments" (Meisel, 1979: 128). The massive 1984 Conservative victory may have permanently altered this traditional pattern of party politics, particularly given the strong Tory majority in the 1988 election as well. However, only time will tell whether the Tory victories have produced a realignment of the party system or simply a temporary aberration in the traditional pattern of Liberal party dominance in the modern era.

The second characteristic of the party system is that it is **federal** in structure, paralleling the federal organization of government. While our main focus is on the national party system, the federalization of party politics has an important bearing on which party wins power in Ottawa. Federalism has created 11 arenas for the party battle. Moreover, the parties have been differentially successful in these various political contests. For example, while the Liberal party may have been the normal governing party in Ottawa between 1921 and 1984, it had become either the major opposition party in provinces like Quebec and Ontario, or had been, for all practical purposes, eliminated from the partisan battle, as in Alberta and British Columbia. With the defeat of the Trudeau government in 1979, not a single Liberal government existed in Canada. By contrast, the Conservatives, the normal opposition party in Ottawa, had become the most successful party in provincial politics, controlling Alberta, Ontario, New Brunswick, Nova Scotia, Prince Edward Island, and Newfoundland (some analysts would also include British Columbia, since it was controlled by the Social Credit party, a Conservative analogue).

The 1984 Tory victory in national politics immediately helped to produce Liberal victories in the provincial arena. In Ontario, the Liberals won power in the 1985 election, after more than four decades in the political wilderness. In Quebec, a resurrected Robert Bourassa led the provincial Liberals into office in 1986 in a smashing victory over the Parti Québécois. In addition, there have been Liberal provincial election successes in Prince Edward Island, New Brunswick, and Newfoundland (and almost in Manitoba), plus reelection victories in Ontario and Quebec. Thus, the Tory victories in national politics in 1984 and 1988 have helped to rejuvenate the provincial Liberal organizations. How long this reversal of roles of success in national or provincial politics for the Tories and Grits remains in place or develops further is one of the most intriguing questions of the Canadian party system.

The impact of federalism on the minor parties has been even greater than on the Liberals and Conservatives. Federalism has helped to promote minor parties, while at the same time it has limited their ultimate national success. By creating provincial units that are worth contesting for, given their powers in the Canadian system, federalism has encouraged new parties at the provincial level of government. However, even if a party wins control of a provincial government, it may find it difficult to expand successfully into the national party system. For example, it is difficult to conceive how the Parti Québécois might be extended either to other provinces or into control of the national government in Ottawa. The minor parties, such as the Progressives, the CCF, and Social Credit, have been primarily provincial success stories which

> In British Columbia federalism has had a very visible impact on party politics. The effects of federal pressures and the strength of the left have driven national and provincial party systems so far apart that there are, in effect, two distinct party systems in federal and provincial politics (Blake et al., 1989: 3).

have failed in the national party arena. Thus, federalism promotes the emergence of new parties around the provincial units, while at the same time it inhibits their expansion into national politics.

In addition to having an important effect on the success of the political parties in the various political arenas, federalism also influences a party's structure and ideology. The national parties are themselves federal organizations: for example, "it is an important part of Liberal mythology that the party, like the country itself, is a federation" (Wearing, 1981: 81). As federal structures, the party organizations have ended up granting considerable power to their provincial components. The result has been that Canada's national parties are decentralized around the provincial organizations and unity of effort, ideology, and personnel is rarely achieved.

A policy that is in the interest of the national party may be detrimental to provincial party success. For example, the emphasis of the federal Liberal party under Pierre Trudeau on the themes of national unity and bilingualism may have been good politics during a national election, but such themes were not very successful in provincial elections, as the provincial Liberal parties in Western Canada discovered. In a similar vein, the federal Conservatives' attempt in 1979 to placate Alberta by moving to the world price for oil produced an unofficial split between the national party organization and its Ontario wing under Premier Bill Davis. Such inconsistencies have sometimes led to the setting up of completely distinct party organizations for the national and provincial arenas. For example, the provincial Ontario wing of the Liberal party established its own structure in 1976, as had the Quebec component in the 1960s. In April 1989, as a way of handling the independence issue, the Quebec NDP split from the national NDP structure.

Even without a formal split between the national and provincial wings, federalism has an important bearing on party policy and platforms. There is no necessary agreement on policy or ideology between the party units that operate at each level of government. A Liberal provincial government or a Conservative one cannot assume ideological congruence from their federal counterparts, or vice versa. For example, while in the early 1980s Pierre Trudeau (national leader of the Liberal party) and Claude Ryan (leader of the provincial Liberal party in Quebec) were both Liberals, their positions on constitutional reform were diametrically opposed. Similarly, while national Liberal leader John Turner supported the Meech Lake accord, several provincial Liberal premiers were strongly opposed to it in 1988 and 1989. Such disagreements are typical and widespread within all the party organizations.

One result is that, regardless of party label, provincial parties often campaign against Ottawa during provincial elections, rather than against the opposition provincial parties. For example, existing provincial governments, in announcing an election, typically ask their electorates for a strong mandate so as to increase their bargaining power with Ottawa — a tactic as true of the New Brunswick Liberals as it is of the Alberta Conservatives or the Newfoundland Conservatives. For example, in the Manitoba provincial election of March 1986, NDP Premier Howard Pawley campaigned against the financial cutbacks of the Mulroney government, rather than taking on the provincial Tories directly over such issues as French language rights in the province. A similar pattern was

> Quebec politics, not unlike the murderous butler in British mysteries, is on the move again. The strange bedfellows of Canadian politics [Mulroney and Bourassa] are none other than the leaders of the arch-rival Liberals and Conservatives. "Les bleus" and "les rouges" used to fight like cats and dogs in Quebec. But not any more. Not since the "sacred alliance" took shape soon after the election of both men (Latouche, 1989: 20).

evident in the Tory election call by Don Getty in Alberta in February 1988.

The result of such a system is a pattern of "federal-provincial schizophrenia" within the Canadian party organizations (Black, 1979: 90). In some instances it may turn into paranoia, where the party at one level of government may actually campaign against the party at the other level, as when "in the early part of the Second World War, Liberal Premier Hepburn of Ontario openly cooperated with the Conservatives in an attempt to oust the Liberal government of Prime Minister Mackenzie King" (Smiley, 1980: 146). And the federal Liberal party, despite public protestations to the contrary, did not seem overly embittered by the defeat of the Quebec provincial Liberals by the Parti Québécois in the 1981 provincial election. The provincial Liberals returned the favour in 1984, when much of the party organization worked for the federal Conservatives during the September campaign. This pattern repeated itself in the 1988 election, with Robert Bourassa "openly" backing the free trade initiative of the federal Conservatives. Such examples show that important aspects of internal and external party relations in Canada are affected by the federal nature of the political system — a factor that is "so obvious as to be almost taken for granted, and yet so important that it can scarcely be overestimated" (Whitaker, 1977: 402).

The third characteristic of the Canadian national party system is its **regional** and

sectional basis. Each of the national parties has regional strongholds and regional wastelands. For that reason it has often been suggested that "in reality, a Canadian national election is a series of regional contests, with the party competitors in each region varying in strength from coast to coast" (Landes, 1981: 105).

The traditional regional nature of the Canadian party system was clearly demonstrated by the 1980 election results (see Table 9.2). In the Atlantic region, the party battle was dominated by the Liberals and Conservatives, although the NDP did have pockets of strength, such as industrialized Cape Breton in Nova Scotia. Historically, the NDP has won only a single seat in Newfoundland in a general election, has never obtained a seat in either New Brunswick or Prince Edward Island, and was only competitive in a few of the Nova Scotia constituencies. Thus, in the overwhelming number of Atlantic seats, the election was a Conservative-Liberal confrontation.

In the 1960s and 1970s, the Quebec ridings in federal elections have been primarily contests between Liberal and Social Credit candidates. The NDP has never won a seat in a general election in Quebec and until 1984 the Conservatives have been lucky to win several—in 1980, they survived in only a single constituency. Particularly since Mackenzie King's sweep of all the federal seats in 1921, Quebec was typically the bastion of Liberal dominance. In 1980, the Liberals won 74 of 75 constituencies, wiping out the Social Credit party in the process.

In Ontario, the three parties were more evenly matched than in any other region, especially in the metropolitan and industrialized sections of the province. However, because of the workings of the electoral system, out of a possible 95 seats, the NDP won only six seats in 1979 and five seats in 1980. Ontario is a crucial region in federal elections not simply because of its large number of seats, but, more importantly, because many of these constituencies are swing ridings. A **swing riding** is one in which party

strengths are evenly matched, so that a small change in the popular vote can change or swing the victory from one party to the other. Thus, the distribution of seats in Ontario usually determines whether the Liberals or Conservatives will win the national election. For example, in 1979, the Conservatives obtained 57 seats to 32 for the Liberals and formed a minority government, while in 1980, the Liberals gained 52 seats to 38 for the Conservatives in winning a majority government. Given their traditional lack of support in Quebec, these swing ridings in Ontario were particularly crucial for the Conservatives in the 1960s and 1970s.

The final regional battle took place in Western Canada. Since John Diefenbaker's electoral sweep in 1958, the Conservative party has become strongly based in the Prairie provinces, and in the 1970s in British Columbia as well. In the 1980 contest, the Conservatives picked up 49 seats in the four Western provinces, compared to 26 seats for the NDP and only two for the Liberals, who were blanked out in Saskatchewan, Alberta, and British Columbia. Western Canada was, thus, in most constituencies, a two-way contest between the dominant Conservatives and their main challenger, the NDP.

More dramatic than the 1980 election results themselves was the impact of regionalism on the ensuing composition of the various party caucuses. The Liberal party remained the party of Central Canada (i.e., Quebec and Ontario). Half of the Liberal party caucus was elected from Quebec (74 of 147 seats), with 85 percent from Ontario and Quebec (126 of 147). The Conservatives were regionally imbalanced as well, with 50 percent of its caucus based in Western Canada (if we include the North, a total of 51 out of 103 seats in 1980) and less than 1 percent of its caucus in the House from Quebec. The greatest regional imbalance was evident for the NDP—it was locked out of representation in six out of 10 provinces, with 80 percent of its caucus from three Western provinces (26 of its 32 seats).

TABLE 9.2 1980 FEDERAL ELECTION RESULTS

PROVINCE	SEATS WON FOR EACH PARTY			
	Conservative	*Liberal*	*NDP*	*SC*
Newfoundland	2	5	0	0
Nova Scotia	6	5	0	0
New Brunswick	3	7	0	0
Prince Edward Island	2	2	0	0
Atlantic Total	13	19	0	0
Quebec	1	74	0	0
Ontario	38	52	5	0
Manitoba	5	2	7	0
Saskatchewan	7	0	7	0
Alberta	21	0	0	0
British Columbia	16	0	12	0
Western Total	49	2	26	0
Northwest Territories/Yukon	2	0	1	0
Total Seats (282)	**103**	**147**	**32**	**0**

The 1984 federal election altered, at least temporarily, the regional basis of party strength (see Table 9.3: 1984 election results are in the parentheses). The crushing Tory victory simply overrode traditional regional patterns. While maintaining their dominance in Western Canada over the NDP (58 to 17 seats, with the Liberals gaining only two MPs), the Tories doubled their seats in Atlantic Canada by comparison to 1980 (25 versus 13 seats four years earlier). In Ontario the Tories gained nearly 30 seats, while in Quebec they went from only one seat in 1980 to 58 seats in 1984. In Quebec, the previous Liberal-Social Credit battle became a Liberal-Conservative one. The NDP, while losing only two seats nationally, gained eight seats in Ontario. The Liberals were decimated, losing 107 seats, with only 40 seats in the entire country. The 1984 Conservative sweep temporarily abated the most obvious impacts of regional

> If dynasties come for a crush of reasons, dynasties die one reason at a time. It starts like a slump. The immense momentum of winning slows; the slump doesn't end. The momentum turns. Everything that fits doesn't fit. Obligation turns cranky; expectations and attitude disappear (Dryden, 1984: 243).

party support. If past history is any guide, such patterns would not remain quiescent for long.

The 1984 contest also changed the composition of the party caucuses. The NDP still failed to gain representation from six provinces, while its Western component declined and its Ontario base expanded. The dependence of the Liberal party on Central Canada increased to 78 percent of its seat total (31 out of 40 seats), while its Atlantic Canada base fell by two-thirds (from 19

TABLE 9.3 1988 CANADIAN FEDERAL ELECTION RESULTS
(1984 election results in parentheses)

PROVINCE	SEATS WON BY EACH PARTY					
	Conservative		Liberal		NDP	
Newfoundland	2	(4)	5	(3)	0	(0)
Nova Scotia	5	(9)	6	(2)	0	(0)
New Brunswick	5	(9)	5	(1)	0	(0)
Prince Edward Island	0	(3)	4	(1)	0	(0)
Atlantic Total	12	(25)	20	(7)	0	(0)
Quebec	63	(58)	12	(17)	0	(0)
Ontario	46	(67)	43	(14)	10	(13)
Manitoba	7	(9)	5	(1)	2	(4)
Saskatchewan	4	(9)	0	(0)	10	(5)
Alberta	25	(21)	0	(0)	1	(0)
British Columbia	12	(19)	1	(1)	19	(8)
Western Total	48	(58)	6	(2)	32	(17)
Northwest Territories/Yukon	0	(3)	2	(0)	1	(0)
Total Seats (295) (282)	**169**	**(211)**	**83**	**(40)**	**43**	**(30)**

to seven seats). Central Canada emerged as the strongest region in the Tory caucus, with 60 percent of the Conservative seats (125 out of 211). Such regional influences on the party system, in terms of representation and caucus composition in 1980 and 1984, carry important implications for the ability of our political parties to successfully perform their electoral and governing functions.

The 1988 election marked the clear reemergence of the regional factor in Canadian voting patterns, as the Tory sweep of 1984 was replaced by a strong majority victory. The 1984 and 1988 elections represented the first time in 40 years that a single party won back-to-back majority governments, perhaps indicating that a major realignment of the federal party system has taken place.

In the Atlantic area, while it retained its

Liberal-Conservative dominance, the parties switched roles: the Liberals won 20 of 32 seats, with the Tories declining from 25 in 1984 to 12 in 1988. The NDP retained its position of ineffectiveness in eastern Canada by not winning a single seat, even though it put up a solid showing in a number of ridings.

The most significant result was in Quebec, where the Tories actually increased their seats from 58 to 63, while the Liberals lost 5, declining from 17 to 12. The NDP continued to be locked out of any real significance in the competitive party battle between the Conservatives and Liberals in Quebec. However, the NDP did achieve an "historic first" in Quebec when consumer-advocate Phil Edmonston won the Chambly by-election as an NDP candidate (February 12, 1990). Given the "Solid South" pattern of voting in Quebec (i.e., Quebec tends to vote strongly for one party), the province of Quebec remains the key to whether or not the Tories will emerge as Canada's normal governing party.

The 1988 election saw major gains for the Liberals in Ontario, as they increased their seat total to 43 (from 14). The NDP made slight gains (up three to 13), while the Tories lost 21 seats. While more evenly matched in terms of voting support than any other region of the country, with respect to seats, Ontario in 1988 was basically a battleground between the Conservatives and the Liberals.

In Western Canada the longstanding trend of the party contest between the Conservatives and New Democrats was clearly evident in 1988 (48 seats for the Tories and 32 for the NDP). Despite increasing popular support, the Liberals won only six seats, up from two in 1984; however, all four seats were gained in Manitoba. The Liberals remained at zero seats in Alberta and Saskatchewan, with only marginal representation in British Columbia (one seat, John Turner's).

Finally, with respect to the 1988 election, we must recognize the growth of a series of generally right-wing protest parties, which, according to some estimates, made the difference between winners and losers in as many as 50 of the 295 ridings. The most important of these was the Reform Party, founded in 1987 and based in Western Canada. In 1988 it won over 15 percent of the vote in Alberta, gained about 275 000 votes in the four Western provinces, and placed second in nine of the 25 Alberta constituencies. Although it won no seats in the general election, it did win a by-election shortly thereafter. Of all the new minor and/or fringe parties, the Reform Party is the one to watch in the immediate future, as it seeks to make inroads into the traditional Tory-NDP battle in Western Canada.

Based on the 1988 seat totals, the Tories are the only real "national" party in Canadian politics, lacking representation in only one province, Prince Edward Island. The Liberals lack a solid party base in the West, with only good representation in Manitoba. The NDP lacks representation in five provinces, with only one seat in a sixth (Alberta). These figures demonstrate a strong regional bias within the various party caucuses. For example, 32 of the 43 NDP seats are from Western Canada, while two-thirds of the Tory caucus is from Central Canada (109 out of 169 seats). The Liberals are currently based in Ontario and Atlantic Canada. Given the volatility of the Canadian electorate in recent years, these results may indicate temporary regional variations. If they persist through the next election, they will indicate a fundamental shift in the alignment of the Canadian party system.

The fourth characteristic of the national party system concerns the typical pattern of interaction among the parties. The party system from 1921–1984 was **centre-based**, with the Liberal party monopolizing the midpoint of the political spectrum (Alford, 1963; Horowitz, 1968). As a general ideological classification of the federal parties, the following placement would seem to be an appropriate summary of party positions over the past several decades: as a social democratic party, the New Democratic Party is on the left; the Liberals are in the centre, usually on the left of centre but flexible enough to move to the right of centre if political conditions require it; the Progressive Conservatives are a centre-right party; and Social Credit is on the right of the political continuum. With the gradual demise of Social Credit, the party system in the 1960s and 1970s was composed of a large centre party challenged from both the left and the right.

Since the majority of voters are in the centre of the political spectrum, the major parties both seek to occupy that position. However, once a party has gained control of the centre, it is difficult to dislodge, which is a key reason why a single party has dominated the federal government since the 1920s. In appealing to the centre, the winning party must find a theme that rallies

To be a Liberal is first and foremost to be an elected representative, a person whose leitmotif, whose supreme will, is to provide opportunities for development and progress for all Canadians. In such a situation, anything can be justified. If the development of individual Canadians is to be achieved through socialization, the Liberal Party can turn socialistic. If the development of individual Canadians is to be achieved through a turn to the right through a strengthening in the industry, the Liberal Party can turn to the right. If in order to promote our development the Liberal Party thinks we have to be communistic, we shall be communistic. This is what it is all about to be a Liberal. To be a Liberal is to be open to all ideas (Liberal MP Pierre Gimaiel, January, 1982).

people to its cause, while at the same time making it difficult for the opposition parties to disagree with it. The current Liberal party discovered such a theme in its emphasis on national unity, just as Macdonald's National Policy worked for the Conservatives in the 19th century. When the electorate does not feel that it is the key issue, as in 1979, the Liberal party fares badly. When the national unity theme is paramount, as in 1968, the Liberals win a majority victory. The opposition parties are put in the unenviable position either of arguing against a theme such as national unity, and thus appearing unpatriotic, or of trying to distinguish their policy from that of the Liberals in the minds of the electorate, a difficult undertaking.

Having established a key theme such as national unity as the basis of their political dominance, the centre-based party then utilizes several tactics: first, it ignores new policy options or issues, hoping that they will disappear so that no action is required; second, if a new issue is gaining public acceptance, the centre party seeks to undercut it by reemphasizing their key theme; and third, if the first two tactics fail, the dominant party takes over or co-opts the issue, remaking it in its own image.

As a result, if the challenge to the centre party is from the left, the party moves left; if the challenge is from the right, the party moves right. The centre party thus establishes a moving equilibrium: its position on the left-right spectrum may change, but its placement between the other parties does not. Between 1921–1984, this technique was exemplified by the Liberal shuffle: three moves left, five right, three left, and one right produces a lot of action, but the party ends up in the same place as it started. Movement becomes mistaken for leadership, with the retention of power the ultimate party goal.

This pattern was first developed for the Liberals under Mackenzie King and has served as the party's most significant operating principle ever since. For example, in addressing the national Liberal meeting in the spring of 1978, Pierre Trudeau was asked by a reporter whether the party was moving to the right in preparation for the next federal election. Trudeau responded that the Liberal party was the party of the "radical centre" and would remain so.

Thus, after years of extensive federal government expansion, by the mid-1970s Trudeau had announced government cutbacks, promised a tightening up of welfare and unemployment benefits, increased military expenditures with the purchase of new tanks and planes, and even curtailed the federal government's bilingualism programs. In effect, the Liberal party in the 1979 campaign ran against its first 10 years in office in an attempt to move to the right of the political spectrum to undercut growing Conservative strength. By contrast, in the 1972–1974 period the Liberal party moved left, passing such legislation as the 1974 Federal Election Expenses Act and establishing Petro-Canada, in order to acquire NDP support in Parliament and to undercut NDP strength in the electorate. While the move to the right was not immediately successful in the 1979 election, it did lay the foundation for the Liberals' return to power within a year. The move to the left in the early 1970s had an even more immediate impact — NDP strength in the 1974 election was cut in half from its 1972 seat total. Such tactics allowed the Liberal party to dominate national politics between 1921–1984 by occupying the "triumphant centre" of the Canadian political spectrum (Horowitz, 1968: 29–44). As Mackenzie King (quoted in Morton, 1950: 22) said in 1921, the "Liberal party with its traditions and aspirations offers a means of escape from both extremes, neither of which is in the national interest."

This centre-based model of the Canadian party system provides a possible explanation for the Tory triumphs in 1984 and 1988. Although a series of factors obviously contributed to the Liberal downfall, an important component of that debacle was that the Tories replaced the Grits as the occupier of the centre position in the political spectrum. Failure to deal adequately with economic problems alienated both working and middle class support, while their constitutional stand alienated the home province of the federal Liberals. Combined with John Turner's inept performance as leader, such factors allowed the Tories, under the Irish charm of Brian Mulroney, to move leftward to become the centre party, instead of a centre-right coalition. Thus, the Conservatives not only held their traditional areas of support in 1984, but added to it the key provinces of Ontario and Quebec. In 1988, although they lost support in Atlantic Canada, the Tories significantly increased their hold on Quebec. As a result, the Liberal party's rebuilding effort will be based on regaining the centre position in the Canadian political spectrum, while the Tories will seek to make that spot their permanent political home. The outcome of this battle will largely determine the structure of the party system for many years.

The Canadian party system is, therefore, best described by four key characteristics: it is competitive, federal, regional, and centre-based. However, underlying each of these attributes is the social, economic, and political diversity of the country. For example, federalism was adopted as a principle of government to help ensure the preservation of the two main cultural groups at the time of Confederation. Not surprising, then, is the finding that such diversity continues to exist and is channeled through the party system, exemplified by the regional basis of party support. Diversity also helps to explain the importance of the centre-oriented strategy of party politics, with a dominant party regularly challenged from both ends of the political spectrum. Finally, diversity makes it impossible for one party to represent all of the social, economic, and political interests of the nation, thereby promoting the development and maintenance of a competitive party system.

THE SELECTION OF NATIONAL PARTY LEADERS

The characteristics of the individual parties and the party system have had a significant impact on both the type of leader chosen and the process of selection. Electorally-oriented parties in a competitive party system, for the most part, prefer leaders who promise the chance of electoral success. Moreover, the significance of our national party leaders is enhanced because Canadian politics has always been leader-oriented (Perlin, 1980: 13–27). The history of Canadian politics is very much a history of its political leaders, such as John A. Macdonald, Sir Wilfrid Laurier, Mackenzie King, Pierre Trudeau, John Turner and Brian Mulroney.

The success of any political party in winning votes and elections is directly linked to the appeal of its leader, the leader's personality, and the policies enunciated by that leader. One reason Pierre Trudeau dominated national

> Joe Clark has an image like the dog food
> that won't sell (Tory MP Elmer MacKay,
> January 20, 1983).

politics for a decade and a half was that his personal appeal, his intellect, and his style far outshone other party leaders, such as Joe Clark, David Lewis, and Robert Stanfield. Moreover, political parties often make the question of leadership the focus of their election strategy, as the federal Liberals did with Trudeau on several occasions (e.g., the 1979 theme that "a leader must be a leader") and as the Ontario Progressive Conservative party did with Bill Davis in the 1981 provincial campaign. If Canadian politics is indeed leader-oriented, then it is important to know how those leaders are selected.

National party leadership selection is also significant because, in a democratic political system, we expect our party leaders to be chosen

according to certain political principles. For example, the selection process is representative (several thousand delegates are selected to attend from the various local, provincial, and national party organizations), open (public in nature and covered by the press and media), competitive (several candidates seek the leadership, thereby giving the delegates a choice between leaders), based on the majority principle (the first candidate to receive a majority of votes is declared the new leader of the party), with votes cast using the individual secret ballot (a way of guaranteeing the political equality of each delegate). While the general public may not be directly involved in the selection of party leaders, the national party leadership selection process is used as a way of giving a small group of party members a direct voice in the choice of their particular leader.

All major parties in Canada now select their leaders through a **national party leadership convention**, which is a gathering of party

Source: Reprinted from *The Leader-Post* (Regina, Saskatchewan). By permission of the paper and Brian Gable.

> National conventions are often times political parties display their innards in public (Windsor, 1986: A2).

> What I don't understand is, why was 67 percent not enough? (Prince Charles to Joe Clark, June 20, 1983).

members from across the country who meet to choose the individual who will become their new leader. In this way, the current practice of leadership conventions varies from the older Canadian tradition of having the party members in Parliament select the leader, a pattern that was used until 1919 in the Liberal party and until 1927 by the Conservatives.

Certain general rules of the selection process are typically employed by the various political parties, although specific details vary between parties or from one leadership convention to the next. The first thing a party must do is the obvious one of deciding to have a leadership convention. In some cases, the decision is straightforward, as when a leader resigns or announces the intention to do so as soon as a successor has been picked (e.g., Lester Pearson's decision to resign as Liberal party leader in 1967, John Turner's similar decision in 1989, and Ed Broadbent's announcement in 1989). However, a party leader who wants to retain the position may be forced to call a leadership convention against his or her will (e.g., John Diefenbaker's position in the mid-1960s). Those not satisfied with their party leader may make use of the **leadership review process**. Under certain conditions, the major party constitutions allow delegates to the national meetings to propose and vote on a resolution that asks for a leadership review. If such a resolution passes with a majority vote, the party then calls a leadership convention. Thus, the party members who select their leader may have the final say over how long he or she remains at the head of the party. For the Tories, after they had replaced Clark with Mulroney in 1983, the rules of the leadership review process were changed,

so that an automatic review only occurs at the first general party meeting after an election loss.

Even if a leadership review resolution does not pass, a strong minority vote in favour of it is a clear indication to the party leader that the rank and file members are unhappy. In 1981, for example, 33 percent of the delegates to the national Progressive Conservative meeting voted in favour of a leadership review. Two years later a similar vote on the leadership question put Joe Clark in the position of calling a leadership convention. Technically, Clark did not have to do so, since the leadership review vote had not passed with a majority.

As the Clark example illustrates, a strong, but less than majority, vote may be enough to force a review process to be undertaken. In New Brunswick in 1985, a challenge to the continued leadership of Richard Hatfield in the Tory party ran into a new problem. The specific results of the vote on the leadership question were not made public. All the convention was told was that the motion in favour of the review had not passed. Such a tactic, of course, prevented Hatfield from facing more pressure for a leadership review, as had happened earlier to Joe Clark.

Once a decision to call a leadership convention has been made, the next order of business is to determine how the delegates to the national party leadership convention will be selected. The rules for delegate selection are important; if they are biased towards a particular candidate or region, for example, they may end up predetermining who has the best chance of winning. A party usually sends several delegates from each local constituency organization, a number of representatives from the provincial party organizations, and a group of delegates from the national party organization. Delegates are included from the party's youth and women's organizations, the elected members of the party in both the provincial and national legislatures, and senators and privy councillors. On occasion defeated candidates from the past election, as well as delegates-at-large appointed by the party leadership, have been given the right to participate. The delegate selection process produces a gathering of several thousand party members, who then choose the party's new leader.

Both the 1983 and 1984 Conservative and Liberal leadership conventions gave ample evidence of a very significant change in the delegate selection process within the major parties. At least in theory and in practice through the 1960s, delegates from the constituency level were seen as "independent" electors who would attend the leadership convention and, after listening to the speeches and meeting the candidates, decide for whom they would vote. However, current practice suggests an opposite pattern, with delegates running as slates pledged to a particular candidate at the constituency level. Once selected, these delegates then attend the leadership convention as pledged backers of a particular candidate. Thus, the way to win national support is to pack the local delegate selection meetings so that your slate will win, even if that means having "instant party members" (i.e., 10-year olds and winos) voting for your cause.

The next stage is the nomination of candidates. In most cases, individuals seeking the position of party leader have announced their candidacy long before the convention begins, in order to have time to win the backing of delegates to the convention. Party leadership contests now last from several months up to a year before the convention, are widely covered by the news media, and can cost a candidate at least several hundred thousand dollars in expenses. For the 1990 Liberal leadership contest, a total of $1.7 million per candidate was set

as the limit. To be officially nominated, a party usually requires the candidate to be a known party member and to have his or her nomination papers signed by a given number of party members (about 50 delegates attending the convention). Few restrictions are placed on who can run for the party leadership, although "frivolous" candidates (those with no party support or those unknown to the party) may be denied the right to enter the contest. These few restrictions have not prevented a large number of people from being nominated for their party's leadership: nine candidates on the first ballot in the 1968 Liberal meeting and 12 candidates in the 1976 Progressive Conservative leadership convention. In 1983 eight candidates received votes on the first ballot at the Conservative convention, while in 1984 for the Liberals seven candidates contested the first ballot.

Once the candidates have been nominated, they are given the opportunity to address the delegates. Following the speeches by the candidates, the voting procedure begins, according to the following rules. First, the voting is done by secret, individual ballot. Since no one else knows how they have voted, delegates are free from political intimidation by a leadership candidate. The secret ballot has also produced an effect known as the **Flora syndrome**, named after Flora MacDonald's Tory leadership bid in 1976. The Flora syndrome refers to a delegate publicly declaring support for one candidate, and then voting differently in the privacy of the voting booth. Thus, it is often difficult to accurately predict the outcome of a leadership contest.

The secret ballot increases the importance of the individual delegate, since a vote from Newfoundland counts as much as a vote from an Ontario delegate. As well, since no candidate can win simply as a regional spokesman or "favourite son," each leadership hopeful must appeal to the delegates on a national or country-wide basis. For example, a candidate from the largest province, Ontario, cannot win solely as a favourite son candidate, even if all of the delegates from Ontario vote for him or her, because the Ontario delegation comprises only about one-third of the total number of participants.

A second operating rule is that each successive ballot (first ballot, second ballot, third ballot, etc.) is held almost immediately. As soon as the first ballot is finished, the second ballot begins, with only a short interval between. Ballots are held until one nominee receives a majority of votes cast. The quick succession of ballots means that candidates have very little time to decide whether they will remain in the contest or to make deals with the other candidates.

A third rule allows for the elimination of minor candidates after each ballot (e.g., those candidates not receiving a minimum number of votes, such as 50) and for the elimination of the least-placed candidate (e.g., the candidate with the fewest votes, once all minor candidates are no longer in the contest). This third operating rule helps to ensure a relatively quick decision by the convention. For example, in the 1968 Liberal convention, the original nine candidates from the first ballot were reduced to three by the fourth ballot, while in the 1976 Progressive Conservative meeting, 12 first-ballot nominees were cut to two by the fourth ballot. In the 1983 Conservative race, eight first ballot candidates were reduced to a field of two by the fourth ballot. For the Liberals in 1984, seven first ballot candidates dwindled to a list of three by the second and final ballot.

The victory of Joe Clark in the 1976 Conservative contest illustrates that the eventual winner need not be the most popular on the first ballot. Clark won because most of the candidates who were eliminated between ballots threw their support to him. For example, between the first and second ballots, Gillies, Stevens, Grafftey, and Fraser withdrew and supported Clark, while Hellyer withdrew and gave his support to Wagner. Between the second and third ballots, MacDonald withdrew and

supported Clark, while Horner and Nowlan aligned themselves with Wagner.

However, more important than how many leadership candidates withdraw and give their support to a remaining candidate is the loyalty of their delegates. Since delegates use the secret ballot, leadership candidates cannot guarantee how their supporters will vote after they have withdrawn or been eliminated from the contest. Because of the quick succession of ballots, all a leadership candidate can do is to ask supporters to cast their future ballots for a specific candidate, or to make some sort of symbolic gesture, such as sitting with a remaining candidate. However, many delegates simply ignore such a request and vote for their own choice anyway. In the 1976 Tory convention, for example, even though Jack Horner moved to the camp of Claude Wagner, it is doubtful that many of his delegates from rural Alberta voted for Wagner on subsequent ballots. The result of such voting rules is to make it possible for a relatively unknown and politically inexperienced candidate to win the leadership of a major Canadian political party.

Leadership selection in the New Democratic Party is based on a different philosophy than that of the two parliamentary parties. As an extra-parliamentary party that seeks to control its leader, the NDP requires that the party leader chosen "is to be held accountable for his term as leader by the members of his party meeting in convention, and he is expected to ensure that the party convention policy decisions are implemented once he and his colleagues have gained power" (Courtney, 1973: 174). As a result of this view, the party leader must automatically seek reelection at the NDP's biennial convention, thus eliminating the traditional need to push for a leadership review process, as in the Liberal and Conservative parties. However, in fact, no serious challenge to the party leader has ever developed within the NDP, thus resulting in a secure tenure of office. For example, in the July 1981 NDP meeting,

Direct Democracy and the Parti Québécois: In replacing René Lévesque as party leader in the fall of 1985, the PQ, for the first time in Canadian history, tried direct democracy rather than a party convention to choose a new leader. All 160 000 party members were eligible to vote, with about 100 000 actually participating. Across the province 900 polling stations were used in this mini-election, with Pierre-Marc Johnson winning on the first ballot. If a second ballot had been needed, it would have taken place a week later, again with all party members eligible to vote. This new format appears unlikely to be adopted soon by the national parties of Canada. However, the Ontario provincial Conservative party adopted (February 1989) a similar direct-ballot proposal, which was used to select its new leader (Michael Harris) in 1990.

Alternation between French and English Canadians in the largely ceremonial office of Governor-General symbolizes the partnership between two national cultures; rigid alternation in the leadership of a national party institutionalizes and may inflame a national divide (Martin, 1989: 164).

while 37 percent of the delegates voted against their leader's stand on the constitutional issue, discontent over policy did not result in a challenge to Ed Broadbent's continuing leadership of the party.

Although all federal parties use the national party leadership convention to select their leaders, the type of leader chosen by the parties has differed historically between the Liberals and Conservatives (Smiley, 1968; Courtney, 1973; Perlin, 1980). In the Liberal party, candidates from Ontario and Quebec dominate. Conservatives are more likely to select nominees from either Western Canada or the Maritimes. Thus, the regional nature of the party system and party support is reflected within the parties, as well as between them in election campaigns.

Until Brian Mulroney and Joe Clark, Conservatives have relied on those who were veterans of elective office, especially on people who have served as provincial premiers. Liberals, in contrast, have rarely chosen a leader who has ever contested a provincial election and have been receptive to candidates who have had little polit-

ical experience. In this sense, the Liberals have been more pragmatic than the Conservatives in the selection of their leaders, even accepting a candidate such as Trudeau, who had vehemently attacked the Liberal party shortly before joining it or John Turner, who had left the cabinet for nearly a decade. Such pragmatism is also evident in the Liberal party's alternation between French and English leaders (King, St. Laurent, Pearson, Trudeau, Turner, Chrétien): the party of Ontario and Quebec rarely forgets where its power base lies. By contrast, Conservatives, until their selection of Brian Mulroney, have failed to appeal to Quebec in terms of their leadership selection, as exemplified by Claude Wagner's defeat in their 1976 convention.

The type of leader selected varies not only between parties, but with other forms of leadership selection as well. For example, since the adoption of the national party leadership convention, the role of the party caucus has greatly diminished, thereby increasing the opportunity for the selection of outsiders. It is highly doubtful that Joe Clark, Pierre Trudeau, John Turner or Brian Mulroney would have been chosen to lead their parties if the party caucus method had been used.

Moreover, being selected by a national party convention has enhanced the power of the leader over his or her party caucus, since leaders now argue that they can only be removed by such a convention. However, if a leader is removed, as Diefenbaker was in the 1967 Conservative convention, then the caucus is likely to become split between the supporters of the old and new leaders, as Robert Stanfield discovered. After his ouster, Diefenbaker remained a member of the party caucus, "emitting all the baleful radiance of a whore at a family wedding" (Young, 1978: 290).

Finally, if the major parties are electoral coalitions, then the basic factor in leadership selection is whether the new leader can enhance the party's electoral prospects. As a result, the leaders so picked have been pragmatic politicians, nonideological in outlook, with their primary goal that of electoral victory. Those leaders who cannot produce such results immediately come under attack, with internal party conflict over leadership replacement usually occurring after an electoral defeat. In an atypical pattern, because Liberal party leader John Turner's standing with his party was so low, there were several tries, shortly before the 1988 election, to replace him as leader and, at least, one serious attempt even after the campaign had started. Since Canadian politics is leader-oriented and because the easiest way to change a party's image is to select a new leader, the Conservative party, as the usual losing party in federal elections, has had a history of internal party conflict over questions of leadership, a pattern dubbed the **Tory syndrome** (Perlin, 1980). The Conservative and Liberal national party leadership conventions of the 1980s and 1990s illustrate many of these trends.

The Tories choose a leader — June, 1983

In Canadian politics, issues have almost always been secondary to concerns about leadership. With the emergence of television as the dominant mechanism in the electoral process, campaigns have increasingly become, in the past two decades, leadership-based media contests. Therefore, to help change a party's electoral prospects, turnover or replacement of a party leader has become a common practice in the battle for power.

Such was the situation immediately confronting Joe Clark after his 1980 election loss. However, questions about Clark's leadership abilities had actually begun several years earlier, shortly after his winning the Conservative leadership convention of 1976. Quite simply, Clark had not been able to assert effective control over either his caucus or party organization. These problems, combined with a public image of his ineptitude and ineffectiveness, led to Clark's defeat in the 1980 election and the ensuing attempts to unseat him as party leader.

The first attempt to get a leadership review process under way was thwarted in 1981 when, at the party convention in Ottawa, 66.1 percent of the delegates voted against a leadership convention. However, the vote two years later in Winnipeg, with the almost identical results of 66.9 percent rejecting a leadership review, produced a leadership convention in June 1983. A two-thirds vote against a leadership review process was not enough politically because it did not put to rest the rising discontent within the party, nor did it clear the air in time for the next general election, which was expected in 1984. Thus, although Clark was not required by the party rules to call a new leadership convention, he did so anyway. Interestingly, after forcing a leadership review on former Prime Minister Clark, the Conservatives ended their 1983 convention by altering the party rules to make such leadership challenges much more difficult to carry out in the future. Paradoxically, at the time that he was politically forced to hold a leadership review, Joe Clark had a healthy 15-percentage-point lead over the Liberals in the public opinion polls.

The internal party leadership battle occupied centre stage for the next six months, as Joe Clark sought to maintain his party's leadership. Clark was challenged by three major contestants from inside the Conservative caucus (John Crosbie, Michael Wilson, David Crombie) and one major candidate outside Parliament (Brian Mulroney). Mulroney had lost to Joe Clark in

TABLE 9.4   1983 CONSERVATIVE LEADERSHIP CONVENTION

CANDIDATES	BALLOT			
	First	*Second*	*Third*	*Fourth*
Joe Clark	1091	1085	1058	1325
Brian Mulroney	874	1021	1036	1584
John Crosbie	639	781	858	—
Michael Wilson	144	—	—	—
David Crombie	116	67	—	—
Peter Pocklington	102	—	—	—
John Gamble	17	—	—	—
Neil Fraser	5	—	—	—

TABLE 9.5   1984 LIBERAL LEADERSHIP CONVENTION

CANDIDATES	BALLOT	
	First	*Second*
John Turner	1593	1862
Jean Chrétien	1067	1368
Don Johnston	278	192
John Roberts	185	—
Mark MacGuigan	135	—
John Munro	93	—
Eugene Whelan	84	—

the 1976 leadership race and had never before run for elective office, but he was a well-known party organizer from Quebec. After a bitter campaign and after four ballots at the leadership convention, Brian Mulroney emerged as the new Conservative leader (Table 9.4). The change in Tory leadership was one factor which helped to convince the Liberals that they too would be better off with a new leader for the next election.

The coronation of John Turner — June, 1984

Pierre Elliott Trudeau had "promised" that the 1980 campaign would be his last. With the patriation battle over in 1982 and with the Conservative's choice of a new leader in 1983, party and public pressure began to grow for Trudeau to fulfill that promise. On 29 February, 1984 he announced his imminent retirement, thus setting in motion a national Liberal leadership contest (June 1984) and a short-lived turnaround in public support for the Liberal party. By the time of the convention in June, the Liberals had managed to gain a 10 percent lead over the Conservatives in the public opinion polls.

The leadership convention was basically a battle between John Turner and Jean Chrétien. Turner, the frontrunner, had been a key figure in the early Trudeau years, holding such important portfolios as Justice and Finance. Long seen as the heir apparent, he resigned from the cabinet in 1975 because of disputes over policy and personality conflicts with Trudeau. The resulting ill will between Turner and Trudeau was one reason why Trudeau decided to remain as leader in December 1979, after the parliamentary defeat of the Clark government. Trudeau wanted to make sure that John Turner would not become leader of the Liberal party. By contrast, Jean Chrétien had emerged in the late 1970s as one of Pierre Trudeau's most trusted lieutenants, taking on any task that his leader might require of him. The other leadership aspirants, even though some had been cabinet ministers for many years, were minor players in the party contest.

The easy second ballot victory for John Turner at the Liberal leadership convention can be explained by a number of factors (Table 9.5). First, Turner had been away from active politics for nearly a decade and thus could argue that his selection represented change while, at the same time, providing a way for the Liberals to retain power. Second, Turner's reputation as an effective minister and potential leader had increased, not diminished, in his years since active politics. Third, the party hierarchy wanted above anything else a winner and John Turner's image had always been what they wanted. Finally, the Liberal party tradition of alternating French and English leaders clearly worked in favour of John Turner and against Jean Chrétien. Thus, John Turner had finally succeeded in his long-held ambition to replace Pierre Trudeau as both Liberal party leader and Prime Minister of Canada.

The 1990 Liberal leadership convention

Following his second massive electoral defeat in 1988, it was only a matter of time before John Turner would have to relinquish the mantle of Liberal party leadership. Finally ending months of speculation, John Turner announced his intention to resign on May 3, 1989, having served five years as Liberal leader. The party's national executive decided in June to hold the leadership convention a year later in Calgary between June 19-23, making it the longest convention race in Canadian political history. Delegates (5200 of them) would be selected after February 15, 1990 in Ontario and after March 1, 1990 in the rest of the country. Each leadership candidate would be allowed to spend a maximum of $1.7 million, with the total cost of the convention estimated at $25 million.

The clear frontrunner to replace John Turner was former Trudeau political ally and cabinet minister Jean Chrétien, who had finished second in the previous leadership race in 1984. The only real challenge came from novice Quebec MP, Paul Martin, Jr., son of longtime Liberal party stalwart, cabinet member, and twice-defeated Liberal leadership candidate, Paul Martin, Sr. The key battle between these two candidates would be in Quebec. The three other official candidates were all junior members of the Liberal caucus: Sheila Copps, Thomas

Wappel, and John Nunziata. Several potential leaders withdrew from the race early on: Lloyd Axworthy, MP from Manitoba, due to his inability to raise sufficient funds and Clifford Lincoln, former Quebec environment minister, after his loss in the federal by-election in the Montreal riding of Chambly on February 12, 1990. Other possible candidates decided not to enter the fray: MP Dennis Mills and Ontario Premier David Peterson.

The leadership race consisted of a series of national debates held across the country and the battle for delegates at the constituency level, with the latter being, by far, the most important ingredient. The party again faced the problem of "instant members" at the delegate selection meetings, with the meetings often stacked by one or the other of the leader's supporters. On a national basis, particularly in Quebec, the Chrétien forces were far superior and won the delegate battle. While Sheila Copps gained considerable media coverage, she was not well-organized at the grassroots level and was unable to turn public support into elected delegates. Both Thomas Wappel, mainly an anti-abortion candidate, and John Nunziata were minor players in the contest. Thus, the strong (57 per cent) first ballot victory for Jean Crétien was no surprise (see Table 9.6).

Overall, the leadership race was dull, given Chrétien's early and large lead, and overshadowed by the debates and conflict over the Meech Lake accord, which died on June 22,

TABLE 9.6 1990 LIBERAL LEADERSHIP CONVENTION

CANDIDATES	FIRST BALLOT
Jean Chrétien	2652
Paul Martin	1176
Sheila Copps	499
Thomas Wappel	167
John Nunziata	64

Source: Reprinted from *The Leader-Post* (Regina, Saskatchewan). By permission of the paper and Brian Gable.

1990, one day before the leadership vote. As an anti-Meech candidate, Chrétien would face tough problems in the future in winning support in Quebec, where a strong majority had backed the Meech Lake accord.

The 1989 NDP leadership convention

Although the NDP won more seats in the 1988 election than ever before (e.g., 43) and its popular vote reached a new high of 20.4 percent, the federal election was a great disappointment, leaving the party demoralized and lacking a sense of direction. In the interelection period (1984–1988), the NDP had found itself leading in the public opinion polls and fantasizing about forming a majority government. Thus, the 1988 results were a deep disappointment to the party and its leader, Ed Broadbent.

One result was that in March of 1989, Ed Broadbent, a 20-year veteran of the House of Commons and 14-year leader of the NDP, announced his retirement. Having led his party through four elections, and even though many in the party wanted him to continue, the former political science professor decided it was time to move on. After a delay of several months, a leadership convention was scheduled in Winnipeg for November, with the actual voting to take place on December 2, 1989, by the approximately 2400 delegates.

The leadership race can only be described as lacklustre, generating little enthusiasm either in the party or the country. A significant factor was the failure of major figures in the NDP to enter the leadership contest. For example, the following NDP "stars" refused to seek the leadership mantle: Bob Rae, former federal MP and current leader of the Ontario NDP; Bob White, president of the Canadian Auto Workers; Stephen Lewis, former Ontario NDP leader and former Canadian Ambassador to the United Nations; Roy Romanow, NDP

TABLE 9.7 1989 NDP LEADERSHIP CONVENTION

CANDIDATES	BALLOT			
	First	*Second*	*Third*	*Fourth*
Dave Barrett	566	780	947	1072
Simon de Jong	315	289	—	—
Roger Lagasse	53	—	—	—
Steven Langdon	351	519	393	—
Howard McCurdy	256	—	—	—
Audrey McLaughlin	646	829	1072	1316
Ian Waddell	213	—	—	—

leader in Saskatchewan; Marion Dewar, former MP and Mayor of Ottawa; and Ed Schreyer, former Premier of Manitoba and former Governor-General.

Those who did run (see Table 9.7) were all from the NDP federal caucus, except for Roger Lagasse. These seven candidates were dubbed by many pundits as the NDP's second string, or as the "seven dwarfs." The leading contender was Audrey McLaughlin, NDP MP from the Yukon and the only woman in the race. Her main challenger was Dave Barrett, NDP MP and former Premier of British Columbia, who entered the race late, just two months before the leadership vote. The other caucus members trying for the leadership (Steven Langdon, Simon de Jong, Howard McCurdy, and Ian Waddell) each had their own strengths and base in the party, but were seen as being unable to beat either McLaughlin or Barrett. As a precursor to the convention, the seven leadership candidates participated in 15 debates held across the country.

By the time the convention opened, it was clearly a two-way race between McLaughlin and Barrett. However, Audrey McLaughlin's uninspiring address to the convention was in sharp contrast to the energetic speech of Dave Barrett, a rousing orator. Partly as a result, McLaughlin's first ballot total over Barrett was much less than expected, leading to speculation that the former B.C. premier might overtake her on later ballots. Although Barrett moved to within 49 ballots on the second round, McLaughlin widened her lead by the third ballot, winning it decisively on the fourth.

An interesting, and controversial, aspect of the 1989 NDP leadership race was the CBC taping of some of the major contenders in their negotiations with each other. In particular, an apparent negotiation between Barrett and de Jong was recorded, showing that de Jong would give his support to Barrett when he was eliminated. In fact, de Jong ended up backing McLaughlin. The resulting furor made it unlikely that the news media, particularly the CBC, will be able to convince candidates to wear microphones at future leadership conventions.

For the NDP, the selection of Audrey McLaughlin, the first woman to lead a national party in North America, reorients the party's direction for the 1990s. The convention clearly shifted power within the NDP to its Western contingent and to its provincial organizations.

PARTY FINANCE

As primarily electoral organizations, it is not surprising to find that the major expenses facing the parties are campaign expenditures. As a fundraiser who worked for both the Conservatives and Liberals, Israel Tarte's statement (quoted in Dawson, 1970: 478) that "elections are not won by prayers alone" points to the importance of financial considerations in the success of a political party. Changes in campaign techniques in recent decades, in particular the emphasis on costly mass media advertising, have greatly increased the necessity for party funds. Parties also need money to carry the organization through the inter-election period, an especially vulnerable situation for opposition parties.

The pattern of party finance differs between

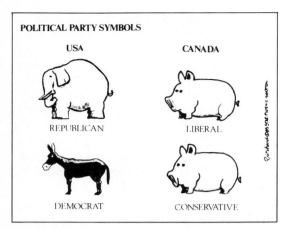

POLITICAL PARTY SYMBOLS

USA   CANADA

REPUBLICAN   LIBERAL

DEMOCRAT   CONSERVATIVE

Source: Portfolio 85: The Year in Canadian Caricature, CROC Publishing, 1985. By permission of Denny Pritchard, *Star-Phoenix.*

the cadre and mass party types. Traditionally, the cadre parties (Liberal and Conservative) have relied on contributions from the corporate sector, with large donations from relatively few sponsors. In contrast, mass parties have taken a grass-roots funding approach, depending on small donations from numerous individuals or on union support.

In the initial years of Confederation, party leaders had to concern themselves directly with matters of party finance. The inevitable soon occurred: a party leader, John A. Macdonald, was involved in questions of party funding and corruption. The Pacific Scandal brought the downfall of the Conservative government and almost wrecked Macdonald's career. Consequently, party leaders have since sought to isolate themselves from matters of party finance by having specific party organizers for fundraising activities. These **bagmen**, who are often appointed to patronage positions such as the Senate, operate outside of the party leader's sight, so that when the political scandal eventually hits, the party leader is able to disassociate himself or herself from any involvement in political wrong doing. Seeing no evil allows the party

leader to profess innocence, while the party's bagman may be charged with criminal wrongdoing by the government controlled by his party and left to defend himself, as Liberal Senator Louis Giguère discovered in the Sky Shops Affair.

This pattern of fundraising by the Liberals and Conservatives, based on large corporate donations, has endured, in slightly modified form, to the present. The financial backing thus received helped to reinforce the dominance of the two major parties, since new parties were often hard-pressed for cash. Moreover, because the extra-parliamentary parties represented a challenge to the existing social and economic interests of Central Canada, they neither wanted, nor were they typically offered, corporate largesse. As a result, they sought a new means of party finance, attempting to use the mass-funding techniques of the European social democratic parties.

This grass-roots approach centred on two sources of potential party income: annual dues from individual members and contributions from trade unions and interest groups. The initial attempts at mass-funding through individual contributions were not particularly successful, usually leaving the party perpetually short of funds, as the experience of the CCF demonstrates. However, dues-paying members combined with labour union contributions have helped to give the NDP a more solid financial base than its predecessor. In the 1960s, trade union financial support for the NDP amounted to approximately 40 percent of party funds, allowing the party to challenge the financial dominance of the Liberals and Conservatives (Paltiel, 1970: 56–61). The most successful mass-funding party in Canadian history (at least in its early years) is the Parti Québécois, which not only sent back corporate donations in the 1973 and 1976 provincial election campaigns, but proceeded to make such contributions to parties illegal after they became the government in 1976.

The traditional pattern of party finance for the Liberals and Conservatives utilized several basic techniques, although these practices were regularly denied by the party bagmen. The essential first step in fundraising was to select bagmen who had access to the financial and corporate elite: as Mackenzie King (quoted in Wearing, 1981: 63) put it, "you need million-aires to get money from millionaires." These fundraisers would then visit wealthy individuals and corporate executives for their annual contri-butions. A longtime practice was for the dona-tions to be split 60 percent for the government party and 40 percent for the opposition. Now that the record of party finance is public knowl-edge, a 50/50 split is often seen among the major corporate donors. Such contributions thus ensured that no matter which party won the next election, the individual or corporation, hav-ing donated to the party coffers, could count on access to the political leaders.

If such donations were not readily given, the governing party could institute the practices of toll-gating and kickbacks (Wearing, 1981: 58–64). In **toll-gating**, government con-tracts or business would be allocated to those firms that had given to the party coffers, while a **kickback** scheme meant that once a firm had received government work, a certain percent-age would be returned to the ruling party, usually by way of campaign contributions. Advertising agencies and their lucrative con-tracts with government departments often provide suitable examples of this point. Finally, the party in power could also use patronage appointments to bolster party finances. Those receiving such appointments are often expected to contribute a portion of their salaries to the party that appointed them. These practices clearly favour the party in power, with electoral defeat often creating a crisis of party finance. For example, the defeated Liberals found them-selves $3.5 million in debt after the 1984 con-test, and an estimated $6-7 million in debt after their second consecutive election loss in 1988.

The major change in this traditional pattern of party finance came with the passage of the 1974 Election Expenses Act, which attempts both to regulate party fundraising activities and to provide public subsidies for election expenses. The adoption of such a measure has an interesting political lineage: the Liberal minority government between 1972 and 1974 needed the backing of the NDP caucus to stay in power and election finance reform was one payoff for the NDP's continuing support. Not surprisingly, the 1974 reforms have greatly benefitted the NDP, putting the party on a more equal financial footing with the major parties. We would also suggest a further reason for the 1974 Election Expenses Act: campaign expendi-tures were increasing so rapidly that all of the parties feared their inability to raise adequate funds in future elections. As a result, the parties collectively turned to public funding and pro-ceeded to raid the public treasury without greatly changing the existing practices of party finance.

One requirement of the Election Expenses Act is that the parties have to file an annual financial report with the Chief Electoral Officer. The first reports, which covered the 1974–1975 fiscal year, indicated that it cost about $2 million to operate a national party in a non-election year (*The Globe and Mail*, February 10, 1976 and February 11, 1976). By the beginning of the 1980s, that annual figure for party spending had reached $4 to $5 million; by the late 1980s, that figure stood somewhere between $6 and $10 million for each party to operate on a national level. Moreover, the corporate sector, with few exceptions, gave exactly the same contribution to both major parties. The differences between cadre and mass party funding approaches were also evident in these early reports (1974–1975): while 6 400 individuals contributed to the Con-servatives and 9 900 to the Liberals, 28 000 per-sons made a donation to the NDP. While approximately 30 percent of Conservative funds and 50 percent of Liberal funds came from

Source: Guy Badeaux (ed.), *1988 Portfolio: The Year in Canadian Caricature*, Montreal: Eden Press, 1988. By permission of Adrian Raeside.

individuals, 85 percent of NDP donations originated from party members.

By the time of the 1984 election, these figures had increased dramatically. The data for the major parties show that contributions came to nearly $42 million, with the Conservatives spending nearly $20 million, the Liberals $11 million, and the NDP over $6 million. A total of 114 485 individuals gave to the Tories, 35 631 to the Liberals, and 81 261 to the NDP. The success of the Tories in party finance reflected not only the expectation that they would form the government, but also their lead in using the new techniques, such as direct-mail solicitations. After the Liberal defeat, for example, John Turner admitted that his party was 10 years behind the times in the manner in which it organized itself.

Party fundraising, as might be expected, became more difficult after the election year in 1984. In 1985, the Tories raised $14.5 million,

the Liberals $5.6 million, and the NDP $10.2 million. Thus, in 1985 the three main parties raised about $30 million—a decline of $12 million from their 1984 figure. By 1986, however, party fundraising rebounded, with the main party competitors collecting about $33 million; in the election year of 1988, that total soared to nearly $50 million.

In addition to requiring an annual report, the Election Expenses Act seeks to limit the amount of money that parties and candidates can spend, provides for the disclosure of the sources of party and candidate incomes, grants subsidies for candidate expenses and party media advertising, and establishes a tax credit for people contributing to party funds (Paltiel, 1975). Although the Act was in effect as of August 1, 1974, the first election to which these provisions applied was the 1979 contest. The July 1974 election was conducted under the traditional pattern of party finance—an example of "once more for old-times sake" before the reform legislation became applicable.

The impact of the Election Expenses Act can be seen in the extent of public subsidies to parties and candidates in the 1979 and 1980 election campaigns (Seidle and Paltiel, 1981: 275–276). Subsidies to the parties came to $4.5 million and to $17 million for the various candidates. From 1974 to 1980, public support for election expenses had totalled close to $50 million.

While the 1974 Election Expenses Act represents a considerable improvement over past practices, its effectiveness is open to challenge. For example, the limits on party and candidate expenditures were set relatively high, so that if the Act had applied to the 1974 election, no party would have exceeded them. Moreover, before the Act was applied the first time, these limits were raised in 1977 and the base year for indexing the spending ceilings was changed from 1974 to 1976, which added a possible $23 million to potential party and candidate costs. Since that change was made, an automatic escalator clause has also been inserted to handle the problem of inflation. In other words, limits which are set so high that no party approximates them in no way curtail party spending in campaigns. In fact, since the public now subsidizes these expenses, the costs of the campaigns have soard to unprecedented levels.

A second defect concerns the amount of individual contributions: any donation over $100 must be disclosed, but no limit is put on how much can be given. Thus, the financial dependence on small groups of financial backers has not been greatly undercut. Contrary to what might be expected, the largest single donation from an individual to a political party has gone to the NDP. Irene Dyck from Calgary contributed $216 000 in 1984 to the Socialist cause, a decline from her 1983 largesse of $453 000. In 1989 her contribution was $147 668.

Third, the enforcement provisions for violations of this Act are weak — it is up to the public or the various parties to lay complaints with the Chief Electoral Officer. With the "live and let live" attitudes of the parties, few violations will be investigated. Given these limitations of the 1974 Election Expenses Act, the traditional pattern of party finance remains largely in place, with public funding grafted on. The parties successfully raided the public treasury without giving the public effective control over the area of party finance. Whether this pattern continues will depend, in part, on the results of the Royal Commission on Electoral Reform and Party Financing, which began its hearings in 1990.

PARTY FUNCTIONS

Party finance is significant because it helps to determine whether a party will be successful in carrying out its electoral functions: money cannot buy electoral victory, but electoral victory is difficult to achieve without it, given the expensive nature of modern campaigns. Canadian parties are electoral organizations not only in the sense of aiming for victory, but also because they are important actors in organizing the electorate. For example, parties help to get the individual voters on the appropriate polling lists, provide the voters with information on the issues of the contest, and help to stimulate voter interest and participation. Parties are also the key structure in recruiting candidates for office, thus providing the electorate with someone to vote for or against, as the case may be. As Dalton Camp (1979: 231) has observed, the "essentials of Canadian politics are few: the system needs enough good men to make it work and enough fools to make it interesting."

Parties also help to structure the electorate by serving as political objects with which people can identify. These partisan attachments are some of the earliest linkages an individual develops with the political system. Although individual partisan attachments may vary, in the aggregate they help to structure the partisan

> Early Canadian political history includes a number of election riots, even some in which participants were killed. The 1988 election never reached that level of confrontation, but . . . enough noses were punched or heads gashed to push Canadian elections back into the category of a blood sport (Boyer, 1989: 72).

> The role of the party today is to get organized every two or four years in order to return a government to power. The role of party militants is to supply applause for party leaders, to serve as background for the 11 o'clock television news (Williams, 1980: 7).

coloration of the electorate; there is a reservoir of support for the parties, which they receive regardless of the issues or leaders in a particular campaign.

In addition to serving as objects of individual emotional ties, parties help to structure the electorate, because the major socioeconomic cleavages of society differentiate the group bases of partisan support in the Canadian polity. Historically, different regions, religious, ethnic, and linguistic groups have become linked with specific parties. The way these groups align themselves with the parties gives historical continuity to the party system. The most obvious example of this point was the usual preference of French-Canadians for the Liberal party between 1921 and 1984. Such group bases of party support reveal that the Canadian "party system is organized around the usual regional, religious, and social class oppositions to which is added a specific linguistic cleavage" (Laponce, 1972: 284).

The party that wins the election undertakes, in addition to its electoral functions, a number of what can be called governing functions. In the Canadian parliamentary system, the governing party is the key mechanism for achieving the fusion of the executive and legislative branches of government. Walter Bagehot's famous description of the mid-19th century British cabinet as "the hyphen which joins—the buckle which fastens—the executive to the legislative part of the state" is obsolete since the advent of parties. It is the party that lays the foundation

for the fusion of executive and legislative powers, and only after the party does so can an institution such as the cabinet implement the fusion of powers on a day-to-day basis. In the modern era, cabinet government is predicated on party government; Walter Bagehot's buckle has a party label. Failure to realize this relationship has often led to a denigration of the significant role parties play in the governing process.

Parties help to organize the government in several ways. It is the electoral success of a party, in terms of it winning more seats than any other party in the legislature, which provides the group basis of government organization. Except in rare circumstances, the leader of the party with the largest block of legislative seats is asked by the formal executive to form a government. Thus, control of the legislature gives the party control of the executive.

While it is true that once a government has been formed, the cabinet may dominate the party caucus and the legislature, the legislative base of the cabinet is often lost sight of. In a parliamentary system, the political executive retains office only as long as it has legislative support, and that support is provided by the party organization through the principle of party discipline. Only when a **free vote** is called (i.e., when party discipline is relaxed and the legislative members decide on an individual basis how to vote) does the group basis of legislative power momentarily recede. Interestingly, Joe Clark became an advocate of free votes after his brief term of office as Prime Minister, but did

> Patronage is the outward and visible sign of an inward and spiritual grace, and that is power (Benjamin Disraeli).

> Patronage is the pornography of politics, enticing to some, repulsive to others, justified as inevitable, condemned as immoral, a practice seldom considered a fit subject for polite discussion (Simpson, 1988: 6).

not advocate their use after becoming a part of the Mulroney cabinet after the 1984 election victory.

An additional governing function of the successful party is that it directly provides the personnel to fill the cabinet portfolios. Except for the one experience of coalition government during the First World War, all subsequent cabinets have been formed by the individuals from a single party. In this way, the party literally takes over physical control of the government by placing its members in positions of executive authority. Moreover, the cabinet, once formed, controls thousands of further job appointments to the various departments and agencies of government. Through the use of patronage appointments, the governing party oozes its way through the structure of government, linking unto itself the disparate realms of power and influence.

Patronage is the interstitial glue of politics, fusing together the otherwise inchoate elements of government. A good example of this process was evident when the Conservatives won power in 1979. After securing office, the party set up, under one of its defeated candidates Jean Pigott, a screening process for all government appointments. A list of all jobs over which the government had appointment power was prepared, so that when vacancies occurred these positions would be filled by people with Conservative party ties. When the Tories returned to power in 1984, a modified version of this placement system was again used to control appointments for the roughly 3 500 jobs filled by prime ministerial discretion. Moreover, a longstanding practice in Canadian politics has been to appoint a political minister for each province, who oversees and directs the filling of vacant federal governmental positions within his or her province. By such mechanisms, parties seek to organize the disparate structures of government into a working, if not necessarily a cohesive, organization.

A final governing function of parties is to contribute to policy direction and leadership for the political system. In most cases, the parties play only a small role in this process. Once a government is formed, the policy process is dominated by the cabinet and bureaucracy, with the party organizations relegated to a minor role. However, parties are an essential basis for the implementation of policy, because they provide the necessary support in the legislature for its passage. In addition, parties may play a policy-making role by providing the party platforms for election campaigns. Overall, however, the party organizations have a limited role in the policy process, serving instead as supporters of policy decided elsewhere.

While all parties have various electoral functions, it is only the winning party that directly participates in the several governing functions. However, the opposition parties are indirectly involved through their participation in the legislature, which can be used to attack or to suggest changes in government policy. Although no minor party has ever formed a government in Ottawa, they have often acquired limited governing functions because of the frequent occurrence of minority governments. As a result, minor parties have sometimes had a direct impact on government policy, which has enhanced their role as innovators in the Canadian party system.

Comparing Parties and Party Systems

Britain and the United States are two examples of competitive party systems. In these polities, current practices reflect the origin and development of the individual parties.

BRITISH POLITICAL PARTIES

Historically, what were to become parties first emerged in the European context, with Britain leading in the development of these new political mechanisms. By the middle of the 17th century, factions, the forerunners of the modern party organizations, were present within the legislature. However, the importance of these new groups was not immediately appreciated, as evidenced by the labels Tories and Whigs, nicknames "given in a spirit of derision," since "Tories were bandits on the highways of Ireland" and the "Whigs a band of Scottish insurgents in 1648" (Duverger, 1972: 78). By the middle of the 19th century, the factions had developed into the parties of the modern era. With the Reform Act of 1832, these parties expanded from their legislative birthplace to seek greater support among the electorate, in the process establishing party structures at the local level and cohesive groups within Parliament. Adopting the names Conservatives and Liberals, instead of Tories and Whigs, the two initial parties of parliamentary origin dominated the party system for three-quarters of a century.

However, parties of extra-parliamentary origin have had a major impact on British politics in the 20th century. The most significant event was the formation of the Trade Union Congress in 1900, which aimed at establishing a mass-

> I believe that without party, Parliamentary Government is impossible (Benjamin Disraeli).
>
> British government would be fundamentally changed if parties were absent from the voter's mind (Butler and Stokes, 1976: 13).
>
> Setting aside the party myths and the inter-party propaganda, it is clear that the primary function of the mass organizations of the Conservative and Labour parties is to sustain the two competing teams of parliamentary leaders between whom the electorate as a whole may periodically choose (McKenzie, 1967: 642).

based, socialist, working-class party. Adopting the name Labour Party in 1906, this group gradually emerged as a challenger to the Liberals and Conservatives. By the 1920s it had become the second largest party in Parliament, replacing the Liberals, with the first Labour government formed in 1923. With the long-term decline of the Liberal party from the 1930s to the early 1980s, Britain has had primarily a two-party battle between the Conservatives and the Labourites.

In addition to the expansion of the Labour party in the early decades of the present century, Britain experienced the growth of a series of nationalist parties based on the regional and cultural concerns of Ireland, Scotland, and Wales. The most significant nationalist party was the Irish, which held 80 seats in the House of Commons from 1910 to 1918 and eventually succeeded in gaining Home Rule or independence for Ireland, although the Protestant areas remained within Britain as Northern Ireland. More recently, the 1970s and 1980s saw seats in the Commons obtained by both the Scottish Nationalist Party (SNP) and the Welsh Nationalist Party (Plaid Cymru). In addition to these nationalist parties, other groups such as the

Communist Party and the National Front (a neo-fascist group) have competed in recent elections, but have had little electoral success and no great impact on the longstanding parties in British politics.

While the internally created parliamentary parties (Liberal and Conservative) and the externally created parties (especially the Labour party) show the characteristics of the cadre and mass type of parties, respectively, British parties have some unique features as well, which reflect certain attributes of societal and governmental organization. Most important is the fact that Britain is both parliamentary and unitary, with the parties reflecting the resulting centralization of power. For example, while the Liberals and Conservatives may be traditional in organization, they are "rigid elitist parties" in operation (Duverger, 1972: 7). In comparison to Canadian parties, the British parties are also more centralized in structure, recruitment, and leadership. British parties are also more ideological than their Canadian counterparts; parties run on explicit platforms or party manifestos that they are expected to implement if they acquire office. Thus, the major parties in Britain in the 1990s (Labour and Conservative) can be classified as ideological in content and programmatic in function. One result of programmatic and centralized parties was the early development of unified groups within Parliament, with strict party discipline being seen historically as one of the hallmarks of British party organization. Although party discipline was increasingly challenged in the late-1970s and 1980s, the Labour and Conservative parties in the 1990s are still basically unified and cohesive organizations in Parliament, except on rare occasions.

In addition to their more ideological style and centralized structure, British parties are less regional than their Canadian analogues. Although there is a regional basis of party support even within England itself, the Labour and Conservative parties are more national in composition traditionally than either of the two

> Party, not Parliament, determines the control of British government . . . . The slow pace of change and the very limited deviations from collective party discipline are a caution against the bark of dissent as evidence of a break in the bars of the iron cage of party government (Rose, 1983: 282, 298).

major Canadian parties (Drucker, 1979: 217). Moreover, the centralized nature of the political system has forced nationalist parties to compete for seats in the national legislature. The result has been a greater impact of new parties in British than Canadian politics, although the appearance of such parties in Britain has been less frequent. In Canada, federalism has helped to contain nationalist sentiment, exemplified by the Parti Québécois and its power in provincial politics, while in Britain, nationalist emotion led to the granting of Home Rule for Ireland. Although the characteristics of the major parties are reflective of the general origin and development of the cadre (Conservative) and mass (Labour) types, their evolution in the British milieu has produced these unique features as well. The British parties remain, however, electorally oriented parties: "the goal of the British political party is to win elections" (Finer, 1980: 167).

The party system in Britain since the Second World War can be described as competitive in nature, dominated by two major parties, but challenged by both the growth of new parties and a corresponding decline in public support for themselves (Drucker, 1979). The two major parties have controlled governmental office since 1945, with no other party participation, and, unlike in Canada, election results have regularly produced majority governments, except for the February 1974 contest. Moreover, during the 1960s and 1970s, the two main parties have alternated in office, although the Conservatives have more often been the government

> Although many people enjoy themselves in opposition more than they do on the government back benches, the Labour Party is no longer what I called it and what it was — the natural party of government (former Prime Minister Harold Wilson, January, 1984).

> The Conservatives at their annual conference sing "Land of Hope and Glory" and drape the platform with the Union Jack; Labour delegates at their conference sing "The Red Flag," and the Union Jack is never anywhere to be seen (King, 1985: 32).

party since 1945. At the end of Margaret Thatcher's third term in office, the Conservatives will have governed for 30 years since 1945. However, the traditional turnover pattern makes the British party system more competitive than the Canadian.

In addition to its competitive nature, the two-party battle between the Conservative and Labour parties, and party alternation in office (at least until Margaret Thatcher's three terms in office), the British party system is further characterized by the historical dominance of the Conservative party: from 1885 to 1945 the Conservatives "were in government for almost 75 percent of the time" (Gamble, 1979: 26). The normal governing party in British politics is the Conservative party, while in Canada in the modern era it has been the Liberals (1921–1984). Moreover, the tactics of both parties have been similar, with their appeals to national unity.

The cleavage basis of the British party system in the 20th century has been the class division, which replaced the predominant religious cleavage of the 18th and 19th centuries (Butler and Stokes, 1971: 95–134). The transformation of the cleavage basis from religion to class had a significant influence on the party system: it destroyed the basis of Liberal party support and allowed for its replacement by the Labour party. In contrast, the continuing significance of the religious, ethnic, linguistic, and regional cleavages in Canada has been a key factor in the modern dominance of the Liberal party from 1921–1984 and has prevented the

expansion of the NDP, which appeals to voters on the basis of class considerations.

The traditional British method of picking party leaders is through selection by their respective party caucuses. If the leader of a British party resigns, members of the party caucus meet and vote from among those candidates who have declared themselves for the office. Successive ballots are held until one candidate has achieved a majority. For example, in October 1980, James Callaghan resigned as leader of the Labour party. In November, British Labour MPs selected as their new leader, Michael Foot, after two ballots of the party caucus.

There are several advantages to choosing party leaders this way. First, only current members of Parliament have a chance of being selected, thus ensuring that the leader chosen will be well-known, at least to the party. However, selection by the party caucus has a corresponding disadvantage of producing a closed process: it is practically impossible for an unknown to win, despite the example of Margaret Thatcher. The second advantage of the British practice is that a decision can be reached on a new leader in a matter of weeks (days or hours, if necessary). For example, in 1975 the Conservatives announced their leadership call on January 24, with the first ballot held on February 4. Because no one had a majority on the first ballot, a second and final one was held a week later on February 11. Thus, the entire process of leadership selection took less than three weeks. In contrast, the Canadian pattern now takes at least several months to complete, and sometimes longer. For example, a year

TABLE 9.8 BRITISH CONSERVATIVE PARTY
LEADERSHIP SELECTION — 1975

First Ballot	Thatcher	130
	Heath	119
	Fraser	16
Second Ballet	Thatcher	146
	Whitelaw	79
	Howe	19
	Prior	19
	Peyton	11

intervened between Liberal leader John Turner's decision to step down and the June 1990 Liberal leadership convention. The third advantage of caucus selection is that the candidate so selected to lead the party in Parliament will have majority support in the caucus. By contrast, in Canada, a leader selected by the convention method may find that he or she lacks the support of a significant section of the parliamentary caucus. Finally, in the Tory race in 1975, new nominations were called for between each ballot, thus allowing additional candidates to enter the race after it had already begun (Table 9.8). In Canada, candidates must be nominated at the beginning and cannot enter the contest for just the later ballots.

Although the caucus is the key element in the party leadership selection process, there are some interesting differences between the British parties. Prior to 1965, the Conservatives did not take an explicit vote; instead, a leader "emerged" from the ranks of the party caucus. While this was a somewhat mysterious process even to party insiders, the system worked well until the 1960s, when no clear-cut leader appeared. As a result, reforms adopted in 1965 provide for an actual vote among Conservative Members of Parliament. This method of leadership selection, especially prior to the reforms of the 1960s, reinforced the leader's control: the

"most striking feature of the Conservative party organization is the enormous power which appears to be concentrated in the hands of the Leader" (McKenzie, 1967: 21). Initially the British Conservative leader, once selected, was not required to face reelection by the party organization; however, since 1975, reelection is required at the annual meeting. In December of 1989, Margaret Thatcher, for the first time in 14 years, faced an official challenge to her leadership. However, she easily defeated Sir Anthony Meyer, by a vote of 314 to 33.

The selection and power of the Labour party leader reflects the extra-parliamentary origins of the party. In such a mass-based, ideological party, the party organization seeks to exert control not only over the party caucus, but over the party leader as well. At least in theory, both the leader and caucus are subject to the organization's directives and policy decisions; in fact, in most cases, the parliamentary leader and caucus have managed to retain a considerable measure of autonomy from the extra-parliamentary organization. One way of seeking to ensure control of the leaders has been the traditional practice of making them stand for annual reelection by the party organization, although in practice they are almost never opposed. The result has been to place Labour leaders in a less dominant position within the party hierarchy than their Conservative counterparts, particularly when the Labour party is in opposition. Although subject to outside advice and interference, if not control, by the extra-parliamentary organization, the party leader, prior to the 1980s, was always chosen by the caucus, using a voting procedure similar to that of the Conservatives.

The longstanding battle between the parliamentary and extra-parliamentary wings of the Labour party finally became so intense in the fall of 1980 as to provoke a change in the party's leadership selection process. The basic method of leadership selection, beginning in 1981, is based on a widening of the election process to include not only the party caucus but the trade

TABLE 9.9 BRITISH LABOUR PARTY LEADERSHIP SELECTION—1983

	Kinnock	Hattersley	Heffer	Shore
Constituencies	27.45	0.58	1.97	0.00
Unions	29.04	10.88	0.45	0.03
PLP	14.78	7.83	4.29	3.10
Total	71.27	19.29	6.30	3.14

All figures are percentages

unions and constituency parties as well. An electoral college type of mechanism was adopted in January 1981, which gave the party caucus 30 percent of the vote, the constituency associations 30 percent, and the trade unions 40 percent. This new pattern was designed to give the extra-parliamentary wing of the party, dominated by the trade unions and the more leftist elements, control of the leadership selection process in the Labour party (Table 9.9). The first use of the new electoral college mechanism by the Labour party to choose a new leader occurred in 1983, when Neil Kinnock was selected to replace Michael Foot, after the Labour party's disastrous electoral defeat in the general election (Drucker, 1984: Mitchell, 1984).

The 1981 change in the process of selecting the Labour party leader is the most important political development in the British party system since the formation of the Labour party in 1900, for it has had profound effects on the competitive party battle. First, the British Labour party splintered over this issue, with a number of key members and former ministers leaving the party to found a new, centre-based Social Democratic Party. Polls in the winter and spring of 1981 indicated that the new party was initially more popular than either of the major parties. Second, this new party, by aiming at the centre of the political spectrum, was seeking to capitalize on the increasing polarization of the old-line parties in the late 1970s and early 1980s, as the Labour party moved left and the Conser-

vative party moved right. Third, the new party rekindled life into the Liberal party, which had had little influence in the party system for over 50 years. For example, in June 1981 the Liberals and the Social Democrats agreed to a joint strategy for the next general election, in that they decided not to compete against each other at the constituency level.

The initial success of the SDP in 1981 was not continued in 1982 and 1983. Disputes within the Alliance (SDP and Liberals), as well as the Falklands war, undercut the party's popularity in 1982. In 1983 the general election results contained both good and bad news for the new party. In the election, although the Alliance won 26 percent of the vote and 23 seats, the SDP won only six seats. Two of its most prominent members were defeated (Shirley Williams and William Rodgers) and the party now ranked fifth in the House of Commons (at dissolution it was third in terms of seats). By 1985 the SDP was showing signs of renewed popularity in the public opinion polls, as the Conservative party's strength declined. However, the 1987 election

In fact, the most striking feature of those who have broken away from the Liberal and Labour parties to form new parties is not their treachery but their failure. The overwhelming message of their experience is the strength of the adversarial two-party system (Bradley, 1981: 21).

was even more of a disaster than the 1983 contest for the SDP: while the Alliance won 23 percent of the vote and 22 seats, the SDP, as its share of these totals, gained only 5 seats (17 for the Liberals). Over the next few years, the Alliance faced leadership disputes, name changes, declining popular support, and internal policy disagreements.

By 1990, most of the Alliance members of the 1980s had merged to form, first, the Social and Liberal Democrats (SLD), then just simply the Liberal Democrats (October 1989). A small rump group led by David Owen still retained the SDP name. Thus, the challenge mounted by the Alliance in the mid-1980s to the two dominant parties failed; by the early 1990s, the various remnants of the Alliance no longer appeared to be viable alternatives for most of the electorate. Moreover, the Labour Party under Neil Kinnock had moved back towards the centre of the political spectrum by the early 1990s, thus positioning itself to be the main opposition party for the next general election.

Since the rise of the class alignment in the 20th century, the key factor in the social bases of party support in Britain is the class cleavage, with the middle and upper classes supporting the Conservatives and the working class backing the Labour party. However, both major parties appeal to members of all social classes. If party strength corresponded to rigid class support, then the Conservatives would never win an election. However, with about 30 percent of their support coming from the working class, the Conservatives have done well in their contests for office. Moreover, in recent decades, white-collar workers have given substantial support to the Labour party. The basic class patterns of party support in Britain are not evident, however, with respect to the nationalist parties, which appeal to cultural and regional loyalties instead. Thus, unlike the major Canadian parties, which show little class basis, British party support reflects the class divisions of the 20th century.

Patterns of party finance show predictable characteristics in Britain. The Conservative party is dependent on the cadre type of party finance, with individual and business contributions from relatively few donors. The party has been more than able to finance itself, has opposed public subsidies, has been successful in constituency level finance, and, as a result, clearly outspends the Labour party both between and during election contests (McKenzie, 1967: 653–659; Finer, 1980: 105–110). The Labour party is heavily dependent on trade union financial backing, which now accounts for 80 percent of party funds (Birch, 1983: 109). With individual party membership declining and with the local constituency associations unable to raise adequate revenue, the Labour party favours extension of the public financing of parties and election campaigns.

While local campaign costs have been limited since 1948, there is no limit on the amount spent by the national parties (Punnett, 1980: 57). Public subsidies cover such items as free TV party broadcasts, but the parties still need considerable additional funds to support the national party advertising campaign during an election. In a non-election year in the early 1980s, total national party income and costs ran between £2 and £3 million. In the 1983 election year, the Conservatives spent £6.1 million on routine expenses and £3.7 million on the general election, while the corresponding figures for the Labour party are £4.1 and £2.1 million, respectively (Pinto-Duschinsky, 1985: 330, 333). For the 1987 contest, these figures had risen to £6.9 million and £8.7 million for the Conservatives and to £7.0 million and £4.4 million for the Labour party. In contrast to the Canadian pattern, the major donors to the Labour and Conservative causes do not contribute to both parties, a reflection, perhaps, of the more ideological and class-based party system in Britain.

While British parties have developed certain unique features of structure, style, and interaction, we should not lose sight of the fact that British parties, like their counterparts in other competitive polities, continue to be significant governing mechanisms.

AMERICAN POLITICAL PARTIES

Reflective of the political culture's suspicion of power and its concentration is the traditional American attitude towards political parties: at best, parties are viewed in an ambivalent manner; at worst, they are perceived as downright detrimental to democracy. In his famous Farewell Address, George Washington sought to alert the American public to "the baneful effects of the Spirit of Party," and even Thomas Jefferson (quoted in Hofstadter, 1972: 2, 123), who was later instrumental in the development of the longest-lasting political party in history — the Democratic party — remarked that "If I could not go to heaven but with a party, I would not go there at all." However, this aversion to parties was overcome, as in other countries, due to practical considerations, primarily the need to govern in a system of fragmented power.

The initial parties were of legislative origin, created in the early years of the 19th century. However, it was not until the era of Jacksonian democracy in the 1830s that the parties emerged as necessary ingredients of the governing process. The 19th-century origin of the American parties is crucial in understanding their structure, organization, and attributes.

American parties are the preeminent examples of the cadre type of political party: "highly decentralized, status-quo oriented, and win-centered" (Blank, 1980: 55). The goal of electoral victory has produced another attribute of American parties — they are usually nonideological. Ideological specificity repels rather than attracts voters, thereby typically leading to similar policy views for both the Republican and Democratic parties and to the charge that the

two parties are interchangeable in office. When a party becomes ideologically distinct from the main trends of public opinion, as the Republicans did with Barry Goldwater in 1964 and the Democrats achieved with George McGovern in 1972, a massive electoral defeat occurs. Although Ronald Reagan may have begun and sustained his political career by his image as a "man of the right," his years as governor of California and his 1980 and 1984 presidential election victories demonstrated his ability to moderate his views and to move to the centre of the political spectrum in the search for electoral victory. As a result, American parties appeal to a wide social and economic base; they are heterogeneous in makeup, not class-based. Party membership is not clearly defined; membership cards, annual dues, and agreement with a party's policy positions are basically unknown in the American context.

In terms of structure, the parties are extremely decentralized and power resides at the state and local levels. National party coalitions are created around the presidential contest every four years — between such events, the parties survive on a local base. The decentralization of power is evident in terms of party finance, membership and recruitment. This dispersal of power is a reflection of several of the key principles of the American system of government, namely federalism and the separation of powers. The decentralized pattern has been greatly strengthened in the 20th century by the use of the primary method of candidate selection, which has countered the centralizing or nationalizing trends with respect to some aspects of American politics. If anything, the parties are more decentralized now than they have ever been.

Within the parties, the decentralization of power is reflected in the lack of strong party cohesion both inside and outside of the legislature. While party members share a common label, they rarely share a common purpose. American parties are highly factionalized, with

> There are obstacles to the renewal of political parties, however, and one towers over all others: the average officeholder hates a strong party, unless she or he happens to control it (Burns, 1984: 58).

> . . . parties are the custodians of our political standards. They bring coherence and continuity to our democratic practices. Strong rival parties watch each other, and the public interest is safer. Weak parties invite chaos (Theodore Sorenson, former aide to President John F. Kennedy, February, 1987).

candidates forming their own organizations in their bids for elective office. If successful, candidates thus owe little loyalty to the party organization but considerable loyalty to the group that helped them to win power. Candidate-centred groups have been strengthened by the use of the primary method of nomination for office, where the party can no longer even control who runs under its party label.

The effects of the decentralized pattern are clearly evident in the legislature, where party discipline is weak, particularly in any comparison with a parliamentary system. Party members, with almost total immunity from retribution from their party leaders, can vote as they wish, for the simple reason that the party leadership has few political resources to turn against them. Party unity is often dependent on the issue being considered. Moreover, each party contains both liberal and conservative factions, which may desert their party leadership on specific matters of public policy. Majorities are often forged across, rather than within, party lines. For example, Republican President Ronald Reagan, despite the fact that the House of Representatives had a solid Democratic majority, was able to win large cuts in government programs in his first few months in office in 1981 by aligning Republicans and conservative Democrats together in a working majority. This cross-party alliance was the key to Ronald Reagan's success with Congress during both terms of his presidency.

The two long-dominant major American parties, therefore, can be described as cadre parties, election-oriented, nonideological, heterogeneous in social composition, decentral-

ized, with weak party unity. These attributes are reflected in and conditioned by the nature of the party system. The American party network is competitive, dominated by the two major parties, and highly discriminatory against new or minor parties.

The electoral battle between Democrats and Republicans, however, has not been, from an historical point of view, an equal battle. One party, as in Britain and Canada, has tended to dominate for long periods: the Republicans from the time of the Civil War to the 1920s, the Democrats from the 1930s to the 1960s, with the 1970s showing a more balanced competitive pattern, at least in presidential elections. If anything, however, the Republicans have once again emerged as the dominant party in presidential elections, given their victories in 1980, 1984, and 1988.

The two-party competition focuses on control of the centre of the political spectrum. However, unlike the Canadian system, where the centre is regularly occupied by one party, the centre of the political spectrum in American politics is up for grabs — either party may occupy it, and both usually try to do so. The battle for the political centre is a key reason why the Democrats and Republicans are nonideological and socially diverse parties.

One of the most often described characteristics of the American party system is that it is a two-party system, dominated by the Republicans and Democrats since the middle of the 19th century. However, it is not true to say that only two parties exist — many parties officially

> The national Democratic leadership is going so far left, they've left America (Ronald Reagan, July 25, 1984).

compete, for example, in a presidential election. What is significant is that these other parties rarely affect the pattern of competition between the two major parties, exemplified by the failure of John Anderson's National Unity Ticket in 1980, which received only 7 percent of the popular vote and no delegates in the Electoral College. New parties or minor parties are regularly formed, but their success is limited.

Minor parties usually emerge around a specific issue or are based on a particular ideology, thereby limiting their appeal to the majority of the American electorate. If such a party begins to show signs of electoral success, its programs and leaders may be co-opted by one of the major parties, whose nonideological stance allows for considerable flexibility and pragmatism in such matters. Moreover, the decentralized structure and weak cohesion of the major parties often entices new groups to work within one of the major parties, instead of forming a new party (e.g., Goldwater within the Republican party in 1964, McGovern within the Democratic party in 1972). The most successful new groups or movements in American politics have been those that have worked within the existing parties.

In addition, the rules of the electoral system are designed to discourage minor parties. New parties, for example, find it difficult to get their names on the ballot: in the 1968 presidential race, "George Wallace had a staff of twenty-five lawyers traveling from state to state researching election laws, filing suits, and getting petition signatures to meet local requirements" (Huckshorn, 1980: 70). Moreover, the plurality electoral formula used in the United States makes it difficult for a minor party to win legislative seats even when it wins a sizable share of

the popular vote. For these reasons, since the Civil War minor parties have rarely disturbed the two-party battle between Republicans and Democrats.

Why do minor parties develop in the first place and what accounts for their relative electoral success in a system such as the Canadian and their failure in others like the American? The reason for new parties in both systems is the same — social and economic diversity. The way these new groups operate varies because of the differing institutional contexts in Canada and the United States. It is wrong to assume that Canada has produced more minor parties than the United States — on a numerical basis it has not. However, Canada has produced more minor parties that have affected the pattern of competition in the party system. The basic explanation for Canada is that diversity, combined with federal and parliamentary principles and party discipline, encourages the formation of new parties. In contrast, the decentralized parties and the various election laws, which discriminate against new groups in the American system, make it likely that they will work within one of the existing party organizations. In Canada, a George McGovern or a Barry Goldwater would have formed a new political party; in the United States, they simply seized control of the existing party structures.

Given the characteristics of the major American parties and the party system, the essential aim in selecting party leaders is to win elections. The American parties have been in the forefront of developing new mechanisms of leadership selection, although it is open to question whether these new techniques have improved the quality of the nominees for political office. The current system of leadership selection is an amalgam of historical practice, containing elements of caucus, convention, and primary techniques. The most significant aspect of the change from one method to the next has been the desire to give the public, rather than the party bosses, control of the nomination and leadership selection process. In contrast to the Canadian system of party members meeting in a national party leadership convention, or the traditional British pattern of the parliamentary caucus casting a ballot, current American practice aims at providing an opportunity for involving the mass public in choosing party leaders.

American party leaders are selected through a two-stage process: first, delegates are chosen to attend a national party convention and second, the national party convention selects the party leader. Unfortunately, what seems straightforward at first glance is exceedingly complex, since each of the 50 states sets its own rules for delegate selection, procedures which may change (and they usually do) from one election to the next.

The first stage of leadership selection uses two basic approaches — the primary and caucus techniques. The most important of the two methods of delegate selection is the presidential primary, which in 1988 picked about 75 percent of the delegates to the national conventions and was used by about 30 states. A **presidential primary** is an election *among party members to choose their delegates to the national convention*, which in turn selects the party's presidential candidate. Those candidates seeking their party's nomination enter a number of that party's presidential primaries. Generally, if a candidate wins 30 percent of the vote in a primary, he or she will receive approximately 30 percent of that state's delegates to the national convention. By winning significant strength in the primaries, a candidate can win the party's nomination for president.

Presidential primaries are held between February and June in an election year. These primaries have become the crucial component in the party leadership contest, since a candidate can win enough delegates to be guaranteed a first ballot nomination victory at the leadership convention. In recent decades, all party leaders have won first ballot convention victories; in other words, the real decision-making power in winning party leadership is the delegate selection process, with the convention simply ratifying the choice already made.

The second method of delegate selection to the national convention is the caucus technique. The term caucus, as used in the American presidential system of delegate selection, is not the same as a caucus in a parliamentary system. In Britain and Canada, a party caucus means the group of party members in the legislature. In the American delegate selection process, caucus means a meeting of party members from the mass public who decide on their delegates to the national convention. These caucus meetings begin at the local or precinct level and work their way up through district, county, and state-wide conventions. About 20 states used this procedure in the 1988 presidential race to pick about 25 percent of the total delegates. While it allows for public participation, the caucus method of delegate selection usually involves far fewer rank-and-file party members than does the primary technique.

Several aspects of the American delegate selection process need to be emphasized: first, at the mass level, party members are given the right to participate in the selection of the party leader in both the primary and caucus states and second, at the elite level, anyone has the right to run for the leadership of the party. Both these characteristics emphasize the extent to which the political party, as an organization, has lost control of the nomination process: it controls neither who participates in the delegate selection mechanisms nor who can run for the leadership of the party. Such a pattern of selection might be characterized as "garage-sale politics": one never knows in advance who will show up to offer items for sale or to purchase the goods presented. The only thing that is definite is that few Van Gogh's will ever be found among the dusty artifacts of life, or, as one writer phrased it, "the primary-dominated system of nomination is an unqualified disaster" (McWilliams, 1981: 170).

> The political convention is thus an event:
> something to watch, not something to do.
> Like the Super Bowl or Derby, it is some-
> thing to view on the screen, with a beer in
> one hand and a tally sheet in the other (Bar-
> ber, 1984: 54).

Following the primaries and caucuses, each party holds its national convention during the summer months of July or August. The conventions previously held centre-stage in the selection of party leaders; the satirist H.L. Mencken once said that there is "nothing quite as entertaining as a hanging or a good convention." In recent decades, there is nothing quite as boring as a national convention, because it has lost the effective power of choice — it merely ratifies the winner determined by the primaries and caucuses. Only if the primaries and caucuses fail to coalesce behind a single candidate would the national convention reacquire effective decision-making power.

The operating rules of an American national convention differ significantly from those utilized in the Canadian national party leadership conventions. First, balloting is open, not secret, and done by states, rather than by individuals. Until the reforms of the 1970s, this rule meant that large blocs of votes could be controlled by party leaders and that deals between leaders and state delegations could be arranged, because a state voted as a group in favour of one or the other candidates, a procedure known as the **unit rule**. Although the unit rule no longer applies, voting is still done on a state-by-state basis, with delegates openly declaring their support for one of the nominees. Second, such a voting procedure is cumbersome, with the interval between ballots at least several hours, if not longer. Third, there is no rule for the elimination of candidates between ballots, so that a nominee can stay in the race until someone receives a majority vote. The result, historically, has been long conventions, with the 1924 Democratic meeting holding 103 ballots. These rules of procedure make an American convention very different from a Canadian national party leadership convention.

Although we have assumed that a party's presidential nominee is the party's leader, in non-presidential election years, especially for the party that loses the presidential race, there is no set way of deciding the question of leadership. For example, after the Democratic defeat in the 1988 presidential contest, who was the leader of the Democratic party? Democrats would likely have agreed on only one thing — that Michael Dukakis was no longer their leader. The decentralized structure and fragmented power of the American parties means that the party's legislative leaders in the Senate or House of Representatives, as well as the various leaders in state politics, have as legitimate a claim on that role as the party's defeated presidential nominee.

The dominance of the Republican and Democratic parties has traditionally been reflected in the extent of partisan attachments: electors overwhelmingly identify with the two main parties. A chief characteristic of partisan loyalties in the United States is their public nature — most people are not reluctant to declare which party they support. Moreover, the strength of these partisan ties to the two main parties has often been cited as one important reason why minor parties have had little success at the polls; if people already have an emotional commitment to either the Republicans or Democrats, then it is difficult for a new party to gain adherents.

The extent of partisan attachments gives each of the major parties a pool to draw on in any particular election. While appealing to the wider electorate, the Republicans and Democrats have traditional groups that support them. Each party seeks to put together a large enough coalition of such groups to win power: the "supporters of the two American political parties have been distinguished from each other by economic, religious, and national-ethnic differences" (Nie et al., 1979: 213).

The social bases of party support in recent decades can be summarized as follows. First, the higher one's position in the social class hierarchy, the more likely is one to be a Republican. Second, with respect to religion, Jews are more Democratic than Catholics, who in turn are more Democratic than Protestants. Third, minority groups, particularly racial and the more recent immigrant groups, show a marked proclivity to support the Democratic party. Fourth, regional differences, noticeably the South as a bastion of Democratic strength and Republican dominance in the Middle West and Northeast, have declined in recent years. Thus, the American parties, while socially diverse, do not appeal equally to all major groups in the polity. Although the majority Democratic coalition has been severely weakened during the past two decades, the Republican party has not been able to transform discontent with the Democrats into majority party status for itself, even when they win the presidency. Instead, more and more Americans are declaring themselves to be Independents (particularly true in the 1960s and 1970s), so that in many surveys more individuals claim such a status than those willing to specify the Republicans or Democrats as the party of their attachment.

The socially diverse support base of the two major parties is not reflected, however, in the area of party finance. As the preeminent cadre parties, the Republicans and Democrats have long depended on corporate backing and large individual contributions. Similar to other systems, the area of party finance has been regularly associated with major political scandals, with Watergate being only the major recent example from among many. Party finance is particularly important in American politics because of the large number of officials selected through the election process. With over 500 000 people chosen for government service in a pres-

idential election year, the amount of money spent by the parties and candidates quickly accumulates into the hundreds of millions of dollars. For example, in the national races alone in the early-1980s, the total campaign costs were over half-a-billion dollars. By 1990, that figure stood at $1 billion spent on the national, state, and local elections every four years during a presidential-election year. Such expenditures have rapidly escalated, given the heavy emphasis on television advertising in both presidential and congressional elections.

The cost of campaigns, along with the Watergate scandal, produced a climate of reform in the United States in the early 1970s. Although regulation of campaign donations had been on the books since the 1920s, such laws were regularly ignored or violated, given their very weak enforcement provisions. The reforms of the 1970s have put more effective limits on contributions and spending for both individual candidates and parties. In a major departure from past practice, the United States in 1974 adopted provisions (the Federal Election Campaign Act) for the public financing of presidential election campaigns. A party's presidential nominee who accepts public money is prevented from obtaining private donations for general election expenses. A second major reform concerns the development of **political action committees**, or PACs for short. PACs may be formed by any group to support a particular cause, candidate, or party. By the mid-1980s, PACs had become the major source of political funding in the American system. In the 1988 election, based on a count by the Federal Election Commission, there were 9 100 PACs, which contributed $120 million to the various candidates and parties.

The characteristics of the American parties and the party system thus reflect certain unique patterns of origin, development, and operation. However, in broad comparisons with other political systems, the American parties show basic similarities with their counterparts in Canada and Britain, the most important attribute being the competitive nature of these three party systems.

Political Opposition and Party Futures

Political parties can perform any number of roles or functions in the political process. In our consideration of parties in Canada, Britain, and the United States, we have focused on two basic tasks of the party organizations, which we designated as their electoral and governing functions. The origin, development, and characteristics of the individual parties and party systems in each country have resulted in different techniques in the performance of these functions. However, a third task of parties in democratic systems is to provide the essential structural means to oppose the government of the day.

PARTIES AND POLITICAL OPPOSITION

For those who have grown up in a democratic system, the acceptance of the idea of a political opposition institutionalized through the role of competitive parties appears normal. Historically, however, and even for the vast majority of current political systems, this is not the case. While political opposition functions may be carried out by various political mechanisms, such as an independent judiciary, interest groups, or a free press, the primary organizational agent of political opposition is the political party (Ionescu and de Madariaga, 1972: 52–62).

The distinguishing characteristic between competitive party systems (Canada, Britain, and the United States) and a party-state system (China, the Soviet Union through the late 1980s) turns on the role of parties: in the first

> The two-party system of modern parliaments uses the psychological structure of opposing armies (Canetti, 1966: 188).

instance, organized opposition challenges for power, in the second it does not. While opposition exists in all systems, in a party-state pattern it is unorganized and takes place in private within or through the single party organization; in a competitive party system, opposition is organized and occurs in public, primarily through the battle for office. Elections by themselves do not make a system democratic, but elections with organized parties competing for power add immeasurably to such a result. Given the allure of the democratic ideal in the 20th century, party-states nominate candidates for office and hold elections—events which in no way change their classification as totalitarian systems.

Political opposition is not only significant in that it provides for a competitive struggle for power, but also because it is one way of handling the conflict that lies at the basis of politics: "political opposition . . . is the most advanced and institutionalized form of political conflict" (Ionescu and de Madariaga, 1972: 16). Allowing people and groups to contest for power through legitimate channels, such as the party system, increases the likelihood that violence will not be resorted to. Conversely, when the opposition feels that it cannot fairly contest for power through the party system, then violence and coercion may become the reciprocal tools of opposing and governing, as reflected in the events leading to the 1970 FLQ Crisis in Canada. Providing organized political opposition continues to be an important function of the political parties in the democratic systems of Canada, Britain, and the United States.

POLITICAL PARTY FUTURES

Predicting the future of political institutions, such as political parties, is very risky. However, the past can at least tell us that some events are more likely in the future than others. And an historical appreciation of the origins and functions of political parties cannot only help us to understand their present status, but it can keep us from denigrating the present because of our ignorance of the past. In recent years, a common criticism of parties in democratic systems is that they are failing to perform adequately. Implicit in most such assessments is the view that previously parties were more effective and more efficient in carrying out their electoral and governing functions. Critics have gone so far as to suggest the possible demise of parties altogether (and they sometimes seem more than pleased by such a prospect)!

Such views fail to appreciate either the historical or contemporary contributions of political parties to the political process. Historically, parties, while not the sole creators, contributed strongly to the development of the democratic polity. Currently, the nomination of candidates, the selection of leaders, the organizing of election campaigns, the raising of party funds, and, for the successful party, the burdens and rewards of office are no small feat. In fact, it would be difficult to conceive how other institutions might carry out these functions if the parties were to disappear. The disparagement of parties indicates, perhaps, that we expect too much of them, on the basis of a false analogy that in the past they somehow performed better. Reformers are perpetually upset with the nature of the democratic parties.

Concern with the supposedly declining role of parties in democratic systems is evident in Canada, Britain, and the United States. Concomitant with such negative views are a number of more specific party-related developments, including a decline in the trust and confidence

> When parties are absent or . . . have become Cheshire cats of which very little is left but the smile, pathologies multiply (Burnham, quoted in Wattenberg, 1984: xiii).

the public has in political institutions in general and parties in particular, and an erosion of partisan attachments for the major parties and a growth in support for either new parties or for being independent from partisan ties. However, such developments need not herald the end of the significant role of political parties in democratic systems. What they do portend are some possible future changes in the way the parties perform their traditional electoral, governing, and opposition functions.

Summary

1. Political parties are a way of giving the mass of people control over their leaders in democratic systems and a means of elite control over the masses in totalitarian systems. Parties may be classified according to their origin (internally versus externally created parties), their structure (cadre versus mass parties), and their ideology (programmatic versus pragmatic parties). Party systems are either competitive or non-competitive, while a one-party situation is classified as a party-state system. All parties serve both electoral and governing functions; parties in democratic systems also provide a political opposition function.

2. The major Canadian parties are electorally-oriented coalitions, pragmatic in style, parliamentary in origin, structurally decentralized around the provincial units, and cohesive in the legislature. The minor parties since the 1920s have been, by contrast, extra-

parliamentary in origin, programmatic in style, ideological in appeal, and political movements as well as partisan organizations. The Canadian party system is competitive, federal, regional, and centre-based. Party leaders are chosen by national party leadership conventions, with party finance the key remaining area of political corruption.

3. British political parties are more centralized, ideological, class-based, and programmatic than their Canadian counterparts. The British party system is competitive between two major parties (Conservative and Labour), but challenged by nationalist parties (Scottish Nationalist Party and the Plaid Cymru) and by minor parties, such as the long-established Liberal party or the rise and decline of the Social Democratic Party in the 1980s. Party leaders have been selected traditionally by the party caucuses, although the Labour party broke with tradition and decided in 1981 to begin using an electoral college type of selection procedure.

4. The major American parties (Republicans and Democrats) are cadre parties, election-oriented, nonideological, heterogeneous in social composition, decentralized, with weak party unity. The American party system is competitive, dominated by the two major parties, and highly discriminatory against new or minor parties. Party leaders are selected at national party conventions, but the key area of choice is the delegate selection process, which is now dominated by the presidential primaries. Unlike Canada or Britain, the mass public may be involved in the selection of party leaders in the United States.

5. Despite some obvious shortcomings, parties, especially the competitive parties in democratic systems, continue to be important political institutions. However, the way in which the existing parties carry out their traditional electoral, governing, and opposi-tion functions may change in the future, as the parties adapt to a changing environment.

Recommended Readings

Political Parties: Theoretical

DAHL, ROBERT A., ed. (1966) *Political Oppositions in Western Democracies*. New Haven: Yale University Press.

_____ ed. (1973) *Regimes and Oppositions*. New Haven: Yale University Press.

DUVERGER, MAURICE (1964) *Political Parties: Their Organization and Activity in the Modern State*. London: Methuen and Co.

HOFSTADTER, RICHARD (1972) *The Idea of a Party System*. Berkeley: University of California Press.

IONESCU, GHITA and ISABEL DE MADARIAGA (1972) *Opposition: Past and Present of a Political Institution*. London: Penguin Books.

LENIN, V.I. (1902, 1947) *What Is to be Done?* Moscow: Progress Publishers.

MICHELS, ROBERT (1962) *Political Parties: A Sociological Study of the Oligarchical Tendencies of Modern Democracies*. New York: Collier Books.

OSTROGORSKI, MOISEI (1902, 1964) *Democracy and the Organization of Political Parties*. New York: Anchor Books.

PANEBIANCO, ANGELO (1988) *Political Parties: Organization and Power*. Cambridge: Cambridge University Press.

RANNEY, AUSTIN (1962) *The Doctrine of Responsible Party Government: Its Origins and Present State*. Urbana: The University of Illinois Press.

RIKER, WILLIAM H. (1962) *The Theory of Political Coalitions*. New Haven: Yale University Press.

ROSE, RICHARD (1984) *Do Parties Make a Difference?* London: Macmillan, 2nd ed.

SARTORI, GIOVANNI (1976) *Parties and Party Systems: A Framework for Analysis*. London: Cambridge University Press.

SCHATTSCHNEIDER, E.E. (1942) *Party Government*. New York: Holt, Rinehart and Winston.

VON BEYME, KLAUS (1985) "Karl Marx and Party Theory," *Government and Opposition* (Winter), Volume 20, Number 1, pp. 70–87.

WARE, ALAN (1987) *Citizens, Parties and the State: A*

Reappraisal. Princeton, N.J.: Princeton University Press.

—— ed. (1987) *Political Parties: Electoral Change and Structural Response*. Oxford: Basil Blackwell.

WILSON, JAMES Q. (1973) *Political Organizations*. New York: Basic Books.

ZARISKI, RAPHAEL (1986) "The Legitimacy of Opposition Parties in Democratic Political Systems: A New Use for an Old Concept," *The Western Political Quarterly* (March), Volume 39, Number 1, pp. 29–47.

Political Parties: Comparative

BUDGE, IAN, DAVID ROBERTSON and DEREK HEARL, eds. (1987) *Ideology, Strategy and Party Change: Spatial Analyses of Post-War Election Programmes in 19 Democracies*. Cambridge: Cambridge University Press.

CLARKE, HAROLD et al. (1985) "Issue Volatility and Partisan Linkages in Canada, Great Britain, the United States, and West Germany," *European Journal of Political Research* (September), Volume 13, Number 3, pp. 237–263.

DUVERGER, MAURICE (1972) *Party Politics and Pressure Groups: A Comparative Introduction*. New York: Thomas Y. Crowell.

EPSTEIN, LEON D. (1967) *Political Parties in Western Democracies*. New York: St. Martin's Press.

HILL, RONALD J. and PETER FRANK (1986) *The Soviet Communist Party*. Boston: Allen and Unwin, 3rd ed.

LAWSON, KAY and PETER H. MERKL, eds. (1988) *When Parties Fail: Emerging Alternative Organizations*. Princeton, N.J.: Princeton University Press.

RANDALL, VICKY, ed. (1988) *Political Parties in the Third World*. London: Sage Publications.

WARE, ALAN (1989) "Parties, Electoral Competition and Democracy," *Parliamentary Affairs* (January), Volume 42, Number 1, pp. 1–22.

Canadian Parties

ANGELL, HAROLD M. (1987) "Duverger, Epstein and the Problem of the Mass Party: The Case of the Parti Quebecois," *Canadian Journal of Political Science* (June), Volume 20, Number 2, pp. 363–378.

ARCHER, KEITH (1989) "Review Article: On the Study of Political Parties in Canada," *Canadian Journal of Political Science* (June), Volume 22, Number 2, pp. 389–398.

BASHEVKIN, SYLVIA V. (1985) *Toeing the Lines: Women and Party Politics in English Canada*. Toronto: University of Toronto Press.

BLAKE, DONALD E., R.K. CARTY and LYNDA ERICKSON (1989) "Federalism, Conservatism and the Social Credit Party in B.C.," *BC Studies* (Spring), Number 81, pp. 3–23.

BRENNAN, J. WILLIAM, ed. (1984) *Building the Cooperative Commonwealth: Essays on the Democratic Socialist Tradition in Canada*. Regina: Canadian Plains Research Centre.

BRODIE, JANINE and JANE JENSON (1988) *Crisis, Challenge and Change: Party and Class in Canada Revisited*. Ottawa: Carleton University Press.

CARTY, R.K. (1989) "Is There Political Life After Losing the Race?" *Journal of Canadian Studies* (Summer), Volume 24, Number 2, pp. 116–127.

CHRISTIAN, W. and C. CAMPBELL (1983) *Political Parties and Ideologies in Canada*. Toronto: McGraw-Hill Ryerson, 2nd ed.

COURTNEY, JOHN C. (1973) *The Selection of National Party Leaders in Canada*. Toronto: Macmillan of Canada

FRASER, GRAHAM (1984) *PQ: René Lévesque and the Parti Quebecois in Power*. Toronto: Macmillan of Canada.

GAGNON, ALAIN G. and A. BRIAN TANGUAY, eds. (1989) *Canadian Parties in Transition: Discourse, Organization and Representation*. Scarborough, Ontario: Nelson Canada.

GOLDFARB, MARTIN and THOMAS AXWORTHY (1988) *Marching to a Different Drummer: An Essay on the Liberals and Conservatives in Convention*. Toronto: Stoddart Publishing.

LANDES, RONALD G. (1984) "In Defence of Canadian Political Parties." Paper presented to the annual meeting of the Canadian Political Science Association, Guelph, Ontario.

MARTIN, PATRICK et al. (1983) *Contenders: The Tory Quest for Power*. Scarborough, Ontario: Prentice-Hall Canada.

MCCALL-NEWMAN, CHRISTINA (1982) *Grits: An Intimate Portrait of the Liberal Party*. Toronto: Macmillan of Canada

PERLIN, GEORGE C. (1980) *The Tory Syndrome:*

Leadership Politics in the Progressive Conservative Party. Montreal: McGill-Queen's University Press.

_____ ed. (1988) *Party Democracy in Canada: The Politics of National Party Conventions.* Scarborough, Ontario: Prentice-Hall Canada.

QUINN, HERBERT F. (1984) "Political Resurrection in Quebec: The Re-election of Robert Bourassa as Liberal Leader," *Dalhousie Review* (Spring), Volume 64, Number 1, pp. 115-124.

SMITH, DAVID E. (1981) *The Regional Decline of a National Party: Liberals on the Prairies.* Toronto: University of Toronto Press.

SNIDER, NORMAN (1985) *The Changing of the Guard: How the Liberals Fell from Grace and the Tories Rose to Power.* Toronto: Lester and Orpen Dennys.

STANBURY, W.T. (1986) "The Mother's Milk of Politics: Political Contributions to Federal Parties in Canada, 1974–1984," *Canadian Journal of Political Science* (December), Volume 19, Number 4, pp. 795–821.

THORBURN, HUGH G., ed. (1985) *Party Politics in Canada.* Scarborough, Ont.: Prentice-Hall Canada, 5th ed.

WEARING, JOSEPH (1988) *Strained Relations: Canadian Parties and Voters.* Toronto: McClelland and Stewart.

WHITAKER, REGINALD (1977) *The Government Party: Organizing and Financing the Liberal Party of Canada 1930–1958.* Toronto: University of Toronto Press.

WINN, C. and J. MCMENEMY, eds. (1976) *Political Parties in Canada.* Toronto: McGraw-Hill Ryerson.

British Parties

BALL, ALAN (1981) *British Political Parties: The Emergence of a Modern Party System.* London: Macmillan.

BEER, SAMUEL (1982) *Modern British Politics: Parties and Pressure Groups in the Collectivist Age.* New York: W.W. Norton.

BRADLEY, IAN (1981) *Breaking the Mould? The Birth and Prospects of the Social Democratic Party.* Oxford: Martin Robertson.

COOK, CHRIS (1984) *A Short History of the Liberal Party, 1900–84.* London: Macmillan.

DRUCKER, HENRY, ed. (1979) *Multi-Party Britain.* London: Macmillan Press.

_____ (1984) "Intra-Party Democracy in Action: The Election of Leader and Deputy Leader by the Labour Party in 1983," *Parliamentary Affairs* (Summer), Volume 37, Number 3, pp. 283–300.

FINER, S.E. (1980) *The Changing British Party System, 1945–1979.* Washington, D.C.: American Enterprise Institute for Public Policy Research.

INGLE, STEPHEN (1987) *The British Party System.* New York: Basil Blackwell.

JOHNSTON, R.J. (1986) "A Further Look at British Political Finance," *Political Studies* (September), Volume 34, Number 3, pp. 466–473.

KAVANAGH, DENNIS (1985) "Power in British Political Parties: Iron Law or Special Pleading?" *West European Politics* (July), Volume 8, Number 3, pp. 5–22.

MCKENZIE, ROBERT (1967) *British Political Parties: The Distribution of Power Within the Conservative and Labour Parties.* London: Heinemann Educational Books.

MESSINA, ANTHONY M. (1987) "Postwar Protest Movements in Britain: A Challenge to Parties," *The Review of Politics* (Summer), Volume 49, Number 3, pp. 410–428.

PELLING, HENRY (1985) *A Short History of the Labour Party.* London: Macmillan, 8th ed.

PINTO-DUSCHINSKY, MICHAEL (1981) *British Political Finance 1830–1980.* Washington, D.C.: American Enterprise Institute for Public Policy Research.

_____ (1985) "Trends in British Political Funding in 1979–1983," *Parliamentary Affairs* (Summer), Volume 38, Number 3, pp. 328–347.

_____ (1989) "Trends in British Party Funding 1983–1987," *Parliamentary Affairs* (April), Volume 42, Number 2, pp. 197–212.

ROSE, RICHARD (1983) "Still the Era of Party Government," *Parliamentary Affairs* (Summer), Volume 36, Number 3, pp. 282–299.

SHAW, ERIC (1989) "The Labour Party and the Militant Tendency," *Parliamentary Affairs* (April), Volume 42, Number 2, pp. 180–196.

WHITELY, PAUL (1983) *The Labour Party in Crisis.* London: Methuen.

American Parties

DREW, ELIZABETH (1983) *Politics and Money: The New Road to Corruption.* New York: Macmillan.

ELDERSVELD, SAMUEL J. (1982) *Political Parties in American Society.* New York: Basic Books.

EPSTEIN, LEON (1986) *Political Parties in the American*

Mold. Madison, Wisconsin: The University of Wisconsin Press.

GODWIN, R. KENNETH (1988) *The Direct Marketing of Politics: $1 Billion of Influence*. Chatham, N.J.: Chatham House Publishers.

KEEFER, SCOTT and CLIFF ZURKIN (1983) *Uninformed Choice: The Failure of the New Presidential Nominating System*. New York: Praeger.

LADD, EVERETT CARLL (1987) "Party Reform and the Public Interest," *Political Science Quarterly* (Fall), Volume 102, Number 3, pp. 355–369.

LOWI, THEODORE J. (1983) "Toward a More Responsible Three-Party System: The Mythology of the Two-Party System and Prospects for Reform," *PS* (Fall), Volume 16, Number 4, pp. 699–706.

POLSBY, NELSON W. (1983) *Consequences of Party Reform*. Oxford: Oxford University Press.

PRICE, DAVID E. (1984) *Bringing Back the Parties*. Washington, D.C.: Congressional Quarterly Press.

ROYKO, MIKE (1971) *Boss: Richard J. Daley of Chicago*. New York: New American Library.

SABATO, LARRY J. (1988) *The Party's Just Begun: Shaping Political Parties for America's Future*. Glenview, Illinois: Scott, Foresman and Company.

SCARROW, HOWARD A. (1986) "Duverger's Law, Fusion, and the Decline of American 'Third' Parties," *The Western Political Quarterly* (December), Volume 39, Number 4, pp. 634–647.

SHAFER, BYRON E. (1984) *Quiet Revolution: The Struggle for the Democratic Party and the Shaping of Post-Reform Politics*. New York: Basic Books.

SORAUF, FRANK J. and PAUL ALLEN BECK (1988) *Party Politics in America*. Glenview, Illinois: Scott, Foresman and Company, 6th ed.

WATTENBERG, MARTIN P. (1984) *Decline of American Political Parties, 1952–1980*. Cambridge, Mass.: Harvard University Press.

CHAPTER 10

The Electoral Process: Political Recruitment and Elections

The entrance to public life is not through the gate of truth or honour (Smith, 1891: 178).

I don't care who does the electing, so long as I do the nominating (American politician, Boss Tweed).

A vote is only an avowal of support at a particular time, very often of support with reservations. The count of votes tells no one how far voters will follow the victorious candidate, or for how long, or in what direction (Kelley, 1983: 4).

Every election is a contest between heritage and impulse, as the verities of the past compete with the risks of the future (Newman, 1988: 29).

THE ORCHESTRATED cacophony of an election campaign is at once both the most visible and most vital ingredient of the public's role in the political process of democratic systems. Unfortunately, few voters understand either the mechanics or the consequences of the electoral process, both of which have a profound impact on the distribution of influence and power in the polity.

The Nature of Elections and Political Recruitment

Elections have become an important characteristic of all forms of government in the 20th century. However, there is considerable variation in the structure and functions of the electoral process in different types of political systems. In democratic systems, elections are competitive: that is, several candidates openly contest for power, with the winning party acquiring control of government through a peaceful and public transfer of power. In totalitarian systems, elections are non-competitive: only one party runs a single candidate for each office. The real political battle is carried on in private among the political elites, with elections serving to ratify or legitimate the selection

> Electoral institutions are among the most important instruments of governance available to the modern state. Elections delimit mass political activity, popular influence, and access to power. Elections transform the potentially disruptive energy of the masses into a principle source of national power and authority. Governments rule through electoral institutions even when they are sometimes ruled by them (Ginsberg, 1986: 10).

> We cannot fool all of the people some of the time, or even some of the people all of the time — but if we can fool a majority of the people at election time, that's all the time we need (Charles McKenzie, Rhinoceros Party of Canada, September 1988).

already made by the single party. As a senior Soviet parliamentary official explained in June 1988: "in actual fact there is no possibility of choice in elections." In autocratic systems, elections may include several candidates or parties, but the result is never in doubt. The dominant party is assured of winning either through intimidation or electoral manipulation, exemplified by the success of the Islamic Republican Party in controlling the electoral process in post-revolutionary Iran.

In democratic polities, the basic function of elections is to select those individuals who will govern and direct the political process until the next campaign. By choosing the governors and forcing them to return to the people at regular intervals for a renewed mandate, the mass public indirectly influences the content and direction of public policy. The public's role in the electoral process is often misunderstood because the connection between the governors and governed is assumed to be immediate and direct — most often it is not.

Elections are a blunt instrument of popular control, because they are infrequent and party-based. Between elections, the selected elite has a relatively free hand in governing, although they must always keep their eye on levels of public support if they wish to retain office in the future. Governments are most responsive before an election campaign, usually providing new programs or promises of future improvements in public policy. After an election, governments may undertake unpopular measures (e.g., raising their own salaries, wage-and-price controls, tax increases to reduce the deficit), in

Those who deny that elections in a democratic context can have significant implications for the makeup of a nation's ruling circle and the character of its policies are merely being foolish (Ginsberg, 1982: viii).

... in a modern mass democracy the ultimate political decisions concern not what the rulers shall do but who the rulers shall be. Determining who shall rule through periodic elections of public officials remains the sovereign people's weapon-of-last-resort for influencing what government does (Ranney, 1965: vii).

Victor Biaka-Boda, who represented the Ivory Coast in the French Senate, decided to let the people of the hinterlands know where he stood on the issues, one of which was their lack of food. His constituents ate him (*Time*, quoted in Wicks, 1982: 101).

Mandate, schmandate. The mandate is that I am here and you're there (John F. Kennedy, quoted in Ladd, 1985: 19).

the hope that their effects on the public will be forgotten or forgiven by the time a new mandate is sought. Given this pattern, it is not unreasonable to suggest that governments should face the wrath of the electorate on a yearly basis. One reason why minority governments in Canada have typically been more responsive than many majority ones can be attributed, at least in part, to this electoral connection.

In the modern era, elections are party contests for power, not simply a series of individual battles in the various constituencies. Moreover, each party usually takes a stand on a series of issues, so that the electorate may have difficulty in determining which party to select. For example, if you think Party A is on the correct side of two issues, and Party B reflects your sentiments on two others, for which do you cast your ballot?

Many people — quite likely a majority of voters — determine their choice of party on factors other than policy, including items such as religion, family ties, social class, personality, looks, and charisma. No wonder then that it is often an indirect impact that elections make on public policy. The electorate chooses their leaders, who in turn decide the content of the political agenda. Thus, voters rarely grant a specific mandate to any party with respect to the content of public policy, even though winning parties usually act as if their program has, in fact, received the public's benediction.

While the broad purposes and structures of electoral politics are similar in parliamentary and presidential systems, they differ on several important characteristics. In a parliamentary context, election time periods are variable within a maximum tenure of office, typically five years. Election writs are issued after the formal executive grants a dissolution of Parliament, but the formal executive only acts on the initiative of the political executive. Individuals are eligible to vote if they meet minimum standards of age and citizenship and have their name included on the voters' list as a result of an enumeration process. Candidates for public office must qualify as a voter and also be nominated by a number of their fellow citizens, with most nominees running under a party label. The selection of candidates is carried out by the parties at the local or constituency level, usually without direct intervention from national party headquarters. Election campaigns are of short duration, in most cases.

In a presidential system, elections are constant (e.g., every four years for the American presidency, every two years for the House of Representatives) and constitutionally prescribed: there is no leeway in the election call, since it is mandated by law. While historically the parties have exercised power over candidate selection in the United States, the introduction of the primary technique has undercut the role of parties in the nomination process. Moreover, citizens must take the initiative to have their names included on the list of eligible voters due to a registration, rather than an enumeration, procedure. Election campaigns may be very long: even though the formal American campaign extends from Labor Day to the first Tuesday in November in presidential elections, the informal campaign starts in January, and, in some cases, up to a year or more before that (i.e., nearly two years in total). Some would argue that, in fact, the 1992 presidential race started on election day in 1988; that is, an election period that is four years long. The different election procedures utilized in presidential and parliamentary systems help to determine the types of parties that will compete and the kind of candidates nominated for public office.

Through the election campaign, the public decides which set of party leaders will govern, while a second important election ingredient, and one prior to the election itself, is the nomination and selection of party candidates. Even though an individual may contest office as an independent, the nomination process is overwhelmingly a party matter, and will be so treated in the ensuing analysis. Parties are the prime agents in the **political recruitment process**, a concept that refers to those "processes that select from among the several million socially favored and politically motivated citizens comprising the political stratum those several thousand who reach positions of significant national influence" (Putnam, 1976: 46).

One factor, often overlooked, in getting people to run for office is what happens to them when they leave office. In rigid totalitarian systems, such as the Soviet Union under Stalin, loss of office often meant loss of life. For example, even though he begged for mercy, former KGB chief Lavrenti Beria was shot in 1953. In democratic systems loss of office does not involve loss of life. Instead we pay our politicians to leave quietly and peacefully, by offering pensions as a reward for past service. For example, Canadian MPs who have served for six years start receiving their pension the day they leave office; those who have not served six years receive severance pay of six months salary. Sometimes other benefits are also available. Upon René Lévesque's retirement, the Parti Québécois gave him thousands of dollars of airline tickets, presumably so he would be out of the country during the provincial election campaign. Successful politicians also find that they are asked to serve as representatives on corporate boards of directors. Former Premier Bill Davis of Ontario was appointed as a director of numerous businesses, including Ford Motor Company, Canadian Imperial Bank of Commerce, Honeywell Limited, Inter-City Gas Corporation, and The Seagram Company — among others. Similarly, when former Alberta Premier Peter Lougheed left elective politics, he was named to the following boards of directors: Norcen Energy Resources; Biotechnica Canada; Princeton Developments; Bombardier; Brascan; and Northern Telecom Limited.

The political recruitment process is significant because, by determining who stands for office, it ultimately selects the makers of public policy. Moreover, it should not be overlooked that in many democratic polities nomination is tantamount to election, given the existence of safe seats for each party. A **safe seat** for a party is a constituency in which that party has consistently won with large vote pluralities over the other parties. Under normal circumstances, the party's candidate will win, no matter who that candidate happens to be. In these situations, the real electoral choice is made by the party at the constituency nomination meeting, not in the general election. At the federal level in Canada, during a normal election, probably 50 to 60 percent of the seats in the House of Commons could be so classified, with an even higher figure applicable in Britain (two-thirds to

> Politics is perhaps the only profession for which no preparation is thought necessary (Robert Louis Stevenson, 1882).
>
> The disproportionate advantage of male, educated, high-status elite recruits increases as we move up the political stratification system. The "law of increasing disproportion" seems to apply to nearly every political system; no matter how we measure political and social status, the higher the level of political authority, the greater the representation for high-status social groups (Putnam, 1976: 33).

three-quarters). In American national legislative elections, incumbents traditionally win re-election between 80 and 90 percent of the time. In 1986 the success rate of incumbents seeking reelection to the House of Representatives reached the incredible rate of 98.4 percent.

While theoretically it is possible for a considerable portion of the public to become involved in the process of political recruitment, either by becoming a candidate or by helping to nominate one, no known instance of such involvement has ever been observed. Instead, from among the many, few directly participate in the candidate selection process, with fewer still ever chosen to become official candidates. The recruitment process can be symbolized, perhaps, as a funnel, with the mouth of the funnel representing the electorate and the narrow end, those nominated and elected to public office. The further into the funnel one moves, the fewer are the number of people involved, but the greater is their power in the political recruitment process. Those individuals who are directly involved in the choice of candidates are often referred to as the **selectorate**, typically a small group in most democratic polities. The selectorate at the constituency level in parliamentary systems may range from several hundred to several thousand delegates in those

ridings in which there is a battle for the nomination.

Since the nomination of candidates is an internal party matter with limited mass participation, the recruitment of candidates in a parliamentary system can be classified as **closed**. In contrast, the American presidential system has an **open** recruitment process. The use of primaries to nominate party candidates allows for extensive public participation in the selection process. Moreover, the primaries permit almost anyone a try at gaining the nomination, although in many cases it is the party-backed individual who wins.

The nature and operation of the recruitment process, therefore, reveal much about the political stratification of the polity, for the ability of the selectorate to control who leads ultimately determines the content of public policy. Moreover, those who recruit and are recruited are never a mirror image of society, but represent, instead, the political elite. A paradox is thus created: representative government is often composed of individuals unrepresentative of some of the major sectors of the sociopolitical milieu. If this discrepancy becomes too great, then the legitimacy of the polity itself might be called into question.

Political Recruitment in Canada

Although parties have traditionally controlled both the recruitment and nomination of candidates for public office in Canada, the fiction was long maintained that those candidates were simply individuals rather than party representatives. For example, it was not until the 1972 federal election that a candidate's party affiliation was included on the ballot. As private organizations, the parties determine their own recruitment and selection procedures. The result, historically, has been for a pattern of elite control of the political recruitment process.

The legal qualifications to be a candidate are minimal. Generally speaking, any person qualified to vote — that is, any elector — has the right to stand for nomination and election to public office. However, certain classes of people, such as those who have violated provisions of the Canada Elections Act in the previous campaign or government contractors, are excluded. A separation between the federal and provincial arenas is maintained in the recruitment process at this point, since members of one level of government cannot be officially nominated or contest the election at the other level without resigning from their current office. For example, before former Premier Gerald Regan entered federal politics as an official Liberal candidate in the 1980 election, he resigned his seat in the Nova Scotia House of Assembly. Since the eligible electorate in the 1979, 1980, and 1984 federal elections was about 16 million and slightly more than 17 million in 1988, the potential number of candidates is very large indeed.

A second set of legal requirements, in addition to being qualified as an elector, must be met before an individual is officially nominated. Nomination papers, properly executed, must be filed before the date set for nominations to end. Although some minor differences exist between federal and provincial requirements, the general pattern is that candidates must have their nomination papers signed by a number of qualified electors (25 in federal contests) in their electoral district. When the nomination papers are filed, a fee or deposit (federally it is $200) must be paid. This procedure was designed to prevent frivolous candidates from running for office, but in practice it does not appear to be a serious impediment to those with electoral ambitions: in recent federal elections, about 1 600 individuals have been officially nominated. Given that 295 seats are being contested in the House of Commons, this number averages out to approximately five to six candidates for each constituency. Finally, the nomination papers must contain a witnessed declaration by the candidate that he or she is willing to stand for election to public office.

To choose from a potential 17 million candidates approximately 1 600 who will actually contest for office in a federal election campaign reveals that the political recruitment funnel in Canada narrows quickly and precipitously. Between the potential and actual candidates stands the selectorate, the party activists who involve themselves in the nomination process. Although there are no exact figures on the size of the Canadian selectorate, a rough approximation can be calculated as follows. If we assume that in future federal elections all three parties (Liberal, Conservative, NDP) nominate candidates in all 295 constituencies and that each party also holds a constituency nomination meeting attended by about 300 people, then the size of the Canadian selectorate is a quarter of a million electors (295 constituencies $\times$ 3 parties = 885 meetings $\times$ 300 average attendance = 265 500 individuals). Such a figure would represent 1.6 percent of the eligible electorate (265 500 divided by 17 million). Adding the smaller parties to these calculations would only increase the totals by a marginal amount.

We would suggest that this figure greatly exaggerates the number of electors who are effectively involved in the recruitment process. Most recruitment decisions are taken by the party elite before the nomination meetings are held, so that in many constituency contests only one individual is presented for consideration. While party rules allow for more than one name to be presented, so that the process appears to be competitive and democratic, a contested nomination is usually a sign that the political elite has either refused to coalesce around a single candidate or that, even when it has, some individual or group in the party fails to recognize the legitimacy of such backroom decisions. Thus, the vast majority of individuals who attend their party's constituency nomination

I started off as a truck driver on the north shore of the St. Lawrence River. When I was driving a truck, John Turner was dancin' with Princess Margaret. I tell you this, there are more truck drivers in Canada than ballroom dancers (Brian Mulroney, July 7, 1984).

POLITICAL RECRUITMENT: CANADIAN-STYLE

Source: Andy Donato, *The Toronto Sun*, July 5, 1981. By permission: Canada Wide Feature Service and Andy Donato.

meeting are not really given an effective voice in the political recruitment process: their task, instead, is to legitimate the choice of the party elite. The effective Canadian selectorate, therefore, might range all the way from one (e.g., the party leader) to several hundred or more, depending on the historical period, the competitiveness of the electoral district, and the extent of the political elite's control over the party organization.

The traditional pattern of political recruitment has been for the party leader and a few key party organizers in each constituency to control the process. To this day, the leadership of the Quebec wing of the federal Liberal party, which has its own separate constitution, is allowed to reserve ridings for star candidates, thus obviating the need to even hold nomination meetings. Perhaps the longest lasting example of a party leader's control over the recruitment and nomination process at both the provincial and federal levels occurred in Newfoundland under Liberal Premier Joey Smallwood (1975: 186).

> For a hundred years in Newfoundland, the leader of a political party exercised an authority that disappeared in mainland Canada long ago. It was the leader of the party who personally selected and appointed every individual candidate of the party in each election.

Those involved in picking nominees often try to bring in some high profile candidates. For example, Ambassador Ken Taylor of Iranian hostage crisis fame was offered a safe seat for the 1984 contest by both the Liberals and Conservatives. However, Taylor turned down these offers to go into private business with Nabisco.

Although the number of federal candidates that must be nominated tends to preclude a leader's control over all of them, party leaders may still play a significant role, either directly or indirectly through their key aides. The following description of the role of Jim Coutts, then principal secretary to Prime Minister Trudeau, in the recruitment of some highly visible Liberal candidates in the 1970s illustrates this point.

> Above all Coutts is indispensable because his own greatest strength is Trudeau's greatest weakness: the management and the manipulation of people.

Coutts, particularly in recent years, has become Trudeau's talent scout and fixer, doing for him what Trudeau cannot or will not do for himself. He recruited Jack Horner, the Conservative frontbencher, a transient success that turned into stupendous failure because Horner, simply by leaving, transformed the Tory caucus into a united team. He tried to recruit Ed Schreyer to the cabinet and almost succeeded. He recruited John Evans, the former president of the University of Toronto, a much-heralded political comet, until he was brought down in the 1978 Rosedale by-election. He recruited as a Liberal candidate Maurice Strong, a former chairman of Petro-Canada until Strong, recognizing his ineptitude for politics, withdrew. He lured three Conservative M.P.s — Claude Wagner, Jack Marshall, and Bob Muir into the Senate, thus opening up by-elections in promising constituencies (Gwyn, 1980: 173).

Control by the current leader and the other members of the party elite has often been highly visible in the recruitment of a new party leader, a statement that is particularly applicable to the federal Liberal party. For example, Mackenzie King chose Louis St. Laurent (Whitaker, 1977:171–178) who in turn selected Lester Pearson (1973: 299–303). While not as open about his preference for a successor as previous Liberal leaders, the record seems clear that Prime Minister Pearson favoured Pierre Trudeau as his replacement (Radwanski, 1978: 79–87). One of the paradoxes of Trudeau's leadership of the Liberal party was his inability to find a successor: those who wanted it he shunted aside, such as John Turner for almost a decade, while those he seemed to favour, such as Maurice Strong, John Evans, Donald Macdonald, and Jim Coutts, were either unwilling or unable to gain both party and electoral support. Similarly, John Turner played no significant role in the selection of his successor at the June 1990 Liberal leadership convention.

While the role of the party leader may be strong, the trend in recent decades is for increasing decentralization, with much of the control over political recruitment residing with the executive of the party's local constituency association. Although control is most often localized, a party leader may take the rare decision to disassociate himself and his party from a particular candidate, as Robert Stanfield, leader of the Progressive Conservative party, did in 1974 when he refused Leonard Jones of Moncton, New Brunswick the right to run as a party candidate. A similar situation occurred in March 1979, when Prime Minister Trudeau refused to accept two Manitoba Liberal candidates who had been openly critical of their leader. In October of 1988, Prime Minister Mulroney announced that he would not sign the nomination papers of Sinclair Stevens, thus ending his candidacy for the Tories — even though he had won the York-Simcoe constituency nomination in July.

A leader may help to parachute a candidate into a local riding, but most such cases have been unsuccessful in Canadian politics. In **parachuting**, a local association may have no obvious candidate or they may desire one with more national stature, so that the party leader may bring in an outsider to receive the nomination. Because there is no legal residency requirement at the constituency level (i.e., a qualified elector may seek the nomination in any of the 295 ridings), such practices are possible. However, political tradition works strongly in favour of a local candidate, so that most candidates either live in the constituency they represent or close by.

The local executive of a party's constituency organization attempts to maintain control of the recruitment process by several different methods. First, and most effectively, the local party elite must keep tabs on the sentiment within the constituency organization, so that they know about and are able to defuse possible challenges to their control of the recruitment process. Second, the party elite must work out behind the scenes the candidate to be nominated and then ensure his or her success by coalition-building among the disaffected elements of the party organization. Third, if a contested nomination meeting is expected, then the rules of the game are often changed to limit last-minute memberships, to put an age requirement on those able to vote (e.g., 18), and to restrict access of the challengers to party membership lists.

A wise constituency executive never assumes that the obvious will happen — to do so may mean political failure. For example, a number of longtime MPs were denied their party's nomination in preparation for the 1984 contest, such as 27-year-veteran Tory MP Marcel Lambert in the Edmonton West constituency. These internal party battles were particularly noticeable in the safe seats for the various parties, where nomination means almost certain victory.

If the above caveats are not followed, then a constituency nomination meeting will become uncontrollable, as many outside, underaged, and recently-arrived party members vote for the party's candidate. For example, in the Trudeaumania of 1968, the Liberal association in the Davenport riding found that its membership "rose from 150 to 5 445 in a few weeks," with the outcome "determined by non-residents and ten-year-olds who, under the rules, could not be debarred from voting" (Beck, 1968: 401).

A sudden surge in party membership at the constituency level prior to a nomination meeting indicates that the political elite's control is being challenged and that the nomination process will likely be a competitive one. For example, in the Liberal constituency association of Rosedale in the spring of 1978, membership swelled from 100 to 2 000 as Ann Cools and Dr. John Evans vied for the nomination. The candidate of the party elite, Dr. John Evans, was a touted successor to Pierre Trudeau and won the nomination for the 1978 by-election. The fact that he had to contest vigorously for it shows the power of the local constituency association in the political recruitment process. Dr Evans was defeated in the by-election and

decided not to stand for the later contests, which resulted in the nomination going to Ann Cools.

Although the executive of the local constituency association has considerable leeway and thus potential influence in the recruitment process, a national party leader may, through influence, challenge the local results. In what seems destined to become a classic case of the Canadian political recruitment process, then Conservative leader Joe Clark, while suffering an initial setback, succeeded in 1977 in taking a nomination away from Stan Schumacher and thus forcing him to leave the Conservative caucus.

The unusual scenario began in 1976 with Joe Clark's selection as national party leader. As a moderate in the party, Clark was seen as suspect by right wing members of the Tory caucus. Moreover, the fact that Clark had defeated Jack Horner, a fellow Albertan and close ally of Schumacher, aggravated the Clark-Schumacher relationship. Because of the electoral redistribution, which gave Alberta two additional seats for the 1979 election, the boundaries of many districts were greatly altered. The new leader wanted to run in the Bow River constituency, because it contained his hometown. However, Schumacher also had a legitimate claim on the Bow River riding, since it included part of his old electoral district. One must remember that all of the Alberta seats went Tory in 1974 and were expected to so again in the next election, so Clark and Schumacher were both expected to be returned to the Commons, no matter in which riding they received the nomination.

The Battle of Bow River received national attention from August to October 1976, at which point Joe Clark, realizing the Schumacher forces had control of the local constituency association, withdrew from the race. However, the Battle of Bow River was not over, for a year later, when the official nomination meeting was held, Stan Schumacher lost, not to Joe Clark, but to Gordon Taylor, a former Social Credit member of the Alberta legislature. The constituency

> . . . while candidates for federal political office are coming to represent the Canadian populace more widely, over the past two decades elected MPs have increasingly come from selective economic backgrounds (Guppy et al., 1987: 420–423).

> The continued relegation of women to the status of perennial political menials represents a serious flaw in our system of leadership selection, and, ultimately, in our democratic representation (Brodie, 1985: 122).

meeting was packed by new members—Schumacher charged that they were from outside the riding as well, meaning loyal to the national leader. There then ensued more bickering, as the local constituency executive (i.e., Schumacher forces) ruled that the first meeting had been improperly held and ordered a new one. That decision was itself overturned by the party's provincial executive loyal to Clark and later upheld by the national party executive. If the new leader was unsuccessful in getting the Bow River nomination, he was able, nonetheless, to prevent his opponent from getting it. This case is very revealing in that Joe Clark could more easily win the national leadership of the Conservative party than he could his party's constituency nomination in his hometown!

The recruitment and nomination process, as well as the nature of the selectorate, demonstrate the "law of increasing disproportion." Nominees and elected representatives are not a mirror image of Canadian society, but are individuals from the better-off segments of society in terms of education, occupation, social class, and most other basic socioeconomic attributes. As one study concluded, "Canadian MP's, in comparison to a cross section of the population, have always had elite social and political backgrounds" (Kornberg et al., 1980: 5). Moreover, the largest contingent of public officials have traditionally been lawyers—usually about one-third of the total, although this figure has declined during the past decade.

The most glaring deficiency of the political recruitment process is the virtual exclusion of women: " . . . Canadian women remain conspic-

uously absent from Canadian legislatures" (Brodie and Vickers, 1981: 324). After the 1988 federal election, the number of women in the House of Commons rose to 39 (out of 295), up from 29 (out of 282) after the 1984 contest. In fact, while women make up over 50 percent of the population, in the 20th century less than one percent of elected representatives at both the federal and provincial levels have been women.

Many reasons can be advanced for the causes of this pattern, the most obvious of which is simply discrimination against females: "Male dominance in politics generally and in elite political institutions in particular is an established fact" (Kornberg et al., 1979: 186). In particular, male dominance and control over the party nomination process is an especially important explanation for why so few women ever get elected to the House of Commons. The unrepresentative nature of the candidates nominated and elected and the relatively closed procedures utilized are the bases for the conclusion that "candidate selection seems to be one area of Canadian party politics which departs widely from the democratic ideal" (Qualter, 1970: 76).

The Election Process in Canada

If the recruitment and nomination of political candidates departs from the democratic ideal, how can an election between candidates so selected be seen as contributing to the

The 1984 Liberal Campaign: Seldom, if ever, in Canadian political history has a major party conducted a campaign of such sustained ineptitude (Simpson, 1985: 15).

It wasn't a very nice election [1988], but it was, for once, an important one. The voters were actually offered a choice between two starkly different futures. That's what elections are supposed to do, but that's not how Canadian politics customarily works (Frum, 1989: 40).

democratic nature of the larger political system? The key is in the choice between candidates and their respective parties. The overall system is democratic because it gives people a choice between competing candidates and not because those candidates have been necessarily selected in a democratic manner. The electoral battle in democratic polities allows the public to choose their governors at regular intervals — it rarely allocates to the ordinary citizen a role in selecting who those competitors will be. Between election campaigns, the individual is given few opportunities to influence the course of events. As former Prime Minister Pierre Trudeau said on several occasions during his long tenure in office, if the people do not like government policy, then they can kick out that government at the next election. Such a view implies, of course, that attempts by the public to control their governors between campaigns may not be seen as a particularly legitimate activity by the political elite.

In Canada, the life of any Parliament is limited to a maximum term of five years. Based on political tradition, majority governments usually return to the people after four years. Governments seek a new mandate when they perceive that the time is auspicious for success, which usually means, in the modern era, that the public opinion polls are in their favour. Minority governments may be forced into an election after only a short term in office, if they suffer defeat in the legislature (e.g., the federal Conservatives in December 1979). However, most minority governments hold an election when they feel they can gain a majority (e.g., the federal Liberals in 1968 and 1974). Since the Second World War, minority governments have

been of limited duration, not usually because of their lack of support in the legislature, but as a result of their desire to fashion a majority in a new election or of their belief that, if an election were to be forced by the opposition, they would be reelected.

The five-year maximum life of Parliament may be extended under special circumstances, if the decision for such an action is not opposed by more than one-third of the members of the House of Commons. Only once (during the First World War) was this extension provision utilized, so that over six years intervened between the federal elections of 1911 and 1917. Because to extend the life of Parliament requires, in effect, a two-thirds vote in its favour and because the official opposition party (or opposition parties in total) normally has at least one-third of the seats in the Commons, it is politically improbable that a government could take such action simply to avoid an anticipated defeat at the polls (Table 10.1).

The mechanics of the election process are relatively straightforward. Having requested

TABLE 10.1   1988 CANADIAN ELECTION RESULTS

Party	% of Votes	# of Seats	% of Seats
Conservative	43	169	57
Liberal	32	83	28
NDP	20	43	15
Other	5	0	0

Source: Reprinted from the *Times-Colonist* (Victoria, British Columbia). By permission of Adrian Raeside.

and received a dissolution of Parliament from the formal executive, the prime minister and cabinet instruct the chief electoral officer to issue the election writs for each constituency. The election procedure in each riding is under the direction of the returning officer, whose job it is to prepare the voters' list, to make ready the necessary ballots, and to receive the nomination papers from those individuals who seek to be recognized as official candidates in the election. The tasks of the returning officer also include designating the various polling stations in each constituency, which may range from several dozen to upwards of 500, supervising the vote on election day, counting the ballots, and then

> . . . one needs the disposition of a test pilot and the arse of a cowboy to endure modern life on the campaign trail (Camp, 1979: 215).

declaring a particular candidate elected. Thus, the returning officer in each riding is responsible for the administration of the election in a fair and nonpartisan manner.

Of major significance for the citizen is the preparation of the voters' list. At the federal level, and for most provinces, the list is prepared by an **enumeration** process, that is, a door-to-door registration of urban voters after the election writs have been issued. In rural areas, voters' lists are open, in that exclusion from them does not prevent a person from voting. Enumerators are patronage positions, with two required in urban ridings (one from each of the two leading parties in that constituency in the last election) and one in rural settings. Given the number of individuals and households that must be contacted in short order, there is considerable pressure on the enumerators to proceed as quickly as possible. The result is some inaccuracy in the voters' lists, since enumerators rarely inquire as to the citizenship, age, or residency of the individuals who happen to be at home when they knock on the door. Contrary to correct procedure, enumerators often add to the list the names of individual family members who are not at home. It is thus possible to get one's name on the voters' list without meeting all of the legal requirements for voting. However, if your name is improperly registered on the voters' list, you are still not entitled to vote.

Although the current practice of having enumerators from both major parties in the urban ridings prevents most corrupt practices, in the past, control of the enumeration process has been used for partisan purposes. For example, what was known as the **graveyard vote** could be used to swing the results in closely contested ridings. If the government controlled the choice of enumerators, they could then list dead people on the voters' list and have a party worker show up on election day to cast the ballot. More than anything else, what probably prevents such practices in recent decades is simply the size of the constituencies: so many names would have to be manipulated that it would be obvious to the parties contesting the election.

A related historical practice was to have the same person register more than once, using slightly different spellings of his or her name. Such techniques were widespread in Western Canada, particularly after the large waves of immigration from Eastern Europe in the 20th century. For example, in Manitoba, the government often traded beer and favours in exchange for votes, a practice made possible because "undecipherable Slavic names made voters' lists elastic and impersonation unchallengeable" (Peterson, 1978: 66). While such practices have largely disappeared and while the voters' lists appear to be reasonably accurate, the major remaining deficiency seems to be the number of individuals whose names appear who do not meet all of the legal qualifications for voting.

The preparation of voters' lists is carried out each time a federal election is called. Thus,

Canadian elections are based on what is known as a **temporary voters' list**, because it is used only for a single election before being discarded. A rare exception to this practice occurred in 1980, with the unexpected defeat of the Clark government. The 1979 voters' lists were used in 1980 as well, with the normal enumeration period spent in revising and updating the records. Such a practice, however, did not serve as a precedent for the introduction of a **permanent voters' list**, which would be continued from one election to the next. At the federal level a permanent voters' list has only been tried once. Such a procedure was passed by Parliament in 1934 and used in the 1935 election, but, because of complaints, the use of a permanent list was abolished in 1938.

The use of a temporary voters' list has had one major impact on the nature and organization of election campaigns in Canada, namely, to make them lengthy. Because the enumerators in urban areas must begin their canvass about seven weeks before the election date (45 days before polling day) and because it takes some time to get enumerators appointed and trained, the duration of a federal campaign has to be nearly two months long (a minimum of 50 days). In the 1988 federal election, the thirty-third parliament was dissolved on October 1, with the vote on November 21 and the election writs returned on December 12. The only practical way to shorten the election period is to utilize a permanent voters' list. Instead of a seven- or eight-week contest, an election campaign might be held in four to six weeks. Shorter federal campaigns would likely be welcomed by the parties and their candidates, and probably joyously received by the public as well. In fact, shorter provincial campaigns are already evident in Canada. The 1989 Alberta provincial election was called on February 20, with the vote 29 days later, on March 20.

A further significant element of the electoral process concerns the way in which citizens cast their ballots and the way votes are counted in

Joey Smallwood and Lester Pearson on the Campaign Trail: Smallwood was totally committed to politics, and knew everything about political tactics—especially, his envious opponents would say, the trickier kind. He used to smile at these accusations and put them down to jealousy. Never did I campaign in Newfoundland without a motorcade from the airport at St. John's to the hotel with, naturally, many more cars than there were in the welcome for the Tory leader the week before. Then there would be a drive through the streets in an open car. On one occasion the weather was so atrocious, with cold and sleeting rain pelting down, that I assumed the drive would be called off. My mistake. We started at the appointed time with the leaders in the lead in an open car. Joey insisted that I sit up with him at the back so that everybody could look at me. So far as I could see 'everybody' was 'nobody' because the streets were empty. He assured me, however, that faces were pressed against every pane of glass and that I should wave and smile enthusiastically for their benefit. I felt foolish, and was miserably soaked and cold. At one point our road went through a cemetery and I thought that here, at least, I would be able to get down and crouch from the elements for a few moments. 'No, no,' said Joey, 'stay up there and wave. Some of your most faithful voters are in there' (Pearson, 1973: 22).

determining the winning party. Although other patterns have been experimented with in several provinces, the basic system currently used is the single-member district with a plurality electoral formula. The **single-member district** means that only one candidate is elected from each riding, while the **plurality electoral formula** refers to the fact that the person with the most votes in each riding wins (in other words, a plurality is not necessarily a majority).

Based on the 1971 census figures, the number of single-member districts in the House of Commons came to 282, an increase from the 264 seats that was the total used until the 1979 election. After each census, an automatic revision in the number and distribution of seats among the provinces is carried out. However, a time lag always exists, so that the 1984 federal election was based on constituencies drawn as a result of the 1971 census. The allocation of provincial seat totals was initially outlined by a series of rules specified in the 1867 Constitution Act (Section 51), with several modifications since that initial allocation. Although the rules are complex, seats in the House of Commons are primarily distributed on a population basis, with certain safeguards for Quebec and the

The Conservative victory demonstrated that Montreal is the political capital of Canada, and that the party that taps both the Toronto financial community and Quebec's "native son" commitment is unbeatable (Steed, 1988: xvii).

smaller provinces. For example, Quebec is assigned a given number of seats, with the other provincial seat allocations determined from that base.

The current distribution of seats for federal elections was determined by the 1981 census. The initial allocation would have increased the number of seats in the House of Commons to 310, with further increases for each census (369 seats after the census in the year 2001). However, because of cost and other political considerations, in late 1985 the Conservative government passed legislation to slow the rate of growth in the membership of the House of Commons. Instead of 310 seats, the 1981 census, under the revised formula, has produced 295 MPs. The redistribution based on the 1991 census will not affect the constituencies until

TABLE 10.2   PROVINCIAL SEATS IN THE HOUSE
OF COMMONS

Province	CENSUS		
	1961*	1971**	1981***
Ontario	88	95	99
Quebec	74	75	75
British Columbia	23	28	32
Alberta	19	21	26
Saskatchewan	13	14	14
Manitoba	13	14	4
Nova Scotia	11	11	11
New Brunswick	10	10	10
Newfoundland	7	7	7
Prince Edward Island	4	4	4
Northwest Territories	1	2	2
Yukon	1	1	1
Total	**264**	**282**	**295**

*Results first applied in the 1968 election.
**Results first applied in the 1979 election.
***Results first applied in the 1988 election.

the mid-1990s. The next election (in about 1992, assuming a four-year period for the Tory majority election in 1988) will still be based on the 1981 census figures. The provincial distribution of these seats is indicated in Table 10.2.

Several significant patterns are revealed by these data. First, the dominance of Ontario and Quebec is clear, since together they receive, on the basis of the 1971 census, 170 seats out of 282 or 60 percent of the total of all elected representatives to the national legislature. Second, although somewhat delayed in their impact, shifting population growth patterns are also apparent. For example, the four Atlantic provinces, while retaining the same number of seats in 1961, 1971, and 1981, are in fact losing, on a proportional basis, representation in the Commons (32 seats out of 264 in 1961 and 32 seats out of 295 as result of the 1981 figures).

In contrast, the four Western provinces, most notably British Columbia and Alberta, are gaining seats. Third, Central Canada, especially Ontario, continues to gain seats as well. Although the West is gaining seats at a slightly faster rate than Central Canada, it will be many decades before the electoral dominance of Ontario and Quebec is seriously challenged.

When provincial seat allocations are altered due to population changes, then an **electoral redistribution** takes place, that is, a redrawing of the constituency boundaries. Historically, federal redistributions take place after each census, although for the provincial legislatures several decades might pass before such a procedure is undertaken. The consequence of infrequent redistributions is a situation known as **malapportionment**. Because of population shifts, some constituencies may end up with many more voters than others, thus undercutting the supposed equality of each citizen's vote. Until recent decades, malapportionment favoured those parties with a rural base, since urban ridings would usually be more densely populated. In the past 30 years, the major population trend has been to the suburbs, so that these areas have typically been underrepresented in the legislatures. Since, traditionally, provincial redistributions are usually decided upon by the government of the day, the decision to reallocate constituency boundaries often carries important political consequences. If a party feels that it would benefit, then a redistribution will occur. In contrast, if the party in power perceives that a redistribution will undercut its base of support, then it will be postponed as long as possible. Interestingly, in May of 1989, the British Columbia government was ordered by the Chief Justice of the B.C. Supreme Court, Madam Justice Beverley McLachlin, to redraw the province's electoral boundaries because of obvious malapportionment among the constituencies. Such an order, as a result of an action by the B.C. Civil Liberties Association under Section 3 of the Charter of Rights and Freedoms, heralds the potential end of excessive mal-apportionment in the provincial legislatures.

A closely related technique to that of malapportionment is the practice of **gerrymandering** constituency boundaries, that is, the drawing of the boundaries to maximize the political support of your party and to minimize that of the other parties. The name derives from American history: in 1812, Governor Elbridge Gerry of Massachusetts redistributed electoral boundaries in such a way that the electoral map looked like a salamander, hence the word gerrymander. The way the process works can be illustrated as follows. If the constituencies are not required to be of equal population size (i.e., malapportionment), then put as many of the opposing party's areas of strength in as few ridings as possible. Concurrently, spread your own political support over as many constituencies as possible, but in such a way as to ensure a majority position within each one.

Even when the ridings must be of roughly equal size, constituency boundaries can still be drawn in such a way as to help some parties and hinder others. Throughout Canadian history, gerrymandering has been a regular feature of political life. However, at the federal level, since 1964, such practices have been greatly minimized, with nonpartisan boundary commissions now responsible for the redrawing of constituency boundaries during the redistribution process. At the provincial level, however, a number of provinces have retained the traditional practice of the government controlling when and how redistributions take place. As a result, gerrymandering remains an accepted practice of provincial politics.

A final distinction concerning the Canadian electoral process is the difference between a general election and a by-election. A **general election** results from a dissolution of Parliament, so that all seats in the House of Commons are contested in a nationwide election. A **by-election** is an election in a single constituency to fill a vacancy that has developed between

> ... the only certainty they face—from the moment of their election—is that sooner or later they are going to be defeated and thereafter largely ignored (Michael Pitfield, quoted in Troyer, 1980: 6).

general elections. A vacancy may occur as a result of a member's death or resignation from the legislature. When notified of a vacancy by the speaker of the House, the prime minister, within six months, can select the date of the by-election. Although the prime minister must act within the six-month limit, the actual date of the by-election can be anytime in the future, up to the holding of the next general election. Thus, a prime minister can quickly call by-elections in those vacant constituencies the party feels confident of winning, and postpone, at least for a while, those in ridings the party is likely to lose.

The results of a by-election sometimes register the prevailing national political sentiment, sometimes shifts in it, or sometimes serve simply as a means of venting the electorate's anger against the government of the day. Consequently, opposition victories in by-elections do not accurately predict the results of the next general election. For example, the provincial Liberal party in Quebec won an impressive series of by-election victories after the general election of 1976, but ended up losing the provincial general election of 1981. However, after their 1981 loss, the Liberals once again won every by-election until the next general election, which they won in 1986. The protest aspect of by-elections helps to account, at least in part, for the federal Liberals' extensive losses in the 15 by-elections held in October 1978 and for the win by the separatist candidate in the Alberta provincial by-election in Olds-Didsbury in February 1982.

The victorious party in the by-election often interprets the result as an indicator of political trends, while the losing party dismisses it as an aberrant result due to local or other special features not likely to be repeated in a general election. By-elections take on added significance if the government is in a minority position or if it has only a slim majority. In these situations, the loss of several by-elections might cost the government its right to remain in office.

Britain's Electoral Process

The recruitment and nomination of candidates for the British House of Commons reflects several unique attributes. If the Canadian recruitment process is closed, then the British one is even more so. Candidate selection is a private, internal party matter, a practice which the major parties seem bent on retaining. A consequence of this tightly controlled recruitment process is that the British selectorate, under normal circumstances, is quite small. The selectorate's power, however, is extensive, because up to 75 percent of the seats in the House of Commons are safe ones.

The control of the national and local party elites over the recruitment process is clearly demonstrated by the practice of **short listing**, which works as follows. When a constituency organization for a party is looking for a candidate, those who wish to have the nomination indicate their desire to the executive of the local organization. Other names may be brought forward by the national party office or by members in the local organization. From this pool of possible candidates, which may be anywhere from a few people to many, a short list of the most desirable candidates is prepared. The short list typically contains up to half a dozen names and is prepared by a screening committee of local party officials. This screening committee may contain one to two dozen members and is often described "as the most critical single stage of the entire selection process" (Ranney, 1975: 42).

The short-listed individuals then appear before a meeting of local party members, usually several hundred, known as the **selection conference**, a group roughly similar to the constituency nomination meeting in Canada. After listening to a presentation by each potential candidate, the selection conference votes for one person, who becomes the party's candidate for public office. A final step involves the approval of the candidate by the national party organization. With rare exception, the procedure puts the control of the recruitment and nomination of candidates effectively in the hands of the party elite.

In addition to the closed nature of the recruitment process, several other characteristics of British practice are worthy of mention. Although similar to Canada in not requiring candidates to be residents of the constituency in which they seek office, the British nonresidency rule has resulted in a considerable movement of possible candidates between constituencies from one election to the next, in contrast to the Canadian convention. In fact, there is a pecking order among constituencies for each party in terms of the likelihood of victory. Before gaining a nomination in a safe seat, positions that are usually reserved for the party leaders and incumbent MPs, individuals will contest an election in a constituency in which they have almost no chance of winning. If a candidate makes a credible showing, he or she may be given the opportunity to run in a more winnable constituency in the next election — and so on, until gaining a seat in the Commons. Except as a result of an electoral redistribution, such movements by candidates between ridings are rare in Canadian politics.

A second distinctive aspect of the recruitment process in Britain is the early selection of candidates prior to an election call. All major parties select a considerable portion of their candidates well in advance of an expected general election, so that they are ready to do battle on short notice. This early selection of candidates is, in part, a reflection of the brief election campaigns in Britain: the parties cannot waste half of the official campaign simply getting their candidates chosen. In contrast, Canadian parties, especially the Liberals and Conservatives, select most of their candidates for office after a dissolution of Parliament has been granted. The initial weeks of a Canadian campaign have traditionally been an exercise in political recruitment, not a battle focused on the other parties.

A third important attribute of the candidate selection process in Britain concerns the potential role of the national party leader and organization. In comparison to their Canadian counterparts, British parties are not only well-organized, but also highly centralized. At least in theory, this centralization of party organization extends to the candidate selection process. For example, as outlined above, after being named as the party's nominee by the selection conference at the constituency level, the candidate must still be approved by the national party headquarters, a practice true of both the Labour and Conservative parties. Moreover, the national parties maintain lists of possible candidates that the local parties are expected to consult and use, whenever feasible. The national party offices may even recommend to a specific constituency particular candidates they wish to be considered.

The centralization of national party control over the candidate selection process, however, is more apparent than real. Most nominations are decided by the local parties without interference from the national organization. While the national party leadership can step into the process and reject a locally selected candidate, this rarely happens. It would be most accurate to see national party control as a reserve power that is rarely exercised. For example, in 1983 the Conservatives attempted to prevent right-wing elements from winning control over and nominations in the local constituencies by

> I think one of the major problems of a woman politician in either Great Britain of the United States, where the image of women is changing, is a certain conflict between what is seen by people to be the image of a politician and what is seen to be the image of a woman (Shirley Williams in Holtzman and Williams, 1987: 26).

requiring that potential parliamentary candidates reveal whether or not they had ever been members of any other political organization.

These characteristics of the British candidate selection process help to quickly narrow the political recruitment funnel. From a population of nearly 57 million, over 43 million individuals are qualified as electors and thus, also, as potential candidates for public office. For the 1979 election, the narrowly-based selectorate reduced this large number of potential candidates to 2576 official candidates, who then competed in the general election. In 1983 a total of 2579 people ran for public office, which produced, on average, about four candidates per constituency. For the 1987 election, 2327 individuals stood for selection to the House of Commons.

The closed nature of the candidate selection process, not surprisingly, has resulted in nominees for public office who are unrepresentative of the socioeconomic characteristics of British society. Even more so than in Canada, the British political process is male-dominated, a statement that remains true, despite Margaret Thatcher's success in becoming Prime Minister in 1979, 1983 and 1987. In 1983, for example, 11 percent of all candidates in the general election were women, with 23 elected to office (3.5 percent of the total). In 1987, these figures rose slightly: 14 percent of candidates were women, with 41 elected to office (6.3 percent of the total). In order to help overcome such results, in 1981 a multi-party organization known as the 300 Group was formed to try and increase the

> General elections are the locks on the stream of British democracy, controlling the flow of the river and its traffic (Sir Lewis Namier, 1952: 183).

number of women in British party politics. The motto of the 300 Group is as follows: "A woman's place is in the House . . . of Commons."

Further, education from one of the elite public schools (comparable to the private schools of Canada) characterizes the candidates of both the Conservative and Labour parties, especially the former. In one study, the "Oxbridge" connection (university education from Oxford or Cambridge) was found to have been true of all prime ministers, 72 percent of all cabinet ministers, 37 percent of all Members of Parliament, but less than 1 percent of the total British population between 1955 and 1974 (Putnam, 1976: 35). Other socioeconomic considerations reveal a similar pattern, so that one researcher concluded that "whatever else MPs may be representative of, it is not the social composition of their constituents, nor even the social composition of their own voting supporters" (Pulzer, 1972: 70). The class-based and deferential aspects of Britain's political culture are clearly revealed in the "law of increasing disproportion," which characterizes the results of the candidate selection process.

The mechanics of a British election resemble those of a Canadian one, with a few significant exceptions. The power to precipitate an election resides with the prime minister, who requests a dissolution of Parliament from the Queen. Because Britain has typically had majority governments since the Second World War, the prime minister has had considerable leeway in such matters. The only recent exception would be the defeat of the Callaghan government on a nonconfidence motion on March 28, 1979. Rather than giving the leader of the opposition party a chance to form a government, a dissolu-

tion of Parliament was sought and received by the Labour Prime Minister.

The length of the ensuing election campaign is revealing: only six weeks passed between the defeat of the Labour government in the Commons and the first meeting of the new Parliament under the victorious Conservative leader, Margaret Thatcher (Punnett, 1980: 33–34). The official campaign was even briefer: Parliament was dissolved on April 7, election notices were published on April 11, with the actual vote taking place on May 3, 1979. Thus, the official campaign was only four weeks long, one-half of the duration of a typical Canadian election! A similar time period occurred during the 1987 contest, with the election announced on May 11 and the vote on June 11. The short electoral battle reflects the impact of a permanent voters' list and the tradition in British politics of quickly resolving disputes about which party shall lead the country.

The general election, since 1983, is contested in 650 single-member districts, which utilize a plurality electoral formula. Considerable malapportionment exists: in 1983, the largest constituency had over 94 000 members, with the smallest one containing under 23 000 electors. Although boundary commissions were first created in 1944, their work is not carried out at regular intervals (approximately every 10 to 15 years). Since their recommendations must be put into effect by the government, the implementation of a distribution scheme is a political decision. The last redistribution occurred in the early 1980s, an allocation that is likely to remain in place until the mid-1990s. Historically, blatant gerrymandering was a common political technique, but one that has receded in the modern era of British politics. The latest electoral redistribution was first utilized for the 1983 election. The results for the 1987 general election are presented in Table 10.3.

The nature of British parties has had an important impact on election campaigns. The ideologically-distinct and class-based parties,

TABLE 10.3   1987 BRITISH ELECTION RESULTS

Party	Votes	%	Seats	%
Conservative	13 760 583	42.3	376	57.8
Labour	10 029 807	30.8	229	35.2
Liberal and Social Democratic Party Alliance	7 341 633	22.5	(17) (5) 22	3.4
Ulster Unionists and Loyalists	400 430	1.2	13	2.0
Scottish National Party	416 473	1.3	3	0.5
Social Democratic and Labour Party	154 087	0.5	3	0.5
Plaid Cymru	123 599	0.4	3	0.5
United Ireland	102 683	0.3	1	0.2

which offer the voters a clear choice between their programs, give the British citizen a greater possibility of making a connection between his/ her vote and public policy than is true in Canada. Moreover, the shortness of the campaign period means that the parties have little opportunity to change a person's voting intention. Elections in Britain, more often than not, simply register public sentiment as it existed prior to the campaign. As a result, British election campaigns are "quiet in comparison with campaigns in most other democratic countries" (Birch, 1983: 75).

American Elections

A characterization of the electoral process that certainly does not apply to the United States is that it is quiet. In contrast to Britain, election campaigns are noisy, lengthy, expensive, and nearly continuous in the American polity. Moreover, the doctrines of individualism and popular sovereignty have been extended to the internal operations of the political parties themselves, so that a considerable portion of the public has

the potential to become involved in the political recruitment process. Candidates for public office are nominated by an election method known as the direct primary—one of the most unique aspects of the American political arena. However, involvement in the process of candidate selection, as well as frequent elections, do not necessarily lead to effective control of public policy. The traditional nonideological nature of the American political parties and the dominance of two competitive parties in the national party system have resulted in election campaigns that choose leaders, not the content of public policy.

> *Proclamation for the first American federal election in 1788:* Hear ye, Hear ye, Hear ye, the poll of this election is opened, and all the manner of persons attending the same are strictly charged and commanded by the authority, and in the name of the people of this state, to keep the peace thereof, during their attendance at this election, upon pain of imprisonment.

Percentage of Americans who say they day-
dream about being rich: 52

About being elected to political office: 6.

Source: Harper's Magazine (August, 1984), p. 11.

In the American presidential system, elections are mandated by law, so that the executive
has no control over when they are held. No
matter what the state of the economy or world
affairs happen to be, the election process continues. For example, the November 4, 1980 presidential election was held, much to the despair
of the incumbent Carter administration, on the
one-year anniversary of the seizing of the American diplomats by the revolutionary government
in Iran, a timing that was less than auspicious
for the Democratic party, which was seeking
reelection. Elections take place in single-member districts, under a plurality electoral formula.
The election of the president is accomplished
through the electoral college, which is a special
and complex variation of this basic format.

The practice of malapportionment has long
characterized the American electoral process,
although its worst effects have been minimized
in the last three decades. Because the constituency boundaries of the congressional districts
in the United States House of Representatives
are drawn by the respective state legislatures,
which means, in fact, that they are drawn by
the majority party in that state, manipulation of
constituency size used to be a common political
practice. However, in 1964, the Supreme Court
ruled malapportionment among congressional
districts unacceptable and ordered a redrawing
of their boundaries on the principle of "one man,
one vote." The result has been a virtual elimination of malapportionment in the lower House
and an increase in the number of seats from
both the urban and suburban areas. However,
malapportionment is guaranteed in the Senate,
since each state receives two seats: a senator

from Maine represents one million constituents, but a senator from California 26 million.
An electoral redistribution for the House of
Representatives now takes place after each
decennial census, with the Midwest and Northeast losing seats and the South and West gaining
them. Unlike in Canada, where seats are often
added to the Commons during a redistribution,
the size of the House of Representatives
remains constant: if some states are to gain
seats, others must lose them.

Although a reduction in malapportionment
minimizes, somewhat, the leeway for gerrymandering the constituency boundaries, it has
certainly not eliminated this finely-honed practice from American politics. Gerrymandering,
once described as "ingenious exercises in political geography" (Key, 1964: 302), has particularly characterized state legislatures, serving as
one means, for example, of discrimination
against minority groups, especially blacks. An
almost sure sign that district boundaries have
been gerrymandered is their misshapen outline:
often districts were drawn right down to the
individual block or house, instead of following
more natural dividing lines, such as major
streets, county boundaries, or geographical par-
titions such as rivers.

Probably the most unusual, as well as the
most significant, aspect of the American electoral process concerns the potential role of the
ordinary citizen in the candidate selection procedures. Most candidates are now nominated
through the use of direct primaries — a technique that remains uniquely American. A **direct
primary** is an election among party members
that selects that party's candidates for the general election. The direct primary was developed
as a means of undercutting boss rule and giving
to the ordinary citizen control over the nominees for political office. First adopted by the state
of Wisconsin in 1903, the direct primary is the
basic mechanism of political recruitment,
although limited elements of older practices
(e.g., conventions, caucuses) still remain. The

> A national campaign is better than the best circus (H.L. Mencken, American satirist).

thrust of the direct primary has been to democratize the candidate selection process, both in terms of the individuals who may seek office and in respect to the size of the selectorate. As a result, the American recruitment process, at least in theory, is the most open in the world. Presidential primaries, which are used in the selection of presidential candidates, are a special version of the direct primary technique.

While the direct primary provides the potential for the average citizen to become involved in the candidate selection process, it also means that a political party may not be able to control who runs under the party label. For example, in March 1986 in the Democratic primary in the state of Illinois, two candidates who were followers of Lyndon LaRouche won the Democratic nomination for state-wide office. Mr. LaRouche, who has run three times for President, is an extreme right-wing ideologue who believes that the Queen of England is a drug pusher and that Henry Kissinger is a Communist agent. However, his two candidates, because they won the Democratic primary, became the official Democratic nominees for the general election.

Election campaigns in the United States are, therefore, a two-step process: first, a series of primary elections to select the party nominees for each office and second, a general election in which the various party candidates, so selected, compete with each other. Primary elections for all elective officers are normally held on the same day, usually several months, at least, before the general election. The typical pattern of primaries is as follows: on primary election day, a voter, who is registered as a Democrat, will be given a ballot containing the names of all those seeking the Democratic nomination for each office. The candidate receiving the most votes in the Democratic primary for each office

(i.e., a plurality system) becomes the officially recognized Democratic candidate in the ensuing general election. A similar procedure is followed for Republican voters on primary day. Thus, a primary election is best seen as an internal party election by party activists and supporters of their candidate, who will then compete in the general election against the official candidates of the other parties.

Although the intent of the direct primary was to give the general public or at least party members a role in the candidate selection process, its effect in practice has been far from that ideal. For example, the rate of participation in primaries is usually a small percentage of those eligible, ranging anywhere from 10 percent in some cases upwards to 70 or 80 percent in others. The right to participate does not necessarily lead to actual participation. At the candidate level the law of increasing disproportion still operates: few ordinary citizens are likely to enter the battle for a party's nomination. Again, although the legal right is there, other factors work to limit a citizen from seeking and gaining nomination through the primary route. A major factor in this regard is a financial one: it may cost several hundred thousand dollars or more to run a primary campaign for a major political office. Without public funding for nomination campaigns, few citizens can afford the attempt to gain their party's nomination, let alone pay for the costs of the general election if they happen to be successful at step one.

Even though the direct primary has enlarged the number of citizens who participate in the selectorate, the effectiveness of the public's involvement is open to challenge. The primary mechanism has introduced public competition into the candidate selection process, by giving party members a chance to select which individual from the party's political elite will compete in the general election under the party label. Whether such a result, to an outside observer, is worth the cost and complex method of primary elections is not important, for it seems to be so to the American citizenry: "The American political tradition caps decisions made by popular vote with a resplendent halo of legitimacy" (Key, 1956: 133).

Although the American polity has enshrined the principle of popular sovereignty throughout its election process by electing more public officials in more elections on a more frequent basis than any other democratic polity in the world, neither the rate of political participation in voting nor the effectiveness of popular control over government has necessarily been improved. The potential avenues for active political participation are widespread, but, in reality, the average citizen plays a more modest role. For example, only 50 percent of the eligible electorate voted in the 1988 presidential election. Likewise, as in other countries, elections are primarily a means of choosing government leaders, not a particularly effective technique for controlling the content of public policy: "To choose a government is not to choose governmental policies" (Pomper, 1968: 51).

Comparing Electoral Processes

The nature, operation, and consequences of a polity's electoral process reflect the party and constitutional context within which it operates. In turn, elections condition and modify both the party and constitutional systems. As a result, the type of electoral process utilized by a particular country is often a good indicator of the nature of the overall political regime. Competitive elections characterize democratic systems, while non-competitive ones are typically associated with the autocratic and totalitarian political systems. Within the democratic variety, presidential and parliamentary systems differ with respect to both the political recruitment process and the mechanics of their election campaigns.

In making a comparative analysis of the

> To see a group of countries with similar electoral values and machinery is not necessarily to see a group of countries where the same sort of election is occurring (Pammett, 1988: 125).

recruitment and nomination of candidates for public office, the nature of the selectorate must be a critical concern. The group that has the effective power and influence to serve in this capacity has the ability to control the kinds of candidates from among which the public will choose their governors. While all systems reflect the law of increasing disproportion, the basis of that inequality may be education in one system, race in another, and religion in a third. The open or closed nature of the recruitment process will determine the size and composition of the selectorate, as well as the type of individual chosen for public service. As a result, a country's political stratification system is clearly revealed by the operation and consequences of the political recruitment process.

Comparing election campaigns in democratic polities focuses on such matters as their timing, length, and electoral formula. Further aspects that often have significant political consequences include the problems of malapportionment and gerrymandering, as well as the frequency and partisanship of electoral redistributions. While governments and oppositions typically seek mandates from the public for the content of policy during an election battle, rarely does the public clearly register its policy preferences. Elections are a largely unrefined tool of public control over the content of the political agenda. Instead, elections allow the governed to choose which members of the political elite will govern them.

> All students of politics are, perforce, students of politicians (Fenno, 1986: 3).

Summary

1. The most significant difference between elections in democratic and totalitarian systems is the degree and effectiveness of the choice presented to the voter: in the former, the choice is real, in the latter, it is merely apparent.
2. In parliamentary systems, the election call, within a five-year maximum, is at the prerogative of the political executive, except in rare circumstances. Elections are party-based, of relatively short duration, with either a temporary or permanent voters' list prepared by an enumeration of eligible participants. Presidential systems operate elections under fixed time constraints, put the burden of involvement on the citizen to register to vote, and are typically lengthy. A two-stage election process is utilized in the United States, with stage one selecting party candidates and stage two allowing the voter in a general election to choose between the party candidates so selected.
3. Political recruitment is the process of finding and nominating candidates for public office. Given the number of safe seats in democratic polities, nomination for office is often tantamount to election. The selectorate in any system is usually small, as the political elite attempts to control the holders of public office by determining which individuals are nominated to contest an election. Whether operating in a closed or open pattern, the political recruitment process produces candidates who are often unrepresentative of some of the major socioeconomic interests of society. Generally, any person who is qualified as an elector is also legally entitled to run for and serve in public office.
4. Canadian elections are competitive, relatively lengthy, and based on single-member districts, which utilize a plurality electoral formula. Voters' lists are temporary and constituencies are allocated among the provinces primarily on a population basis, with federal electoral redistributions required after each decennial census. In the process of redistributing electoral districts, malapportionment and gerrymandering have been greatly reduced at the federal level. The selectorate in Canada is small, although more decentralized now than in the past. In most cases, effective control resides at the local level, although a national leader can, at times, challenge and overturn the decisions so made. The process of candidate recruitment can diverge rather sharply from the democratic ideal.
5. British campaigns are short, based on a permanent voters' list, called at the request of the prime minister, and are quiet, but usually decisive, in that they typically produce majority governments. Candidate selection is a secretive, internal party matter, under the control of the party's elite through the use of such practices as short listing. Centralization of national party control over candidate selection exists in theory, but is rarely exercised in practice: local ridings have considerable autonomy to choose the candidate they desire.
6. American elections are noisy, lengthy, expensive, and nearly continuous. Popular sovereignty is imbedded in the two-stage election process through the use of the direct primary technique to nominate candidates for public office. Extensive avenues for political participation have not resulted, however, in high rates of actual involvement. The American election process, as in Canada and Britain, chooses the governors of the polity, not the priorities of the political agenda.

Recommended Readings

The Electoral Process: General

BIRNBAUM, PIERRE (1985) "Universal Suffrage, the Vanguard Party and Mobilization in Marxism,"

Government and Opposition (Winter), Volume 20, Number 1, pp. 53–69.

BRADY, DAVID W. et al. (1988) "The Electoral Antecedents of Policy Innovations: A Comparative Analysis," *Comparative Political Studies* (January), Volume 20, Number 4, pp. 395–422.

BUTLER, DAVID and AUSTIN RANNEY, eds. (1978) *Referendums: A Comparative Study of Practice and Theory*. Washington, D.C.: American Enterprise Institute for Public Policy Research.

_____ HOWARD R. PENNIMEN, and AUSTIN RANNEY, eds. (1981) *Democracy at the Polls: A Comparative Study of Competitive National Elections*. Washington, D.C.: American Enterprise Institute for Public Policy Research.

EULAU, HEINZ and MOSHE M. CZUDNOWSKI, eds. (1976) *Elite Recruitment in Democratic Polities: Comparative Studies Across Nations*. New York: Halsted Press Division, John Wiley and Sons.

GALLAGHER, MICHAEL and MICHAEL MARSH, eds. (1988) *Candidate Selection in Comparative Perspective: The Secret Garden of Politics*. London: Sage.

GELB, JOYCE (1989) *Feminism and Politics: A Comparative Perspective*. Berkeley: University of California Press.

GINSBERG, BENJAMIN (1982) *The Consequences of Consent: Elections, Citizen Control and Popular Acquiescence*. Reading, Mass.: Addison-Wesley.

_____ (1986) *The Captive Public: How Mass Opinion Promotes State Power*. New York: Basic Books.

HAMILTON, RICHARD F. (1982) *Who Voted for Hitler?* Princeton, N.J.: Princeton University Press.

HARROP, MARTIN and W.L. MILLER (1987) *Elections and Voters: A Comparative Introduction*. London: Macmillan.

HOLTZMANN, ELIZABETH and SHIRLEY WILLIAMS (1987) "Women in the Political World: Observations," *Daedalus* (Fall), Volume 116, Number 4, pp. 25–33.

KAASE, MAX (1987) "On the Meaning of Electoral Change in Democratic Polities," *Political Studies* (September), Volume 35, Number 3, pp. 482–490.

PAMMETT, JON H. (1988) "A Framework for the Comparative Analysis of Elections Across Time and Space," *Electoral Studies* (August), Volume 7, Number 2, pp. 125–142.

POWELL, G. BINGHAM, JR. (1986) "American Voter Turnout in Comparative Perspective," *American Political Science Review* (March), Volume 80, Number 1, pp. 17–43.

PRZEWORSKI, ADAM and JOHN SPRAGUE (1986) *Paper Stones: A History of Electoral Socialism*. Chicago: the University of Chicago Press.

RANDALL, VICKY (1988) *Women and Politics: An International Perspective*. Chicago: The University of Chicago Press, 2nd ed.

ROSE, RICHARD and HARVE MOSSAWIR (1969) "Voting and Elections: A Functional Analysis," pp. 69–97 in Charles F. Cnudde and Deane E. Neubauer, eds., *Empirical Democratic Theory*. Chicago: Markham Publishing.

SABATO, LARRY J. (1981) *The Rise of Political Consultants: New Ways of Winning Elections*. New York: Basic Books.

Canada's Electoral Process

BECK, J.M. (1968) *Pendulum of Power: Canada's Federal Elections*. Scarborough, Ontario: Prentice-Hall Canada.

BRODIE, JANINE (1985) *Women and Politics in Canada*. Toronto: McGraw-Hill Ryerson.

_____ (1989) "The 'Free Trade' Election," *Studies in Political Economy* (Spring), Volume 28, pp. 175–182.

FORSTER, BEN, MALCOLM DAVIDSON and R. CRAIG BROWN (1986) "The Franchise, Personators, and Dead Men: An Inquiry into the Voters' Lists and the Election of 1891," *Canadian Historical Review* (March), Volume 67, Number 1, pp. 17–41.

FRASER, GRAHAM (1989) *Playing for Keeps: The Making of the Prime Minister, 1988*. Toronto: McClelland and Stewart.

FRIZZELL, ALAN, JON H. PAMMETT and ANTHONY WESTELL (1989) *The Canadian General Election of 1988*. Ottawa: Carleton University Press.

GUPPY, NEIL, SABRINA FREEMAN and SHARI BUCHAN (1987) "Representing Canadians: Changes in the Economic Backgrounds of Federal Politicians, 1965–1984," *The Canadian Review of Sociology and Anthropology* (August), Volume 24, Number 3 pp. 417–430.

HUNTER, ALFRED A. and MARGARET A. DENTON (1984) "Do Female Candidate's 'Lose Votes'? The Experience of Female Candidates in the 1979 and 1980 Canadian General Elections," *The Canadian Review of Sociology and Anthropology* (November), Volume 21, Number 4, pp. 395–406.

KAPLAN, GERALD, MICHAEL KIRBY and HUGH SEGAL

(1989) *Election: The Issues, The Strategies, The Aftermath*. Scarborough, Ontario: Prentice-Hall Canada.

KORNBERG, ALLAN, JOEL SMITH, and HAROLD D. CLARKE (1979) *Citizen Politicians-Canada: Party Officials in a Democratic Society*. Durham, North Carolina: Carolina Academic Press.

LANDES, RONALD G. (1981) "The Canadian General Election of 1980," *Parliamentary Affairs* (Winter), Volume 38, Number 1, pp. 86–96.

_____ (1985) "The Canadian General Election of 1984," *Parliamentary Affairs* (Winter), Volume 38, Number 1, pp. 86–96.

PALDA, KRISTIAN S. (1985) "Does Canada's Election Act Impede Voters' Access to Information?" *Canadian Public Policy* (September), Volume 11, Number 3, pp. 533–542.

PENNIMAN, HOWARD R., ed. (1975) *Canada at the Polls: The General Election of 1974*. Washington, D.C.: American Enterprise Institute for Public Policy Research.

_____ (1981) *Canada at the Polls, 1979 and 1980: A Study of the General Elections*. Washington, D.C.: American Enterprise Institute for Public Policy Research.

_____ (1988) *Canada at the Polls, 1984: A Study of the Federal General Election*. Durham, North Carolina: America Enterprise Institute, Duke University Press.

SIMPSON, JEFFREY (1984) *Discipline of Power: The Conservative Interlude and the Liberal Restoration*. Toronto: Macmillan of Canada.

WOODCOCK, GEORGE (1986) "Voter's Block: What if They Called an Election and Nobody Came?" *The Canadian Forum* (February), Volume 65, Number 754, pp. 5–9.

Britain's Electoral Process

BUTLER, DAVID and DENNIS KAVANAGH (1984) *The British General Election of 1983*. London: Macmillan.

GALBRAITH, JOHN W. and NICOL C. RAE (1989) "A Test of the Importance of Tactical Voting: Great Britain, 1987," *British Journal of Political Science* (January), Volume 19, Number 1, pp. 126–136.

GEEKIE, JACK and ROGER LEVY (1988) "Reselection, Activism and the Labour Party," *The Political Quarterly* (October-December), Volume 59, Number 4, pp. 478–485.

GREENWOOD, JOHN (1988) "Promoting Working-Class Candidature in the Conservative Party: The Limits of Central Office Power," *Parliamentary Affairs* (October), Volume 41, Number 4, pp. 456–468.

MILLER, W.L. (1984) "There was No Alternative: The British General Election of 1983," *Parliamentary Affairs* (Autumn), Volume 37, Number 4, pp. 364–384.

MUGHAN, ANTHONY (1986) *Party and Participation in British Elections*. London: Frances Pinter.

NORRIS, PIPPA (1987) "Four Weeks of Sound and Fury . . . The 1987 British Election Campaign," *Parliamentary Affairs* (October), Volume 40, Number 4, pp. 458–467.

_____ and JONI LOVENDUSKI (1989) "Women Candidates for Parliament: Transforming the Agenda?" *British Journal of Political Science* (January), Volume 19, Number 1, pp. 106–115.

PENNIMAN, HOWARD R., ed. (1975) *Britain at the Polls: The Parliamentary Elections of 1974*. Washington D.C.: American Enterprise Institute for Public Policy Research.

_____ (1981) *Britain at the Polls, 1979: A Study of the General Elections*. Washington, D.C.: American Enterprise Institute for Public Policy Research.

RANNEY, AUSTIN (1965) *Pathways to Parliament: Candidate Selection in Britain*. Madison, Wisconsin: University of Wisconsin Press.

VALLENCE, ELIZABETH (1984) "Women Candidates in the 1983 General Election," *Parliamentary Affairs* (Summer), Volume 37, Number 3, pp. 301–309.

_____ (1988) "Two Cheers for Equality: Women Candidates in the 1987 General Elections," *Parliamentary Affairs* (January), Volume 41, Number 1, pp. 86–91.

American Elections

ARGERSINGER, PETER H. (1986) "New Perspectives on Election Fraud in the Gilded Age," *Political Science Quarterly* (Winter), Volume 100, Number 4, pp. 669–687.

CARROLL, SUSAN J. (1985) *Women as Candidates in American Politics*. Bloomington, Indiana: Indiana University Press.

CRONIN, THOMAS E. (1988) "Public Opinion and Direct Democracy," *PS* (Summer), Volume 21, Number 3, pp. 612–619.

_____ (1989) *Direct Democracy: The Politics of Initiative, Referendum, and Recall.* Cambridge, Mass.: Harvard University Press.

FRANKOVIC, KATHLEEN A. (1985) "The 1984 Election: The Irrelevance of the Campaign," *PS* (Winter), Volume 18, Number 1, pp. 39–47.

GOLDMAN, PETER and TOM MATTHEWS (1989) *The Quest for the Presidency 1988.* New York: Touchstone Books.

HERSHEY, MARJORIE RANDON (1984) *Running for Office: The Political Education of Campaigners.* Chatham, N.J.: Chatham House Publications.

LANCASTER, THOMAS D. (1986) "Electoral Structures and Pork Barrel Politics," *International Political Science Review* (January), Volume 7, Number 1, pp. 67–81.

LUNTZ, FRANK I. (1988) *Candidates, Consultants, and Campaigns: The Style and Substance of American Electioneering.* New York: Basil Blackwell.

MAGELBY, DAVID B. (1988) "Taking the Initiative: Direct Legislation and Direct Democracy in the 1980s," *PS* (Summer), Volume 21, Number 3, pp. 600–611.

MARTIN, JANET M. (1989) "The Recruitment of Women to Cabinet and Subcabinet Posts," *The Western Political Quarterly* (March), Volume 42, Number 1, pp. 161–172.

MCCLAIN, PAULA D. (1988) "Arizona 'High Noon': The Recall and Impeachment of Evan Mecham," *PS* (Summer), Volume 21, Number 3, pp. 628–638.

MITCHELL, GEORGE (1988) "How Media Politics Was Born," *American Heritage* (September/October), Volume 39, Number 6, pp. 34–41.

POMPER, GERALD M. et al. (1989) *The Election of 1988: Reports and Interpretations.* Chatham, N.J.: Chatham House Publishers.

REICHLEY, A. JAMES, ed. (1987) *Elections American Style.* Washington, D.C.: The Brookings Institution.

SCHLOZMAN, KAY L., ed. (1986) *Elections in America.* Boulder, Colorado: Westview Press.

SHAFER, BYRON E. (1989) "The Election of 1988 and the Structure of American Politics: Thoughts on Interpreting an Electoral Order," *Electoral Studies* (April), Volume 8, Number 1, pp. 5–21.

SORAUF, FRANK J. (1988) *Money in American Elections.* Glenview, Illinois: Scott Foresman.

WATTENBERG, MARTIN P. (1987) "The Hollow Realignment: Partisan Change in a Candidate-Centered Era," *Public Opinion Quarterly* (Spring), Volume 51, Number 1, pp. 58–74.

CHAPTER 11
Comparing Electoral Systems

As former Chancellor of the Exchequer Denis Healey told the 1982 Labour Conference: "Now comrades there is a problem here. General elections do not change the laws of arithmetic" (quoted in Rose, 1984: xxxii).

While it is probably the fate of man forever to pursue the better gadget, the power of man as an inventor seems to have found its real focus in the electoral system, where his passion for politics is wed to his passion for gadgetry (Milnor, 1969: 71).

ONE OF THE MOST important consequences of election campaigns and the competitive party struggle in democratic political systems is the actual physical control of the political structure gained by the victorious political party. Control of the political structure provides the winning party numerous political resources that it can use to maintain itself in office. These political resources include such items as the right to dispense patronage and government appointments, the ability to dominate media coverage, the right to determine the course of public policy and to focus the public's attention on certain priority areas, and the acquisition of the role of representative for the country in international affairs. One important power is the ability of the victorious party to modify the "rules of the political game" before the next electoral contest. Possible changes in the rules of the electoral process are rarely neutral or evenhanded in their effects on party competition. Nevertheless, this overt manipulation of the electoral system is often a common feature and tradition in the party battle in democratic political systems.

There are numerous Canadian examples, both historical and contemporary, of the redrawing of electoral boundaries. One of the most blatant historical examples of electoral manipulation is the famous gerrymander of 1882 by the Conservatives under John A. Macdonald (Beck, 1968: 40–41). The redrawing of electoral boundaries can often be utilized most effectively against individual opposition candidates. For example, when in 1945 the riding of Montreal Cartier elected a Communist Member of Parliament, its boundaries were extensively redrawn in 1947, resulting in a Liberal victory in that riding in the 1949 federal election (Winn and McMenemy, 1976: 119). However, if the party in power is too obvious and blatant in attempting to rid itself of a particular opposition member, it might find the voters returning that member anyway. For example, the federal Liberals tried on several occasions in the late 1940s and early 1950s to rid themselves of John Diefenbaker through the use of a gerrymander, but each time the voters sent Diefenbaker back to the Commons (Newman, 1973: 29–30).

Such manipulation of the electoral process is not unique to the Canadian polity. For example, electoral manipulation has been more prevalent in France, which has tried several different types of electoral systems since the Second World War. General Charles de Gaulle himself was not above electoral chicanery. In designing the Fifth Republic's Constitution, de Gaulle modified the electoral system for National Assembly elections from the Fourth Republic's system of proportional representation and returned France to a system of single-member districts with a two-ballot structure previously utilized in the Third Republic. This tradition of electoral manipulation was continued by French President François Mitterand (leader of the Socialist Party), when he changed the electoral system for the National Assembly from a two-ballot structure back to proportional representation before the legislative elections in 1986. This attempt, at least, proved unsuccessful: the Conservative parties still won the election, but by only a very narrow margin. However, the centre-right coalition was strong enough to immediately reinstitute a two-ballot structure after acquiring office. The two-ballot system was used in the French legislative elections of June 1988.

The Significance of Electoral Systems

Although such blatant manipulation of the electoral process has declined in recent decades in most democratic political systems, the fact that so much effort has been invested in such exercises leads us to consider the strategic political importance of electoral systems. If the rules of the electoral process had little impact on the

> In a really equal democracy, every or any section would be represented, not disproportionately, but proportionately. A majority of the electors would always have a majority of the representatives; but a minority of electors would always have a minority of the representatives (Mill, 1861:190).
>
> The voter seeks a consensus which the electoral system prevents him from achieving. That is the nub of the criticism of the plurality system (Bogdanor, 1981: 205).

political and party systems, then there would be little, if any, incentive to make such changes.

Probably the most significant consequence of electoral systems is their impact on the allocation of political power and influence within the political system. Since they transfer the percentage of popular vote won by the parties in the election into possible governmental control in terms of seats in the legislature, electoral systems help to determine which party actually wins an election campaign. As a result, electoral systems have important long-term effects on political parties' chances of gaining control of the political structure through the electoral mechanism. For example, some systems of electoral law prevent certain kinds of political parties from competing, thereby eliminating any chance for them to gain political power through normal democratic channels. In West Germany, Article 21 of the Basic Law (the Constitution of the Federal Republic of Germany) prohibits political parties that seek "to impair or abolish the free and democratic basic order" of the state (Burkett, 1975: 17). Parties of both the left and right have been banned under this provision: the Communist Party, for example, was outlawed between 1956 and 1969 as a legitimate competitor in the West German party system. Other systems, such as the Canadian, are generous in allowing almost any type of party to compete in the electoral battle. The victories

of the Parti Québécois in the 1976 and 1981 provincial elections in Quebec are ample evidence of this point.

However, to compete in Canadian federal elections, political parties must meet certain minimum requirements. These regulations are designed to prevent parties that have no electoral base from either appearing on the ballot or from receiving public monies for their campaign expenditures. The democratic nature of the Canadian electoral process probably does not suffer greatly from the elimination of such fringe groups as the Nude Garden Party as a combatant in federal elections. Thus, by helping to determine which parties are eligible to compete and which parties will be rewarded with seats in the legislature, the first major consequence of electoral systems is their impact on the distribution of political power and influence in the polity.

A second effect of electoral systems is their important interface with the political party systems. The traditional view has been that specific kinds of electoral systems are a major factor in producing certain types of party systems. The most commonly held view is that the plurality electoral system tends to produce a two-party system, while proportional representation helps to generate a multi-party system (Duverger, 1964). While this hypothesis on the relationship between the electoral and party systems has generated considerable controversy, most current interpretations admit that the nature of a country's electoral system does have an important bearing on the type of political party system that emerges (Rae, 1971).

A third consequence of electoral systems is that all types tend to favour large parties over small parties in the allocation of legislative seats. Electoral systems appear to be cognizant of the Biblical injunction: "For whosoever hath, to him shall be given; but whosoever hath not, from him shall be taken away" (quoted in Rae, 1971: 134). As a result, electoral systems tend to favour the status quo parties, since new parties representing new ideas and ideologies are

Proportional Representation In Israel: A good example of how PR helps to multiply parties can be seen in the 1988 Israeli election for the legislature (the Knesset). With one electoral district of 120 and using a PR system which advantages small parties, neither of the two major parties could win a majority (Likud had 40 seats and the Labour Alignment had 39). Thirteen other parties won at least one seat, but no more than six. Thus, fifteen parties were represented in the legislature. Moreover, 12 additional parties contested the election, but did not gain any representation, for a total of 27 parties competing in the Israeli general election of 1988.

usually small to begin with. However, as a general rule, plurality systems discriminate far more heavily against most small parties than do the proportional representation electoral systems.

A fourth result of electoral systems is a practical one: that is, the problems they present for using national opinion polls to predict the results of forthcoming elections. The percentage of national popular support for a party does not necessarily translate into the percentage of seats that party will win in the election, especially under a plurality electoral system. One reason former Prime Minister Trudeau decided not to call an election in the spring and early summer of 1978 was the realization of this important point. Even though at the time the Liberals were leading the Conservatives by a small margin in the national polls, the fact of their overwhelming support in Quebec meant that they might lose the election because of the distribution of sentiment in the rest of the country, particularly in Southern Ontario and British Columbia. In other words, public opinion polls can give an accurate account of national views, but they are a very poor base for predicting election outcomes in terms of legislative

seats. The reason for this is clear: it is the distribution of political preferences within the various electoral constituencies, not the national pattern, which will determine the election winner. Only if a poll were carried out within all or perhaps within a representative sample of constituencies could any serious attempt be made to predict the election results in terms of the number of seats that might be won by any political party.

Types of Electoral Systems

Up to this point in our analysis of electoral systems, we have dealt with their overall importance, without getting into the specifics of the various types. As a starting point, we need to consider a few basic concepts. What do we mean when we talk of electoral law? The following definition will serve as our basic guide.

Electoral laws are those which govern the process by which electoral preferences are articulated as votes and by which these votes are translated into distributions of governmental authority (typically parliamentary seats) among the competing political parties (Rae, 1971: 14).

In other words, electoral law is concerned with both the method of voting and the counting of those votes. As such, electoral law has to deal with two basic issues: first, how many candidates are to be elected in each constituency and second, the method for translating the percentage of popular votes into the number of seats won by each party in the legislature. These two issues can be referred to as dealing with the magnitude of the electoral districts and with the selection of an appropriate electoral formula. Using these criteria, we will analyze the two basic types of electoral systems: the single-member district with a plurality electoral formula and multi-member districts with a pro-portional representation electoral formula.

DISTRICT MAGNITUDES

In relation to our first criterion, the **magnitude of the electoral district**, our concern is with the number of people elected in each constituency, or, in other words, the number of seats to be filled within a given electoral district. In **single-member electoral districts**, only one candidate is elected, no matter how many candidates are running for office in that constituency. In contrast, in **multi-member constituencies**, two or more members are elected, with the number selected depending on the electoral law of the country. Countries that use the single-member district (i.e., a district magnitude of one) include Canada, Britain, and the United States. Political systems using multi-member electoral districts include the Scandinavian countries, France in the Fourth Republic, Italy, Israel, and Austria. The magnitudes of these electoral districts may range from a minimum of two upward to the total number of seats in the legislature. For example, Israel considers the country as one large electoral district and thus ends up with a district magnitude of 120.

ELECTORAL FORMULA

Our second criterion of electoral systems concerns the electoral formula for translating the popular vote into seats won in the legislature. There are two basic types of electoral formula: plurality and proportional representation.

Under a **plurality electoral formula**, the percentage of popular votes won by a party rarely equals the percentage of legislative seats obtained: in fact, there is often a rather large discrepancy between the two. The reason for this discrepancy is evident if we take a look at the mechanics of the plurality formula. A

TABLE 11.1   PLURALITY FORMULA — MAJORITY VICTORY

MANICOUAGAN RIDING, QUEBEC — 1984*

Party	% of Vote
PC	72
Liberal	24
NDP	2

*Conservative leader Brian Mulroney's riding

plurality formula means that the party and/or candidate with the largest number of votes wins the seat or constituency (Table 11.1). A plurality winner is not necessarily a majority winner. When only two candidates run for a specific office, the winner will have both a plurality and a majority. For example, let us assume that a constituency has 60 000 voters and that two parties contest the election. If Party A wins 40 000 votes and Party B wins 20 000 votes, then Party A has received both a plurality (more votes than any competitor) and a majority victory (at least 50 percent plus one). However, if three or more parties contest the election, then the winner often ends up with a plurality, but not a majority victory (Table 11.2). In our example, let us assume that three parties contest the election, with the following breakdown of the popular vote: Party A receives 25 000 votes, Party B 20 000, and Party C 15 000. Under these conditions, Party A still wins the constituency, but the outcome is a plurality, not a majority victory.

When this kind of distortion within a particular riding is multiplied throughout the entire number of constituencies, some rather strange results can occur. A party can win on a national basis a respectable share of the popular vote, but end up with a small number of legislative seats. Such a result is especially true of a party whose support is spread rather evenly across the country (what is called a pattern of diffuse or generalized electoral support). In Canadian

**TABLE 11.2   PLURALITY FORMULA—
PLURALITY VICTORY**

VANCOUVER QUADRA RIDING, B.C.—1984*

Party	% of Vote
PC	38
Liberal	44
NDP	17

*Liberal leader John Turner's riding

A rather odd anomaly of proportional representation occurred in the June 1987 Italian general election. Running under the Radical Party label, Ilona Staller, better known to her fans as Cicciolina ("the little fleshy one"), was elected to Italy's Chamber of Deputies. Well known in Italy's pornography industry, Cicciolina campaigned by appearing barebreasted at many of her party rallies. It is doubtful that advocates of PR have such a situation as this in mind when they use the concept of "fair representation."

federal elections, the New Democratic Party particularly feels the impact of this characteristic of the plurality electoral formula.

Moreover, because of such distortions, a party can actually lose an election in terms of legislative seats obtained, even though it has received a greater percentage of the popular vote than its opponents. Such was the fate of the Liberal party in Quebec in the 1966 provincial election and of the Conservative party in the February 1974 British general election. In the 1979 Canadian federal election, the Liberal party received 40 percent of the popular vote compared to 36 percent for the Conservatives on a national basis, but the Conservatives, who won 136 seats to the Liberals' 114, formed the government. Because the electoral formula can sometimes turn winners into losers and vice versa, it is clear that the electoral system is an important factor in the obtaining of political power in any political system.

The second major type of electoral formula, that of **proportional representation**, attempts to eliminate the distortion found in plurality systems. Proportional representation electoral formulas seek to have the percentage of popular votes received by a party equal the percentage of seats won by that party in the legislature. The translation of popular support into legislative seats is determined by a specific type of proportional representation electoral formula: the two most common types are the **highest average** and the **greatest remainder** formulas.

The actual calculations using these formulas can become very complex, so our examples will simply assume that proportional representation would equalize the percentage of votes and seats won by each party. It is also necessary to remember that proportional representation electoral formulas operate in multi-member constituencies.

Let us assume that a constituency with 100 000 voters selects 10 members to the legislature and that the breakdown of the party vote is as follows: Party A receives 60 000 votes, Party B 30 000 votes, and Party C 10 000 votes. The allocation of legislative seats under proportional representation would thus be distributed among the three parties in the resulting pattern: Party A would win six seats, Party B would obtain three seats, and Party C would elect one legislative member. In this example, each party's share of the popular vote equals its share of legislative seats, although in any real system this perfect equality is never reached.

Having calculated the number of seats won by each party, we must now determine which candidates have been selected. The most common type of candidate selection under proportional representation is the **list system**. In our sample constituency, 10 members are to be elected. Each party contesting the election in this constituency would nominate up to 10 candidates before election day and list them on the party's nomination papers in order from one to 10. Once the number of seats won by each party is determined, then the specific members elected are chosen, in descending order, from that party's list of candidates. In our example, Party A elected six members, thus, those candidates in positions one through six on Party A's list of candidates would become Party A's elected members from this riding. A similar allocation procedure would occur for Party B and Party C. As this example demonstrates, the basic difference between plurality and proportional representation electoral formulas is in their effects on the allocation of legislative seats: plurality systems often show a great distortion between popular support and legislative representation, while proportional representation seeks to equalize a party's electoral support with the size of its parliamentary contingent.

The Canadian Electoral System

In both federal and provincial elections, the Canadian electoral system is an example of the single-member district and plurality electoral formula. The plurality or, as it is sometimes called, the "first-past-the-post" system, is the only type of electoral system ever used in federal elections, although several Western provinces (Manitoba, Alberta, and British Columbia) have in the past experimented with other forms in provincial elections. For example, between 1924 and 1956, a preferential voting system was used in provincial elections in Alberta. Like other political systems that use the single-member district and plurality electoral formula, the Canadian electoral system regularly distorts the relationship between a party's popular support and the size of its parliamentary representation. The most glaring recent example of this distortion occurred in New Brunswick in 1987, when the provincial Liberals under Frank McKenna

captured all 58 seats in the legislature with 60 percent of the popular vote. The only other time a shut-out happened was in the 1935 provincial election in Prince Edward Island.

Such a distortion is also evident in the national vote and seat totals for the political parties in the last five federal elections (see Table 11.3). For example, the Liberals in 1974 gained a 10 percent reward from the electoral system, the Conservatives in 1979 received 12 percent, and the Liberals in 1980 gathered 8 percent. In other words, the difference (column 4) between the percentage of a party's popular vote (column 2) and the percentage of a party's seat share (column 3) represents the effect of the electoral system in translating popular support into parliamentary representation. In 1984 this bias of the electoral system gave the Conservatives an extra 25 percent of the total seats in the House of Commons, while in 1988 the Tories received a 14 percent advantage.

Examples of the various parties' fortunes in 1980 should help to clarify the effects of the electoral system in Canada. Even though the Liberal party was advantaged on a national basis by the plurality system, it still was discriminated against in specific provinces. For example, the Liberals received over 20 percent support in the three Western provinces of Alberta, Saskatchewan, and British Columbia (over half a million votes), yet they gained no seats in these electoral contests. Similarly, the Conservatives obtained over 350 000 votes in Quebec, but managed to grasp only one seat out of 75. Analogous patterns emerged in the 1984 election as well. The Liberals, for example, obtained 18 percent of the vote in Saskatchewan, but received no seats. Meanwhile, in Ontario, where they took 30 percent of the vote, they only won 14 out of 95 seats. In contrast, the Conservatives greatly benefited from the working of the plurality formula. For example, in Nova Scotia, where they won 51 percent of the vote, the Tories captured 9 out of 11 seats.

TABLE 11.3 CANADIAN ELECTION RESULTS — 1974, 1979, 1980, 1984, 1988

	# of seats	% of votes	% of seats won	electoral system bias %
1974 election				
Liberal	141	43	53	+ 10
PC	95	35	36	+ 1
NDP	16	15	6	− 9
SC	11	5	4	− 1
1979 election				
Liberal	114	40	40	0
PC	136	36	48	+ 12
NDP	26	18	9	− 9
SC	6	5	2	− 3
1980 election				
Liberal	147	44	52	+ 8
PC	103	33	37	+ 4
NDP	32	20	11	− 9
SC	0	2	0	− 2
1984 election				
Liberal	40	28	14	− 14
PC	211	50	75	+ 25
NDP	30	18	11	− 7
SC	0	1	0	− 1
1988 election				
Liberal	83	32	28	− 4
PC	169	43	57	+ 14
NDP	43	20	15	− 5
Other	0	5	0	− 5

On a national basis in Canada, therefore, the "first-past-the-post" system is usually biased in favour of the major parties, particularly the largest party in terms of votes, at the same time that it may discriminate against the major parties in particular regions of the country. In contrast, the present electoral system has disadvantages for the New Democratic Party on both a national and regional basis. The NDP's strength, while fairly widespread (20 percent of the vote in the 1980 election, 18 percent in 1984 and 20 percent in 1988), is distributed in a pattern of generalized or diffuse support. In other words, the NDP's support is spread too evenly across too many constituencies for it to gain a fair allocation of seats in the legislature. Minor parties like the NDP with diffuse support are typically discriminated against by a plurality electoral formula. For example, in 1980 in Ontario the Liberals won 52 seats with 42 percent of the popular vote, but the NDP, with 22 percent support from the Ontario electorate, gained only five seats. In the 1980 election the NDP received no seats in six provinces, even though it gained as much as 21 percent of the vote in a province like Nova Scotia. In 1988 the NDP gained no seats in five provinces and only 1 seat in Alberta. Thus, under the present plurality system, the New Democratic Party is heavily disadvantaged on both a national and a regional basis.

The plurality system, however, works to the advantage of minor parties that exhibit strong regional or sectional voting support. The Social Credit party over several decades (the 1960s and 1970s) benefited the most from this pattern. For example, in the 1968 federal election, Social Credit won 4.4 percent of the popular vote and 14 legislative seats, while the NDP obtained 17 percent of the popular vote (four times that of Social Credit), but only 22 seats (eight more seats than Social Credit). However, Social Credit's popular support declined to the point where it received no legislative seats in either the 1980 or 1984 contests. For all practical purposes, Social Credit is no longer a force in national politics, nominating only nine candidates (out of a possible 295) in the 1988 federal election.

In addition to these national and regional effects on the seat allocations for the political parties, the plurality electoral system in Canada also has a number of other important political consequences (Cairns, 1968). First, in contrast to other political systems, such as Britain, which utilize the plurality formula, in Canada the present electoral system does not produce majority governments on a regular basis. For example, the last eight federal elections have witnessed an almost regular alternation between minority (1965, 1972, 1979) and majority governments (1968, 1974, 1980, 1984, 1988). In the last quarter century Canada has experienced six minority and six majority administrations. The 1980s are unique in having produced three consecutive majority administrations.

The electoral system also contributes to the public's misperception about the nature of the various political parties' status as national political organizations. The public perceives the

parties in terms of their parliamentary representation, not in terms of their electoral or voting support. For example, in 1980 the Liberals were locked out of support in the three most Western provinces in terms of seats, but not in terms of popular voting support, which was over 20 percent. Similarly, the Conservatives' lack of support in Quebec in 1980 and the NDP's failure to gain representation in six provinces in both 1980 and 1984 and in five provinces in 1988 is only true in terms of seats, not with respect to voting support. All three federal parties are more national in scope than the plurality electoral system has led us to believe.

Third, the plurality electoral system reinforces the sectional and regional basis of the Canadian political system, because it tends to reward those parties that have established regional strongholds. The most obvious example is the Liberal party's previous dominance of Quebec: in 1980, the Liberals won 74 of 75 seats (99 percent of the seats), but in terms of votes they won only 68 percent of popular support. Similarly, the Tories won all 21 seats in Alberta, on the basis of 66 percent support from the electorate in 1980.

Finally, the plurality system affects the process of governing. For example, the previously discussed nature of the regional composition of the cabinet is influenced by the workings of the plurality system. By preventing adequate regional Liberal representation from the West and Conservative representation from Quebec in the House of Commons, the plurality electoral system forced the 1979 Clark government and the 1980 Trudeau administration to use the Senate as a temporary base for cabinet selection. Likewise, it is not entirely coincidental that Alberta, which has not elected a Liberal member to the House of Commons since 1968, was in the forefront of federal-provincial conflict during the Trudeau years. Thus, the present plurality electoral system, in addition to its effect on the translation of popular support into parliamentary representation, has a number of

... the present electoral system, with its built-in bias towards regionalism, is dangerous and destructive of Canadian unity, as well as plain unfair (Stewart, 1973: 234).

Proportional representation, as envisaged by the Pepin-Robarts commission, serves not the public, but the political parties (editorial, *The Globe and Mail*, February 27, 1980, p. 6).

TABLE 11.4 ALTERNATIVE ELECTORAL SYSTEMS 1988 (SEATS)

	Plurality	*Limited PR**	*Full PR***
Liberal	83	115	94
PC	169	212	127
NDP	43	63	59
Other	0	5	15
Total	295	395	295

*The limited proportional representation figures are based on the following calculations. An additional 100 seats in the House of Commons are allocated on the basis of the parties' national vote totals (percentage). Thus, the Liberals would gain 32 seats, the Conservatives 43, and the NDP 20. Minor parties would all obtain a total of about five seats, since they had over 4 percent of the total vote in 1988.

**The full proportional representation figures are obtained by multiplying the party's percentage of the popular vote times 295 seats.

important consequences for the operation of the Canadian political system.

The above effects of the plurality electoral system in the Canadian context have generated numerous proposals for electoral reform. Those reform proposals that have received the greatest attention in the past few years can be broken down into two basic types: limited proportional representation and full proportional representation.

While varying on specifics, **limited proportional representation** proposals suggest adding a given number of seats (ranging from 50 to 100) to the present number of seats in the House of Commons and then distributing these additional seats on a proportional basis among the various political party competitors (Task Force on National Unity, 1979: 104–106; Broadbent, 1980, 1978; Landes, 1980: 2–10; Smiley, 1978: 84–87; Irvine, 1979: 64–67). The allocation of these additional seats would generally correspond to the various parties' popular support and would be calculated under some system of proportional representation, either on a national, regional, or provincial basis. As a result, the Canadian electoral system would become a "mixed" system: most constituencies would be selected under the present plurality formula, while the additional seats would be based on some kind of proportional representation.

The primary effect of such a reform would be to increase the regional seat representativeness of all three federal parties: no party would be entirely lacking in legislative representation from any region of the country. As an example of a limited proportional representation plan (LPR for short), we present in Table 11.4 one possible allocation based on the 1988 election results. Such limited proportional representation proposals are a "conservative" way of achieving regional representation without greatly disturbing the overall election results in terms of seats won in the regular single-member plurality contests.

All of the proposed limited proportional representation schemes, however, leave basically untouched the inequities produced by the plurality electoral formula in the initial single-member ridings. For those who believe that a party's vote share should equal its share of legislative seats, the obvious answer is to adopt some form of full proportional representation (Irvine, 1979; Quebec Liberal Party, 1980: 46). Under such a plan, a party's legislative representation would approximately equal its share of the popular vote. Table 11.4 includes an allocation of parliamentary seats for 1988 if a full proportional representation formula had been utilized.

The effects of full proportional representation on the parliamentary strength of the political parties would be dramatic. First, the smaller political parties in recent federal elections would be advantaged under any system of full proportional representation. For example, in the 1979 election, Social Credit would have doubled its parliamentary seats (from six to 12) and in 1980 would have survived as a political party with four seats (compared to zero under the plurality system). Even more significant would be the results of full proportional representation for the New Democratic Party: it would become overnight a major force in federal politics, with a possible 51 seats (compared to the actual 30 seats) in the 1984 contest and 59 seats in 1988 (compared to the actual number of 43). More importantly, not only would the NDP's parliamentary representation greatly increase in any typical election, it would also often hold the balance of power within the House of Commons: either the Conservatives or Liberals could govern with the support of the NDP. It is clear that the primary beneficiary of any system of full proportional representation would be the New Democratic Party.

The impact of full proportional representation on the Liberal and Conservative parties, at least from their point of view, would be detrimental: the seat leader under the present plurality system would face major losses. For example, in 1979, the Conservatives would have lost 30 seats, would have found their position as the largest party eliminated, and would not have formed the government (based on the assumption that the largest party in terms of seats would be asked to form a government). In 1980, the Liberals, the leading party under the plurality system, would have lost about 20 seats under any full proportional representation scheme. While remaining the largest parliamentary party, the Liberals would have become a minor-

ity, instead of a majority, administration. In 1984, the Conservatives would have lost their huge majority (declining from 211 to 141 seats), giving up 70 seats and becoming an almost-majority government. In 1988, the Tories would have dropped to a clear-cut minority position of 127 seats.

A further result of proportional representation would be a dramatic change in the internal regional composition of the three national parties. All three parties would become national parties in the sense of receiving seats throughout the regions. The Liberals would typically gain strong support in the West and the Conservatives would regularly gain a base of support in Quebec. The major winner in terms of regional representation would be the NDP: it would typically gain representation in every province except Prince Edward Island. For the Liberals and Conservatives, increased regional representation under proportional representation has the price of the reduction in their total number of parliamentary seats. For the NDP, increased regional representation is combined with a major increase in its legislative caucus. Such consequences would seem to make the adoption of full proportional representation by either a Conservative or Liberal administration very unlikely.

The British Electoral System

Like Canada, Britain uses the single-member district (650) and plurality electoral formula for elections to the House of Commons. As might be expected, then, many of the consequences of the plurality electoral system are similar in Canada and Britain (see Table 11.5). For example, in Britain, a party that loses the popular vote can end up winning the largest allocation of parliamentary seats, as the Labour Party did in the February 1974 election. Likewise, the

TABLE 11.5   BRITISH ELECTION RESULTS—1974, 1979, 1983, 1987

	# of seats	% of vote	% of seats	Effects of the Electoral System %	# of seats under full PR
February 1974					
Labour	301	37	47	+10	236
Conservative	297	38	47	+ 9	242
Liberal	14	19	2	−17	123
Other					
SNP	7	2	1	− 1	12
Plaid Cymru	2	1	0	− 1	3
Ulster Loyalist	11	1	2	+ 1	8
October 1974					
Labour	319	39	50	+11	250
Conservative	277	36	44	+ 8	227
Liberal	13	18	2	−16	116
Other	26	6	4	− 2	41
SNP	11	3	2	− 1	18
Plaid Cymru	3	1	1	0	4
Ulster Loyalist	10	1	2	+ 1	9
1979 election					
Labour	268	37	42	+ 5	233
Conservative	339	44	53	+ 9	277
Liberal	11	14	2	−12	88
Other	17	6	3	− 3	36
1983 election					
Labour	209	28	32	+ 4	182
Conservative	397	42	61	+19	279
Liberal/SDP	23	25	4	−21	165
Other	21	4	3	− 1	24
1987 election					
Labour	229	31	35	+ 4	202
Conservative	376	42	58	+16	273
Alliance (Liberal–SDP)	22	23	3	−20	149
Other	23	4	4	0	26

plurality system typically works to the advantage of the major parties and discriminates heavily against those parties with generalized or diffuse support (the Liberals and the Social Democrats). For example, the Liberals won 19 percent of the popular vote in the February 1974 contest, but gained only 2 percent of the legislative seats. In 1987 the Alliance (Liberal

On the morning after the election [1983] millions of people woke up both metaphorically and literally to discover that our electoral system was totally incapable of reflecting their viewpoint (Owen, 1983: 16).

The prime minister sits in triumph in Downing Street not on a surge of popular support but as the result of unjust electoral arrangements (editorial, *The Sunday Times*, June 12, 1983: 16).

Former Labour Party Leader Michael Foot on Electoral Reform (June 5, 1983): We in the Labour party and myself especially are bitterly opposed to a system of proportional representation because I believe that it would destroy the connection between the MP and his own constituency which I regard as being one of the essential protections of our democracy in this country.

and Social Democratic Parties) won 23 percent of the popular vote, but ended up with only 3 percent of the seats. In other words, the Alliance was denied 127 seats by the plurality system. In contrast, small parties with strong sectional or regional support (i.e., the Scottish Nationalist Party or the Welsh Nationalist Party) usually fare much better under the plurality formula than the Liberals. For example, the Ulster Loyalists, with only 1.2 percent of the national vote, won 11 seats in February 1974, while the Liberals, with 19.3 percent public support, gained only 14 seats in the House of Commons. Thus, in both Canada and Britain, the plurality system advantages the major parties (in Canada, the Liberals and the Conservatives; in Britain, the Labour and Conservative parties); discriminates against those parties with generalized or diffuse support (in Canada, the New Democratic Party; in Britain the Liberal and Social Democratic Parties); and either aids parties with strong sectional or regional support or at least does not discriminate against them with the same intensity as it does against those parties with diffuse support (in Canada, the Social Credit party; in Britain, typically the various nationalist parties).

The differential effects of the plurality system in the British and Canadian contexts can be seen with respect to two areas: first, the creation of majority governments and second, the regional composition of the major parties. Although simi-

lar to Canada in that the winning party rarely has a majority of the vote (the last election where a party won more than 50 percent of the vote took place in 1931), in contrast to Canada, the plurality formula in Britain regularly produces majority governments in terms of parliamentary seat allocations. In the postwar era (1945–1987), 13 elections have been contested, with majority governments resulting in 12 cases. The only exception was the February 1974 election, although the October 1974 Labour majority was so small that it became a minority government within a couple of years through defections, retirements, and deaths. Majority governments have occurred in Britain because, until the 1974 elections and the rise of several nationalist parties, minor parties have received a small number of legislative seats, while in Canada, minor parties have consistently fared much better under the plurality system. In the 1960s and 1970s Canada's four-party system (Liberal, Conservative, New Democratic

On grounds of *fairness*, it is hard to deny their case: PR would produce a fairer distribution of seats. But to claim because of this that PR would be more *democratic* is altogether different, for most PR advocates fail to acknowledge the extent to which their alternatives would undermine important democratic principles (Hain, 1986: 2).

Party, Social Credit), combined with the effects of the plurality formula, helped to prevent the regular formation of majority governments, a situation that was modified in the 1980s (three consecutive majority elections in 1980, 1984, and 1988).

A second difference between the plurality system in Britain and Canada concerns the regional nature of a political party's legislative representation. In the Canadian context, the combination of the plurality system with the regional bases of party support has often resulted in a party receiving no legislative seats from certain regions of the country (i.e., the Liberal party in Alberta has obtained no seats in the last six federal elections). In Britain, parties have regional strongholds, but a party is rarely discriminated against to such an extent that it receives no legislative representation from a region (Drucker, 1979: 216–217). For example, even though the Labour party has typically dominated the other parties in the constituencies in Scotland and Wales, the Conservative party continues to receive a block of seats in these regional battles: 16 seats in Scotland and eight seats in Wales in the October 1974 election (Punnett, 1980: 60–61). However, the trend of the 1980s was for a regionalization of party support in Britain between the North (increasingly Labour) and the South (increasingly Conservative). For example, in the 1987 general election, the Conservatives won 24 percent of the vote in Scotland compared to 42 percent for the Labour Party, while in England the Tories won 46 percent and Labour 30 percent (Kendrick and McCrone, 1989). Thus, in both countries, the plurality electoral system helps to build and to sustain regional party strongholds, but the extent of this pattern is greater in Canada than in Britain.

Proposals for electoral reform in Britain have centred, as in Canada, on alternatives that would increase the equality between a party's share of the popular vote and its share of legislative seats. The most commonly advocated reform

> For the debate on electoral reform, seemingly part of an abstract constitutional argument, is in reality a debate about the distribution of political power in Britain. Its resolution therefore will depend not on the abstract merits of the arguments deployed, but upon the outcome of the party struggle (Bogdanor, 1987: 120).

calls for the adoption of the single transferable vote or STV for short (Scammon, 1975: 165–176; see also Norton, 1984: 96–102). While the details of such a plan are beyond the scope of our concern here, the STV system, or any specific proportional representation scheme, would greatly alter the electoral fortunes of the various political parties. Since the major parties are as unlikely to commit political hari-kari in Britain as they are in Canada, prospects for the adoption of any system of proportional representation or of the STV do not seem likely.

The American Electoral College

As in Canada and Britain, the electoral system used in the United States is the single-member district, plurality electoral formula mechanism. For example, in selecting members for the House of Representatives, there are 435 congressional districts, with one member elected in each. For Senate elections, each district corresponds to a state's boundaries, with the person with the most votes (i.e., a plurality) winning a place in the national legislature. In electing a president, a special version of the single-member district, plurality formula is used—the electoral college.

The **electoral college** is only used in selecting the president and vice-president of the United States once every four years, but it is

> It would be as unnatural to refer the choice of a Chief Magistrate to the people, as it would, to refer a trial of colours to a blind man (Virginia delegate George Mason at the American constitutional convention).

> The electoral college is a paradigm of the American democracy because it is based on popular votes aggregated state by state: thus it is both democratic and federal. This outcome is fitting because our Constitution created a democratic federal republic (Best, 1986: 19).

one of the unique aspects of American election practices. It was initially designed to provide an indirect method of electing the American president. The people would elect members of the state legislatures, who in turn would elect the individuals to serve in the electoral college. The members of the electoral college thus chosen would then select the president and vice-president. The ordinary citizen was, therefore, twice removed from direct involvement in the presidential election process. However, as the idea of popular sovereignty became enshrined in the American political culture, the people were granted a somewhat greater say. The people now select the membership of the electoral college when they cast their ballot in the presidential election in November once every four years. Moreover, the electoral college has become a formality, with the real decision made by the people in the presidential election. Although it need not always be the case, the electoral college in the modern era merely ratifies the outcome of the popular vote registered at the polls.

The structure of the electoral college is roughly based on population, since each state receives presidential electors equal to its number of members in the national legislature. For example, since the 1980 census, California has two senators and 45 congressmen, so it has 47 votes in the electoral college. The total number of votes in the electoral college is 538 (a figure equivalent to 100 senators plus 435 representatives plus three votes for the District of Columbia). To win, a candidate must receive a majority of votes, that is, a total of 270 (Table 11.6).

When American citizens cast their ballots in

TABLE 11.6 ELECTORAL COLLEGE—
MINIMAL WINNING COALITION

1.	California	47
2.	New York	36
3.	Texas	29
4.	Pennsylvania	25
5.	Illinois	24
6.	Ohio	23
7.	Florida	21
8.	Michigan	20
9.	New Jersey	16
10.	Massachusetts	13
11.	North Carolina	13
12.	Any other state (a minimum of 3 votes)	3
	Total =	270

the presidential contest, they are really selecting their state's representatives in the electoral college. Each party or candidate in the presidential race draws up a list of people willing to serve as presidential electors. This slate of delegates is listed after the name of the presidential candidate on the ballot. If a candidate wins the popular vote (i.e., a plurality) in that state, then his or her electors become the state's delegation to the electoral college.

Moreover, the election in each state is based on the **unit rule**, a special version of the plurality formula. A candidate who wins the popular vote in a state wins all of the state's vote in the electoral college. In other words, in each state, a presidential election is based on a "winner take all" principle. For example, in 1976 the presidential outcome would have been altered (e.g., Ford elected rather than Carter) if 5559 voters in Ohio and 3687 voters in Hawaii had voted for Ford. These changes, because of the unit rule, would have given Ford the 25 Ohio votes and the four Hawaii votes in the electoral college, producing a narrow Republican victory (270 votes for Ford versus 268 votes for Carter). Thus, the presidential vote in November determines the composition of each state's slate of delegates in the electoral college.

The next step is for the presidential electors who have been selected to meet and cast their ballots for the president and vice-president. The electors meet in their respective state capitals in December and cast their secret ballots, which are then sent on to the president of the American Senate (i.e., the current vice-president of the United States). In early January, a joint meeting of the House of Representatives and Senate is held to count the ballots and to officially declare a winner. Thus, the president and vice-president are not technically elected until the votes of the presidential electors are counted by Congress, although for all practical purposes they are elected in November.

However, a further complicating factor might arise. If two candidates or parties are competing in a presidential election, then the electoral college will produce a majority winner as a result of the workings of the unit rule. However, if more than two candidates compete and if the electoral college vote is splintered among three or more parties, then nobody may receive a majority of votes when Congress counts the ballots in January. If no majority is received, then the House of Representatives selects the president from among the three who received the most electoral college votes, with the Senate choosing the vice-president. This result has never happened in the 20th century, but it is a possibility when more than two parties gain a significant share of the electoral college vote.

The effects of the electoral college on presidential politics are many, even though its opera-

---

Citizen knowledge of the Electoral College
The following are the responses by American citizens to questions asking them to discuss the Electoral College (Michener, 1969: 39):

One man said: "Every boy and girl should go to college and if they can't afford Yale or Harvard, why, Electoral is just as good, if you work."

A sporting type said: "The guys at the bar poor-mouth Electoral somethin' awful. Wasn't they mixed up in a basketball scandal or somethin'?"

---

tion has largely become a formality in deciding who wins. First, a party can win the presidency by winning the vote in about the 12 largest states. The presidential candidate with the largest national popular vote does not necessarily win a majority of presidential electors in the electoral college (Table 11.7). Second, the Democrats and Republicans will most often select as their presidential and vice-presidential candidates individuals from these largest states. This custom, even though somewhat attenuated, is based on the assumption that such candidates will win their home states in the presidential election. For example, in 1960, the Democrats chose John F. Kennedy from Massachusetts and Lyndon B. Johnson from Texas; this pattern was repeated in 1988 when Michael Dukakis from Massachusetts chose Senator Lloyd Bentsen of Texas as his running mate. It used to be an assumption of American presidential politics that, to win the presidency, a candidate needed victories in the big-city states of the Northeast (i.e., New York, New Jersey, Michigan, etc.). However, with the population shift of recent decades to the South and West, since 1980 it is possible to win the electoral college with votes from just the South and West.

TABLE 11.7   ELECTORAL COLLEGE—CREATING MAJORITIES

	% of vote	Electoral College vote	% of Electoral College
1968 election			
Richard M. Nixon	43.4	301	56
Hubert H. Humphrey	42.7	191	36
George C. Wallace	13.5	46	8
*1976 election**			
Jimmy Carter	50.1	297	55
Gerald R. Ford	48.0	240	45
1984 election			
Ronald Reagan	58.8	525	98
Walter Mondale	40.6	13	2
1988 election			
George Bush	54	426	79
Michael Dukakis	46	112	21

*Total of electoral votes for the two major candidates is only 537 instead of 538 because a Republican elector from the state of Washington deserted his party's nominee and cast his ballot instead for Ronald Reagan.

Such a shift in the voting strength of states in the electoral college is good news for the Republicans and conservatives in American politics. Third, election campaigns are centred around the largest states, since that is where most of the electoral college votes are determined. Thus, the electoral college not only helps to influence the kind of person nominated for president, but also the nature of American presidential campaigns.

> If the electoral college operated only as a neutral and sure means of counting and aggregating votes, it would likely be the subject of little controversy. The electoral college, however, is neither certain in its operations nor neutral in its effects (Longley, 1986: 22).

Comparing Electoral Systems

In comparing electoral systems, several basic criteria are significant: first, the kind of electoral system used; second, the effects of the electoral system on the party system; and third, how electoral reform is achieved. These three areas are interdependent, since the type of electoral system influences the type of party system created, both of which in turn condition the prospects for electoral reform.

Suggestions for electoral reform are evident in most democratic political systems. Yet most electoral reform proposals have died because of their expected political consequences, real or apprehended. Once a particular electoral system is adopted and used, a pattern of interests develops around its workings and effects; these interests then become opposed to further political change. Those political groups that benefit from the current system will obviously be opposed to and suspicious of political reform efforts, while those political interests disadvantaged by current practices will be the most vociferous champions of political change. In either case, self-interest, not abstract political principles of democracy or equality, determines a group's attitude toward reform proposals. Using Canada as our example, we will analyze the expected political results of adopting either a limited or a full proportional representation electoral formula.

All considerations of alternative electoral systems make one crucial assumption, namely, that voter preferences will remain the same under new election mechanics as they were in previous elections. For example, in Table 11.2 and Table 11.3 we based our estimates of the effects of proportional representation in Canada and Britain on the voting patterns of recent campaigns. Such an assumption, of course, is false: as Duverger (1964) noted several decades ago, the first effect of any electoral reform is to modify not only the distribution of seats, but also the distribution of votes.

It is probably fair to hypothesize that the greater the difference between the new electoral formula and the present system, the greater the change in the actual distribution of the vote. On this basis, limited proportional representation would produce minimal changes in voter preferences: probably 1 to 2 percent of the national vote. The NDP would likely benefit slightly, since the so-called "wasted votes" would at least be rewarded in the allocation of the additional seats in the House of Commons. Under full proportional representation, the NDP would likely, over several elections, increase its base of popular support. It would immediately become a major party under any full proportional representation formula, which might then serve as a foundation for NDP expansion to

> A major purpose of elections is to supply a stable institutional framework for the expression of various viewpoints. Even if imperfect, a long-established existing electoral system may satisfy this purpose better than could a new and unfamiliar system, even if it be inherently more advantageous (Taagepera and Shugart, 1989: 49).

challenge the dominance of the two old-line parties. A three-party system, similar to that found in Ontario at the provincial level, might result. A change to full proportional representation could lead, over a series of elections, to a realignment of the federal party system along European lines of development (Duverger, 1972: 40–76).

A second possible consequence of electoral reform is a change in the number of parties competing in the federal party system and their relative share of the popular vote and legislative seats. The possible splintering of the national party system under full proportional representation is probably less likely than most observers acknowledge. The Canadian electorate in recent years has shown no predilection for either forming or supporting parties that would be serious challengers to the existing party competitors. In fact, with the demise of Social Credit in the 1980 election, the federal party system has been consolidated, in the sense that the total vote share of the three largest parties is now at a 30-year peak (i.e., in 1989). The only possible exception on the horizon to this conclusion might be the growth of the Reform Party in Western Canada in the late 1980s. Although it failed to elect any candidates in the general election in 1988, the Reform Party did win a seat in a federal by-election in Alberta soon thereafter. However, while individual, provincial, and regional voting patterns can shift fairly quickly, the national levels of voting support for the three national parties have typically stayed fairly constant over long periods of time. Therefore, it is unlikely that a change to even

Liberal MP Lloyd Axworthy on "Wasted Votes": Frankly, the only thing that boggles me . . . is that I for the life of me can't understand people in this region [British Columbia] really voting for the NDP. Because frankly, voting for the NDP federally is like voting for a eunuch to go into a harem. They can talk a lot but they don't get much action and it just really doesn't make sense when it comes down to it (*Mail-Star*, February 25, 1980, p. 15).

full proportional representation would fracture the federal party system by producing a new party or a series of new partisan coalitions (see, for example, Duverger, 1964: 228–255; Rae, 1971: 148–176; Sartori, 1976).

A third important result of a change in the electoral formula might be in the kind of government (i.e., majority or minority) that results. Systems of limited proportional representation would rarely change the majority-minority decision currently found. In contrast, a proportional representation formula would institutionalize minority governments as the typical Canadian pattern: given the historical voting patterns, it would be rare for any party to end up with a majority of the popular vote and a resulting majority of legislative seats. For example, Pierre Trudeau, while winning three majority governments under the current plurality system, would always have experienced minority governments under any of the full proportional representation schemes. Thus, the proper question seems to be not what kind of government would full proportional representation produce, but, instead, what would be the stability of the resulting minority situations?

Stability of such minority governments could be assessed on two grounds: first, the frequency of dissolutions of the House and the calling of new elections and second, the frequency of defeats in Parliament and the formation of a new government without resort to new elections.

Perhaps paradoxically, full proportional representation would likely lead to more stable governments than the plurality system with respect to the first criterion. Since a party's national vote rarely fluctuates by more than several percentage points between elections and since proportional representation fairly faithfully reflects in seats a party's share of the popular vote, a return to the people in new elections would rarely change a party's relative standing. Thus, opposition parties or the government might be much less motivated to force new elections than under the current plurality system.

With respect to the second criterion, parliamentary defeats of the governing party might occur on a fairly regular basis. However, in light of the 1968 constitutional precedent concerning the defeat of a minority government, these defeats would not necessarily lead to the resignation of the government. If parliamentary defeats and/or changes in government began to occur on a regular basis, it is possible that some form of coalition government might develop. However, given the previous single federal experience with coalition government, it is unlikely that a coalition government along European lines (i.e., with cabinet portfolios given to the minor party or parties) would be set up. More probable would be agreements to support, for limited time periods, a major party in Parliament by the NDP in return for favourable legislation. Thus, even with respect to the criterion of parliamentary defeats, proportional representation would not necessarily lead to unstable governments in the Canadian context: much would depend on the ability and willingness of the party leaders to make such a system viable.

A change in the electoral system, particularly to full proportional representation, would also greatly alter the internal composition and thus the power of various factions within the political parties. For example, at least until 1984, it was not in the political interest of the Quebec Liberal caucus to change to a proportional

Nothing in political life requires a party to work for the greater representation of its opponent, especially when its political interest can be bolstered by an argument that has been so successful in the past (Scammon, 1975: 176).

Electoral reform proposals have in some cases become reminiscent of the eternal search for the better mousetrap, forgetting in the process that no matter how good the mousetrap becomes, one still ends up catching a mouse (Landes, 1980: 34).

representation electoral formula: first, based on the 1980 figures, about 25 percent of its members would have lost their seats and, thus, would have played a reduced role within the federal Liberal party. The role of the Quebec Liberal caucus in retaining Pierre Trudeau as the Liberal leader for the 1980 election demonstrates the importance of these internal party considerations. After the 1980 election, the Quebec Liberal caucus had a majority of seats (74/147) in a majority government (147/282): under proportional representation they would have been a minority faction in a minority government. A similar case could be made for the role of the West within the Conservative party. Moreover, even though the New Democratic Party would gain seats under proportional representation, the power basis within the party caucus would shift away from Western towards Central and Eastern Canada. Such reflections indicate likely opposition to full proportional representation from the dominant factions within all of the existing federal parties.

The above analysis of the political context and consequences of electoral reform in Canada raises a number of significant considerations which apply to electoral reform efforts in most democratic political systems. First, a change in the electoral system will modify not only the distribution of seats among the parties, but the distribution of votes as well. Second, a change in the electoral formula will have a bearing on the number of political parties that continue to exist or that are likely to develop in the future. In other words, the type of electoral system adopted by a political system has an important bearing on the type of political party system that emerges. Third, electoral systems not only help to determine the minority or majority status of governments, but their resulting stability as well. Finally, the electoral system influences a party's organizational structure and the internal power of the various party factions. Such conclusions support the view that "the electoral system affects the political life of a country mainly through the parties" (Duverger, 1951: 314).

Summary

1. Electoral systems are significant elements of the political process because they help to determine the election winner, influence the number of parties that develop, and affect the internal composition of the political parties.
2. Two basic types of electoral systems can be identified: first, single-member districts with a plurality electoral formula and second, multi-member districts with a proportional representation formula. The plurality format usually distorts the relationship between a party's popular vote and its strength in the legislature, while proportional representation seeks to equalize a party's vote and seat share.
3. The Canadian electoral system is an example of the plurality type: it benefits the larger parties and minor parties with regional support, but is a disadvantage to minor parties with diffuse or generalized support. Full proportional representation would greatly help the NDP, but, for that very reason, it is a most unlikely occurrence.
4. Britain's plurality formula has effects similar

to those of its Canadian counterpart, greatly aiding the larger parties and sectional parties, but discriminating against those parties, such as the Liberals, which have traditionally received generalized support.

5. The American electoral college, a special variation of a plurality system, is used to elect the president and vice-president. Although it has typically become a formality in American politics, with the real choice made by the people when they cast their presidential vote, it continues to influence the nomination of presidential candidates and the nature of presidential electoral strategies.

6. Electoral reform often carries with it important political consequences for the existing parties. As a result, electoral reform is often blocked by the current major parties in an attempt to protect their own political dominance in the polity.

Recommended Readings

Electoral Systems: General

BALINSKI, MICHEL L. and H. PEYTON YOUNG (1982) *Fair Representation: Meeting the Ideal of One Man, One Vote*. New Haven: Yale University Press.

BLAIS, ANDRÉ (1988) "The Classification of Electoral Systems," *European Journal of Political Research* (January), Volume 16, Number 1, pp. 99–110.

_____ and R.K. CARTY (1988) "The Effectiveness of the Plurality Rule," *British Journal of Political Science* (October), Volume 18, Number 4, pp. 550–553.

BOGDANOR, VERNON (1984) *What Is Proportional Representation? A Guide to the Issues*. London: Basil Blackwell.

_____ and DAVID BUTLER, eds. (1983) *Democracy and Elections: Electoral Systems and Their Consequences*. New York: Cambridge University Press.

BRAMS, STEVEN J. and PETER C. FISHBURN (1983) *Approval Voting*. Boston: Birkhauser.

CARSTAIRS, ANDREW MCLAREN (1980) *A Short History of Electoral Systems in Western Europe*. London: George Allen and Unwin.

DOBELL, W.M. (1986) "Updating Duverger's Law," *Canadian Journal of Political Science* (September), Volume 19, Number 3, pp. 585–595.

DUMMETT, MICHAEL (1985) *Voting Procedures*. Oxford: Oxford University Press.

DUVERGER, MAURICE (1951) "The Influence of the Electoral System on Political Life," *International Social Science Bulletin* (Summer), Volume 3, Number 2, pp. 314–365.

GROFMAN, BERNARD and AREND LIJPHART, eds. (1985) *Electoral Laws and Their Political Consequences*. New York: Agathon Press.

LIJPHART, AREND (1985) "The Pattern of Electoral Rules in the United States: A Deviant Case Among the Industrial Democracies," *Government and Opposition* (Winter), Volume 20, Number 1, pp. 18–28.

LONGLEY, LAWRENCE D. (1988) "The Politics of Electoral Reform in Great Britain and the United States," *Parliamentary Affairs* (October), Volume 41, Number 4, pp. 527–535.

MILNOR, A.J. (1969) *Elections and Political Stability*. Boston: Little, Brown and Company.

PAINE, NEIL R. (1988) "Voting Procedures: A Substitute Proposal," *British Journal of Political Science* (January), Volume 18, Number 1, pp. 140–141.

RAE, DOUGLAS W. (1971) *The Political Consequences of Electoral Laws*. New Haven: Yale University Press, rev. ed.

RULE, WILMA (1987) "Electoral Systems, Contextual Factors and Women's Opportunity for Election to Parliament in Twenty-Three Democracies," *The Western Political Quarterly* (September), Volume 40, Number 3, pp. 477–498.

SHAMIR, MICHAL (1985) "Changes in Electoral Systems as 'Interventions': Another Test of Duverger's Hypothesis," *European Journal of Political Research* (March), Volume 13, Number 1, pp. 1–10.

TAAGEPERA, REIN and MATHEW S. SHUGART (1989) "Designing Electoral Systems," *Electoral Studies* (April), Volume 8, Number 1, pp. 49–58.

The Canadian Electoral System

CAIRNS, ALAN C. (1968) "The Electoral System and the Party System in Canada, 1921–1965," *Canadian Journal of Political Science* (March), Volume 1, Number 1, pp. 55–80.

CARTY, R.K. (1985) "The Electoral Boundary Revolution in Canada," *The American Review of Canadian Studies* (Autumn), Volume 15, Number 3, pp. 273–287.

COURTNEY, JOHN C. (1980) "Reflections on Reforming the Canadian Electoral System," *Canadian Public Administration* (Fall), Volume 23, Number 3, pp. 427–457.

_____ (1988) "Parliament and Representation: The Unfinished Agenda of Electoral Redistributions," *Canadian Journal of Political Science* (December), Volume 21, Number 4, pp. 675–690.

HESKETH, BOB (1987) "The Abolition of Preferential Voting in Alberta," *Prairie Forum* (Spring), Volume 12, Number 1, pp. 123–143.

IRVINE, WILLIAM P. (1979) *Does Canada Need a New Electoral System?* Kingston, Ontario: Institute of Intergovernmental Relations, Queen's University.

LANDES, RONALD G. (1980) "Alternative Electoral Systems for Canada." Paper presented to the annual meeting of the Canadian Political Science Association, Montreal, Quebec.

The British Electoral System

ALDERMAN, G. (1978) *British Elections: Myth and Reality*. London: Batsford.

BOGDANOR, VERNON (1981) *The People and the Party System: The Referendum and Electoral Reform in British Politics*. Cambridge: Cambridge University Press.

_____ (1987) "Electoral Reform and British Politics," *Electoral Studies* (August), Volume 6, Number 2, pp. 115–121.

CHANDLER, A. (1982) "The Plurality Vote: A Reappraisal," *Political Studies*, Volume 30, Number 1, pp. 87–94.

FINER, S.E. (1975) *Adversary Politics and Electoral Reform*. London: Wigram.

HAHN, PETER (1986) *Proportional Misrepresentation: The Case Against PR in Britain*. England: Wildwood House.

JOHNSTON, R.I. (1986) "Constituency Redistribution in Britain: Recent Issues," pp. 277–288 in Bernard Grofman and Arend Lijphart, eds., *Electoral Laws and Their Political Consequences*. New York: Agathon Press.

The American Electoral College

BEST, JUDITH A. (1986) "The Electoral College: A Paradigm of American Democracy," *This Constitution* (Fall), Number 12, pp. 19–22.

HESS, STEPHEN (1988) *The Presidential Campaign*. Washington, D.C.: The Brookings Institution, 3rd ed.

KESSEL, JOHN H. (1988) *Presidential Campaign Politics: Coalition Strategies and Citizen Response*. Chicago: The Dorsey Press, 3rd ed.

KING, ANTHONY (1981) "How Not to Select Presidential Candidates: A View from Europe," pp. 303–328 in Austin Ranney, ed., *The American Elections of 1980*. Washington, D.C.: American Enterprise Institute for Public Policy Research.

LONGLEY, LAWRENCE D. (1986) "The Electoral College: Archaic, Uncertain, Unfair," *This Constitution* (Fall), Number 12, pp. 22–25.

MICHENER, JAMES A. (1969) *Presidential Lottery*. Greenwich, Conn.: Fawcett Crest.

ORREN, GARY R. and NELSON W. POLSBY, eds. (1987) *Media and Momentum: The New Hampshire Primary and Nomination Politics*. Chatham, N.J.: Chatham House Publishers.

POLSBY, NELSON W. and AARON WILDAVSKY (1988) *Presidential Elections: Strategies of American Electoral Politics*. New York: Charles Scribner's Sons, 7th ed.

REITER, HOWARD, L. (1985) "The Limitations of Reform: Changes in the Nominating Process," *British Journal of Political Science* (October), Volume 15, Part 4, pp. 399–417.

12 Political Behaviour: Socialization and Participation

The entire man is, so to speak, to be seen in the cradle of the child (de Tocqueville, 1835).

American students have been conditioned from infancy to think of themselves as citizens of one of the world's great powers. Canadians are conditioned from infancy to think of themselves as citizens of a country of uncertain identity, a confusing past and a hazardous future (Frye, 1980: B1).

Voting is a form of tribal dance around the ballot box in which as many as possible should participate (Laponce, 1969: 45).

IN RECENT CANADIAN federal elections, about 13 million voters dutifully trudged to the polls to cast their ballots for their favorite candidates and parties (a cynic might suggest that they had voted for their least objectionable preference). Unless one makes the probably unwarranted assumption that such behaviour is a reflection of inherited lemming-like traits on the part of the Canadian voter, we are left with the basic question of all social scientific endeavour: why did this pattern occur? At first glance, the answer appears to be deceptively simple: since human behaviour is learned, political behaviour is likewise the result of the learning process.

The attempt to understand adult political beliefs and behaviour has thus led back to an investigation of their origins and development, that is, to a concern with the **political socialization process**. The basic assumption of political socialization research is that the initial learning of political values and ideas in childhood and adolescence influences, to a greater or lesser extent, the later political values and behaviour of adults: "political ideas — like the consumption of cigarettes and hard liquor — do not suddenly begin with one's eighteenth birthday" (Niemi, 1973: 117). Although political learning may begin in childhood, it is also important to remember that it is continuous throughout a person's life. While many orientations and attitudes may be formed in childhood and adolescence, actual experience with and participation in politics as an adult may modify

> The Tchaikovsky Conservatory, the Soviet Union's premier institution of music and probably one of the finest in the world, requires each week that its students attend three hours of lectures on the history of the Communist Party . . . (Shipler, 1983: 253).

and change previously held ideas. In addition to being continuous and beginning early, the political socialization process, for most people, is also cumulative in nature: that is, the orientations acquired later in life are grafted onto and mixed with those adopted in childhood and adolescence. It is difficult to discard years of learning, political or otherwise, and to start over with a fresh set of beliefs.

Different types of political systems utilize various techniques in attempting to control the learning of political values by the young. In democratic systems, the political socialization process is usually indirect and implicit. Few parents consciously seek to teach their offspring a particular set of political beliefs. Instead, children usually acquire values similar to those of their parents from observing the values parents exhibit in their own behaviour. Even when children are exposed to political content in the educational process, there is usually an attempt to avoid partisan debate. In contrast, both autocratic and totalitarian systems seek explicit control of the political socialization process by directly using state-controlled institutions, such as the school system and mass media, to forge a common set of political values among their citizens. How far this process had gone in the

> **Political Math — Cuban Style**
> (Fagen, 1964: 68).
>
> *Problem 1:* A medicine which cost $4.75 before the Revolution can now be bought for $3.16. How much less do we pay for this product?
>
> *Problem 2:* There have been 3000 lynchings in the United States in the last 20 years. What has been the average number of lynchings per year in that country?

> The rise of "spin control" in politics, postmodernism in the arts, and media studies in the academy all reflect the fact that *how* we learn about events — the selection, shape, and sequence of information we encounter — affects our responses to them (Cornfield and Yulof, 1988: 185).

Soviet Union was revealed in June 1988, when, as a result of the recent reforms, it was admitted that existing history textbooks were inaccurate and that history exams were thus cancelled. Whether state-directed or not, the various agents of the political socialization process (i.e., family, schools, peer groups, mass media) affect individuals in all political systems. For most individuals, political beliefs reflect a mixture of the influence of socialization agents and personal experiences with the political system.

By the time people reach the age of formal participation in the political process, perhaps best illustrated by the right to vote, their political values, beliefs, and behaviour are generally established. Although a small segment of the public may be politically active in their adolescent years, most are not, a pattern carried over into their adult years. Outside of voting in elections, most citizens participate only intermittently in the political process. The types of political behaviour an individual can use to influence leaders can run the gamut from the unconventional (riots, protest meetings, terrorism) to the conventional (participation in community affairs, campaign activity, running for office) to more passive modes of participation, such as simply voting. Moreover, a segment of any electorate is likely to be apathetic and, thus, does not participate in either conventional or unconventional political activity (Milbrath and Goel, 1977: 18–19). Although the concept of political behaviour contains a number of kinds of activity, our main focus will be on voting behaviour, because it is the dominant mode by which most citizens seek to influence the operation of their political system.

Acquiring Political Beliefs: The Political Socialization Process

While the specific mechanisms utilized in the political socialization process vary from one

> Peace issues are the great life-and-death issues of the age . . . . It is a calamity that peace education is not automatically part of every curriculum (Stephen Lewis, Canada's Ambassador to the United Nations, April 21, 1986).

country to the next, there are many similarities between political systems of each major type. After considering the political socialization process in Canada, we will briefly consider the nature of political learning in Britain and the United States.

POLITICAL SOCIALIZATION IN CANADA

Politics is not an especially salient focus of concern for the average citizen, a situation which reveals much about the nature of the political socialization process. For most Canadian youth, the learning of political orientations is indirect and implicit and perhaps based on the assumption that "politics, like sex, should be learned in the streets rather than the classroom" (White et al., 1972: 193). However, the acquisition of political beliefs begins early on a wide variety of topics.

The learning of political information centres initially on political leaders rather than on political institutions (Landes, 1976). By junior high school most children can correctly identify the prime minister, although provincial and local leaders are less well-recognized. Identification of political executives (prime minister, premiers) far exceeds that of the formal executive positions (governor general, lieutenant governors). However, understanding of the more complicated aspects of the political system, such as the job or role of these political leaders, reveals a minimum level of knowledge. For example, the Canadian Student Awareness Survey (Hurtig, 1975) found that 68 percent of high school seniors were unable to name the governor general, 61 percent were unable to name the BNA Act as Canada's Constitution, and 70 percent had little or no idea what percentage of Canada's population was French-Canadian. Similarly, a 1989 study of first-year political science and journalism students at Laval University found that 80 percent had no real understanding of the 1970 October Crisis — a seminal event in Quebec's political evolution (Aubin, 1989: A8). Thus, the average Canadian adolescent would appear to have a rather low level of political knowledge. As one researcher phrased these findings, "I feel as though someone out there waged a war on knowledge, and I've been shell-shocked by the 'Ignorants'. Knowledge of Canadian geography is almost nonexistent, political awareness unbelievable, cultural knowledge abysmal" (Hurtig, 1975: 10).

Even though levels of political information are low, children and adolescents still develop an emotional tie to political leaders and the political system. The typical pattern is for the child to personalize the political system (i.e., to perceive politics in terms of leaders) and to develop supportive attitudes and positive feelings toward the polity. For example, a comparative study of English-Canadian and American school children, grades four through eight, found that the Canadian child's affective (i.e., emotional) response to government in terms of benevolence, dependability, and leadership was greater than for his or her American counterparts (Landes, 1977: 68). Although the initial pattern of political affect is usually positive or supportive of the political regime, typically the level of political affect declines during the adolescent years and may even turn into feelings of alienation and cynicism. A particularly important affective tie is the child's early attachment to a specific political party. However, the development of party orientations among young people shows significant regional variations, with the West having the lowest and the Maritimes dis-

playing the highest rate of partisan attachments (Gregg and Whittington, 1976: 78).

In addition to information, affect, and partisan ties, political socialization research has found that the major themes of Canada's political culture are reflected in the political learning process. By the adolescent years, for example, strong patterns of regional loyalties are evident. As Johnstone (1969: 22) concluded, "during the adolescent years Canadian young people become aware of the important sectional, regional, and provincial interests in Canadian life," so that the "adolescent years . . . could be characterized as the period of emergent sectionalism." With respect to the dualism theme, a number of studies have discovered that English-Canadian and French-Canadian youth are taught different political values in the political socialization process (Lamy, 1975; Forbes, 1976). For example, an analysis of English- and French-Canadian history textbooks found that almost totally contradictory pictures of individuals and events were presented (Trudel and Jain, 1970). Such findings led one observer to conclude that "political socialization in Canada, then, seems to be for young French and English Canadians a process of socialization into discord . . . (Lamy, 1975: 278). Finally, the continentalism theme reveals the American impact on the learning of political values in Canada. For example, the American domination of the mass media has meant that many children are socialized to American rather than Canadian political values. Students often learn little of the Canadian political tradition, but much about American history and politics. As one student in the Canadian Student Awareness Survey concluded, "Never heard of them, so they must be Canadian" (Hurtig, 1975: 13). Combined with the early development of regional loyalties and English-French differences in political outlooks, the American penetration of the political learning process certainly exacerbates the development of a Canadian national identity.

An interesting example of how subtle American

influences can be through the mass media was demonstrated by the way in which *Time* magazine (which is widely read in Canada) reported on the results of the 1984 general election. The cover of the September 17, 1984 issue showed a picture of Brian Mulroney, with him indicated as the "Prime Minister-Elect." Of course, in a British parliamentary system, the people do not elect the prime minister directly. A person becomes prime minister after he is successful in forming a government, after being asked to do so by the governor general. In other words, there is no such position in Canadian politics as "prime minister-elect," which is an interpretation based on the presidential-style system of American politics.

The content of the political socialization process is influenced by the nature of the socialization agents utilized. Although specific political orientations such as partisan attachments may be passed from parents to children, as a general pattern, "most Canadian families, however, are not consciously involved in politically socializing their members" (Kornberg et al., 1979: 228). The family's impact is most apparent in providing the child with certain circumstances of birth (e.g., a social class position, a place of residence in a particular region of the country) which may look nonpolitical to begin with, but which have important consequences for what the child eventually is taught and learns about his or her political environment. In addition, the influence of the family as an agent of political socialization depends in part on the homogeneity of the family unit. If the mother and father have the same political outlooks, then their effect on the child will be greater than if their political beliefs contradict each other. Finally, while the Canadian family in the 1990s remains an important agent in the political socialization process, it is increasingly in competition with the other intermediaries in the learning process.

The significance of schools as the second agent of socialization is suggested by the fre-

> . . . Baie-Comeau was not an egalitarian society. The Mulroneys had a good life, but they didn't call the shots . . . . Brian wanted to call the shots. And politicians were the people with clout. So despite his family's lack of political involvement or interest, he would make politics his life (Murphy et al., 1984: 27).

> . . . Trudeau spent all his formative years with one foot in each of Quebec's two major linguistic and cultural groups, differing from most of the children of his generation in his lack of total identification with either side (Radwanski, 1978: 45).

> [Mackenize] King's special regard for his mother . . . did not stem merely from the fact that she was his mother. She was also William Lyon Mackenzie's daughter, and this was very important. King was constantly and acutely conscious that he was his grandfather's political heir (Stacey, 1985: 68).

quent battles over attempts to censor school textbooks and reading materials. For example, in British Columbia in 1987, foresters were upset and complained to the Ministry of Education over what they saw as a bias in how their industry was being portrayed in a grade 8 science textbook. Censorship disputes are concerned with which community forces will control the content presented by the school as an agent of socialization: "some people fear that insidious professors or evil books may politically subvert the young" (Jaros, 1973: 113).

The role of Canadian schools as agents of political socialization can be summarized with respect to the following major points. First, since under the 1867 Constitution Act (Section 93) education is made an exclusive provincial jurisdiction, "political socialization via the schools is fragmented because of the ten different provincial systems" (Ogmundson, 1976: 181). Second, as a public agent, the schools provide for most Canadians the only "exposure to formal political socialization by an instrument of the state . . . " (Kornberg et al., 1979: 228). Third, the extent of explicit political exposure through the schools is minimal, confined mainly to history and civics courses. Fourth, what little political content is presented is done so in nonpartisan terms, stressing a consensus version of Canada's political experience. Fifth, the result of the schools' efforts is an uninformed citizenry: "most high school graduates lack basic knowledge of Canadian political studies" (Symons, 1978: 50).

A third important element in the political socialization process in recent decades is the mass media, especially television. The potential impact of the mass media rests on two considerations: first, the nearly universal access most people have to newspapers, magazines, and television and second, the ability of the mass media to bypass other intermediaries of socialization and to provide information directly to children and adolescents. Thus, it is not surprising to find that children and adolescents depend on television and the mass media for political news and for help in understanding political events. The mass media have also made available to young children some of the harsher realities of political life, including wars, riots, revolutions, and assassinations. While these events usually occur in other countries, the fact that they are presented in the Canadian media means that such tragic events are helping to mold the political values and beliefs of our children.

Although other agents, such as peer groups or one's personal contacts with the political regime, may be significant shapers of political values, we will conclude our discussion of the political socialization process in Canada by emphasizing that the content of political learning is heavily influenced by the nature of the socializing agents. For example, the promotion and perpetuation of regional loyalties and French-English differences have been constitutionally facilitated by providing that education is an exclusive jurisdiction of the provincial governments. Likewise, the creation of a common national identity has been hindered not only by provincial control of education, but also by the dominance of the mass media. In addition, the indirect nature of political socialization through such agencies as the family and the minimal levels of political content presented to the child through the formal political socialization agent of the schools has meant the production of an uninformed citizenry. Any reform of this situation must contemplate major changes in both the content and agents of political learning.

THE BRITISH AND AMERICAN PATTERNS

Since our general statements about the nature of the political socialization process in Canada apply to most democratic systems, we will focus here on only a few of the distinctive characteristics of political learning in Britain and the United States.

With respect to the content of political socialization in Britain, two areas are significant: deferential attitudes toward political authority and the early acquisition of partisan identifications. As we indicated in the discussion of Britain's political culture, deference and a class-based social structure have long been cited as distinguishing attributes. While all political systems seek to instill respect for authority, the British stands out among democratic ones in this regard, perhaps best reflected in popular support for the monarchy. While such a pattern may be true of England, it is often forgotten that this view does not apply equally well to Great Britain, where sectors of the young may develop anti-English and nationalistic views (e.g., Northern Ireland, Scotland).

A second significant aspect of content in the

political learning process concerns partisan identifications. While the saying that English children are born as "either a little Liberal or else a little Conservative" would have to be modified since the rise of the Labour and nationalist parties in British politics, it does emphasize the historical importance of learning a partisan attachment in the British context. Partisanship is acquired early and influences a person's attitudes and behaviour in the adult years.

> Partisanship over the individual's lifetime has some of the quality of a photographic reproduction that deteriorates with time: it is a fairly sharp copy of the parents' original at the beginning of political awareness, but over the years it becomes somewhat blurred, although remaining easily recognizable (Butler and Stokes, 1976: 31).

The transmission of partisan attachments from parents to children reveals the continuing importance of the family as an agent of socialization in Britain. Moreover, interest in politics and political activity is often the result of family influence. One fascinating study of British prime ministers has argued, for example, that "the long and meandering road that ends at 10 Downing Street begins its course in an unhappy home," with "the most eminent British political leaders ... distinguished, to an exceptional degree, by childhood bereavement and personal isolation" (Berrington, 1974: 345). Thus, the family in Britain remains an important agent in the political socialization process, particularly with respect to political activity and leadership recruitment. A second distinctive agent of political learning in Britain is the school system, especially the public schools, which are in fact private institutions. The educational system is class-based, with those receiving a university education, especially from the most prestigious schools, dominating the political process (Hall, 1969). Such an educational system helps to reinforce the deferential attitudes and class basis of the British political culture.

In the American socialization process, two agencies have developed unique attributes. First, the school system has traditionally been utilized as a means of developing a homogeneous political culture, as a key agency in achieving the American melting pot. The large waves of immigrants of the 19th and 20th centuries were to be molded into Americans — social differentiation was discouraged in the search for the common man. The school system was a vital element of this process, teaching people a common language, history, and culture, often through specialized civics courses. Although the school system is probably not as influential today as it once was, it remains an important shaper of values, given the relatively high political content in many American schools.

A second significant agent in American political learning is the mass media. The early and widespread use of television in the United States, combined with a political process that encourages and demands coverage, has given the mass media an increasingly important role in the learning of political values. Wars, assassinations, elections, and state occasions, such as a presidential inauguration, receive extensive media exposure. Moreover, even children's programs on television have a high level of political content, as a perusal of Saturday morning shows quickly reveals. For example, one major American network in the late 1970s was less than indirect in its approach, interspersing traditional cartoons with political ones on "how a bill becomes a law" or how the United States became an independent country through a revolution, with the cartoon figures, in Hollywood fashion, doing a song-and-dance act about "no more king, no more king." As a result, the news media are "a significant determinant of children's political attitudes and patterns of political participation" (Conway et al., 1981: 175).

With respect to the content of the political socialization process, the United States is highly nationalistic and patriotic, with an emphasis on the goodness of the American way of life and its values. National loyalty is inculcated early, through symbols such as the flag and through recitation of the Pledge of Allegiance. Extensive study of American history is compulsory, with historical figures such as Washington and Lincoln receiving almost saintly status. The uniqueness of the American political experiment is stressed, with an emphasis on the special nature of the land and its people. The typical interpretation of events stresses consensus, downplaying the differences that might separate any group from the mainstream of American political life. Thus, it is not surprising to find, as an example of censorship, that in 1987 a United States federal judge in Alabama banned 32 textbooks from the public schools because they "illegally promoted the religion of secular humanism." A second distinguishing attribute of the political socialization process in the United States is the dominant role of the president in the child's initial perception of politics. This dominance of the presidency is in part a reflection of the consensus image of American politics and the strong sense of nationalism, of which the presidency is a key symbol.

> When Castro said that all revolution is an extraordinary process of education, he was saying that in a relatively short time Cubans must learn an almost totally new set of political values and practices (Fagen, 1969: 2).

tained in the school curriculum. Moreover, such systems place an emphasis on both adult and childhood political learning.

The result of the political socialization process for the individual is the learning and acceptance of the main elements of his or her country's political culture. From the perspective of the political system, political socialization processes are significant for their impact on the stability and continued existence of the political regime. All polities seek to influence, if not to control directly, both the agents and content of political education: "the stakes are simply too high for those in control not to attempt to influence who learns what, especially as that learning affects basic political values" (Dawson et al., 1977: 10).

CONSEQUENCES OF POLITICAL SOCIALIZATION

Although each polity may have some unique characteristics with respect to the process of political learning, the goal of political socialization in all systems is to produce loyal citizens who accept the legitimacy of the existing political institutions. To accomplish such an objective, however, different kinds of systems place varying emphasis on and control over both the content and agencies of the political learning process. In democratic systems, political education is most often implicit and indirect, with little political content taught directly to the child. In totalitarian systems, the process is state-controlled, centralized, explicit, and direct, with a high level of political content con-

Citizen Participation: Voting Behaviour

The impact of the political socialization process is such that by the time people are old enough to vote, their views about and desire to become involved in politics are already well-established. Given the impact of the democratic ideal in the 20th century, people are encouraged to participate in the political process. Although many kinds of political activity are available to the individual, voting is the supreme act of participation for most citizens, especially those in democratic systems.

The rationale for voting can be viewed from the perspective of the overall political system

> In his reflective moments even the most experienced politician senses a nagging curiosity about why people vote as they do (Key, 1966: 1).

> I never vote for anyone. I always vote against (American humorist, W.C. Fields).

or from that of the individual participant. In the democratic age, voting has become both a symbol of mass participation in the polity and a process for establishing the legitimacy of the political system. Participation through voting is a way of developing and enhancing a person's support for the political system: if one feels that one can influence political decisions by voting, one will be less likely to seek changes in the political structure. The legitimacy of the political system and the individual's corresponding support for it are important consequences of the voting process. From the individual's perspective, voting is also significant because, in democratic systems, it is the primary means by which he or she both selects those who govern and seeks to influence their behaviour.

FACTORS INFLUENCING PARTICIPATION

Even though a person in a participant political culture may have adopted or learned the need to vote as a result of the political learning process, many other factors influence both the frequency and form of that involvement. On a general level, we can identify four major influences on voting participation: legal, social, political, and personal factors.

With respect to legal influences, the 20th century has witnessed a gradual reduction of prohibitions to near minimum levels. However, it was not until 1984 that women were finally granted the right to vote in Liechtenstein, and 1989 in Jordan. In Canada it was not until 1988 that those citizens with a mental disease were declared eligible to vote by the Federal Court.

While not everyone can vote, restrictions are few and generally limited only by age (usually 18), residency (usually six months to one year), citizenship (usually limited to citizens only), and registration requirements. The latter factor is often overlooked, but the differences between an enumeration process in a parliamentary system such as Canada and an individual registration procedure as in the United States affect the rate of voting turnout (Glass et al., 1985).

Other legal requirements sometimes influence the extent of voting as well. For example, in most democratic systems, voting is voluntary. Once people have met the requirements of age, residency, citizenship, and registration, they are entitled to vote, but may choose not to do so. However, some democratic systems, such as Australia, have adopted **compulsory voting**, whereby people are legally required to exercise their franchise, otherwise they face a small fine. By the 1990s, about 20 countries penalized their citizens for not voting.

Even if one meets all legal requirements, the remaining social, political, and personal factors may circumscribe an individual's political activity. Social characteristics include such things as a person's occupation, education, religion, social class, ethnicity, and region of residence. These factors are often classified as the basic sociopolitical cleavages that divide the political community. Membership in a particular ethnic, class, religious, linguistic, or regional group often has important political consequences. The various sociopolitical groups differentially participate in the political process and as a result wield different degrees of influence in the decision-making process. For example, one leading comparative study concluded that the "political advantage of those citizens more advantaged in socioeconomic terms is found in all nations . . ."

(Verba et al., 1978: 1). In a similar vein, political advantage accrues to particular ethnic, class, linguistic, and regional groups in all societies.

By political factors we mean the impact of leaders, policies, parties, and events on one's desire to participate. For example, a new leader may galvanize people into participating in the political system. If a particularly salient issue comes to the forefront during a campaign or if people perceive the outcome of the vote to be especially crucial, then participation increases. A political crisis or a referendum on a controversial issue may be the means for taking politics more seriously than in the past. Finally, identifying with a specific political party is often an incentive to increased participation. Such political factors suggest that the political process itself, in terms of its leaders, policies, and parties, has a significant bearing on citizen participation.

The personal characteristics of the individual citizen, which in most cases are psychological, are the final factor influencing political involvement. For example, a major incentive to participation are feelings of **political efficacy**, that is, the belief or view that one is capable of influencing the political process. Those persons with high levels of political efficacy participate at a much greater rate than those with low levels. By contrast, those individuals who are cynical, apathetic, or alienated tend to withdraw from active participation in the polity. Such personal characteristics are often developed before the individual becomes old enough to vote and, for the most part, demonstrate the results of the socialization process.

These legal, social, political, and personal factors all influence rates of voting participation, although their specific impact may vary from one individual to another and from one political system to another.

THE CANADIAN VOTER

An important point of analysis concerns the problem of how many people participate in Canadian elections in comparison with the number of people who are eligible. Political activity was initially limited to white, adult males. Women were finally granted the suffrage in federal elections in 1918. Property qualifications were eliminated by the early decades of the 20th century. The age requirement for federal elections was reduced from 21 to 18 in 1970, with the age standard for participation in provincial elections now standing at either 18 or 19. In relation to the citizenship criterion, until 1970 Canadian citizens or British subjects residing in Canada could vote federally, but since 1975, only Canadian citizens are eligible. Landed immigrants cannot vote, which also means that they are excluded from political office, since to qualify as a candidate a person must be qualified as an elector. Residency requirements have traditionally been 12 months, with a person's residence defined as where he/she was living when the election was called. Legal discrimination has been virtually eliminated from voting criteria, although it was as late as 1950 that Inuit (then called Eskimos) were enfranchised and only in 1960 that discrimination against Indians was removed from the federal franchise. While such legal considerations as age, sex, citizenship, and residence have prevented otherwise eligible adults from voting throughout most of Canadian history, their elimination or reduction to minimal levels during the 20th century means that in the 1990s few individuals are disenfranchised. If an adult Canadian citizen does not vote, it is usually not the result of explicit legal barriers to political participation.

The extent of voter participation is usually measured as the percentage of those individuals on the voters' list who in fact cast a ballot on election day. Over the past several decades in federal elections, the rate of voter turnout has been about 75 percent, although in three consecutive elections (1958, 1962, 1963) it reached a high of 79 percent. In provincial elections, voter turnout has exceeded the federal average in some provinces, such as Saskatchewan and Prince Edward Island, while in others, such as Alberta, it has been considerably lower. Although these rates of voter participation are high, when asked whether they have voted in an election, a greater percentage of the electorate claims to have done so than the turnout rates indicate. Such inflated figures appear to be a reflection of the participation theme of Canada's political culture: good citizens are supposed to vote, so that when they do not, they are reluctant to admit it. Although voter participation is extensive, it must also be remembered that for "most Canadians political participation is confined to voting in periodic elections" (Clarke et al., 1979: 321).

The high percentage of Canadians who vote means that most of the basic sociopolitical cleavages do not differentiate significant groupings in terms of rates of participation. The variation in voting turnout among these groups has in most cases been small, leading one researcher to conclude that Canadians "lived in a political melting-pot" which produced similar attitudes toward participation (Laponce, 1969: 178). For example, the social factors of ethnicity, religion, gender, and age produce few differences in rates of voter participation (Welch, 1975). Even as pervasive an influence as regionalism seems to have little effect on political participation (Mishler, 1979: 58). In contrast, indicators of social class, such as occupation and education, are related to varying rates of participation: "It appears that Canadians who have a higher level of economic and social resources with which to participate in politics are more likely to do so" (Van Loon, 1970: 390). Although most of the basic sociopolitical cleavages have little impact on the rate of voting, their influence on the total electoral process is significant because of their strong association with partisan attachments, what we previously labeled as the social basis of party support.

A further set of factors that influences participation is political in nature, by which we refer to the impact of parties, policies, and leaders. For example, an individual's attachment to a political party is a spur to activity, since parties

> Part of political mythology is that elections are called in order to resolve policy differences and that, when the smoke of battle has cleared, an incoming government will have a mandate to implement specific policies. But cases in which this actually happens are extremely rare (Clarke et al., 1984: 171–172).

are so intimately involved in the electoral process. A commitment to a party increases a citizen's interest, knowledge, and activity, while a lack of partisan beliefs is most often found among the inactive segment of the electorate. Moreover, if the parties in a campaign are closely competitive, more voters will be drawn into the electoral process. For example, the battles between Diefenbaker and Pearson in 1962 and 1963 had turnouts of 79 percent, while their respective contest in 1965 aroused less interest and a voter participation rate of 75 percent. Similarly, the 1980 election attracted half a million fewer voters than only nine months earlier in May 1979. Part of the reason for the lower turnout seems to have been the expected Liberal victory in 1980, given their 20-point lead in the public opinion polls when the election started. If the citizen views the results of an election as a foregone conclusion, then the incentive to vote is greatly diminished.

With respect to policies, most people do not participate as a direct result of a single important issue. Rarely does an issue appear, which by itself provokes an increase in political participation. A possible exception is the "independence option" in Quebec politics, which seems to have so polarized the provincial political community that high rates of participation resulted. Likewise, the dominance of the free trade issue in the 1988 federal election campaign could also be seen in this light. More typically, issues are significant with respect to specific and usually small segments of the electorate, so that their impact on overall voting percentages is small or negligible.

OLD ELECTION STRATEGY | NEW ELECTION STRATEGY

BRIAN&MILA | BRIAN&MOOLAH

PRITCHARD

Source: Reprinted from *The Star-Phoenix* (Saskatoon, Saskatchewan). By permission of Dennis Pritchard.

A final example of a political factor that influences participation is the appeal of a particular leader. A new leader may attract people into the political arena by the strength of personality or the policies for which he or she stands. However, a strong personality may also offend many people, so that the overall impact on the extent of political activity is little changed. For example, while it is clear that Trudeau brought many new people into Liberal party ranks during the 1968 campaign, the percentage of those voting in 1968 (76 percent) was only 1 percentage point greater than in 1965 (75 percent).

Psychological attitudes towards politics, which we have classified as personal factors, have consistently been found to influence politi-

> The colonial mentality is probably more deeply ingrained in the Canadian consciousness than in the national outlook of any other country. Such a mentality is not conducive to political participation (McDonald, 1977: 459).

cal participation. For example, individuals who have an interest in political matters, who have developed an adequate knowledge about their political system, or who have a feeling that a good citizen should be active in politics, have much higher rates of participation than those who do not exhibit such views (Van Loon,

1970: 394–396). Similarly, those citizens who feel that they can influence the political system are most prone to political activism (Mishler, 1979: 76). These findings reflect the importance of perception in the world of politics: if people think they have a meaningful role in it, they are more likely to participate in the polity.

In examining the four factors that influence political participation (legal, social, political, and personal), we have discovered some items that usually have little impact (e.g., age, sex, legal requirements such as citizenship) and others with more specific political consequences (e.g., education, partisanship, efficacy and interest). Voting participation in Canada is high, but voter turnout tells us about the quantity of participation, not its quality. Recent assessments of the quality of participation have been somewhat pessimistic. However, given the extent of citizen participation in most polities, a comparative view would be mildly encouraging: while "the structure and quality of citizen participation in political life fall far below the democratic ideal, it is also apparent that Canada approaches much closer to this ideal than the great majority of the world's nation-states" (Mishler, 1981: 140).

THE BRITISH VOTER

Throughout the 19th century, the right to participate in electoral politics was severely limited in Britain, although the series of Reform Acts did increase the percentage of adults voting from roughly 5 to 30 percent. Women were granted the right to vote in 1918, although there was a higher age qualification for women (30) than for men (21). Moreover, women were initially entitled to vote only if their husbands met the property qualifications then in existence. The age qualification for women was lowered to 21 in 1928, a legal restriction that stood for both men and women for 40 years until 1969, when adulthood was defined as 18. Although over the last century and a half "the extent of the fran-

chise has been the most important constitutional issue" in Britain (Birch, 1983: 65), it is no longer an area of controversy, since there are now only minimal legal restrictions on the franchise.

An interesting historical aspect of legal qualifications and voting in Britain concerns the use for certain groups of **plural voting**, that is, where one individual was legally entitled to vote more than once. For example, between 1918 and 1948, owners of a business could vote in both the constituency where their business was located and in the constituencies where they lived, if separate constituencies were involved. As well, since the 14th century Britain had allowed a limited number of special university seats in the Commons. University graduates were entitled to two ballots: one for the university seats and one in their constituency of residence. Reforms adopted in 1948 abolished both types of plural voting, so that each elector is now entitled to only a single vote.

A further distinctive aspect of the legal qualifications in Britain concerns the electoral register. As in Canada, the government has assumed the responsibility for registering people to vote. However, instead of making up a new list when an election is called, Britain maintains a **permanent voters' list**, which is revised once a year in the fall and which indicates those eligible to vote as of October 10 of that year. This electoral register goes into effect the following February for a one-year period. Most studies have suggested that the electoral register thus produced is quite accurate, with about 95 percent of those eligible to vote contained on the voters' list.

Minimal legal restrictions and a permanent voters' list have helped to produce high levels of voter turnout in British national elections. As a percentage of those included on the electoral register, the 1979 election had a turnout of 76 percent, which is the average turnout in general elections since 1945. The highest level of voting occurred in 1950, with an 84 percent turnout, and the lowest rate was seen in 1970 with just

72 percent participating. The 1983 British general election had a participation rate of just under 73 percent, which rose to over 75 percent in the 1987 contest. On an average percentage basis, these figures indicate a slightly higher rate of participation in British than in Canadian general elections since the Second World War. However, such differences are very small and can probably be accounted for by the infrequency of British elections and the use of the permanent voters' list.

The impact of the various social, political, and personal factors on voter participation in Britain is comparable to that found in other democratic systems. For example, the higher one's social class, occupation, education, and income, the greater is one's political involvement. Similarly, urban rather than rural residents, middle-aged rather than either very young or very old voters, and men rather than women demonstrate greater rates of voter turnout, although such differences may be small. As in Canada, the impact of these sociopolitical cleavages, the most important of which is social class in Britain, is mediated by an individual's party identification. Feelings of political efficacy, as well as having a partisan attachment, also increase the rate of political activity. With respect to political factors, closely competitive or marginal seats have a higher turnout rate than safe seats. The nature of the party system contributes to voter participation as well: programmatic parties, one of which typically forms a majority government, should enhance the value of the individual's vote.

Since the legal requirements prevent few eligible voters from participating, the reasons for nonvoting must be found in a combination of the effects of the social, political, and personal factors. In most British elections, about 25 percent of the eligible voters do not participate. The causes for such a pattern of abstention may reflect a conscious decision by voters that none of the relevant parties or candidates running for office represents their interests. Nonvoting may also reflect low feelings of efficacy or the belief that a single vote will not make any difference on the outcome of a general election. Low participation may also illustrate that people are so alienated from the political regime that they do not want to involve themselves in the political process, while for others nonparticipation may exemplify satisfaction with the polity, so that voting is not necessary. While the causes of nonvoting at the individual level are complex, from the viewpoint of comparative analysis, the total rate of abstention is revealing for what it demonstrates about the stability of the polity and the general attitudes towards political activity. The rate of nonvoting in Britain in this comparative perspective is low: the same conclusion cannot necessarily be advanced with respect to political participation in the American system.

THE AMERICAN VOTER

The study of political behaviour in the United States has revealed a fundamental paradox: while the opportunities for participation are multiple, the rate of political activity is much lower than in other democratic systems. This paradox is, in large part, the result of a unique combination of legal restrictions, which tend to disenfranchise a significant segment of potential voters.

While the general historical trend has been for a removal of most legal restrictions on the right to vote, so that most adults over 18 are now enfranchised, the extension of the suffrage has produced bitter battles in the political arena. Some of these conflicts have become so salient that they have been resolved through the process of constitutional amendment. If we discount the first 10 amendments, since they constitute the American Bill of Rights, of the remaining 16 amendments, five have been concerned with extensions of the suffrage: the Fifteenth Amendment (1870) prohibited discrimination in voting privileges based on race;

> Nonvoting, in short, is almost entirely concentrated among the unregistered . . . . In effect, restrictive registration procedures are the functional equivalents of earlier property and literacy qualifications (Piven and Cloward, 1988: 869).

> The American legal and institutional environment is inhibiting to voter participation (Powell, 1986: 36).

> The key disfranchising features of the Southern registration laws were the amount of discretion granted to the registrars, the specificity of the information required of the registrant, the times and places set for registration, and the requirement that a voter bring his registration certificate to the polling place (Kousser, 1974: 48).

the Nineteenth Amendment (1920) extended the right to vote to women; the Twenty-Third Amendment (1961) granted residents in the American Capital the franchise; the Twenty-Fourth Amendment (1964) prohibited the use of the poll tax; and the Twenty-Sixth Amendment (1971) lowered the age of participation to 18 in all elections. These constitutional amendments have been a significant factor in eliminating some of the gross injustices that prohibited significant segments of the population from voting.

Two legal restrictions, however, have remained as important factors in nonvoting even through the modern era: registration and residency requirements. Unlike in the process of enumeration used in most democratic systems, the American voter is responsible for getting his or her name on the voters' list and for keeping it there. The individual must make the effort to register to vote by going to the proper government office, usually several weeks before the actual election. Moreover, states may remove a name from the electoral register if a person fails to vote in several consecutive elections. While the emphasis on the individual's role in registering to vote is a reflection of the individualism theme of the American political culture, its impact on voter participation is significant, since a quarter or more of the population may disenfranchise themselves by failing to register. Because those not registered tend to come from groups which have traditionally supported the Democratic party, a priority for the Democratic party in the 1984 and 1988 presidential elections was to get as many people registered to vote as possible.

Historically, registration procedures have been specifically used as a cover for racial discrimination, especially against blacks in the American South, through poll taxes and literacy tests (Kousser, 1974). A **poll tax** is a tax, usually only several dollars, which must be paid before a person casts a ballot. Even though the amount was small, it effectively disenfranchised poor blacks and whites. **Literacy tests** (e.g., ability to read, knowledge of the Constitution) could be rigorously applied against minority groups and not applied at all to majority group members.

The result of such practices was that a large segment of the potential electorate in the South could not vote until the end of the 1960s. Elimination of such discrimination began with the outlawing of the poll tax in 1964 and, more significantly, with the passage in 1965 of the Voting Rights Act, which allowed the federal government to send in people to register potential voters in the Southern states. The effects were dramatic: "in Mississippi, for example, the black registration rate jumped from 8.3 percent in 1965 to 67.6 percent in 1970, and the white rate from 57.9 percent to 92.2 percent" (Milbrath and Goel, 1977: 131). Although flagrant abuses of the registration system, such as the discriminatory use of poll taxes and literacy tests, have been abandoned, the need to register before voting remains a major impediment to Americans' political participation in the 1990s.

A second important continuing legal restriction is the residency requirement, which has been quite lengthy in the American system. A **residency requirement** specifies that a person must have resided within an electoral district for a given period of time before being entitled to vote. The longer the residency requirement, the more people are disenfranchised. In addition, residency qualifications often apply to the state, local, and precinct levels, with a different time period for each level. The state residency qualification has typically been a year. Although there was a trend toward shorter residency requirements in the 1970s, at least for national elections, they continue to be a significant participation hurdle for many Americans.

In addition to the legal requirements, several political factors unique to the American system seem to discourage high levels of citizen involvement. For example, both frequent elections and complicated ballots appear to limit participation. Some voters may simply become weary of voting on an almost regular basis and so decide to participate differentially in various kinds of contests. Thus, we find voter turnout highest in presidential election years, lower in congressional election years, and lower still in state and local contests. In addition, American ballots are often long, with the voter being asked to decide on contests for national, state, and local offices, as well as various referendums and tax-related proposals. The ballot in some of the larger states may be several columns wide and several feet long, asking the voter to make numerous separate voting decisions. The result is that, as the voter goes through the ballot, more and more of the contests are not judged: faced by voter fatigue or lack of knowledge of the issues, the voter leaves the end of the ballot blank.

Frequent elections, numerous contests, lengthy ballots, registration requirements, and residency qualifications are some of the most distinctive legal and political factors that influence voter participation in the American system. The bearing of the social and personal attributes on voting is similar to those already discussed for the Canadian and British systems. For example, with respect to personal characteristics, those who feel a strong or intense psychological involvement in the political arena are more likely to participate, as well as those with partisan attachments and feelings of political efficacy. In relation to social attributes, those characterized by more education, higher personal incomes, middle age, as well as those who are white, male, non-Southern, and Jewish usually have the highest rates of voting turnout (Hill and Luttberg, 1980: 91). Such findings are consistent with the view that a "major force leading to participation . . . is associated with social status and the civic attitudes that accompany it" (Verba and Nie, 1972: 336).

Given such considerations, it is not surprising that voting turnout is low and, in fact, has been declining in recent decades. For example, turnout in presidential elections in the early 1960s was about 62 percent, while by 1984 it had dropped to 55 percent and to just over 50 percent in the 1988 presidential contest.

THE ROLE OF THE CITIZEN IN THE POLITICAL PROCESS

Our analysis of voting behaviour and the typical factors that influence political activity demonstrates that in the last century all three countries have extended, with few exceptions, the right to participate to most adult citizens over the age of 18. Bitter political fights often occurred over the successive expansions of the electorate, while the right to vote remained a key domestic political issue well into the 20th century. Although voting rates are typically high in democratic systems, any optimistic conclusion about the impact of individual involvement must be tempered by the realization that for most

> The spread of the franchise has not brought a great deepening of political knowledge, nor a growth of public spirit. Like universal education, universal suffrage, though cherished in theory, has brought indifference upon itself (Moore, 1987: 22).

> Democracy is ultimately a form of self-protection, a political system in which you have the best chance of preventing someone else from imposing his or her will on you (DiClerico and Uslaner, 1984: 133).

citizens, most of the time, voting is their only mode of political activity.

If most individuals only participate through voting, what does this say about the role of the citizen in the political process? In democratic systems, voting is usually voluntary and occurs in a free election process characterized by competition between two or more parties fighting for control of governmental office. The individual's vote is thus a means of choosing between leaders or groups of leaders and only rarely indicates a specific choice of policy. It is through their role in selecting the leaders of the polity that most citizens have an indirect say in decision-making. While such a function may be a far cry from the role perceived for the citizen among the writings of the classical democratic theorists (Pateman, 1970), it nevertheless remains a highly significant one, especially when we consider the alternatives.

Given the appeal of the democratic ideal in the modern age, even totalitarian systems seek to nominate candidates and to hold elections. Such elections may even achieve an almost 100 percent turnout of the electorate. However, the key point of comparison is the concept of choice. For example, participation in totalitarian countries is not voluntary, but expected: nonparticipation is usually interpreted by the state as evidence of dissent, if not downright disloyalty. Moreover, when citizens vote there is usually no choice presented on the ballot: they are merely ratifying choices already made by the sole party. Elections in such systems are a way of legitimating the regime and its leaders, not a means of citizen influence on or control over

the polity: as a consequence "those regimes often appear to be purer than Ivory Soap in voter turnout and approbation" (LaPalombara, 1974: 424). Almost perfect rates of turnout occur when such participation has no bearing on control of the polity: voting in a totalitarian system does not determine who governs. Voting does select who governs in a democratic system, even though such participation is intermittent and rarely controls policy in any direct fashion.

While democratic systems grant most citizens the right or opportunity to participate, individuals from the various social classes, regions, religions, and racial groups differentially involve themselves in the polity. Political activity, such as voting, is seen here as a political resource with which to increase an individual's or group's power and influence in the political process. The sectors of the electorate that vote often select as their leaders those who adopt policies to favour the very groups that elected them to office in the first place. Nonparticipation is not only a consequence, but also a cause, of the nature of political inequality found in democratic systems (Verba et al., 1978).

One reason why the suffrage extensions produced such intense political controversies is a reflection of this conclusion: newly enfranchised groups would make use of their vote to ensure more responsive leaders and policies and thereby reduce the existing inequalities in the system. Those groups that benefited from the existing social and political arrangements were thus opposed to the enfranchisement process, while those who desired change argued for universal adult suffrage. The movement to universal adult suffrage has not, however, produced equality in the social, economic, or political spheres. While democratic systems have created the opportunities for extensive citizen participation, a major challenge in the years ahead is to translate more of the potential for involvement into actual participation.

Summary

1. The learning of political beliefs through the political socialization process is one explanation for adult political values and behaviour. In democratic systems, the political learning process is indirect and implicit, while in totalitarian systems it is direct, explicit, and state-controlled.

2. Although political learning begins early in Canada, by high school graduation very few individuals show very much interest in or knowledge about their political system. Initial contact with the political regime is personalized through identification with political leaders and political parties. As the child matures, the major values of Canada's political culture are acquired, especially the attitudes associated with regionalism and dualism. American influence is particularly evident with respect to two agents, the schools and the mass media. The creation of a common national identity has been inhibited by the fragmented and indirect nature of the political learning process.

3. While similar to Canada in their political socialization processes, both Britain and the United States show some unique traits. With respect to content, Britain stresses deferential attitudes toward political authority and early acquisition of partisan attachments, while the public schools are an important agent of political learning and recruitment. In the United States, the schools and the mass media are significant agents of social-

ization, with an emphasis on a common national identity and national loyalty.

4. Citizen participation may take many forms, although the basic mode in modern systems is by voting in elections. Four major influences (legal, social, political, and personal) determine rates of participation in democratic systems. While legal restrictions are now minimal, the social, political, and personal factors keep many people from political involvement.

5. Rates of voting are greater in Canada and Britain than in the United States. In all three polities, participation is greater among the better-off, among those with partisan attachments, and among those with feelings of political efficacy. The use of an enumeration process in parliamentary systems encourages participation, while the registration process in the United States disenfranchises an important segment of the electorate. Nonvoting can reflect various attitudes, ranging from the cynical and alienated to the apathetic, to satisfaction with the political system.

6. Participation in totalitarian systems is nearly 100 percent, but voting in such a polity is an act of legitimation rather than one of popular control. In democratic systems, voting is a choice between sets of leaders that determines who will govern, although it rarely involves a decision on specific policies or issues.

Recommended Readings

Political Socialization

AVIS, GEORGE, ed. (1987) *The Making of the Soviet Citizen: Character Formation and Civic Training in Soviet Education*. London: Croom Helm.

BERRINGTON, HUGH (1972) "Review Article: The Fiery Chariot: British Prime Ministers and the Search for Love," *British Journal of Political Science* (October), Volume 4, Number 4, pp. 345–369.

BRONFENBRENNER, URIE (1970) *Two Worlds of Child-hood: U.S. and U.S.S.R.* New York: Simon and Schuster.

COLES, ROBERT (1986) *The Political Life of Children.* Boston: The Atlantic Monthly Press.

DAWSON, RICHARD E., KENNETH PREWITT, and KAREN S. DAWSON (1977) *Political Socialization.* Boston: Little, Brown and Co., 2nd ed.

JENNINGS, M. KENT (1984) "The Intergenerational Transfer of Political Ideologies in Eight Western Nations," *European Journal of Political Research* (September), Volume 12, Number 3, pp. 261–276.

_____ and RICHARD G. NIEMI (1981) *Generations and Politics: A Panel Study of Young Adults and Their Parents.* Princeton, N.J.: Princeton University Press.

LANDES, RONALD G. (1976) "The Use of Role Theory in Political Socialization Research: A Review, Critique, and Modest Proposal," *International Journal of Comparative Sociology* (March-June), Volume 17, Numbers 1–2, pp. 59–72.

_____ (1977) "Political Socialization Among Youth: A Comparative Study of English-Canadian and American School Children," *International Journal of Comparative Sociology* (March-June), Volume 18, Numbers 1–2, pp. 63–80.

_____ (1988) "Political Education and Political Socialization," pp. 15–20 in Jon H. Pammett and Jean-Luc Pepin, eds., *Political Education in Canada.* Halifax: The Institute for Research on Public Policy.

_____ and JOSEPH JABBRA (1979) "Partisan Identity Among Canadian Youth: A Case Study of Nova Scotian Adolescents," *Journal of Commonwealth and Comparative Politics* (March), Volume 17, Number 1, pp. 60–76.

_____ (1981) "The Impact of Socio-Political Cleavages on Support for Democratic Orientations Among Canadian Adolescents in Nova Scotia," *The Indian Political Science Review* (July), Volume 15, Number 2, pp. 158–174.

MACDONALD, L. IAN (1984) "The Education of Brian Mulroney," *Saturday Night* (November), Volume 99, Number 11, pp. 21–33.

MACKENZIE, W.J.M. (1978) *Political Identity.* Middlesex, England: Penguin Books.

MERELMAN, RICHARD M. (1986) "Revitalizing Political Socialization," pp. 279–319 in Margaret G. Hermann, ed., *Political Psychology.* San Francisco: Jossey-Bass.

MINNS, DANIEL RICHARD (1984) "Voting as Influential

Behavior: Child and Adolescent Beliefs," *American Politics Quarterly* (July), Volume 12, Number 3, pp. 285–304.

NIMMO, DAN and JAMES E. COMBS (1983) *Mediated Political Realities.* New York: Longman.

PAMMETT, JON H. and MICHAEL S. WITTINGTON, eds. (1976) *Foundations of Political Culture: Political Socialization in Canada.* Toronto: Macmillan.

_____ and JEAN-LUC PEPIN, eds. (1988) *Political Education in Canada.* Halifax: The Institute for Research on Public Policy.

PELLETIER, GERARD (1984) "The Political Awakening of Pierre Elliott Trudeau," *Saturday Night* (March), Volume 99, Number 3, pp. 50–55.

SEARING, DONALD D. (1986) "A Theory of Political Socialization: Institutional Support and Deradicalization in Britain," *British Journal of Political Science* (July), Volume 16, Number 3, pp. 341–376.

SHORISH, M. MOBIN (1988) "The Islamic Revolution and Education in Iran," *Comparative Education Review* (February), Volume 32, Number 1, pp. 58–75.

STACEY, BARRIE (1977) *Political Socialization in Western Society: An Analysis from a Life-Span Perspective.* New York: St. Martin's Press.

Political Behaviour

BAKER, PAULA (1984) "The Domestication of Politics: Women and American Political Society, 1780–1920," *The American Historical Review* (June), Volume 89, Number 3, pp. 620–647.

BARBER, BENJAMIN (1984) *Strong Democracy: Participatory Politics for a New Age.* Berkeley, California: University of California Press.

BASHEVKIN, SYLVIA B., ed. (1985) *Canadian Political Behaviour: Introductory Readings.* Toronto: Methuen.

BLAKE, DONALD E. (1984) "The Electoral Significance of Public Sector Bashing," *BC Studies* (Summer), Number 62, pp. 29–43.

BUTLER, DAVID and DONALD STOKES (1976) *Political Change in Britain.* New York: St. Martin's Press, 2nd college ed.

CLARKE, HAROLD D., JANE JENSON, LAWRENCE LEDUC and JON H. PAMMETT (1980) *Political Choice in Canada.* Toronto: McGraw-Hill Ryerson, abr. ed.

CONWAY, MARGARET M. (1985) *Political Participation in*

the United States. Washington, D.C.: Congressional Quarterly Press.

CREWE, IVOR and DAVID DENVER, eds. (1985) *Electoral Change in Western Democracies: Patterns and Sources of Electoral Volatility*. New York: St. Martin's Press.

ETZIONI-HALEVY, EVA (1986) "Radicals in the Establishment: Towards an Exploration of the Political Role of Intellectuals in Western Societies," *Journal of Political and Military Sociology* (Spring), Volume 14, Number 1, pp. 29–40.

FORD, FRANKLIN L. (1985) *Political Murder*. Cambridge, Mass.: Harvard University Press.

GLASS, DAVID et al. (1985) "Voter Turnout: An International Comparison," pp. 345–360 in Ronald G. Landes, ed., *Canadian Politics: A Comparative Reader*. Scarborough, Ontario: Prentice-Hall Canada.

GLAZER, AMIHAI and BERNARD GROFMAN (1989) "Must Liberals Always Vote for Liberals and Need the More Competent Candidate Always Be Preferred?" *British Journal of Political Science* (January), Volume 19, Number 1, pp. 154–159.

HAPPY, J.R. (1986) "Voter Sensitivity to Economic Conditions: A Canadian-American Comparison," *Comparative Politics* (October), Volume 19, Number 1, pp. 45–56.

HEATH, ANTHONY and SARAH MCDONALD (1988) "The Demise of Party Identification Theory?" *Electoral Studies* (August), Volume 7, Number 2, pp. 95–107.

HUNTINGTON, SAMUEL P. and JOAN M. NELSON (1976) *No Easy Choice: Political Participation in Developing Countries*. Cambridge, Mass.: Harvard University Press.

JACKMAN, ROBERT W. (1987) "Political Institutions and Voter Turnout in the Industrial Democracies," *American Political Science Review* (June), Volume 81, Number 2, pp. 405–423.

KITSCHELT, HERBERT P. (1986) "Political Opportunity Structures and Political Protest: Anti-Nuclear Movements in Four Democracies," *British Journal of Political Science* (January), Volume 16, Number 1, pp. 57–85.

KLEPPNER, PAUL (1984) *Who Voted? The Social Contours of Electoral Turnout, 1870–1980*. New York: Praeger.

MILBRATH, LESTER W. and M.L. GOEL (1977) *Political Participation: How and Why Do People Get Involved in Politics?* Chicago: Rand McNally, 2nd ed.

MISHLER, WILLIAM (1979) *Political Participation in Canada: Prospects for Democratic Citizenship*. Toronto: Macmillan of Canada.

NIE, NORMAN H., SIDNEY VERBA and JOHN R. PETROCIK (1979) *The Changing American Voter*. Cambridge, Mass.: Harvard University Press, enlarged ed.

OPP, KARL-DIETER (1986) "Soft-Incentives and Collective Action: Participation in the Anti-Nuclear Movement," *British Journal of Political Science* (January), Volume 16, Number 1, pp. 87–112.

PAMMETT, JON H. (1987) "Class Voting and Class Consciousness in Canada," *Canadian Review of Sociology and Anthropology* (May), Volume 24, Number 2, pp. 269–290.

PATEMAN, CAROL (1970) *Participation and Democratic Theory*. London: Cambridge University Press.

PIVEN, FRANCES FOX and RICHARD A. CLOWARD (1988) *Why Americans Don't Vote*. New York: Pantheon Books.

POOLE, KEITH T. and L. HARMON ZEIGLER (1985) *Women, Public Opinion, and Politics: The Changing Political Attitudes of American Women*. New York: Longman.

ROBERTSON, DAVID (1984) *Class and the British Electorate*. Oxford: Basil Blackwell.

ROSE, RICHARD, ed. (1980) *Electoral Participation: A Comparative Analysis*. Beverly Hills: Sage.

SCARBOROUGH, ELINOR (1985) *Political Ideology and Voting*. Oxford: Oxford University Press.

SQUIRE, PEVERILL, RAYMOND E. WOLFINGER, and DAVID P. GLASS (1987) "Residential Mobility and Voter Turnout," *American Political Science Review* (March), Volume 81, Number 1, pp. 45–65.

VERBA, SIDNEY, NORMAN H. NIE, and JAE-ON KIM (1978) *Participation and Political Equality: A Seven-Nation Comparison*. London: Cambridge University Press.

WOLFINGER, RAYMOND E. and STEVEN J. ROSENSTONE (1980) *Who Votes?* New Haven: Yale University Press.

CHAPTER 13

Political Behaviour: Interest Groups

All polities are pressure cookers. They differ in all sorts of ways — and many of the differences between them reflect the differences in the pressures they contain, in the way the "cooker" has been designed or has found a durable shape, and in how they respond to the changing force and direction of the pressures (Gould, 1973: 242).

And I concede your point too, that it's likely we heard more from the vested interests than we did from the little taxpayer who didn't have . . . the high-paid lawyers to speak for him . . . . I suppose in participatory democracy there will always be some whose voice is louder than others . . . (Trudeau, quoted in Lewis, 1972: iv).

. . . the first rule of politics: Every one, and every group, want more than they deserve, and demand more than they want (White, 1982: 231).

THE INDIVIDUALISTIC outlook of Western society, symbolized by the role of the citizen in the electoral process (i.e., voting), has obscured, at times, the important place of groups in the polity. While the immediate impact of a single vote might be minimal, individuals in democratic systems soon discovered that, by combining forces with other like-minded citizens, they could enhance their influence in the political process. These groups or collectivities of individuals "who share common material concerns" and who seek to influence the political process to deal with their shared priorities are called **interest groups** (Burnham, 1983: 158).

Interest groups have traditionally played a significant role in the democratic electoral process by providing money for candidates and parties. However, such groups are probably even more important in the inter-election period as a means for connecting citizens with their government. In the modern era interest groups have expanded their role in the political process, often at the expense of both political parties and the individual citizen. Interest groups have become crucial not only to the practice of democratic politics, but to the theory of liberal democracy as well, best exemplified by the theory of pluralism or pluralist democracy. **Pluralism** might be defined as the view that the competitive battle of group and individual self-interest somehow produces the public good. Such a competitive battle is greatly influenced by both the political structure and the political culture of a particular polity.

The Nature of Interest Groups

Several difficulties confront the political analyst in dealing with the role and impact of interest groups in the political process. First, political terminology has often been confusing and inconsistent, with interest groups variously

> Political pluralism describes a society in which power is widely distributed among numerous groups arrayed in shifting patterns of conflict, competition, and cooperation (Plano et al., 1982: 92).
>
> Amongst the laws which rule human societies there is one which seems to be more precise and clear than all the others. If men are to remain civilized, or to become so, the art of associating together must grow and improve, in the same ratio in which the equality of condition is increased (de Tocqueville, 1835).

referred to as pressure groups or lobbies. While some writers have tried to distinguish differences between these concepts, we will broadly use the term interest group to include all such related concepts. Second, we must distinguish between interest groups and political parties. The primary distinction is that parties are organizations that run candidates for public office, while interest groups are organizations that seek to influence those people selected to govern by the election process. Interest groups may be intimately involved in the electoral battle by providing money, by campaigning in favour of or against a particular policy, or by backing a specific candidate or party; but they use such techniques to influence or control those in government rather than by becoming the government itself. Third, although interest groups may cross national borders and lobby in other systems, most interest groups are domesticated organisms (see, for example, Gotlieb et al., 1984). Thus, our focus will be on the power and role of interest groups inside particular political systems.

A final problem for political analysis is the relationship between interest groups and liberal democracy: can interest groups exist in non-democratic systems? Our view is that interest groups, as previously defined, are democratic creatures, fundamentally dependent on the political and civil liberties of freedom of speech and freedom of association. Thus, we reject the view that interest groups exist in totalitarian systems such as the Soviet Union (Skilling and Griffiths, 1971). While "interests," based on factors such as the economy, religion, region, class, ethnicity, or bureaucratic structures are endemic and universal, interest groups are not so ubiquitous. Interest groups are a democratic phenomenon. Thus, our focus will be on an analysis of interest group politics in the liberal democracies of Canada, Britain, and the United States.

WHY INTEREST GROUPS?

No social or political system is homogeneous in makeup — diversity is a basic fact of life. As Aristotle (Barker, 1962: 151) observed, "the polis . . . is an aggregate of many members," and the size of the polis and its varying interests have expanded greatly since Aristotle's time. This diversity can be channeled into the political process by a number of mechanisms, including the political parties, voting patterns, political culture, or interest groups. Thus, the potential bases for interest group formation are coterminous with reality: almost any factor (religion, region, class, political idea) can spur a group's formation. Interest groups can range from the obvious (business, farm, labour, and consumer associations) to the sublime (the Flat Earth Research Society, which has 3000 members worldwide). Interest group creation and behaviour also reflect the problem of scarcity perceived through the filters of self-interest. Political conflict grows out of both diversity and scarcity and interest groups are one way of participating in that competitive battle, whether it concerns ideas (peace, abortion) or material interests (money, beneficial tax laws, direct government subsidies).

When a reporter asked President Harry Truman in 1948, "Would you be against lobbyists who are working for your program?," the President replied, "We probably wouldn't call these people lobbyists. We would call them citizens appearing in the public interest."

TYPES OF INTEREST GROUPS

Under the general rubric of interest groups lie a series of different types of organizations. Most traditional interest groups are economic in nature, that is, they represent particular sectors of the economy, especially producer groups. Such associations include business, farm, labour and professional organizations and they have long dominated the interest group process. These groups are often designated as **special-interest groups**.

A more recent phenomenon is interest groups espousing the general interest or the public's interest, such as that of consumers. These associations are typically fewer in number, poorer in their financial base, and not as well-organized as the special-interest groups. However, **public-interest groups**, such as Greenpeace or Common Cause, can be successful in particular areas of concern.

A third type of interest group focuses not on economic matters but on ideas. In the past decade or two, these groups have become particularly noticeable, with groups forming both in favour of or against particular policy positions. Classic examples of these **single-issue interest groups** would be those concerned with issues such as abortion, capital punishment, and disarmament.

The latest entrants into the pressure group arena, and ones still largely confined to the American polity, are the **political action committees** (PACs). The political action groups select particular candidates that they want either elected or defeated and, instead of channeling the money through a political party—the traditional pattern of special-interest groups—they spend money on behalf of "their" candidate directly. These political action committees have mushroomed in significance in the American system in the past two decades: for many candidates they are now the most important source of campaign largesse. Until the 1988 federal election, the impact of PACs on the Canadian election process had been slight. The emergence of PACs, as well as the rapid expansion of the more traditional groups, has created the paradox of Madison's dilemma.

Madison's dilemma

In a democratic polity, with freedom of speech and freedom of association, interest groups will battle for their own self-interest. **Madison's dilemma** (Berry, 1984: 1–15), what he called "curing the mischiefs of faction," is thus created: who looks after the public's interest or those segments of society not included in the interest group contest? The answer to that question tells us much about the nature of liberal or pluralist democracy in the modern era.

The political resources needed to compete fairly in the interest group contest are, of course, not distributed evenly: the "flaw in the pluralist heaven is that the heavenly chorus sings with a strong upper-class accent" (Schattschneider, 1960: 35). Significant political resources such as time, money, and access are more available to some interests than to others.

> The latent causes of faction are thus sown in the nature of man; and we see them everywhere brought into different circumstances of civil society. . . . But the most common and durable source of factions has been the various and unequal distribution of property (James Madison, *The Federalist Papers*, Number 10).

Thus, interest group politics are not neutral in their effects: they help the advantaged over the disadvantaged, the rich over the poor, the organized over the unorganized. In the process the public interest becomes distorted or ignored. Critics argue that the resulting pattern can be called **interest-group liberalism**:

> It is interest-group liberalism because it sees as both necessary and good a policy agenda that is accessible to all organized interests and makes no independent judgment of their claims. It is interest-group liberalism because it defines the public interest as a result of the amalgamation of various claims (Lowi, 1979: 51).

INTEREST GROUP FUNCTIONS

As with other political institutions, interest groups can perform a variety of functions (Berry, 1984: 6–8). Our concern with why interest groups develop and with Madison's dilemma indicates that interest groups serve participation and representation roles. Interest groups provide a mechanism by which the citizen can participate in the polity both during and between election campaigns. In so doing the individual seeks to have his priorities represented in government, in order to protect his own or his group's self-interest. As an outgrowth of both participation and representation, a third consequence becomes apparent, namely, a policymaking function. Representation and participation are not ends in themselves, but are ultimately designed to affect the content of public policy. Finally, interest groups are involved in a bureaucratic function: once public policy has dealt with your concerns, does the government effectively implement and administer the legislative program? How a program works on a day-to-day basis is often of much greater consequence than the letter of the law. Successful groups monitor as well as propose program or policy changes. In carrying out the

> A man will fight harder for his interests than his rights (Napoleon Bonaparte).

representation, participation, policy-making, and bureaucratic functions, interest groups utilize a variety of techniques.

METHODS OF INFLUENCE

The crucial problem for interest groups is access to those decision-makers who are making public policy which affects the group and its members. The methods of influence, therefore, aim at guaranteeing the interest group access to key decision-makers.

One way of ensuring potential governmental responsiveness is through the electoral pocketbook: money may not directly buy policy (except in cases of political corruption), but it is likely to guarantee an opportunity to make one's case to the policy-makers. A typical example of this approach is through campaign finance. The electoral process in the modern era is incredibly expensive and politicians need money not only to run for office but to stay reelected. Campaign contributions are, therefore, an important means of access to decision-makers. Other related techniques based on money may be used as well: free travel, vacations, low-cost loans, and, sometimes, outright bribery. Things which money can buy — such as the proverbial wine, women, and song — have been known to make their way into the interest group process as well.

An additional means of influence for interest groups is their control of information. Governments often depend on interest groups for the information on which government policy is based. Collecting and presenting data to the government, even if government might suspect its accuracy, allows the interest group some impact in the decision-making process. Testimony before legislative committees, meetings with key bureaucrats, and annual reports or briefs to government are all part of the information process.

Our emphasis on access and information leads to an often misunderstood perception of interest group activity. Unlike the electoral process, publicity and the mobilization of public opinion may not be a very effective technique for specific interest groups. As a general rule of thumb, the most successful interest groups are the least visible ones. Behind the scenes negotiations with key political and bureaucratic elites are a preferred and more effective strategy than public confrontations extensively covered by the mass media. While publicity may have beneficial results for some groups, the general pattern is the opposite: like resignations from the cabinet, appeals to the court of public opinion are usually admissions of political weakness, not political strength.

EXPLAINING INTEREST GROUP SUCCESS

Before we can identify the factors which make for interest group success, we must first decide on what "success" means in an interest group context. Given our definition of interest groups, we assume that the primary criterion of success is favourable public policy, meaning policy compatible with an interest group's goals. A second measure of influence would be the ability of a group to get particular candidates elected to office or to be influential in the naming of individuals to the relevant bureaucratic positions. A third criterion of interest group influence would be the group's ease of access to the key political and bureaucratic elites. These three criteria of success all focus on the actual impact of an interest group on the political process. Thus, we consider the organizational survival of an interest group, in and of itself, to be a poor indicator of interest group success. The ultimate goal of interest group behaviour is to change the content and decisions of the political agenda; its penultimate goal is to determine who the decision-makers will be; its tertiary goal is to influence the relevant politicians and bureaucrats in the political decision-making process.

Interest group success is determined by the interaction of three fundamental factors: the political structure, the political culture, and the internal characteristics of the interest group itself. The most influential groups are those which find means for meshing group concerns with larger movements of opinion (i.e., political culture) in such a way as to make effective use of existing political institutions (i.e., political structure).

Internal group characteristics would include such factors as the number of members, the number of active members, the political resources, such as time and money, which members are willing to commit to the cause, and the intensity of belief with which members adhere to the goals of the organization. Particularly important would be the skills of political leadership displayed by the organization's officers, including communication and fundraising abilities. What such internal characteristics point to is the fact that while it may be relatively easy to start an organization, it is an entirely different matter — and a complex one at that — for that organization to become an effective and influential participant in the political process. A myriad of groups exists; only a small proportion have much impact on the political agenda.

One basic way in which a polity's political culture influences interest group behaviour is in terms of the legitimacy of such activity. Political attitudes define whether such behaviour should take place at all: for example, lobbying and lobbyists are political terms with negative connotations. A political culture based on the idea of popular sovereignty is more compatible with extensive interest group activity than one based on parliamentary sovereignty. Key themes of a country's political culture, such as deference, elitism, or individualism, affect the formation, activity, and success of interest groups.

Intermingling with the political culture and the organization's internal characteristics is the political structure. Particularly crucial is the impact of the separation of powers or fusion of powers principles, that is, whether groups find themselves operating in a presidential or a parliamentary structure. A successful group has to know how the political structure works and where power resides before it can affect the content of public policy. For example, developing a good relationship with a powerful committee chairman in the American legislature is often an important technique of interest group influence; in Canada, committee chairmen are not key actors in the parliamentary process and, thus, such a relationship would be a sign of ineffective group tactics. In a parliamentary system access to cabinet members or key bureaucratic positions is a surer route to power than intimate involvement in the legislative process.

An additional component of the political structure which affects the behaviour of interest groups is the federal or unitary structure of the polity. In a unitary system, such as Britain, the number of sites at which interest groups contest is reduced, while in a federal system, such as Canada, the number of points for interest group activity is increased. If both levels of government in Canada are concerned with an interest group's policy area, then that organization may have to operate in 10 provincial capitals, as well as in Ottawa. The more sites at which interest groups have to participate in order to protect their concerns or achieve their goals, the harder it is for them to affect the decision-making process. Thus, the political structure largely defines the arena of the interest group battle, as well as helping to determine matters of strategy and tactics.

Interest Groups Triumphant: The American Pattern

It is by no means coincidental that interest groups are more significant and widespread in the American polity than in any other comparable system. Several factors have produced such a pattern. First, key elements of the American political culture, such as individualism and popular sovereignty, encourage interest group formation and serve to legitimate their behaviour and influence. Second, the constitutional system which explicitly protects, in the First Amendment, the rights of free speech, press, and assembly, as well as the right to "petition the Government for a redress of grievances," buttresses and protects interest group activities. Third, a political structure which fragments and decentralizes political power has meant that a consequence unforeseen by the Framers of the Constitution "was to make it relatively easy for pressure groups to influence decisions on behalf of objectives that are often narrow and highly particularistic" (Dahl, 1982: 190). This confluence of political beliefs, constitutionally-guaranteed rights, and a fragmented political structure has generated, particularly in the twentieth century, a literal explosion of interest group formation and activity.

Interest group influence on the political process has often been seen, by both foreign observers and internal critics alike, as a distinguishing feature of American government. Particularly disconcerting has been the traditional linkage between interest groups and political corruption, as illustrated in the following example:

> *The Diversity of Interest Groups*: The 1987 National Trade and Professional Association of the United States lists over 6500 groups, including the following:
>
> **Accordion Teachers' Guild**
> **Aromatic Red Cedar Closet Lining Manufacturers' Association**
> **Association of Tongue Depressors**
> **Frozen Onion Ring Packers Council**
> **Pressure Sensitive Tape Council**
> **Society for Investigative Dermatology**

In the early 1800s, one of the best-known lobbyists was a gent named Edward Pendleton, who operated a gambling house on Pennsylvania Avenue, within an easy hike of the Capitol, where congressmen were bribed in the form of fixed winnings (Sherrill, 1984: 296).

Whether dealing with the Teapot Dome Scandal of the 1920s or the Watergate Scandal of the 1970s, this connection between interest groups and political corruption has neither abated nor been adequately dealt with by reforming the political system.

Periodic demands for reforms to limit interest group behaviour have often had, in fact, the opposite result, namely, an increase in interest group activity and influence. For example, reform efforts in the early 20th century, such as the introduction of direct primaries to nominate candidates for public office, have not only weakened the political parties, but, as an unintended consequence, strengthened the importance of interest group representation. In the American polity, the strength of political parties and interest groups is inversely related (Chase et al., 1980: 82–89). More recently, reforms by Congress, which attempted to undercut the excesses of the seniority system and the power of committee chairmanships, have resulted in a further decentralization of power and a corresponding increased role for lobbyists in the legislative process. As one critic observed, "There are so many lobbyists today largely because there are so many opportunities to lobby" (Easterbrook, 1984: 72). While there are approximately 7000 registered lobbyists in Washington, the actual figure (i.e., including unregistered lobbyists) is in the range of 20 000 or 37 lobbyists per legislator. As a result, a new development has occurred: lobbyists now lobby other lobbyists. Lobbying has become a growth sector of the American economy.

The historically important and greatly expanding role of interest groups in the United States has affected not only the practice of politics, but the American theory of liberal

> Everybody in America has a lobby (former Speaker of the House of Representatives, Tip O'Neill).
>
> Pressure groups have played a remarkable role in American politics, but they have played an even more remarkable role in American political theory (Schattschneider, 1975: 21).
>
> . . . residents of Indiana last year contributed $296 to B-PAC, the bowling political action committee. B-PAC tries to entice politicians to adopt a more pro-bowling stance (Owen, 1985: 80).

famous definition of elections as "the competitive struggle for the people's vote" would illustrate such a change. Finally, group theory, by definition, reduces the importance of the individual's role in the political process: groups become the determining actors in the political arena. The development and functions of interest groups have, therefore, changed not only the practice of democratic politics, but the conception of liberal democracy as well. Such modifications of both theory and practice may have advantages and disadvantages associated with them (Dahl, 1982; Lowi, 1979; Macpherson, 1977). A more detailed look at American interest groups will highlight several of these significant problem areas.

democracy as well. If any approach to political science is decidedly American in outlook, it must surely be the group theory of politics, as commonly incorporated into the theory of pluralist democracy (Dahl, 1956; Garson, 1978). As British political scientist Bernard Crick (1959: 188) has observed, "By the 1900s the unity of American experience and the stress on tactical considerations of politics in a federal system gave a meaning to politics that was radically unlike the ideological and doctrinal struggles of Europe." In what is now considered a classic example of political analysis, Arthur F. Bentley (1908), in his book *The Process of Government*, defined that new meaning and approach to politics in group terms: "When the groups are adequately stated, everything is stated. When I say everything, I mean everything."

Pluralist theory, based on the interest group perspective, made several significant changes to traditional or classical democratic theory. First, the public interest became defined as the end product of competitive self-interest, perhaps best exemplified by Harold Lasswell's (1958) definition of politics as "who gets what, when, and how." Second, the election process came to be conceived more in terms of means than of ends. Joseph Schumpeter's (1950: 269)

THE PATTERN OF AMERICAN INTEREST GROUPS

As one might suspect from the preeminent capitalist society, the basis of most traditional interest groups has been economic, with an emphasis on producer groups. These special-interest groups, formed around the business and farming sectors, dominated interest group politics in the 19th century, although by the end of that period they were challenged by the growing labour movement. Corporate interests were particularly influential in the legislative process, receiving tax breaks and favourable policy in return for campaign contributions and sometimes political payoffs. Examples of such groups would include the American Farm Bureau Federation, the AFL-CIO, and the National Association of Manufacturers. These groups are the big-hitters of the interest group battle because of their longevity, their large membership, and their money, which has traditionally been channeled through the parties in electoral contests.

Single-issue interest groups have appeared intermittently throughout American history. Historically, the abolitionists opposed to slavery

Gray Power: An American Interest Group:
One of the most influential, and now the largest, special-interest group in the United States, AARP (The American Association for Retired Persons) has 27 million members, making it larger than the AFL-CIO and many countries. With an annual membership fee of $5, AARP, during 1988, expanded by the rate of 8000 members per day. During the presidential contest in 1988, it spent over $8 million on advertising and a get-out-the-vote campaign. This special-interest group has two key issues: Social Security and long-term health care. Since the number of elderly has increased eightfold since 1900, compared to a three-fold rise in the general population, the influence of AARP is likely to increase in the years ahead.

in pre-Civil War days, the suffragettes who fought for women's right to vote, and the prohibitionists opposed to alcohol have all had considerable impact on American politics, as did the anti-Vietnam War groups in the late 1960s. More recently, the anti-abortion or right-to-life groups have gained considerable attention from the media and from some political leaders such as Ronald Reagan. These groups have not been as significant as the special-interest groups in the long run, because the public's interest in such issues ebbs and flows and because single-issue groups are frustrated by the bargaining and compromising required to be successful in the American polity. Moral issues and fervently held ideals tend to preclude conciliation, while the special-interests concerned primarily with economic rewards can more easily gain access to, control over, and compromise within the legislative and executive branches of government.

Public-interest groups or people's lobbies really began to flourish in the 1960s, perhaps best exemplified by the various organizations created by Ralph Nader in the area of consumer protection and by Common Cause with respect to governmental reform. A public-interest group is concerned with how government decisions affect the general welfare, not the narrower outlook of most groups centred on material self-interest. A public-interest group, however, does not deal with all issues that might affect the public, but instead focuses on one or two particular areas of expertise. For example, Common Cause, started by John W. Gardner, previously head of the Carnegie Foundation and former American Secretary of Health, Education, and Welfare under Lyndon Johnson, was founded in 1970, had a membership of 200 000 people within two years, and concentrated on particular issues of the governmental process (McFarland, 1984: 6–10). Among its principal successes are included support for changes in American campaign financing and a role in the elimination of the oil depletion allowance, a major tax loophole long held sacred by the oil industry. As a general rule, however, neither the single-issue groups nor the public-interest groups can match, on a long-term basis, the money, access, and influence of the special-interest groups.

The most important recent change in the pattern of interest representation in the American system has been the development of political action committees (PACs). Although PACs, such as the AFL-CIO's political education organization COPE, have existed for some time, these groups really mushroomed as a result of the reform legislation concerning party and campaign finance in the 1970s. Rather than simply giving money to a political party, PACs work directly in favour of or against a particular candidate, regardless of that candidate's party label. Because of a loophole in the reform legislation (the law limits what candidates and parties spend, but not what others may spend on their behalf), PACs became the most important source for interest group campaign contributions and the largest single source of campaign fundraising for many seeking legislative office by the late 1980s.

Lobbying techniques

Money, access, and lobbying techniques are all intimately related. The more traditional special-interest groups still concentrate on campaign contributions, on gaining access to legislators in the key spots in the decision-making process, and on developing personal ties to the power-brokers through lunches, gifts, and sometimes bribes. One rather ingenious way of giving money to officials, which is legal, is to pay them an "honorarium" for making a speech to your organization. If the fee or honorarium is excessively high, then it reflects a campaign contribution or a hold on the legislator out of all relationship to his effort — in other words, something very close to resembling a good old-fashioned bribe.

Public-interest groups and single-issue groups, while they may utilize these techniques as well, have a tendency to turn to the public through media campaigns, protest marches, or mass letter-writing projects. Threats of electoral retribution are sometimes used, but as a general rule most groups are not large enough or organized sufficiently to make such a threat credible. Money and access remain the keys to interest group success.

A specific technique, which has remained one largely utilized in the American system, is to use the courts to challenge government practices or legislation. Because the court system operates under the principle of full judicial review, litigation may be an effective tool for some interests. The most notable success in this area was the use of the courts by the NAACP (National Association for the Advancement of Colored People) and various civil rights organizations to attack racial discrimination and its effects. However, litigation is often both a very lengthy as well as an expensive process for which most groups are not prepared.

> It was Justin Dart, longtime friend of President Reagan and head of Dart Industries, who once observed that talking to politicians "is a fine thing but with a little money they hear you better" (Sabato, 1985: 122).

In addition to the above techniques, major interest groups have sometimes used longer-term strategies to influence the policy process. One rather hidden but effective technique is the **revolving door syndrome** between governmental personnel, interest group representatives, and government regulatory positions. Government agencies typically depend on industry or interest groups being regulated to provide personnel for the relevant government departments. However, individuals know that their government service is likely to last only a year or two, at the end of which they will again be seeking employment in the private sector. Such a career opportunity structure is likely to dull the reform instincts of all but the most ardent idealists. Moreover, former Congressmen, legislative assistants, or even White House aides typically become lobbyists as a kind of end of career promotion pattern. For example, in early January 1985, Michael Deaver, long-time aide to Ronald Reagan and Deputy Chief of Staff during Reagan's first term, left his White House post to head his own public relations firm. Interestingly, Mr. Deaver's first client was the Canadian government, which acquired his services for a retainer of $105 000 (US) per year. Moreover, a number of legislators defeated in the November, 1984 election switched sides and became lobbyists. For example, Illinois Republican Congressman John Erlenborn, who as a 10-term legislator wrote much of the pension-plan legislation passed in recent years, became a lobbyist, at three times his previous salary, for the companies affected by that same legislation (*Time*, January 28, 1985, p. 36).

Of Madison's dilemma and iron triangles

The rapid expansion of interest group formation and activity in the last decade has created a paradox for American democracy: the more special interests are represented, the less well-represented are the individual citizens and groups who are left out of the pressure group game. In particular, the traditional organizations used in the process of representation, namely the political parties, have been decimated, both organizationally and as representative institutions. Madison's dilemma in American politics has created a system of **dual representation**, whereby the ordinary citizen is represented through the election process by selecting legislative members, while interests and groups have developed their own representation process, that is, the pressure group game (Wootton, 1985: 328–340). Moreover, this interest group activity has overwhelmed and taken control of the traditional pattern of legislative representation.

Nowhere is this development more clearly demonstrated than in the **iron triangles** of American politics. The tripartite composition of the iron triangles includes the following: first, the relevant government department or agency; second, the corresponding legislative committee of Congress which deals with the legislation affecting that department or agency; and third, the interest groups concerned with that particular policy area. These three components bargain and work with each other to develop policy to deal with their priorities, thereby bypassing presidential control of the executive branch and, often as well, the public interest. Power that is separated by constitutional prescription is united by iron triangle tactics based on complementary self-interests. As a result, the role of the individual citizen in and the representative nature of American democracy are further diminished.

Senator John Tower as an "iron triangle": In many ways, the career of former Senator John Tower of Texas illustrates, in one person, all of the links in an iron triangle in American politics. Having served as a United States Senator for several terms, Senator Tower joined the Reagan administration as the chief strategic arms negotiator during the START talks in Geneva. He then returned to the United States and spent two years as a lobbyist for several major defence contractors, earning close to $1 million in fees. Following the 1988 presidential election, George Bush nominated John Tower as Secretary of Defense. However, the Senate refused to confirm Tower's nomination. If he had been confirmed, Tower would have completed all of the legs of the iron triangle: executive department, key senator, and interest group representative.

INTEREST GROUPS INCARNATE: AN EXPLANATION

To understand the important and growing role of interest groups in the American polity, we must look to several interrelated factors. First, the American Constitution protects fundamental political and civil liberties which provide the bases for potential interest group development and involvement in the political process. Second, the general fragmentation of political power in the United States, while it has often prevented government from acting in the public interest, has, at the same time, encouraged interest group activity, particularly in the area of material self-interest. The separation of powers principle between branches of government, as well as the further fragmentation and decentralization of authority within each branch, has unwittingly enhanced interest group access and provided a political structure amenable to manipulation. In particular, the legislative process, in terms of both the election of legislators and the passage of legislation, has expanded the opportunity structure for interest group activity. Finally, the political culture of liberalism, with its emphasis on individualism, equality of opportunity, and popular sovereignty, intersects with the institutional structure to provide a congenial environment for the pattern of interest group dominance of the American polity.

> Nothing so characterizes contemporary Canadian affairs as the multiplicity of interest groups. . . . Increasingly, citizens press their claims through interest groups rather than political parties (Simpson, 1989: A6).

Interest Groups in Canada

Given elements of both Canada's parliamentary political structure and its elitist and deferential political culture, it is not surprising to find that the traditional view of interest groups has centred on their nonimportance, both in practical and academic contexts.

> Thus a good deal of Canadian political history has been written as if divisions of the population along such lines as these did not exist. Political leaders, anxious to broaden the group interest basis of support of the parties they led, have joined with the student of politics in this conspiracy of silence (Clark, 1963: 65).

It was not until the 1970s that a number of studies of interest groups began to appear (Kwavnick, 1972; Presthus, 1973). Even at that time, however, it was still necessary to make the argument that interest groups were essential to both the operation and understanding of the political process in Canada. For example, Presthus (1973: 10–11) asserted that interest groups had been "comparatively neglected" and that they were, in fact, "more powerful and operationally essential than the parties."

The extent of interest group activity can be seen in a number of ways. For example, Presthus (1973: 355), in preparing his samples based on those groups listed in the telephone directories, discovered approximately 1200 groups in the major metropolitan areas of both Toronto and Montreal. Thus, an accurate listing of all provincial and federal interest groups in Canada would likely number in the thousands. While some of these groups predate Confederation (e.g., Société Saint-Jean-Baptiste founded in 1834 in Quebec), most interest groups reflect the social and economic concerns of more recent decades (e.g., the Committee for an Independent Canada, the Canadian Coalition on Acid Rain, the Friends of Public Broadcasting). Although often unperceived by the ordinary citizen, interest groups make themselves felt on a daily basis in the political process.

The functions and types of interest groups in Canada are fairly typical of most liberal democracies, as modified by the workings of a parliamentary system. Business and corporate interests predominate with respect to influence, access, and money. Consumer groups have traditionally been poorly organized and relatively unsuccessful. For example, the 40-year-old Consumers Association of Canada faced a $1-million debt in 1988 and had to receive emergency aid of $300 000 from the federal government in order to survive. Unlike the American pattern (e.g., Common Cause), public-interest groups have been neither very visible nor successful. Single-issue groups, such as the pro-life group Campaign Life, have become increasingly apparent in recent years, but, as yet, have not achieved the successes of their American counterparts. Political action committees have been restricted in their impact because of the nature of the parliamentary party system, at least until the mid-1980s. Historically, interest groups have sought to work through the party system electorally and

"... no we're opposed to Free Trade ... the Pro-Life group has moved over there between the Capital Punishment marchers and the Women's Rights bunch ..."

Source: Reprinted from the *Toronto Star*, by permission of The Toronto Star Syndicate.

A 1981 study by the Economic Council of Canada found that business and professional lobby groups spent more than $122 million promoting their interests, compared with $2 million a year mustered by public-interest groups (McQuaig, 1985: 72).

through the bureaucracy in the inter-election period. One distinguishing feature of Canadian interest group formation has been the number and salience of groups dealing with nationalism and the bicultural cleavage. These groups range from the establishment of the Orange Order in Ontario in 1830 to the Committee for an Independent Canada nearly a century-and-a-half later.

Given the range and number of interest groups, almost every sector of society now has its own special representative body. In the 1960s and early 1970s, the federal government, because it found it to be of help in the policy-making process, even went so far as to provide "seed" money with which to form new interest groups. Government-sponsored groups proved to be quite influential in such areas of public

Government Funding of Canadian Interest Groups: An outstanding example of this pattern is the federal government's monetary support for multicultural groups, which has amounted to nearly $200 million over the last 18 years (1971–1989). In the mid-1980s, government support was about $18 million a year. Grants included in the 1986–1987 budget contained the following items: $350 000 to McGill University for a chair in Urdu language and culture; $850 000 to various Jewish groups; and $650 000 to a number of Ukrainian associations.

A second prominent example of government subsidies to interest groups involves the feminist movement in Canada. Funded through the Secretary of State's budget is the Women's Program, which by 1989 was giving $13 million a year to various groups "promoting the status of women." The largest women's lobby, the National Action Committee on the Status of Women (NAC), receives half a million dollars a year from Ottawa.

Canadian Lobbyists: "They are supplicants in a city built to serve power, but they are a privileged breed. They know whom to ask. How to ask. And when to ask for it. What they seek they often get" (MacQueen, 1986: 14).

policy debate as potential gas-and-oil development in the North (e.g., the Berger Commission Report). One example of this practice occurred in April 1985, when the federal government announced a $25 000 grant to support a peace convention, even though the various peace groups had been strongly and vociferously opposed to the government's foreign and defence policies. In 1987 the federal government supported more than 500 interest groups with grants totalling about $155-million (Simpson, 1989: A6). In many respects, this connection between the government and interest groups is the Canadian version of the iron triangles of American politics. However, although we have a myriad of groups, no one would be likely to suggest that all interests are represented, equally or otherwise. Participation in

most interest groups remains a pleasure and prerogative of the middle and upper classes.

The participation of interest groups in policy-making centres on the executive branch (Faulkner, 1982), because interest groups have an acute sense of smell when tracking the scent of power. Interaction with the bureaucracy and not with MPs is the goal of most groups and one reason why interest group activity is not highly visible to the untrained eye. Moreover, producer groups, such as the various farm associations, often aid in implementing government policy.

Occasionally, an interest group will become involved in an educative role as well. For example, in early 1985 the Canadian Bankers' Association widely advertised and distributed a game ("Money In Your Life") about banking that they had developed for 9 to 13-year-olds. One suspects that, in addition to teaching young people such things as how interest rates are determined, the game was an attempt to offset adverse publicity that Canadian banks had received in recent years because they were the most profitable banks in the world. The educative function of "Money In Your Life" was not entirely altruistic.

For the most part, Canadian interest groups have utilized the standard techniques of lobbying characteristic of such activity in liberal democracies. However, unlike in the American system where the influence of parties and interest groups is inversely related, in Canada we have had strong parties characterized by rigid party discipline and highly influential interest groups at the same time. The reason for this traditional pattern would seem to be that, for the most part, interest groups have worked within the parties and through the party system, not in opposition to it. The parliamentary structure, based on the fusion of powers principle, combined with broadly based brokerage parties, has provided a congenial atmosphere for interest group activity, access, and influence.

In addition, the parliamentary structure has meant that emotional appeals to the court of public opinion have not been a particularly effective technique for most groups. However, some exceptions are worthy of mention. For example, women's and native rights groups were successful in pressuring the federal and provincial governments to reinsert constitutional guarantees of their rights during the patriation battle in the fall of 1981. Similarly, a group such as Greenpeace has been instrumental, despite government opposition, in undercutting the annual seal hunt in Canada. In both of these cases, however, one factor stands out: the appeal to public opinion worked because the interest groups were able to galvanize the public on the issue. In these cases, the public responded (in the Greenpeace situation — the international public) and only then did government policy respond. In other words, turning to public opinion is often a last-ditch effort and a high-risk strategy at the same time. If the public does not respond, then the interest group is, quite literally, dead in the water.

Although the traditional method of Canadian interest group activity has been to focus on the government rather than the public, the Canadian Charter of Rights and Freedoms has already begun to modify that pattern. Groups, particularly public-interest ones, that lack access or find that government policy has already gone against them, can now turn to the judiciary and litigation in an attempt both to stop government actions and to gain publicity for their cause. For example, in 1983 a coalition of 26 peace and disarmament interest groups, led by Operation Dismantle, challenged the federal government's decision to allow the testing of the American cruise missile in Canada. This court challenge was based on the Charter (especially Section 7) which proclaimed that "Everyone has the right to life, liberty and security of the person and the right not to be deprived thereof except in accordance with the principles of fundamental justice." The anti-cruise groups argued that a new weapon system and the resulting increased possibility of nuclear war might have something to do with the "security of the person." While a lower court judge initially agreed, the cruise challenge was later rejected by the Federal Court of Appeal. The cruise tests were begun in 1984. Although the tests were not stopped, this court challenge focused significant attention on the nuclear question for many months and gave the disarmament movement a public forum that would have been denied them in pre-Charter days.

The Charter of Rights also has had an impact on the development of political action committees in Canada. The 1974 Election Expenses Act channeled money from the public purse through the political parties, candidates, or their official agents, thus preventing the growth of political action committees along American lines. Just to make sure that no PAC-like clones would develop, the parties amended the Canada Elections Act in the fall of 1983 (Bill C-169) to prevent groups other than parties from spending funds during an election campaign. The bill, which became effective on May 17, 1984, was supported by all three national parties and passed the House of Commons after only 40 minutes of debate. However, a special interest lobby, the National Citizens' Coalition, challenged that law, because they felt it violated at least several sections of the new Charter (i.e., freedom of speech and association). An Alberta court agreed, so that the Chief Electoral Officer announced that he would not prosecute such groups during the 1984 campaign until the law was clarified. The matter was still unresolved by the time of the 1988 federal election, so that

A CANADIAN INTEREST GROUP IN ACTION

CONGRATULATIONS WOMEN OF CANADA!

On January 8, 1983, the women of Canada organized protests in 19 cities and towns across the country to demonstrate against the introduction of Playboy programming on Pay-TV.

On January 18, 1984, we repeated these protests in 31 communities when the CRTC failed to include "sex" in its regulations prohibiting abusive comment or abusive pictorial representations on the basis of race, religion or creed.

During 1983 and 1984 we wrote thousands of letters and signed hundreds of petitions urging our elected officials to take action to stem the proliferation of pornography in Canadian society.

In two short years we have achieved the following results:
— Statements in the 1983 and 1984 Speeches from the Throne affirming that pornography has no place in Canadian society.
— The establishment of a Parliamentary Sub-Committee on Sexually Abusive Broadcasting which recently issued its report supporting our concerns.
— The establishment of a Special Committee on Pornography and Prostitution (the Fraser Committee).
— Revised CRTC regulations prohibiting abusive programming on the basis of sex.
— The passing of by-laws in many Canadian municipalities regulating the conditions of sale and lease of pornographic materials.
— And hundreds of local initiatives in hundreds of communities which have raised the awareness of the public and encouraged debate and discussion on the negative impact of pornography.
We've done well, women of Canada!

There's lots more to do but this January 18 let's celebrate our victories.
On January 19 we'll get back to work. Please support our efforts by joining the Coalition ($15) or making a contribution.

Canadian Coalition Against Media Pornography, P.O. Box 1075, Station B, Ottawa, Ontario K1P 5R1

Source: The Globe and Mail, January 18, 1985, p. 3. By permission of the Canadian Coalition Against Media Pornography.

for the first time special-interest groups made a quantum leap forward in their participation in the electoral contest. For example, the free trade issue galvanized such groups, with the Pro-Canada Network spending about $1 million and the Canadian Alliance for Free Trade and Job Opportunities about $1.5 million. Unless the loophole created by the court ruling is closed, special-interest groups will continue to expand rapidly along American lines (i.e., PACs). Thus,

the Charter might allow for significant PAC development in the years ahead. That growth potential will, however, be limited by the strength of the parliamentary parties and party discipline.

Because the manner and means of protecting basic civil and political liberties in the Charter is more of an American than a British mechanism, it should not be surprising to find that the results of the Charter will be to move Canadian interest group patterns along American lines as well. The cruise missile and political action committee examples indicate such a development is already under way. How far it proceeds remains conjectural at this point, but an unintended consequence of the Canadian Charter of Rights and Freedoms will likely be an expanded pattern of interest group activity.

> Now that the Charter is part of the constitution we may expect a substantial number of issue-groups, from environmentalists to pro- and anti-abortion groups, to fight their battles in the courts, which will greatly enhance their capacity to mobilize public opinion (Mallory, 1984: 8).

EXPLAINING THE CANADIAN PATTERN

Both the basic political beliefs or themes of the political culture, as well as the parliamentary political structure, influence the pattern and tactics of Canadian interest groups. Each in turn affects the success of the organizations in the political process.

Political culture affects interest group behaviour in a number of ways. Political beliefs help to define the legitimacy of such organizations. In Canada, while interest group activity has, quite likely, always been important, the legitimacy of such activity, in the public's eye, has not always been benign. In a system of parliamentary sovereignty, group influence has been seen as undercutting that basic principle of government. Traditionally, a quasi-participative political culture has not enhanced nor legitimated such activity on the part of the ordinary citizen, acting either alone or in concert. Interest group activity is tainted by an aura of popular sovereignty, a belief which is still not particularly well-accepted in Canada even in the early 1990s. Moreover, the elitist strain in Canada has helped to downplay interest group growth as well, particularly single-issue and public-

> Access, which was once the right of a citizen and the obligation of a minister, is now being peddled for a fee (Senator Michael Pitfield, April 13, 1989).

interest groups. What has resulted, historically then, has been a predominant pattern of special-interest groups working outside of public view and interacting with the bureaucratic and political elites in the development of public policy.

Matters of strategy and organization are also greatly affected by the structure of the political system. The federal principle of organization has several consequences. For example, single-issue groups may be particularly affected by the distribution of powers between the levels of government. Since the federal level was given jurisdiction over criminal law, groups wishing to change the criminal law must deal with the national government and develop a national organization and movement or protest base. The issues of capital punishment and of prostitution control cannot be dealt with by the provincial governments. Getting the national government to act is often, of course, much more difficult to do than dealing with the lesser units in the federal system. If jurisdiction in a policy area is shared, as in agriculture, then the interest groups are forced to deal with 11 governments, rather than just one. Moreover, federalism affects an interest group's own organization, not just its tactics. Most groups in Canada's federal system are themselves organized as federations, so as to parallel the structure of government.

In addition to federalism, the parliamentary structure has an important bearing on interest groups. Most interest groups discovered long ago that parliamentary sovereignty was a myth. As a result, little time is spent lobbying backbenchers or opposition members. Instead, interest group activity typically focuses on cabinet ministers and the bureaucracy in the

Registering Canadian Lobbyists: On June 12, 1989, the federal government published regulations affecting the registration of lobbyists. Effective September 1, an estimated 15 000 persons registered under the Lobbyists Registration Act. However, since the registrar has no enforcement power, registration will be voluntary and will only involve sending in a business card once a year for most lobbyists. Thus, the Act seems destined to be ineffective.

relevant government departments. It should be kept in mind that the bureaucracy itself is structured to represent many of the major interests in Canadian society to start with: the Department of Agriculture, the Department of Consumer and Corporate Affairs, or the Ministry of State for Small Business. Moreover, the cabinet, because of the representation principle, reflects the major interests in Canadian affairs too. Thus, interacting with the relevant minister and the key bureaucrats in the appropriate government departments or agencies is how successful interest groups operate. The reason interest group activity has been difficult to spot is not that it does not take place, but that it occurs out of view of the ordinary citizen. If the political executive is the repository of power in the political structure, then it is also the key site which determines interest group success.

Canada's parliamentary structure, disciplined parties, and powerful bureaucracy are the reasons why, unlike in the American system, iron triangles have not developed. Interest groups in Canada do not seek to bypass the political executive but to control it or influence it. Legislative committees have little power, reflecting Parliament's overall position. With the legislature and bureaucracy both under the control of the political executive, an interest group either deals with that reality or it does not deal at all. Wishful thinking has no bearing on interest group reality. As C.E.S. Franks (1983: 205)

has put it, "There is no Canadian counterpart to the powerful union in the United States of interest groups, Congressional committees and bureaucracy."

A key prerequisite to interest group success is an understanding of the political structure and the skill to mesh interest group concerns with movements of public opinion. Some interest groups have been very successful in Canada; others have not been (Berry, 1974). While interest groups will continue to influence the Canadian polity and while that influence may grow as a result of the Charter, Canada's parliamentary democracy has not yet been taken over by interest group expansion or dominance. Interest groups are fewer, less visible, and less successful overall in Canada than in the United States (Ostry, 1980: 31).

The Pattern of British Interests

The basis for interest group behaviour in Britain can be traced back nearly eight centuries to the Magna Carta in 1215, which guaranteed people the right to petition their government. Moreover, the term lobby itself is of British origin, in that the phrase was coined to describe the pressure put on Members of Parliament in the lobby of the House of Commons before a vote was cast. However, interest groups began to make themselves particularly felt in the political process in the early decades of the 19th century.

Initially, interest group activity was not seen as legitimate, because it was perceived as threatening the role of Parliament and the doctrine of parliamentary supremacy: as Gladstone put it in 1867, these groups were "agencies out of doors." In the 19th century, in a system in which few adults had the right to participate, it is not surprising to find that public pressure groups might not be well-received either. However, this "pressure from without," that is, public pressure on Parliament, had achieved a number of successes by the end of the century, including some significant reforms in social and economic policy (Hollis, 1974: 5). Interest groups had become an accepted means of public influence and were increasingly incorporated into the party system (e.g., they operated through the major parties).

> Pressure from without had both stretched the arena of government and access to government, and in the process had thrown up feminist groups for the rights of prostitutes, evangelicals on the wrongs of prostitutes, public health on the diseases of prostitutes, Shaftesbury and Gladstone on refuges for prostitutes, and sabbatarians for no prostitution on Sundays. Victorian political life was engagingly pluralist (Hollis, 1974: 26).

INTERESTS OF THE REALM

A unique feature of the pattern of British interests, and one which reflects a historical tradition, is the "interests of the realm" (Verney, 1976: 191–196). Traditional interests of the realm would include the Royal Society, the City of London, and the Church of England, while more recent examples would be illustrated by the British Broadcasting Corporation, the National Coal Board, and British Railways.

Current interests of the realm are brought into existence by an act of Parliament or by royal charter, are concerned usually with the public interest, are outside of direct government control by Parliament, and are used in particular in relation to key sectors of the economy. In this regard, the closest Canadian analogue to these interests of the realm would be the semi-autonomous crown corporations, such as the CBC or Via Rail. The British interests of the realm are important actors in the political process, as demonstrated by the role of the National Coal Board in the bitter and lengthy miners' strike in 1984 and 1985. However, our main

focus will be on more typical types of groups in the British polity.

TYPES OF GROUPS

As in most liberal democracies, the major sectors of the economy are the bases for interest group formation. These special-interest groups would include the Confederation of British Industries (CBI), the National Federation of Building Trade Employers, the British Medical Association, and the Association of University Teachers. Particularly important in the pattern of British interest group activity are the trade unions, which have a membership of over 11 million and are organized as a national federation known as the Trades Union Congress (TUC). Because of the class and ideological basis of 20th century British politics, the special-interest groups have traditionally developed close partnerships with the major parties. For example, most business groups are associated with the Conservative party, while the labour movement, through the TUC, is formally linked to the Labour party. Unlike most Canadian and American interest groups which seek to influence all the major parties, because one never knows for sure which party will win the election, British interests make their electoral choice before the ballots are cast. Special-interests in Britain do not act in opposition to the party system, but in conjunction with it.

Public-interest groups have not had many victories in the British polity, although rare successes do occur, such as the achievements of the National Campaign for the Abolition of Capital Punishment. The lack of public-interest group success reflects the strength of the more traditional special-interests and the incorporation of those special-interests in the policy-making process. As a result, governments tend to perceive the public interest through the eyes of the special-interests.

What are categorized as single-issue groups

in Canada and the United States are more typically called **promotional** or **cause** groups in Britain. Such groups have had a long history. For example, the Committee for the Abolition of the Slave Trade was begun in 1807. In more recent times, these groups have included both pro- and anti-abortion groups, both pro and con groups with respect to Britain's role in the Common Market, and the League Against Cruel Sports (an animal welfare association). As in Canada and the United States, such groups are rarely any match for the special-interest groups.

Political action committees are not a British phenomenon, because of the historical close relationship between interest groups and the party system. PACs are a means of doing an end run around the parties: however, in Britain there is no need to do so. For example, a group, such as the Confederation of British Industries, actually sponsors many Conservative party candidates and MPs and contributes financially to the party as well. This pattern of sponsoring MPs is particularly important for the Labour party, given the direct connection between it and the Trades Union Congress (Muller, 1977). In fact, pressure groups may not only work through the party system, but actually control it, in the sense that the parties become subordinate to the pressure groups (Duverger, 1972: 119). In such a system, political action committees are not needed.

CORPORATISM AND FUNCTIONAL REPRESENTATION IN BRITAIN

The development and success of interest group activity during the 19th and early 20th centuries led to a further enhancement and elaboration of their role. In particular, interest groups became widely accepted as legitimate and were explicitly incorporated into the decision-making process (Panitch, 1977). This cooptation of major social and economic interests directly within the policy-making machinery of government is

known as **corporatism** or **functional representation** (Leys, 1983: 275–279). Although it is true that "governments have always struck bargains with barons" (Richardson and Jordan, 1979: 192), what corporatism does is to involve interest groups in the internal process of governing, both in terms of deciding policy and in implementing it as well. While interest groups in Canada and the United States, by and large, operate to bring pressure on or to influence the government, in corporatism or functional representation, the groups become part of the government. Interest groups have evolved in Britain from being "pressures from without" Parliament to being key actors within the executive decision-making process. However, the myth of parliamentary sovereignty remains.

> The role of groups is rarely acknowledged officially — the doctrine of parliamentary supremacy is still invoked — but in practice much public policy is influenced or even determined by interest groups (Jacobs et al., 1983: 56).

Such a pattern of functional representation has also been classified as **collectivism** or the **new group politics** (Beer, 1982a, 1982b). It is the consequence of three basic facts about modern government: first, government's growth and expansive nature; second, an increasing centralization of power in government; and third, the location of that decision-making power in the executive. The new group politics is a direct result of such developments: "the 'realities of governing' that led Governments and parties to bargain with organized producers and the 'realities of winning power' that led them to bid for the support of groups of consumers among the voters" (Beer, 1982a: 318–319).

Interest groups, corporatism, and policy-making

The consequences of corporatism and, by implication, of the influence of interest groups in

Britain are many. Moreover, such a pattern has developed in a unitary political structure in which the civil service, known as Whitehall, had already acquired considerable power. Thus, corporatism is both a cause and consequence of the concentration of political power in the political executive.

Specifically, corporatism or functional representation has lead ultimately to an undercutting of Parliament's role in the policy process, to a diminuation of the functions of the political parties, and to an enhancement of the power of the political executive. As a result, interest groups focus their efforts on the political executive and bureaucracy. The average citizen, who is represented through the geographically-based constituencies in the House of Commons, is shunted aside by the workings of corporatism (except, of course, for those people represented by the functional groups). The "symbiotic relationship between groups and government" (Richardson and Jordan, 1977: vii) has clearly enhanced the power of interest groups in the British polity and made it difficult to successfully govern without, at least, their grudging cooperation. Former Prime Minister Edward Heath discovered this fact in his 1974 confrontation with the unions (i.e., he lost that struggle, his position as PM, and, ultimately, his role as leader of the Conservative party to Margaret Thatcher).

> Probably the greatest limitation on a Prime Minister and his government comes from the various power blocs in the community, their power being largely negative; to refuse to cooperate, to strike, to fail to participate or to follow new rules (Mackintosh, 1982: 89).

| I have never regarded politics as the arena of morals; it is the arena of interests (Aneurin Bevan on British politics). |

Comparing Interest Groups

Interest groups have developed as a means to fulfill or to carry out certain basic tasks in the political process. These functions include participation, representation, policy-making, and implementation. Therefore, the mix of functions performed by interest groups, and the way in which those functions are carried out, are important bases for comparing interest group behaviour. In the modern era, interest groups have become particularly important mechanisms for involving people (or, at least, a segment of them) in the political process: "Interest and pressure groups are the living 'public' behind the parties" (Friedrich, 1968: 454).

A second basis for comparing group behaviour is the types of organizations prevalent in any system. We focused on four different types of groups: special-interest groups, public-interest groups, single-issue groups, and political action committees. The presence and influence of these groups varies from one system to another.

A third concern in any analysis of group patterns is the techniques of influence utilized. These methods of influence can range from contributing money during electoral contests, to providing information to government, to wining and dining key legislators and bureaucrats. In systems with constitutionally-guaranteed rights, litigation may be used as well.

In seeking to account for the functions, types, and techniques of interest group activity, several factors can be utilized as explanatory tools. First, organizational characteristics, such as the size of the group and the motivation of its membership, aid in accounting for interest group success. Second, the nature of the political structure (e.g., federal or unitary, presidential or parliamentary) helps to determine interest group strategies, tactics, and internal organization. Third, the political culture conditions the

> Group politics, far from being a bitter strug-
> gle, as some writers have assumed, is an
> exercise in mutual accommodation. The
> Hobbesian war gives way to a more limited
> type of competition whose sanction lies in
> the ubiquitous instinct of organizational
> self-preservation (Kwavnick, 1972: 3).

legitimacy of interest group access and influence, as well as the responsiveness of the policy
process to its proposals. Thus, interest group
systems differ not only with respect to functions, types, and techniques, but also in relation
to the factors responsible for such characteristics (e.g., organizational criteria, the political
structure, and the political culture).

> Instead of a battlefield, the scene of group conflict
> has become a kind of market in which relatively
> autonomous forces contend according to certain
> rules of the game, by virtue of which nobody is a
> permanent winner or loser (Dahrendorf, 1959: 67).

Summary

1. Interest groups are representative creatures
   reflecting the struggle for competitive advantage, usually material in nature, in liberal-
   democratic polities. Such organizations involve citizens in the political process, both
   during and between election campaigns.
   However, as Madison's dilemma shows, not
   everyone benefits equally from a pattern of
   interest-group liberalism.
2. In democratic regimes, special-interest
   groups based on producer segments of the
   economy have been the most successful in
   terms of access and favourable public policy.
   Public-interest groups are less successful
   and less pragmatic, although they have
   achieved results in particular areas of public
   policy. Single-issue groups have proliferated
   in recent decades, but they are no match, on

a long-term basis, for the special-interests.
Political action committees have been a particularly American phenomenon, although
the Canadian Charter of Rights and Freedoms provides the potential for similar developments in the future.
3. Access to governmental decision-makers is
   a key problem for interest groups, with the
   ultimate goal being favourable public policy
   from those decision-makers. Interest group
   success is dependent on three interrelated
   criteria: organizational composition, political
   structure, and political culture.
4. American interest groups have expanded
   greatly in the last few years and continue
   as significant elements in the struggle for
   power. As a result, many theories of liberal
   democracy are now group-centred, with pluralism being the primary example. Special-
   interest groups have long been associated
   with political corruption and scandals. The
   most important recent development has
   been the use of political action committees.
   Constitutionally-guaranteed rights, a political culture based on popular sovereignty, and
   a fragmented political structure have all
   enhanced the role of interest groups in the
   American system.
5. Canadian interest groups have traditionally
   been less visible, but not necessarily less
   important, than their American counterparts. The parliamentary political structure
   and a party system with strong party discipline has resulted in interest groups focusing
   their attention on the political executive and
   the bureaucracy. Consequently, iron triangles are not a Canadian phenomenon, with
   political action committees limited in their
   impact as well.
6. The British system is unique in the extent
   to which interest groups have been formally
   coopted and incorporated into the decision-
   making process (e.g., corporatism or functional representation). The doctrine of parliamentary sovereignty remains in place, but

the power of choice has passed to the political executive and Whitehall. While Canadian and American groups work through the party system, Britain has developed a pattern in which certain groups are explicitly and directly linked to particular parties (e.g., the TUC and the Labour party). In this pattern of collectivism, the ability to govern is heavily dependent on the relationship between the prime minister and the interest group system.

Recommended Readings

Interest Groups: General and Comparative

BENTLEY, A.F. (1908) *The Process of Government*. Chicago: University of Chicago Press.

BERGER, SUZANNE D., ed. (1981) *Organizing Interests in Western Europe*. London: Cambridge University Press.

CLAWSON, ALAN, ed. (1985) *Organized Interests and the State: Studies in Meso-Corporatism*. Beverly Hills, California: Sage Publications.

DUVERGER, MAURICE (1972) *Party Politics and Pressure Groups: A Comparative Introduction*. New York: Thomas Y. Crowell.

GOULD, JULIUS (1973) "Interests and Pressures," *Government and Opposition* (Spring), Volume 8, Number 2, pp. 242–258.

GRADY, ROBERT C. (1986) "Reindustrialization, Liberal Democracy, and Corporatist Representation," *Political Science Quarterly*, Volume 101, Number 3, pp. 415–432.

GRANT, WYN, ed. (1987) *Business Interests, Organizational Development and Private Interest Government*. Berlin: Walter de Gruyter.

OLSON, MANCUR (1965) *The Logic of Collective Action*. Cambridge: Mass.: Harvard University Press.

PANITCH, LEO (1977) "The Development of Corporatism in Liberal Democracies," *Comparative Political Studies* (April), Volume 10, Number 1, pp. 61–90.

SCHATTSCHNEIDER, E.E. (1975) *The Semisovereign People: A Realist's View of Democracy in America*. New York: Holt, Rinehart and Winston.

STREECK, WOLFGANG and PHILIPPE C. SCHMITTER, eds. (1985) *Private Interest Government: Beyond Market and State*. London: Sage.

TRUMAN, DAVID B. (1951) *The Governmental Process*. New York: Knopf.

WILSON, JAMES Q. (1973) *Political Organizations*. New York: Basic Books.

Canadian Interest Groups

COLEMAN, WILLIAM D. (1985) "Analysing the Associative Action of Business: Policy Advocacy and Policy Participation," *Canadian Public Administration* (Fall), Volume 28, Number 3, pp. 413–433.

CRITTENDEN, DANIELLE (1988) "REAL Women Don't Eat Crow," *Saturday Night* (May), Volume 103, Number 5, pp. 27–35.

FAULKNER, J. HUGH (1982) "Pressuring the Executive," *Canadian Public Administration* (Summer), Volume 25, Number 2, pp. 240–253.

FILLMORE, NICK (1986) "The Right Stuff: An Inside Look at the National Citizen's Coalition," *This Magazine* (June/July), Volume 20, Number 2, pp. 4–11, 19.

—— (1989) "The Big OINK – How Business Won the Free Trade Battle: A Case Study," *This Magazine* (March-April), Volume 22, Number 8, pp. 13–20.

FULTON, M. JANE and W.T. STANBURY (1985) "Comparative Lobbying Strategies in Influencing Health Care Policy," *Canadian Public Administration* (Summer), Volume 28, Number 2, pp. 269–300.

GOTLIEB, ALLAN E., ROY T. COTTIER and R.G.P. STYLES (1984) "Canadian Business Representation in the United States," *Behind the Headlines* (September), Volume 42, Number 1, pp. 1–25.

KARDAM, NUKHET (1983) "Interest Group Power and Government Regulation: The Cases of the Mining and Insurance Industries During the Period of New Democratic Party Government in British Columbia, 1972–1975," *BC Studies* (Winter), Number 60, pp. 48–74.

KWAVNICK, DAVID (1972) *Organized Labour and Pressure Politics: The Canadian Labour Congress 1956–1968*. Montreal: McGill-Queen's University Press.

MALVERN, PAUL (1985) *Persuaders: Influence Peddling, Lobbying and Political Corruption in Canada*. Toronto: Methuen.

PRESTHUS, ROBERT (1973) *Elite Accommodation in Canadian Politics*. Toronto: Macmillan of Canada.

PROSS. A. PAUL, ed. (1975) *Pressure Group Behaviour in Canadian Politics*. Toronto: McGraw-Hill Ryerson.

_____ (1986) *Group Politics and Public Policy*. Toronto: Oxford University Press.

American Interest Groups

ADLER, MARSHA NYE (1988) "The Politics of Censorship," *PS* (Winter), Volume 21, Number 1, pp. 18–24.

BERRY, JEFFREY M. (1984) *The Interest Group Society*. Boston: Little, Brown and Company.

CIGLER, ALLAN J. and BURDETT A. LOOMIS, eds. (1983) *Interest Group Politics*. Washington, D.C.: CQ Press.

COOK, CONSTANCE EWING (1984) "Participation in Public Interest Groups: Membership Motivations," *American Politics Quarterly* (October), Volume 12, Number 4, pp. 409–430.

DENZAU, ARTHUR T. and MICHAEL C. MUNGER (1986) "Legislators and Interest Groups: How Unorganized Interests Get Represented," *American Political Science Review* (March), Volume 80, Number 1, pp. 89–106.

GAIS, THOMAS L., MARK A. PETERSON and JACK L. WALKER (1984) "Interest Groups, Iron Triangles and Representative Institutions in American National Government," *British Journal of Political Science* (April), Volume 14, Part 2, pp. 161–165.

GRADY, ROBERT C. (1984) "Juridicial Democracy and Democratic Values: An Evaluation of Lowi's Alternative to Interest-Group Liberalism," *Polity* (Spring), Volume 16, Number 3, pp. 404–422.

LOWI, THEODORE J. (1979) *The End of Liberalism: The Second Republic of the United States*. New York: Norton, 2nd ed.

MANSBRIDGE, JANE J. (1986) *Why We Lost the ERA*. Chicago: The University of Chicago Press.

MCFARLAND, ANDREW S. (1984) *Common Cause: Lobbying in the Public Interest*. Chatham, N.J.: Chatham House Publishers.

_____ (1987) "Interest Groups and Theories of Power in America," *British Journal of Political Science* (April), Volume 17, Number 2, pp. 129–147.

SABATO, LARRY J. (1985) *PAC Power: Inside the World of Political Action Committees*. New York: W.W. Norton and Company.

TESH, SYLVIA (1984) "In Support of 'Single-Issue' Politics," *Political Science Quarterly* (Spring), Volume 99, Number 1, pp. 27–44.

WOOTTON, GRAHAM (1985) *Interest Groups: Policy and Politics in America*. Englewood Cliffs, N.J.: Prentice-Hall.

British Interest Groups

BEER, SAMUEL H. (1982) *Britain Against Itself: The Political Contradictions of Collectivism*. New York: W.W. Norton.

_____ (1982) *Modern British Politics: Parties and Pressure Groups in the Collectivist Age*. New York: W.W. Norton.

BYRNE, PAUL (1987) "The Campaign for Nuclear Disarmament: The Resilience of a Protest Group," *Parliamentary Affairs* (October), Volume 40, Number 4, pp. 517–535.

DOIG, ALAN (1986) "Influencing Westminster: Registering the Lobbyists," *Parliamentary Affairs* (October), Volume 39, Number 4, pp. 517–535.

GRANT, WYN and DAVID MARSH (1977) *The Confederation of British Industry*. London: Hodder and Stoughton.

HOLLIS, PATRICIA, ed. (1974) *Pressure from Without in Early Victorian England*. London: Edward Arnold.

MARTIN, ROSS M. (1980) *TUC: The Growth of a Pressure Group 1868–1976*. Oxford: Clarendon Press.

MULLER, WILLIAM D. (1977) *The 'Kept Men'? The First Century of Trade Union Representation in the British House of Commons, 1874–1975*. Brighton: Harvester Press.

WOOTTON, GRAHAM (1975) *Pressure Groups in Britain, 1720–1970*. London: Allen Lane.

PART FOUR

Evaluating the Canadian Political Experiment

Is is commonly said that Canada produces more politics to the acre than any other country (Smith, 1891: 178).

Where is the Canadian who, comparing his country with even the freest countries, would not feel proud of the institutions which protect him (Sir Wilfrid Laurier)?

The second-largest country in the world, Canada was created by another foreign power for reasons of its own that had little to do with Canadian desires and nothing to do with natural geographical boundaries. And so, beset by political handicaps, a harsh climate, and a divisive geography, a disparate Canada, with one-tenth as many people as its American neighbor in 110 percent of the space, set out to build a modern, independent country in the economic, military, and cultural shadow of the world's two superpowers, the United States and the Soviet Union, both next door. The fact that it accomplished this task at all without a military revolution, without a civil war, and without the overthrow of any government denotes an impressive amount of skill and grace. But it was also accomplished without much attention even within Canada (Malcolm, 1985: xi).

Canadian Politics at Work: The 1982 Canada Act

Only connect (Forster, 1910).

Changing a constitution confronts a society with the most important choices, for in the constitution will be found the philosophical principles and rules which largely determine the relations of the individual and of groups to one another and to the state (Scott, 1977: ix).

After . . . living with a constitutional Charter of Rights and Freedoms the only safe thing to say is that it has turned out to be not nearly as bad as its opponents feared it might be nor nearly as great as its promoters promised it would be (Russell, 1985: 368).

No discussion of constitutional matters in Canada should take place without ready access to a copy of Lewis Carroll's standard reference work, Through the Looking Glass and What Alice Found There *(Cook, 1987: 817).*

TO COMPREHEND the interconnections of political life is, at once, both the most necessary and most difficult task of political analysis. The various elements of the body politic represent a pattern, not of random discord, but of discordant harmony. The continuous interdependence of institutions and processes makes the polity complex and, therefore, difficult to understand, but it need not be beyond reason.

One way of bringing together the various ingredients of the political system into a coherent whole is to analyze a significant piece of legislation with respect to both the structures and processes of the polity. While no single political event is typical, the Constitution Act or Canada Act of 1982 (and its political child, the Meech Lake accord) provides an excellent example of many of the political relationships and concepts discussed separately in the previous chapters. Although the terms Canada Act and Constitution Act refer to the same basic document, there is one important difference between them. The Canada Act is the piece of legislation that was passed by the British Parliament, while the Constitution Act is that portion of the Canada Act that was proclaimed on April 17, 1982. The Constitution Act is the Canada Act minus the opening preamble to the Queen. In our analysis, we have used the term Canada Act in discussions of the patriation process, but the term Constitution Act in discussing specific provisions or references to how that statute will affect Canadian politics in the future.

Because it provides the Canadian polity with a new constitutional base, an understanding of the Constitution Act is essential for analyzing future developments in the political system. As a leading constitutional writer once put it: "We have a rendezvous with the BNA Act. It's going to come someday" (Scott, quoted in McWhinney, 1979: 137). That someday has now come and gone — whether or not it was a rendezvous with destiny remains to be seen. However, given both the process used and the provisions contained in the 1982 Constitution Act, one thing does seem certain: Canadian politics will never be the same again.

1982 Canada Act: Major Provisions

Although the immediate gestation period of the Canada Act was approximately two years, its content seems destined to be as well-known by the public as that of its predecessors, such as the BNA Act of 1867 and the 1960 Bill of Rights. To help counter such a situation and to set the basis for our discussion of the passage and implications of the Canada Act, it is necessary, therefore, to outline its major provisions. Table 14.1 presents a summary of the Canada Act.

Following the preamble, which humbly requests the Queen to act, on our behalf, one last time by laying before the British Parliament the Canada Act of 1982, the Canadian Charter of Rights and Freedoms is specified. The Charter begins with its own minipreamble, affirming that "Canada is founded upon principles that recognize the supremacy of God and the rule of law," which is followed by a series of political, legal, and language rights in Sections 1 through 34. Approximately one-half of the Canada Act is devoted to these basic civil and political liberties. However, perhaps prophetic in its long-range implications for the Charter is Section 1, which limits these rights and freedoms before they are even recognized: "the rights and freedoms set out in it subject only to such reasonable limits prescribed by law as can be demonstrably justified in a free and democratic society." In other words, the basic rights protected by the Charter can be limited by law, as long as that limitation is demonstrably justified in a free and democratic society.

Sections 2 through 5 protect some of the basic civil and political liberties, such as the freedoms of speech, assembly, religion, and voting. Section 6 represents a new addition to the

"...WELL THEN... IF NOT A RATIFIED CONSTITUTIONAL ACCORD, WHAT DO YOU FEEL FORMS THE HEART AND SOUL OF THE CANADIAN PSYCHE?..."

Source: Brian Gable, *Gable: The Editorial Cartoons of Brian Gable*. Saskatoon: Western Producer Prairie Books, 1987. By permission of the *Regina Leader Post*.

traditional list of human freedoms, in that mobility rights are explicitly recognized for the first time in Canada. At the insistence of the federal government, mobility rights were included in an attempt to prevent the "balkanization" of the polity, so that the provinces could not continue to pass legislation designed to hinder interprovincial migration. The necessity of including mobility rights in the Charter reflects the strength of regionalism, as well as an attempt to limit it in the years ahead. However, some restrictions on mobility rights are allowed, if a province's rate of employment is below that of the national average.

The legal rights of Canadian citizens contained in Sections 7 through 14 begin with the "right to life, liberty, and security of person and the right not to be deprived thereof except in accordance with the principles of fundamental justice." However, such "principles of fundamental justice" are left undefined, so that the judiciary will be required to specify their nature through the decisions they are called upon to make in the course of constitutional litigation. The series of legal rights protected include the right to be free against unreasonable searches or seizures, arbitrary detention and imprisonment, or any cruel and unusual treatment or punishment. One's right to counsel, reasonable bail (not to be denied "without just cause"), and trial ("within a reasonable time") are also specified. Protection against self-incrimination, except in perjury cases, and of being tried a second time for an alleged crime after an initial acquittal are also contained in the section on legal rights. These provisions are basic ones for protecting the individual against the possible abuses of state power.

TABLE 14.1 — BASIC PROVISIONS OF THE CANADA ACT

Section	Content	Section	Content
Preamble	Request to the Queen to submit the Patriation Resolution to the British Parliament for passage.		females, Charter to be interpreted so as to protect the multicultural heritage of Canada)
Constitution Act			
PART ONE: CHARTER OF RIGHTS AND FREEDOMS		Sections 32–34	Application of Charter (applies to both federal and provincial governments, but an opting out or notwithstanding clause is included)
Section 1	General guarantee of rights and freedoms		
Section 2	Fundamental Freedoms (religion, speech, etc.)	PART TWO: RIGHTS OF ABORIGINAL PEOPLES	Existing aboriginal and treaty rights of aboriginal peoples recognized and affirmed.
Sections 3–5	Democratic Rights (voting, yearly sitting of Parliament)	PART THREE: EQUALIZATION AND REGIONAL DISPARITIES	Both levels commit themselves to promote the well-being of Canadians, to further economic development, to provide essential public services, and to maintain equalization payments.
Section 6	Mobility Rights (rights of citizens to enter and leave country, to move between provinces)		
Sections 7–14	Legal Rights (protection against unreasonable search and seizure, right to counsel, etc.)	PART FOUR: CONSTITUTIONAL CONFERENCE	Required meeting of all first ministers within one year of the passage of this Act.
Section 15	Equality Rights (protects against discrimination on the basis of race, national or ethnic origin, colour, religion, sex, age, or mental or physical disability)	PART FIVE: AMENDING PROCEDURE	Details of procedure specified, with several different types of formulas used, depending on which sections of the Constitution are to be amended.
Sections 16–22	Official Languages (protection of bilingualism in the federal government and New Brunswick)	PART SIX: AMENDMENT TO THE BNA ACT OF 1867	Protection of provincial powers over natural resources reaffirmed by adding Section 92A to the BNA Act of 1867.
Section 23	Minority Language Educational Rights (where numbers warrant, education to be provided for from public funds in language first learned by the child)	PART SEVEN: GENERAL	Housekeeping provisions: Constitution of Canada declared to be the supreme law of the land; all BNA Acts are now to be renamed as the Constitution Acts; English and French versions of the Constitution Act are equally authoritative.
Section 24	Enforcement (right to appeal to the courts if rights in the Charter are violated)		
Sections 25–31	General (protection of aboriginal rights and equality of males and		

> By and large, it will colour our political culture, moving us significantly in the direction of the United States. A country dedicated in the preamble of its constitution to "peace, order and good government" will give way to a Canadian society much more concerned with the American dream of "life, liberty and the pursuit of happiness" (Cheffins and Johnson, 1986: 130).

The equality rights contained in Section 15 guarantee that "every individual is equal before and under the law and has the right to equal protection and equal benefit of the law without discrimination and, in particular, without discrimination based on race, national or ethnic origin, colour, religion, sex, age or mental or physical disability." Most of these rights were included in the 1960 Bill of Rights, although the Charter has added protection on the grounds of ethnic origin, age, and mental or physical disability. However, government programs designed to overcome the effects of previous discrimination (i.e., "affirmative action" programs) are allowed. Unlike most provisions of the Canada Act, which became effective as soon as the new Constitution was formally proclaimed, the array of equality rights specified in Section 15 of the Charter could not be applied for three years (April 17, 1982 to April 17, 1985) from the date of the Constitution Act's proclamation (Section 32, Subsection 2). Since many of these rights fell within the areas of traditional provincial jurisdiction, the provinces wanted time to accommodate their existing legislation to those new provisions.

> Of the various *Charter* guarantees, the assurance of equality and non-discrimination is most likely to affect Canadians on a day-to-day basis (Boyer, 1985: 1).

The inclusion of the age clause is of interest and, although primarily aimed at the mandatory retirement deadline of 65, it might also be interpreted to protect the rights of young people. The basic social and economic reason for this age provision is that people are living longer and, as a result, the social protection programs, such as the Canada Pension Plan, will be in financial difficulty in the years ahead unless their funding is improved. One way of achieving that end, of course, is to have people working for more years, that is, past the traditional retirement age of 65. Therefore, from this vantage point, the outlawing of discrimination based on age, rather than acting as an extension of human freedom, might be its exact opposite: the state has laid the constitutional foundation for prolonging individuals' obligations to the state by keeping them working and paying taxes for more years. The expansive nature of government may follow you, quite literally, to your grave.

Protection of Canada's two official languages is contained in Sections 16 through 22, which basically entrench in the Constitution the existing language rights as previously specified in the federal government's Official Languages Act and New Brunswick's version of that Act. Entrenchment enhances the extent of language protection, since constitutional provision for it is less immune to future change than legislative statutes. The official languages are recognized with respect to the procedures of the courts, legislatures, and bureaucracy, although in the latter case only where numbers warrant. Quebec is not included in these provisions, but language protection continues in that province under Section 133 of the BNA Act of 1867 (now the Constitution Act of 1867). However, language protection in Quebec is not extended under this provision to an individual's dealings with the bureaucracy—only language use in the courts and the legislature is specified for Quebec in the 1867 Act. Thus, the combination of the Constitution Acts of 1867 and 1982 guarantees language protection in dealings with the federal government and the provinces of New Brunswick and Quebec. However, given the bilingual belt thesis, the major flaw in this pattern of language protection is the obvious exclusion of the province of Ontario.

Language protection is extended to the educational system by Section 23 of the Charter. Citizens of Canada have the right to education in their mother tongue, where numbers warrant, and to have such instruction paid for out of public funds. The background of this aspect of the Charter is complex, raising the whole issue of minority rights and language use throughout Canadian history. Its inclusion, at the insistence of the federal government, was a reaction to the politicization of the language issue in Quebec during the 1960s and 1970s and the passage in 1977 of Bill 101 by the Quebec government. Section 23 attempts, in effect, to correct, even if somewhat belatedly, an oversight in the original BNA Act.

Contained in Section 93 of the BNA Act of 1867 is protection for the separate school systems desired by the minority religious groups in each province. As Eugene Forsey (1974: 244–245) has pointed out, it was likely assumed by the Fathers of Confederation that a Protestant separate school system in Quebec would in fact be English-speaking, while such a separate school system in English Canada would in fact be Catholic and, thus, by implication French-speaking. However, a literal reading of Section 93 allows a provincial government to determine the language of instruction, as long as the separate school system itself is not attacked. By including Section 23 in the Charter of Rights, the federal government was explicitly challenging the language legislation in Quebec and the attempt by the Parti Québécois to make Quebec a unilingual French-speaking province.

Not surprising, therefore, was the rejection of the Canada Act by the government of Quebec, with Section 23 being a primary reason for its

> Contrary to first impressions, the principal impact of the Charter of Rights and Freedoms is not the creation of new rights, but rather a new way of making decisions about rights in which judges will play a central and authoritative role (Morton and Pal, 1985: 222).

refusal. However, in order to minimize the possible negative reaction to the Canada Act among the French-speaking populace in Quebec, minority language educational rights in Section 23(1)(a) will not apply in that province until they are proclaimed, at some future date, by the Queen or governor general (procedure specified in the Charter, Section 59, Subsections 1 and 2). Such a proclamation cannot be issued until it has been authorized by the legislative assembly or government of Quebec. However, once Quebec agrees to Section 23(1)(a), it cannot reverse itself at a later date, because the override clause does not apply to Section 23 of the Charter.

The enforcement of the Charter of Rights is allocated to the judiciary by Section 24. Anyone who feels that their fundamental rights and freedoms have been infringed or denied "may apply to a court of competent jurisdiction to obtain such remedy as the court considers appropriate and just in the circumstances." This explicit recognition of the role of the courts in protecting fundamental rights increases the potential for a more activist judiciary in Canada, if citizens are willing to challenge possible violations of the Charter by bringing them to the attention of the judicial branch.

Sections 25 through 31 of the Charter, labelled General, are a miscellaneous group of provisions not easily accommodated in the previous sections. Section 25 guarantees aboriginal rights, including those that might accrue by means of future land claims settlements. Section 28 specifically recognizes the equality of "male and female persons." These two provisions, at first glance, appear to duplicate the bar against discrimination on the basis of sex and national or ethnic origin contained under Section 15 on equality rights. However, Section 15 did not take effect until three years after the Charter was proclaimed (i.e., April 17, 1985) and, more importantly, unlike Section 15, the protections of Sections 25 and 28 cannot be overridden using Section 33 of the Charter. Thus, these two provisions were applied immediately between 1982 and 1985 and cannot be taken away by legislative fiat at some future point. Also contained within the miscellaneous category is an extension of the Charter to the Yukon and Northwest Territories (Section 30), a proviso that the Charter "shall be interpreted in a manner consistent with the preservation and enhancement of the multicultural heritage of Canadians" (Section 26), an assertion that "nothing in this Charter extends the legislative powers of any body or authority" (Section 31), and, in case some rights may have been overlooked, a claim that lack of inclusion of any such rights in the Charter cannot be taken to mean that they do not exist (Section 26).

The final major section of the Charter of Rights concerns its application. Section 32 specifically enforces the Charter on both the federal and provincial levels of government, as well as on the Yukon and Northwest Territories, although the equality rights of Section 15 are delayed for three years. Most significant is Section 33, which allows either the federal or provincial governments to override any rights specified in Section 2 or Sections 7 to 15 of the Charter of Rights. Thus, Section 33 continues the practice of placing the principle of parliamentary supremacy over the application of fundamental freedoms, whether these freedoms are entrenched in the Constitution or not. The use of the override or notwithstanding clause is limited to five years, although it may be reenacted repeatedly in a series of five-year terms. There is no apparent means by which an over-

ride action by either the federal or provincial legislatures can be legally challenged by the citizen. The recourse to a misuse of this power must be effected by defeating the government at the next election, rather than through a process of constitutional litigation.

Parts Two through Four of the Canada Act are relatively brief and straightforward. The "existing aboriginal and treaty rights" are "recognized and affirmed" in Part Two, along with a definition of the concept of "aboriginal peoples of Canada" (i.e., Indian, Inuit, and Métis). Part Three reflects the impact on the Canadian polity of regionalism, in that the federal and provincial governments commit themselves, very generally, to the reduction of regional disparities through equalization payments to the provinces. No formula for determining equalization grants or funding levels is included, thereby protecting the flexibility of the governments involved in negotiating these matters. Quite likely, the federal and provincial governments will continue to have different views of what constitutes "sufficient revenues" to the provinces. Part Three was a major concession by the federal government to the poorer provinces in order to try and win their grudging acceptance of the constitutional reform package.

Part Four requires that the prime minister convene a conference of first ministers within one year of the proclamation of the Constitution Act. Part Four also mandates that matters affecting Canada's aboriginal peoples must be considered by this conference, that representatives from these groups must be invited to attend so as to participate in the discussions of these matters, and that elected representatives of the Yukon and Northwest Territories will also be in attendance to discuss any matters that directly affect them. For the first time, there is a legal requirement that someone other than the federal and provincial political executives be involved in the process of constitutional negotiation.

A crucial addition to Canada's constitutional

structure is Part Five of the Canada Act, which specifies amending clauses for future constitutional reform efforts. Thus, a major flaw of the BNA Act of 1867 has finally been corrected. However, the amendment of the Constitution Act is complex; in fact, five different procedures are prescribed. For example, within certain limits, the existing right of the provinces to determine their own structure and operation, as well as the power of the federal government to do likewise, is recognized in Sections 45 and 44, respectively. A third variation concerns an amendment that affects at least two provinces, but not all (Section 43). In this situation, a proclamation by the governor general is required, after "resolutions of the Senate and House of Commons and of the legislative assembly of each province to which the amendment applies." The fourth amending procedure (Section 41) differs from the third in that the unanimous consent of all provinces must be obtained with respect to any amendments to the offices of the formal executive (Queen, governor general, lieutenant governor), the composition of the Supreme Court, the use of the English or French languages within a province, and the right of a province to have at least the same number of members in the House of Commons as it has senators.

The most general amending procedure, and the fifth possible alternative, is contained in Section 38, which will likely become the heart of the amending process in Canada. Under this technique an amendment is proclaimed by the governor general when authorized by "resolutions of the Senate and House of Commons" and by "resolutions of the legislative assemblies of at least two-thirds of the provinces that have, in the aggregate, according to the then latest general census, at least 50 percent of the population of all the provinces." However, even if it is passed under these conditions, the remaining provinces may opt out of any such amendment. If the amendment opted out of transfers powers in the education or cultural fields to Ottawa,

then the provinces are entitled to financial compensation. These amending procedures, particularly Section 38, represent a major change in the nature of constitutional reform in Canada, transforming a process based on convention into one based on constitutional prescription.

An important alteration of the Senate's role in the amending process is contained in Section 47, which gives the upper chamber a suspensive veto of 180 days with respect to all amending procedures except those relating to either the provincial or federal levels changing their own structure and operation. If a resolution authorizing an amendment is passed by the House, but is not passed within 180 sitting days of Parliament by the Senate, then the House can pass the resolution a second time, at which point the amending procedure moves ahead. Because the Senate can be effectively bypassed, if necessary, what Section 47 does is to give ultimate control of the basic amending processes to the House of Commons. The Senate can even be gotten around with respect to amendments that change both the powers of and method of selecting members of the upper house.

Part Six of the Canada Act amended the original British North America Act of 1867 by adding a definition of and additional protection for provincial control over natural resources (Section 92A). The newly emerging wealth of Alberta, Saskatchewan, and British Columbia and the hoped-for wealth of the Atlantic provinces is based on the natural resource sector, one which these provinces fear the federal government covets. Thus, part of the tradeoff for the Charter of Rights wanted by the federal government was enhancement of provincial control over the natural resource sector.

The final part of the Canada Act (Part Seven, Sections 52 through 60) is another catchall series of provisions: how the Canada Act can be cited, the fact that the English and French versions are considered equally authoritative, and that the Constitution of Canada is the "supreme law of Canada."

Our survey of the major provisions of the Canada Act might lead one to conclude that it is the Rubik's Cube of Canadian politics: what appears simple at first glance is, in fact, an extremely complex constitutional document with many significant implications for the future direction of the polity. While it is a consolidation of a number of existing constitutional provisions, the 1982 Canada Act, by itself, is not a comprehensive constitutional document — elements of the 1867 BNA Act and the 1960 Bill of Rights remain as significant ingredients of the total constitutional context in Canada. A considerable portion of the 1982 Canada Act is simply a repetition of existing constitutional enactments. For example, most of the Charter of Rights was already contained in the 1960 Bill of Rights.

However, a number of new elements have been added, including the mobility rights and minority language educational rights in the Charter, the entrenchment of fundamental freedoms in the Constitution, and the Charter's applicability to both levels of government. Outside of the Charter, the Canada Act has also added protection of aboriginal rights, enhanced provincial control over the natural resource sector, and provided a series of constitutionally-designated amending procedures. The major provisions of the Canada Act each represent the result of political accommodations between the federal and provincial governments in the struggle for influence and power in the future Canadian polity. The process used in passing the Canada Act clearly reveals this political nature of constitutional reform.

Passage of the Canada Act: A Political Analysis

The political bargains struck, the provisions contained in — as well as those left out — and the longrun implications of the Canada Act all demonstrate its significance for the future of

> The dustbin of recent history is littered with discarded constitutions cast aside after brief and withering exposure to reality. Constitutions capable of responding and adapting to the perils of change have sufficient scarcity value to be treated with the deference appropriate to rare achievements. All the more curious, therefore, has been the detached, unappreciative Canadian attitude to one of the most durable and successful constitutions in the world (Cairns, 1970: 483).

Canadian politics. Moreover, the passage of the patriation resolution illustrates many of the conclusions reached in our analysis of the institutions and processes of the Canadian polity. In order to connect our discussion more closely to the actual workings of the political arena, we present in this section a brief political analysis of the passage of the Canada Act. The steps in the passage of the act are outlined in Table 14.2.

One of the major incentives for undertaking constitutional reform, of course, was the perceived inadequacy of the BNA Act of 1867 and other features of constitutional government in Canada (i.e., no entrenched bill of rights). The key provisions of the Canada Act, therefore, are designed to specify and fill in some of the significant gaps in the structure and practice of Canadian constitutionalism. These innovations include a series of amending procedures and an entrenched Charter of Rights, which apply to both the federal and provincial levels of government. Such changes have expanded and helped to codify the nature of constitutional government in Canada.

The impact of federalism was pervasive on both the process and content of the Canada Act. The immediate cause of the constitutional reform effort was the attempt to show Quebec, after the concept of sovereignty-association had been defeated in May 1980, that a renewed federalism could accommodate Quebec's aspirations. However, the rejection of the new Constitution by the Parti Québécois government was inevitable: how could a party and government, whose central purpose was to secede from Canada and form an independent country, agree to any renewal of a federal structure they had so long despised? A renewed federalism would undercut the logic and necessity for independence: politically, René Lévesque could not become a new Father of Confederation.

The importance of federalism was also revealed in the stands taken on the question of patriation by both the federal and provincial governments. Although Prime Minister Trudeau asserted, in his address to the nation on October 2, 1980, that his patriation proposal was a "people's package," which would not alter the existing balance of power between the levels of government, the reaction to his plan showed otherwise. The majority of provinces were opposed, not only because they rightly saw that many of the provisions of the Charter of Rights were dealing with matters of property and civil rights over which they wanted to retain control, but also because of their view that, if the Canada Act was to be accepted as initially proposed, the future of the federal system would be weighted in favour of Ottawa.

In many ways, the Canada Act illustrates a reassertion of Ottawa's influence and power in the federal system—an outgrowth, no doubt, of Trudeau's view that the political system had become too decentralized in the 1960s and 1970s. By threatening unilateral patriation, the federal government forced the provinces to accommodate, although it ultimately had to do so as well: that threat, however, was a significant political resource that was skillfully utilized by Ottawa. Moreover, there seems little doubt that the Canada Act has altered some of the fundamental rules of the political contest, which will ultimately affect the balance of power in the federal system.

The bitter antagonisms produced during the confrontations over the Canada Act soured federal-provincial relations for a few years. Most disquieting was the isolation of Quebec under the PQ government. For example, in protest over the Canada Act, the Parti Québécois government adopted a policy of not participating in other than "essential" federal-provincial negotiations. Even before the Canada Act passed the British Parliament, Prime Minister Trudeau had asserted that cooperative federalism was dead (*The Globe and Mail*, February 27, 1982). With such conflicts, the pattern of executive federalism could not long continue unaffected. Distrust of the federal government became pervasive among the provincial premiers, illustrated by the evident hostility during the unsuccessful First Ministers' Conference on the economy held in February 1982.

Only one major addition to the allocation of powers specified in Sections 91 and 92 of the BNA Act was contained in the Canada Act: Part Six amended Section 92 of the BNA Act by strengthening provincial control over the natural resource sector. Notable by their absence were any representatives from the local level of government. The Canada Act was a federal-provincial confrontation in which the local level neither participated nor was recognized: Canada's federal structure remains bipartite.

A further impact of federalism was its influence on the political strategies of both the national and provincial governments. The national government needed some provincial allies to bolster its position, which it found in its tacit alliance with Conservative Premiers Bill Davis of Ontario and Richard Hatfield of New Brunswick. Ontario's backing was crucial, so that both the provinces opposed and the national government sought its support. It should be remembered that Bill Davis played a crucial role in 1979 and 1980 in discrediting the national Conservative administration of Joe Clark. Moreover, during the 1980 campaign, the national Liberal party ran ads in Ontario that quoted Bill Davis and other Ontario cabinet

TABLE 14.2 — PASSAGE OF THE CANADA ACT

Date	Event	Date	Event
1927–1979	A series of unsuccessful reform efforts, including several by Prime Minister Pierre Trudeau.	October 24, 1980	Closure imposed by Liberals to end the initial debate of 11 days on the Patriation Resolution.
May 1979	General election defeat of the Trudeau Government; the Conservatives form their first government since 1963, giving constitutional reform a low priority.	November 6, 1980	Joint Committee begins hearings on the Resolution. Extension of Committee hearings to February 6, 1981 agreed to on December 2, 1980. Justice Minister Jean Chrétien revises Charter of Rights on January 12, 1981.
February 1980	Liberals return to power with a majority.		
May 20, 1980	Quebec referendum on sovereignty-association. The ''No'' side wins, with Trudeau pledging to keep his promise for significant constitutional changes.	February 3, 1981	Manitoba Court of Appeal rules 3 to 2 that the Patriation Resolution is legal.
		February 12, 1981	Joint Committee reports, with 65 proposed amendments to the Canada Act.
May–August 1980	A summer of constitutional negotiations fails to produce an accord, but a final attempt will be made during a Constitutional Conference in September.	February 17, 1981	Debate resumes in the Commons, with Tories stalling for time to allow the judiciary to rule on the constitutionality of the Canada Act. Conservative filibuster begun on March 24, 1981.
September 8–13, 1980	A six-day Constitutional Conference ends in total failure—no agreements on any major reforms are reached.	March 30, 1981	Newfoundland Court of Appeal decides 3 to 0 against unilateral patriation.
October 2, 1980	Prime Minister Trudeau addresses the nation, says he will proceed immediately to unilaterally patriate the Constitution, with a Charter of Rights and an amending formula.	April 8, 1981	A deal is struck among the parties in the House to end debate, if the patriation proposals are sent to the Supreme Court for a review of the constitutionality of the Canada Act.
October 6, 1980	Patriation Resolution introduced in Parliament; debate begins immediately on it. The NDP supports the measure, with Conservatives vowing protracted opposition.	April 15, 1981	Quebec Court of Appeal rules 4 to 1 in favour of the federal government's proposals.
		April 23, 1981	Final votes in the Commons on the various amendments to

TABLE 14.2   CONTINUED

Date	Event	Date	Event
	the Canada Act. Final approval delayed until the Supreme Court rules.		outcry, the federal government and the nine provinces reach an agreement on including women's and aboriginal rights in the Charter.
April 28–May 5, 1981	Supreme Court hears arguments on the appeals stemming from Manitoba, Newfoundland, and Quebec decisions on the constitutionality of the Canada Act.	December 2, 1981	Canada Act passes the House of Commons by a vote of 246 to 24. Quebec moves to challenge the Act in the courts—flags in Quebec lowered to half-mast.
September 28, 1981	Supreme Court decision rules that the Canada Act is legal, but violates the constitutional customs and conventions of the Canadian political system. Both sides claim victory.	December 8, 1981	Senate passes Canada Act by a vote of 59 to 23. Special ceremony held to present the Canada Act to the Governor General at Government House.
October, 1981	Intense bargaining as both sides seek a political settlement. A final Constitutional Conference is decided upon for November.	December 9, 1981	Patriation Resolution delivered to the Queen by Governor General's Secretary and by Justice Minister Jean Chrétien.
November 2–5, 1981	Constitutional Conference, after several days of stalemate, begins to work out a compromise among the participants. Tentative agreement reached in a late-night session between the federal government and nine provinces.	December 1981 to March 1982	British Parliament approves Canada Act. The Act is tabled in the Commons on December 21, 1981 and approved at Second Reading on February 18, 1982, by a vote of 334 to 44. House of Lords approves on March 25, with Royal Assent granted on March 29, 1982.
November 5, 1981	Constitutional Accord is announced and is introduced in the Commons. Quebec denounces the agreement. Special protection of women and aboriginal rights not included in the compromise plan.	April 17, 1982	Home At Last, Oh Lord, Home At Last! Queen proclaims Constitution Act in Ottawa. Quebec stages a series of counter-demonstrations.
November 23, 1981	After several weeks of public		

ministers in their opposition to the Clark budget of December 1979.

The alliance of Ottawa and Ontario should be seen for what it was — the central heartland seeking to retain its leading role in the Canadian polity. Only a rejuvenated national government could possibly protect the declining dominance of Ontario in the 1970s. The price of Ontario's support was high and undercut the integrity of the national Liberal leader: Ontario would not be included in the bilingual protection contained in Sections 16 through 22 of the Charter of Rights. The province with the largest number of French-speaking citizens outside of Quebec would retain its unilingual posture — a perfect illustration that constitutions are exercises in life, not in logic.

The pattern of executive dominance of the Canadian polity is clearly revealed in the negotiations for the passage of the Canada Act. The constitutional reform process and the political career of Pierre Trudeau became inextricably linked from the mid-1960s onward. For example, Trudeau first rose to national attention as Justice Minister under Prime Minister Lester Pearson. Particularly crucial was the federal-provincial conference on constitutional reform held in February 1968, during which Justice Minister Trudeau, on national television, spurned a special-status solution to Quebec's aspirations. Even before then, his writings on French-Canada and the constitution had brought Trudeau to the attention of the Liberal party hierarchy, resulting in his eventual cooptation into the Liberal fold for the 1965 campaign. Appointment as parliamentary secretary to Prime Minister Pearson and then later elevation to the Justice portfolio put Trudeau in a crucial political role as far as constitutional matters were concerned (Radwanski, 1978: 81–91).

Throughout his many years as Prime Minister, constitutional change was a primary concern for Trudeau, if not always for the nation which he governed. During his initial stay in office, two major attempts at constitutional

reform were unsuccessful: the review between 1968 and 1971, which ended with Quebec's rejection of the Victoria Charter (i.e., the tentative agreement on constitutional reform reached at the 1971 Constitutional Conference held in Victoria, B.C.), and the review that began in 1974 and continued on through the presentation of constitutional reform proposals in 1978, entitled "A Time for Action," which also foundered from lack of provincial support.

Although Trudeau sought to make constitutional reform and national unity the primary issue in the 1979 federal election, he was unsuccessful. The election of Joe Clark put constitutional reform on a backburner. It was only the surprise defeat of the Conservative budget that provided the opportunity for Trudeau to return to once again undertake his pet project of revising the Canadian constitutional context. According to Trudeau, his brief respite in the role of opposition leader "rejuvenated his spirits" for the long ordeal ahead (*The Globe and Mail*, February 23, 1982).

A fortuitous conjunction of circumstances occurred with the holding of the sovereignty-association referendum in Quebec on May 20, 1980. The intervention of the Prime Minister and the federal Liberal party on the side of the "No" forces was a significant factor in the defeat of the referendum. As a rationale for rejecting sovereignty-association, Trudeau promised major constitutional change in a "renewed federalism," although the specifics of these reforms were left largely undefined. Trudeau then held that his promise was sacred, one that had to be met, thus allowing him to cajole English Canada into accepting the need for a revised Canadian constitution. The fact that Quebec did not want the reforms — they were supported by neither the Parti Québécois nor the provincial Liberals — appeared to be ignored by English Canada: Trudeau had become, once again, the sole defender of Quebec's interests in the federal system.

A final factor prompting constitutional reform

THE MACPATRIATION BROTHERS

The MacPatriation Brothers

Source: Roy Peterson, *Drawn and Quartered: The Trudeau Years, 1984.*
By permission: Roy Peterson and *The Vancouver Sun.*

was Trudeau's sense of history. Having "promised" that the 1980 campaign would be his last, it was now or never with respect to a new constitution. The push for constitutional revision was instigated, led, and controlled by Trudeau. Despite considerable dissatisfaction from within the Liberal caucus and party organization, the troops rallied behind their leader's third and, presumably, final attempt to achieve constitutional sainthood. Thus, personal motives finally meshed with political circumstances to produce a climate hospitable for constitutional reform. In politics, the timing of political actions is a crucial ingredient of influence and power. It is likely that Trudeau's place in Canadian history

will be written largely in terms of his ability to seize the political opportunity, which he himself helped to create, to give the country a patriated and revised constitution.

Not only was the constitutional reform process executive-dominated, it was controlled by the 11 political executives. Federal and provincial political executives were the key actors in the constitutional drama, to the exclusion of almost everyone else. An explicit concern of the political executives was to keep the reform negotiations to themselves; they steadfastly rejected any suggestion, such as a referendum or an election, which might bring the public into the constitutional discussions. Moreover,

> The reality of Canadian politics is that it is conducted within narrow limits of probability, so that the power of government is contained well short of adventure and innovation. What remains is the power of governance over the ambitions of others, the small change of preferment and perquisite — old vestments and titles for new men (Camp, 1979: 143).

control over future constitutional revisions by the political executives is clearly maintained in the various amending procedures specified in the Constitution Act. A further illustration that constitutions benefit those who write them can be seen in the refusal by the provincial political executives to recognize local governments as a separate level of government in the Canadian federal state.

Typical of his general position in the polity, the formal executive played a symbolic and ceremonial role in the passage of the Canada Act. For example, the transmission of the Patriation Resolution from Canada to Britain and back was technically carried out by the formal executives or their representatives (e.g., the secretary to the governor general). While Governor General Schreyer likely discussed the progress of the constitutional review process with Prime Minister Trudeau during their weekly meetings, he is unlikely to have altered the intent of the government on the contents of the measure. In an interview after the passage of the Canada Act in Canada, Governor General Schreyer maintained that, if a constitutional agreement had not been reached between the federal government and the nine provinces, he had been prepared to step in and block unilateral patriation by dismissing the government from office, thereby forcing a general election on the issue (*The Globe and Mail*, January 22, 1982).

The ensuing outcry over such a suggestion is instructive. Governor General Schreyer was roundly criticized for publicly making such views known; this action was itself a breach of political propriety. More importantly, expert opinion held that such a move would have been politically unacceptable. For example, Eugene Forsey (*The Globe and Mail*, February 2, 1982) concluded that whether "the situation would have been exceptional enough to warrant dismissing the Government and holding an election is, to say the least, doubtful." Quebec Premier René Lévesque was more blunt in his assessment, saying that "Governor General Schreyer should go back to his normal occupation — sleeping — and stop making noises about the constitution" (*The Globe and Mail*, January 23, 1982). Prime Minister Trudeau then stepped in, asserting that no such threat, or even any discussion of its possibility, had ever been made to him by the formal executive (*The Globe and Mail*, January 27, 1982). The significant point raised by this fracas is the difference between the formal executive's legal powers and his actual role in the political process. While legally entitled to take such a measure, it seems unlikely, from a political perspective, that Governor General Schreyer could have successfully forced an election in this situation.

The Constitution Act seems unlikely to change the formal executive's role in the political process. For example, while under the new amending procedures such changes take place on the issuance of a proclamation by the Governor General, he or she only so acts when authorized to do so by the political executive, after the appropriate resolutions have been passed by the various legislatures. However, the Canada Act may allow for an enhancement of the Governor General's role in the years ahead. The formal executive's nonpolitical role has been necessary in the past so as to preclude foreign interference in the domestic political battle. By cutting the remaining ties to Britain, the Canada Act might allow the formal executive a somewhat greater political role and more leeway to become involved in the political affairs of the nation

(McWhinney, *The Globe and Mail*, February 6, 1982).

The task of the Canadian Parliament in the constitutional reform process was initially designed to be a subservient one, although it did not turn out that way. Crucial to the patriation plan was the gaining of a majority government by the Liberal party in the 1980 federal election. A majority situation, with strict party discipline imposed on the governing caucus, would ensure the quick and easy passage of the Canada Act through the House of Commons. Even though the government majority was small (147 out of 282 seats), party discipline guaranteed that it was big enough to force unilateral patriation through, if necessary, with only Liberal party support. Thus, the need to compromise with the opposition parties was minimal and closure could always be utilized.

If the 1980 election had produced, instead, a minority Liberal government, it seems likely that unilateral patriation would not even have been attempted. Too many compromises would have been needed to gain the support of at least one of the opposition parties in the Commons, with the government possibly facing a defeat over the measure, if no such agreement could have been reached. In addition to its majority in the Commons, the Liberals' huge majority in the Senate appeared to ensure the upper chamber's quick approval of the Patriation Resolution. Given a majority in both Houses, it is no wonder that suggestions for deciding the issue through a free vote, a referendum, or a new federal election were rejected outright by the Liberal government.

The nature and importance of party discipline was clearly revealed in the passage of the Canada Act, although significant breaks in its application occurred within all three parties. For example, at third reading in the House of Commons on December 2, 1981, the vote was 246 in favour of the Canada Act, with 24 opposed. Since the three parties were in support of the Patriation Resolution at this point, all 24 votes

against represent breaks in party unity: five for the Liberals, 17 for the Conservatives, and two for the New Democrats (plus one abstention). In the Senate, the final vote on December 8, 1981, was 59 to 23, with mainly Conservatives opposed, although five Liberals ignored party cohesion as well.

Considering the emotional nature of the reaction to the Canada Act, both pro and con, it is difficult to assess the significance of these breaks in party unity. However, it seems unlikely that they will be viewed, in retrospect, as a precursor for any general diminution of the power of party discipline in the normal workings of Parliament. Moreover, the number of individuals willing to break party ranks may have been greater than most people expected, simply because all parties were supporting the final version of the Patriation Resolution. For the Conservatives, lack of party unity would do little to affect their overall political position. Opposition parties are usually less likely to impose strict party discipline than is a governing party. And less than 100 percent party unity neither threatened the Liberal government's hold on office nor the success of the measure itself; thus, some tolerance of dissent was possible.

The real test of party discipline in the House would have come if no compromise solution had been reached between the federal government and nine of the provinces at the Constitutional Conference in November, because then any breaks in party cohesion among the Liberals might have cost them office. Rejection of party discipline was more evident in the Senate than in the House, a result, quite likely, of a senator's more secure tenure, based on appointment rather than election. Moreover, the overwhelming Liberal dominance of the upper house made the vote as close to a sure thing as possible.

Parliamentary procedures and tactics had not been as complex and controversial since the great Pipeline Debate 25 years earlier. Several techniques are particularly worthy of mention: the imposition and use of closure, the

Conservatives' filibuster, and the role of the speaker in attempting to maintain order and impartiality throughout. Although Prime Minister Trudeau had promised full and extensive debate on his unilateral patriation scheme, the Liberal government also sought to have the measure passed as quickly as possible (the initial date was January 1, 1981). Early in the parliamentary battle, the Liberals were quite willing and able to impose order on the proceedings; by the end of it, however, their control was beginning to dissipate. For example, to move the Patriation Resolution past second reading and forward to the committee stage, closure was imposed in the early morning hours of October 24, 1980. The outcry from the press and at least some elements of the public was so great, that the government was increasingly reluctant, as the patriation battle dragged on, to resort to such measures. One major reason for such reticence concerned the legitimacy of the Canada Act itself: if significant constitutional reform was achieved by brute imposition of the government's majority position in the Commons, would the people and the provinces accept the results of unilateral patriation?

The Liberal party's reluctance to force anything as momentous as the Canada Act through Parliament in a matter of weeks gave the Conservatives a chance to effectively utilize the last bastion of opposition influence in the Commons — namely, time. The goal of the Conservatives was to delay passage of the Canada Act for as long as possible, in the hopes of wringing concessions from the Liberal government. Moreover, a lengthy debate in Parliament was necessary to see whether or not public opinion could be mobilized against the measure, as well as to give the provinces opposed to it a chance to challenge the constitutionality of the Patriation Resolution in the courts and ultimately in the Supreme Court of Canada.

By making full use of the opposition's right to debate and discuss each aspect of the resolution, the Conservatives not only delayed its passage

for over a year (from October 1980 to December 1981), but, more importantly, forced major revisions in the content of the Canada Act. Most indicative of this pressure was the filibuster during March 1981, which delayed action until the Newfoundland Court of Appeal ruled against the federal plan. This court decision, in conjunction with the Tory filibuster, forced the government to delay final passage of the Patriation Resolution until the Supreme Court could rule on its constitutionality. The opposition's power to delay the process gave it a limited ability to shape the substance of the reforms.

Throughout the emotion-charged and lengthy debates, the ability of Speaker Jeanne Sauvé, as well as her impartiality, were put to the test on numerous occasions: given the circumstances, she performed well. The difficult nature of the task of the speaker was clearly revealed when closure was imposed to end debate at second reading. The debate raged on until the early morning hours and when the vote finally came, with the deputy speaker presiding, the tension in the Commons almost spilled over into physical confrontations, as several Conservatives literally charged towards the speaker's chair, and one Liberal member crossed the centre aisle to confront opposition leader Joe Clark. Probably the most significant decision made by Speaker Sauvé was the one not to end the Conservative filibuster in March 1981, a move that asserted her independence from the government of which she had been a former member. Moreover, by allowing the debate to continue, Speaker Sauvé bolstered her support among the opposition parties, in addition to protecting the legitimacy of the Canada Act itself. Without the acquiescence of the speaker, the Tory filibuster could have been quickly ended.

Although Parliament ultimately became involved in altering the content of the Canada Act, it should not be overlooked that throughout much of the process, it was effectively bypassed. Symbolic, perhaps, of Parliament's intended role was the date of the federal-provincial agreement. November 5 is Guy Fawkes Day in Britain, named after the 17th-century radical who attempted to blow up Parliament. After a constitutional agreement was reached on November 5, 1981, Prime Minister Trudeau rejected attempts by the federal opposition parties to bring about further changes, on the grounds that any alterations by the national Parliament might lead to a breakdown of the federal-provincial agreement! When native and women's rights were reinserted into the Canada Act in November, it was done by Parliament, but only after the federal and provincial governments had agreed to such modifications. A pattern of executive federalism between levels of government leads to a denigration of the role and powers of the national Parliament.

The nature of the Canadian judicial process greatly influenced the political strategies of the contending parties in the patriation battle. Most revealing was the attempt by both those supporting and those opposed to the Canada Act to keep the judiciary from becoming initially involved: the political executives did not want to relinquish their control over the constitutional reform process to the courts. This strategy on the part of the federal government was clearly outlined in the Kirby memorandum, which was "leaked" to the premiers and the press during the Constitutional Conference in September 1980.

Named after its author, Michael Kirby, who was then secretary to the cabinet for federal-provincial relations, the Kirby analysis argued that the federal government should proceed quickly with unilateral patriation before any court challenges could be mounted. Only an assumption that the courts might rule against the patriation resolution could serve as the basis for such a strategy. Moreover, the Kirby memorandum, which is an excellent example of political analysis, was amazingly prescient in its description of the strengths and weaknesses of the political positions of the provinces opposed to the unilateral patriation move. A suspicious

person might even suggest that the Kirby memorandum was purposely distributed by the Quebec delegation on the first day of the Constitutional Conference so as to preclude any agreement. Failure of the Constitutional Conference in September 1980 provided, of course, the necessary rationale for unilateral patriation in October, without the federal government having to make any compromises with the provinces at all.

The reluctance to involve the judiciary was also evident among the eight provinces originally opposed to the Canada Act. Although they had threatened possible court action throughout the period of negotiations, it was only after the federal government seriously moved on unilateral patriation that the opposing provinces turned to the judicial strategy as their last resort. Court challenges were mounted by the opposing provinces in Manitoba, Newfoundland, and Quebec, in the hope that at least one such challenge would be successful, or alternatively, that they would provide a means for ultimately appealing the case to the Supreme Court of Canada. Throughout the patriation battle, the federal government, meanwhile, sought to prevent a court ruling on the constitutionality of its reforms. Only after the adverse ruling by the Newfoundland Court of Appeal did the federal government finally relent, agreeing not to pass the Patriation Resolution until the Supreme Court could consider it.

The judiciary was being asked to rule on the validity of constitutional reform by the federal government when Ottawa had not first obtained provincial consent for such changes. In other words, the Supreme Court was brought in to arbitrate which levels of government had the right to decide and to be involved in both the process and content of constitutional amendment — one of the classic concerns of a pattern of limited judicial review. Because the Patriation Resolution had not yet passed Parliament and, as it turned out, was not yet in its final form, the Supreme Court did not rule on the validity of the Canada Act as passed on December 8, 1981, but on an earlier version of it.

Thus, the fact that the judiciary does not have a self-starting mechanism is clear throughout — the courts could only act on the initiative of others in the political process. Moreover, the Supreme Court did not have to accept the need to issue a ruling on the case at all — it could have decided that the Patriation Resolution was a political problem and have refused to render a decision. In fact, when arguments were first made before the Supreme Court in April 1981, the federal government so argued, in the vain hope that a judicial decision might still be averted. Right to the bitter end the federal government sought to limit the exercise of judicial power.

The slow-moving nature of the court system was quite likely another reason why the federal government sought to prevent the judicial branch from becoming involved in the constitutional reform process. There was a five-month period between hearing arguments on the constitutional issue and getting a decision from the Supreme Court. Perhaps symbolic of the Supreme Court's role was the way the decision was announced. In order to enhance the visibility of the Supreme Court, public access was provided as the Chief Justice rendered the decision. However, technology refused to cooperate — the microphones were so poor that the content of the decision was not immediately evident, which added to the confusing nature of the decision itself. What the Supreme Court decided, in broad outline, was that the federal government's constitutional reforms were legal, while at the same time they violated some of the important customs and conventions of Canadian constitutional practice. For example, provincial agreement was a custom, not a legal necessity of constitutional reform, but that agreement did not need to be unanimous ("substantial agreement" by the provinces was left undefined).

The typical reluctant exercise of power by the

judiciary is clearly demonstrated: the Supreme Court arbitrated the case in such a way that both sides could claim victory. Appeal to the Supreme Court did not settle the matter; it forced the federal and provincial governments back to the negotiating table in order to achieve a political, rather than a legal, settlement of the controversy. In that sense, the referee of the federal system sent both parties into an overtime, sudden-death period — the Constitutional Conference of November 1981. The consequence of the Supreme Court ruling was to make necessary a politically-determined process of constitutional reform, a conservative result that is consistent with the traditional pattern of limited judicial review and judicial restraint.

In addition to the specific role of the courts in the passage of the Canada Act, a long-term consideration must be whether the Patriation Resolution will alter the role of the judiciary in the political process. While some features of the Constitution Act create the potential for a more activist judiciary (e.g., an entrenched Charter of Rights applying to both levels of government), others seek to limit judicial power (e.g., the override provision). One of the main complaints of the opposing provinces was that the Canada Act, as initially proposed, would expand judicial power and, thus, by implication, undercut not only provincial power, but the principle of parliamentary supremacy. The override provision of Section 33 was devised to limit judicial involvement, as is the assertion in Section 1 of the Charter of Rights that rights and freedoms can be prescribed by law, if such limitations can be "demonstrably justified in a free and democratic society."

Moreover, the judicial branch, except in reference cases, only enters the political battle through litigation — cases must be brought before the courts before they can do anything. Judicial personnel will only slowly change, and there is no guarantee that new court appointments will be any more "activist" in orientation

> The power of the Canadian judiciary has historically been quite different from its counterpart in the United States. Canada's judges do not have an activist tradition and they bring a different philosophical orientation to their task. Predictions about the *Charter* should thus be grounded in Canadian experience and tradition (MacKay, 1985).

than those whom they replace. One highly symbolic appointment was the selection on March 3, 1982 of Bertha Wilson to the Supreme Court—the first woman ever so appointed in the Court's history. This appointment reflects, perhaps, the initial impact of the Canada Act, which protected, in two separate provisions, the equality of men and women. How could an all-male Supreme Court maintain its legitimacy in deciding future cases involving matters of sexual equality?

In the preceding analysis of the Canada Act, we have briefly dealt with the impact that basic political structures (i.e., the constitution and the three branches of government) had on its content and passage. In addition, the political processes of the Canadian polity also significantly shaped the constitutional reform battle.

The overall context, as well as the specific strategies of the contending parties, reflected some of the main themes of the Canadian political culture. Most important was the role of custom and convention and the various participants' use and interpretation of it. The half-century process of constitutional failure reflected a longstanding assumption that unanimity among the participants was preferred in matters of constitutional reform. Thus, a single province such as Quebec in 1971 could stop the Victoria Charter from going forward. This assumption about the importance of consensus was wrongly interpreted by the provinces to mean that unilateral patriation by the federal government could not be achieved. The provinces clearly thought that the federal government was bluffing, but, in a major challenge to political tradition, the Liberal government went ahead after the Constitutional Conference failed in September 1980. This bold move by Ottawa put the opposing provinces on the defensive, and it took them many months to recover their momentum. As Justice Minister Jean Chrétien said on the day of the Supreme Court decision, "conventions change." The flexibility of tradition has been an important means of constitutional adaptation in Canada. Thus, the Canada Act has not only transformed several key aspects of convention into law, but in the process altered its content.

The difficulty of achieving constitutional reform is an obvious reflection of the fragmented nature of Canada's political culture, while the isolation of Quebec, with its distinctive subculture, reveals the continuing strength and problems of both dualism and regionalism. The debate over the amending formulas was another illustration of regionalism, since all provinces initially wanted to retain a veto as a symbolic sign of their equality in the federal system. On this point, at least, there was some accommodation. Elitism was epitomized by the political executives' dominance of the constitutional reform process, while the fear of continentalism was expressed in the desire not to turn the Canadian judiciary into a replica of the activist American one, which is based on the principle of full judicial review. Finally, the notion that Canada can be held together by a process of elite accommodation has been sorely tested. Not only has Quebec been isolated in the federal system as the only province not initially willing to accept the Canada Act, but the attempted unilateral patriation and resulting two-year political battle did little to cement the system together at the leadership level. At probably no time in modern Canadian political history have the political elites been more in conflict than between 1980–1982, operating under a pattern that could be called contentious self-righteousness.

The constitutional review process created a number of internal problems for each of the political parties. Two such areas of particular importance were questions regarding party leadership and federal-provincial party relations. For the Liberals, successful completion of the constitutional quest generated anew speculation about Pierre Trudeau's anticipated retirement. Once constitutional reform had been achieved, there would be little rationale for his continued stewardship: the question was not "if," but "when" his retirement would come. The dominance of the leader in the Liberal party structure, however, did not make such a result inevitable: the decision to exit would be Pierre Trudeau's, not that of the party organization. Such a decision was in fact made by Trudeau on February 29, 1984.

For the Conservatives, questions of the continuing leadership of Joe Clark served as a backdrop to the constitutional reform process. Clark's decision to vigorously oppose unilateral patriation and his considerable success in doing so enhanced his stature within the Conservative party and in the country as well. By the time the Canada Act had been sent to Britain, Clark had survived an initial challenge to his leadership and had emerged with his party leading the public opinion polls. While the Conservatives' public support in the winter of 1982 had to be attributed, in part, to the neglect of the economy by the Liberals during the two-year review process, some of it undoubtedly reflected their role as a "viable opposition" and possible alternative government during the passage of the Canada Act. Joe Clark's role in the patriation debate, particularly his defence of Quebec, will likely be remembered as his finest hour—although not fine enough, from his party's perspective, to keep him from being ousted as leader in 1983.

Although the continued leadership of Ed Broadbent was not in question, his actions in committing the New Democratic Party to support of the Liberals' unilateral patriation caused serious dissent within the party organization.

Apparently without consulting his caucus, Broadbent threw his support behind Trudeau. The ensuing outcry was so great, particularly from the party's Saskatchewan members, that party discipline was challenged, and the NDP's constitutional critic, Lorne Nystrom, resigned from his assigned task. By the end of the patriation battle, however, Broadbent was consulting his caucus before committing his party's support to amendments of the Canada Act during the course of parliamentary debate. In this respect, the NDP was similar to the old-line parties: the party leaders, by and large, determined their party's stand on the patriation question.

Matters of federal-provincial party relations were more complex than those of leadership and possibly had greater long-term effects. Each of the parties suffered serious federal-provincial strains. For example, while provincial Liberal leaders in the West rejected Trudeau's patriation plan, more serious was the challenge from Quebec Liberal leader Claude Ryan. Beginning with the October Crisis of 1970, the Trudeau-Ryan relationship had never been overly friendly. The federal Liberal party's move to unilaterally patriate seriously weakened the appeal of the provincial party in Quebec, so much so that, contrary to their impressive string of by-election victories and a several-year lead in public opinion polls, the provincial Liberals were defeated by the Parti Québécois in the spring 1981 provincial election. Claude Ryan directly attributed his party's loss to the federal Liberals and their constitutional reforms. When the agreement of November 5, 1981, which isolated Quebec, was reached, Claude Ryan condemned it and then helped to write a resolution in the Quebec National Assembly that reasserted the powers and privileges of that province in the federal system. In response, the federal Liberal party in Quebec openly questioned the competence of its provincial counterpart.

Federal-provincial strains in the Conservative

party were most apparent with respect to Ontario and to a lesser extent with New Brunswick. Most provinces in the 1980–1982 period were controlled by Conservative governments that were opposed to the unilateral patriation plan. However, the Conservative government in Ontario under Bill Davis supported the national Liberal government of Pierre Trudeau, thereby creating a serious split within the party. This Ontario desertion was particularly significant because the province is not only the largest, but also crucial for any Conservative victory in a national election. The rejection of Clark by Ontario voters in 1980 guaranteed his defeat: Ontario's alliance with the federal Liberals continued this convenient relationship between Bill Davis and Pierre Trudeau. For example, immediately after Ottawa moved to unilaterally patriate the constitution, Ontario Premier Bill Davis held a news conference at which he not only backed the plan, but attacked those who rejected it on "narrow partisan grounds" — a not too subtle reference to the federal Conservatives. Moreover, Premier Davis publicly called on all Members of Parliament and senators — especially those from Ontario — to support the Patriation Resolution (*The Globe and Mail*, October 4, 1980). These attacks did little for the credibility of either the national Conservative party or its leader. In addition, it seems likely that the alliance between Davis and Trudeau during the patriation battle was a major reason why Bill Davis found that he had little support outside of Ontario when he contemplated running for the leadership of the national party in 1983.

Internal division in the New Democratic Party centred on the split in the party between its Western and Ontario wings. While its leader and a considerable portion of its voting support were from Ontario, its seats were from the Western provinces: 26 of the NDP's 32 seats in the 1980 election. This east-west division in the NDP was exacerbated by the federal-provincial split over the Canada Act. NDP Premier of Saskatchewan, Allan Blakeney, disagreed with his federal counterpart, Ed Broadbent, and opposed Trudeau's unilateral patriation scheme. Thus, the only elected NDP government in the country broke with its national party over the Canada Act, as it was initially presented to Parliament.

The final major aspect of the constitutional reform process that is illustrative of the workings of the Canadian polity is the electoral mechanism and the public's role therein. Although the contending parties often argued that they represented the public, no government had, in fact, a specific electoral mandate from which to proceed. For example, only the most partisan could interpret the Liberal victory in the 1980 election as a mandate for constitutional reform. The public rejected the Clark Conservative government, particularly with respect to its budget — it did not select Trudeau in order to bring about constitutional change. All the governments spoke eloquently of their right to interpret and to defend the public's interest in the reform process, while none of them were elected to office on any such grounds. Only when the patriation battle was well underway in 1981 did the Conservative government of Bill Davis in Ontario and the PQ Government of René Lévesque in Quebec hold provincial elections that might be so interpreted. The perceived mandates of the political executives to negotiate constitutional change were more apprehended than real.

The public was initially excluded from any direct involvement in the process of constitutional reform. After public and opposition attacks, the government finally consented to public hearings by a Joint Parliamentary Committee. However, only indirectly through the mass media and public opinion polls was the ordinary citizen given any attention. Media advertising campaigns, and extensive ones at that, were conducted by both the federal and provincial governments. Private party polls, as well as the Gallup ones, were widely cited. In fairly typical fashion, the same public opinion

> There is little cause for national self-congratulation in the Constitution Act, 1982 and the procedures by which it became a part of the constitution . . . . The damage done to our legal, political and constitutional order outweighs the gains (Smiley, 1983: 93).

> Charter litigation is a boom industry, but like all industries, its products vary in quality (Hutchinson, 1987: A7).

results were interpreted to support both those in favour and those opposed to unilateral patriation. Perceived public support was a political resource that both sides sought to manipulate to their own advantage. However, since the public was largely excluded from the two-year constitutional reform process, it is quite likely that the ordinary citizen will return the favour by ignoring the final product. The Canada Act was primarily the result of a political confrontation between the federal and provincial political elites that was carried out in the name of the public interest.

The Impact of the 1982 Constitution Act

While some political prognosticators predicted that the 1982 Constitution Act might have almost revolutionary consequences on the political process, others felt that it might end up having little effect, as did the Bill of Rights of 1960. Both views, given the first decade of the 1982 Constitution Act, have turned out to be wrong. At this point, the long-term results of the 1982 Constitution Act, especially the impact of the Charter of Rights and Freedoms, remain problematical. However, some evident trends of judicial interpretation and legal usage have already emerged.

After looking at how often the 1982 Constitution Act has been utilized, we will take an overview of several key cases. Our concern is not

with a comprehensive look at each part of the 1982 Constitution Act, but a more modest investigation of some of its major provisions and their initial application and interpretation by the judiciary. Finally, we will consider the long-term implications of the 1982 Constitution Act, especially the Charter of Rights and Freedoms.

OVERALL IMPACT – THE NUMBERS GAME

From the day of its proclamation on April 17, 1982, the Constitution Act has had an important effect, at least on the legal profession. It now seems to be almost obligatory for each case to have a Charter argument, including those cases that were already before the courts in April 1982. Many of these initial usages of the Charter were "last try" arguments, in that people had nothing to lose and possibly much to gain from appealing to the new Constitution Act. As a result, there was an explosion of Charter-related cases after April 1982. While most of these cases lost with respect to their interpretations of the Charter, they did demonstrate the intellectual ingenuity of the legal profession, at the same time that they tested the patience of the judiciary.

In its first year, over 500 cases had arguments related to the Charter, with about 750 usages in its first three years of existence. However, these figures underestimate the total, since many lower court cases, which include Charter arguments, are not very visible. As a result, one estimate puts the probable number of Charter-related cases, in the first three years of its existence, at 1500 (Russell, 1985: 369). By early 1989, that figure was estimated to be in the range of 4000 cases. However, few had reached the Supreme Court level, which had only decided four such cases by the summer of 1985 and about 50 cases by 1988. This modest output of the Supreme Court on Charter-related cases will not last long, as literally dozens of cases will reach its docket in the next few years. For example, by the summer of 1989, the number of Supreme Court cases based on the Charter had already doubled to 100. Such figures indicate that a Charter-related argument has become a status symbol for lawyers, even if it is not yet a legal obligation.

This initial array of Charter cases has caused a certain element of confusion in the legal system, as the various provincial courts have given, at times, contradictory interpretations of the 1982 Constitution Act. Gradually, however, as the Supreme Court considers cases, a national pattern will emerge, since Supreme Court decisions are applicable in all of the provinces. Diversity of judicial interpretation will only last until the Supreme Court decides. Thus, it is apparent that the 1982 Constitution Act, and especially the Charter, will have a nationalizing, if not necessarily a unifying, impact on Canadian politics. For example, even though Quebec was not a party to the constitutional accord, the 1982 Constitution Act and Supreme Court decisions based thereon still apply to that province.

The necessity for having the Supreme Court settle various issues raised by the Constitution Act led the federal government to announce a program of helping to pay the legal costs of Charter-related cases. In September 1985, the federal government expanded its Court Challenges Program to include cases relating to the equality rights provision (Section 15) of the Charter. A total of $9 million was allocated for such legal support during the period of 1985–1989 (about $2 million per year). These funds, to prevent any apparent government control or conflict of interest, would be administered by the Canadian Council on Social Development. Interestingly, however, such funding was not made available to parties wishing to intervene in a court challenge. While the Court Challenges Program may eventually help to unify the judicial application of the 1982 Constitution Act, its most immediate impact was to increase the number of Charter-related cases with which the judiciary had to deal. As former Saskatchewan Attorney General Roy Romanow put it in a speech in March 1982, the "scope for challenge is mind-boggling."

THE 1982 CONSTITUTION ACT IN ACTION

The vast array of cases so far have concerned the rights and privileges contained in the Charter and, of those, most have dealt with criminal cases. In fact, one might easily have concluded, in the initial year following the proclamation of the 1982 Constitution Act, that the main beneficiaries were alleged prostitutes, drug dealers, and ex-Nazis. A few examples will illustrate the current emphasis of Charter interpretation.

In Section 2 of the Charter, fundamental freedoms, such as those of religion, press, and association, are protected from governmental interference. Several of the more prominent Charter-related cases fall into this category. For example, a controversial area has been the question of businesses operating on Sundays in contravention of the federal Lord's Day Act. In the Big M Drug Mart case, decided in April of 1985, the Supreme Court upheld a lower court decision which had overturned the Lord's Day Act because it violated the Charter's guarantee of freedom of religion. However, in a 1986 decision, the Supreme Court upheld Ontario's

> **Because the Charter has elements of both continuity and change with Canadian political tradition, interpretation becomes a matter of emphasis (Morton, 1987: 33).**

Sunday closing legislation (the Retail Business Holidays Act), because it was written in totally secular terms, thus primarily avoiding the issue of freedom of religion. In other Section 2 related cases, the Supreme Court has determined that freedom of association does not necessarily include the right to strike. Finally, the language question in Quebec, which resulted in several court challenges, based on the protection of freedom of expression in Section 2(b), led the Supreme Court to overturn provincial legislation, only to find the province responding by invoking the override provision (Section 33) of the Charter (see discussion of the language issue and the notwithstanding clause in the next section).

The democratic rights protected by Sections 3–5 of the Charter have produced relatively few court cases, although some are of particular relevance to the operation of Canadian elections. Traditionally, certain classes of people, such as prisoners or the mentally infirm, have been denied the right to vote. Quebec has been the only province to allow inmates to vote in provincial elections. A number of challenges have been made to federal and provincial restrictions on prisoners' voting rights, with only partial success and conflicting results to date. For example, prisoners in Saskatchewan being held for trial were granted the right to vote, and those on probation in British Columbia were also allowed the right to participate as a result of Charter challenges. With respect to mentally handicapped and mentally ill patients, a ruling by the Federal Court of Canada on October 17, 1988 (during the federal election) granted them the right to vote in the November 21, 1988 election. This ruling affected approximately 50 000 potential voters across the country.

Over the years the political activities of civil servants have been regulated by both provincial and federal governments, under the rationale that a "neutral" civil service cannot be openly composed of those directly involved in partisan activities. A number of court cases in this area have produced conflicting results to date. By and large, however, the courts have generally upheld the right of governments to restrict the openly-partisan activities of their respective bureaucrats.

One extremely important area for the future impact of the Charter on the electoral process concerns the equality of population size of electoral constituencies. In British Columbia in 1989, the provincial Supreme Court ruled that provincial electoral boundaries had to be drawn so as to promote and protect the equality of each citizen's vote. If such a view extends to the other provincial governments and the federal government as well, its potential implications could be extremely important for the operation of the Canadian electoral process.

A series of legal rights are protected in Sections 7–14 of the Charter and have produced an avalanche of court challenges. In its initial impact, the Charter cases have dealt, to a large extent, with the question of procedural fairness in the Canadian justice system.

The right to a trial "within a reasonable time" has been the basis for having charges dismissed in several provinces. In Quebec, a Superior Court judge in November of 1983 quashed charges against seven current or former members of the RCMP who had been accused of stealing the PQ membership list back in 1973, because a decade (1973 to 1983) without a trial was deemed contrary "to within a reasonable time." The right to counsel was the basis for an April 1, 1986, Supreme Court decision in which a New Brunswick woman's confession of murdering her husband was ruled as inadmissible evidence because she had "waived" her right to counsel while drunk. A charge of marijuana possession against a woman was dismissed by the Supreme Court of Ontario (May 1985) because the woman had been strip-searched after an arrest for a minor theft. In May 1985, the Supreme Court of Canada ruled that police have a constitutional obligation to inform drivers of their right to legal counsel when they have agreed to take a breathalyser test for impaired driving.

An interesting application of the Charter concerns Section 11, which states that a person has the right "to be presumed innocent unless proven guilty according to law." Under this protection, the so-called "reverse-onus" clause of the Narcotic Control Act (Section 8) was ruled unconstitutional by the Supreme Court of Canada (March 1986). Given that provision, a person accused of possessing a certain amount of drugs was assumed to be trafficking, unless he or she could prove otherwise. Previously, several provinces had already held that the "reverse-onus" provision was unacceptable under the Charter.

While the Charter, as illustrated above, has been used to protect an individual's rights in criminal cases, not all of the court rulings have necessarily expanded such rights. For example, in April 1986, the Ontario Court of Appeal ruled that provisions in the federal Young Offenders Act that deny a young person a trial by jury do not violate any of the provisions of the Charter. In a similar vein, the Supreme Court of Canada (March 1986) decided that the restriction in Ontario of civil servants getting involved in politics does not contravene any Charter protections. Thus, the pattern, so far, of judicial decision and discretion is a mixed one. The Charter has been most effective with respect to procedural rights in the criminal law area, with a more modest impact for other Charter provisions.

One of the most important cases considered to date by the Supreme Court of Canada concerns the testing of the cruise missile. The government of Pierre Trudeau agreed to let the American military carry out cruise missile tests over Canadian territory. However, a number of peace groups, led by Operation Dismantle, challenged the government's decision with respect to Section 7 of the Charter, which guarantees the "security of the person." Arguing

> The Charter of Rights and Freedoms has begun to transform Canadian politics. Most obviously, by entrenching judicial review, the Charter has redefined the institutional balance of power among legislature, executive and judiciary (Sniderman et al., 1989: 259).

that the cruise missile would increase the likelihood of nuclear war, thereby undercutting the security of the person, the peace groups challenged Ottawa's right to take such decisions, even in the areas of foreign policy and national defence. Ultimately, the Supreme Court of Canada rejected the view (May 1985) proposed by Operation Dismantle.

However, the significance of the cruise decision does not reside in whether or not the tests were allowed to go ahead, but in what the Supreme Court of Canada asserted was its right in making such a decision. The Supreme Court declared its prerogative to review cabinet decisions, a view which has potentially far-reaching implications for the scope of judicial review. The secrecy of cabinet decision-making is no longer sacrosanct, since the judiciary can now review its results, including regulations and orders-in-council.

The "security of the person" provision of Section 7 also served as the basis for the Supreme Court's decision in January 1988 on the abortion question. The case concerned Dr. Henry Morgentaler and his associates, who had been convicted of giving abortions, contrary to section 251 of the federal Criminal Code. On appeal to the high court, Morgentaler argued that the abortion law violated the rights and security of the person of the pregnant woman. The Supreme Court agreed and declared Canada's abortion law to be unconstitutional, setting off another round of emotional political controversy on the issue.

With the coming into force in 1985 of the

GROUPS THROUGHOUT CANADA CELEBRATE
IMPLEMENTATION OF EQUAL RIGHTS LAW ....

WOMEN   HANDICAPPED   ELDERLY   ETHNIC GROUPS

LAWYERS

Source: Portfolio 85: The Year in Canadian Caricature, CROC Publishing, 1985.
Reproduced by permission of Mike Graston, *Windsor Star*.

equality rights provision (Section 15) of the Charter, the potential Charter challenges increased exponentially. Section 15 included such important and sometimes controversial issues as mandatory retirement and male-female equality. It will likely take a number of court decisions, and many years, before a clear and consistent pattern of interpretation is available from the court system.

By itself, the initial response to Section 15 has been significant. The provinces and the federal government have sought to bring provincial and federal practices into conformity with the equal rights section. The beginning step in this pro-

cess was a review of existing laws and regulations, usually followed by an omnibus bill making the desired corrections. For example, the government of Alberta in 1985 brought forward the Charter Omnibus Act to deal with these matters. However, critics of this process argued that most of the omnibus bills dealt with trivial changes, leaving many key issues still to be resolved by the courts. For some provinces that charge was particularly correct. Fear of Charter challenges based on Section 15 did, however, force governments to act in some areas; for example, the federal government in March 1985 abolished the practice of mandatory retirement in the federal civil service. Controversies growing out of Section 15 issues will likely be with us, and high on the political agenda, for many years to come.

The first equality rights section decision made by the Supreme Court occurred in February 1989. The particular situation (the Andrews Case) concerned the provision of British Columbia's law requiring that lawyers be citizens. The Supreme Court decided that the law was unconstitutional because it barred an entire class of people from employment, thus violating the equality rights guaranteed by Section 15. However, more important than the specifics of this case was the attitude that the Supreme Court displayed towards Section 15, namely, a rather generous interpretation of this provision and its application.

While the impact of the Charter in its first decade has been extensive and impressive, the Charter contains one serious drawback, namely, the override provision contained in Section 33. This provision allows the federal and provincial governments the ability to bypass the Charter — and court decisions based on it — under certain conditions.

SECTION 33 — OVERRIDING THE CHARTER

Even in its first decade of operation, the Charter has laid the basis for a more activist judiciary. However, the extent of judicial review may be limited in the long run by the possible willingness of the federal and provincial levels to use Section 33 to override the fundamental rights of Sections 2 and 7 through 15. The override provision basically asserts that parliamentary supremacy is superior in law to sections of the Charter, if Parliament so decides.

In the first eight years of the Charter's existence (1982–1990), the federal government did not use the power contained in Section 33. The first province to invoke the override power to declare a single law exempt from the Charter was the province of Saskatchewan. On January 31, 1986 the legislature in Saskatchewan sent striking members of the government employees union back to work. A more significant use of Section 33 involved the PQ government in Quebec. As a protest of the fact that they had not agreed to the Constitution Act, from April 17, 1982 onward every single piece of legislation passed by the Quebec National Assembly was made exempt from the relevant provisions of the Charter. Moreover, the PQ government made its override exemption retroactive, so that past legislation was free from Charter challenges as well.

With the defeat of the Parti Québécois in the December 2, 1985 provincial election, Quebec's position on Section 33 altered. By the spring of 1986, the new provincial Liberal government indicated that they would stop the practice of exempting all legislation from the Charter. The blanket or omnibus use of Section 33 was not renewed in 1987. Moreover, it was made clear that the Charter of Rights and Freedoms would be given precedence over Quebec's own human rights legislation. It seems unlikely that any government, at least in the immediate future, will make use of the wholesale or blanket override of the Charter.

The first specific use of Section 33 by Quebec occurred in February 1984, in order to protect the French-only sign provision of Bill 101. The provincial government in Quebec faced immediate court challenges over its language legislation, with the strategy of not dealing further with the language law until the Supreme Court had considered the matter. On December 15, 1988, the Supreme Court issued its ruling in the Quebec Sign Case (Quebec v. Ford et al.). The Supreme Court found the provincial language legislation of 1984 to be in violation of both the Canadian and Quebec Charters. Two days later, the Liberal government of Premier Robert Bourassa decided to bring in legislation permitting "French only signs outside but

> Prime Minister Brian Mulroney addressing the House of Commons (April 7, 1989) on the "notwithstanding" clause of the Charter of Rights:
>
> "You [Liberals] paid a price that was much too high for Canada and for the fundamental rights of Canadian citizens. It was the greatest price that a federal Parliament has ever been called upon·to pay in regard to the protection of fundamental liberties, of religion, of association."

bilingual signs inside" in the province of Quebec (Bill 178). This legislation allowed the use of the override provision as a means of bypassing the Supreme Court ruling. Needless to say, this action became a political storm centre, pushing language rights once again to the forefront of Canada's political agenda and throwing the ratification process of the Meech Lake accord into limbo.

The current applications of Section 33 reveal several important patterns. First, outside of Quebec and the contentious policy area of language rights, the override provision of the Charter has been modestly used in its first decade of existence. Whether this trend will continue is difficult to assess, but wholesale invocation or frequent applications of Section 33 appear to be unlikely. Second, as the Supreme Court increasingly decides Charter-related cases in the 1990s, the temptation to invoke the override provision may increase. However, pressure from the public and vocal interest groups may keep this trend modest. Finally, provincial governments, in particular, will use Section 33 when it is in their interests to do so in order to protect their power and privilege in the Canadian federal system.

CONCLUSION ON THE CANADA ACT

This brief overview of some of the important court decisions based on the Charter reveals a conflicting pattern of interpretation. Certainly the role of the courts as the umpires of the federal system and interpreters of the Charter has been enhanced. Protection of individual rights and procedural fairness of the justice system have been promoted, although the courts have been more modest in their explicit challenges to legislative supremacy. The number of cases involving Charter issues since 1982 has been substantial, but in some areas it is still too early to determine definite trends of interpretation.

Our discussion of the content of the Canada Act reveals that its major provisions represent a series of political compromises between the federal and provincial governments. While some new features were added, such as an entrenched Charter of Rights and a series of amending formulas, most of the Canada Act is a refinement of existing arrangements. In fact, the 1982 Constitution Act may be misnamed — it does not provide Canada with a new, comprehensive constitution. What it does, primarily, is to consolidate existing provisions into one Act and make a series of amendments to others. Thus, a more accurate title might have been the Constitutional Amendment Act of 1982.

The passage of the Patriation Resolution seems consistent with our analysis of how the basic political structures and processes of the Canadian polity actually operate. As our brief survey of its application has suggested, the long-term impact of the Constitution Act may be to alter some of the traditional institutional and political relationships (e.g., the political role of the judiciary). In particular, the potential for a more activist judiciary has not only been put

> The ultimate effect of the Charter will depend primarily on the integrity of those who are involved in its application, secondly on the procedures through which it is interpreted and applied, and lastly on the instrument itself (Greene, 1989: 228).

> After five years of the Charter's life, the judiciary hasn't gone berserk and struck down laws right and left. It just hasn't happened. So the alarm is, up until now, a false alarm (Canadian Supreme Court Justice, Mr. Antonio Lamer, April 1987).

> Canadians are almost obsessed with changing their constitution . . . . Canadians are . . . apt to believe that they have a marvelous country if only they could find the ideal constitution (Russell et al., 1989: 681).

into place, but has also been put into practice. How far this pattern develops will depend, to a great extent, on how the judiciary itself interprets key provisions of the Charter of Rights and Freedoms. As one assessment has it "we have put a little more faith in the courts and a little less faith in the people" (Mallory, 1984: 8).

The Meech Lake Accord

Given the difficult battle to patriate the Constitution and to add a Charter of Rights to the Canadian constitutional system, as well as the political repercussions of the 1980–1982 period, it might seem likely to expect a generation to pass before such issues were raised again. However, in Canada constitutional reform is a never-ending treadmill, the leitmotif of the political process. As in no other modern democratic system, in Canada the politics of our constitution are the constitution of our politics.

The popular term, the Meech Lake accord — named after the place where the original agreement was negotiated — is technically incorrect. Instead, the proper term is the Constitution Amendment, 1987. In fact, the Meech Lake accord consists of three documents: first, the original agreement in principle of April 1987 (the 1987 Constitutional Accord); second, the Resolution presented to Parliament to authorize the agreement; and, finally, the actual constitutional changes needed to implement the 1987 Constitutional Accord (the Constitution Amendment, 1987). (Both the 1987 Constitutional Accord and the Constitution Amendment, 1987 are reproduced in the Appendix for the

reader's convenience.) Thus, the 1987 constitutional negotiations did not produce a new Canadian constitution; instead, they produced a series of proposed amendments to the Constitution Act, 1867 and the Constitution Act, 1982.

After the 1987 Constitutional Accord of April 1987 and the detailed contents were agreed to in the Constitution Amendment, 1987 in June, the ratification process was allowed three years to complete (until June 23, 1990 — 3 years from the date of the first legislature to approve it). The initial response to the Meech Lake accord was quite favorable. However, as provincial governments and leaders were changed (Manitoba, New Brunswick, Newfoundland) and as the deadline drew near, considerable opposition to the proposal developed by 1989. The last few months (January to June, 1990) of the ratification process were extremely contentious with the Meech Lake accord failing to receive provincial approval by Manitoba and Newfoundland. However, even though the Meech Lake accord has been defeated, the proposal and its rejection are still highly significant, for it will set the tone and direction of Canadian politics in general and constitutional negotiations in particular for many years to come.

THE CONTENT OF THE MEECH LAKE ACCORD

The primary constitutional problem facing Canadian politics in the mid-1980s was how to draw Quebec back into the constitutional family. Because it was the only province not to sign the 1982 Canada Act, most politicians felt it essential, as soon as possible, to have Quebec

> Whereas the Constitution Act [1982] primarily addressed the relationship between citizens and their governments, the Accord attempts to redefine the relationship among governments in the Canadian federal state. In the long run, changes to that relationship could have a profound impact on the character of Canadian political life . . . (Gibbins, 1988: 3).

become a full partner in the federal polity. Although not a top priority on the political agenda between 1982 and 1987, this problem of Quebec led to another round of constitutional negotiations which culminated in the 1987 Constitutional Accord — much to everyone's surprise. After outlining its major provisions, we will briefly discuss the process and implications of the Meech Lake accord and its rejection.

Over half of the 1987 Constitution Amendment consists of proposed revisions to the Constitution Act, 1867. First, Quebec was recognized as constituting "a distinct society" and Canada was recognized as a bicultural society composed of French-speaking and English-speaking citizens, both inside and outside of Quebec. The "distinct society" clause was seen as crucial by Premier Bourassa to Quebec's future participation in and support for the federal system. However, critics of the Meech Lake accord saw the "distinct society" clause as providing recognition of a special status for the province of Quebec.

The second major change to the 1867 Constitution Act concerned the method of selecting senators. The traditional method, selection by the prime minister, would have been replaced by a process which gave the provinces a significant role in choosing members of the upper House of the national legislature. When a senate vacancy occurred, the government of the province (i.e., premier) in which that vacancy existed would have submitted a list of names to the Queen's Privy Council for Canada (i.e., prime

minister) of those who might be summoned to the Senate. The prime minister would have selected the nominee from that list.

In many ways, this proposed procedure merely specified in law what has happened in practice for many years (see Chapter six). However, by formalizing the process and the provinces' role in it, the prime minister would have relinquished some of his power in this area. Contrary to popular impressions, under the Meech Lake accord, the provinces would not have appointed members to the senate, but only would have recommended the names from which the prime minister would have chosen. There was nothing to force a prime minister to act. If he was not happy with the list of names submitted, he could have refused to appoint any, leaving the senate seat vacant until a suitable name had been put forward by the province.

In an attempt to speed up the process of senate reform, the province of Alberta, which wants the Senate to be an elected body, used an election to determine their first senate nominees. The first senate election in Canadian history was held on October 16, 1989. Six candidates vied for the position, with Stan Waters, representing the newly formed regional protest party — the Reform Party — easily winning over his rivals. On October 20, Alberta Premier Don Getty submitted his list of nominees to Prime Minister Mulroney. Even though at this point the Meech Lake accord had not been formally ratified, the Prime Minister had agreed to follow its provisions regarding Senate appointments. Even though selected under its auspices, Stan Waters was, in fact, opposed to the Meech Lake accord, calling it a "seriously-flawed document." However, Prime Minister Mulroney did not immediately act to appoint Stan Waters to the Senate, although he later did.

A third major change to the Constitution Act, 1867 would have affected the process of immigration. The federal government was committed to negotiating an agreement concerning immigration and the admission of aliens with any province which requested such an agreement. Thus, the provinces would have been given a direct role in the federal policy area of immigration—one which they initially held under the 1867 British North America Act.

A fourth area of constitutional reform that would have been made by the Meech Lake accord related to the judiciary. The Supreme Court of Canada, along with its composition and structure, would have been entrenched in the Constitution. For example, the Supreme Court was specified as consisting of nine justices (a Chief Justice of Canada and eight other judges), with three of these justices admitted from the bar of Quebec. A significant modification was made in the selection of Supreme Court judges. As with senate appointments, the Queen's Privy Council of Canada—for all practical purposes the prime minister—would have chosen the judges from lists of names provided by the provinces.

A further change was proposed in the area of shared-cost programs. A province would have been able to opt-out of any shared-cost program within the powers of exclusive provincial jurisdiction and receive "reasonable compensation" from the federal government. However, such compensation would have been given to the province only if it had carried "on a program or initiative that is compatible with the national objectives."

Finally, a first ministers' conference on the "economy and such other matters as may be appropriate" was now constitutionally required at least once a year. Thus, the first ministers' conferences, which in the past had been based on convention, would have been mandated by constitutional prescription.

In addition to these six amendments to the 1867 Constitution Act, several changes would also have been made by the Meech Lake accord to the 1982 Constitution Act. Sections 40–42 of the 1982 Constitution Act were modified, extending the range of areas for which provinces would have received financial compensa-tion and over which each province would have had a veto (since unanimous consent would have been required). For example, unanimous consent would have been needed for any changes to "the powers of the Senate and the method of selecting Senators," "the Supreme Court of Canada," and "the establishment of new provinces." Previously these areas of reform only required support of two-thirds of the provinces with 50 percent of the nation's population. Thus, each province would have had a veto over crucial areas of potential constitutional reform.

A second modification concerned the necessity for yearly constitutional conferences. Beginning in 1988, a yearly constitutional conference was mandated, along with its agenda: senate reform, the fishery, and "other matters as are agreed upon."

If these changes to the 1867 and 1982 Constitution Acts had been made, the Meech Lake accord would have altered the direction of Canadian federalism. In contrast to Pierre Trudeau's vision of Canada and the centralizing tendencies of his rule and the 1982 Canada Act, the now defeated Meech Lake accord, by enhancing the role and power of the provinces, would have created a decentralizing pattern in the federal polity.

PROCESS OF THE MEECH LAKE ACCORD

Although constitutional reform was not high on the political agenda after the adoption of the 1982 Canada Act, there was widespread recognition of the need to have Quebec accept the revised constitution. Quebec was therefore the crucial province in developing the Meech Lake accord, even though the process was arduous and complicated. The process of the Meech Lake accord is outlined in Table 14.3. Here we will comment on how the agreement was initially achieved, as well as on several key points in the unsuccessful ratification process.

TABLE 14.3 PROCESS OF THE MEECH LAKE ACCORD
(Constitution Amendment, 1987)

Date	Event
August 6, 1984	In his nomination speech, Brian Mulroney promises to bring Quebec into the constitution.
September 4, 1984	Landslide election for the Conservatives; constitutional reform given only slight attention during the campaign.
December 2, 1985	Former Premier Robert Bourassa and the provincial Liberals win the Quebec provincial election; Premier Bourassa willing to negotiate with the federal government on constitutional reform.
November 1986	First Ministers' Conference in Vancouver agrees to try and gain a constitutional settlement with Quebec.
March 1987	Quebec refuses to attend the constitutional conference on aboriginal rights.
January–April 1987	Behind-the-scenes negotiations between federal and provincial leaders show promise of a possible compromise.
April 30, 1987	Agreement on "matters-of-principle" at Meech Lake (1987 Constitutional Accord).
May 27, 1987	Former Prime Minister Pierre Trudeau intervenes in the debate, strongly condemning the accord.
June 3, 1987	Details of the constitutional compromise specified (Constitution Amendment, 1987).
June 23, 1987	Quebec National Assembly passes the accord.
September 23, 1987	Saskatchewan approves the accord.
October 13, 1987	New Brunswick election: the Liberals and Frank McKenna win, with an anti-Meech Lake position.
October 26, 1987	The House of Commons passes the accord.
December 7, 1987	Alberta approves the accord.
April 21, 1988	Senate amends the accord.
April 26, 1988	Manitoba election produces a minority Conservative government.
May 13, 1988	PEI approves the accord.
May 25, 1988	Nova Scotia approves the accord.
June 22, 1988	House of Commons rejects senate amendments, passes the accord for the second time.
June 29, 1988	Ontario and British Columbia both approve the accord.

TABLE 14.3 Continued

Date	Event
July 7, 1988	Newfoundland approves the accord.
December 15, 1988	Supreme Court overturns Quebec's language legislation, Bill 101.
December 16, 1988	Debate on the accord begins in the Manitoba legislature.
December 18, 1988	Quebec invokes Section 33 of the Charter in bypassing the Supreme Court decision.
December 19, 1988	In response to the events in Quebec, and in order to save his minority government, Manitoba Premier Gary Filmon suspends the Meech Lake debate.
April 20, 1989	Newfoundland election: provincial Liberals, led by Clyde Wells, elected on an anti-Meech Lake platform.
September 25, 1989	Premier Bourassa wins reelection in the Quebec provincial election.
October 1989	Manitoba and New Brunswick issue reports on the accord which demand major changes in the powers given to Quebec. The Meech Lake accord appears dead.
November 1989	First Ministers' Conference to try and gain final ratification of the accord fails.
March 21, 1990	Premier McKenna of New Brunswick proposes a "companion resolution" in conjunction with the accord.
March 26, 1990	Prime Minister Mulroney sends the McKenna proposal to a special all-party Commons committee for public hearings.
April 6, 1990	Newfoundland legislature rescinds its approval of the Meech Lake accord.
May 17, 1990	House of Commons committee issues its report, calling for passage of the accord, with other constitutional changes to be dealt with later.
May 22, 1990	In protest over possible changes to the Meech Lake accord, Lucien Bouchard, the Prime Minister's Quebec lieutenant, resigns from the cabinet and the Conservative party.
June 3, 1990	Start of a week of intense negotiations to try and save the accord.
June 9, 1990	A tentative revision of the Meech Lake accord is announced, with the legislatures in Manitoba, New Brunswick and Newfoundland to try and ratify the accord by the June 23 deadline.
June 16, 1990	New Brunswick legislature unanimously passes the accord.
June 22, 1990	The Meech Lake accord dies, after the Manitoba legislature is prevented from proceeding by NDP member Elijah Harper and Premier Clyde Wells of Newfoundland refuses to have the legislature hold a vote on the accord.
June 23, 1990	As the ratification deadline passes, Canada's constitutional and political future is thrown into doubt.

> Tonight Canada is whole again, the Canadian family is together again, and the nation is one again (Prime Minister Brian Mulroney, announcing the Meech Lake accord, June 1987).
>
> . . . a constitutional document which — if it is accepted by the people and their legislators — will render the Canadian state totally impotent. That would destine it, given the dynamics of power, to eventually be governed by eunuchs (former Prime Minister Pierre Elliott Trudeau, commenting on the Meech Lake accord, May 1987).

> Brian Mulroney will get a place in history for having pulled this off . . . . People will see that it was the Conservative party which got unanimity, and which is truly the party of national unity (Senator Lowell Murray, quoted in Gray, 1987: 15).
>
> Mulroney simply gave the premiers everything they said they wanted, and as a bonus threw in the assurance that anything they get in the future will also be exactly what they want. He then announced this surrender as a triumph of statesmanship (Fulford, 1987: 5).

Although Prime Minister Brian Mulroney had indicated in the 1984 election the need to bring Quebec back into the constitutional process, very little actual happened on the matter in 1984 and 1985. However, behind-the-scenes negotiations began to bear fruit in 1986, leading to a First Ministers' Conference at Meech Lake in late April 1987. After five years of refusing to accept the new constitution of 1982 and after also rejecting any other area of constitutional reform until its concerns had been met, Quebec agreed to the 1987 Constitutional Accord which recognized Quebec as a "distinct society" (April 30, 1987). However, the details of the agreement still had to be specified. Following a hard month of bargaining, the final deal was struck (Constitution Amendment, 1987) on June 3, 1987, with ratification by all provinces and the federal government to be completed within three years.

The initial reaction to the Meech Lake accord was generally favourable: all three national leaders endorsed it, along with all of the premiers, who had, of course, just negotiated it. Gradually, however, opposition to the accord began to build, and political circumstances, such as elections, began to change the prospects for ratification. New governments and new premiers not committed to the accord were elected in several

provinces (New Brunswick, Newfoundland). Moreover, the new minority Conservative government in Manitoba withdrew its support (i.e., decided not to try and push the accord through its legislature) after Quebec invoked Section 33 of the Charter in order to override the Supreme Court's decision on Bill 101 in December of 1988. However, by late 1989 the accord had been ratified by the federal government and eight provinces (all except Manitoba and New Brunswick), even though the newly elected Premier of Newfoundland was threatening to rescind the province's earlier acceptance of the accord.

Opposition to the accord centred on several key points. First, the recognition of Quebec as a distinct society caused concern among English Canadians in particular, for it seemed to confer a special status on the province of Quebec. Second, the ability of the provinces to opt-out of national programs, with financial compensation guaranteed, appeared to limit the national role of the federal government, particularly in relation to the "have-not" provinces. Third, the provinces were given considerably more power in areas like senatorial and judicial appointments. Moreover, the changes in the amending procedures gave each province a veto power over crucial areas of future constitutional

> Constitutions are not really fit subjects for leisurely contemplation. The shaping of them is like no other political act; it goes to the root of a nation's self-image (Sheppard and Valpy, 1982: 7).

reform. In effect, each province, and not just Quebec, was given more power, symbolized by the veto for every province (i.e., a "special-status for all" solution). Fourth, the Yukon and Northwest Territories were opposed to the accord, because each existing province now held a veto over the admission of new provinces, making it unlikely that such new provinces might soon be created.

Support for the accord was based on the need to accommodate Quebec and to have that key province accept the revised 1982 Constitution. Moreover, for those who felt that the federal system had become too centralized in recent decades, the decentralization of Canadian federalism promoted by the accord was viewed as a positive, not a negative, trend. In addition, most of the provinces (i.e., the premiers) liked the accord because it enhanced their status and prestige in the Canadian federal system.

One of the most dramatic moments in the ratification process was the intervention of former Prime Minister Pierre Trudeau into the national debate on the Meech Lake accord. Having kept a self-imposed silence since leaving office, Trudeau finally "went public," because the accord stood diametrically opposed to his vision of Canada and his achievements in the 1982 Constitution Act. On May 27, 1987, Trudeau condemned the accord in articles in *La Presse* and the *Toronto Star*. Similar views were later expressed by Trudeau in his appearance before the parliamentary committee on August 27, 1987. The former Prime Minister argued that the accord would give special status to Quebec, undercut the power of the federal govern-

Source: Guy Badeaux (ed.), *Portfolio 87: The Year in Canadian Caricature*. Montreal: Ludcom, 1987. By permission of Susan Dewar.

ment to respond to national needs and purposes, and prevent future constitutional reform.

As a result of Trudeau's intervention, the mobilization of public opinion by various interest groups (labour, women, minorities, and the territories), and the turnover in several provincial election campaigns (Manitoba, New Brunswick, Newfoundland), what looked like an easy ratification process in June of 1987 had become a problematical one by the spring of 1990.

From a constitutional perspective, the winter and spring of 1990 were particularly grueling.

Numerous meetings, bilateral negotiations, press statements and public protest put Meech Lake at the top of the nation's political agenda. The key issue was whether or not Quebec would agree to any revisions to the Meech Lake accord in order to placate the objections of the premiers of Manitoba, New Brunswick and Newfoundland before the June 23 deadline was reached. Quebec's position was clear — no changes to Meech Lake, with other areas of reform to be considered only after it had been passed. Premier Bourassa felt that Quebec had already negotiated and compromised in good faith in order to get the Meech Lake accord; thus, no other revisions could be tolerated. Given the growing nationalist sentiment in Quebec, this was an understandable political position to take. What Quebec did not recognize, however, was the outrage in English-Canada over the use of section 33 in relation to Bill 101 (December, 1988); it was at that point that public opinion in the rest of Canada turned against Quebec and the accord. As a sign of this negative reaction, Newfoundland, on April 6, 1990, rescinded its approval of the Meech Lake accord, thus putting one more rather large nail in the accord's coffin.

The months of April and May saw further negotiations to try and save the Meech Lake accord, with Quebec continuing to refuse to discuss any further changes and the remaining provinces (Manitoba, Newfoundland, New Brunswick) just as stubbornly rejecting its approval without such changes. In an attempt to preempt the federal government from backing any revisions to the accord, Prime Minister Mulroney's Quebec lieutenant and cabinet officer, Lucien Bouchard, resigned from the caucus and cabinet, sending political shock waves through the nation. Bouchard's resignation and hero's welcome back in Quebec effectively eliminated any immediate compromise by Quebec and the federal government on the Meech Lake accord. In a last ditch effort to save the constitutional package, Prime Minister

Mulroney invited the 10 premiers to dinner on June 3, a meeting which extended into a week-long marathon bargaining session.

On June 9, it appeared that the Meech Lake accord had been miraculously saved. The first ministers agreed to some modest changes of the future constitutional reform process, but first, the provinces of Manitoba, New Brunswick and Newfoundland would pass the accord. Then, on the question of Senate reform, the federal and provincial governments would seek an unanimous agreement within 5 years. If no such agreement was reached, Ontario would relinquish six of its Senate seats, and New Brunswick and Nova Scotia one each, with Manitoba, Saskatchewan, Alberta and Newfoundland gaining one each and British Columbia granted two additional senators. The "distinct society" clause and the "Canada clause" would both be clarified, with issues such as aboriginal rights dealt with in the next round of constitutional talks.

With the June 23 deadline drawing near, time was of the essence. New Brunswick approved the accord on June 16, thus leaving the fate of Meech Lake to the legislatures in Manitoba and Newfoundland. In Manitoba, the minority Conservative government had previously agreed with the opposition parties to have a public hearing process before ratifying any proposal. With the procedural delaying tactics of NDP member Elijah Harper (the only aboriginal member of the Manitoba legislature), Manitoba would not meet the deadline. Premier Clyde Wells had promised either a referendum or free vote in the legislature, finally deciding on the latter alternative.

When it became clear that Manitoba would need extra time to approve the accord, the federal government proposed, on June 22, 1990, a complicated move to buy more time by extending the deadline. This process would have meant asking the Supreme Court to rule if the deadline could be moved back to September 23, three years from the date that the second province had approved the accord, with Quebec then passing the accord a second time. However, Premier Wells rejected this plan and then adjourned the Newfoundland legislature without the promised free vote on the accord. Thus, Meech Lake was finally dead—one day before its deadline.

While the repercussions from the defeat of the Meech Lake accord would be many, one thing could be certain: Quebec's role in the Canadian political system would never be the same again. The neverending story of constitutional reform would remain in place as the leitmotif of the Canadian polity.

Recommended Readings

The 1982 Canada Act

AXWORTHY, THOMAS S. (1986) "Colliding Visions: The Debate over the Canadian Charter of Rights and Freedoms, 1980–81," *The Journal of Commonwealth and Comparative Politics* (November), Volume 24, Number 3, pp. 239–253.

BANTING, KEITH and RICHARD SIMEON, eds. (1983) *And No One Cheered: Federalism, Democracy and the Constitution Act*. Toronto: Methuen.

BENDER, PAUL (1983) "The Canadian Charter of Rights and Freedoms and the United States Bill of Rights: A Comparison," *McGill Law Journal*, Volume 28, Number 4, pp. 811–866.

BOYER, J. PATRICK (1985) *Equality for All: Report of the Parliamentary Committee on Equality Rights*. Ottawa: Supply and Services.

CHANDLER, MARSHA A. (1986) "Constitutional Change and Public Policy: The Impact of the Resource Amendment (Section 92A)," *Canadian Journal of Political Science* (March), Volume 19, Number 1, pp. 103–126.

CHEFFINS, RONALD I. and PATRICIA A. JOHNSON (1986) *The Revised Canadian Constitution: Politics as Law*. Toronto: McGraw-Hill Ryerson.

GREENE, IAN (1989) *The Charter of Rights*. Toronto: James Lorimer and Company.

KNOPFF, RAINER (1987) "What Do Constitutional Equality Rights Protect Canadians Against?"

Canadian Journal of Political Science (June), Volume 20, Number 2, pp. 265–286.

KOME, PENNY (1983) *The Taking of Twenty-Eight: Women Challenge the Constitution*. Toronto: Women's Educational Press.

LASELVA, SAMUEL V. (1983) "Only in Canada: Reflections on the Charter's Notwithstanding Clause," *Dalhousie Review* (Autumn), Volume 63, Number 3, pp. 383–398.

MALLORY, J.R. (1984) "The Charter of Rights and Freedoms and Canadian Democracy," *The Timlin Lecture*. University of Saskatchewan, Saskatoon.

MANDEL, MICHAEL (1989) *The Charter of Rights and the Legalization of Politics in Canada*. Toronto: Wall and Thompson.

MANNING, MORRIS (1983) *Rights, Freedoms and the Courts: A Practical Analysis of the Constitution Act, 1982*. Toronto: Emond-Montgomery Publications.

MEEKISON, J. PETER et al. (1985) *Origins and Meaning of Section 92A: The 1982 Constitutional Amendment on Resources*. Halifax: Institute for Research on Public Policy.

MILNE, DAVID (1982) *The New Canadian Constitution*. Toronto: James Lorimer and Company.

MORTON, F.L. (1987) "The Political Impact of the Canadian Charter of Rights and Freedoms," *Canadian Journal of Political Science* (March), Volume 20, Number 1, pp. 31–55.

NURGITZ, NATHAN and HUGH SEGAL (1983) *No Small Measure: The Progressive Conservatives and the Constitution*. Ottawa: Deneau.

RUSSELL, PETER H. (1985) "The First Three Years in Charterland," *Canadian Public Administration* (Fall), Volume 28, Number 3, pp. 367–396.

_____RAINER KNOPFF and TED MORTON, eds. (1989) *Federalism and the Charter: Leading Constitutional Decisions, A New Edition*. Ottawa: Carleton University Press.

SHEPPARD, ROBERT and MICHAEL VALPY (1982) *The National Deal: The Fight for a Canadian Constitution*. Toronto: Macmillan.

The Meech Lake Accord

BAINES, BEVERLEY (1987) "Gender and the Meech Lake Committee," *Queen's Quarterly* (Winter), Volume 94, Number 4, pp. 807–816.

CAMPBELL, ROBERT M. (1989) "Eleven Men and a Constitution: The Meech Lake Accord," pp. 227–314 in Campbell and Leslie A. Pal, *The Real Worlds of Canadian Politics: Cases in Process and Policy.* Peterborough, Ontario: Broadview Press.

COOK, RAMSAY (1987) "Alice in Meechland or The Concept of Quebec as 'A Distinct Society'," *Queen's Quarterly* (Winter), Volume 94, Number 4, pp. 817–828.

FULFORD, ROBERT (1987) "Surrenduring Canada," *Saturday Night* (August), Volume 102, Number 8, pp. 5–7.

GIBBINS, ROGER, ed. (1988) *Meech Lake and Canada: Perspectives from the West.* Edmonton: Academic Printing and Publishing.

IGNATIEFF, MICHAEL (1987) "The Longest Shadow," *Saturday Night* (October), Volume 102, Number 10, pp. 25–32.

LITHWICK, N. HARVEY and ALLAN M. MASLOVE (1989) "The Sum of the Parts: Free Trade and Meech Lake," pp. 25–51 in Katherine A. Graham, ed. *How Ottawa Spends 1989–90; The Buck Stops Where?* Ottawa: Carleton University Press.

MUNRO, GARY (1989) "Constitutional Change in Canada: The Meech Lake Accord," *The Journal of Commonwealth and Comparative Politics* (July), Volume 27, Number 2, pp. 201–217.

MURRAY, LOWELL (1988) "The Process of Constitutional Change in Canada: The Lessons of Meech Lake," *Choices* (February). Halifax: Institute for Research on Public Policy.

SCHWARTZ, BRYAN (1987) *Fathoming Meech Lake.* Winnipeg: Legal Research Institute, University of Manitoba.

WHYTE, JOHN D. and IAN PEACH, eds. (1989) *Re-forming Canada? The Meaning of the Meech Lake Accord and the Free Trade Agreement for the Canadian State.* Kingston, Ontario: Institute of Intergovernmental Relations, Queen's University.

CHAPTER 15

The Canadian Polity: A Comparative Assessment

A government may deserve to be credited not only with the positive successes it has achieved, but with the negative success of having escaped evils that have vexed other nations living under somewhat similar conditions (Bryce, 1921: 42).

The remedy for these ills, however, does not lie in institutional reform but in political action, participation and commitment by more of the populace. Failing that, Canada is condemned like other countries to the most unhappy of fates: it has the government it deserves (Franks, 1983: 206).

There is part of the Hippocratic oath that doctors have to swear that says the first obligation of the physician is to do no harm. Then after that, if he is sure he is doing no harm, he can start seeing if he can do a little good. Maybe not a bad rule for political reformers too (Austin Ranney, quoted in Sabato, 1985: 173).

STUDYING THE POLITICS of one's own country should be an enjoyable experience, and at the same time it is a necessary prerequisite for effective participation in the polity. Knowledge and understanding are fundamental ingredients of a politically-educated citizenry. While no book — and, especially, no textbook — can answer all of the questions about the polity, it can present a basis for students to arrive at their own conclusions about the nature, advantages, and disadvantages of their political system.

Comparing the Canadian, British, and American Political Systems

A comparative approach to the Canadian polity was adopted as a particularly appropriate task, given the historical and contemporary impact of Britain and the United States on the origin and evolution of the institutions and processes of the political system. Moreover, a comparative perspective facilitates an appreciation of the Canadian polity by delineating the similarities and differences among the political structures and procedures of these three governments. In political analysis, the more specific the basis of comparison, the greater the differences appear to be. Conversely, the broader the comparison, the larger are the perceived similarities. As a way of summarizing the discussion, Table 15.1 presents a brief topic-by-topic comparison of the major characteristics of government and politics in the Canadian, British, and American polities.

The conclusions arrived at in any comparison depend, of course, on the unit of analysis, that

> More appealing than knowledge itself is the feeling of knowing (Boorstin, 1983: 92).

is, on which particular aspect of the polity is being investigated. A comparative analysis might focus on political institutions, as we did in Part Two, or on political processes, as we did in Part Three. The goals of comparative political analysis are multiple, not the least of which is a better understanding of not just the world, but of ourselves. Comparison is a way of discovering similarities as well as differences, both of which can help to overcome one of the "marked characteristics" of the political community, namely, the "Canadian preference, in spite of the clearness of our physical climate, for living constantly in an atmosphere of mental haze" (Underhill, 1960: 118). While the problems facing the political system are, quite likely, immune to any quick-fix solutions, they will never be successfully dealt with unless we think reflectively about their nature and resolution.

A basic assumption of our analysis has been that one can only understand the political process by studying it. The goals of comparative analysis include description, explanation, and prediction. While our analysis has focused on descriptions and explanations of the institutions and processes of these three democratic polities, our final concern is to venture forth into the area of political reform. It is in the expected consequences of different patterns of political change that prediction becomes an essential tool of political analysis. However, political reformers must be cognizant of the fact that a political system is a pattern of interconnections that may well be, from an historical perspective, accidental in nature.

The result of such a view is to realize that changes in political institutions and processes may have two consequences: first, immediate or proximal effects and second, long-term or distal effects. The **proximal effect** of political reform alters the nature and operation of a specific institution or process, while the **distal effect** may transform the pattern of relationships between various institutions and processes.

TABLE 15.1 GOVERNMENTAL AND POLITICAL CHARACTERISTICS OF THE CANADIAN, BRITISH, AND AMERICAN POLITIES

Basis of Comparison	Canada	Britain	United States
1. *Constitution*	Constitutional government based on a federal and parliamentary structure. Federalism has become decentralized in recent decades. The 1982 Canada Act has added an entrenched Charter of Rights and amending clauses to the Constitution. Constitutional conventions remain an integral part of the overall pattern of Canadian constitutionalism.	Constitutional government based on a series of documents and on political traditions. Britain is both unitary and parliamentary, which leads to a concentration of political power. In practice, the concentration of power is limited by the conventions of the polity.	Constitutional government based on the view of political power as evil. American constitutionalism seeks to limit and fragment power by such devices as the separation of powers, checks and balances, federalism, and a Bill of Rights. Presidential and federal in structure, with American federalism now highly centralized.
2. *Executives*	A dual executive structure, with the formal executive performing primarily symbolic tasks. The political executive dominates the political process.	A dual executive structure, with an hereditary monarch as the formal executive. Political executive predominates even more than in Canada, although prime ministerial government is constrained by the collegial nature of cabinet government.	A single executive, with the president carrying out both the symbolic and political functions of executive power. The American cabinet is of minor importance in the political process.
3. *Bureaucracies*	A crucial element of the Canadian policy-making process. Policy is incremental in nature and administered by generalists, with ideology of little importance.	Whitehall, along with the political executive, dominates the political process. Professional civil servants, with a generalist education, predominate.	The American version is less professionally trained and more partisan based than in either Canada or Britain. Bureaucratic power is enhanced by the separation of powers principle.
4. *Legislatures*	Bicameral structure, with an appointed Senate playing a minor legislative role. The House of Commons dominates and is based on direct election with the government of the day responsible to it.	Bicameral legislature, with an appointed House of Lords and a directly elected House of Commons. The Lords has been a minor legislative body in the 20th century, with the government responsible to the Commons.	Bicameral structure, with both parts equal in theory as well as in practice. Executive not responsible to the legislature. American legislature has retained an important policy-making role.

TABLE 15.1 Continued

Basis of Comparison	Canada	Britain	United States
5. *Judiciaries*	Reluctant participants traditionally in the political process, the courts operate under the principle of limited judicial review and judicial self-restraint. Constitution Act, 1982 has made the judiciary more activist in outlook. On the whole, civil liberties have been weakly protected by the courts in Canada, a situation the Charter of Rights has helped to rectify.	Given the principle of parliamentary sovereignty, judicial review is unknown. A redress of grievances is a political, not a judicial concern. Civil liberties, historically, have been protected by the freedom to do that which is not proscribed by law.	The most powerful judicial branch in any democratic system, the American courts operate on the principle of full judicial review. The judiciary is activist in outlook and intimately involved in the political process. Civil liberties protected in the Bill of Rights, but sometimes ignored, historically, in practice.
6. *Political Culture*	Characterized by the themes of elitism, regionalism, dualism, and continentalism, the political culture is fragmented.	Political values of deference, consensus, and traditionalism predominate in a relatively homogeneous or integrated political culture.	Liberalism is triumphant, with an emphasis on individualism, popular sovereignty, and political moralism. Political power is seen as inherently evil.
7. *Political Parties*	Major parties are pragmatic in style, election-centred, parliamentary in origin, structurally decentralized, and cohesive in the legislature. The party system is competitive, federal, regional, and centre-based.	Parties are more centralized, class-based and programmatic than in Canada. The British party system is competitive between the Labour and Conservative parties, with the early-1980s challenge by the Social Democrats now a largely spent force.	Parties are election-centred, decentralized, non-ideological, with weak party unity.The party system is competitive between the Republicans and Democrats, but highly discriminatory against minor parties.
8. *Electoral Process*	Elections are competitive, lengthy, and based on temporary voters' lists. Recruitment is primarily a party matter, with the selectorate small in size.	Elections are competitive, short, and based on a permanent voters' list. Candidate selection is a secretive and closed process, under the direction of the party elite.	Elections are competitive, lengthy, nearly continuous, and based on individual voter registration. The direct primary allows members of the mass public to become involved in the nomination of candidates for public office.

TABLE 15.1 Continued

Basis of Comparison	Canada	Britain	United States
9. *Electoral Systems*	Based on single-member districts, with plurality election, the electoral system rewards the major parties and those minor parties with regional support. Electoral reform is unlikely, since it would benefit the NDP.	Based on single-member districts and the plurality formula, the electoral system discriminates most seriously against the minor parties. As in Canada, electoral reform is unlikely.	Traditional dominance of Republicans and Democrats depends, in part, on the plurality electoral formula. Selection of the president through the electoral college mechanism is a particular variation of the plurality format.
10. *Political Behaviour*	Political learning begins early, but does not result in a politically-educated citizenry. In terms of voting turnout, participation is high, but between elections political activity is minimal.	Political learning is class-based and deferential in outlook. Participation is extensive during a general election, but weaker between campaigns.	Political learning is more explicit than in Canada and Britain, with an emphasis on national loyalty. Opportunities for participation not matched by actual behaviour.
11. *Interest Groups*	Less visible than their American counterparts, Canadian interest groups focus their attention on the executive. A strong party system has traditionally limited the role of interest groups.	Unique in that interest groups have been formally co-opted into the policy process. Unlike the U.S. and Canada, major interest groups are specifically linked to particular parties.	Expanding greatly in the past several decades, American interest groups play an important and highly visible role. The most important recent development has been the growth of PACs as electoral participants.

A polity is a patterned set of interactions, that is, a system of behaviour. As a result, it is nearly impossible to reform a single structure or mechanism by itself. For example, a change in how party leaders are chosen may alter the chances various individuals or groups have of winning control of that party (a proximal effect). However, such a change by one party is also likely to have an impact on the way other parties select their leaders, on the competitive relationship between the parties, and, ultimately, on the direction of public policy (distal effects). A further example of the proximal and distal effects of political reform would be the representation principle of cabinet composition. Adoption of that operating guide from 1867 onward influenced not only the makeup of the cabinet (a proximal effect), but the political function of the cabinet (a distal effect). Moreover, the representation principle has altered the institutional relationship between the cabinet and the Senate, helping to make the former the key decision-making body and the latter increasingly superfluous to the political process.

Pierre Trudeau when questioned by a Commons Committee about his views on Canada adopting a presidential form of government: "I'd be happy to give you a course in comparative government at some other time" (November 4, 1980).

> A political system is an accident. It is an accumulation of habits, customs, prejudices, and principles that have survived a long process of trial and error and of ceaseless response to changing circumstances (Banfield, 1980:148).

> . . . the best advice remains "caveat reformator": let the reformer beware (Sabato, 1985: 192).

Before any specific ideas for political reform can proceed, we must be clear, first of all, in our understanding of what currently exists and second, in our view of the kind of polity we wish to produce through any proposed political reforms. Thus, to discuss political reform is to deal with the normative aspects of the polity, that is, the shape of the polity yet to come. Our basic perspective is that of liberal-democracy, in that we prefer that type of polity to all others; at the same time, we wish to improve the way specific institutions and processes operate. As Winston Churchill is reputed to have said, liberal-democracy is the worst form of government ever invented — except for all other types yet tried. A brief assessment of the liberal-democratic nature of the current Canadian polity will provide the basis for a few suggested reforms.

The Liberal-Democratic Nature of the Canadian Polity: Prospects for Reform

In discussing political reform, we are going to use a very different type of comparison: instead of comparing three existing systems with each other, we will compare one existing polity — in this case, the Canadian system — with an ideal system, that of "classical democracy." The purposes or goals of comparison remain the same; the focus is simply altered. However, it is well to keep in mind the remarks of George Bernard

Shaw that reformers mistakenly believe that "change can be achieved by brute sanity." Rather than sanity, the political context typically constrains and circumscribes the nature and extent of political reform.

Few people would disagree that because of its "long experience of competitive politics and free elections, Canada has one of the oldest continuously functioning democratic political systems in the world" (Cairns, 1981: 1). Certainly by comparison to most existing systems, such an assessment is accurate. However, in relation to the democratic ideal, the Canadian polity remains deficient. In the political world of the classical democratic theorists, the individual citizen was concerned, interested, and knowledgeable about the polity, with active political participation a natural outgrowth of such characteristics. Political elites were responsive to the mass public, with elections conferring mandates for the implementation of public priorities. The electoral process was competitive and open and political dissent was a fundamental ingredient of the political system.

The Canadian political world of the 1990s is very far from this romanticized picture of a democratic utopia: " . . . with respect to the democrats' requirements that political man be imbued with a developed sense of civic activism, research in Canada has confirmed what long had been suspected, that the interests of the average citizen range from crabgrass to hockey but rarely to politics" (Mishler, 1979: 6). In our view, it is in its participative aspects that the democratic nature of the Canadian political process is weakest. The structural organization of the polity is democratic in form, but often lacking in the substance of active and widespread political involvement. Thus, our suggestions for

> Most Canadians, throughout their history, have been proud of the fact that they do not think reflectively about the profound questions of politics (Christian and Campbell, 1974: 1).

political reform will largely centre on increasing and making more viable the role of the citizen in the political affairs of the nation.

With respect to the Constitution, several significant changes would be desirable, even if, for political reasons, their adoption seems unlikely. First, once the 1982 Constitution Act has been in place for a number of years, the override provision in relation to Sections 2 and 7 through 15 of the Canadian Charter of Rights and Freedoms should be deleted. Fundamental rights should be recognized as fundamental in fact, or, at least, be restricted only under carefully defined conditions. On either criterion, the general override power of the federal and provincial governments is unacceptable on democratic grounds. Second, citizens should be incorporated into the process of constitutional reform by requiring a national referendum on any major changes before they are proclaimed by the governor general. If nothing else, this change in procedure would increase the legitimacy of the final product. Third, the Canadian Constitution should be consolidated into a single document, instead of being parceled out into a series of constitutional statutes. Such a revision would allow easier understanding of the Constitution by the ordinary citizen. Moreover, we should require a constitution written in plain English or French, as the case may be.

While the principle of federalism is likely to remain in place, the way it operates is open to reform. As a process, federalism can only be effective if the political elites at the federal and provincial levels want it to work: too often, the other level of government serves as a political scapegoat for any problems, which in turn

reduces the accountability and the responsibility of both levels of government. Unfortunately, one cannot constitutionally require either good judgment or common sense from the political leaders of the federal and provincial levels of government. Moreover, competent leadership cannot be electorally guaranteed.

However, one way of increasing the political sensitivity of leaders is to remove the impediments to office that have tended to limit political careers to one or the other levels of government. A broader mixture of leaders electorally experienced in both political arenas could greatly facilitate the adaptability and flexibility of the federal system. One of the most disturbing trends of recent years has been the inability, as well as the apparent unwillingness, of federal and provincial leaders to empathize with each other — the result has been a confrontation style of politics. The intermingling of federal and provincial political career patterns would be a start in removing some of the obstacles to a more cooperative brand of federalism.

In relation to the pattern of executive federalism, which has removed so much that is vital in federalism from the purview of the electorate, we would suggest that any agreements between the two levels of government be ratified by a resolution of their respective legislatures. These resolutions would either accept or reject the agreements as negotiated; however, such a process would inform the public — or, at least, a segment of it — of what important issues were being decided behind closed doors. Such a change would also have the desirable effect of bringing the legislative branch of government back into the daily workings of the federal system, even if only in a minimal way.

It is unlikely that any reforms could be designed that would effectively involve the mass public in the normal workings and decision-making processes of the executive and legislative branches of government. Instead, we would propose means by which governmental personnel would be made more responsible and thus more responsive to the concerns of the citizenry. We propose, therefore, that governments, as well as specific elected officials, be subject to a recall procedure. While the actual details of this procedure would have to be carefully specified, it would clearly put a government in continual fear of electoral retribution — not necessarily at the election four or five years hence, but much sooner. Nothing is more apt to make a government responsive than possible loss of office. The major flaw in the electoral process is that elections are too infrequent and usually at the discretion of the government. Under the recall procedure, they need not be. A similar procedure might also be adopted for individual members of the legislature and the bureaucracy.

A major problem in relation to the judicial branch of government is the enforcement of individual civil and political liberties. Freedoms are only as good as their application in practice; they are not self-enforcing mechanisms. While the Charter of Rights guarantees many basic freedoms, it may take years and cost thousands of dollars for a citizen to use the judicial alternative for a redress of grievances all the way up to a Supreme Court judgment. The structures, procedures, and personnel of our judiciary need improvement, particularly now that the Charter has increased the significance of the courts in our political system. At a minimum, more judges and more courts are required.

Three significant reforms should be considered in relation to the election process: complete public funding of election campaigns at the constituency level, regularization of the political nomination process, and closing the loophole in the political finance legislation which allows for special-interest group funding of election expenses. Having legally recognized the existence of political parties and their role in the electoral process, the public now needs to be encouraged to participate in that most vital of party functions, the political recruitment process. Nomination of candidates for public office

> A familiar and rueful Canadian joke holds that, while Canada had hoped to achieve a synthesis of British governance, French culture, and American know-how, it has been left, instead, with the residue of British know-how, French governance, and American culture (Friedenberg, 1980: 107).

is too important a democratic task to be left entirely in the hands of the party elites. Rules covering the holding of and procedures utilized in constituency nomination meetings by the parties should be incorporated into the Canada Elections Act. Meetings should be publicly advertised well in advance, membership requirements at the local level should be clearly defined, and the vote conducted by the Chief Returning Officer in that constituency. Eligibility requirements to vote at nomination meetings should be the same as those to be an elector in the general election, plus both party membership and residency in the constituency. These kinds of changes would create the potential for more widespread participation in the nomination process, while at the same time it would limit a party role to party members resident in that constituency who can vote in the general election.

To encourage a more representative cross-section of Canadian society to stand for election to public office, the full cost of campaigns at the constituency level should be paid for from the public treasury. Under current law, about one-third of a candidate's expenses are reimbursed, but given the cost of modern campaigns — even with the limits on constituency expenses — most citizens cannot afford to compete in the electoral process. The salaries and pensions of MPs are now quite generous, but most people are not wealthy enough to become serious contenders for public office. The problem is not the remuneration for holding public office, but the cost of getting there.

A third electoral reform concerns the role and growth of special-interest groups as campaign contributors, a problem particularly evident in the 1988 contest. Because of a court ruling, third-party political funding of electoral contests is now allowed. In order to prevent the emergence and dominance of American-style PACs, which would undercut the role of both parties and citizens in the political process, this situation must be eliminated as soon as possible.

Although numerous other reforms might be proposed, a final consideration must be dealt with. If it is in the interest of the political elites to keep the nature and extent of mass participation limited and if current mass political beliefs are generally deferential in nature, how can political change be achieved? This paradox is the Catch-22 of Canadian politics. The answer is simply an unrelenting demand from the public for political change. The constitutional review process might be instructive in this regard. The political elites were not only willing to ignore the public's role in the process, but to negotiate away fundamental freedoms such as sexual equality and native rights. However, it was public protest that forced the reinsertion of those provisions back into the 1982 Canada Act,

because of the political elites' fear of possible electoral retribution. Fear is a great motivator of people and governments. Agnes McPhail (quoted in McPhee, 1980: 149), the first woman elected to the Canadian House of Commons, put it rather succinctly: "the way to get things out of a government is to back them to the wall, put your hands to their throats, and you will get all they have."

In addition, it is often assumed that the Canadian elite is a cohesive and unified group, which it is not. Political reform has been achieved, as in the case of the extension of the suffrage, when a segment of the political elite realized that it was in its own political interest to act. It is this combination of changing public perceptions about the nature of the political process and the self-interest of a segment of the political elite that can bring about substantial movements of political reform. Change may be slow, incremental, and infrequent in liberal-democracies, but it does occur and at a faster pace than most critics are willing to admit. Such reforms, intended to increase the participation of the average citizen in the political process will, if adopted, have the effect of encouraging more reform, at a faster rate, in the future.

CONSTITUTION ACT, 1982

PART I

CANADIAN CHARTER OF RIGHTS AND FREEDOMS

Whereas Canada is founded upon principles that recognize the supremacy of God and the rule of law:

Guarantee of Rights and Freedoms

1. The *Canadian Charter of Rights and Freedoms* guarantees the rights and freedoms set out in it subject only to such reasonable limits prescribed by law as can be demonstrably justified in a free and democratic society.

Fundamental Freedoms

2. Everyone has the following fundamental freedoms:

(a) freedom of conscience and religion;

(b) freedom of thought, belief, opinion and expression, including freedom of the press and other media of communication;

(c) freedom of peaceful assembly; and

(d) freedom of association.

Democratic Rights

3. Every citizen of Canada has the right to vote in an election of members of the House of Commons or of a legislative assembly and to be qualified for membership therein.

4. (1) No House of Commons and no legislative assembly shall continue for longer than five years from the date fixed for the return of the writs of a general election of its members.

(2) In time of real or apprehended war, invasion or insurrection, a House of Commons may be continued by Parliament and a legislative assembly may be continued by the legislature beyond five years if such continuation is not opposed by the votes of more than one-third of the members of the House of Commons or the legislative assembly, as the case may be.

5. There shall be a sitting of Parliament and of each legislature at least once every twelve months.

Mobility Rights

6. (1) Every citizen of Canada has the right to enter, remain in and leave Canada.

(2) Every citizen of Canada and every person who has the status of a permanent resident of Canada has the right

(a) to move to and take up residence in any province; and

(b) to pursue the gaining of a livelihood in any province.

(3) The rights specified in subsection (2) are subject to

(a) any laws or practices of general application in force in a province other than those that discriminate among persons primarily on the basis of province of present or previous residence; and

(b) any laws providing for reasonable residency requirements as a qualification for the receipt of publicly provided social services.

(4) Subsections (2) and (3) do not preclude any law, program or activity that has as its object the amelioration in a province of conditions of individuals in that province who are socially or economically disadvantaged if the rate of employment in that province is below the rate of employment in Canada.

Legal Rights

7. Everyone has the right to life, liberty and security of the person and the right not to be deprived thereof except in accordance with the principles of fundamental justice.

8. Everyone has the right to be secure against unreasonable search or seizure.

9. Everyone has the right not to be arbitrarily detained or imprisoned.

10. Everyone has the right on arrest or detention

(a) to be informed promptly of the reasons therefor;

(b) to retain and instruct counsel without delay and to be informed of that right; and

(c) to have the validity of the detention determined by way of *habeas corpus* and to be released if the detention is not lawful.

11. Any person charged with an offence has the right

(a) to be informed without unreasonable delay of the specific offence;

(b) to be tried within a reasonable time;

(c) not to be compelled to be a witness in proceedings against that person in respect of the offence;

(d) to be presumed innocent until proven guilty according to law in a fair and public hearing by an independent and impartial tribunal;

(e) not to be denied reasonable bail without just cause;

(f) except in the case of an offence under military law tried before a military tribunal, to the benefit of trial by jury where the maximum punishment for the offence is imprisonment for five years or a more severe punishment;

(g) not to be found guilty on account of any act or omission unless, at the time of the act or omission, it constituted an offence under Canadian or international law or was criminal

according to the general principles of law recognized by the community of nations;

(h) if finally acquitted of the offence, not to be tried for it again and, if finally found guilty and punished for the offence, not to be tried or punished for it again; and

(i) if found guilty of the offence and if the punishment for the offence has been varied between the time of commission and the time of sentencing, to the benefit of the lesser punishment.

12. Everyone has the right not to be subjected to any cruel and unusual treatment or punishment.

13. A witness who testifies in any proceedings has the right not to have any incriminating evidence so given used to incriminate that witness in any other proceedings, except in a prosecution for perjury or for the giving of contradictory evidence.

14. A party or witness in any proceedings who does not understand or speak the language in which the proceedings are conducted or who is deaf has the right to the assistance of an interpreter.

Equality Rights

15. (1) Every individual is equal before and under the law and has the right to the equal protection and equal benefit of the law without discrimination and, in particular, without discrimination based on race, national or ethnic origin, colour, religion, sex, age or mental or physical disability.

(2) Subsection (1) does not preclude any law, program or activity that has as its object the amelioration of conditions of disadvantaged individuals or groups including those that are disadvantaged because of race, national or ethnic origin, colour, religion, sex, age or mental or physical disability.

Official Languages of Canada

16. (1) English and French are the official languages of Canada and have equality of status and equal rights and privileges as to their use in all institutions of the Parliament and government of Canada.

(2) English and French are the official languages of New Brunswick and have equality of status and equal rights and privileges as to their use in all institutions of the legislature and government of New Brunswick.

(3) Nothing in this Charter limits the authority of Parliament or a legislature to advance the equality of status or use of English and French.

17. (1) Everyone has the right to use English or French in any debates and other proceedings of Parliament.

(2) Everyone has the right to use English or French in any debates and other proceedings of the legislature of New Brunswick.

18. (1) The statutes, records and journals of Parliament shall be printed and published in English and French and both language versions are equally authoritative.

(2) The statutes, records and journals of the legislature of New Brunswick shall be printed and published in English and French and both language versions are equally authoritative.

19. (1) Either English or French may be used by any person in, or in any pleading in or process issuing from, any court established by Parliament.

(2) Either English or French may be used by any person in, or in any pleading in or process issuing from, any court of New Brunswick.

20. (1) Any member of the public in Canada has the right to communicate with, and to receive available services from, any head or central office of an institution of the Parliament or government of Canada in English or French, and has the same right with respect to any other office of any such institution where

(a) there is a significant demand for communications with and services from that office in such language; or

(b) due to the nature of the office, it is reasonable that communications with and services from that office be available in both English and French.

(2) Any member of the public in New Brunswick has the right to communicate with, and to receive available services from, any office of an institution of the legislature or government of New Brunswick in English or French.

21. Nothing in sections 16 to 20 abrogates or derogates from any right, privilege or obligation with respect to the English and French languages, or either of them, that exists or is continued by virtue of any other provision of the Constitution of Canada.

22. Nothing in sections 16 to 20 abrogates or derogates from any legal or customary right or privilege acquired or enjoyed either before or after the coming into force of this Charter with respect to any language that is not English or French.

Minority Language Educational Rights

23. (1) Citizens of Canada

(a) whose first language learned and still understood is that of the English or French linguistic minority population of the province in which they reside, or

(b) who have received their primary school instruction in Canada in English or French and reside in a province where the language in which they received that instruction is the language of the English or French linguistic minority population of the province,

have the right to have their children receive primary and secondary school instruction in that language in that province.

(2) Citizens of Canada of whom any child has received or is receiving primary or secondary school instruction in English or French in Canada, have the right to have all their children receive primary and secondary school instruction in the same language.

(3) The right of citizens of Canada under subsections (1) and (2) to have their children receive primary and secondary school instruction in the language of the English or French linguistic minority population of a province

(a) applies wherever in the province the number of children of citizens who have such a right is sufficient to warrant the provision to them out of public funds of minority language instruction; and

(b) includes, where the number of those children so warrants, the right to have them receive that instruction in minority language educational facilities provided out of public funds.

Enforcement

24. (1) Anyone whose rights or freedoms, as guaranteed by this Charter, have been infringed or denied may apply to a court of competent jurisdiction to obtain such remedy as the court considers appropriate and just in the circumstances.

(2) Where, in proceedings under subsection (1), a court concludes that evidence was obtained in a manner that infringed or denied any rights or freedoms guaranteed by this Charter, the evidence shall be excluded if it is established that, having regard to all the circumstances, the admission of it in the proceedings would bring the administration of justice into disrepute.

General

25. The guarantee in this Charter of certain rights and freedoms shall not be construed so as to abrogate or derogate from any aboriginal, treaty or other rights or freedoms that pertain to the aboriginal peoples of Canada including

(a) any rights or freedoms that have been recognized by the Royal Proclamation of October 7, 1763; and

(b) any rights or freedoms that may be acquired by the aboriginal peoples of Canada by way of land claims settlement.

26. The guarantee in this Charter of certain rights and freedoms shall not be construed as denying the existence of any other rights or freedoms that exist in Canada.

27. This Charter shall be interpreted in a manner consistent with the preservation and enhancement of the multicultural heritage of Canadians.

28. Notwithstanding anything in this Charter, the rights and freedoms referred to in it are guaranteed equally to male and female persons.

29. Nothing in this Charter abrogates or derogates from any rights or privileges guaranteed by or under the Constitution of Canada in respect of denominational, separate or dissentient schools.

30. A reference in this Charter to a Province or to the legislative assembly or legislature of a province shall be deemed to include a reference to the Yukon Territory and the Northwest Territories, or to the appropriate legislative authority thereof, as the case may be.

31. Nothing in this Charter extends the legislative powers of any body or authority.

Application of Charter

32. (1) This Charter applies

(a) to the Parliament and government of Canada in respect of all matters within the authority of Parliament including all matters relating to the Yukon Territory and Northwest Territories; and

(b) to the legislature and government of each province in respect of all matters within the authority of the legislature of each province.

(2) Notwithstanding subsection (1), section 15 shall not have effect until three years after this section comes into force.

33. (1) Parliament or the legislature of a province may expressly declare in an Act of Parliament or of the legislature, as the case may be, that the Act or a provision thereof shall operate notwithstanding a provision included in section 2 or sections 7 to 15 of this Charter.

(2) An Act or a provision of an Act in respect of which a declaration made under this section is in effect shall have such operation as it would have but for the provision of this Charter referred to in the declaration.

(3) A declaration made under subsection (1) shall cease to have effect five years after it comes into force or on such earlier date as may be specified in the declaration.

(4) Parliament or the legislature of a province may re-enact a declaration made under subsection (1).

(5) Subsection (3) applies in respect of a re-enactment made under subsection (4).

Citation

34. This Part may be cited as the *Canadian Charter of Rights and Freedoms*.

1987 CONSTITUTIONAL ACCORD

WHEREAS first ministers, assembled in Ottawa, have arrived at a unanimous accord on constitutional amendments that would bring about the full and active participation of Quebec in Canada's constitutional evolution, would recognize the principle of equality of all the provinces, would provide new arrangements to foster greater harmony and cooperation between the Government of Canada and the governments of the provinces and would require that annual first ministers' conferences on the state of the Canadian economy and such other matters as may be appropriate be convened and that annual constitutional conferences composed of first ministers be convened commencing not later than December 31, 1988.

AND WHEREAS first ministers have also reached unanimous agreement on certain additional commitments in relation to some of those amendments;

NOW THEREFORE the Prime Minister of Canada and the first ministers of the provinces commit themselves and the governments they represent to the following:

1. The Prime Minister of Canada will lay or cause to be laid before the Senate and House of Commons, and the first ministers of the provinces will lay or cause to be laid before their legislative assemblies, as soon as possible, a resolution, in the form appended hereto, to authorize a proclamation to be issued by the Governor General under the Great Seal of Canada to amend the Constitution of Canada.

2. The Government of Canada will, as soon as possible, conclude an agreement with the Government of Quebec that would

  (a) incorporate the principles of the Cullen-Couture agreement on the selection abroad and in Canada of independent immigrants, visitors for medical treatment, students and temporary workers, and on the selection of refugees abroad and economic criteria for family reunification and assisted relatives,

  (b) guarantee that Quebec will receive a number of immigrants, including refugees, within the annual total established by the federal government for all of Canada proportionate to its share of the population of Canada, with the right to exceed that figure by five percent for demographic reasons, and

  (c) provide an undertaking by Canada to withdraw services (except citizenship services) for the reception and integration (including linguistic and cultural) of all foreign nationals wishing to settle in Quebec where services are to be provided by Quebec, with such withdrawal to be accompanied by reasonable compensation.

and the Government of Canada and the Government of Quebec will take the necessary steps to give the agreement the force of law under the proposed amendment relating to such agreements.

3. Nothing in this Accord should be construed as preventing the negotiation of similar agreements with other provinces relating to immigration and the temporary admission of aliens.

4. Until the proposed amendment relating to appointments to the Senate comes into force, any person summoned to fill a vacancy in the Senate shall be chosen from among persons whose names have been submitted by the government of the province to which the vacancy relates and must be acceptable to the Queen's Privy Council for Canada.

SCHEDULE

CONSTITUTION AMENDMENT, 1987

Constitution Act, 1982

1. The *Constitution Act, 1867* is amended by adding thereto, immediately after section 1 thereof, the following section:

Interpretation

"2.(1) The Constitution of Canada shall be interpreted in a manner consistent with

(a) the recognition that the existence of French-speaking Canadians, centred in Quebec but also present elsewhere in Canada, and English-speaking Canadians, concentrated outside Quebec but also present in Quebec, constitutes a fundamental characteristic of Canada; and

(b) the recognition that Quebec constitutes within Canada a distinct society.

Role of Parliament and legislatures

(2) The role of the Parliament of Canada and the provincial legislatures to preserve the fundamental characteristic of Canada referred to in paragraph (1)(a) is affirmed.

Role of legislature and Government of Quebec

(3) The role of the legislature and Government of Quebec to preserve and promote the distinct identity of Quebec referred to in paragraph (1)(b) is affirmed.

Rights of legislatures and governments preserved

(4) Nothing in this section derogates from the powers, rights or privileges of Parliament or the Government of Canada, or of the legislatures or governments of the provinces, including any powers, rights or privileges relating to language.

2. The said Act is further amended by adding thereto, immediately after section 24 thereof, the following section:

Names to be submitted

"25.(1) Where a vacancy occurs in the Senate, the government of the province to which the vacancy relates may, in relation to that vacancy, submit to the Queen's Privy Council for Canada the names of persons who may be summoned to the Senate.

Choice of Senators from names submitted

(2) Until an amendment to the Constitution of Canada is made in relation to the Senate pursuant to section 41 of the *Constitution Act, 1982*, the person summoned to fill a vacancy in the Senate shall be chosen from among persons whose names have been submitted under subsection (1) by the government of the province to which the vacancy relates and must be acceptable to the Queen's Privy Council for Canada."

3. The said Act is further amended by adding thereto, immediately after section 95 thereof, the following heading and sections:

"Agreements on Immigration and Aliens

Commitment to negotiate

95A. The Government of Canada shall, at the request of the government of any province, negotiate with the government of that province for the purpose of concluding an agreement relating to immigration or the temporary admission of aliens into that province that is appropriate to the needs and circumstances of that province.

Agreements

95B. (1) Any agreement concluded between Canada and a province in relation to immigration or the temporary admission of aliens into that province has the force of law from the time it is declared to do so in accordance with subsection 95C(1) and shall from that time have effect notwithstanding class 25 of section 91 or section 95.

Limitation

(2) An agreement that has the force of law under subsection (1) shall have effect only so long and so far as it is not repugnant to any provision of an Act of the Parliament of Canada that sets national standards and objectives relating to immigration or aliens, including any provision that establishes general classes of immigrants or relates to levels of immigration for Canada or that prescribes classes of individuals who are inadmissible into Canada.

Application of Charter

(3) The *Canadian Charter of Rights and Freedoms* applies in respect of any agreement that has the force of law under subsection (1) and in respect of anything done by the Parliament or Government of Canada, of the legislature or government of a province, pursuant to any such agreement.

Proclamation relating to agreements

95C.(1) A declaration that an agreement referred to in subsection 95B(1) has the force of law may be made by proclamation issued by the Governor General under the Great Seal of Canada only where so authorized by resolutions of the Senate and House of Commons and of the legislative assembly of the province that is a party to the agreement.

Amendment of agreements

(2) An amendment to an agreement referred to in subsection 95B(1) may be made by proclamation issued by the Governor General under the Great Seal of Canada only where so authorized.

(a) by resolutions of the Senate and House of Commons and of the legislative assembly of the province that is a party to the agreement; or

(b) in such other manner as is set out in the agreement.

Application of sections 46 to 48 of *Constitution Act, 1982*

95D. Sections 46 to 48 of the *Constitution Act, 1982* apply, with such modifications as the circumstances require, in respect of any declaration made pursuant to subsection 95C(1), any amendment to an agreement made pursuant to subsection 95C(2) or any amendment made pursuant to section 95E.

Amendments to sections 95A to 95D or this section	95E. An amendment to sections 95A to 95D or this section may be made in accordance with the procedure set out in subsection 38(1) of the *Constitution Act, 1982*, but only if the amendment is authorized by resolutions of the legislative assemblies of all the provinces that are, at the time of the amendment, parties to an agreement that has the force of law under subsection 95B(1)."

4. The said Act is further amended by adding thereto, immediately preceding section 96 thereof, the following heading:

"General"

5. The said Act is further amended by adding thereto, immediately preceding section 101 thereof, the following heading:

"Courts Established by the Parliament of Canada"

6. The said Act is further amended by adding thereto, immediately after section 101 thereof, the following heading and sections:

"Supreme Court of Canada"

Supreme Court continued	101A.(1) The court existing under the name of the Supreme Court of Canada is hereby continued as the general court of appeal for Canada, and as an additional court for the better administration of the laws of Canada, and shall continue to be a superior court of record.
Constitution of Court	(2) The Supreme Court of Canada shall consist of a chief justice to be called the Chief Justice of Canada and eight other judges, who shall be appointed by the Governor General in Council by letters patent under the Great Seal.
Who may be appointed judges	101B.(1) Any person may be appointed a judge of the Supreme Court of Canada who, after having been admitted to the bar of any province or territory, has, for a total of at least ten years, been a judge of any court in Canada or a member of the bar of any province or territory.
Three judges from Quebec	(2) At least three judges of the Supreme Court of Canada shall be appointed from among persons who, after having been admitted to the bar of Quebec, have, for a total of at least ten years, been judges of any court of Quebec or of any court established by the Parliament of Canada, or members of the bar of Quebec.
Names may be submitted	101C.(1) Where a vacancy occurs in the Supreme Court of Canada, the government of each province may, in relation to that vacancy, submit to the Minister of Justice of Canada the names of any of the persons who have been admitted to the bar of that province and are qualified under section 101B for appointment to that court.
Appointment from names submitted	(2) Where an appointment is made to the Supreme Court of Canada, the Governor General in Council shall, except where the Chief Justice is appointed from among members of the Court, appoint a person whose

name has been submitted under subsection (1) and who is acceptable to the Queen's Privy Council for Canada.

Appointment from Quebec

(3) Where an appointment is made in accordance with subsection (2) of any of the three judges necessary to meet the requirement set out in subsection 101B(2), the Governor General in Council shall appoint a person whose name has been submitted by the Government of Quebec.

Appointment from other provinces

(4) Where an appointment is made in accordance with subsection (2) otherwise than as required under subsection (3), the Governor General in Council shall appoint a person whose name has been submitted by the government of a province other than Quebec.

Tenure, salaries, etc. of judges

101D. Sections 99 and 100 apply in respect of the judges of the Supreme Court of Canada.

Relationship to section 101

101E.(1) Sections 101A to 101D shall not be construed as abrogating or derogating from the powers of the Parliament of Canada to make laws under section 101 except to the extent that such laws are inconsistent with those sections.

References to the Supreme Court of Canada

(2) For greater certainty, section 101A shall not be construed as abrogating or derogating from the powers of the Parliament of Canada to make laws relating to the reference of questions of law or fact, or any other matters, to the Supreme Court of Canada.

7. The said Act is further amended by adding thereto, immediately after section 106 thereof, the following section:

Shared-cost program

"106A.(1) The Government of Canada shall provide reasonable compensation to the government of a province that chooses not to participate in a national shared-cost program that is established by the Government of Canada after the coming into force of this section in an area of exclusive provincial jurisdiction, if the province carries on a program or initiative that is compatible with the national objectives.

Legislative power not extended

(2) Nothing in this section extends the legislative powers of the Parliament of Canada or of the legislatures of the provinces."

8. The said Act is further amended by adding thereto the following heading and sections:

"XII — Conferences on the Economy and Other Matters

Conferences on the economy and other matters

148. A conference composed of the Prime Minister of Canada and the first ministers of the provinces shall be convened by the Prime Minister of Canada at least once a year to discuss the state of the Canadian economy and such other matters as may be appropriate.

XIII — References

Reference includes amendments

149. A reference to this Act shall be deemed to include a reference to any amendments thereto."

Constitution Act, 1982

9. Sections 40 to 42 of the *Constitution Act, 1982* are repealed and the following substituted therefor:

Compensation

"40. Where an amendment is made under subsection 38(1) that transfers legislative powers from provincial legislatures to Parliament, Canada shall provide reasonable compensation to any province to which the amendment does not apply.

Amendment by unanimous consent

41. An amendment to the Constitution of Canada in relation to the following matters may be made by proclamation issued by the Governor General under the Great Seal of Canada only where authorized by resolutions of the Senate and House of Commons and of the legislative assembly of each province:

(a) the office of the Queen, the Governor General and the Lieutenant Governor of a province;
(b) the powers of the Senate and the method of selecting Senators;
(c) the number of members by which a province is entitled to be represented in the Senate and the residence qualifications of Senators;
(d) the right of a province to a number of members in the House of Commons not less than the number of Senators by which the province *was* entitled to be represented on *April 17, 1982*;
(e) the principle of proportionate representation of the provinces in the House of Commons prescribed by the Constitution of Canada;
(f) subject to section 43, the use of the English or the French language;
(g) the Supreme Court of Canada;
(h) the extension of existing provinces into the territories;
(i) notwithstanding any other law or practice, the establishment of new provinces;
(j) an amendment to this Part."

10. Section 44 of the said Act is repealed and the following substituted therefor:

Amendments by Parliament

"44. Subject to section 41, Parliament may exclusively make laws amending the Constitution of Canada in relation to the executive government of Canada or the Senate and House of Commons."

11. Subsection 46(1) of the said Act is repealed and the following substituted therefor:

Initiation of amendment procedures

"46.(1) The procedures for amendment under sections 38, 41 and 43 may be initiated either by the Senate or the House of Commons or by the legislative assembly of a province."

12. Subsection 47(1) of the said Act is repealed and the following substituted therefor:

Amendments without Senate resolution

"47.(1) An amendment to the Constitution of Canada made by proclamation under section 38, 41 or 43 may be made without a resolution of the Senate authorizing the issue of the proclamation if, within one hundred and eighty days after the adoption by the House of Commons of a resolution authorizing its issue, the Senate has not adopted such a resolution and if, at any time after the expiration of that period, the House of Commons again adopts the resolution."

13. Part VI of the said Act is repealed and the following substituted therefor:

"Part VI
Constitutional Conferences

Constitutional conference

50.(1) A constitutional conference composed of the Prime Minister of Canada and the first ministers of the provinces shall be convened by the Prime Minister of Canada at least once each year, commencing in 1988.

Agenda

(2) The conferences convened under subsection (1) shall have included on their agenda the following matters:
(a) Senate reform, including the role and functions of the Senate, its powers, the method of selecting Senators and representation in the Senate;
(b) roles and responsibilities in relation to fisheries; and
(c) such other matters as are agreed upon."

14. Subsection 52(2) of the said Act is amended by striking out the word "and" at the end of paragraph (b) thereof, by adding the word "and" at the end of paragraph (c) thereof and by adding thereto the following paragraph:

"(d) any other amendment to the Constitution of Canada."

15. Section 61 of the said Act is repealed and the following substituted therefor:

References

"61. *A reference to the Constitution Act, 1982, or* a reference to the *Constitution Acts 1867 to 1982*, shall be deemed to include a reference to *any amendment thereto*."

General

Multi-cultural heritage and aboriginal peoples

16. Nothing in section 2 of the *Constitution Act, 1867* affects section 25 or 27 of the *Canadian Charter of Rights and Freedoms*, section 35 of the *Constitution Act, 1982* or class 24 of section 91 of the *Constitution Act, 1867*.

CITATION

Citation

17. This amendment may be cited as the *Constitution Amendment, 1987*.

BIBLIOGRAPHY

ABERBACH, JOEL D., ROBERT D. PUTNAM and BRET A. ROCKMAN (1981) *Bureaucrats and Politicians in Western Democracies*. Cambridge, Mass.: Harvard University Press.

ABRAHAM, HENRY J. (1985) *Justices and Presidents: A Political History of Appointments to the Supreme Court*. New York: Oxford University Press, 2nd ed.

—— (1986) *The Judicial Process: An Introductory Analysis of the Courts of the United States, England and France*. New York: Oxford University Press, 5th ed.

AKERMAN, JEREMY (1977) *What Have You Done For Me Lately? A Politician Explains*. Windsor, Nova Scotia: Lancelot Press.

ALBROW, MARTIN (1970) *Bureaucracy*. London: Macmillan.

ALDERMAN, R.K. and J.A. CROSS (1985) "The Reluctant Knife: Reflections on the Prime Minister's Power of Dismissal," *Parliamentary Affairs*, Volume 38, Number 4, pp. 387–408.

ALFORD, ROBERT R. (1963) *Party and Society: The Anglo-American Democracies*. Chicago: Rand McNally.

ALLISON, GRAHAM T. (1971) *Essence of Decision: Explaining the Cuban Missile Crisis*. Boston: Little, Brown and Company.

ALMOND, GABRIEL A. and G. BINGHAM POWELL, JR. (1978) *Comparative Politics: System, Process and Policy*. Boston: Little, Brown and Company, 2nd ed.

—— and SIDNEY VERBA (1965) *The Civic Culture: Political Attitudes and Democracy in Five Nations*. Boston: Little, Brown and Co.

ATWOOD, MARGARET (1972) *Survival*. Toronto: Anansi.

BAGEHOT, WALTER (1867, 1963) *The English Constitution*. London: Collins, The Fontana Library.

BAILEY, F.G. (1988) *Humbuggery and Manipulation: The Art of Leadership*. Ithaca, New York: Cornell University Press.

BAILYN, BERNARD (1968) *The Origins of American Politics*. New York: Alfred A. Knopf.

BAKVIS, HERMAN (1989) "Regional Politics and Policy in the Mulroney Cabinet, 1984–88: Towards a Theory of the Regional Minister System in Canada," *Canadian Public Policy* (June), Volume 15, Number 2, pp. 121–134.

BANFIELD, EDWARD C. (1980) "In Defense of the American Party System," in Robert A. Goldwin, ed., *Political Parties in the Eighties*. Washington, D.C.: American Enterprise Institute for Public Policy Research, pp. 133–149.

BARBER, BENJAMIN R. (1984) "The Conventions: Unconventional Democracy," *Psychology Today* (July), Volume 18, Number 7, pp. 52–54.

BARBER, JAMES DAVID (1985) *The Presidential Character: Predicting Performance in the White House*. Englewood Cliffs, New Jersey: Prentice-Hall, 3rd. ed.

BARKER, ERNEST (1944) *The Development of Public Services in Western Europe: 1660–1930*. Oxford: Oxford University Press.

—— ed. (1962) *The Politics of Aristotle*. New York: Oxford University Press.

BAY, CHRISTIAN (1968) "Needs, Wants, and Political Legitimacy," *Canadian Journal of Political Science* (September), Volume 1, Number 3, pp. 241–260.

BEALEY, FRANK (1988) *Democracy in the Contemporary State*. Oxford: Clarendon Press.

BECK, J. MURRAY, ed. (1964) *Joseph Howe: Voice of Nova Scotia*. Toronto: McClelland and Stewart.

—— (1968) *Pendulum of Power: Canada's Federal Elections*. Scarborough, Ontario: Prentice-Hall Canada.

—— (1977) "The Maritimes: A Region or Three Provinces?" Paper presented at the annual meeting of The Royal Society of Canada, Fredericton, New Brunswick.

BEER, SAMUEL H. (1973) "The British Political System," in Samuel H. Beer et al., eds., *Patterns of Government: The Major Political Systems of Europe*. New York: Random House, 3rd ed., pp. 119–329.

—— (1982a) *Modern British Politics: Parties and Pressure Groups in the Collectivist Age*. New York: W.W. Norton.

—— (1982b) *Britain Against Itself: The Political*

Contradictions of Collectivism. New York: W.W. Norton.

BEGIN, MONIQUE (1988) "Debates and Silences — Reflections of a Politician," *Daedalus* (Fall), Volume 117, Number 4, pp. 335–362.

BELL, DAVID V.J. (1975) *Power, Influence and Authority: An Essay in Political Linguistics*. New York: Oxford University Press.

_____ and LORNE TEPPERMAN (1979) *The Roots of Disunity: A Look at Canadian Political Culture*. Toronto: McClelland and Stewart.

BENN, TONY (1980) "The Case for a Constitutional Premiership," *Parliamentary Affairs*, Volume 33, Number 1, pp. 7–22.

_____ (1982) *Arguments for Democracy*. Middlesex, England: Penguin Books.

BENSEL, RICHARD FRANKLIN (1984) *Sectionalism and American Political Development 1880–1980*. Madison, Wisconsin: University of Wisconsin Press.

BENTLEY, A.F. (1908) *The Process of Government*. Chicago: University of Chicago Press.

BERGER, THOMAS R. (1981) *Fragile Freedoms: Human Rights and Dissent in Canada*. Toronto: Clarke, Irwin and Company.

BERNARD, ANDRE (1978) *What Does Quebec Want?* Toronto: James Lorimer and Company.

BERNSTEIN, EDUARD (1899, 1961) *Evolutionary Socialism: A Criticism and Affirmation*. New York: Schocken Books.

BERRINGTON, HUGH (1974) "Review Article: The Fiery Chariot: British Prime Ministers and the Search for Love," *British Journal of Political Science*, Vol. 4, No. 3 (July), pp. 345–370.

BERRY, GLYN R. (1974) "The Oil Lobby and the Energy Crisis," *Canadian Public Administration* (Winter), Volume 17, Number 4, pp. 600–635.

BERRY, JEFFREY M. (1984) *The Interest Group Society*. Boston: Little, Brown and Company.

BEST, JUDITH A. (1986) "The Electoral College: A Paradigm of American Democracy," *This Constitution* (Fall), Number 12, pp. 19–22.

BIERCE, AMBROSE (1911, 1958) *The Devil's Dictionary*. New York: Dover Publications.

BIRCH, ANTHONY H. (1983) *The British System of Government*. London: George Allen and Unwin, 6th ed.

BLACK, CHARLES (1963) *Perspectives in Constitutional Law*. Englewood Cliffs, N.J.: Prentice-Hall.

BLACK, EDWIN R. (1979) "Federal Strains Within a Canadian Party," in Hugh Thorburn, ed., *Party Politics in Canada*. Scarborough, Ontario: Prentice-Hall Canada Inc., 4th ed., pp. 89–99.

BLAKE, DONALD E., R.K. CARTY and LYNDA ERICKSON (1989) "Federalism, Conservatism, and the Social Credit Party in B.C.," *BC Studies* (Spring), Number 81, pp. 3–23.

BLANK, ROBERT H. (1980) *Political Parties: An Introduction*. Englewood Cliffs, N.J.: Prentice-Hall.

BLONDEL, JEAN (1973) *Comparative Legislatures*. Englewood Cliffs, N.J.: Prentice-Hall.

_____ (1987) *Political Leadership: Towards a General Analysis*. London: Sage.

BOGDANOR, VERNON (1981) *The People and the Party System: The Referendum and Electoral Reform in British Politics*. Cambridge: Cambridge University Press.

_____ (1987) "Electoral Reform and British Politics," *Electoral Studies* (August), Volume 6, Number 2, pp. 115–121.

_____ (1988) "Britain: The Political Constitution," pp. 53–72 in Bogdanor, ed. *Constitutions in Democratic Politics*. Aldershot, England: Gower Publishing.

BOORSTIN, DANIEL J. (1983) *The Discoverers*. New York: Random House.

BORK, ROBERT H. (1986) "Judicial Review and Democracy," *Society* (November/December), Volume 24, Number 1, pp. 5–8.

BOURGAULT, JACQUES and STEPHANE DION (1989) "Governments Come and Go, But What of Senior Civil Servants? Canadian Deputy Ministers and Transitions in Power (1867–1987)," *Governance* (April), Volume 2, Number 2, pp. 124–151.

BOYER, J. PATRICK (1985) *Equality for All: Report of the Parliamentary Committee on Equality Rights*. Ottawa: Supply and Services.

_____ (1988) "Robust Democracy: The Canadian General Election of 1988," *The Parliamentarian* (April), Volume 70, Number 2, pp. 72–76.

BRADLEY, IAN (1981) *Breaking the Mold? The Birth and Prospects of the Social Democratic Party*. Oxford: Martin Robertson.

BRADSHAW, KENNETH and DAVID PRING (1972) *Parliament and Congress*. London: Quartet Books.

BRADY, ALEXANDER (1947) *Democracy in the Dominions: A Comparative Study in Institutions*. Toronto: University of Toronto Press.

BRENNAN, WILLIAM J., JR. (1987) "Interpreting the Constitution," *Social Policy* (Summer), Volume 18, Number 1, pp. 24–28.

BROADBENT, EDWARD (1978) "Opening Statement" to the Joint Senate-House of Commons Committee on the Constitution (August 15). Ottawa: New Democratic Party of Canada.

—— (1980) "Statement on Electoral Reform." Ottawa: New Democratic Party of Canada.

BRODIE, JANINE (1985) *Women and Politics in Canada*. Toronto: McGraw-Hill Ryerson Limited.

—— and JILL VICKERS (1981) "The More Things Change... Women in the 1979 Federal Campaign," in Howard R. Penniman, ed., *Canada at the Polls, 1979 and 1980: A Study of the General Elections*. Washington, D.C.: American Enterprise Institute for Public Policy Research, pp. 322–336.

BROGAN, D.W. (1956) *The American Character*. New York: Time Incorporated.

—— (1960) *Politics in America*. New York: Anchor Books, Doubleday.

BROWN, IAN (1985) "Climbing the Tower of Bureaucratic Babel," *The Globe and Mail* (March 5), p. 7.

BROWN, ROBERT CRAIG (1980) "Fishwives, Plutocrats, Sirens and Other Curious Creatures: Some Questions About Political Leadership in Canada," pp. 149–160 in Kenneth Carty and W. Peter Ward, eds., *Entering the Eighties: Canada in Crisis*. Toronto: Oxford University Press.

BRYCE, JAMES (1888, 1959) *The American Commonwealth, Volume One*. Lewis M. Hacker, ed. New York: G.P. Putnam's Sons.

—— (1921) *Canada: An Actual Democracy*. Toronto: Macmillan Co. of Canada.

BRYDEN, DAVID P. (1988) "How to Select a Supreme Court Justice: The Case of Robert Bork," *The American Scholar* (Spring), Volume 7, Number 2, pp. 201–217.

BUCHANAN, JAMES M. (1977) "Why Does Government Grow?" in Thomas E. Borcherding, ed., *Budgets and Bureaucrats: The Sources of Government Growth*. Durham, N.C.: Duke University Press, pp. 3–18.

BUNCE, VALERIE (1981) *Do New Leaders Make a Difference? Executive Succession and Public Policy under Capitalism and Socialism*. Princeton, New Jersey: Princeton University Press.

BURKETT, TONY (1975) *Parties and Elections in West Germany*. New York: St. Martin's Press.

BURNHAM, WALTER DEAN (1983) *Democracy in the Making: American Government and Politics*. Englewood Cliffs, N.J.: Prentice-Hall.

BURNS, JAMES MACGREGOR (1984) "Coming to the Aid of the Party," *Psychology Today* (July), Volume 18, Number 7, pp. 56–62.

—— et al. (1984) *Government by the People*. Englewood Cliffs, N.J.: Prentice-Hall, 12th ed.

BUTLER, DAN and BRUCE D. MACNAUGHTON (1984) "More or Less for Whom? Debating Directions for the Public Sector," in Michael S. Whittington and Glen Williams, eds., *Canadian Politics in the 1980s*. Toronto: Methuen, pp. 1–32.

BUTLER, DAVID and DONALD STOKES (1976) *Political Change in Britain*. New York: St Martin's Press, 2nd college ed.

CAIRNS, ALAN C. (1968) "The Electoral System and Party System in Canada, 1921–1965," *Canadian Journal of Political Science*, Vol. 1, No. 1 (March), pp. 55–80.

—— (1970) "The Living Canadian Constitution," *Queen's Quarterly*. Vol. 77, No. 4 (Winter), pp. 483–498.

—— (1981) "The Constitutional, Legal, and Historical Background," in Howard R. Penniman, ed., *Canada at the Polls, 1979 and 1980: A Study of the General Elections*. Washington, D.C.: American Enterprise Institute for Public Policy Research, pp. 1–23.

CALLWOOD, JUNE (1985) "Running Up Against the Legislative Wall," *The Globe and Mail* (May 17), p. 11.

CAMERON, DAVID M. (1971) "Regional Integration of the Maritime Provinces," *Canadian Journal of Political Science*, Vol. 4, No. 1 (March), pp. 24–25.

CAMP, DALTON (1979) *Points of Departure*. Ottawa: Deneau and Greenberg.

—— (1984) "Reforming the Senate: a Political Game that Never Ends," *The Gazette*, March 8, p. B3.

CAMPBELL, COLIN (1977) "Interplay of Institutionalization and Assignment of Tasks in Parliamentary and Congressional Systems: House of Commons and House of Representatives," *International Journal of Comparative Sociology*, Vol. 18, Nos. 1–2 (March-June), pp. 127–153.

—— (1978) *The Canadian Senate: A Lobby from Within*. Toronto: Macmillan of Canada.

—— (1988) "Review Article: The Political Roles of Senior Government Officials in Advanced Democracies," *British Journal of Political Science* (April), Volume 18, Number 2, pp. 243–272.

_____ and GEORGE J. SZABLOWSKI (1979) *The Super-bureaucrats: Structure and Behaviour in Central Agencies*. Toronto: Macmillan of Canada.

CANETTI, ELIAS (1966) *Crowds and Power*. New York: Viking Press.

CARELESS, J.M.S. (1970) *Canada: A Story of Challenge*. Toronto: Macmillan of Canada, 3rd ed.

CASSIRER, ERNST (1946) *The Myth of the State*. New Haven: Yale University Press.

CHANDLER, MARSHA A. and WILLIAM M. CHANDLER (1979) *Public Policy and Provincial Politics*. Toronto: McGraw-Hill Ryerson Ltd.

CHASE, HAROLD W. et al. (1980) *American Government in Comparative Perspective*. New York: Franklin Watts.

CHEFFINS, R.I. and R.N. TUCKER (1976) *The Constitutional Process in Canada*. Toronto: McGraw-Hill Ryerson, 2nd ed.

_____ and P.A. JOHNSON (1986) *The Revised Canadian Constitution: Politics as Law*. Toronto: McGraw-Hill Ryerson.

CHRISTIAN, WILLIAM and COLIN CAMPBELL (1974) *Political Parties and Ideologies in Canada*. Toronto: McGraw-Hill Ryerson.

CHURCHILL, WINSTON (1949) *Their Finest Hour*. London: Cassell.

CLARK, IAN D. (1985) "Recent Changes in the Cabinet Decision-making System in Ottawa," *Canadian Public Administration*, Volume 28, Number 2, pp. 185–201.

CLARK, S.D. (1963) "Group Interests in Canadian Politics," pp. 64–78 in J.H. Aitchison, ed., *The Political Process in Canada*. Toronto: University of Toronto Press.

CLARKE, HAROLD D. et al. (1981) *Political Choice in Canada*. Toronto: McGraw-Hill Ryerson.

_____ et al. (1984) *Absent Mandate: The Politics of Discontent in Canada*. Toronto: Gage.

CLEROUX, RICHARD (1986) "Speaker under Siege," *The Globe and Mail*. February 13, p. A1.

COLEMAN, WILLIAM D. (1983) "A Comparative Study of Language Policy in Quebec: A Political Economy Approach," pp. 21–42 in Michael M. Atkinson and Marsha A. Chandler, eds., *The Politics of Canadian Public Policy*. Toronto: University of Toronto Press.

COMMAGER, HENRY STEELE (1984) "Tocqueville's Mistake," *Harper's Magazine*, Volume 269, No. 1611, pp. 70–74.

CONWAY, MARGARET M. et al. (1981) "The News Media in Children's Political Socialization," *Public Opinion Quarterly*, Vol. 45, No. 2 (Summer), pp. 164–178.

COOK, RAMSAY (1987) "Alice in Meechland or The Concept of Quebec as 'A Distinct Society'," *Queen's Quarterly* (Winter), Volume 94, Number 4, pp. 817–828.

COOPER, BARRY (1984) "Western Political Consciousness," pp. 213–238 in Stephen Brooks, ed., *Political Thought in Canada*. Toronto: Irwin Publishing.

CORNFIELD, MICHAEL and DAVID ALASTAIR YALOF (1988) "Innocent by Reason of Analogy: How the Watergate Analogy Served Both Reagan and the Press During the Iran-Contra Affair," *Corruption and Reform*, Volume 3, Number 2, pp. 185–206.

CORRY, J.A. (1947) *Democratic Government and Politics*. Toronto: University of Toronto Press.

COSER, LEWIS A. (1970) *Men of Ideas: A Sociologist's View*. New York: The Free Press, Part Two, "Intellectuals and the House of Power," pp. 133–243.

COURTNEY, JOHN C. (1969) "In Defense of Royal Commissions," *Canadian Public Administration* (Summer), Volume 12, Number 2, pp. 198–212.

_____ (1973) *The Selection of National Party Leaders in Canada*. Toronto: Macmillan of Canada.

CRICK, BERNARD (1964) *In Defense of Politics*. Baltimore, Maryland: Penguin Books.

_____ (1967) *The American Science of Politics: Its Origins and Conditions*. Berkeley, California: University of California Press.

_____ (1973) *Basic Forms of Government: A Sketch and a Model*. London: Macmillan Press.

CROSSMAN, RICHARD H.S. (1972) *The Myths of Cabinet Government*. Cambridge, Mass.: Harvard University Press.

CURTIS, MICHAEL (1978) *Comparative Government and Politics: An Introductory Essay in Political Science*. New York: Harper and Row, 2nd ed.

D'ACQUINO, THOMAS et al. (1983) *Parliamentary Democracy in Canada: Issues for Reform*. Toronto: Methuen.

DAHL, ROBERT (1956) *A Preface to Democratic Theory*. Chicago: University of Chicago Press.

_____ (1961) *Who Governs? Democracy and Power in an American City*. New Haven: Yale University Press.

_____ (1970) *After the Revolution?* New Haven: Yale University Press.

_____ (1982) *Dilemmas of Pluralist Democracy: Autonomy vs. Control*. New Haven: Yale University Press.

_____ (1984) *Modern Political Analysis*. Englewood Cliffs, N.J.: Prentice-Hall, 4th ed.

DAHRENDORF, RALF (1959) *Class and Class Conflict in Industrial Society*. Stanford: Stanford University Press.

DAWSON, RICHARD E. et al. (1977) *Political Socialization*. Boston: Little, Brown and Co., 2nd ed.

DAWSON, R. MACGREGOR (1970) *The Government of Canada*, rev. by Norman Ward. Toronto: University of Toronto Press, 5th ed.

DE JOUVENEL, BERTRAND (1962) *On Power: Its Nature and the History of Its Growth*. Boston: Beacon Press.

DE TOCQUEVILLE, ALEXIS (1835, 1945) *Democracy in America*. Phillips Bradley, ed. New York: Vintage Books.

DEL GUIDICE, DOMINIC and STEPHEN M. ZACHS. (1976) "The 101 Governments of Metro Toronto," in Lionel D. Feldman and Michael M. Goldrick, eds., *Politics and Government of Urban Canada: Selected Readings*. Toronto: Methuen, 3rd ed., pp. 285–295.

DERTHICK, MARTHA (1989) "The Enduring Features of American Federalism," *The Brookings Review* (Summer), Volume 7, Number 3, pp. 34–38.

DEUTSCH, KARL W. (1968) *The Analysis of International Relations*. Englewood Cliffs, N.J.: Prentice-Hall.

DEVINE, DONALD J. (1972) *The Political Culture of the United States*. Boston: Little, Brown and Company.

DICKSON, MR. CHIEF JUSTICE BRIAN (1985) "The Judiciary: Law Interpreters or Law-makers," pp. 213–218 in Ronald G. Landes, ed., *Canadian Politics: A Comparative Reader*. Scarborough, Ontario: Prentice-Hall Canada.

DICLERICO, ROBERT E. and ERIC M. USLANER (1984) *Few Are Chosen: Problems in Presidential Selection*. New York: McGraw-Hill.

DION, LEON (1976) *Quebec: The Unfinished Revolution*. Montreal: McGill-Queen's University Press.

DJILAS, MILOVAN (1957) *The New Class: An Analysis of the Communist System*. New York: Praeger Publishers.

DOERN, G. BRUCE (1983) "The Liberals and the Opposition: Ideas, Priorities and the Imperatives of Governing Canada in the 1980s," pp. 1–36 in Doern, ed., *How Ottawa Spends: The Liberals, the Opposition and Federal Priorities 1983*. Toronto: James Lorimer and Company.

_____ (1985) "The Canadian Cabinet: Priorities and Priority Setting in the Trudeau Era," pp. 81–111 in Ronald G. Landes, ed., *Canadian Politics: A Comparative Reader*. Scarborough, Ontario: Prentice-Hall Canada.

DOGAN, MATTEI and DOMINIQUE PELASSY (1984) *How to Compare Nations: Strategies in Comparative Politics*. Chatham, New Jersey: Chatham House Publishers.

DOHERTY, MICHAEL (1988) "Prime-Ministerial Power and Ministerial Responsibility in the Thatcher Era," *Parliamentary Affairs* (January), Volume 41, Number 1, pp. 49–67.

DOWNS, ANTHONY (1957) *An Economic Theory of Democracy*. New York: Harper and Row.

DRUCKER, H.M., ed. (1979) *Multi-Party Britain*. London: Macmillan Press.

_____ (1984) "Intra-Party Democracy in Action: The Election of Leader and Deputy Leader by the Labour Party in 1983," *Parliamentary Affairs* (Summer), Volume 37, Number 3, pp. 283–300.

DRYDEN, KEN (1984) *The Game*. Toronto: Totem Books.

DUCHACEK, IVO (1973) *Rights and Liberties in the World Today: Constitutional Promise and Reality*. Santa Barbara, California: ABC-CLIO Press.

DUNCAN, GRAEME (1987) "Understanding Ideology," *Political Studies* (December), Volume 35, Number 4, pp. 649–659.

DUNN, BRIAN A. (1989) "The Governor-General: The Changing of the Guard," *The New Federation* (Spring/May), Volume 1, Number 3, pp. 10–13.

DUVERGER, MAURICE (1951) "The Influence of the Electoral System on Political Life," *International Social Science Bulletin*, Vol. 3, No. 2 (Summer), pp. 314–365.

_____ (1964) *Political Parties: Their Organization and Activity in the Modern State*. London: Methuen and Co.

_____ (1972) *Party Politics and Pressure Groups: A Comparative Introduction*. New York: Thomas Y. Crowell.

_____ (1974) *Modern Democracies: Economic Power versus Political Power*. Hinsdale Ill.: The Dryden Press.

DYE, THOMAS R. (1977) *Politics in States and Communities*. Englewood Cliffs, N.J.: Prentice-Hall, 3rd. ed.

EASTERBROOK, GREGG (1984) "What's Wrong With

Congress?" *The Atlantic Monthly* (December), Volume 254, Number 6, pp. 57–84.

Economic Council of Canada (1977) *Living Together: A Study of Regional Disparities*. Ottawa: Supply and Services Canada.

EDELMAN, MURRAY (1985) "Political Language and Political Reality," *PS* (Winter), Volume 18, Number 1, pp. 10–19.

ELLUL, JACQUES (1972) *The Political Illusion*. New York: Vintage.

EPSTEIN, LEON D. (1967) *Political Parties in Western Democracies*. New York: Praeger Publishers.

EULAU, HEINZ (1963) *The Behavioural Persuasion in Politics*. New York: Random House.

FAGEN, RICHARD R. (1964) *Cuba: The Political Content of Adult Education*. Stanford, California: The Hoover Institution.

_____ (1969) *The Transformation of Political Culture in Cuba*. Stanford, California: The Hoover Institution.

FAULKNER, J. HUGH (1982) "Pressuring the Executive," *Canadian Public Administration* (Summer), Volume 25, Number 2, pp. 240–253.

FENNO, RICHARD F. (1986) "Observation, Context, and Sequence in the Study of Politics," *American Political Science Review* (March), Volume 80, Number 1, pp. 3–15.

FINER, S.E. (1980) "Princes, Parliaments, and the Public Service," *Parliamentary Affairs* (Autumn), Volume 33, Number 4, pp. 353–372.

_____ (1980) *The Changing British Party System, 1945–1979*. Washington, D.C.: American Enterprise Institute for Public Policy Research.

_____ (1983) "Perspectives in the World History of Government - a Prolegomenon," *Government and Opposition* (Winter), Volume 18, Number 1, pp. 3–22.

_____ and MICHAEL STEED (1978) "Politics of Great Britain," in Roy C. Macridis, ed. *Modern Political Systems: Europe*. Englewood Cliffs, N.J.: Prentice-Hall, 4th ed., pp. 27–92.

FLAHERTY, DAVID H. (1988) "Who Rules Canada?" *Daedalus* (Fall), Volume 17, Number 4, pp. 99–128.

FLETCHER, MARTHA (1977), "Judicial Review and the Division of Powers in Canada," in J. Peter Meekison, ed., *Canadian Federalism: Myth or Reality*. Toronto: Methuen, 3rd. ed., pp. 100–123.

FORBES, H.D. (1976) "Conflicting National Identities Among Canadian Youth," in Jon H. Pammett and Michael S. Whittington, eds., *Foundations of Political Culture: Political Socialization in Canada*. Toronto: Macmillan, pp. 288–315.

_____ ed. (1985) *Canadian Political Thought*. Toronto: Oxford University Press.

FORCESE, DENNIS (1978) "Elites and Power In Canada," in John H. Redekop, ed., *Approaches to Canadian Politics*. Scarborough, Ontario: Prentice-Hall Canada, Inc., pp. 302–322.

FORSEY, EUGENE (1974) *Freedom and Order: Collected Essays*. Toronto: McClelland and Stewart.

_____ (1985) "The Role and Position of the Monarch in Canada," pp. 53–62 in Ronald G. Landes, ed., *Canadian Politics: A Comparative Reader*. Scarborough, Ontario: Prentice-Hall Canada.

FORSTER, E.M. (1910, 1955) *Howard's End*. Hammondsworth, England: Penguin Books.

FOTHERINGHAM, ALLAN (1981) "On Mangling Language," *Maclean's*, Vol. 94, No. 6 (February 9), p. 60.

FRANKFORT, HENRI et al. (1949) *Before Philosophy*. Baltimore: Penguin Books.

FRANKS, C.E.S. (1983) "Borrowing from the United States: Is the Canadian Parliamentary System Moving Toward the Congressional Model," *The American Review of Canadian Studies* (Autumn), Volume 13, Number 3, pp. 201–214.

_____ (1985) "Debates and Question Period in the Canadian House of Commons: What Purpose Do They Serve?" *The American Review of Canadian Studies* (Spring), Volume 15, Number 1, pp. 1–15.

_____ (1986) "Reform of the Canadian House of Commons," *The American Review of Canadian Studies* (Winter), Volume 16, Number 4, pp. 399–412.

FRASER, JOHN (1980) *The Chinese: Portrait of a People*. New York: Summit Books.

_____ (1988) "Diary: Crowning Around With Mulroney While Sauve Is Elbowed Aside," *Saturday Night* (April), Volume 103, Number 4, pp. 9–10.

_____ (1989) "Why Can't Quebec Listen to Sense?" *Saturday Night* (April), Volume 104, Number 4, pp. 13–16.

FRIEDENBERG, EDGAR Z. (1980) *Deference to Authority: The Case of Canada*. White Plains, N.Y.: M.E. Sharpe, Inc.

FRIEDRICH, CARL J. (1968) *Constitutional Government and Democracy: Theory and Practice in Europe and America*. Waltham, Mass.: Blaisdell Publishing Co., 4th ed.

—— (1974) *Limited Government: A Comparison*. Englewood Cliffs, N.J.: Prentice-Hall.

FRIENDLY, FRED W. and MARTHA J. ELLIOTT (1984) *The Constitution: That Delicate Balance*. New York: Random House.

FRUM, DAVID (1988) "Who's Running the Country, Anyway?" *Saturday Night* (October), Volume 103, Number 10, pp. 57–66.

—— (1989) "Double Dealing," *Saturday Night* (March), Volume 104, Number 3, pp. 40–50.

FRYE, NORTHROP (1980) "Canada's Emerging Identity," *Toronto Star*, June 28, pp. B1 and B4.

FULFORD, ROBERT (1987) "Surrendering Canada," *Saturday Night* (August), Volume 102, Number 8, pp. 5–7.

GAMBLE, ANDREW (1980) "The Conservative Party," in H.M. Drucker, ed., *Multi-Party Britain*. London: Macmillan Press, pp. 25–53.

GARSON, DAVID (1978) *Group Theories of Politics*. Beverly Hills, California: Sage Publications.

GERTH, H.H. and C. WRIGHT MILLS, eds. (1958) *From Max Weber: Essays in Sociology*. New York: Oxford University Press.

GIBBINS, ROGER (1982) *Regionalism: Territorial Politics in Canada and the United States*. Toronto: Butterworths.

—— (1985) *Conflict and Unity*. Toronto: Methuen.

—— (1988) "Introduction to Constitutional Politics," pp. 3–8 in Gibbins, ed. *Meech Lake and Canada: Perspectives from the West*. Edmonton: Academic Printing and Publishing.

GIGANTES, SENATOR PHILIPPE DEANE (1985) "The Senate as Asset: a View from the Inside," *The Globe and Mail*, February 14, p. 7.

GINSBERG, BENJAMIN (1982) *The Consequences of Consent: Elections, Citizen Control and Popular Acquiescence*. Reading, Mass.: Addison-Wesley.

—— (1986) "Elections, Liberty, and the Consequences of Consent," pp. 10–18 in Ginsberg and Alan Stone (eds.), *Do Elections Matter?* Armonk, New York: M.E. Sharpe.

GLASS, DAVID et al. (1985) "Voter Turnout: An International Comparison," pp. 345–360 in Ronald G. Landes, ed., *Canadian Politics: A Comparative Reader*. Scarborough, Ontario: Prentice-Hall Canada.

GOULD, JULIUS (1973) "Interests and Pressures," *Government and Opposition* (Spring), Volume 8, Number 2, pp. 242–258.

GRAY, CHARLOTTE (1987) "Clever Lowell Murray," *Saturday Night* (November), Volume 102, Number 11, pp. 13–17.

—— (1988) "Politics: Bureaucratic Blues," *Saturday Night* (February), Volume 103, Number 2, pp. 11–13.

—— (1989) "How the West Won," *Saturday Night* (June), Volume 104, Number 6, pp. 15–17.

GREENE, IAN (1989) *The Charter of Rights*. Toronto: James Lorimer and Company.

GREEN, MARK J. et al. (1972) *Who Runs Congress?* Toronto: Bantam Books.

GREENSTEIN, FRED I. (1988) "Introduction: Toward a Modern Presidency," pp. 1–6 in Greenstein (ed.), *Leadership in the Modern Presidency*. Cambridge, Mass.: Harvard University Press.

GREGG, ALLAN and MICHAEL S. WHITTINGTON (1976) "Regional Variation in Children's Political Attitudes," in David J. Bellamy et al., eds., *The Provincial Political Systems: Comparative Essays*. Toronto: Methuen, pp. 76–85.

GUPPY, NEIL, SABRINA FREEMAN and SHARI BUCHAN (1987) "Representing Canadians: Changes in the Economic Backgrounds of Federal Politicians, 1965–1984," *The Canadian Review of Sociology and Anthropology* (August), Volume 24, Number 3, pp. 417–430.

GWYN, RICHARD (1985) *The 49th Paradox: Canada in North America*. Toronto: McClelland and Stewart.

HAIN, PETER (1986) *Proportional Misrepresentation: The Case Against PR in Britain*. Hants, England: Wildwood House.

HALL, RON (1969) "The Family Background of Etonians," in Richard Rose, eds., *Studies in British Politics*. London: Macmillan, 2nd ed., pp. 67–77.

HALPERIN, MORTON (1974) *Bureaucratic Politics and Foreign Policy*. Washington, D.C.: The Brookings Institution.

HAMILTON, WILLIE (1975) *My Queen and I*. Don Mills, Ontario: Paperjacks.

HEALD, DAVID (1988) "The United Kingdom: Privatization and Its Political Context," *West European Politics* (October), Volume 11, Number 4, pp. 31–48.

HENIG, JEFFREY R., CHRIS HAMNETT and HARVEY B. FEIGENBAUM (1988) "The Politics of Privatization: A Comparative Perspective," *Governance* (October), Volume 1, Number 4, pp. 442–468.

HILL, DAVID B. and NORMAN R. LUTTBERG (1980) *Trends*

in American Electoral Behaviour. Itasca, Ill.: Peacock Publishers.

HILSMAN, ROGER (1979) *To Govern America*. New York: Harper and Row.

HINCKLEY, BARBARA (1978) *Stability and Change in Congress*. New York: Harper and Row.

HOCKIN, THOMAS A. (1973) "Adversary Politics and the Functions of Canada's House of Commons," in Orest M. Kruhlak et al., eds., *The Canadian Political Process: A Reader*. Toronto: Holt, Rinehart and Winston, rev. ed., pp. 361–381.

_____ (1976) *Government in Canada*. Toronto: McGraw-Hill Ryerson Ltd.

HODGETTS, TED (1985) "The Deputy Ministers' Dilemma," pp. 139–145 in Ronald G. Landes, ed., *Canadian Politics: A Comparative Reader*. Scarborough, Ontario: Prentice-Hall Canada.

HOFSTADTER, RICHARD (1948) *The American Political Tradition*. New York: Vintage Books.

_____ (1972) *The Idea of a Party System: The Rise of Legitimate Opposition in the United States 1780–1840*. Berkeley: University of California Press.

HOLLIS, PATRICIA, ed. (1974) *Pressure from Without in Early Victorian England*. London: Edward Arnold.

HOLTZMAN, ELIZABETH and SHIRLEY WILLIAMS (1987) "Women in the Political World: Observations," *Daedalus* (Fall), Volume 116, Number 4, pp. 25–33.

HOOD, CHRISTOPHER, with ANDREW DUNSIRE and LYNN THOMSON (1988) "Rolling Back the State: Thatcherism, Fraserism and Bureaucracy," *Governance* (July), Volume 1, Number 3, pp. 243–270.

HOROWITZ, GAD (1968) *Canadian Labour in Politics*. Toronto: University of Toronto Press.

HUCKSHORN, ROBERT J. (1980) *Political Parties in America*. North Scituate, Mass.: Duxbury Press.

HUNTINGTON, SAMUEL P. (1981) *American Politics: The Promise of Disharmony*. Cambridge, Mass.: Belknap Press of Harvard University Press.

HURTIG, MEL (1975) *Never Heard of Them . . . They Must be Canadian*. Toronto: Canadabooks.

HUTCHINSON, ALLAN C. (1987) "Veil of secrecy on top judges should be lifted," *Globe and Mail* (March 6), p. A7.

INGLEHART, RONALD (1988) "The Renaissance of Political Culture," *American Political Science Review* (December), Volume 82, Number 4, pp. 1203–1230.

IONESCU, GHITA and ISABEL DE MADARIAGA (1972) *Opposition: Past and Present of a Political Institution*. London: Penguin Books.

IREMONGER, LUCILLE (1970) *The Fiery Chariot: A Study of British Prime Ministers and the Search for Love*. London: Seeker and Warburg.

IRVINE, WILLIAM P. (1979) *Does Canada Need a New Electoral System?* Kingston, Ont.: Institute of Intergovenmental Relations, Queen's University.

_____ (1980) "Librl, Pcons, Ndpty, Pcrd, Rhino," *Report* (July/August), p. 22.

JACK, MALCOLM (1985) "Parliament's Role as a Check on Government," *Parliamentary Affairs* (Summer), Volume 38, Number 3, pp. 296–306.

JACOBS, DAN N. et al. (1983) *Comparative Politics*. Chatham, N.J.: Chatham House Publishers.

JAROS, DEAN (1973) *Socialization to Politics*. New York: Praeger Publishers.

JOHNSON, CHALMERS (1983) *Revolutionary Change*. London: Longman, 2nd ed.

JOHNSTON, R.I. (1986) "Constituency Redistribution in Britain: Recent Issues," pp. 277–288 in Bernard Grofman and Arend Lijphart, eds., *Electoral Laws and Their Political Consequences*. New York: Agathon Press.

JOHNSTONE, JOHN C. (1969) *Young People's Images of Canadian Society*. Ottawa: Queen's Printer.

JONES, PETER (1989) "Review Article: Re-examining Rights," *British Journal of Political Science* (January), Volume 19, Number 1, pp. 69–96.

JOY, RICHARD J. (1972) *Languages in Conflict: The Canadian Experience*. Toronto: McClelland and Stewart.

_____ (1985) "Canada's Official Language Populations, as Shown by the 1981 Census," *American Review of Canadian Studies* (Spring), Volume 15, Number 1, pp. 90–96.

JUDGE, DAVID, ed. (1983) *The Politics of Parliamentary Reform*. London: Heinemann Educational Books.

KARP, WALTER (1988) "In Defense of Politics," *Harper's Magazine* (May), Volume 276, Number 1656, pp. 41–49.

KAVANAGH, DENNIS (1972) *Political Culture*. London: Macmillan.

_____ (1980) "Political Culture in Great Britain: The Decline of the Civic Culture," in Gabriel A. Almond and Sidney Verba, eds., *The Civic Culture Revisited*. Boston: Little, Brown and Co., pp. 124–176.

KEEFE, WILLIAM J. and MORRIS S. OGUL (1985) *The American Legislative Process: Congress and the*

States. Englewood Cliffs, N.J.: Prentice-Hall, 6th ed.

KELLEY, STANLEY (1983) *Interpreting Elections*. Princeton, New Jersey: Princeton University Press.

KENDRICK, STEPHEN and DAVID MCCRONE (1989) "Politics in a Cold Climate: The Conservative Decline in Scotland," *Political Studies* (December), Volume 37, Number 4, pp. 589–603.

KEY, V.O., JR. (1956) *American State Politics: An Introduction*. New York: Alfred A. Knopf.

—— (1964) *Politics, Parties, and Pressure Groups*. New York: Thomas Y. Crowell, 5th ed.

—— (1966) *The Responsible Electorate: Rationality in Presidential Voting 1936–1960*. Cambridge, Mass.: The Belknap Press.

KILBOURN, WILLIAM (1988) "The Peaceable Kingdom Still," *Daedalus* (Fall), Volume 117, Number 4, pp. 1–29.

KING, ANTHONY (1985) "Margaret Thatcher's First Term," pp. 1–38 in Austin Ranney (ed.), *Britain At the Polls, 1983*. Durham, N.C.: Duke University Press.

KIRBY, MICHAEL J.L. (1985) "Is There a Conservative Resurgence in Canada?" Paper presented to the Atlantic Provinces Political Science Association, Wolfville, Nova Scotia.

KORNBERG, ALLAN and WILLIAM MISHLER (1976) *Influence in Parliament: Canada*. Durham, N.C.: Duke University Press.

—— et al. (1979) *Citizen Politicians – Canada: Party Officials in a Democratic Society*. Durham, N.C.: Carolina Academic Press.

—— et al. (1980) "Parliament and the Representational Process in Contemporary Canada," in Harold D. Clarke et al., eds., *Parliament, Policy and Representation*. Toronto: Methuen, pp. 1–24.

KOUSSER, J. MORGAN (1974) *The Shaping of Southern Politics: Suffrage Restriction and the Establishment of the One-Party South 1880–1910*. New Haven: Yale University Press.

KRISLOV, SAMUEL (1974) *Representative Bureaucracy*. Englewood Cliffs, N.J.: Prentice-Hall.

KWAVNICK, DAVID (1972) *Organized Labour and Pressure Politics: The Canadian Labour Congress 1956–1968*. Montreal: McGill-Queen's University Press.

LADD, EVERETT C. (1986) "The Foreign Policy Record:

Reagan's Sphere of Influence," *Public Opinion* (Summer), Volume 9, Number 2, pp. 3–5.

LAMY, PAUL G. (1975) "Political Socialization of French and English Canadian Youth: Socialization into Discord," in Elia Zureik and Robert M. Pike, eds., *Socialization and Values in Canadian Society: Volume One – Political Socialization*. Toronto: McClelland and Stewart, pp. 263–280.

LANDES, RONALD G. (1976) "The Use of Role Theory in Political Socialization Research: A Review, Critique, and Modest Proposal," *International Journal of Comparative Sociology*, Vol. 17, Nos. 1–2 (March-June), pp. 59–72.

—— (1977) "Political Socialization Among Youth: A Comparative Study of English-Canadian and American School Children," *International Journal of Comparative Sociology*, Vol. 18, Nos. 1–2 (March-June), pp. 63–80.

—— (1979) "The Federal Political Culture in Canada." Paper presented to the annual meeting of the Canadian Political Science Association, Saskatoon, Saskatchewan.

—— (1980) "Alternative Electoral Systems for Canada." Paper presented to the annual meeting of the Canadian Political Science Association, Montreal, Quebec.

—— (1981) "The Canadian General Election of 1980," *Parliamentary Affairs*, Vol. 34, No. 1, pp. 95–109.

—— (1984) "In Defence of Canadian Political Parties." Paper presented to the annual meeting of the Canadian Political Science Association, Guelph, Ontario.

—— (1985) "Public Perceptions of the Canadian Parliament," pp. 206–210 in Landes, ed., *Canadian Politics: A Comparative Reader*. Scarborough, Ontario: Prentice-Hall Canada.

LAPALOMBARA, JOSEPH, ed., (1963) *Bureaucracy and Political Development*. Princeton, New Jersey: Princeton University Press.

—— (1974) *Politics Within Nations*. Englewood Cliffs, N.J.: Prentice-Hall.

—— and MYRON WEINER, eds. (1966) *Political Parties and Political Development*. Princeton, N.J.: Princeton University Press.

LAPONCE, J.A. (1969) *People vs. Politics*. Toronto: University of Toronto Press.

—— (1972) "Post-dicting Electoral Cleavages in Canadian Federal Elections, 1949–68: Material for a Footnote," *Canadian Journal of Political Science*, Vol. 5, No. 2 (June), pp. 270–286.

_____ (1985) "Protecting the French Language in Canada: From Neurophysiology to Geography to Politics: The Regional Imperative," *The Journal of Commonwealth and Comparative Politics* (July), Volume 23, Number 2, pp. 157–170.

LASKI, HAROLD J. (1940) *The American Presidency*. New York: Grosset and Dunlap.

LASKIN, BORA (1959) "An Inquiry into the Diefenbaker Bill of Rights," *Canadian Bar Review*, Vol. 37, pp. 77–134.

LASSWELL, HAROLD (1958) *Politics: Who Gets What, When, How?* Cleveland: Meridian Books.

_____ and ABRAHAM KAPLAN (1950) *Power and Society: A Framework for Political Inquiry*. New Haven: Yale University Press.

LATOUCHE, DANIEL (1989) "Politics and the Mulroney/Bourassa Alliance," *The New Federation* (Spring/May), Volume 1, Number 3, pp. 20–22.

LAURIER, SIR WILFRID (1985) "Political Liberalism," pp. 134–151 in H.D. Forbes, ed., *Canadian Political Thought*. Toronto: Oxford University Press.

LAWSON, KAY, ed. (1980) *Political Parties and Linkage: A Comparative Perspective*. New Haven: Yale University Press.

LAXER, JAMES (1985) "Who's Left?" *Saturday Night*, Volume 100, Number 3, pp. 11–17.

LEMCO, JONATHAN (1986) "Senate Reform: A Fruitless Endeavor," *The Journal of Commonwealth and Comparative Politics* (November), Volume 24, Number 3, pp. 269–277.

LEVESQUE, RENE (1968) *An Option for Quebec*. Toronto: McCelland and Stewart.

LEWIS, DAVID (1972) *Louder Voices: The Corporate Welfare Bums*. Toronto: James Lewis and Samuel.

_____ (1981) *The Good Fight: Political Memoirs 1909–1958*. Toronto: Macmillan, a Division of Gage.

LEYS, COLIN (1983) *Politics in Britain*. Toronto: University of Toronto Press.

LIGHTBODY, JAMES (1989) "With Whom the Tolls Dwell: The Great Edmonton Telephone Dispute, 1984–1987," *Canadian Public Administration* (Spring), Volume 32, Number 1, pp. 41–62.

LINDBLOM, CHARLES E. (1977) *Politics and Markets: The World's Political Economic Systems*. New York: Basic Books.

LIPSET, SEYMOUR MARTIN (1970) *Revolution and Counterrevolution: Change and Persistence in Social Structures*. New York: Anchor Books.

_____ (1986) "Historical Traditions and National Characteristics: A Comparative Analysis of Canada and the United States," *The Canadian Journal of Sociology* (Summer), Volume 11, Number 2, pp. 113–155.

LITTLE, BRUCE (1985) "New Solitudes in the Capital," *Report on Business*, Volume 2, Number 6, pp. 32–38.

_____ (1985) "Switch in Power Makes Politicians Versatile Actors," *The Globe and Mail*, January 29, p. B8.

LOWENBERG, GERHARD and SAMUEL C. PATTERSON (1979) *Comparing Legislatures*. Boston: Little, Brown and Co.

LONGLEY, LAWRENCE D. (1986) "The Electoral College: Archaic, Uncertain, Unfair," *This Constitution* (Fall), Number 12, pp. 22–25.

LOWI, THEODORE J. (1979) *The End of Liberalism*. New York: Norton, 2nd ed.

MACINTOSH, JOHN P. (1982) *The Government and Politics of Britain*. London: Hutchinson, 5th ed., revised and updated by Peter Richards.

MACIVER, R.M. (1965) *The Web of Government*. New York: The Free Press, rev. ed.

MACKAY, WAYNE (1981) "Reflections on the Canadian Supreme Court." Lecture given to the Saint Mary's University Law Society, Halifax, Nova Scotia.

MACKINNON, FRANK (1973) *Postures and Politics: Some Observations on Participatory Democracy*. Toronto: University of Toronto Press.

_____ (1976) *The Crown in Canada*. Calgary, Alberta: McClelland and Stewart West, Glenbow-Alberta Institute.

MACKINTOSH, GORDON H.A. (1985) "A Fateful Prorogation: The Death of Constitutional Proposals in Manitoba," *The Parliamentarian* (April), Volume 66, Number 2, pp. 60–66.

MACPHERSON, C.B. (1977) *The Life and Times of Liberal Democracy*. Oxford: Oxford University Press.

MACQUEEN, KEN (1986) "The Power Brokers," *Maclean's* (February 24), Volume 99, Number 8, pp. 14–16.

MACRIDIS, ROY C. (1955) *The Study of Comparative Government*. New York: Random House.

_____ (1980) *Contemporary Political Ideologies: Movements and Regimes*. Cambridge, Mass: Winthrop Publishers.

MAKIN, KIRK (1989) "Patronage cited in 50% of Tory judicial appointments," *The Globe and Mail* (June 3), p. A1.

MALCOLM, ANDREW H. (1985) *The Canadians.* Toronto: Fitzhenry and Whiteside.

MALLORY, J.R. (1954) *Social Credit and the Federal Power in Canada.* Toronto: University of Toronto Press.

—— (1971) *The Structure of Canadian Government.* Toronto: Macmillan of Canada.

—— (1984) "The Charter of Rights and Freedoms and Canadian Democracy," *The Timlim Lecture.* University of Saskatchewan, Saskatoon.

MARCH, ROMAN R. (1974) *The Myth of Parliament.* Scarborough, Ont.: Prentice-Hall Canada.

MARSHALL, GEOFFREY (1988) "Canada's new Constitution (1982): Some lessons in constitutional engineering," pp. 156–170 in Vernon Bogdanor, ed., *Constitutions in Democratic Politics.* Aldershot, England: Gower Publishing.

MARTIN GED (1989)"The 'Principle of Alternation' in the Leadership of the Liberal Party of Canada: An Unhelpful Myth," *The Round Table* (April), Volume 78, Number 310, pp. 158–164.

MATHESON, W.A. (1976) *The Prime Minister and the Cabinet.* Toronto: Methuen.

MAYO, HENRY B. (1960) *An Introduction to Democratic Theory.* New York: Oxford University Press.

MCCAFFREY, JEFFREY (1984) "Canada's Envelope Budgeting System," *The American Review of Canadian Studies* (Spring), Volume 14, Number 1, pp. 45–62.

MCCALL-NEWMAN, CHRISTINA (1982) *Grits: An Intimate Portrait of the Liberal Party.* Toronto: Macmillan, a division of Gage Publishing.

MCDONALD, VIRGINIA (1977) "Participation in the Canadian Context," *Queen's Quarterly* (Autumn), Volume 84, Number 3, pp. 457–475.

MCFARLAND, ANDREW S. (1984) *Common Cause: Lobbying in the Public Interest.* Chatham, N.J.: Chatham House Publishers.

MCGRATH, JAMES (1985) *Report of the Special Committee on Reform of the House of Commons.* Ottawa: Queen's Printer.

MCILWAIN, CHARLES HOWARD (1947) *Constitutionalism: Ancient and Modern.* Ithaca, New York: Great Seal Books, Cornell University Press, rev. ed.

MCKENZIE, ROBERT (1967) *British Political Parties: The Distribution of Power Within the Conservative and Labour Parties.* London: Heinemann Educational Books.

MCMENEMY, JOHN (1980) *The Language of Canadian Politics.* Toronto: John Wiley and Sons Canada.

MCMONAGLE, DUNCAN (1988) "System of 'little laws' condemned by Ontario panel," *The Globe and Mail* (June 27), A4.

MCNAUGHT, KENNETH (1975) "Political Trials and the Canadian Political Tradition," in Martin L. Friedland, ed., *Courts and Trials.* Toronto: University of Toronto Press, pp. 137–161.

—— (1983) "History and the Perception of Politics," in John H. Redekop, ed., *Approaches to Canadian Politics.* Scarborough, Ont.: Prentice-Hall Canada, 2nd ed., pp. 89–100.

MCPHEE, NANCY, ed. (1980) *The Book of Insults: Ancient and Modern.* Markham, Ontario: Penguin Books of Canada.

MCQUAIG, LINDA (1985) "Big Business's Soft-Talking Lobbyist," *Report on Business Magazine* (March), Volume 1, Number 3, pp. 68–72.

MCRAE, KENNETH, ed. (1974) *Consociational Democracy: Political Accommodation in Segmented Societies.* Toronto: McCelland and Stewart.

MCROBERTS, KENNETH and DALE POSGATE (1980) *Quebec: Social Change and Political Crisis.* Toronto: McClelland and Stewart, rev. ed.

MCWHINNEY, EDWARD (1979) *Quebec and the Constitution 1960–1978.* Toronto: University of Toronto Press.

—— (1982) "Giving the Governor-General a More Active Role to Play," *The Globe and Mail* (February 6).

—— (1987) "Judicial Review in a Federal and Plural Society: The Supreme Court of Canada," pp. 63–74 in John R. Schmidhauser (ed.), *Comparative Judicial Systems: Challenging Frontiers in Conceptual and Empirical Analysis.* London: Butterworths.

MCWILLIAMS, WILSON CAREY (1981) "The Meaning of the Election," in Gerald M. Pomper, ed., *The Election of 1980: Reports and Interpretations.* Chatham, New Jersey: Chatham House Publishers, pp. 170–188.

MEISEL, JOHN (1979) "The Decline of Party in Canada," in Hugh G. Thorburn, ed., *Party Politics in Canada.* Scarborough, Ontario: Prentice-Hall Canada, 4th ed.

MENCKEN, H.L. (1922, 1963) *In Defense of Women*. New York: Time.

MERRIAM, CHARLES E. (1934, 1964) *Political Power*. New York: Collier Books.

MICHELMANN, HANS J. and JEFFREY S. STEEVES (1985) "The 1982 Transition in Power in Saskatchewan: the Progressive Conservatives and the Public Service," *Canadian Public Administration* (Spring), Volume 28, Number 1, pp. 1–23.

MICHENER, JAMES A. (1969) *Presidential Lottery*. Greenwich, Conn.: Fawcett.

MILBRATH, LESTER W. and M.L. GOEL (1977) *Political Participation: How and Why Do People Get Involved in Politics?* Chicago: Rand McNally, 2nd ed.

MILL, J.S. (1861, 1948) *On Liberty and Considerations on Representative Government*, R.B. McCallum, ed. Oxford: Basil Blackwell.

MILNOR, A.J. (1969) *Elections and Political Stability*. Boston: Little, Brown and Co.

MISHLER, WILLIAM (1979) *Political Participation in Canada: Prospects for Democratic Citizenship*. Toronto: Macmillan of Canada.

_____ (1981) "Political Participation and Democracy," in Michael S. Whittington and Glen Williams, eds., *Canadian Politics in the 1980's*. Toronto: Methuen, pp. 126–141.

MITCHELL, AUSTIN (1984) "A College Education: Electing Labour's Leader," *The Parliamentarian* (April), Volume 65, Number 2, pp. 104–116.

MITCHELL, WILLIAM C. *The American Polity: A Social and Cultural Interpretation*. New York: The Free Press.

MONIERE, DENIS (1981) *Ideologies in Quebec: The Historical Development*. Toronto: University of Toronto Press.

MOORE, CHARLES (1987) "Why Vote? *The Spectator* (May 2), Volume 258, Number 8286, pp. 21–23.

MORGAN, JANET (1981) "The House of Lords in the 1980s," *The Parliamentarian* (January), Volume 62, Number 1, pp. 15–19.

MORTON, DESMOND (1974) *NDP: The Dream of Power*. Toronto: Hakkert.

MORTON, F.L. (1987) "The Political Impact of the Canadian Charter of Rights and Freedoms," *Canadian Journal of Political Science* (March), Volume 20, Number 1, pp. 31–55.

_____ and LESLIE A. PAL (1985) "The Impact of the Charter of Rights on Public Administration,"

Canadian Public Administration (Summer), Volume 28, Number 2, pp. 221–243.

MORTON, W.L. (1950) *The Progressive Party in Canada*. Toronto: University of Toronto Press.

MUELLER, CLAUS (1973) *The Politics of Communication: A Study in the Political Sociology of Language, Socialization, and Legitimation*. New York: Oxford University Press.

MULLER, WILLIAM D. (1977) *The 'Kept Men'*. Brighton: Harvester Press.

MURPHY, BRUCE ALLEN (1983) *The Brandeis/Frankfurter Connection: The Secret Political Activities of Two Supreme Court Justices*. New York: Anchor Press, Doubleday and Company.

MURPHY, RAE et al. (1984) *Brian Mulroney: The Boy from Baie-Comeau*. Halifax: Formac Publishing.

NAMIER, SIR LEWIS (1952) *Avenue of History*. London: Hamish Hamilton.

NEELY, RICHARD (1981) *How Courts Govern America*. New Haven: Yale University Press.

NEUSTADT, RICHARD E. (1980) *Presidential Power: The Politics of Leadership from FDR to Carter*. New York: John Wiley and Sons.

NEWMAN, PETER C. (1973) *Renegade in Power: The Diefenbaker Years*. Toronto: McClelland and Stewart.

_____ (1979) *Bronfman Dynasty: The Rothchilds of the New World*. Toronto: Seal Books.

_____ (1979) "Three Remedies for a Liberal Party that Can Never Again Win with Pierre Trudeau," *Maclean's*, Vol. 92, No. 49 (November 26), p. 3.

_____ (1984) "Introduction," in Roy Peterson, *Drawn and Quartered: The Trudeau Years*. Toronto: Key Porter Books.

_____ (1985) "Canada's National Ailment: Inferiority Complex," *The Globe and Mail* (August 19), p. 7.

_____ (1988) "A Radical Mandate; Canadians Choose a New Political Order," *Maclean's* (December 5), Volume 101, Number 50, pp. 29–30.

NIE, NORMAN H. et al. (1979) *The Changing American Voter*. Cambridge, Mass.: Harvard University Press, enlarged ed.

NIEMI, RICHARD G. (1973) "Political Socialization," in Jeanne N. Knutson, ed., *Handbook of Political Psychology*. San Francisco: Jossey-Bass Publishers, pp. 117–138.

NORTON, PHILIP (1982) *The Canadian Constitution in Flux*. Oxford: Martin Robertson.

NUTTER, G. WARREN (1978) *Growth of Government in*

the West. Washington, D.C.: American Enterprise Institute for Public Policy Research.

OAKESHOTT, MICHAEL (1962) *Rationalism in Politics and Other Essays.* London: Methuen and Co.

OBLER, JEFFREY (1981) "Legislatures and the Survival of Political Systems: A Review Article," *Political Science Quarterly,* Vol. 96, No. 1 (Spring), pp. 127–139.

ODDO, GILBERT L. (1979) *Freedom and Equality: Civil Liberties and the Supreme Court.* Santa Monica, Calif: Goodyear Publishing.

OGMUNDSON, RICK (1976) "The Sociology of Power and Politics: An Introduction to the Canadian Polity," in G.N. Ramn and Stuart D. Johnson, eds., *Introduction to Canadian Society: A Sociological Analysis.* Toronto: Macmillan, pp. 157–211.

OLIVER, DAWN (1989) "Law, Convention and Abuse of Power," *The Political Quarterly* (January), Volume 60, Number 1, pp. 38–49.

OZLESZEK, WALTER J. (1978) *Congressional Procedures and the Policy Process.* Washington, D.C.: Congressional Quarterly Press.

ORNSTEIN, M.D. and H.M. STEVENSON (1984) "Ideology and Public Policy in Canada," *British Journal of Political Science* (July), Volume 14, Part 3, pp. 313–344.

OSTROGORSKI, MOISEI (1902, 1964) *Democracy and the Organization of Political Parties.* Seymour Martin Lipset, ed. New York: Anchor Books.

OSTRY, SYLVIA (1980) "Government Intervention: Canada and the United States Compared," *Policy Options* (March), Volume 1, Number 1, pp. 26–31.

OWEN, DAVID (1983) "Justice for the Voters of Britain," *The Times,* June 19, p. 16.

OWEN, DAVID (1985) "The Fifth Estate," *The Atlantic Monthly* (July), Volume 256, Number 1, pp. 26–31.

PAINE, ROBERT (1981) *Ayatollahs and Turkey Trots: Political Rhetoric in the New Newfoundland-Crosbie, Jamieson, and Peckford.* St. John's: Breakwater.

PALTIEL, K.Z. (1970) *Political Party Financing in Canada.* Toronto: McGraw-Hill.

—— (1975) "Campaign Financing in Canada and Its Reform," in Howard R. Penniman, ed., *Canada at the Polls: The General Election of 1974.* Washington, D.C.: American Enterprise Institute for Public Policy Research, pp. 181–208.

PAMMETT, JON H. (1988) "A Framework for the Comparative Analysis of Elections Across Time and Space," *Electoral Studies* (August), Volume 7, Number 2, pp. 125–142.

PANITCH, LEO (1977) "The Development of Corporatism in Liberal Democracies," *Comparative Political Studies* (April), Volume 10, Number 1, pp. 61–90.

—— (1981) "Elites, Classes and Power in Canada," in Michael S. Whittington and Glen Williams, eds., *Canadian Politics in the 1980's.* Toronto: Methuen, pp. 167–188.

PARKINSON, C. NORTHCOTE (1957) *Parkinson's Law.* Boston: Houghton Mifflin.

PATEMAN, CAROL (1970) *Participation and Democratic Theory.* London: Cambridge University Press.

PATTERSON, C.A. (1979) "Trudeau Was Great Prime Minister and Leader," *The Mail Star* (Halifax), December 15.

PEARSON, LESTER B. (1973) *Mike: The Memoirs of the Rt. Hon. Lester B. Pearson, Volume 2.* John A. Munro and Alex I. Inglis, eds. Scarborough, Ont.: Signet Books.

PELTASON, J.W. (1979) *Corwin and Peltason's Understanding the Constitution.* New York: Holt, Rinehart and Winston, 8th ed.

PERLIN, GEORGE C. (1980) *The Tory Syndrome: Leadership Politics in the Progressive Conservative Party.* Montreal: McGill-Queen's University Press.

PETERS, B. GUY (1981) "The Problem of Bureaucratic Government," *The Journal of Politics* (February), Volume 43, Number 1, pp. 56–82.

PETERSON, THOMAS (1978) "Manitoba: Ethnic and Class Politics," in Martin Robin, ed., *Canadian Provincial Politics.* Scarborough, Ont.: Prentice-Hall Canada, 2nd ed., pp. 69–115.

PINCHER, CHAPMAN (1986) *The Secret Offensive.* London: Sidgwick and Jackson.

PINTO-DUSCHINSKY, MICHAEL (1985) "Trends in British Political Funding 1979–1983," *Parliamentary Affairs* (Summer), Volume 38, Number 3, pp. 328–347.

PIOUS, RICHARD M. (1979) *The American Presidency.* New York: Basic Books.

PIPES, SALLY and MICHAEL WALKER (1984) *Tax Facts 4: The Canadian Consumer Tax Index and You.* Vancouver: The Fraser Institute, 4th ed.

PIRAGES, DENNIS (1976) *Managing Political Conflict.* New York: Praeger Publishers.

PIVEN, FRANCES FOX and RICHARD A. CLOWARD (1988) "National Voter Registration Reform: How It

Might Be Won," *PS* (Fall), Volume 21, Number 4, pp. 868–875.

POLSBY, NELSON W. and AARON WILDAVSKY (1986) *Presidential Elections: Strategies of American Electoral Politics*. New York: Charles Scribner's Sons, 6th ed.

POMPER, GERALD M. (1968) *Elections in America: Control and Influence in Democratic Politics*. New York: Dodd, Mead and Co.

POWELL, G. BINGHAM, JR. (1986) "American Voter Turnout in Comparative Perspective," *American Political Science Review* (March), Volume 80, Number 1, pp. 17–43.

PRESTHUS, ROBERT (1962) *The Organizational Society: An Analysis and a Theory*. New York: Vintage Books.

—— (1973) *Elite Accommodation in Canadian Politics*. Toronto: Macmillan of Canada.

—— (1981) "Mrs. Thatcher Stalks the Quango: A Note on Patronage and Justice in Britain," *Public Administration Review*, Vol. 41, No. 3 (May/June), pp. 312–317.

PULZER, PETER G. (1972) *Political Representation and Elections in Britain*. London: George Allen and Unwin, 2nd ed.

PUNNETT, R.M. (1977) *The Prime Minister in Canadian Government and Politics*. Toronto: Macmillan of Canada.

—— (1980) *British Government and Politics*. London: Heinemann, 4th ed.

PUTNAM, ROBERT D. (1976) *The Comparative Study of Political Elites*. Englewood Cliffs, N.J.: Prentice-Hall.

QUALTER, TERENCE H. (1980) *The Election Process in Canada*. Toronto: McGraw-Hill Ryerson.

Quebec Liberal Party (1980) *A New Canadian Confederation*. Montreal: The Quebec Liberal Party.

RADWANSKI, GEORGE (1978) *Trudeau*. Scarborough, Ont.: Signet.

RAE, DOUGLAS W. (1971) *The Political Consequences of Electoral Laws*. New Haven: Yale University Press, rev. ed.

RANNEY, AUSTIN (1965) *Pathways to Parliament: Candidate Selection in Britain*. Madison, Wisc.: University of Wisconsin Press.

—— (1975) "Selecting the Candidates," in Howard R. Penniman, ed., *Britain at the Polls: The Parliamentary Elections of 1974*. Washington, D.C.:

American Enterprise Institute for Public Policy Research, pp. 33–60.

RASMUSSEN, JORGEN S. (1984) "Is Parliament Revolting?" pp. 20–47 in Donley T. Studlar and Jerold L. Waltman, eds., *Dilemmas of Change in British Politics*. London: Macmillan.

—— (1987) "Constitutional Aspects of Government Formation in a Hung Parliament," *Parliamentary Affairs* (April), Volume 40, Number 2, pp. 139–153.

REDEKOP, JOHN H. (1978) "Continentalism: The Key to Canadian Politics," in Redekop, ed., *Approaches to Canadian Politics*. Scarborough, Ont.: Prentice-Hall Canada, pp. 28–57.

—— ed. (1983) *Approaches to Canadian Politics*. Scarborough, Ont.: Prentice-Hall Canada, 2nd ed.

REID, ESCOTT (1979) "The Rise of National Parties in Canada," in Hugh G. Thorburn, ed., *Party Politics in Canada*. Scarborough, Ont.: Prentice-Hall Canada, 4th ed., pp. 12–20.

REVEL, JEAN-FRANCOIS (1978) *The Totalitarian Temptation*. Middlesex, England: Penguin Books.

RICHARDSON, J.J. and A.G. JORDAN (1979) *Governing Under Pressure: The Policy Process in a Post-Parliamentary Democracy*. Oxford: Martin Robertson.

RIDLEY, F.F. (1988) "There is No British Constitution: A Dangerous Case of the Emperor's Clothes," *Parliamentary Affairs* (July), Volume 41, Number 3, pp. 340–361.

ROBERTS, PAULA (1986) "Bureaucracy: A Ministerial Portfolio," *The Atlantic Monthly* (June), Volume 257, Number 6, pp. 22, 24.

ROBERTSON, GORDON (1989) "The Global Challenge and Canadian Federalism," *Canadian Public Administration* (Spring), Volume 32, Number 1, pp. 124–134.

ROCHAN, THOMAS R. (1984) "The Creation of Political Institutions: Two Cases from the Netherlands," *International Journal of Comparative Sociology* (September/December), Volume 25, Number 3–4, pp. 173–188.

ROELOFS, H. MARK (1986) "The American Polity: A Systematic Ambiguity," *The Review of Politics* (Summer), Volume 48, Number 3, pp. 323–348.

ROMANOW, ROY, JOHN WHYTE, and HOWARD LEESEN (1984) *Canada . . . Notwithstanding: The Making of the Constitution 1976–1982*. Toronto: Carswell/Methuen.

ROSE, RICHARD (1982) *The Territorial Dimension in Government: Understanding the United Kingdom*.

Chatham, New Jersey: Chatham House Publishers.

—— (1983) "Still the Era of Party Government," *Parliamentary Affairs* (Summer), Volume 36, Number 3, pp. 181–299.

—— (1984) *Do Parties Make a Difference?* London: Macmillan Press, expanded 2nd ed.

—— (1986) *Politics: England*. Boston: Little, Brown and Co., 4th ed.

—— (1987) "Steering the Ship of State: One Tiller but Two Pairs of Hands," *British Journal of Political Science* (October), Volume 17, Number 4, pp. 409–433.

—— and GUY PETERS (1978) *Can Government Go Bankrupt?* New York: Basic Books.

—— and EZRA N. SULIEMAN, eds. (1981) *Presidents and Prime Ministers*. Washington, D.C.: American Enterprise Institute for Public Policy Research.

ROSENBAUM, WALTER A. (1975) *Political Culture*. New York: Praeger Publishers.

ROSSITER, CLINTON (1963) *The Political Thought of the American Revolution*, volume three of *Seedtime of the Republic*. New York: Harcourt, Brace and World.

ROTH, DAVID F. and FRANK L. WILSON (1980) *The Comparative Study of Politics*. Englewood Cliffs, N.J.: Prentice-Hall, 2nd ed.

RUSH, MICHAEL (1982) "Parliamentary Committees and Parliamentary Government: The British and Canadian Experiences," *The Journal of Commonwealth and Comparative Politics* (July), Volume 20, Number 2, pp. 138–154.

—— (1983) "Parliamentary Reform: The Canadian Experience," pp. 147–164 in David Judge, ed., *The Politics of Parliamentary Reform*. London: Heinemann Educational Books.

RUSSELL, PETER (1975) "Judicial Power in Canada's Political Culture," in Martin L. Friedland, ed., *Courts and Trials*. Toronto: University of Toronto Press, pp. 75–88.

—— (1985) "The First Three Years of Charterland," *Canadian Public Administration* (Fall), Volume 28, Number 3, pp. 367–396.

—— RAINER KNOPFF and TED MORTON, eds. (1989) *Federalism and the Charter: Leading Constitutional Decisions, A New Edition*. Ottawa: Carleton University Press.

SABATO, LARRY J. (1985) *PAC Power: Inside the World of Political Action Committees*. New York: W.W. Norton and Company.

SAFIRE, WILLIAM (1978) *Safire's Political Dictionary*. New York: Ballantine Books.

—— (1980) *On Language*. New York: Times Books.

SARTORI, GIOVANNI (1976) *Parties and Party Systems: A Framework for Analysis*. London: Cambridge University Press.

SAWATSKY, JOHN (1989) *The Insiders: Power, Money, and Secrets in Ottawa*. Toronto: McClelland and Stewart.

SCAMMON, RICHARD N. (1975) "The Election and the Future of British Electoral Reform," in Howard R. Penniman, ed., *Britain at the Polls: The Parliamentary Elections of 1974*. Washington, D.C.: American Enterprise Institute for Public Policy Research, pp. 163–176.

SCARROW, HOWARD A. (1969) *Comparative Political Analysis: An Introduction*. New York: Harper and Row.

SCHATTSCHNEIDER, E.E. (1942) *Party Government*. New York: Holt, Rinehart and Winston.

—— (1969) *Two Hundred Million Americans in Search of a Government*. New York: Holt, Rinehart and Winston.

—— (1975) *The Semisovereign People*. New York: Holt, Rinehart and Winston.

SCHLESINGER, ARTHUR M., JR. (1974) *The Imperial Presidency*. Toronto: Popular Library.

SCHULTZ, RICHARD (1984) "Regulatory Agencies," in Michael S. Whittington and Glen Williams, eds., *Canadian Politics in the 1980's*. Toronto: Methuen, pp. 434–448.

SCHUMPETER, JOSEPH A. (1950) *Capitalism, Socialism and Democracy*. New York: Harper and Row.

SCHWAM, ALLEN, ed. (1979) *Would You Buy a Used Country from This Man? Trudeau's Ten Years in Cartoons*. Toronto: Coles Publishing Company.

SCHWARTZ, MILDRED A. (1974) *Politics and Territory: The Sociology of Regional Persistence in Canada*. Montreal: McGill-Queen's University Press.

SCOTT, FRANK R. (1977) *Essays on the Constitution: Aspects of Canadian Law and Politics*. Toronto: University of Toronto Press.

SEIDLE, F. LESLIE and KHAYYAM ZEV PALTIEL (1981) "Party Finance, The Election Expenses Act, and Campaign Spending in 1979 and 1980," in Howard R. Penniman, ed., *Canada at the Polls, 1979 and 1980: A Study of the General Elections*. Washington

D.C.: American Enterprise Institute for Public Policy Research, pp. 226–279.

SHENKER, ISRAEL (1988) "Lording It Over England," *The New York Times Magazine* (May 8), pp. 34–36, 82–85.

SHEPPARD, ROBERT and MICHAEL VALPY (1982) *The National Deal: The Fight for a Canadian Constitution*. Toronto: Macmillan of Canada.

SHERRILL, ROBERT (1984) *Why They Call It Politics: A Guide to America's Government*. New York: Harcourt Brace Jovanovich, 4th ed.

SHIPLER, DAVID K. (1983) *Russia: Broken Idols, Solemn Dreams*. Middlesex, England: Penguin.

SHOGAN, ROBERT (1982) *None of the Above; Why Presidents Fail—And What Can Be Done About It*. New York: New American Library.

SILVERSTEIN, MARK (1984) *Constitutional Faiths: Felix Frankfurter, Hugo Black, and the Process of Judicial Decision Making*. Ithaca: Cornell University Press.

SIMEON, RICHARD and DAVID J. ELKINS (1974) "Regional Political Cultures in Canada," *Canadian Journal of Political Science*, Vol. 7, No. 3 (September), pp. 397–437.

SIMPSON, JEFFREY (1980) *Discipline of Power: The Conservative Interlude and the Liberal Restoration*. Toronto: Personal Library.

_____ (1983) "Another Punch at Canada's Bag," *The Globe and Mail*, January 18, p. 5.

_____ (1984) "The Long Goodbye," *The Globe and Mail*, November 28, p. 6.

_____ (1985) "The Vincible Liberals," pp. 15–28 in Alan Frizzel and Anthony Westell, eds., *Canadian General Election of 1984: Politicians, Parties, Press and Polls*. Ottawa: Carleton University Press.

_____ (1988) *Spoils of Power: The Politics of Patronage*. Toronto: Collins.

_____ (1989) "The Pressure Gauge," *The Globe and Mail* (March 15), p. A6.

_____ (1989) "The Age of the Interest Group," *The Globe and Mail* (December 6), p. A6.

SKILLING, H. GORDAN and FRANKLYN GRIFFITHS, eds. (1971) *Interest Groups in Soviet Politics*. Princeton, N.J.: Princeton University Press.

SMALLWOOD, JOSEPH R. (1975) *I Chose Canada, Volume II: The Premiership*. Scarborough, Ontario: Signet Books.

SMILEY, DONALD V. (1968) "The National Party Leadership Convention in Canada: A Preliminary Analy-

sis," *Canadian Journal of Political Science*, Vol. 1, No. 4, pp. 379–397.

_____ (1978) "Federalism and the Legislative Process in Canada," in W.A.W. Neilson and J.C. MacPherson, eds., *The Legislative Process in Canada*. Montreal: Institute for Research on Public Policy, pp. 73–87.

_____ (1980) *Canada in Question: Federalism in the Eighties*. Toronto: McGraw-Hill Ryerson, 3rd ed.

_____ (1983) "A Dangerous Deed: The Constitution Act, 1982," pp. 74–95 in Keith Banting and Richard Simeon, eds., *And No One Cheered*. Toronto: Methuen.

SMITH, GOLDWIN (1891) *Canada and the Canadian Question*. Toronto: Hunter, Rose and Company.

SMITH, GORDON (1980) *Politics in Western Europe: A Comparative Analysis*. London: Heinemann Educational Books, 3rd ed.

SMITH, HEDRICK (1988) *The Power Game: How Washington Works*. New York: Random House.

SNIDERMAN, PAUL M., JOSEPH F. FLETCHER, PETER H. RUSSELL, and PHILIP E. TETLOCK (1989) "Political Culture and the Problem of Double Standards: Mass and Elite Attitudes Toward Language Rights in the Canadian Charter of Rights and Freedoms," *Canadian Journal of Political Science* (June), Volume 22, Number 2, pp. 259–284.

STACEY, C.P. (1985) *A Very Double Life*. Halifax: Formac Publishing.

STEED, JUDY (1988) *Ed Broadbent: The Pursuit of Power*. Markham, Ontario: Penguin Books Canada.

STEVENS, GEOFFREY (1979) "The Word is 'Mess'," *The Globe and Mail*, November 30, p. 6.

STEVENSON, GARTH (1979) *Unfulfilled Union: Canadian Federalism and National Unity*. Toronto: Macmillan of Canada.

STEWART, WALTER (1971) *Shrug: Trudeau in Power*. Toronto: New Press.

_____ (1973) *Divide and Con--Canadian Politics at Work*. Toronto: New Press.

SYMONS, THOMAS H.B. (1978) *The Symons Report*. Toronto: The Books and Periodical Development Council.

TAAGEPERA, REIN and MATTHEW S. SHUGART (1989) "Designing Electoral Systems," *Electoral Studies* (April), Volume 8, Number 1, pp. 49–58.

TARSCHYS, DANIEL (1988) "Tributes, Tariffs, Taxes and Trade: The Changing Sources of Government

Revenue," *British Journal of Political Science* (January), Volume 18, Number 1, pp. 1–20.

Task Force on National Unity (1979) *A Future Together*. Ottawa: Minister of Supply and Services.

THORBURN, HUGH G. (1979) "The Development of Political Parties in Canada," and "Interpretations of the Canadian Party System," in Thorburn, ed., *Party Politics in Canada*. Scarborough, Ont.: Prentice-Hall Canada Inc., 4th ed., pp. 2–11 and 34–56.

TROYER, WARNER (1980) *200 days: Joe Clark in Power*. Toronto: Personal Library.

TRUDEAU, PIERRE ELLIOTT (1968) *Federalism and the French Canadians*. Toronto: Macmillan of Canada.

TRUDEL, MARCEL and GENEVIEVE JAIN (1970) *Canadian History Textbooks*. Ottawa: Queen's Printer.

TRUMAN, TOM (1971) "A Critique of Seymour M. Lipset's Article, 'Value Differences, Absolute or Relative: The English-Speaking Democracies'," *Canadian Journal of Political Science*, Vol. 4, No. 4 (December), pp. 497–525.

TUCHMAN, BARBARA W. (1984) *The March of Folly: From Troy to Vietnam*. New York: Alfred A. Knopf.

TUFTE, EDWARD R. (1978) *Political Control of the Economy*. Princeton, N.J.: Princeton University Press.

UNDERHILL, FRANK H. (1960) *In Search of Canadian Liberalism*. Toronto: Macmillan of Canada.

VALPY, MICHAEL (1981) "Above and Beyond the Hurly Burly," *The Globe and Mail*, December 12, p. 10.

_____ (1981) "Make LOVE, Not War," *The Globe and Mail*, June 25, p. 6.

VAN LOON, RICK (1970) "Political Participation in Canada: the 1965 Election," *Canadian Journal of Political Science*, Vol. 3, No. 3 (September), pp. 376–399.

VERBA, SIDNEY et al. (1978) *Participation and Political Equality: A Seven-Nation Comparison*. London: Cambridge University Press.

_____ and NORMAN H. NIE (1972) *Participation in America: Political Democracy and Social Equality*. New York: Harper and Row.

_____ and GARY ORREN (1985) *Equality in America: The View from the Top*. Cambridge, Mass.: Harvard University Press.

VERNEY, DOUGLAS V. (1976) *British Government and Politics: Life Without a Declaration of Independence*. New York: Harper and Row, 3rd ed.

VON BEYME, KLAUS (1985) "Karl Marx and Party Theory," *Government and Opposition* (Winter), Volume 20, Number 1, pp. 70–87.

WALD, KENNETH D. (1988) "Advance by Retreat? The Formation of British Labour's Electoral Strategy," *Journal of British Studies* (July), Volume 27, Number 3, pp. 283–314.

WALDEN, KEITH (1982) *Visions of Order: The Canadian Mounties in Symbol and Myth*. Toronto: Butterworths.

WAPSHOTT, NICHOLAS and GEORGE BROCK (1983) *Thatcher*. London: Futura.

WATTENBERG, MARTIN P. (1984) *Decline of American Political Parties, 1952–1980*. Cambridge, Mass.: Harvard University Press.

WEARING, JOSEPH (1981) *The L-Shaped Party: The Liberal Party of Canada 1958–1980*. Toronto: McGraw-Hill Ryerson.

WEBSTER, DONALD B. (1986) "Free Trade," *The Globe and Mail*, February 13, p. A7.

Weekend Magazine (1977) "Canadians Think the Queen is Just Fine," October 22.

WELCH, SUSAN (1975) "Dimensions of Political Participation in a Canadian Sample," *Canadian Journal of Political Science*, Vol. 8, No. 4 (December), pp. 553–559.

WHEARE, K.C. (1963) *Legislatures*. London: Oxford University Press.

WHITAKER, REGINALD (1977) *The Government Party: Organizing and Financing the Liberal Party of Canada 1930–58*. Toronto: University of Toronto Press.

WHITE, THEODORE H. (1976) *Breach of Faith: The Fall of Richard Nixon*. New York: Dell Publishers.

_____ (1978) *In Search of History*. New York: Warner Books.

_____ (1982) *America in Search of Itself: The Making of the President 1956–1980*. New York: Harper and Row.

WHITE, W.L. et al. (1972) *Introduction to Canadian Politics and Government*. Toronto: Holt, Rinehart and Winston.

WICKS, BEN (1982) *More Losers*. Toronto: McClelland and Stewart.

_____ (1984) *So You Want to be Prime Minister?* Toronto: McClelland and Stewart.

WILDAVSKY, AARON (1984) *The Politics of the Budgetary Process*. Boston: Little, Brown and Company, 4th ed.

WILL, GEORGE F. (1989) "How Reagan Changed America," *Newsweek* (January 9), Volume 113, Number 2, pp. 13–17.

WILLIAMS, BLAIR (1980) "The Decline of Political Parties," *The Globe and Mail*, July 4, p. 7.

WILLIAMS, SHIRLEY (1989) "The New Authoritarianism," *The Political Quarterly* (January), Volume 60, Number 1, pp. 4–9.

WILSON, HAROLD (1977) *The Governance of Britain*. London: Sphere Books.

WILSON, JAMES Q. (1987) "Does the Separation of Powers Still Work?" *The Public Interest* (Winter), Number 86, pp. 36–52.

WILSON, JOHN (1974) "The Canadian Political Cultures: Towards a Redefinition of the Nature of the Canadian Political System," *Canadian Journal of Political Science*, Vol. 7, No. 3 (September), pp. 438–483.

WILSON, V. SEYMOUR (1981) *Canadian Public Policy and Administration: Theory and Environment*. Toronto: McGraw-Hill Ryerson.

WILSON, WOODROW (1885, 1956) *Congressional Government: A Study in American Politics*. New York: Meridian.

WINN, C. and J. MCMENEMY, eds. (1976) *Political Parties in Canada*. Toronto: McGraw-Hill Ryerson.

WINSOR, HUGH (1986) "Should Party Be Equivalent of Sheltered Shop for Women PCs" *The Globe and Mail*, March 17, p. A2.

WOLIN, SHELDON S. (1960) *Politics and Vision: Continuity and Innovation in Western Political Thought*. Boston: Little, Brown and Co.

WOODCOCK, GEORGE (1986) "Voter's Block: What if They Called an Election and Nobody Came?" *The Canadian Forum* (February), Volume 65, Number 754, pp. 5–9.

WOOTTON, GRAHAM (1985) *Interest Groups: Policy and Politics in America*. Englewood Cliffs, N.J.: Prentice-Hall.

WRIGHT, F.J. (1973) *British Constitution and Government*. London: MacDonald and Evans, 2nd ed.

YOUNG, WALTER D. (1969) *The Anatomy of a Party: The National CCF 1932–1961*. Toronto: University of Toronto Press.

_____ (1978) "Leadership and Canadian Politics," in John H. Redekop, ed., *Approaches to Canadian Politics*. Scarborough, Ont.: Prentice-Hall Canada Inc., pp. 282–301.

Subject Index

A

Administrative state, 137
Administrator of Canada, 103
Adversary (fight) system of justice, 211
Advisory (reference) decisions, 219
Alberta Heritage Trust Fund, 7
American constitutionalism
  auxiliary precautions, 88
  Bill of Rights, 91
  checks and balances, 22, 89
  enumerated powers, 90
  federalism, 21, 89
  implied powers, 90
  limitation of power, 87
  residual power clause, 90
  separation of powers, 22, 88
American government
  characteristics, 23, 24
Approaches to political analysis, 58
Auditor general, 14
Autocracy
  characteristics, 19
  defined, 18

B

Bagmen, 290
Bicameral legislatures, 165
Bilingual belt thesis, 244
British constitutionalism
  concentration of power, 86
  elements, 85
British government
  characteristics, 23, 24
Budget expenditure, 13
Bureaucracy
  Britain, 152
  Canada, 142
  characteristics, 137
  defined, 101, 136
  delegated power, 148
  generalists, 148
  and patronage, 158
  role, 137
  United States, 154
By-election, 329

C

Cabinet
  American, 156
  British, 123
Cabinet, Canadian
  composition, 113
  Clark cabinet, 118
  generalists, 148
  inner and outer, 118
  "kitchen", 118
  Mulroney cabinet, 118
  organization, 116
  political ministers, 116
  regional defenders, 115
  representation principle, 114
  resignation from, 113
  shuffles, 112
  structure (*figure*), 147
  Trudeau cabinet, 117
  Turner cabinet, 118
Cadre party, 263
Canada (Constitution) Act of 1982
  amending procedures, 415
  Charter of Rights, 4
  contents, 77, 409
  impact, 430
  override provision, 414, 435
  political analysis, 416
  Senate's suspensive veto, 415
Canadian Bill of Rights
  elements, 75
  limitations, 76
Canadian Charter of Rights and Freedoms
  contents, 77, 409
  override provision, 414
Canadian constitution
  amendment, 79
  Canada Act, 409
  elements, 68
  evolution, 77, 78
  federalism, 68
  financing of, 82
  judicial review, 73
  operation, 81
  structure, 68

Canadian Constitutional Crisis of 1968, 99
Canadian federalism
   conditional grants, 83
   decentralization, 77
   and finance, 82
   reasons for evolution, 78
Canadian government
   characteristics 23, 24
   comparative perspective, 24
   Canadian Judicial Council, 216
   Charismatic authority, 44
   Checks and balances, 22, 89
   Clark government
   defeat of, 3
Classical democracy
   comparison to Canada, 452-453
   description, 452
Classical federalism, 70
Classifications in political analysis, 18
Closure
   in Canada, 176
   defined, 176
Cloture, 201
Collective responsibility, 98
Collectivism, 402
Comparative political analysis
   approaches, 58
   importance for the study of Canada, 58
   nature, 58
   problems of, 59
Compulsory voting, 371
Concurrent jurisdiction, 71
Conditional grants, 83
Confederal systems, 21
Consociational democracy, 248
Constitution Act 1867 (BNA Act)
   allocation of powers, 69
   concurrent jurisdiction, 71
   declaratory power, 71
   disallowance, 72
   exclusive jurisdiction, 70
   limited judicial review, 73
   reservation, 72
   residual power clause, 71
   supremacy clause, 71
Constitutional amendment
   Canada, 79
   general, 66
   new procedures in Canada Act, 415
   "safeguarded" portions, 80
   United States, 91
Constitutional government
   defined, 65
   elements, 66

Constitutions
   bases of comparison, 92
   functions, 65
   political nature, 65
Continentalism, 246

D

Decision-making
   American, 154
   British, 152
   Canadian, 142
   models
      organizational-politics model, 140
      rational-actor model, 139
Declaratory power, 71
Delegated legislative power, 148
Democracy
   defined, 19
Democratic government
   combined classification scheme (*table*), 23
Democratic socialism, 36, 39
Deputy minister, 149
Direct investment, 247
Direct primaries, 334
Disallowance, 72
Dual representation
   interest groups, 393
Dualism, 242
Due process of law, 211

E

Election Expenses Act of 1974, 291
Elections
   bases of comparison, 336
   Britain, 330
   Canada, 323
   functions, 315
   in parliamentary systems, 316
   in presidential systems, 316
   United States, 333
Electoral College, 354
Electoral formulas, 345
Electoral function of parties, 261
Electoral law, 344
Electoral redistribution, 328
Electoral systems
   Britain, 351
   Canada, 347
   consequences, 342
   types, 344
   United States, 354
Elitism, 235
Emergencies Act 1988, 75
Entrenchment, 76

Enumeration, 325
Envelope budgeting system, 145
Environmental Protection Agency (EPA), 15
Equality of condition, 34
Equality of opportunity, 34
Established Program Financing (EPF), 82
Exclusive jurisdiction, 70
Executive branch
    bases of comparison, 129
    functions, 100
    growth, 98
    parliamentary type, 98
    presidential type, 99
    structure in Canada (*figure*), 120
Executive federalism, 81
Executive privilege, 89
Externally created (extra-parliamentary)
        parties, 262

F
Federalism
    Canada, 69
    definition, 21
    United States, 89
Filibuster, 200
Flora syndrome, 282
Formal executive
    Britain, 22
    Canada, 22, 101
    defined, 22, 98
    role, 22, 98, 104
Fragmented political culture, 234
Free trade, 32, 247
Functional representation
    interest groups, 402

G
General election, 329
Gerrymandering, 329, 334
Governing function of parties, 261
Government
    classifications, 18
    defined, 6, 30
    expansive nature, 8
    multiple nature, 6
    necessary nature, 16
        and conflict, 16
        and diversity, 16
    privatization, 15
    reasons for growth, 8
    size, 12
    types, 18
    ubiquitous nature, 5
    varied nature, 17

Government bill, 174
Governor general
    appointment, 102
    functions, 104
Graveyard vote, 326
Greatest remainder electoral formula, 346

H
Highest average electoral formula, 346
House of Commons, Britain
    committees, 192
    party discipline, 193
    passage of legislation, 193
    speaker, 192
    structure, 191
House of Commons, Canada
    closure, 176
    committees, 172
    functions, 178
    oral question period, 177
    party discipline, 171
    party organization, 171
    passage of legislation, 173, 174
    relation to Senate, 166
    role of speaker, 167
    roster system, 178
    structure, 167
    types of bills, 174
House of Lords
    hereditary peers, 194
    life peers, 194
    structure, 194
    suspensive veto, 195
House of Representatives
    committees, 198
    functions, 201
    passage of legislation, 199
    seniority principle, 198

I
Ideology
    definition, 36
    and political culture, 235
    and public policy, 146
    types, 36
Imperial presidency, 100
Incremental decision-making, 148
Indirect democracy, 163
Indirect investment, 247
Influence
    defined, 42
Injunction, 212
Integrated political culture, 234
Interest-group liberalism, 386

Interest groups
  Britain, 400
  Canada, 394
  and corporatism, 402
  defined, 384
  and dual representation, 393
  functions, 386
  interests of the realm, 401
  and iron triangles, 393
  methods of influence, 387
  reasons for, 385
  revolving door syndrome, 392
  types, 385
  United States, 388
Internally created (parliamentary) parties,
  262
Iron triangles
  interest groups, 393

J
Judicial activism, 210
Judicial branch
  bases for comparison, 227
  Britain, 221
  Canada, 212
  political nature, 208
  types of judicial review, 73, 210
  United States, 222
Judicial Committee of the Privy Council
  (JCPC), 213
Judicial independence
  Canada, 215, 216
  defined, 208
  United States, 224
Judicial restraint, 210
Judicial review
  Britain, 221
  Canada, 73, 216
  defined, 73, 210
  full type, 73, 210
  limited type, 73, 210
  United States, 222, 226
Judiciary, American
  election, 224
  judicial review, 73, 210
  patronage, 223
  political role, 227
  senatorial courtesy, 224
  structure, 223
Judiciary, British
  lack of judicial review, 221
  protection of civil liberties, 222
Judiciary, Canadian
  advisory opinions, 219

  effects of, 217
  enforcement of Charter, 221
  federalism, 212
  impact of Canada Act, 220
  operating principles, 215
  patronage-base, 213
  structure, 212
  Supreme Court, 217
  tenure, 214
Just Society, 17

K
Kickback, 291
King-Byng Affair, 107

L
Law of increasing disproportion, 318
Leadership review process, 281
Legal decision
  defined, 54
Legal-regional authority, 44
Legislatures
  bases of comparison, 201
  development, 163
  relation to federalism, 166
  types, 165
Limited judicial review
  defined, 73
Limited proportional representation, 350
List system of proportional representation,
  346
Literacy tests, 377

M
Madison's dilemma, 386
Magnitude of electoral districts, 345
Malapportionment, 328
Mandarins, 152
Marxism, 38
Mass party, 263
Meech Lake Accord
  contents, 4, 437
  defeat of, 444
  ratification process, 439
Ministerialists, 267
Ministerial responsibility, 98
Multi-member electoral districts, 345

N
National party leadership conventions
  Canada, 279
  United States, 306
New group politics, 402
Non-simultaneous elections, 267

O

October Crisis 1970, 3
Office of Management and Budget (OMB), 157
Office of Paperwork Burden, 14
Oral question period, 177
Organizational-politics model, 140
Override provision, Canadian Charter of Rights
    and Freedoms, 414, 435
Overriding (presidential veto), 200

P

Parachuting, 321
Parkinson's Law, 158
Parliamentary privilege, 164
Parliamentary secretaries, 149
Parliamentary sovereignty
    Britain, 191, 193
    Canada, 166
    defined, 163
Parliamentary system
    characteristics (*table*), 23
    defined, 22
Parochial political culture, 233
Parochial priorities, 140
Participant political culture, 233
Party "bagmen," 290
Party discipline
    Britain, 192
    Canada, 171
    defined, 171
    United States, 197
Party finance, 289, 301, 307
Party systems
    competitive, 265
    defined, 263
    non-competitive, 265
    party-state system, 265
Party whips
    Britain, 193
    Canada, 171
    United States, 197
Patronage
    bureaucracy, 138
    Canadian Senate, 183
    defined, 183
    judiciary, 209
Permanent voters' list, 326, 375
Pluralism
    defined, 384
Plurality electoral formula, 327, 345
Plural voting, 375
Policy, 100
Polis, 34
Political Action Committee (PACs), 385

Political analysis
    basic concepts, 40
    basic principles, 51
    behavioural approach, 57
    definition, 30
    historical approach, 57
    institutional approach, 57
    tasks, 31
Political authority
    bases of legitimacy, 44
    definition, 44
    need for, 46
Political convention (custom), 52
Political culture
    American themes, 251
    bases for comparison, 254
    British themes, 249
    Canadian themes, 235
    defined, 233
    types, 233
Political decision
    defined, 54
Political efficacy, 372
Political executives
    Britain, 123
    Canada, 108
    defined, 22, 98
    role, 22, 98, 108
Political function
    defined, 56
Political Influence
    defined, 42
Political language
    connotative aspects, 48
    denotative aspects, 48
    government control, 49
    as a political resource, 51
Political ministers, 116
Political opposition, 308
Political parties
    Britain, 296
    Canada, 267
    defined, 260
    functions, 261
    future, 309
    origin, 260
    party systems, 263
    political opposition, 308
    types, 262
    United States, 302
Political power
    definition, 42
    use of sanctions, 42
Political recruitment

Britain, 330
Canada, 318
closed pattern, 318
defined, 317
open pattern, 318
selectorate, 318
United States, 334
Political reform
distal effects, 448
proximal effects, 448
suggestions for Canada, 452
Political resources
definition, 43
means of influence, 43
Political skill, 43
Political socialization process
Britain, 368
Canada, 365
consequences, 370
defined, 364
United States, 369
Political structure
defined, 56
relation to political functions, 57
Political subculture, 235
Political thought
function, 33
Politics
conservative view, 36
defined, 30, 34
democratic socialist view, 39
development in the West, 33
empirical view, 34
"godfather" function, 33
human basis, 40
ideological definitions, 36
liberal view, 37
normative view, 34
revolutionary view, 38
Polity
defined, 5
Poll tax, 377
Power
defined, 42
Pragmatic parties, 263
Presidency, American
compared to Canada, 128
creation, 126
Executive Office, 156
roles, 126
President pro tempore, 197
Presidentializing parliamentary government, 130
Presidential primary, 305
Presidential system

characteristics (*table*), 23
defined, 22
Prime minister, Britain, 123
Prime minister, Canada
bases of power, 109
control of cabinet, 110
structure of cabinet, 112
Prime ministerial government, 100, 124
Prime Minister's Office (PMO), 117
Private member's bill, 174
Privatization
defined, 15
patterns, 15
Privy Council, 103
Privy Council Office (PCO), 117
Programmatic parties, 263
Proportional representation electoral formula, 346
Province-building, 79
Public-interest groups, 385
Public Accounts Committee, 173
Public Order Temporary Measures Act, 3
Public policy
defined, 100

Q

Quasi-autonomous nongovernmental
organizations (quangos), 152
Quebec
Bill 101, 54, 55, 107
provincial election of 1976, 3
referendum (May, 1980), 3

R

Rational-actor model, 139
Rationalism, 36
Recall of leaders, 454
Regionalism, 238
Regional ministers, 116
Regional political culture
defined, 235
Registration for voting, 371, 377
Representation principle
cabinet selection, 114
defined, 114
effects on cabinet, 116
Republican government, 18
Reservation, 72
Residency requirement, 378
Residual power clause (POGG)
definition, 71
in United States, 90
and War Measures Act, 71
Revolving door syndrome
interest groups, 392

Roster system, 178
Royal commissions, 143
Royal Prerogative, 122

S
Safe seat, 317
Satisficing behaviour, 140
Selection conference, 330
Selectorate, 318
Senate, American
    committees, 198
    filibuster, 200
    functions, 201
    passage of legislation, 199
    seniority principle, 198
    structure, 196
Senate, Canada
    functions, 185
    patronage base, 183
    political uses, 184
    reform, 188
    structure, 183
    suspensive veto,
        in Canada Act, 415
    Triple E, 190
Senatorial courtesy, 224
Seniority principle, 198
Separation of powers
    defined, 22, 88
Short listing, 330
Single-issue interest groups, 385
Single-member electoral districts, 327, 345
Single transferable vote (STV), 354
Speaker of the House
    Britain, 192
    Canada, 167
    United States, 197
Special-interest groups, 385
Standard operating procedures (SOPs), 141
Standing committees
    Britain, 192
    Canada, 172

United States, 198
Stare decisis, 211
Striking committee, 172
Subject political culture, 233
Suffrage, 260
Supremacy clause, 71
Suspensive veto
    Britain, 195
    Canada, 191
    Canada Act (1982), 415
Swing riding, 274

T
Task Force on Program Review, 14
Tax expenditures
    defined, 13
Temporary voters' list, 326
Time and politics, 53
Toll-gating, 291
Tory syndrome, 285
Totalitarian government, 18
Traditional authority, 44, 249
Treasury Board, 145

U
Unicameral legislatures, 165
Unitary systems, 21
Unit rule, 306, 355
University seats, Britain, 375

V
Vice-president, American, 128
Voting behaviour
    Britain, 375
    Canada, 372
    factors influencing, 371
    rationale for voting, 370
    role of citizen, 378
    United States, 376

W
War Measures Act, 3, 47, 74
Whitehall, 152

Name Index

A

Aberbach, Joel D., 135, 137
Abraham, Al, 103, 223
Abraham, Henry J., 211
Acton, Lord, 86
Adams, John, 43
Agnew, Spiro, 126
Aird, John, 103
Aislin (Terry Mosher), 249
Akerman, Jeremy, 29
Albrow, Martin, 136
Alderman, R.K., 125
Alexander, Lincoln, 103
Alford, Robert R., 277
Allison, Graham T., 139
Almond, Gabriel A., 136, 233
Anderson, John, 46, 264, 304
Argue, Hazen, 185
Aristotle, 2, 34, 35, 385
Atkins, Norman, 184
Atwood, Margaret, 246, 249
Aubin, Benoit, 366
Axworthy, Lloyd, 112, 287, 359

B

Badeaux, Guy, 292, 443
Bagehot, Walter, 22, 104, 164, 249, 250, 294
Bailey, F.G., 100
Bailyn, Bernard, 253
Bain, George, 171
Baker, James, 156
Bakvis, Herman, 114, 116
Banfield, Edward C., 451
Barber, James David, 31, 126, 306
Barker, Ernest, 35, 136, 385
Barrett, Dave, 165, 289
Barron, Sid, 144, 264, 395
Bassett, John, 184
Bay, Christian, 45
Bazin, Jean, 190
Bealey, Frank, 34
Beck, Murray, 6, 240, 322, 342
Beer, Samuel H., 194, 195, 250, 402
Bégin, Monique, 47
Bell, David V.J., 47, 233

Benn, Anthony Wedgewood (Tony), 124, 152, 153, 195
Bennett, Bill, 165
Bensel, Richard Franklin, 234
Benson, Edgar, 112
Bentley, Arthur F., 390
Bentsen, Lloyd, 356
Berger, Thomas, 63, 216, 217
Beria, Lavrenti, 317
Bernard, André, 243
Bernstein, Eduard, 40
Berrington, Hugh, 369
Berry, Jeffrey M., 386, 400
Best, Judith A., 355
Bevan, Aneurin, 403
Biaka-Boda, Victor, 316
Bierce, Ambrose, 30, 45, 177
Birch, Anthony H., 122, 194, 222, 301, 333, 375
Bird, Rose, 224
Black, Charles, 63
Black, Edwin R., 273
Blackmun, Harry, 226
Blackwood, John, 81
Blais-Grenier, Suzanne, 99, 112, 113
Blake, Donald E., 272
Blakeney, Allan, 429
Blank, Robert H., 302
Blondel, J., 97, 203
Bogdanor, Vernon, 85, 343, 354
Bonaparte, Napoleon, 387
Boorstin, Daniel, 448
Bork, Robert H., 227
Bosley, John, 168, 169, 170
Bouchard, Lucien, 116, 441, 444
Bourassa, Robert, 3, 113, 245, 249, 272, 273, 435, 438, 440, 444
Bourgault, Jacques, 149
Boyer, J. Patrick, 294, 412
Bradley, Ian, 300
Bradshaw, Kenneth, 191, 193
Brady, Alexander, 25
Brennan, William, 207, 225
Brezhnev, Leonid, 19
Broadbent, Ed, 51, 183, 262, 263, 281, 284, 288, 350, 428, 429

Brodie, M. Janine, 323
Brogan, D.W., 18, 124
Bronfman, Sam, 184
Brown, George, 267
Brown, Ian, 142
Brown, Robert Craig, 46
Brown, Ron, 47
Bryce, James, 25, 57, 237, 447
Bryce, Robert, 104
Bryden, Joseph, 225
Buchanan, James M., 12
Bunce, Valerie, 97, 101
Burke, Edmund, 16
Burkett, Tony, 343
Burnham, Walter Dean, 211, 309, 384
Burns, James MacGregor, 91, 141, 303
Bush, George, 9, 51, 126, 129, 156, 357, 393
Butler, Dan, 11
Butler, David, 296, 298, 369
Butler, R.A., 122
Byng, Lord, 107

C

Cairns, Alan C., 349, 416, 452
Callaghan, James, 58, 153, 298, 332
Callwood, June, 174
Cameron, David M., 240
Camp, Dalton, 119, 189, 293, 325, 422
Campbell, Colin, 452
Campbell, Colin, 117, 138, 173, 187
Canetti, Elias, 46, 54, 308
Caouette, Réal, 45
Caplan, Gerald, 270
Cardow, Cameron (CAM), 247
Careless, J.M.S., 238
Carroll, Lewis, 48, 408
Carter, Jimmy, 125, 126, 129, 141, 154, 223, 252,
   334, 356, 357
Cartier, George Etienne, 237
Cassirer, Ernst, 47
Castro, Fidel, 370
Chandler, Marsha A., 12
Chandler, William M., 12
Charest, Jean, 216
Charles, Prince, 46, 104, 122, 281
Chase, Harold W., 389
Cheffins, R.I., 213, 412
Chernenko, Konstantin, 19
Chouinard, Julien, 213
Chrétien, Jean, 4, 109, 115, 284, 286, 287, 288,
   427
Christ, 45
Christian, William, 452
Churchill, Winston, 43, 100

Clark, Ian, D., 121
Clark, Joe, 3, 4, 8, 31, 51, 69, 107, 110, 114, 115,
   118, 119, 121, 146, 150, 170, 177, 183, 185,
   188, 213, 262, 280, 281, 283, 284, 285, 286,
   294, 322, 323, 326, 349, 417, 420, 424, 428, 429
Clark, S.D., 394
Clarke, Harold D., 241, 373
Cleroux, Richard, 168
Cloward, Richard A., 377
Coates, Robert, 75, 112
Cogger, Michael, 190
Coleman, William D., 48
Commager, Henry Steele, 66
Conway, Margaret M., 369
Cook, Ramsay, 408
Cools, Ann, 190, 322
Cooper, Barry, 239
Copps, Sheila, 164, 287
Cornfield, Michael, 364
Corry, J.A., 25
Cory, Peter, 217
Coser, Lewis A., 43
Cossette-Trudel, Jacques, 38
Cote, Jean-Pierre, 105
Courtney, John C., 145, 283, 284
Coutts, Jim, 184, 185, 320
Crick, Bernard, 18, 19, 20, 37, 38, 66, 390
Crisp, Quentin, 234
Croll, David, 188
Crombie, David, 116, 118, 285, 286
Crosbie, John, 8, 51, 119, 215, 269, 285, 286
Cross, J.A., 125
Cross, James, 3
Crossman, Richard H.S., 153, 193, 222
Crouse, Lloyd, 104
Cullen, Bud, 213
Curtis, Michael, 58

D

D'Acquino, Thomas, 164
Dahl, Robert A., 34, 35, 42, 43, 46, 66, 259, 389,
   390
Dahrendorf, Ralf, 404
Daigle, Joe, 170, 213
Danis, Marcel, 168
Davey, Keith, 183
Davies, Robertson, 234
Davis, Bill, 113, 169, 272, 280, 317, 417, 429
Davis, Jack, 115
Dawson, Richard E., 370
Dawson, R. MacGregor, 51, 56, 185, 289
Deans, Ian, 164
Deaver, Michael, 392
De Bané, Pierre, 82

de Cotret, Robert, 188
de Gaulle, Charles, 51, 342
de Grimm, Baron, 136
de Jong, Simon, 289
de Jouvenel, Bertrand, 5
del Guidice, Dominic, 7
de Madariaga, Isabel, 308
de Tocqueville, Alexis, 2, 66, 232, 363, 384
Derthick, Martha, 90
Deutsch, Karl W., 100
Devine, Donald J., 253
Devine, Grant, 110, 115
Dewar, Marion, 289
Dewar, Susan, 443
Dickens, Charles, 166
Dickson, Brian 186, 207, 214
DiClerico, Robert E., 379
Diefenbaker, John, 45, 110, 115, 171, 172, 186,
    214, 270, 274, 281, 284, 285, 342, 373
Dion, Leon, 243
Dion, Stephane, 149
Disraeli, Benjamin, 163, 295, 296
Djilas, Milovan, 136, 266
Doern, G. Bruce, 148, 237
Doherty, Michael, 125
Dogan, Mattei, 2, 233
Donato, Andy, 110, 187, 218, 320
Douglas, Tommy, 104, 185
Douglas, William O., 224
Downs, Anthony, 261
Drapeau, Jean, 220
Drucker, H.M., 297, 300, 354
Dryden, Ken, 275
Duchacek, Ivo, 65, 66, 67
Dukakis, Michael, 306, 356, 357
Duncan, Graeme, 36
Dunn, Brian A., 110
Duplessis, Maurice, 243
Duverger, Maurice, 51, 126, 163, 262, 296, 297,
    343, 358, 359, 360, 402
Dyck, Irene, 293
Dye, Thomas R., 227

E
Easterbrook, Gregg, 389
Edleman, Murray, 48
Eden, Anthony, 122
Edmonston, Phil, 276
Edwards, Frank A., 83
Elizabeth II, Queen, 4, 335
Elkins, David J., 240, 241
Elliott, Martha J., 89, 223
Epstein, Leon D., 263
Erlenhorn, John, 392

Eulau, Heinz, 58
Evans, John, 321, 322

F
Fagen, Richard R., 364, 370
Fairclough, Ellen, 115
Faulkner, Hugh 173, 396
Feigenbaum, Harvey B., 15
Fenno, Richard F., 336
Fields, W.C., 371
Filmon, Gary 441
Finer, S.E., 1, 136, 250, 297, 301
Fish, Susan, 113
Flaherty, David H., 40
Fletcher, Martha, 219
Flynn, Jacques, 6, 116
Foot, Michael, 298, 300, 353
Forbes, H.D., 66, 366
Forcese, Dennis, 236
Ford, Gerald, 48, 125, 129, 223, 224, 356, 357
Forsey, Eugene, 102, 104, 107, 166, 235, 422
Forster, E.M., 408
Fotheringham, Allan, 51
Fox, Francis, 113
Frankfort, Henri, 33
Frankfurter, Felix 207
Franks, C.E.S., 2, 178, 400, 447
Fraser, John, 48, 108, 136
Fraser, John, 99, 115, 118, 119, 168, 169, 170,
    171, 283
Fraser, Neil, 138, 286
Friedenberg, Edgar Z., 452
Friederich, Carl J., 66, 67, 208, 403
Friendly, Fred W., 89, 223
Frum, David, 221, 324
Frye, Northrop, 363
Fulford, Robert, 442
Fulton, Davie, 215

G
Gable, Brian, 168, 236, 280, 288, 410
Gamble, Andrew, 298
Gamble, John, 286
Gandhi, Mahatma, 45
Gardner, John W., 391
Garrity, W. Arthur, 227
Garson, David, 390
Gerry, Elbridge, 329
Gerth, H.H., 30, 44, 136, 137
Getty, Donald, 164, 273, 438
Ghiz, Joe, 82
Gibbins, Roger, 242, 243, 438
Gibson, Gordon, 109
Gigantes, Philippe Deane, 183

Giguère, Louis, 290
Gillies, Jim, 283
Gimaiel, Pierre, 278
Ginsberg, Benjamin, 315, 316
Gladstone, William, 400
Glass, David, 371
Glube, Constance, 209, 214
Goel, M.L., 365, 377
Goldwater, Barry, 302, 304
Gonthier, Charles, 217
Gorbachev, Mikhail, 19, 23, 127
Gordon, Walter, 112
Gotlieb, Allan, 384
Gould, Julius, 383
Grafftey, Heward, 283
Grafstein, Jerry, 190
Graston, Mike, 434
Gray, Charlotte, 115, 150, 442
Gray, Herb, 113
Green, Mark J., 198
Greene, Ian, 436
Greenstein, Fred I., 128
Gregg, Allan, 366
Griffiths, Franklyn, 385
Guppy, Neil, 323
Guy, Ray, 241
Gwyn, Richard, 30, 246, 321

H
Haig, Alexander, 49
Hain, Peter, 353
Hall, Ron, 369
Halperin, Morton, 139
Hamilton, Willie, 194, 264
Hamnett, Chris, 15
Harle, Graham, 113
Harper, Elijah, 441, 444
Harris, Michael, 284
Hart, Gary, 253
Hart, Johnny, 9
Hastings, Alcee, 225
Hatfield, Richard, 30, 170, 281, 417
Hawkes, James, 173
Hayden, Salter, 183
Heald, David, 15
Healey, Denis, 341
Heath, Edward, 58, 299, 403
Hellyer, Paul, 269, 283
Henderson, Maxwell, 145
Henig, Jeffrey R., 15
Hepburn, Mitchell, 273
Hill, David B., 378
Hilsman, Roger, 197
Hinckley, Barbara, 201

Hitler, Adolf, 20, 45, 49
Hnatyshyn, Ramon, 102, 104, 108
Hockin, Thomas A., 79, 180
Hodgetts, Ted, 149
Hoffer, Eric, 38
Hofstadter, Richard, 87, 89, 302
Hollis, Patricia, 401
Holt, Simma, 173
Holtzman, Elizabeth, 331
Hood, Christopher, 15
Horner, Jack, 283, 321, 322
Horowitz, Gad, 248, 277, 279
Howe, Joseph, 6
Huckshorn, Robert J., 304
Hughes, Charles Evans, 211
Humphrey, Hubert H., 357
Huntington, Samuel P., 51, 252
Hurtig, Mel, 108, 365, 366
Hutchinson, Allan C., 220, 430
Huxley, T.H., 58

I
Inglehart, Ronald, 233
Inman, Elsie, 183
Ionescu, Ghita, 308
Irvine, William P., 350

J
Jack, Malcolm, 191
Jackman, Hal, 184
Jackson, Robert, 211
Jacobs, Dan N., 402
Jain, Genevieve, 366
Jaros, Dean, 367
Jefferson, Thomas, 63, 302
Jerome, James, 169, 170
Johnson, Chalmers, 63
Johnson, Frederick W., 103
Johnson, Lyndon B., 31, 129, 197, 253, 356, 391
Johnson, P.A., 412
Johnson, Pierre-Marc, 284
Johnson, Sam, 31
Johnstone, John C., 366
Jones, Leonard, 321
Jones, Peter, 67
Jordon, A.G., 402, 403
Joy, Richard, 244, 245
Joyal, Serge, 114
Judge, David, 162

K
Kafka, Franz, 139
Kaplan, Abraham, 42
Karp, Walter, 29

Kavanagh, Dennis, 233, 251
Keable, Jean, 219, 220
Keefe, William J., 162
Kelley, Stanley, 314
Kendrick, Stephen, 354
Kennedy, Anthony M., 225, 226
Kennedy, John F., 43, 58, 129, 139, 197, 253, 303, 316, 356
Key, V.O., Jr., 334, 336, 371
Khomeini, Ayatollah, 19
Khrushchev, Nikita, 19
Kierans, Eric, 148
Kilbourn, William, 248
Kindy, Alex, 173
King, Allan, 268
King, Anthony, 298
King, Mackenzie, 54, 107, 114, 217, 238, 273, 274, 278, 279, 284, 291, 321, 367
Kinnock, Neil, 122, 300, 301
Kirby, Michael, 17, 190, 425
Kissinger, Henry, 156, 335
Kornberg, Allan, 167, 182, 323, 367, 368
Kousser, J. Morgan, 377
Krislov, Samuel, 135, 136, 155
Kwavnick, David, 394, 404

L

Ladd, Everett Carll, Jr., 88, 316
Lady Diana Spencer, 46, 104
LaForest, Gerard, 215, 217
Lagasse, Roger, 289
Lalonde, Marc, 72, 219
Lam, David See-Chai, 103
Lambert, Marcel, 322
Lamer, Antonio, 217, 437
Lamontagne, Gilles, 103, 105
Lamoureux, Lucien, 169
Lamy, Paul G., 366
Landes, Ronald G., 31, 163, 235, 241, 259, 274, 350, 360, 365, 366
Lang, Otto, 186
Langdon, Steven, 289
LaPalombara, Joseph, 136, 260, 262, 265, 379
Lapointe, Hugues, 107
Laponce, J.A., 48, 294, 363, 373
Laporte, Pierre, 3
LaRouche, Lyndon, 335
Larson, Edward, 189
LaSalle, Roch, 115
Laski, Harold J., 63, 99, 103
Laskin, Bora, 74, 208, 214, 215, 217, 219
Lasswell, Harold D., 42, 390
Latouche, Daniel, 273
Laurier, Sir Wilfrid, 66, 114, 182, 279, 407

Lawson, Kay, 259
Lawson, Nigel, 123
Laxer, James, 235
LeBlanc, Romeo, 115
Léger, Jules, 102, 103
Lemco, Jonathan, 191
L'Heureux-Dube, Claire, 217
Lévesque, René, 3, 48, 104, 105, 244, 283, 317, 422
Lewis, David, 9, 97, 106, 270, 280, 383
Lewis, Stephen, 288, 365
Leys, Colin, 402
Liani, Dimitri, 30
Ligachev, Yegor, 137
Lightbody, James, 70
Lincoln, Abraham, 370
Lincoln, Clifford, 287
Lindblom, Charles E., 136
Lipset, Seymour Martin, 238, 255
Little, Bruce, 119, 270
Locke, John, 251
Loewenberg, Gerhard, 193
Longley, Lawrence D., 357
Lougheed, Peter, 72, 217, 317
Lower, Arthur, 242
Lowi, Theodore J., 386, 390
Lowther, J.W., 192
Luttberg, Norman R., 378
Lyon, Sterling, 214

M

Macdonald, Donald, 321
MacDonald, Flora, 282, 283
Macdonald, John A., 53, 110, 114, 187, 248, 267, 269, 278, 279, 290, 342
MacDonnell, J.J., 169
MacGuigan, Mark, 148, 213
MacIntosh, John P., 154, 403
MacIver, Robert M., 47
Mackasey, Bryce, 150
MacKay, Elmer, 280
MacKay, Wayne, 214, 427
Mackenzie, William Lyon, 367
MacKinnon, Frank, 98, 105
Mackintosh, Gordon H.A., 106, 175
Macmillan, Harold, 122
Macnaughton, Bruce D., 11
Macpherson, C.B., 390
MacQueen, Ken, 396
Macidris, Roy C., 24, 36
Madison, James, 87, 222, 227, 386, 393
Mailer, Norman, 43
Makin, Kirk, 213
Malcolm, Andrew H., 239, 407

Mallory, J.R., 72, 80, 169, 211, 269, 399, 437
March, Roman R., 171, 172
Marcos, Ferdinand, 265
Margaret, Princess, 320
Marsden, Lorna, 190
Marshall, Geoffrey, 68
Marshall, Jack, 321
Marshall, John, 222
Marshall, Thurgood, 225, 226
Martin, Ged, 284
Martin, Paul, Jr., 287
Martin, Paul, Sr., 184
Marx, Karl, 38
Mason, George, 355
Masse, Marcel, 116
Massey, Vincent, 102
Matheson, W.A., 53, 110, 114
Mayo, Henry B., 19
McCaffrey, Jeffrey, 145, 146
McCall-Newman, Christina, 42, 146
McCarthy, Eugene, 35
McCleave, Robert, 169
McCready, Robert, 170
McCrone, David, 354
McCurdy, Howard, 289
McDonald, Lynn, 174, 182
McDonald, Virginia, 374
McFarland, Andrew S., 391
McGibbon, Pauline, 103
McGovern, George, 302, 304
McGrath, James, 103, 180, 181
McIlwain, Charles Howard, 63
McKenna, Frank, 347, 440, 441
McKenzie, Charles, 315
McKenzie, Robert, 296, 299, 301
McLachlin, Beverly, 217, 289, 328
McMenemy, John, 219, 235, 268, 269, 342
McMillan, Thomas, 239
McMonagle, Duncan, 6
McNaught, Kenneth, 53, 220
McPhail, Agnes, 455
McPhee, Nancy, 455
McQuaig, Linda, 395
McQuarrie, Heath, 185
McRae, Kenneth, 248
McRoberts, Kenneth, 243
McWhinney, Edward, 210, 409, 423
McWilliams, Wilson Carey, 305
Meisel, John, 271
Mencken, H.L., 45, 306, 335
Merriam, Charles E., 98
Meyer, Anthony, 299
Michelmann, Hans J., 101, 150
Michener, James A., 356

Michener, Roland, 102
Mikulski, Barbara, 89
Milbrath, Lester W., 365, 377
Mill, James, 65
Mill, J.S., 343
Miller, Frank, 184
Mills, C. Wright, 30, 44, 136, 137
Mills, Dennis, 287
Mills, Wilbur, 198, 199
Milnor, A.J., 341
Mishler, William, 167, 182, 373, 375, 452
Mitchell, Austin, 300
Mitchell, William C., 86, 252, 253
Mitterand, François, 342
Mondale, Walter, 9, 129, 357
Monière, Denis, 243
Moore, Charles, 378
Moore, Mavor, 238
Morgan, Janet, 195
Morgan, Jim, 113
Morgentaler, Henry, 433
Morris, Edmond, 172
Morse, Wayne, 201
Morton, Desmond, 271
Morton, F.L., 413, 430
Morton, W.I., 279
Moynihan, Daniel, 155
Mueller, Claus, 49
Muir, Bob, 185, 321
Muller, William D., 402
Mulroney, Brian, 4, 13, 14, 15, 17, 44, 45, 51, 53,
    79, 82, 99, 102, 104, 105, 107, 112, 114, 115,
    118, 119, 120, 121, 146, 183, 186, 187, 188,
    213, 214, 217, 246, 262, 279, 281, 284, 285,
    286, 320, 345, 367, 436, 438, 440, 441, 442, 444
Munro, John, 113
Murphy, Bruce Allen, 207
Murphy, Rae, 367
Murray, Lowell, 190, 442

N
Nader, Ralph, 391
Namier, Sir Lewis, 332
Neustadt, Richard E., 89
Newman, Peter C., 31, 43, 109, 142, 168, 170,
    184, 187, 193, 237, 270, 314, 342
Nichols, Marjorie, 82
Nie, Norman H., 307, 378
Nielsen, Erik, 14
Niemi, Richard G., 364
Nixon, Richard M., 126, 127, 129, 156, 225, 226,
    253, 357
Norton, Philip, 153, 354
Nowlan, Pat, 283

Nunziata, John, 287
Nutter, G. Warren, 8, 12, 14
Nystrom, Lorne, 164, 428

O

Oakeshott, Michael, 36, 37, 51
Obler, Jeffrey, 162
O'Connor, Sandra Day, 225, 226
Oddo, Gilbert L., 227
Ogmundson, Rick, 368
Ogul, Morris S., 162
Oleszek, Walter J., 199, 201
Oliver, Dawn, 86
Olivier, Jacques, 103
O'Neill, Tip, 390
Ornstein, M.D., 147
Orren, Gary, 34
Ostrogorski, Moisei, 231
Ostry, Sylvia, 400
Ouellet, André, 113
Owen, David, 353
Owen, David, 390

P

Paine, Robert, 48
Pal, Leslie A., 413
Paltiel, K.Z., 290, 293
Pammett, Jon H., 336
Panitch, Leo V., 236, 402
Papandreou, Andreas, 30
Parkinson, C. Northcote, 158
Parrot, Jean-Claude, 163
Pateman, Carol, 379
Patterson, Arnie, 31
Patterson, Samuel C., 193
Pawley, Howard, 106, 112, 150, 169, 273
Pearson, Lester, 45, 118, 268, 281, 284, 321, 327, 373, 420
Peckford, Brian, 21, 219
Pelassy, Dominique, 2, 233
Peltason, J.W., 89, 222
Perlin, George, 279, 284, 285
Peters, Guy, 2, 9, 137
Peterson, David, 112, 115, 287
Peterson, Roy, 270, 421
Peterson, Thomas, 326
Pigott, Jean, 295
Pinard, Yvon, 213
Pinto-Duschinsky, Michael, 301
Pious, Richard, 126
Pipes, Sally, 13
Pirages, Dennis, 16
Pitfield, Michael, 104, 150, 173, 189, 190, 329, 399

Piven, Frances Fox, 377
Plano, Jack C., 384
Pocklington, Peter, 286
Polsby, Nelson W., 31
Pomper, Gerald M., 336
Ponting, Clive, 138
Pope, Alexander, 135
Pope, Sir Joseph, 17
Popper, Karl, 63
Posgate, Dale, 243
Powell, G. Bingham, 136, 377
Presthus, Robert V., 137, 152, 236, 238, 248, 394
Price, Richard, 138
Priestley, J.B., 254
Pring, David, 191, 193
Pritchard, Denny, 290, 374
Pulzer, Peter G., 332
Punnett, R.M., 109, 164, 194, 301, 332, 354
Putnam, Robert D., 317, 318, 332
Pym, Francis, 123

Q

Qualter, Terence H., 323
Quayle, Dan, 126, 129

R

Radwanski, George, 117, 321, 367, 420
Rae, Bob, 35, 50, 270, 288
Rae, Douglas W., 263, 343, 344, 359
Raeside, Adrian, 151, 179, 189, 266, 292, 325
Ranney, Austin, 316, 330, 447
Rasmussen, Jorgen S., 122, 195
Reagan, Nancy, 140
Reagan, Ronald, 8, 15, 125, 126, 127, 129, 140, 154, 156, 198, 200, 223, 225, 253, 302, 303, 304, 357, 391, 392, 393
Redekop, John H., 57, 58, 247
Regan, Donald, 156
Regan, Gerald, 319
Rehnquist, William H., 225, 226
Reid, Escott, 267
Reid, John, 174
Revel, Jean-François, 18
Rice, Donna, 253
Richardson, James, 113
Richardson, J.J., 402, 403
Richelieu, Cardinal, 50
Ridley, F.F., 65
Riel, Louis, 164
Riggins, John, 129
Ritchie, Roland, 215
Roberts, Paula, 98
Robertson, Gordon, 83, 104
Rochan, Thomas R., 45

Rodgers, William, 300
Roelofs, H. Mark, 253
Rogers, Will, 15
Romanow, Roy, 72, 81, 288, 431
Roosevelt, Franklin, 53, 224, 225
Roosevelt, Theodore, 126
Rose, Fred, 164
Rose, Richard, 2, 9, 22, 123, 158, 193, 232, 263,
    297, 341
Rosenbaum, Walter A., 234
Rossiter, Clinton, 253
Roth, David F., 249
Roy, Fabien, 262
Rush, Michael, 192
Russell, Peter, 213, 218, 408, 430, 437
Ryan, Claude, 273, 428

S

Sabato, Larry J., 16, 31, 392, 447, 452
Safire, William, 29, 49
Sartori, Giovanni, 260, 264, 265, 359
Sauvé, Jeanne, 102, 104, 107, 169, 424
Sawatsky, John, 32
Scalia, Antonin, 225, 226
Scammon, Richard N., 354, 360
Scarrow, Howard A., 24
Schattschneider, E.E., 7, 10, 232, 260, 261, 386,
    390
Schlesinger, Arthur M., 125
Schreiner, Keith, 140
Schreyer, Edward, 102, 104, 105, 107, 108, 289,
    321, 422
Schultz, Richard, 11
Schumacher, Stan, 322, 323
Schumpeter, Joseph A., 390
Schwam, Allan, 25
Schwartz, Mildred A., 239, 240
Scott, Frank R., 26, 408, 409
Seidle, F. Leslie, 293
Servan-Schreiber, Jean-Jacques, 163
Shaw, George Bernard, 40
Shenker, Israel, 194
Sheppard, Robert, 74, 443
Sherrill, Robert, 389
Shields, Jack, 168
Shipler, David K., 364
Shogan, Robert, 1
Shugart, Mathew S., 358
Silverstein, Mark, 223
Simeon, Richard, 240, 241
Simmons, Roger, 110
Simpson, Jeffrey, 31, 54, 107, 118, 186, 295, 324,
    394, 396
Skilling, H. Gordon, 385

Smallwood, Joey, 320, 327
Smiley, Donald V., 70, 73, 81, 245, 273, 284, 350,
    430
Smith, Goldwin, 314, 407
Smith, Gordon, 163
Smith, Hedric, 46, 231
Sniderman, Paul M., 433
Sopinka, John, 217
Sorenson, Theodore, 303
Souter, David, 226
Stacey, C.P., 367
Stalin, Joseph, 19, 317
Staller, Ilona (Cicciolina), 346
Stanfield, Robert, 51, 110, 171, 280, 285, 321
Steed, Judy, 327
Steed, Michael, 250
Steeves, Jeffrey S., 101, 150
Stevens, Geoffrey, 7
Stevens, John Paul, 224, 226
Stevens, Sinclair, 283, 321
Stevenson, Garth, 80, 213, 238
Stevenson, H.M., 147
Stevenson, Robert Lewis, 318
Stevenson, William A., 217
Stewart, Potter, 223
Stewart, Walter, 56, 170, 171, 238, 268, 350
St. Laurent, Louis, 284, 321
Stokes, Donald, 296, 298, 369
Stollery, Peter, 184, 185, 190
Strong, Maurice, 321
Suleiman, Ezra N., 232
Symons, Thomas H.B., 5, 368
Szablowski, George J., 117

T

Taagepera, Rein, 358
Taraki, Noor Mohammed, 49
Tarschys, Daniel, 12
Tarte, Israel, 289
Taylor, Gordon, 322
Taylor, Ken, 320
Tellier, Paul, 119
Tepperman, Lorne, 233
Thatcher, Colin, 110, 164
Thatcher, Margaret, 14, 15, 47, 49, 51, 58, 122,
    123, 124, 125, 138, 152, 153, 192, 195,
    251, 298, 299, 331, 332, 403
Thomas, George, 192
Thorburn, Hugh G., 267, 271
Thorpe, Jeremy, 124
Thurmond, Strom, 201
Tower, John, 393
Troyer, Warner, 329
Trudeau, Pierre Elliott, 3, 4, 8, 12, 14, 17, 30, 31,

43, 45, 48, 51, 54, 55, 74, 75, 78, 82, 104, 106,
109, 112, 113, 115, 114, 117, 118, 119, 120,
121, 145, 146, 150, 151, 173, 176, 178, 179,
183, 185, 187, 188, 190, 213, 214, 216, 217,
238, 241, 243, 246, 262, 268, 271, 272, 273,
278, 279, 280, 284, 286, 287, 320, 321, 322,
324, 344, 349, 360, 374, 383, 417, 420, 421,
422, 424, 425, 428, 429, 433, 439, 440, 442,
443, 451
Trudel, Marcel, 366
Truman, Harry, 129, 385
Truman, Tom, 238
Tuchman, Barbara, 1
Tucker, R.N., 213
Tufte, Edward R., 39
Turner, John, 169, 170
Turner, John, 4, 17, 31, 103, 112, 115, 118, 121,
187, 262, 269, 273, 279, 281, 284, 285, 286,
287, 292, 299, 320, 321, 346
Twain, Mark, 197
Tweed, Boss, 314

U

Underhill, Frank, 246, 448
Unger, Jim, 33
Uslaner, Eric M., 379

V

Valpy, Michael, 74, 84, 107, 108, 443
Vander Zalm, Bill, 82
Van Gogh, Vincent, 305
Vanier, George, 102
Van Loon, Richard, 373, 374
Verba, Sidney, 34, 233, 372, 378, 379
Verney, Douglas V., 84, 221, 401
Vickers, Jill, 323
Von Beyme, Klaus, 261

W

Waddell, Ian, 289
Wagner, Claude, 185, 283, 284, 321
Wald, Kenneth D., 261
Walden, Keith, 46
Walding, James, 169
Walker, Michael, 13
Wallace, George, 264, 304, 357
Wappel, Thomas, 287
Warren, Earl, 226

Washington, George, 302, 370
Waters, Stan, 438
Wattenberg, Martin P., 309
Wearing, Joseph, 272, 291
Weatheril, Bernard, 192
Webb, Beatrice, 40
Webb, Sidney, 40
Weber, Max, 30, 44, 45, 136, 137, 138
Webster, Daniel, 129
Webster, Donald B., 241
Weiner, Myron, 260, 262, 265
Welch, Susan, 373
Wells, Clyde, 441, 444, 445
Wells, H.G., 40
Wheare, K.C., 164
Whitaker, Reginald, 273, 321
White, Bob, 288
White, Byron R., 225, 226
White, Theodore H., 33, 125, 225, 252, 383
White, W.L., 365
Whittington, Michael S., 366
Wicks, Ben, 186, 316
Wildavsky, Aaron, 11, 31, 101, 157
Will, George, 126
Williams, Blair, 294
Williams, Shirley, 38, 124, 152, 300, 331
Wilson, Bertha, 217, 427
Wilson, Cairine, 190
Wilson, Frank L., 249
Wilson, Harold, 54, 84, 124, 130, 153, 298
Wilson, James Q., 89
Wilson, John, 239, 240
Wilson, Michael, 82, 285, 286
Wilson, V. Seymour, 158
Wilson, Woodrow, 196
Windsor, Hugh, 281
Winn, Conrad, 268, 269, 342
Wolin, Sheldon S., 33
Wooton, Graham, 393
Wright, F.J., 85

Y

Young, Walter D., 130, 185, 270, 285
Yulof, David Alastair, 364

Z

Zachs, Stephen M., 7
Zedong, Mao, 67
Ziegal, Jacob, 213